The American Family
VARIETY AND CHANGE

The American Family
VARIETY AND CHANGE

EVERETT D. DYER

Professor of Sociology
University of Houston

McGRAW-HILL BOOK COMPANY

New York St. Louis San Francisco Auckland Bogotá Düsseldorf
Johannesburg London Madrid Mexico Montreal New Delhi
Panama Paris São Paulo Singapore Sydney Tokyo Toronto

This book was set in Helvetica Light by Black Dot, Inc. (ECU).
The editors were Richard R. Wright and Barry Benjamin;
the designer was Joan E. O'connor;
the production supervisor was Donna Piligra.
R. R. Donnelley & Sons Company was printer and binder.

The
American Family
VARIETY AND CHANGE

1 2 3 4 5 6 7 8 9 0 D O D O 7 8 3 2 1 0 9

Library of Congress Cataloging in Publication Data

Dyer, Everett Dixon, date
   The American family.

   Includes bibliographies and index.
    1. Family—United States. I. Title.
HQ536.D93   301.42   78-11907
ISBN 0-07-018540-9

ACKNOWLEDGMENTS

Excerpts from Andrew Billingsley, *Black Families in White America* (Englewood Cliffs, New Jersey: Prentice-Hall, Inc., 1968), pp. 9 and 10. Copyright © by Prentice-Hall, Inc., 1968. Reprinted by permission of publishers.

Excerpts from E. Franklin Frazier, "Ethnic Family Patterns: The Negro Family in the United States," *The American Journal of Sociology*, **53** (1948), pp. 435–436. Copyright © by the University of Chicago Press. Reprinted by permission.

Excerpts from William J. Goode, *The Family* (Englewood Cliffs, New Jersey: Prentice-Hall, Inc., 1963), pp. 1, 4, and 5. Copyright © by Prentice-Hall, Inc., 1963. Reprinted by permission of publisher.

Excerpts from William J. Goode, *World Revolution and Family Patterns* (New York: The Free Press, 1963), pp. 1, 2, 6, and 19. Copyright © 1963 by the Free Press of Glencoe, a Division of the Macmillan Company. Reprinted by permission of Macmillan Publishing Company.

Excerpts from John A. Hostetler, *The Amish Society* (Baltimore: The Johns Hopkins University Press, 1963), p. 138. Copyright © by the Johns Hopkins University Press, 1963. Reprinted by permission.

Excerpts from Joseph A. Kahl, *The American Class Structure* (New York: Rinehart and Company, 1953), pp. 191, 203, 210, and 211. Copyright © 1953, 1954, 1955, 1957 by Joseph A. Kahl. Reprinted by permission of Holt, Rinehart and Winston, and Joseph A. Kahl.

Excerpts from Olaf F. Larson and Everett M. Rogers, "Rural Society in Transition: The American Setting," in James Copp, ed., *Our Changing Rural Society: Perspectives and Trends* (Ames, Iowa: The Iowa State University Press, 1964), pp. 42, 158, and 159. Copyright © by the Iowa State University Press. Reprinted by permission.

Excerpts from Ira L. Reiss, *Family Systems in America,* Second Edition (Hinsdale, Illinois: The Dryden Press, 1976), pp. 431 and 438. Copyright © 1976 by the Dryden Press, a division of Holt, Rinehart and Winston, Inc. Reprinted by permission of Holt, Rinehart and Winston, Inc.

Excerpts from John Scanzoni, *Sexual Bargaining* (Englewood Cliffs, New Jersey: Prentice-Hall, Inc., 1972), p. 163. Copyright © by Prentice-Hall, Inc., 1972. Reprinted by permission of publisher.

Excerpts from Louis Wirth, "Urbanism as a Way of Life," *American Journal of Sociology*, **44** (July 1938), p. 20. Copyright © by the University of Chicago Press. Reprinted by permission.

TO JACQUELINE AND JANETTE

CONTENTS

PART TWO *Family Variations in America*

PART THREE   *Family Change in America*

PREFACE

The general purpose of this book is to present a broad view of the family in America, its past and present, its variations, continuities, and changes. The book is the product of more than twenty years' experience in research in the family area and in teaching courses on the family in several major universities. The book was written to help fill a gap in the textbook literature on the American family. While many fine textbooks have been written on the sociology of the family, including those which have focused on selected aspects of family life differences and family change in the American experience, few if any textbooks have attempted a systematic, in-depth treatment of the American family utilizing the interrelated themes of family variation and family change within a broad historical-social context. The present book has this as its objective.

The book is organized for use as a textbook in college courses on the family where students and instructor are interested not only in current issues and problems confronting the contemporary American family but also in its long-term development, its varied origins and cultural sources, and the processes contributing to its changes over the years. Americans today are showing a renewed interest in the historical and cultural origins—or roots—of their families. Many instructors in courses on the family are devoting more time to historical and cross-cultural materials.

A special feature of the book is the selected readings, one of which appears at the end of each chapter. Articles and essays by prominent family authorities have been carefully selected to complement the text materials presented in each chapter. Each reading, selected for its relevance and reader interest, is prefaced with an introduction by the author of the book.

The book is organized into three main parts. Part One aims to provide perspective on the American family by introducing in Chapter 1 materials on the nature and significance of the family for society and its members. A brief review of the development of the family as a field of study precedes some basic family terminology. This is followed by some cross-cultural variations in family structure, to give the student a basis for understanding family variations in America. Perspective on the American family requires some awareness of its historical background and its cultural sources in the Old World, as well as knowledge of its American history and experience. This is attempted in Chapter 2, first by seeking out some of the Old World sources and origins of American families, then by showing how these early family foundations were built upon and further shaped by colonial influences, by early American frontier and rural influences, then by urban and industrial influences. The twin themes of the book, family variation and family change, are presented in Chapter 2, along with some "ideal-type" family conceptual frameworks to be used throughout the book in analyzing family variation and family change in America.

Part Two is concerned with family variations in America, and seeks to convey some idea of the rich and complex variety of American family life, past and present. This is done by presenting selected ethnic, racial, religious, and social-class variations in America (Chapters 3 and 5), and by comparing family life in rural, urban, and suburban America (Chapter 4).

Part Three deals with family change in America, viewed within a broad historical and social context which includes rural and frontier influences, technological developments and industrialization, urbanization, social mobility, and processes of adjustment and assimilation of more than 50 million American immigrants. More recently, other processes and conditions contributing to family change include various ideological and social movements including equalitarianism, feminism, civil rights, and youth movements. Continuity and cohesiveness between Part Two and Part Three are sustained by examining changes and trends in ethnic, racial, social class, and rural and urban families in modern America (Chapters 7 and 8), building upon what had been developed earlier in Chapters 3 to 5. Chapter 9 is devoted to nontraditional family variations and changes in present-day America. Various unconventional alternative life-styles being experimented with today are reviewed and compared with the older conventional forms of marriage and family life. Chapter 10 attempts to look into the future of marriage, family, and the relations between the sexes in America.

The author wishes to express his gratitude to the many authors whose research and interpretations have proved so valuable to him in the preparation of this book. I am especially grateful to my sociology colleagues who read and criticized the various chapters and whose suggestions were gratefully followed. I also wish to thank Arlene Thomas and Janet Warren of the University of Houston for their excellent typing of the manuscript. Very special thanks go to my wife, Jacqueline L. Dyer, and my daughter, Janette Dyer Bannan, for their research assistance, for editing the entire manuscript, and most of all for their enthusiastic support throughout.

Everett D. Dyer

PART ONE

Perspectives on the American Family

CHAPTER 1

Introduction to the Family

This book is about the family in America, its past and present, its historical and cultural varieties, its continuities and changes. As is true of almost all people, Americans have an abiding interest in the family. Recently there has been a resurgence of interest among Americans in their sources or roots, in the historical and cultural origins of their families. And today there certainly is widespread concern with what is happening to marriage and family in contemporary America. Will marriage and family, as basic social institutions, be able to meet and adapt successfully to the many changes and challenges confronting them today? Or will conventional marriage and family forms possibly pass away and be replaced by new or alternative life-styles? These and other related questions and issues underlie and direct much of the following discussion on the American family throughout the book.

Let us start by examining some of the current issues and problems confronting marriage and family in America today. Then we will broaden the discussion to hear what some of the leading family social scientists have to say about the family in general, in order to seek a broader perspective on the family in America.

American family celebrating Thanksgiving Day. (*USDA photo by Marianne Pernold.*)

Issues and Questions in Marriage and Family Today

SOME CURRENT ISSUES AND QUESTIONS
ON MARRIAGE IN MODERN AMERICA

How important is marriage today to people in America? Is marriage less important now than earlier? Are we as a people becoming disillusioned with marriage? Are we perhaps ready to turn more to other types of intimate association to satisfy our personal needs? While conventional marriage has become the target of some rather vocal critics in recent years, many authorities continue to argue that marriage is still the most highly valued relationship in American society. Americans, according to Richard Udry, are fascinated by sex-pair relationships prior to marriage and outside of marriage, but most of all by sex-pair relationships within marriage. "Contemporary Americans, more than most groups of people, are fascinated with marriage. . . . Americans believe in marriage above all. They marry earlier, remain unmarried less often, and remarry after divorce more frequently and more rapidly than people of any other industrialized nation. They look to their marital relationship for their greatest satisfaction in life."[1]

While Americans may disagree as to the details of what proper marital behavior should be, the goals of marriage are quite clear, Udry argues. Marriage should yield personal happiness; it should be the source of emotional gratification and security, and give the marital partners love and companionship. Marriage is seen as the main source of personal happiness by most Americans.

However, conventional marriage has come in for a good deal of criticism in recent years from several quarters. On the one hand, people holding traditional or conservative views may decry the increasing impermanence of marriage, pointing to the high rates of desertion and divorce. They may blame this on sexual immorality, lax marriage and divorce laws, and early marriage by immature youth who are probably not prepared for marriage and who also have little commitment to permanent marriage.[2] At the opposite pole are those who feel marriage has probably outlived its usefulness, that it is not a panacea for one's personal needs, and that it is time for marriage to give way to more up-to-date forms of intimate relationships. People holding such views see the rising divorce rates as symptomatic of the failure of conventional marriage to .meet the great expectations too many people demand of it. They argue that traditional monogamous marriage, with its assumptions of sexual and emotional exclusivity, has too long been the sole model for the expression of sexuality and intimate affectional relations. Such exclusivity, they claim, is more myth than reality, and human beings need greater freedom for personal expression and growth than this traditional monogamous model allows.[3] They argue that marriage as a normative institution has lost its "taken-for-granted, life long quality," that it now seems to possess an "unprecedented fragility."[4]

SOME ISSUES AND QUESTIONS ON THE FAMILY IN MODERN AMERICA

Is the family itself still of central importance in modern America? Is it adapting and functioning effectively in our fast-changing urban society? Or is the family in America in process of disintegration? Such questions are receiving a good deal of attention today throughout the land. As Margaret Mead recently observed, the "American family is at the center of American concern at the present time; its strengths and weaknesses . . . are being subjected to every kind of scrutiny."[5]

If we accept the assumption stated above by Udry that marriage is still very important to Americans, it follows that they also place considerable value on the "nuclear family," consisting of the husband, the wife, and their children. Certainly this is true. By comparison with other cultures, past and present, Americans place great stress on this immediate small family unit which is oriented around the conjugal or marital union. In many other societies, in fact, kinship ties are more important than marital ties, and the nuclear family unit may be a relatively unimportant group embedded within the larger "extended family."[6]

The widespread concern with the "state of the American family" is being voiced by many different commentators and interpreters in religious, political, and journalistic circles, as well as by social scientists. As Bert Adams notes, to those who are favorably disposed toward conventional marriage and family, what they see happening is a source of dismay. Increasing premarital sex, increasing divorce, widening gaps between parents and children are all seen as fearful symptoms of family disintegration.[7] On the other hand, there are those of a radical persuasion to whom the conventional family is an object of serious criticism. They argue today, as Friedrich Engels did decades ago, that the traditional family is one of the greatest barriers to personal freedom, self-realization, and social equality; that being a very conservative institution, the family holds back needed social changes, thereby creating discontent.

These and many other related issues and problems will be treated more fully throughout this volume as we review and analyze trends, continuities, and changes in marriage and family in the United States. Opinions as to where the American family is headed are indeed disparate. Are conventional marriage and family headed for the breakup feared by the conservatives and desired by certain radicals? Or is something less drastic more apt to be happening, as many calmer and more moderate analysts are predicting?

They see marriage and family as surviving the present rather difficult period of change and adjustment, while moving toward a more flexible structure which will provide greater personal freedom for all members and greater opportunities for personal fulfillment.[8]

SOME SPECIFIC ISSUES, PROBLEMS, AND DILEMMAS IN MARRIAGE AND FAMILY LIVING TODAY

Most issues, problems, and dilemmas in human relationships entail differing viewpoints of those involved, behind which are differing values, norms, and sentiments. Here are some of the salient issues and problems confronting Americans today as they strive to work out their marriage and family relationships.

SOME ISSUES AND PROBLEMS CONFRONTING YOUNG PEOPLE AS THEY APPROACH MARRIAGE AGE   (1) Should one wait until marriage to have sex relations? Is premarital sex all right if a young couple are in love but are not ready yet for marriage? (2) How soon should one get married? Should a young couple live together a while before getting married, in order to test their love, their compatibility, and their commitment? (3) Should young people be completely free to select their own marriage partners, even when their choice may be contrary to the wishes of their parents, and may mean a mixed religious or racial marriage? Those holding a traditional "sacred" value orientation would certainly respond to these questions quite differently from others holding more modern "secular" value orientations. The behavior of young Americans today attests to the wide range of viewpoints on these issues.

SOME ISSUES AND DILEMMAS CONFRONTING MARRIED COUPLES   (1) How many children should a married couple have? Is a large family more desirable, or is it better to have only one or two children—or perhaps none at all, considering the population problem in the world and the uncertainties of the times? What methods of family planning and birth control are acceptable and proper? (2) What are the proper role definitions for husbands and wives? Is there a "natural" or right division of labor—and possibly such a division of authority—in marriage based on gender? What is "woman's place" and what is "man's place" in the American family? For example, should the woman's roles be primarily domestic, while the man supports the family, or should she also be free to pursue a career? If she is employed and they have children, how will the children be cared for? Also, if she is employed and is thus helping to support the family, will her husband become an equal partner with her in the performance of domestic roles? (4) Should a married couple always be faithful to each other? Or are there circumstances and conditions under which extramarital sexual relations are legitimate?

Again, the answers to these and other such questions depend in large part on the value positions held by the husband and the wife, and also on the degree of conviction each has. Strong traditionalists would have no doubt that husband and wife should be ever faithful to each other and that the wife's place is in the home looking after her husband and children, while the avowed "Woman's Libber" would stoutly assert that a wife should not be confined by traditional domestic roles, and that she should be as free as her husband to pursue a career and other outside interests, including extramarital relations. As will be seen in Part Two of this book, today many values and norms pertaining to marriage and family living are undergoing change, so that not only is there a wide range of value positions on these issues held by Americans, but also a great many individuals have mixed feelings and uncertainties as to what is the right or best position for them to take.

SOME ISSUES AND PROBLEMS CONFRONTING AGED FAMILY MEMBERS (1) What is the status of the elderly in American families today? Many societies, past and present, have given special deference, respect, and power to the oldest members of the family, who have had many important family roles to fulfill. In modern America, with its youth orientation, the most rewarding and prestige- and power-yielding roles are apt to be withdrawn from aging family members. A woman's mother role diminishes or vanishes as the children grow up and leave home. The man faces retirement from his job, which has been the main family support and also the principal basis of his prestige and power in the family in our industrial and secular society. (2) Are there any useful and rewarding functions left for aged members of modern urban American families? How may their lives continue to be meaningful and satisfying? (3) How may the physical, social, and psychological changes experienced with the onset of old age be eased to reduce the acute sense of loss apparently felt by many? (4) What are the responsibilities of married children for their aging parents? Many urban couples, separated from their parents by time and distance, appear uncertain on this issue. Here again, traditionalists would be more certain as to what is normatively expected than would those of a more secular-individualistic orientation.

As will be apparent throughout this book, the above-mentioned issues, problems, and dilemmas of marriage and family living today are inevitably linked to the varied historical and cultural sources of the present American family, and to the processes and conditions influencing family change. Many of the changes taking place today in marriage and family may be understood as efforts on the part of Americans to deal with these and other family-related issues and problems.

Viewpoints and Perspectives on the Importance of the Family in Human Society

Before continuing our discussions of the family in America, let us just briefly turn our attention to the larger picture in order to get an understanding of the general nature of the family in human society.

What do some of the leading family sociologists and anthropologists have to say about the general nature of the family?

William Kephart refers to the family as "the remarkable institution."

As the oldest and most universal of all man's social institutions, the family provides a fascinating topic for study. . . . [It is] the institution which concerns itself with love, sexual relationships, marriage, reproduction, socialization of the child, and the various statuses and roles involved in kinship organization. Little wonder that the family is referred to as "the remarkable institution."[9]

Clifford Kirkpatrick says that the family is the outstanding example of a primary group, and is really unique in the way it provides continuity of social life.[10] This continuity has a dual aspect. Biologically, the family is the meeting ground of the generations, where "chromosomes and genes carry on their mysterious processes which create children more or less in the image of their parents."[11] Sociologically, family relationships yield cultural transmission and social continuity over the generations and centuries.

The family, says Margaret Mead, is:

the toughest institution we have. It is, in fact, the institution to which we owe our humanity. We know no other way of making human beings except by bringing them up in a family . . . we know no other way to bring up children to be human beings, able to act like men and women and bring up children, except through the family.[12]

George P. Murdock is widely quoted for his position on the universality of the nuclear family:

The nuclear family is a universal human social grouping. Either as the sole prevailing form of the family or as the basic unit from which more complex familial forms are compounded, it exists as a distinct and strongly functional group in every known society. No exception, at least, has come to light in the 250 representative cultures surveyed. . . .[13]

Some family scholars have questioned Murdock's position on the universality of the nuclear family, but their data are not very impressive and are often drawn from groups that do not constitute independent societies, such as the Nayars, a caste group of south India, where the husband spends more time with his sister's family than with his own wife. Another example would be the kibbutz villages in modern Israel.

Claude Lévy-Strauss sees the family as a linking mechanism in the community, as a creator of new social bonds brought about by the linking of two kinship groups.[14] The nuclear family is an arbitrarily created social unit which serves to link together two previously unrelated kin groups. An exchange takes place between these two kin groups, one providing a woman and the other a man. Since mankind's survival and cultural development depend on this outward expanding of social bonds with other people beyond one's immediate blood relatives, marriage outside the kin group is necessary. This helps explain why in so many societies marriages of young people have been arranged by their parental families or their larger kinship groups.

The following statement from Lévy-Strauss sums up his views:

It is almost a universal feature of marriage that it is originated, not by the individuals, but by the groups concerned (families, lineages, class, et cetera), and that it binds the groups before and above the individuals. . . . Although a marriage gives birth to the family, it is the family, or rather families, which produce marriage as the main legal device at their disposal to establish an alliance between themselves.[15]

William J. Goode describes the uniqueness and strategic significance of the family in human society:

In all known societies, almost everyone lives his life enmeshed in a network of family rights and obligations. . . . A person is made aware of [these] through a long period of socialization during his childhood, a process in which he learns how others in the family expect him to behave, and in which he himself comes to feel this is both the right and the desirable way to act. . . . Philosophers and social analysts have noted that society is a structure made up of *families*, and that . . . a given society can be described by outlining its family relations. The earliest moral and ethical writings suggest that a society loses its strength if people fail in their family obligations.[16]

Throughout history, Goode contends, the family has been recognized as a central element in the social structure. He then identifies what he believes to be the strategic significance of the family, which is its "mediating function in the larger society."[17] The family mediates between the individual and the larger society in ways that no other group or agency does. The family is the principal link between the individual and the other groups which make up human society. This mediating function of the family assures that the individual will have some initial preparation or "anticipatory socialization" for his various roles in the community, and that he will generally be adequately motivated to be a participating and productive member of society. When one is tempted to be lax or to deviate, the family is in a unique position to apply sanctions to make one "straighten up" and "get back on the ball" again. In order to be a going concern and to survive, a society must see that its basic needs are met, and this requires adequately motivated, productive human beings. The family, more than any other group, has the job of providing and sustaining members of society who are generally willing and able to make their necessary contributions.[18] Any given society can tolerate only so many dropouts and deviants and still survive.

The family, Goode asserts, is in certain ways a unique social institution. Other than religion, the family is the only social institution which is formally developed in all societies. Not only does the family perform more important services for society (such as reproduction, care, maintenance, and socialization of the young), but the family also is the main "instrumental foundation" of human society, Goode concludes.

[The] family is the fundamental *instrumental* foundation of the larger social structure, in that all other institutions depend on its contributions. The role behavior that is learned in the family becomes the model or prototype for the role behavior required in other segments of the society. The content of the socialization process is the cultural traditions of the society; by passing them on to the next generation the family acts as a conduit or transmission belt by which the culture is kept alive.[19]

SUMMARY OF VIEWPOINTS AND PERSPECTIVES ON THE IMPORTANCE OF FAMILY

The views expressed by the above authorities convey a clear message that the family is indeed highly important. Its importance or value is seen in what it does for society in general as well as what it does for its individual members. The basic nuclear family unit of husband, wife, and offspring appears to be virtually universal. This is the group that brings new members into the society; it is largely responsible for their care as infants and growing children, and for preparing and motivating them to fit into the social life of the community, willing and able to make their contributions to its well-being and survival.

The family is the place where human biological and cultural heritage meet and are joined in the living and learning new family member. It is the place where the biological being becomes a human and social being. The family not only links the individual to society, it also links two previously unrelated kinship groups through the marriage of a woman from one family to a man from another family, thus creating and maintaining new social bonds. The family is in a sense the main instrumental foundation of the larger society in that other institutions and groups depend upon the family to provide them with people who are willing and able to perform needed roles. And finally, the family is probably the most important social institution for sustaining the culture of a society and for transmitting that culture to the next generation.

The Study of the Family

BRIEF HISTORY OF THE STUDY OF THE FAMILY

Sociologists concerned with the development of interest in the family by specialists and the way the study of the family has advanced over the years have attempted to identify various stages or periods through which this growing interest in the family progressed. With some modifications, the following discussion will be based upon the four stages presented by Harold Christensen: (1) Pre-Research, (2) Social Darwinism and Social Reform, (3) Emerging Science, and (4) Systematic Theory Building.[20] It is recognized that such stages or time periods are really arbitrary divisions selected for their convenience and analytical utility.

1   THE PRE-RESEARCH STAGE (PRIOR TO 1850).   Very little in the way of systematic study of the family seems to have been accomplished before the mid-nineteenth century. This does not mean that prior to that time various people were not deeply interested in the family. Prescientific thought on family issues and concerns may be found in some of the earliest literature, such as the Wisdom Writings of ancient Egypt, the Code of Hammurabi of ancient Babylon, the Chinese Confucian classics, and the Old Testament. This prescientific interest in the family tended to be highly value-oriented and moralistic, frequently expressed in proverbs and exhortations for proper family conduct. Through most of these early writings there stood out a deep concern for family welfare and an implicit view of the importance of the family for the society.

2   SOCIAL DARWINISM; SOCIAL REFORM (1850–1900).   The writings of Charles Darwin influenced a number of historians and early social scientists to attempt to apply evolutionary theory to the course of human and social change. Among others, Edward Westermarck, Friedrich Engels, and Lewis Henry Morgan sought to apply notions of evolutionary change and progress to the family throughout human existence.[21] How did marriage start? Did the early human family arise from a primitive horde when original promiscuity gave way to some kind of group marriage which in time evolved into polygamy and eventually progressed to monogamy? Intriguing ideas all right, but not so easily supported by evidence acceptable to most scientists. The general approach of most of these Social Darwinists was to search the literature for evidence in support of their theories, rather than to undertake field studies. They paid attention mainly to primitive societies, often getting their "evidence" from descriptions and recollections of travelers, ships' captains, and missionaries.

However, by comparison with earlier works, what the Social Darwinists did represented the beginning of a somewhat focused and somewhat empirical effort to study the family in human society, even though their methods were descriptive and impressionistic, and certainly colored by a Western ethnocentric viewpoint of what is best and superior in marriage, namely monogamy.

A contemporary who was an exception to the Social Darwinists was Frederic Le Play, a French scholar who emphasized the need to get out and study actual families using accurate research methods.[22] Le Play helped develop the research interview and the participant-observer methods. His studies of French workingmen's families, focusing on such things as family income and expenditure patterns, were directed toward helping establish national policies on family welfare in France.

Le Play's work relates to the second emphasis in family study which emerged in this period, a growing concern with family problems and with social reform. Paralleling Social Darwinism during the latter part of the nineteenth century and continuing on into the twentieth century was an increasing concern with social problems and the search for ways to alleviate them. The industrial revolution and ensuing urbanization had brought on or intensified social problems such as poverty, exploitation of women, child labor, illegitimacy, divorce, etc. The central position of the family in these deepening problems was quite evident, as publicized by writers such as Charles Dickens. Cries for social reform rang out from the pulpits and in Parliament, supported by a growing number of social scientists who were reacting negatively to the fatalism and evolutionary determinism implied in Social Darwinism. The "humanistic" social scientists, including Auguste Comte in France and Lester Ward and E. A. Ross in the United States, felt that people could, through their own intelligent efforts—especially through the application of new scientific knowledge—work toward the solution of social problems, bring about needed reforms, and improve the quality of life for people and their families. In America, the University of Chicago school of sociology became a leader in this movement, as seen in its extensive research efforts in the following period, efforts that frequently focused on the family and its problems and needs in an urbanizing America.

EMERGING SCIENCE (1900–1950) The concern with social reform and with family problems continued into the twentieth century, but was modified and given new direction by the increasing emphasis on science in the study of the family. This scientific orientation stressed an objective and more value-free stance by the family researcher and the use of more rigorous methodology. Attention shifted from large-scale, loosely defined investigations to more narrowly defined studies, carried out by better-trained researchers who emphasized quantification and statistical analysis. A leader in this scientific study of the family was Ernest W. Burgess of the University of Chicago, who, with his associates and students, conducted studies aimed at obtaining data on mate selection, marital interaction patterns, processes of marital breakup, and problems of aging family members.

In this period the study of the family shifted from broad concerns with the family as a social institution to a more narrow and sharply defined focus on the family as a social group. Attention focused on internal family structure and processes such as dating and courtship, marital adjustment, parent-child relations, and personality development within the family context.

4 SYSTEMATIC THEORY BUILDING (1950 TO THE PRESENT) While the term "systematic theory building" is probably a bit of an overstatement, certainly a strong interest in developing family theory has existed in the last few decades. Family research has expanded rapidly, with more studies being designed and executed systematically with a view toward theory development. More family research has moved beyond enumeration and description toward interpretation of the findings within some larger theoretical context. It has been observed that the label "systematic theory building" may be a bit premature, at least for the decades prior to the 1970s.[23] Up to then, the major efforts were to summarize and synthesize various research findings and then to develop a number of conceptual frameworks which would lead, it was hoped, to the emergence of sound family theory. Since 1970 more effort has been made toward codification and actual theory building.

CONCEPTUAL FRAMEWORKS FOR FAMILY STUDY

What are some of the main conceptual approaches or frameworks being developed by sociologists to enable them to understand better the complexities of family phenomena, and to help guide them toward sound family theory? Professors Reuben Hill and Donald Hansen have identified five such frameworks developed and used by family sociologists: (1) the institutional, (2) the structural-functional, (3) the interactional, (4) the situational, and (5) the developmental.[24]

1 THE INSTITUTIONAL FRAMEWORK This is one of the earliest approaches used in studying the family. It originated with anthropologists and was adapted by sociologists who were interested in the development of the family as a social institution and with comparisons of the family institution over time and across societies.[25] This approach thus has a pronounced historical and cross-cultural perspective. It focuses on what families have in common; it attempts to show what the family does and how it does these things; it compares and relates the family to other institutions in society. Many of the notions in the institutional approach overlap with those found in the

structural-functional approach, which is one reason the former approach has in recent years receded and the latter come more to the fore.

2 THE STRUCTURAL-FUNCTIONAL FRAMEWORK This approach views the family as a social structure or social system which "functions" in certain ways to assure that some of the basic needs of the individual and the society are satisfied.[26] This approach to the family is ahistorical, thus differing from the older institutional approach. The focus of the structural-functional approach is on the manner in which the family structure at any given time and place operates to carry out certain family functions, such as child care and training. This is a rather static approach in that it implies that change or variation from the "normal" marriage and family structural patterns are apt to be viewed as dysfunctional. This issue will be encountered again throughout this book as we examine family change and alternative life-styles.

3 THE INTERACTIONAL FRAMEWORK This approach to family study conceptualizes the family as a social group within which family members interact in generally patterned ways. This is essentially a social-psychological approach since it is concerned with the relations between family members, with how family roles are defined and performed, and the ways family members adjust to one another. Ernest W. Burgess, who helped develop this approach, said, "The family is a unity of interacting personalities."[27] The marital adjustment studies of Burgess and his associates are examples of the application of the interactional approach to family analysis.

4 THE SITUATIONAL FRAMEWORK This conceptualization is now generally thought to be a special type of the interactional approach, since it too is concerned with the relations among family members, but in special kinds of family situations. For example, how do marriage partners react and adjust to a new family situation such as the arrival of their first child? The series of studies done in recent years on "parenthood as crisis" and "transition to parenthood" illustrates the application of this approach.[28]

5 THE DEVELOPMENTAL FRAMEWORK The final approach is also concerned with relations among family members, but it envisions family relations within a longitudinal framework consisting of a number of periods or stages of family life. The family is seen as evolving through a number of fairly distinct stages over its life span.[29] The time span is the life cycle of the nuclear family, and the stages or periods, such as infancy, childhood, adolescence, marriage, parenthood, and old age are the units of analysis. The roles and responsibilities of each family member change and develop as he or she moves through successive stages of the cycle. This approach has an advantage over the previous two approaches in that it enables us to study

family interaction within a time-defined framework, and to observe changing family roles and relationships throughout the whole family cycle.

It should be noted that these conceptual frameworks are not themselves really theories of the family. They are approaches which facilitate analysis and interpretation of family phenomena in a systematic way which is necessary before valid family theory can be developed.[30]

Chapters in the present volume dealing with historical backgrounds and cultural variations in the American family will make use of the structural-functional and institutional frameworks; and when issues of internal family relationships or change are being considered, one or more of the other approaches will be drawn on.

We have now reviewed briefly the way the study of the family evolved over the past century or more, and the conceptual frameworks developed by family social scientists to aid them in studying family phenomena. Now we will conclude this section by noting some of the hazards and difficulties that may be experienced in the study of the family.

SOME DIFFICULTIES IN STUDYING THE FAMILY

Nearly everyone spends most if not all of his or her life as a member of a family. In societies such as ours, each of us is normally first a member of the parental family in which we were born; then later in life we will probably help form a new nuclear family by getting married. We are all thus in a sense experts on the family by virtue of our great personal familiarity with it, and our long and intense experience in family relations. This high personal familiarity with the family can be both a help and a hindrance in our efforts to study the family. It is a definite help in providing us with many insights and a basic understanding of what the family is all about. For example, when we see the word "marriage," we envision two people of the opposite sex joined together according to law, who are sharing a common residence and are sexually accessible to each other. The word "family" will probably mean to the average American two parents with one or more children whom they are rearing.

Yet the very fact that we are so familiar with the family, at least with our family and others in our circle of acquaintances, makes it difficult to see the family in general, that is, to see it in the abstract, apart from the specific cases we know and experience. This is one reason we will need to look at some general definitions of the family, and also attempt to get a broad perspective on the family in human society by making some cross-cultural comparisons.

Clifford Kirkpatrick sees two types of difficulties confronting the individual in the study of the family: first there are emotional obstacles, and then there are intellectual obstacles.[31] Emotional obstacles would include various biases, fears, intimate feelings, and preconceptions about sex and marriage which may color or blur the vision of a person in studying family phenomena. Some feel strongly that behavior as intimate as love and sex should not be subjected to the invasion of cold scientific observation, which may be taken as an invasion of privacy. Kirkpatrick sees intellectual obstacles to the study of the family in the average person's lack of knowledge of family life in societies other than one's own, and even within one's own society beyond one's limited circle of acquaintances. Also, dogmatisms, strongly held beliefs about proper family behavior, and the very complexity of family phenomena make objective study difficult. For many people, the strength of beliefs and sentiments held on matters of sex, marriage, and family is second only to the strength of attitudes held on religious matters.

Toward a Sociology of the Family: Some Basic Family Terminology

DEFINITIONS OF THE FAMILY

What then is the family? Is it possible to set down some definitions that specify the essential nature of the family, that enable us to distinguish the family from other groups and institutions, and that still are sufficiently general to allow for historical and cultural variations? In working toward a general definition of the family, we may ask who does the family include? What are the criteria of family membership. We may also ask what the family does; what are its functions in society? And how are the relations among family members defined and structured?

While any definition attempted would probably not cover all the above points, and would thus fall short of providing a universally valid definition of the family in human society, it should be helpful to look briefly at some attempts by family authorities.

Ernest W. Burgess's early definition of the family has been widely quoted: "A family is a group of two or more persons, joined by ties of marriage, blood, or adoption, who constitute a single household, who interact with each other in their respective familial roles, and who create and maintain a common culture."[32]

This definition addresses some of the questions raised as to family membership and relationships. Families consist of people who are marriage partners, or who are blood relatives, or who have been adopted into the family. These then are the three quite universal criteria for family membership—marriage, blood ties, and adoption. Family members then normally live together in some kind of a dwelling place, and relate to each other day in, day out, in their family statuses and roles, and in the process share a common culture.

One of the most often quoted definitions of the family comes from George Murdock, eminent anthropologist, who said: "The family is a social group characterized by common residence, economic cooperation, and reproduction. It includes adults of both sexes, at least two of whom maintain a socially approved sexual relationship, and one or more children, own or adopted of the sexually cohabiting adults."[33]

Notice that this definition not only specifies the sharing of a common residence, but also identifies two other family characteristics, economic cooperation and reproduction. This helps answer the question of what the family does. Murdock elaborates on the membership notion by specifying adults of both sexes but not limiting them to only one male and one female adult as in the monogamous family. In polygamous families there would be two or more wives or husbands present.

These definitions apply basically to the immediate or *nuclear family*, consisting of marriage partners and their children, which Murdock contends is virtually universal. There are, of course, situations where nuclear families may be incomplete or truncated, as in cases where there are no children or where a parent is missing through desertion, divorce, or bereavement. It is important to point out that these are almost always seen as exceptions to the normal model of a completed nuclear family. Also, as we will be seeing shortly, in many societies the nuclear family exists as a part of a larger *composite family* or kinship group. Even there, the nuclear family tends to be recognized as a distinct unit, frequently having its own living quarters.

These variations and distinctions in family characteristics suggest the need to spend a little more time on a few other family terms and concepts which we will find useful in the coming chapters.

To begin with, it should be helpful to distinguish *marriage* as a concept from *family*. Murdock did this by identifying *marriage* as the complex of customs centering on the sexually cohabiting adults within the family.[34] Marriage defines how such a relationship is established and maintained, and how it may be terminated. In a sense, marriage is a subsystem within the larger system of the family.

It is helpful to distinguish between the family of orientation and the family of procreation.[35] The *family of orientation* is the one in which a person is born

FIGURE 1-1 Families of orientation and procreation. (*Source: W. Lloyd Warner*, "A Methodology for the Study of the Development of Family Attitudes," *Social Science Research Council Bulletin, No. 18, 1933.*)

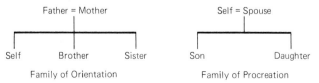

as a son or daughter. It includes one's parents, oneself, and one's siblings, if any. One normally grows up in the family of orientation. At marriage the person creates a new family called the *family of procreation*, in which one is husband or wife and potentially a father or a mother. In our society we are likely to think of the family of procreation as "our own family." It is the family one lives in as an adult, consisting of one's spouse, oneself, and one's children.

The term *nuclear family* may be applied to either the family of orientation or the family of procreation. They both consist of a set of marriage partners and their children. However, in the family of orientation the individual taken as the point of reference is the child (a son or daughter), while in the family of procreation the same individual is now an adult (husband or wife, and potentially a parent).

Nuclear families may be combined into *extended families* through the extension of the parent-child relationship. This produces a family group of three or more generations, including grandparents, parents, and children. The grandparents comprise one nuclear family and the parents and their children a second nuclear family. In traditional China, the ideal (seldom achieved) was to have six generations within the large extended gentry family.

In family structure, priority may be given either to marital ties or to blood ties. Where priority is placed on the marital tie, it is called a *conjugal* system; where blood ties come first, it is called a *consanguine* system. Our typical modern American family system is a conjugal one, where the independent nuclear family is quite free of control by blood relatives. The traditional Chinese extended family was a strong consanguine system, with parent-child ties (especially father-son) far more important than the husband-wife bond.

THE FAMILY AS A SOCIAL INSTITUTION

At the beginning of this chapter, we reviewed a number of viewpoints held by family authorities on the importance or significance of the family in human society. One theme running through many of the statements was that the

FIGURE 1-2 Types of families. (*Source: George Murdock*, Social Structure, *1965.*)

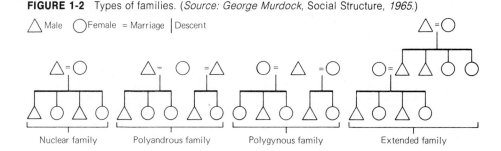

Nuclear family   Polyandrous family   Polygynous family   Extended family

family is one of the major social institutions in society. Some authorities hold, as does Goode, that the family is probably the most important of human social institutions. In any event, a sociological interpretation of the family requires our understanding of the family as a social institution.

A *social institution* may be defined as a system of interrelated customs and norms organized for the purpose of carrying out certain societal functions. To quote Kingsley Davis, a social institution is "a *set* of interwoven folkways, mores, and laws, built around one or more [societal] functions."[36] A key term here is "societal function." In analyzing the way human society works and survives as a going concern, social scientists frequently identify certain basic "societal needs" or "functional requisites" which have to be met for a society to survive. Among those functional requisites frequently named are: (1) Reproduction of new members for the society, (2) provision for care and protection of members, (3) provision for socialization of new members, (4) arrangements for production and distribution of goods and services for members, and (5) provision for accommodating conflicts and for maintaining order.[37] A *societal function*, then, may be defined as a task-oriented activity, usually cooperative, which contributes to the satisfaction of some societal need, such as one of the functional requisites listed above.[38]

Social institutions define and specify how these task-oriented activities are to be carried out. That is, each social institution in a given society consists of a set of interrelated norms and customs (folkways, mores, laws) organized and implemented so as to assure the carrying out of its particular function or functions. Among the basic social institutions are economics, politics and government, religion, education, and family. Economics, for example, has the responsibility for providing the goods and services needed to sustain life and health of the members of a society. As a social institution, economics may be conceptualized as a system of interrelated customs and norms defining how the cooperative activities of manufacturers, wholesalers, retailers, etc., will be carried out so the food, clothing, shelter, energy and other needs of the people will be met. This illustration enables us to complete the picture by pointing out the relationship between social institutions and the actual groups which perform the societal functions. A social institution, as we have said, is a system of interrelated customs and norms. A *social group* consists of two or more human beings who are interacting together. Many social groups have their origin and purpose derived from social institutions. For example, in economics, the task-oriented cooperative activities are actually carried out in formally organized groups such as General Motors, Exxon, Sears, and the corner grocery store.

Now let us apply these concepts to the family as a social institution. When we observe actual families in our community—our own family, our neighbors' families, the Jones family, and the Garcia family—we are looking at the end of a chain, as suggested above. We see groups of human beings interacting in their respective familial roles. We may be aware that certain norms and customs guide and regulate their activities. We may or may not be conscious of the societal functions being carried out by the cooperative behavior of the family members as they interact day in, day out. We are probably less aware of the societal needs or functional requisites which these cooperative family activities are helping to satisfy.

FAMILY FUNCTIONS

What are some of the important functions the family as a social institution performs for society and its members? Family authorities generally agree that among the societal functions of the family would be included: (1) Reproduction, or replacement of the members of a society, (2) care, nourishment, and maintenance of these new members during their infancy and childhood, (3) socialization of the young, and (4) the social placement of these individuals in the community or society.[39] Many other functions have been attributed to the family in whole or in part, depending on the nature of the society in question and the other institutions found there. The family everywhere is an economic cooperative unit, and in many societies the family is or has been the main economic productive unit (such as the traditional farm family). In most modern industrial societies, however, the family is no longer the main economic productive group and so its economic cooperative activities mostly involve the consumption of goods and services. Another important function of the family is "property transmission." The family usually serves as the main agency for transmission of private property from generation to generation in most societies, for example, where parents "will" their property to their children as heirs.

Related to these societal functions performed by the family are a number of *individual-serving functions* which cater directly to the needs of the individual family members.[40] Through the marital relationship the family provides for meeting the sexual needs of its adult members. The family also, through the marital relationship and the parent-child relationship, provides for much of the affectional and emotional needs of its members. And in some societies, such as our own, the family may be expected to satisfy important companionship needs of its members. The family also helps to "stabilize adult personalities," according to Talcott Parsons.[41] A little later on we will see that there are big differences in the number of functions and in the emphasis placed on different family functions when comparing one culture with another. The traditional Chinese family would be an example of a family system of great functionality, while the kibbutz family in modern Israel would be at the opposite extreme, as a family of very little functionality.[42]

Ibans extended family in long house, Borneo. (*Julie Heifetz.*)

FAMILY STRUCTURE

Structural-functional analysis of the family enables us to connect family structure or organization with family functioning. We may say that throughout the history of a given society its family structure has evolved or developed in such a way as to fulfill its functions. Included in the structure of the family (i.e., the nuclear family) are three fundamental social relationships: (1) *The marital relationships*, (2) *the parent-child relationships*, and (3) *the sibling relationships*. These three sets of family relationships, as Kingsley Davis notes, are complicated by two biological factors running through them, age and sex.[43] The marital relationship occurs between a man and a woman who are approximate age peers; thus the relationship is *intra*generational. The parent-child relationship, involving persons of two different generations or age groups, is on the other hand *inter*generational. Americans are quite well aware of the ways this generation difference—or "generation gap"—may affect their relations with their parents or their children. Sibling relations, again, are peer or intragenerational, which tends to make for shared attitudes, sentiments, and interests.

Sex may affect the three fundamental family relationships in a number of ways. Sexuality is of course important in the marital relationship, and the biological differences between male and female largely determine the division of labor in the process of procreating and bearing children. However, a great deal of the division of labor between the sexes in the family and the community is probably more culturally determined than biologically determined. Note the wide variations in how sex roles are defined and played in different societies around the world, as Margaret Mead's studies have shown. Sex differences not only affect the marital relationship but also parent-child and sibling relationships. Mother-son, father-daughter, and brother-sister relations are generally somewhat different—being hedged by sex taboos or restraints—from mother-daughter, father-son, sister-sister, or brother-brother relations.

To conclude this brief discussion of family structure, let us note that each of the three fundamental family relationships is defined by its set of *familial statuses and roles*. The marital relationship is defined by the status-role of "wife" in reciprocity with the status-role of "husband." And so it is with the parent-child relationship, which is defined and activated by the status-roles of "mother" or "father" in relation to the status-roles of "son" or "daughter." The principal status-roles defining sibling relationships are of course "brother" and "sister." Built into these family status-roles are the reciprocal expectations, the rights, privileges, duties, and obligations of each family member with respect to other family members.

While the three fundamental relationships comprising nuclear family structure are quite universal, the ways they may be defined and put into play can be fascinatingly varied, as we shall see next.

Cross-Cultural Variations in Family Structure

Students of the family never cease to marvel at the imaginative and varied ways in which marriage and family have been defined and structured in the different societies around the world, past and present. Evidence compiled by social scientists shows us that, when viewed cross-culturally, variations in family structure are surprisingly great. Why is this so? If we start with a few basic assumptions about the human species, we may wonder why marriage and family patterns are not more alike everywhere. Biologically, *Homo sapiens* is one genus and species, with only minor physical variations (such as racial variations) found within the species. Most authorities agree that these physical variations in and of themselves are not important in determining the structuring of social groups and social relationships such as in marriage and the family. Everywhere on earth there are the two sexes (and probably two sexes are enough) which have to be sorted out into marriage partners. Everywhere people's basic needs are essentially similar, such as the needs for food, shelter, and sex satisfaction; and the processes of reproduction are essentially the same for the whole species.

Why then are there so many different ways throughout the world for getting male and female together, first as marriage partners (mate selection), then for structuring their relationships as marital partners (marriage), then for patterning their relationship with their children (parenthood), and also for organizing the relationships among the children (sibling relationships)? The answer to this question is not simple, of course, and we probably do not as yet have sufficient knowledge to answer it completely. However, there is a good deal of agreement among behavioral scientists that the structure of the family is rooted not just in human biological nature, but probably more importantly in culture and history.[44] This is to say that family structure at a given time and place has to be seen as a part of the larger social structure of that particular society at that juncture in its history. The family structure observed there would reflect the salient cultural values, norms, beliefs, sentiments, and traditions, as well as the social forces and historical processes, that have shaped the various social institutions of that society, including the family. The particular family structure found in each society "makes sense" when seen in its larger social and historical context. For example, the predominant American family of today—the monogamous, independent, small nuclear family—makes sense in modern, mobile, urban, industrial society. And the larger, extended, polyandrous family makes sense in the austere, agrarian society of the Todas of India, where many men have to be away from home tending the herds, and where the sex ratio has long been out of balance, with a surplus of men.

SOME CROSS-CULTURAL VARIATIONS IN MARITAL, PARENT-CHILD, AND SIBLING RELATIONSHIPS

Using the three fundamental sets of relationships found in nuclear family structure, let us next look at some of the principal points of variation found within each.[45]

I Marital relationships
    A Variations in types of marriage
        1 Monogamy
        2 Polygamy
            (a) Polygyny
            (b) Polyandry

Monogamy and polygamy constitute the two principal forms of marriage found throughout the world. In *monogamy*, only one female and one male are allowed to be husband and wife, at least at the same time. *Polygamy*, meaning multiple marriages, has two logical subtypes: (1) *Polygyny*, or multiple wives, and (2) *polyandry*, or multiple husbands. Hypothetically, a third variant here could be *group marriage*, in which several husbands and several wives live together. Such group marriages are very rarely found, according to anthropologists.

Returning to monogamy, variations are possible ranging from societies where virtually absolute monogamy exists to other societies where *serial monogamy* is found. This refers to a situation which stops just short of polygamy, where persons have only one mate at a time but via divorce and remarriage have a series of different marriage partners over the years. An American millionaire, Tommy Manville, is reported to have had fourteen

Newar father and daughters, Katmandu, Nepal. (*Julie Heifetz.*)

different wives over a rather lengthy marriage career. On the other hand, monogamy in some situations can be nearly absolute in the sense that no divorce is allowed and one is expected to keep the same marriage partner for life. Catholic church doctrine has long prescribed this for its members. St. Augustine, an early church father, felt that a good Christian should literally be allowed only one marriage partner in his or her lifetime. His view on this did not prevail however.

In comparing the types of marriage in a world sample of 554 societies, George Murdock finds monogamy in 135 societies, polygyny in 415, polyandry in only 4, and group marriage as an established pattern in none.[46] While these different frequencies are interesting and revealing, they need some explaining. In the monogamous societies, no polygamy would normally be allowed, but in the polygamous societies, while multiple marriages would be normative, monogamous marriages are usually allowed also. In fact, in many polygynous societies the majority of men have only one wife, with only the

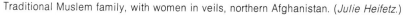

Traditional Muslim family, with women in veils, northern Afghanistan. (*Julie Heifetz.*)

high-status or more affluent men enjoying several wives. Since the sex ratio is approximately equal for most societies most of the time, for fifty men to have two wives would mean that another fifty men would probably be unable to have even one. Muslem societies have traditionally been polygynous, with the Koran allowing a man to have up to four wives. Most societies with a Judeo-Christian tradition are monogamous. The Todas of south India and the Tibetans are among the few people practicing polyandry.

B Variations in the possibility of remarriage
  1 No remarriage possible
  2 Permissive remarriage
  3 Mandatory remarriage

St. Augustine would have forbidden remarriage for a Christian who had lost a spouse through death. Hindu culture has a long tradition of forbidding widow remarriage, although this taboo has been modified in the twentieth century. In America, as in many other modern societies, remarriage is permissible after the death of a spouse, and for those not under a religious restriction, after divorce or annulment. One has considerable freedom of choice in the matter in societies such as ours where personal freedom is highly valued. There are societies, however, where being married is considered so important and such a strong personal obligation that the norms prescribe mandatory remarriage. A practice called the *levirate* requires a brother to marry the widow of his deceased brother. This would normally be found in a polygynous society. A comparable practice called the *sororate* prescribes that a sister marry the widower of her deceased sister.[47]

C Variations in marital authority
  1 Patriarchal
  2 Matriarchal
  3 Equalitarian

A *patriarchal* family is one where the power is vested in the husband-father as is the case in many nuclear family systems, or in the hands of the eldest male as in some large extended family systems. This patriarchal authority pattern has been very prevalent historically and across many cultures. Historical examples would include the ancient Hebrews, Greeks, and Romans as well as the Chinese, the Hindus, the Mohammedans, and Christian societies until fairly recent times. Wherever male dominance exists in the culture, patriarchal authority in the family generally follows, at least officially.[48] Informally, women have exerted considerable power and influence in many formally patriarchal families. The degree of patriarchal power itself may vary, from societies where the father holds virtually absolute power over all members of his family, as was the case of the paterfamilias of the Roman

Large rural Ecuadoran family. (*Roger Nett.*)

Republic, to societies with a mildly patricentric situation where the father is only nominally the head of the family, as in some modern middle-class families in the United States.

Matriarchy, where the wife-mother wields the power in the family, is seldom found in the sense of a woman having full power, or even a high degree of recognized power, in the way a man does in a truly patriarchal family. Even in societies where women have a central and formalized importance, such as where matrilineal descent and property inheritance are found, the family power tends to be in the hands of the males within the female lineage, such as the married woman's brothers.[49]

Equalitarian authority implies a relatively equal or equitable division of power between the husband and the wife. This equalitarian type of family makes sense in societies which emphasize personal freedom and where equal rights for women are strongly advocated. The trend in America today is toward more equality in marriage. The historical change from an earlier American patriarchal family type toward a present-day equalitarian family type is one of the themes in the chapters to follow.

D Variations in choice of marriage partner
  1 Who determines choice of mates
  2 Bases of choice (endogamy and exogamy)
  3 Exchange at marriage

There are two opposite ways in which a marriage partner may be obtained: Either the individuals may find their own mates, or someone else may do it for them, such as their families. The latter method has been far more prevalent throughout history and across cultures. This procedure of the family selecting a mate for sons and daughters is generally called the *arranged-marriage* method. Both parents may be involved in the selection, or perhaps only the father; sometimes a third party is involved, as in the case of the professional go-between in traditional Japan. In India, China, and a good part of the Muslim world, marriages have traditionally been arranged, with the bride and groom having very little voice in the matter of whom they are to marry. These and other societies where this method has existed look upon the marriage as much more than the joining of a man and a woman in wedlock; rather, marriage is seen as an alliance between two families or kin groups which has consequences far beyond the personal satisfaction or happiness of the bride and groom.[50]

In societies such as contemporary America, where little emphasis is placed on kinship ties and where great importance is given the conjugal bond, it makes more sense for each person to have the main say in selecting his or her own marriage partner. One's choice is never completely free, of course, as we'll see next.

All societies define the field of eligible marriage partners. Certain preferential groupings are established within which a mate may or should be chosen. Other groups may be defined as out-of-bounds. *Endogamous* norms specify that one should or even must marry someone within certain groupings, such as one's religious group, one's racial or ethnic group, or one's social class or caste, as in India. *Exogamous* norms specify marriage outside of certain groups, such as one's close blood relatives, or some larger kin group such as a sib. The prohibition against marrying close blood relatives is known as the *incest taboo*, and is a nearly universal restriction found in all human societies.

Claude Lévy-Strauss sees marriage as essentially an *exchange arrangement* whereby the bride and groom each bring a share into the marriage.[51] In arranged marriages especially, the families of the bride and groom enter into a kind of bargaining negotiation through which an agreement is reached as to the nature and the substance of the exchange. Recall the Old Testament example of the arrangement where Jacob was to work seven years for Laban in exchange for his daughter Rachel, but then had to accept Rachel's older sister Leah for his labors since the "sororate" code prescribed that the older sister must be married before the younger sister. (P.S. Jacob then worked another seven years for his true love, Rachel.) In many societies, work or money or property is required as a "bride-price." In others, the family of the bride-to-be has to put up a "groom-price" (dowry) in order to obtain a suitable husband for her. This has long been a practice in high-caste Hindu families. In some societies an equal exchange pattern exists, with the bride and groom each bringing to the marriage money or property of equal value. This practice was observed by C. M. Arensberg and S. T. Kimball in rural Ireland in the 1930s, where the bride was expected to bring to the marriage a dowry equal in value to the value of the farm her husband was to inherit.[52]

    E Variations in residence after marriage
        1 Patrilocal
        2 Matrilocal
        3 Neolocal

Where will the newlyweds live? Since each partner comes from a different family, at least one partner must move at marriage. They can live either with his family of orientation or with hers, or they can move to a new location to set up housekeeping. Or there may be some combination of these possibilities over the years of their marriage. The most common residential pattern around the world is *patrilocal*. Here the bride leaves her parental family and moves in with her husband in the home of his parents. The groom does not have to move; he simply has his new bride join him where he has always lived. Murdock found this patrilocal residential pattern in 146 out of 250 societies surveyed.[53]

Where *matrilocal* residence is the rule, the husband leaves his family of orientation and moves in with his new bride in her parental home. This pattern was found by Murdock to be the rule in 38 out of the 250 societies. He also found a closely related residential practice called *avuncolocal* in eight societies, where the bride and groom move in with the maternal uncle of the groom.[54] In some societies the bride and groom may choose whether they will live with her family or with his family. This is called a *bilocal* residence pattern.

The pattern most familiar to Americans is the *neolocal* or independent residence practice, where the bride and groom set up housekeeping in a new location away from both families of orientation. Compared with patrilocal or matrilocal residence, it is interesting to note that neolocal residence is quite rare. Murdock found it to be the practice in only 17 out of 250 societies.[55] This practice seems to make sense and fits well in societies such as ours which minimize kinship ties and emphasize the marital bond. Neolocal residence seems especially suitable for mobile, middle-class families where the economic and social interests of the young couple are not tied closely to their kin, but rather lie in pursuing their own careers and other personal goals. Occasionally young American couples may live with one set of parents for a time, out of economic necessity perhaps. But they generally look upon this as a temporary arrangement, and feel much relieved when they can move into a home of their own, however humble it may be.

II Children and Parent-Child Relationships
    A Variations in the number of children born
        1 High fertility
        2 Low fertility

Many societies, past and present, have emphasized the value of human fertility. Throughout most of human history the uncertainties and threats to life have made life expectancy so short that it has been necessary for families to have many children in order to assure population replenishment, not to mention growth. Judeo-Christian teachings have admonished the faithful to "be fruitful and multiply." Societies which stress familism and kinship ties, where there is much concern with perpetuating the family name and with having enough heirs to carry on the family name and traditions, are conducive to high fertility. In preindustrial American communities, children were highly valued, partly for these reasons and partly for their economic value in helping with the farm work or with some other family-based economic productivity. Quite the contrary for the majority of urban families today where children, from a strictly economic view, are seen as liabilities, since they have little or no productive role to play in the family situation.

Low fertility seems to accompany not only industrialization and urbanization, but also secularization in general, with its emphasis on individualism and conjugal ties at the expense of familism and kinship ties. Other present-day beliefs, sentiments, and norms contributing to low fertility rates include the rational concern with overpopulation, and the feeling that parents should have only as many children as they can properly support. And of course the dissemination of birth control knowledge and contraceptive techniques has made it easier for more families to plan and limit the number of children born.

    B Variations in parental authority over their children
        1 Very strong authority, up to lifelong duration
        2 Weak authority, ending early

The degree of parental authority over children may range from virtually absolute at one end of a continuum to weak and tenuous at the other end; and the duration of parental authority may extend up to the death of the parent in some societies, while in others the authority may cease at some fixed time, such as when the son or daughter "comes of age." History offers a number of interesting cases of very strong parental authority. The Old Testament description of Abraham about to sacrifice his son on an altar attests to a Hebrew father's power of life or death over his son at that time. In the Roman Republic before the Punic Wars, the family patriarch not only had virtually absolute power in his family but also had control over his sons and unmarried daughters throughout his lifetime. This patriarchal power, called *potestas*, gave the father the authority to control his sons as long as he lived, even after the sons had grown up and had families of their own. There are cases of Roman generals still being under *potestas* after they had become famous and powerful men, but because their fathers still lived they were unable to control their own property or business affairs.[56]

Parental authority over children tends to be weaker and of shorter duration in modern secular societies where kin ties and obligations are weak, and where personal freedom and individual rights are stressed. Peer groups, schools, and the law itself may undermine parental authority over children in modern urban societies. It is logical that the current "human rights" movement should include a children's rights wing. Just how far this "children's liberation" movement may go in the United States is a matter of some conjecture.

    C Variations in types of descent
        1 Patrilineal
        2 Matrilineal
        3 Bilateral

Every society has norms that define the manner in which the individual is related to kinfolk. These norms specify lineage, that is, how the family name is passed down from parents to children, and how biological relatives are identified and delimited. The three most commonly found types of descent are "patrilineal," "matrilineal," and "bilateral."

Patrilineal descent is traced through the male line. At birth the child is assigned to a group of kin who are related through the father's side of the family only. Where this patrilineal descent pattern exists, the most important generational ties or parent-child relationships are normally those of father to son to grandson. Murdock found patrilineal descent in about 40 percent of the 250 societies surveyed. He found matrilineal descent in about 20 percent and bilateral descent in approximately 30 percent of these societies.[57] Patrilineal descent is logically connected with patriarchal authority and patrilocal residence, and has a long history in Western civilization and in many old Eastern civilizations such as India and China.

Matrilineal descent passes the family name and traces relatives through the female line in the family. The children in a matrilineal family would count only their mother's relatives as kin, while disregarding their father's relatives. Matrilineal descent is found in many places throughout the world, such as Melanesia in the Pacific, in Western Africa, and in a number of Southwestern

American Indian groups such as the Navajo and the Zuni. Matriliny seems to be found most frequently in societies which engage in simple agriculture where women play an important role in food production.[58]

Bilateral descent exists where lineage is traced through both the male and the female sides of the family. A limited number of the father's relatives and a limited number of the mother's relatives are included in the kin group. This is the customary practice in the United States where a person is normally considered to be related equally to both parental kin groups. Only in our taking the name of the father's family do we retain a vestige of an earlier patrilineal pattern.

D   Variations in types of inheritance.

Closely related to family descent but not identical with it is family inheritance. Inheritance norms and practices prescribe the manner in which property, land, money, obligations, etc., are passed down from generation to generation within the family or kin group. When possessions are handed down through the male line, as from father to son, it is called *patrilineal* inheritance; when such possessions are passed down through the female line, as from mother to daughter, this is called *matrilineal* inheritance. In some societies one child only may automatically inherit everything, while in other places all survivors may be entitled to a share of the inheritance. A *testamentary* inheritance practice exists where the property owners are free to determine who their heirs will be. The normal procedure in such societies is for the owner to make a "will" specifying the shares each heir is to inherit.

III   Sibling Relationships
A   Variations in the strength of the bond among siblings

The strength of ties between siblings and the nature and extent of mutual obligations between them may vary, from societies where the ties are virtually lifelong to other societies where the bonds between adult siblings are very few, and brothers and sisters feel very little in the way of obligation toward one another.

In strongly familistic societies an individual may not only feel closely bonded to and obligated toward parents (filial piety); additionally, these feelings may be extended to brothers and sisters. This was generally the case in the traditional Chinese extended family. On the other hand, in individual-oriented societies, where independence and social mobility are valued, an individual may feel very little in the way of obligation toward brothers or sisters, especially where they are separated by both geographical and social distance. Only very nominal ties may be retained, such as the exchange of Christmas cards or remembering the birthday of a niece or nephew.

B   Variations in share of inheritance

Cultural variations exist in the sex limitations placed on property inheritance. In some societies only sons may inherit property, while in others only daughters have this right. In certain societies where males may inherit, the eldest son may get the full inheritance. This is known as *primogeniture*. In other male-only societies the youngest son may get it all. This is called *ultimogeniture*, and was practiced in some middle-class English circles at one time. Primogeniture is a long-standing tradition in the British aristocracy.[59] In many modern democratic societies, the practice is for an equal or at least an equitable division of the inheritance to be made among the surviving siblings.

C   Variations in duration of common residence

In some societies brothers may be separated from sisters quite early in childhood, due probably to the strength of the incest taboo. The Papago tribes separate boys and girls at puberty. In most modern Western societies brothers and sisters share a common residence with their parents throughout childhood and adolescence, then separate and go their individual ways at marriage or when leaving home for higher education or jobs. Elsewhere siblings may continue living in the same residence as adults. This would be the case for adult married brothers and unmarried sisters in extended families where patrilocal residence is the rule, such as the Hindu joint family arrangement. In matrilocal-matrilineal societies, such as the Navajo, adult married sisters and unmarried brothers would share a common residence.

The Plan and Content of This Book

The purpose of Part One is to provide a perspective on the family in America. Chapter 1 introduces the reader to the nature and significance of the family for society and its members, stressing the unique nature of the family as a social institution, and the relationship between family functions and family structure. The history and development of the family as a field of study is presented, leading to a review of the various conceptual frameworks being developed by social scientists for family study today. Chapter 1 also introduces cross-cultural variation in family structure to help broaden our perspective.

Perspective on the American family requires knowledge of its historical background and its varied cultural origins in the Old World as well as knowledge of its American experience and history. Chapter 2 is devoted to this effort, first identifying some of the Old World sources of the American family, then showing how these family foundations were built upon and shaped by colonial and early American influences and conditions of life. The twin themes of the book, family variation and family change, are introduced, followed by an explanation of the "ideal-type" conceptual framework which will be used throughout the book to analyze family variation and change in the American family.

Part Two of the book is devoted to family variations in America. It attempts to convey some idea of the immense and complex variety of family life in America, past and present, by reviewing selected ethnic, religious, racial, and social-class family variation (Chapters 3 and 5), and by comparing family life in rural, urban, and suburban America (Chapter 4). The vast majority of American families, past and present, stem from people who came to America from other lands, bringing with them their cultural traditions, including their patterns of family life. (Black American families may be an exception to this, as will be seen in Chapter 3.) Since America has been predominantly a rural society throughout most of its history (until World War I), in order to understand the American family today it is necessary to realize its long rural background and development. Today, of course, most families live in cities or metropolitan areas, and urbanism as a way of life is shaping family structure and relationships virtually everywhere in America, as will be discussed at length in Chapter 4.

Part Three deals with family change in America. Viewed historically, family life has come under many influences: rural and frontier conditions and the westward movement of American population, industrialization, geographic and social mobility, and problems of adjustment and assimilation of more than 50 million American immigrants. Other processes and conditions conducive to family change in America include various ideological and social movements such as expanding democracy and human rights, equalitarianism, feminism, civil rights movements, and youth movements.

In order to sustain continuity and a cohesiveness between Parts Two and Three, Chapters 7 and 8 will examine changes and trends in ethnic, racial, class, and rural and urban families in modern America, building on what had been developed in Chapters 3 to 5.

Chapter 9 is devoted to family changes of an unconventional nature, often referred to as alternative life-styles. The various nontraditional or variant forms being experimented with today by increasing numbers of Americans—such as living together without marriage or joining a commune—will be reviewed and assessed vis-à-vis the older conventional forms of marriage and family living. Finally, Chapter 10 will attempt to look into the future of marriage, family, and the relations between the sexes in America. Will marriage and family as we have known them survive or will they perhaps be replaced by some current or future alternatives? Upon what grounds or bases may projections or predictions of the future of marriage and family be made with any degree of confidence? What do authorities in the area of marriage and family say about these questions? (Feel free to turn to Chapter 10 right away if you are very concerned about these questions—or are just curious.)

Summary

Some current issues and questions on marriage and family in modern America are raised and discussed. While most Americans look to marriage as the main source of personal need satisfaction and happiness, conventional marriage has become the target of critics in recent years. Traditionalists deplore the permissive trends and the increasing impermanence of marriage, and advocates of change say conventional marriage and family have outlived their usefulness and should yield to more up-to-date forms of intimate relationships. Living in a period of great social flux and change, American people are confronted with numerous problems, issues, and dilemmas in everyday marriage and family life.

How important is the family in human society? Its importance or value may be seen in what it does for society and for its individual members. The family brings new members into the society; it is largely responsible for their care and for preparing them for their adult lives in the society. The family links the individual to society, and provides society with people who are willing and able to perform needed roles in other institutions and groups.

The history of the study of the family has been divided into four periods or stages: (1) Pre-Research (prior to 1850), as seen in the writings of philosophers and religious leaders on the proper conduct of family members. (2) Social Darwinism–Social Reform (1850–1900). Here evolutionary theory was applied to family development by the Social Darwinists on the one hand, while on the other hand interest in family problems attending the industrial revolution brought social reform efforts aimed at improving the lot of suffering families. (3) Emerging Science (1900–1950). The twentieth century saw family study become more scientific and the problems studied more narrowly defined. (4) Systematic Theory Building (1950 to the present). A strong interest in developing family theory marks this current period, as evidenced in the effort to develop various conceptual frameworks for family study, including the institutional, the structural-functional, the interactional, the situational, and the developmental frameworks.

Objective study of the family is difficult. Our intense familiarity with and involvement in our own family make it hard to see the family in general and in broad perspective. The student of the family is faced with both emotional and intellectual obstacles.

Some basic family terminology is presented. Definitions of the family by Burgess and Murdock are given and discussed, enabling us to identify the *nuclear family*, consisting of marriage partners and their children, and to distinguish it from larger *composite family* forms or kinship groups. Nuclear families may be combined into *extended families* through the extension of the parent-child relationship whereby two or more nuclear families and three or more generations are living together. In a *conjugal family* system primacy is given the husband-wife relationship, while in a *consanguine* family system blood ties or kinship relationships have priority.

The sociology of the family requires an understanding of the family as a social institution. A *social institution* is a system of customs and norms organized to carry out certain *societal functions*, which in turn contribute to the satisfaction of some *societal needs*. These concepts help us to see the family as a social institution having a number of important functions which it performs for society and its members, including reproduction, care and maintenance of its members, socialization, and social placement of individuals in the society. *Family structures* develop to carry out *family functions*. Basic units of family structure are the *marital relationships*, the *parent-child relationships*, and the *sibling relationships*. Each of these three sets of relationships is defined by its set of *familial statuses and roles*.

Cross-cultural variations in family structure are presented, focusing on the three sets of basic family relationships.

Marital relationships may be *monogamous* or *polygamous*. There are two kinds of polygamy: *polyandry* in which one wife has two or more husbands, and *polygyny* in which a husband has two or more wives. Remarriage is allowed in many societies, required in others, and may not be allowed at all in a few. Marriages may be classified according to the stucturing of family power or authority as *patriarchal, matriarchal,* or *equalitarian*. Some societies such as ours allow a person to choose his or her own marriage partner, while others require the choosing and the arranging to be done by other people, generally one's family. After marriage the newlyweds may live with her family of orientation (*matrilocal* residence) or with his family of orientation (*patrilocal* residence) or move to a new place of their own (*neolocal* residence).

Parent-child relations vary in several ways. First, some societies stress high fertility and encourage parents to bear many children, while at other times and places low fertility is valued and few children are born per family, such as in modern middle-class America. Parental authority over children may be very strong and even last until the parents die or may be weak and end early in the child's life cycle. Family descent and inheritance may be *patrilineal* or *matrilineal*. Also, descent may be *bilateral*, in which case lineage is traced through both the male and female family lines.

Sibling relationships vary considerably too from society to society, such as in the strength and duration of the bonds among siblings, and in the shares of property inherited by sons or daughters. In some societies siblings may be separated in early childhood according to sex, in others they all live together until adulthood, while in others some siblings will continue living together throughout their adult lives.

Notes

1   J. Richard Udry, *The Social Context of Marriage* (New York: J. B. Lippincott Co., 1974), pp. 1–2.

2   William M. Kephart, *The Family, Society, and the Individual* (Boston: Houghton Mifflin Co., 1972), pp. 7–9.

3   R. W. Libby and R. N. Whitehurst, *Marriage and Alternatives* (Glenview, Ill.: Scott, Foresman and Co., 1977), pp. xx–xxiii.

4   Arlene Skolnick and Jerome Skolnick, *Family in Transition* (Boston: Little, Brown & Co., 1971), pp. 2–3.

5 Margaret Mead, "The American Family," in H. Smith., ed., *The Search for America* (Englewood Cliffs, N.J.: Prentice-Hall, 1959), p. 116.

6 Udry, op. cit., pp. 2–3.

7 Bert N. Adams, *The Family* (Chicago: Rand McNally & Co., 1975), pp. 2–3.

8 See Ernest W. Burgess and Harvey Locke, *The Family* (New York: American Book Co., 1945); Dennis Wrong, "The 'Breakup' of the American Family," in Bert N. Adams and Thomas Weirath, eds., *Readings on the Sociology of the Family* (Chicago: Markham Publishing Co., 1971), pp. 434–444.

9 Kephart, op. cit., p. 1.

10 Clifford Kirkpatrick, *The Family* (New York: Ronald Press Co., 1963), p. 4.

11 Ibid., p. 4.

12 Margaret Mead, "The Impact of Cultural Changes on the Family," in *The Family in the Urban Community* (Detroit: The Merrill-Palmer School, 1953), p. 4.

13 George P. Murdock, *Social Structure* (New York: Macmillan Co., 1949), pp. 2–3.

14 Claude Lévy-Strauss, "The Family," in H. L. Shapiro, ed., *Man, Culture and Society* (New York: Oxford University Press, 1956), pp. 261–285.

15 Ibid., p. 270.

16 William J. Goode, *The Family* (Englewood Cliffs, N.J.: Prentice-Hall, 1964), pp. 1–2.

17 Ibid., p. 2.

18 Ibid., p. 3.

19 Ibid., pp. 4–5.

20 Harold Christensen, ed., *Handbook of Marriage and the Family* (Chicago: Rand McNally & Co., 1964). See chap. 1, pp. 3–32.

21 Edward Westermarck, *History of Human Marriage* (1891); Friedrich Engels, *The Origin of the Family, Private Property, and the State* (1902); Lewis Henry Morgan, *Ancient Society* (1877).

22 Frederic Le Play, *The Organization of the Family* (Paris: Dentu, 1870).

23 Adams, op. cit., p. 6.

24 Reuben Hill and Donald Hansen, "The Identification of Conceptual Frameworks in Family Study," *Marriage and Family Living*, 22 (November 1960), pp. 299–311.

25 F. Ivan Nye and F. M. Berardo, *Emerging and Conceptual Frameworks in Family Analysis* (New York: Macmillan Co., 1966), pp. 78–96.

26 Ibid., pp. 52–72.

27 Ibid., p. 97.

28 See E. E. LeMasters, "Parenthood as Crises," *Marriage and Family Living*, 19 (November 1957), pp. 352–355; Everett D. Dyer, "Parenthood as Crises: A Restudy," *Marriage and Family Living*, 25 (May 1963), pp. 196–201; C. M. Russell, "Transition to Parenthood," *Journal of Marriage and Family* (May 1974), pp. 294–301.

29 Evelyn M. Duvall, *Family Development* (New York: J. B. Lippincott Co., 1971).

30 For further discussion of the prospects for family theory, see C. B. Broderick, "Beyond the Five Conceptual Frameworks: A Decade of Development in Family Theory," *Journal of Marriage and Family*, 33 (February 1971), pp. 139–159.

31 Kirkpatrick, op. cit., pp. 8–10. Also see Bernard Farber, "Studying Family and Kinship," in R. W. Habenstein, ed., *Pathways to Data* (Chicago: Aldine Publishing Co., 1970), pp. 50–80.

32   Burgess and Locke, op. cit., p. 8.
33   Murdock, op. cit., p. 1.
34   Ibid.
35   W. Lloyd Warner, "A Methodology for the Study of the Development of Family Attitudes," *Social Science Research Council Bulletin*, No. 18, 1933.
36   Kingsley Davis, *Human Society* (New York: Macmillan Co., 1949), p. 71.
37   J. W. Bennett and Melvin Tumin, *Social Life* (New York: Alfred A. Knopf, 1948), pp. 186–196.
38   Marion Levy, *The Structure of Society* (Princeton, N.J.: Princeton University Press, 1952), p. 56.
39   Davis, op. cit., p. 395. For an excellent functional analysis of the family, see chap. 15. For a thorough recent analysis of family functions, see Robert F. Winch, *The Modern Family* (New York: Holt, Rinehart and Winston, 1971), Chap. 1.
40   Winch, op. cit., pp. 21–23.
41   Talcott Parsons, "The Normal American Family," in M. Barash and A. Scourby, eds., *Marriage and the Family* (New York: Random House, 1970), pp. 198–199.
42   Winch, op. cit., chaps. 2 and 3.
43   Davis, op. cit., pp. 398–399.
44   Goode, op. cit., pp. 8–18; and Davis, op. cit., pp. 397–399.
45   This section closely follows the outline presented by Davis, op. cit., pp. 414–416.
46   George P. Murdock, "World Ethnographic Sample," *American Anthropologist*, 59 (1957), p. 686.
47   Gerald R. Leslie, *The Family in Social Context* (New York: Oxford University Press, 1976), p. 34.
48   Kirkpatrick, op. cit., pp. 80–84.
49   Leslie, op. cit., p. 61.
50   Morris Zeldich, "Cross-Cultural Analysis of Family Structure," in Harold Christensen, op. cit., pp. 469–470.
51   Lévy-Strauss, op. cit., pp. 261–285.
52   C. M. Arensberg and S. T. Kimball, *Family and Community in Ireland (Cambridge: Harvard University Press, 1940)*.
53   Murdock, *Social Structure*, p. 59.
54   Ibid.
55   Ibid.
56   Leslie, op. cit., p. 184.
57   Murdock, op. cit., p. 15.
58   Goode, op. cit., pp. 61–62.
59   Davis, op. cit., pp. 411–412.

SELECTED READING

This article by Professor Goode will serve several purposes. (1) In anticipation of the chapters to follow, it will introduce the present American family as sociologists see it; (2) it will help highlight similarities and differences between American families and those found in other societies around the world; and (3) it will help broaden our perspective on the human family in general.

Goode points out that while Americans live in a wide variety of family arrangements, they still generally follow certain similar patterns. One way to identify and describe these similarities is to compare American family systems with family systems elsewhere in the world. Accordingly, Goode makes a comparison of the American kinship system with kinship systems found in Far Eastern and European societies. He reviews dating, courtship, and mate selection patterns in contemporary American society, and then reviews husband and wife roles and relationships in the United States, comparing them with marital roles found in other societies.

THE CONTEMPORARY AMERICAN FAMILY*

William J. Goode

American Kinship Structure

More than 200 million people in the United States live under such a wide variety of family arrangements that it is impossible to characterize them all by a simple formula. Most do follow similar patterns, however, and we can describe them in a general way by noting how at many points they differ from other family systems of the world.

First, of course, the American system is technically monogamous. It has sometimes been called "serial monogamy," since every year several hundred thousand people divorce and soon remarry, and of course a small percentage of these people may have a succession of spouses over their lifetimes. Nevertheless, the structure of daily marital living is very different from a system in which one man is married to several wives (polygyny) or the much rarer system in which one woman is married to two or more husbands (polyandry), since life with a single spouse is much more intense. In point of fact, in most polygamous systems the ordinary person is usually married to only one spouse; even when marriage to two or more wives is approved, only the powerful and well-to-do have the resources to achieve that blissful state. It should also be kept in mind that in such great civilizations as India, China, Japan, and those Western European countries where monogamy has been the legal norm, the aristocratic and the rich have been able to indulge their wish to enjoy mistresses and concubines without fear of punishment. On the other hand, in all these societies the rules against a woman's enjoying the same privilege have always been very strict.

The American family system is also based on the independent family unit, in which a married couple and their children are expected to live physically separated from their kin and from their parents. In most instances, even older parents prefer to live alone if they have the financial means to do so. Here again our system differs from that of many other societies, such as China, Japan, India, and Arabic Islam, in which a couple might continue to reside for years in either a joint household or under some other kind of shared economic arrangement. To be sure, this kind of living arrangement was always more common among the upper classes, who could more easily afford to take care of a young dependent couple. In most societies a young man has not been able to afford a marriage until he achieved economic independence. Formerly this independence came with owning land; now it comes with holding a job. Nevertheless, in most societies the ideal, if not the universal, practice was one large family unit in which several family units were linked closely together.

Because of the American emphasis upon the independence of the family unit, the age at which people marry in the United States has been somewhat higher than in Eastern countries, though lower than in most European countries. The average age of American males at marriage is approximately twenty-two years of age; that of females is approximately twenty. Thus the majority of American women marry when they are still in their late teens. As noted earlier, the average marital age in the United States was higher fifty years ago. At present, most young women work for a while before they marry. Men who marry young typically have jobs that pay low wages, but they are not as economically dependent upon their parents as rural people were a hundred years ago, when owning land was necessary for making a living.

In the last two decades a slightly new pattern has emerged, which might be considered the spread of an *older* upper-class pattern: middle-class youngsters have married increasingly earlier but remained economically dependent on their parents. In practice this has meant that young men and women who are in college are permitted to marry, but still continue to receive all or most of their income from their parents. Socially, this pattern overlaps with a deviant arrangement, in which a young middle-class couple lives together with the tacit approval and financial support of their parents, who may or may not hope that the two will ultimately legitimate their union by formal marriage.

Although the American system is still patronymic, since the name of the family line comes from the male side, it is neither a patrilineal nor matrilineal society but a *bilateral* one in which kinship is equally traced through both male and female parents. All of the major civilizations that we know of have been patrilineal, in that the lineage is traced primarily through the male line. Modern research, however, clearly reveals that in all major civilizations at least the informal links with the female side have often counted very heavily.

Patrilineal societies are also likely to give far more authority to the male and, in some societies, to the eldest living male ancestor. In the American system the husband does indeed have more authority than the wife, especially in major decisions, but not only do many women manage to achieve considerable influence in all family relations, but the modern movement in favor of liberating women continues to press for still greater decision-making power for wives.

This marks a difference from most other major societies in the past, and of course represents a substantial departure from America's own historical pattern. For years in the United States wives were not permitted to make contracts on their own. If they possessed real estate when they entered the marriage, the husband could legally use that real estate in order to earn money of his own. It was extremely difficult for a woman to leave her own home without being charged with "abandoning her domicile." She could not gain custody of her children, since children belonged to the husband's line. She could not sue. Along with these and many other legal disabilities, the near impossibility of earning an adequate salary by herself meant that the wife ultimately had to obey the authority of her husband, if he chose to exercise it.

The American kinship system has also been one of equal inheritance, as contrasted with those traditional social systems in which all of the family estate went to a single male heir (as in upper-class England and Japan) or in which the males shared equally (as in China), or in which the male received a larger share than the female children (as in Arabic Islam). In the United States the allocation of an inheritance is largely a problem of the more affluent social strata, and indeed our social patterns place less and less importance on the notion of "building an estate for the children."

Although equal inheritance is the legal norm, in fact there are many informal rules which alter this arrangement. If the family owns a business it is likely that a son, not a daughter, will enter it. If there are two sons, it is likely that the son who enters the business will inherit it, with some financial provision being made for the other son. Sons are likely to receive loans or gifts of money, while daughters are more likely to be left trust funds which give them much less autonomy in financial matters.

The American kinship system is also characterized by "free courtship," which in the adolescent phase of dating to some degree resembles the Polynesian societies in its emphasis upon romance. Perhaps the only European societies that come close to it are the Scandinavian ones, though parental influence in the ultimate choice of the spouse may be greater in those countries than in America. In practice, as is well known, our system permits rather early dating, great freedom of physical movement, privacy, and almost no chaperonage whatsoever. In America, too, there is no sharp line between dating and courtship; the social assumption is that people who go together are merely dating unless they announce that they are serious about their future plans.

The informal assumption of our courtship system is that people date one another on the basis of personal attraction. Yet many researchers have shown the extent to which people are actually participating in a kind of limited "marriage market," in which one excludes most of the population and accepts only people with characteristics very similar to one's own. The element of choice in dating is wider than in marriage, but most people never date across broad caste, religious, class, or age lines. Both parents and peer groups support these restrictions, by cajoling, threats of social ostracism, refusals of invitations, and financial inducements. Thus, technically, anyone may marry almost anyone else who is not barred by incest rules, but in fact informal family patterns confine most people within a fairly narrow pool of eligible dating or marriage partners who share a similar background. Moreover, when people do cross these lines successfully, for the most part they do so only when they have already lost some of the traits that are associated with their particular caste, ethnic group, or class. Thus, for example, a girl from the lower class who has gone to college may well have lost most of the social traits of her own class, and have acquired those of the middle class. Similarly, those who cross religious lines are likely to be less intense in their devotion to the religion in which they were reared, and to move in social circles where religion is not considered very important.

Most family systems of the great civilizations have (or have had) either a dowry system or a bride-price system, but the American kinship pattern has dropped this sort of marriage gift. In Western countries the dowry has been fairly standard, and in Europe it is not uncommon even today in some upper-middle-class circles. When it was in full operation, a family with many daughters might be unable to marry all of them off to husbands of the appropriate class, because such husbands would expect an adequate amount of money, and there might not be enough to divide among all the daughters. A family with sons was of course in a more fortunate position. Under some dowry systems, the money actually went to the elders or to the family estate rather than to the husband himself.

Note, however, that both the dowry and the bride-price system ultimately depend upon a high degree of stability in the marriage itself. When elders have no assurance that the marriage they are helping to arrange and pay for will continue for any length of time, they are less likely to be willing to make substantial cash investments in it. In any event, over the past century such arrangements have come to be viewed as degrading, for they suggest that the woman is worthless in herself and is valuable only for the money she brings in.

It could be argued that in fact the American family system does operate under a dowry arrangement, though it is not a legal requirement and is never spoken of as a dowry. It is, however, clear that not only are there strong pressures on the part of both parents to contribute as much money and goods to the young couple as possible, but the bride's family is clearly expected to contribute far more than the groom's. Supposedly, the side with the most money contributes most, but this rule is tempered by the social pressure on the bride's parents to contribute more. Not only are they expected to pay for the wedding and reception, which may be elaborate and expensive, but they are expected in addition to come up with other sums and gifts beyond those expected of the groom's parents.

As with the traditional Japanese and Arabic Islamic family, the American system exhibits a high rate of instability. For technical reasons it is difficult to calculate the rate of this instability with any exactitude. Nevertheless, various estimates suggest that approximately one-fourth of all American marriages end in divorce. The divorce figure is certainly lower in rural areas than in urban areas, lower among Catholics than among Protestants, lower among whites than among blacks.

America's high marital instability has in turn meant a high "turnover"—that is, most of those who become divorced or who lose their spouses through death are likely to remarry. As a consequence, the dating and courtship system is not confined to the young, as it traditionally was in European and earlier American society. Other industrial nations are experiencing rapid increases in their divorce rate, but theirs are not as high as that of the United States. Over the past fifty years the social disapproval of divorce in America has dropped substantially, men can obtain most of the services their wives provide by simply buying them (laundry, housekeeping, and so forth), and wives in turn can support themselves by getting jobs on their own. In very few circles these days would a man or woman be ostracized for seeking a divorce.

Crucial to any account of marriage in contemporary America is the great emphasis that Americans place upon individual happiness. Since the supposed purpose of marriage is "happiness through love," and since any relationship of this kind is not likely to continue to yield the same intense feeling year after year, far more is expected of marriage than it can possibly produce. In fact, most American marriages carry too heavy an emotional burden. In this context, divorce serves as an escape valve for all the tensions of a highly intimate, emotionally overloaded relationship from which far too much has been expected.

Another difference between the American kinship system and that of most great civilizations of the past has to do with the position our system accords the elderly. In traditional societies the eldest male has been viewed as head of the family, a figure endowed with great authority and paid enormous deference. In some societies he was thought to be in touch with the spirits of the dead, to control magic, and to be the possessor of considerable wisdom. In the older societies, where most technical procedures and problems might be relatively simple and similar from one decade to another, very likely the older men did in fact have much useful knowledge.

While American society does not withdraw respect from older people, as is obvious to anyone who looks at the age distributions of powerful or esteemed politicians, judges, or corporate executives, nevertheless age itself commands little deference. In the American kinship system the position of the elderly is ambiguous. Few obligations or responsibilities are prescribed by age. The grandfather of sixty may, if he wishes, move to another state, take up water skiing, go to nightclubs, adopt the newest fashions, or even decide to start a new career without much social disapproval. He may also, if he wishes, play a much more traditionally grandfatherly role, again without much criticism. This arrangement has advantages as well as disadvantages. The older kinsman has in effect earned very little credit. Certainly he cannot rest upon his laurels. If he wishes to keep his kin network alive and active, he will have to take the initiative and continue to contribute to the ongoing flow of affection, services, and funds that characterize family life. He cannot expect his kinsmen to flock around him, as they might once have done to a revered elder. On the other hand, the older kinsman now can shake off some of his traditional responsibilities if he does not wish to maintain them, and can start an almost entirely new life without expecting more than mild joshing or a comment or two about "acting his age."

Mating, Dating, and Courtship

Moving from this broad perspective to a closer view of the American courtship system, its dynamics become clearer. All courtship systems are "marriage markets," but the American version differs from others in the extent to which each individual tries to sell his own wares and carry out his or her own negotiations. In many traditional societies, by contrast, elder kinsmen made these arrangements for younger people.

In America everyone is permitted to marry as early or as late as he chooses. If he chooses early, his marriage may well fall short of his ideal expectations. This would be especially likely if he is upwardly mobile, for a marriage with someone of his own class origin might prove embarrassing once he had moved up into a higher class. If a man marries late, the marriage market will have been severely narrowed, and his ideal spouse may have already married. If a man desires to marry a pretty, rich, talented woman, he is certainly permitted to make the attempt; but if he has no equivalent gifts to offer, he is likely to be rejected. In order to avoid that risk, he may instead court a young woman whose qualities are worth much less in the market than his own. Although kinsmen and friends will usually offer some advice about his choice, there are no official "go-betweens," or matchmakers, whose responsibility is to investigate the prospective bride or groom so as to prevent foolish errors of judgment.

Several processes in the American "free-courtship" system can be distinguished. One is the ordinary market process of supply and demand. Some people ask for more than they can get on the market, and others ask less, but in general brides and grooms are likely to be roughly similar in their traits and assets. A girl who is physically attractive can marry a young man who is less handsome but upwardly mobile. A young man in a higher social class is most likely to marry a woman from his own class, but he may go outside his class to choose someone who has money or beauty. An older man is most likely to marry a woman younger than himself (but still in an older age bracket); but if he is rich or influential, he has a good chance of marrying a much younger woman who is very attractive. In general, marital choices are homogamous: like marry like, and discrepancies are likely to be balanced off.

However, underlying all marital choices is a set of preferences, or values, which tend toward homogamy. Everyone is socialized to value certain traits, and thus a man (and his kinsmen and friends who influence his choices) sees others as more or less attractive to the extent to which they possess these traits. The talented young assistant professor of economics may seem very attractive to his female students, but he may appear pretentious, unmanly, and boring to a lower-class woman. People who have been reared mainly within one ethnic or religious group are not only less likely to meet and date outsiders; they are also less likely to enjoy being in an intimate situation with them. Thus the apparently "free" American system of individual courtship presses toward homogamy.

None of this is meant to deny the importance of love. Indeed, until recently, when their own courtship systems became closer to our own, European social commentators often ridiculed Americans for allowing love so large a role in marital choice. The theme of love has for decades pervaded American movies, popular music, literature, and advertising, and is one of the commonest topics of gossip. Perhaps no other major nation ever gave so prominent a position to love; specifically, only Americans have assumed it to be necessary (if not altogether sufficient) for marriage.

By contrast, in some societies love is viewed as a threat to the orderly processes of mate choice, since the choice of a mate is carried out by elder kinsmen, and so strong an attraction between a young man and woman might well thwart those negotiations. In these societies love is rather to be isolated or curbed, either by marrying young people off very early or by controlling access to jobs or land so as to prevent free choice. In still other societies love is not viewed as an aberration or a threat; instead, it is thought acceptable as long as it does not interfere unduly with the marriage arrangements made by kinsmen. This can usually be accomplished by seeing to it that only young men and women who belong to the appropriate class or kinship line have any opportunity of meeting, and hence of falling in love with one another. Our own society, of choice, permits love a very large role in marital choice, though the extent to which the likelihood of falling in love is constricted by social and economic factors is great.

Some social analysts have argued that love motivates young people, who after all do not know each other very well, to adjust to one another's foibles and idiosyncracies in the early stages of marriage. It also motivates them to leave their parents and establish their own home. This is especially important in that in our system few people have much stake in maintaining the marriage—at least as compared with people living in those systems in which a large kin network may actually have an economic investment in the marriage. Many couples are disappointed when the high excitement of courtship diminishes, leaving them with a drab and rather humdrum existence. Marital counselors and others point out that if the relationship between men and women is pervaded by love before marriage, it is difficult to tell married people afterwards that it is of secondary importance. In any event love will continue to be of central significance to the American marriage far into the future.

Husbands and Wives

A famous actress once protested that what's wrong with getting married is that after the honeymoon husbands always want to go home with their wives. This objection to the day-to-day boredom of marital adjustment is found in many barbed comments from social philosophers, whether professors or cab drivers. On the other hand, every study of marital adjustment reveals that a large majority of husbands and wives claim that they are either "happy" or "very happy" in their marriages. Since the American marriage system encourages maximum closeness between husbands and wives, the opportunities for disagreement are also maximized. How then do they adjust to one another's different behavior in the various areas of married life, such as the division of labor, power and authority, sex, attitudes toward work, and children?

In the traditional Hindu marriage—to look once again at other cultures—a young girl is married in her early teens to an older man and goes to live with her husband's family before the union is finally consummated. Thus she has few resources with which to resist their authority, and is either forced or persuaded to learn the ways to please her husband and his kin. Relieving these pressures somewhat was the custom of fairly long visits to her own relatives, who assured her that her duty was to adjust. In the old Chinese kinship system, the young woman also lost the potential support of her own kin since she moved to the village or area where her husband's family lived, and like the Hindu girl, she was given no options: divorce was nearly impossible, and she found herself surrounded by older and more powerful people who in any dispute were likely to side with her husband. In addition, both systems prescribed certain tasks that were appropriate to males and females. The young husband had his own duties, and these were clearly separate from those of his wife. If each carried out his or her own traditional duties, then there could be little conflict. The amount of daily contact between the young husband and wife was reduced to a minimum. The young wife cooperated with her female relatives and the young husband carried out male tasks with his male relatives. In these ways the importance of the husband-wife bond was reduced.

In most such traditional kinship systems, again in contrast to our own, the notion of "love and happiness" was simply not the aim of married life at all. The officially supported aims of marriage were continuing the family line, honoring ancestors, contributing to the economic well-being of the larger kin unit, or living a harmonious life according to established religious precepts. By setting a much lower standard of emotional attachment between husband and wife, and by emphasizing specific duties and tasks, such systems made it possible for most people to reconcile themselves to the humdrum qualities of daily married life.

The advantage of such a system is that it prescribes actions, rather than a loving emotion. We can *will* conformity to the former, but not the latter. It is also easier to fulfill marital obligations if both husband and wife agree on what those obligations are, but the American system is probably less clear than almost any other in its specification of what each partner in a marriage is supposed to do. There is thus a wider area of action in which conflict is at least potential: each couple must work out for themselves just who is responsible for what. There are husbands who refuse to help at any household task and others who are willing to share in all of these tasks, from cooking to redecorating the home.

It may be objected that the two great areas of "earning a living" and "taking care of the children" are clear role obligations that are divided by sex. Indeed, it is true that it would be difficult to find many homes in which the wife goes out to earn a living, while the husband stays at home to care for the house and children. Yet if a group of men and women were asked individually to write down a fairly complete list of all the tasks in a marriage, designating which ought to be carried out by the husband and which by the wife, it would soon become apparent that even in a fairly homogeneous group, disagreement is likely to be very large and full of tension. Even in a household where both husband and wife know what in general the other expects, both may also harbor considerable resentments about the way these jobs are allocated.

Husbands and wives, of course, begin the adjustment of such differences as early as their first date together and may continue the process throughout their marriage. From their very first meetings, young men and women inform each other by subtle or not so subtle cues or even full-blown philosophical discussions of how they feel about what husbands and wives ought to do, in areas ranging from sexual relations to how many children a couple should have. Although each may be trying to impress the other, or to present his or her best self, the other is generally able to penetrate these disguises to a considerable extent—certainly to the point where it can be ascertained whether the other's views are traditional or radical, egalitarian or patriarchal, flexible or rigid. By the time they have actually begun their married life together, most of the larger issues have at least been confronted in one way or another, if not actually settled.

No matter how intimate their exploration of each other was before marriage, most couples experience the first year of marriage as a set of discoveries. Some of these are delightful, while others create chagrin and dismay. Like all great alterations in status, the change from single to married life holds surprises that few can anticipate. Some men can be effective and masterful in the dating situation, but once married expect to be fully taken care of by their wives. Some young women seem soft and yielding before their marriages, but these traits often turn out to conceal ruthless ambition and a deep need to dominate. On the other hand, some husbands and wives, once the anxieties and tensions of courtship and early marriage are over, enjoy the relaxation of building a home together and the security of an emotional solidarity in which each takes real pleasure in pleasing the other.

Most couples at least strive to make a go of marriage, and most do stay married until the union is broken by death. If few attain the ecstatic bliss portrayed in TV commercials and popular romances, most do manage to work out a tolerable situation. Husbands and wives learn what will anger or soothe the other, what the other can or will not do, and adjusts his or her actions to these realities of the relationship in so far as possible.

The general form of that adjustment is determined by the values brought to bear by the larger society. We are socialized to believe in monogamy and to avoid divorce if possible; we live as couples in independent households; we have two or three children; we give more authority in large decisions to the husband and expect him to earn most or all of the family income; we expect the wife to manage the household and the children; and so on.

Within each class, ethnic group, neighborhood, or social circle still other values and expectations create pressures toward more specific adjustmental patterns: wives with younger children should not hold full-time jobs unless the economic need is great; young parents should keep in close contact with their parents if possible; to maintain their social standing, husbands and wives should encourage and press their children to go to church or synagogue; it may be permissible for the husband to neglect his wife because he works late hours; and so on. Needless to say, in many circles one or more of these items would be rejected.

Husbands and wives also work out still more detailed adjustments of their own, from the choice of friendship and kinship visits, to sexual and other expectations. Moreover, they may (in private or public) simply ignore some of the directives of the larger society. Couples may agree on these personal adjustments from the beginning, or grow into them gradually, but most are the slow result of many trials, tentative probings, disagreements, errors, and successes.

If two people are to adjust, both must yield somewhat, but it is obvious that who yields in which areas is determined by who has the most resources and who has the greatest will to win. The husband or wife who has a lesser stake in the union will care less whether his or her spouse is displeased, and thus have a greater chance of imposing his or her will. The wife whose husband loves her more than she loves him is more likely to have her whims obeyed. Husbands who enjoy fighting will win more often, at least as long as the marriage lasts. Wives with an independent income are in a better position to act autonomously and to gain their ends. It is not surprising, then, to learn that wives make more adjustments in marriage than do husbands, since their resources are less. Lower-class wives enjoy more influence than do wives closer to the upper social strata, since the discrepancy between their earnings and those of their husbands is less. Women who work full time enjoy a stronger voice in family decisions than those who do not. Husbands who are better educated than their wives have more influence than those with less education.

Such factors continue to affect husband-wife relations throughout the life cycle of the family, and vary according to the area of family life. Other things being equal, wives are listened to more in the realms of children's religious education than in choosing family friends; decisions about small purchases than large ones; about where to spend vacations than whether to move elsewhere for a better job opportunity.

Social change has also transformed the areas in which personal adjustments between spouses can or must be made. The American economic and legal systems have given new options to wives, for example: independent ownership and management of property, custody of the children, graduate education, higher-level occupations, and so forth, thus creating new areas for adjustments as well as potential conflicts. A century ago, husbands and wives had almost no chance of getting a divorce, and thus felt a greater need to make a go of the only marriage they were ever likely to have. New choices expand opportunities for both spouses, but also create new problems of getting along together.

An example is the area of sexual relations. Until well after World War I, it is likely that, although sex relations were not satisfying to a high percentage of husbands and wives, the problem of adjustment was minimal. More husbands than wives felt that sexual intercourse was too rare. For a high percentage of wives—the figure varies from one sample to another—possibly as much as one half, the pleasure of orgasm was not a typical experience. As a holdover from the Victorian period, husbands were not greatly concerned with their wives' enjoyment, and many would still have argued at that time that a real lady should tolerate sex but not exult in it. Husbands were not, however, so likely as wives to be satisfied with a marriage in which the degree of sexual pleasure was low, since women expected less of sex, and other areas of family life counted for more in their eyes. In any case, neither husbands nor wives typically felt sex a problem they had to solve. More accurately it might rather be called a burden which many had to live with. Some wives or husbands went to physicians, and others hoped that time and patience might remedy matters, but in general husbands and wives felt that little could be done about sexual difficulties.

Now this situation has changed radically. The pill and other effective contraceptives have largely removed the fear of pregnancy that so often tainted sexual relations in the past. Hundreds of books explain to anyone who can read how to improve their sexual technique. Much of this information trickles from the upper middle class down, and it is explained and disseminated by the mass media, including films. Of their sex lives, wives and husbands are told frequently that they can and should "do something about it." Young people experiment with sex in order to gain pleasure and sexual competence before settling down to married life. It is safe to say that at the present time a far higher percentage of husbands and wives actually derive more pleasure from sex than ever before; yet a far higher percentage of married people also feel frustrated by the need to solve sexual problems that in marriages of fifty years ago would have demanded no special effort because they were not thought capable of solution. Beyond question, far more husbands and wives now expect more pleasure from sex, and may well be disappointed when, as so frequently happens, sex turns out to be no substitute for the need for adjustment in other areas of family living.

CHAPTER 2

Historical Background and Cultural Sources of the American family

To understand the American family, it is necessary to know something of its history and development. Since the history of family development and organization is a big and complex topic, too much so to be treated adequately here, our treatment will have to be limited and selective.[1] While the big majority of American families derive from Western nations and traditions, many American families stem from other historical and cultural traditions such as those of China and Japan. And then there are the varied family patterns of the native American Indian peoples, bearers of the original American culture.

Historical-Cultural Sources and Origins of Family Variations in America

OLD WORLD SOURCES AND ORIGINS

Here we will outline some of the highlights in the history of the Western family. We will go back to the ancient Hebrew, Greek, and Roman civilizations, and move next to the medieval and contemporary periods of Western civilization.

Swedish immigrant family, 1890. (*Fred J. Pearson.*)

The ancient Hebrew family system is probably the earliest direct antecedent to our own family system about which we have much reliable knowledge.[2] The ancient Hebrew family system was an extended type, with strong kinship ties on the male side. The family was strongly patriarchal, with the authority of the father being almost absolute. The biblical story of Abraham's near sacrifice of his son Isaac would indicate that the father literally held the power of life and death. The Hebrew father's power was based on religious beliefs and traditions, as indicated in the Old Testament. God had told Eve, after she had eaten the forbidden fruit, that her husband "shall rule over thee" (Genesis: 4:16). Hebrew children were expected to obey and honor their parents, adhering to the norm of filial piety. The family was also patrilineal, patrilocal, and polygynous, all evidence of the male-centeredness of Hebrew society. Marriage was highly valued, and sons greatly desired in order to perpetuate the family line. It was the wife's sacred duty to provide her husband with sons so that his family name "be not put out of Israel." The husband had the power to divorce his wife, but she had no such right throughout most of the history of the Hebrew family. By the Roman period she had achieved the right to divorce her husband for several specific reasons, such as if her husband refused to support her or if he changed his religion. In the earlier periods, the eldest son normally inherited all the family property. Later, all sons got some with the eldest getting a double portion. Only if there were no sons did a daughter inherit property.[3]

The family system of the ancient Greeks was similar to that of the Hebrews in many ways, being strongly patriarchal, patrilineal, patrilocal, and extended. Although officially monogamous, the Greeks supplemented monogamy with well-established concubinage for the upper classes and prostitution in the lower classes. The power of the Greek patriarch stemmed from his status as trustee of the family lands and property and from his role as priest in the Greek religious practice of ancestor worship. Only sons could inherit property, and the eldest son generally inherited all the landed property. Greek wives, especially in Athens, were confined to the home and generally had very low status. To the Greeks, marriage was a sacred obligation, and celibacy was punishable by law. In the earlier periods of Greek history, divorce was very rare. Later, during the periods of urbanization, both the husband and wife had limited rights of divorce.[4]

In the days of the ancient Roman Republic, probably the strongest patriarchal family ever known anywhere was in existence. The Roman paterfamilias had the power of life and death over his wife and his children. Sons remained under the power (*potestas*) of their father as long as he lived, and daughters until their marriage, when this power was transferred to the hands of their husbands. The family was also patrilocal and patrilineal. Marriage was as important to the Romans as it had been to the Hebrews and Greeks before them. The importance of continuing the family line, coupled with ancestor worship, made marriage both a patriotic and a religious duty. In early Rome, upon the death of the Roman pater, each adult son inherited an equal share of the family property. In later periods, the widow and any adult daughters received equal shares along with the sons, but the daughters were not allowed to sell or dispose of their shares. Following the Punic Wars, Roman civilization began to disintegrate, and family solidarity and discipline weakened. *Potestas* declined, while celibacy, childlessness, divorce, and abortion became common.[5]

EARLY CHRISTIAN INFLUENCES   In many respects the views and policies of the early Christians on marriage and family matters developed in reaction to prevailing conditions among the Romans. Divorce, adultery, infanticide, prostitution, and other "vices of the flesh" were common. Christian leaders sought to resurrect the stern morality codes of earlier times. While some of the church fathers held marriage in high esteem, others saw marriage as essentially a sexual union and thus only slightly more desirable than fornication. This view was stated by St. Paul, who, while championing chastity, conceded that "it is better to marry than to burn."[6] Sexual intercourse was considered a necessary evil rather than a source of pleasure—necessary in order to produce Christian children. By the year 402 A.D., priests and nuns were required to remain single. Second marriages for Christians were condemned, and marriages were declared indissoluble by the Council of Carthage in the year 407.

The early Christian attitude toward women was paradoxical. Men and women were viewed as being equal in the sight of God, both possessing divine souls. Virgins, as "brides of Christ," were assigned important roles in the church convents and in the Christian community. However, women were also closely associated with the evils of sex, and were assumed to be tools of the devil acting as tempters of men. Thus, tainted with "the sin of Eve," women suffered a lowered status which persisted in Christendom until very recently.

MIDDLE AGES   The above view persisted well into the early Middle Ages. Marriage was not yet defined as a holy union, but rather as a concession to the weakness of the flesh. The extended family or kinship group predominated, and the nuclear family had very little identity apart from the larger kinship milieu in which the individuals functioned. These extended kin groups were called the "maegth" in England and the "sippe" on the continent.[7]

Certain developments by the late Middle Ages had profound effects later upon the family in colonial America. An awareness of the value of the nuclear family emerged, accompanied by more privacy for individual family members. The family became glorified and marriage was defined now as a sacrament by the church.[8] Sex outside marriage was a sin, but within marriage sex was blessed by the church. With the increased independence of the nuclear family came an increase in domination of the husband over his wife. This tended to reinforce the traditional subordinate position of women. Another development was the emergence of romantic love as something different from ordinary love. Mainly an upper-class phenomenon, romantic love emerged as a technique whereby young people rebelled against family-controlled mate selection, as well as against the strict religious-based norms which limited sex to marriage.[9] While sources on these matters are limited and not too reliable, it seems likely that during the late Middle Ages upper-strata marriages were generally arranged by the families, while lower-strata marriages were more a matter of personal choice.

THE REFORMATION As the state gained ascendancy over the Catholic church in more European countries, the traditional authority of the church over marriage and family was increasingly challenged by civil authorities. The role of Catholic canon law waned, especially in Protestant nations. The late fifteenth-century Reformation movement resulted in the Protestant view that marriage was not a sacrament but was a civil contract which had the blessing of God. This meant that marriage and divorce should be regulated by the state rather than the church. Although the Catholic church strongly opposed these views, the civil authorities gradually assumed legal control of marriage and family matters in many European countries. In England, the Cromwell Act of 1653 made a civil marriage ceremony before a justice of the peace obligatory. A century later, the Hardwicke Act of 1753 required that public banns be posted before a marriage, and that the marriage ceremony be performed by an Anglican clergyman before witnesses. The officiating clergyman acted as an agent of the state, and was required to keep an exact record of each marriage.[10]

COLONIAL AND FRONTIER BACKGROUNDS

COLONIAL FAMILY PATTERNS In the American colonies family life was shaped both by the European cultural traditions and practices brought over by the settlers and by New World conditions and experiences. The settlers generally came in nuclear families and as single persons rather than in extended family groups. Thus, the nuclear family became the principal social unit early in the colonial period. Dependency on the nuclear family increased with the mobility that characterized the settling of the North American continent. As nuclear families and single individuals, mostly men, moved from place to place, kinship ties were inevitably weakened. Individual choice in mate selection gained an early foothold in the colonies, due partly to the preponderance of settlers from the lower classes in Europe and partly to new freedoms and "supply and demand" in the New World. Romantic love became linked to mate selection in the colonies, especially on the frontiers of settlement, where there was a chronic shortage of women. Despite this unbalanced sex ratio, traditional religious prohibitions against plural marriages were apparently effective in preventing the establishment of polyandry as a practice.

One of the best-known features of official colonial morality was its ethic of sexual repression, especially true in Puritan New England. Severe punishments were often imposed for sex offenses. The extent of deviations from the sex codes is a matter of some conjecture among authorities, however. Arthur Calhoun feels that New World conditions were relatively favorable to chastity, citing early marriage, the lack of "mercenary marriage," and democratic freedom of choice. Others, such as Washington Irving, point to the colonial courtship custom of "bundling" as a practice that resulted in premarital sex and pregnancies out of wedlock.[11] Compared to those in New England, sex standards and practices in the Southern colonies were more variable. Laws and their applications were often less strict. However, a double sex standard was obvious, one for women and another for men. Genteel white women were guarded against premarital and extramarital sexual involvement, while white men enjoyed greater sexual freedom both before and after marriage. White men could have black mistresses, but contacts between black men and white women were forbidden.[12]

In its internal organization, the colonial family resembled its European ancestor quite closely. The family was still patriarchal, with the husband-father legally and actually the head of the family. There are indications, however, that the wife often exercised an informal power in numerous subtle ways, a pattern not too unusual where males held the formal power. The woman's roles were mainly domestic, childbearing, and child rearing, as expressed in the old German "three K's" of *Kirche, Kuchen* and *Kinder* (church, kitchen, and children). The child's status in the colonial family has been said to be represented by the "three R's" of "repression, religion, and respect."[13] Children were expected to be submissive, and to do their share of the work in the family economy, on the farm or in the house. They had to work for the father without pay. And if children worked for an outsider, the father was entitled to their earnings.[14] Neither the child nor the wife-mother had any legal status.

Other similarities between the colonial family and its European predecessor may be seen in its relations to the external world. The nuclear family was quite closely tied to the other institutions in the colonies. The economy depended upon family farms; from 70 to 90 percent of the colonial population lived on these farms. The family was active in many other vital functions—religious, recreational, educational, protective, and medical. In a word, the family was functionally central in the colonial society.[15] The value of the family in the colonies may be seen in the concern of the colonists with keeping family units intact. Divorce laws became very strict, with adultery as the most universal ground for divorce, and the norms and sanctions against desertion were sufficiently strong to keep occurrences to a minimum.

For a more detailed review and analysis of the colonial family, see the article by Seward at the end of this chapter.

FRONTIER INFLUENCES ON THE AMERICAN FAMILY   The development of the American family during the period of the nationalization of the United States was strongly influenced by the conditions of life on the frontier and by pioneering. Calhoun says that the most distinctive factor in American history was "the phenomenon of the westward-moving forefront of settlement."[16] The long persistence of the frontier, as the population moved westward across the North American continent, brought a considerable part of the population under the direct influence of frontier life. Family traditions and customs brought over from Europe were inexorably modified by the rough, open, primitive, and free life on the American frontier.

In many ways pioneer conditions favored early marriage and large families. Calhoun puts it this way:

Inasmuch as the pioneer settler's time was divided mostly between home building and home protection, the psychology of domesticity was supreme; the family was the one substantial social institution in a nation that had discarded hierarchical religion and that had reduced government to a minimum, while business corporations had not yet attained notable development. On the frontier at least this was the case. The field was rather bare for the unmarried man or woman, neither sex could get along comfortably, and women scarcely at all, without a partner.[17]

Nebraska pioneer homestead, 1905. (*Fred J. Pearson.*)

The pressure to marry was strong, and there was little to discourage early marriage as long as abundant and cheap land was to be had, together with equipment and skills for farming or a trade. Kentucky records as early as 1776 show first marriages as young as ages fifteen or sixteen. Large families were desirable because of the free labor of the children and because strong sons helped protect the family from the Indians. Families of twelve or more were frequently mentioned in early records. Adam Smith's reference to early American fecundity is worth quoting:

Those who live to old age, it is said, frequently see . . . there from fifty to a hundred . . . descendants from their own body. Labor is there so well rewarded that a numerous family of children, instead of being a burden, is a source of opulence and prosperity to the parents. The labor of each child before it can leave their house, is computed to be worth a hundred pounds clear gain to them. A young widow with four or five young children, who, among the middling or inferior ranks of people in Europe would have so little chance for a second husband, is there frequently counted as a sort of fortune. The value of children is the greatest of all encouragement to marry.[18]

Abundant land and economic opportunities tended to promote social democracy and impede social-class crystallization on the frontier. Past social gradations diminished in importance, and class considerations in mate selection and marriage were reduced to a minimum. Frontier life promoted individualism, democracy, self-reliance, and ingenuity as traits of the American character, all of which, if not born on the American frontier, were amply nurtured there.[19] Alexis de Tocqueville observed that democratic equality on the frontier tended to obliterate social barriers between young people, thus opening the way to marriage between almost any man and woman.[20] Tocqueville also observed the development of a "clan spirit" on the frontier. Isolation and independence tended to hold the expanding frontier family together. This "kin consciousness" was possible even along with the disposition of the children to leave the parental home early to set up their own homes.[21] It is logical that such familistic ties and loyalties would be strong where survival depended upon mutual cooperation.

Since frontier conditions required family integration, the family tended to remain at least semipatriarchal. At the same time, the value of the labor of the wife and children enhanced their statuses considerably. The seeds of equality between the sexes were being planted on the frontier while women intellectuals back East were beginning to push for equality as a matter of principle.[22] The increasing democratization of the family on the frontier also helped change the patterns of property inheritance. The traditionally favored inheritance privilege for the oldest son, or for sons only, was not compatible with the democratic ideology found on the frontier. The norm developed that all children, girls included, should share equally in the family inheritance.

In adjusting to frontier conditions, the family demonstrated its adaptive qualities. The scope of family functions was broadened, and family solidarity generally strengthened. Family organization, however, became more flexible, with more rights for women and children. An approximation of equality between the wife and the husband developed in many families.

RACIAL, ETHNIC, AND RELIGIOUS BACKGROUNDS AND ORIGINS

The vast majority of American families, past and present, stem from people who migrated to America from Europe, Africa, Asia, and North, Central, and South American nations. The magnitude of these migrations is staggering, with more than 45 million people arriving between 1820 and 1970. Here we will outline briefly the principal racial, ethnic, or national sources of American families, leaving a more systematic presentation for Chapter 4.

AMERICAN INDIANS   It is estimated that in 1492 there were between 700,000 and 1 million Indians in the area that constitutes the forty-eight contiguous states.[23] They included hundreds of different tribes with their separate cultures. Thus, among the historical groups and among contemporary Indian groups may be found many family variations, ranging from the matrilocal and matrilineal Pueblo family type to the patrilineal Algonkians and the patriarchal Papagos of the Southwest.

AFRICANS   The first Africans arrived in 1619 at Jamestown, Virginia, consisting of twenty people with the status of "indentured" servants. With the growth of slavery, many thousands of Negroes were brought to the colonies. By 1790, when the first census was taken in the new United States of America, Negroes were counted at 757,208, constituting about 19.3 percent of the total population, more than 90 percent of them located in the South. By 1860 the number had grown to 4,441,830, or 12.7 percent of the population.[24] In 1808 the United States outlawed slave trade, but some trade continued illegally. However, the chief source of black population growth since 1790 has been natural increase. In 1970 there were 22,673,000 black Americans, making up 11.2 percent of the population. African-Americans came from many different tribal and national stocks. Such diversity in cultural background would normally be expected to result in the transferring of diverse traditional family patterns to America. However, due to the unusual nature of their migration to America, involving forceable capture, separation from family and friends, and being sold into servitude, it became very difficult if not impossible to perpetuate traditional family patterns. The processes and conditions responsible for shaping black family-life variations will be reviewed more thoroughly in Chapter 3.

ASIANS   Census figures show that from 1820 to 1970 there were 1,308,953 Asians, mostly men, who entered the United States, accounting for 2.9 percent of the total immigration during that period.[25] (It should be noted that there was very little immigration between 1783 and 1820; the latter is the year the United States government began to keep official immigration records.) More than 500,000 people came from China; about 365,000 came from Japan, with the remainder from the Philippines, India, Korea, and Southeast Asian countries. Asiatic peoples have generally brought strong family traditions with them. Thus we find Chinese- and Japanese-Americans clinging tenaciously to the family ways of their ancestors after many generations of residence in the United States. Some changes, however, are under way in many of these Oriental-American families, especially since World War II.

EUROPEANS   Between 1820 and 1970 there were 35,914,584 Europeans who came to America, constituting 79.5 percent of the total immigration for this period.[26] Mate immigrants outnumbered females in every nationality, and all immigrant groups contained a disproportionate number of adults. Obviously, the overwhelming majority of American families have a European origin. During the colonial period, most settlers came from the British Isles, France, Spain, and other western European countries. Until the early 1880s, most of the American immigrants still came from western and northern Europe, with English, Irish, German, and Scandinavian peoples predominating. From about 1883 up to World War I the constituency changed. Northern and western European immigrants began to be outnumbered by people from south, central, and eastern Europe, generally referred to as the "New Immigrants." Among them were Italians, Poles, Greeks, Portuguese, Russians, and an assortment of other Slavic peoples. The cultures of these newcomers tended to differ from the majority American culture more significantly than had the cultures of the "Old Immigrants." Whereas the Old Immigrants had been largely Protestant (except for Irish Catholics and some German Catholics), the New Immigrants were overwhelmingly Catholic, Jewish, or Greek Orthodox. The significance of these and other cultural disparities for the adjustment and assimilation of New Immigrant families in the United States will be pursued more fully in Chapter 3.

OTHER AMERICANS   South and Central America, along with Canada, sent 7,469,589 people to the United States between 1820 and 1970, or about 16.5 percent of the total immigration for the 150-year period. Canada led with 3,968,708, followed by Mexico with 1,592,592. Immigration from Mexico has been especially heavy since 1951. Census figures show 753,748 legal immigrants from 1951 to 1970.[27] Mexican-American family patterns will be discussed in Chapter 7.

The richness and variety of family life in nineteenth- and twentieth-century

Three immigrant boys, 1870.
(*Fred J. Pearson.*)

America owe much to these varied racial, ethnic, and national origins of American people. We became a truly heterogeneous nation with heterogeneous family patterns.

SOCIAL-CLASS BACKGROUND OF AMERICAN FAMILIES

Most Americans are somewhat aware of social stratification and the existence of social classes in America. Most are conscious of the fact that even though we proclaim the ideal of social equality, our society is and probably always has been stratified, with categories of people who are ranked differently, some high, some middling, and some low in prestige, power, and material wealth. Certain aristocratic traditions were transferred from the Old World, such as the agrarian tradition of landed gentry which persisted in the Southern colonies.

Such Old World–based class distinctions persisted very strongly in the

South preceding the Civil War, and afterward in modified forms. Families possessing large tracts of land and cultivating large plantations were the recognized aristocrats of the Old South. A visit today to any of these antebellum plantation homes will impress one with the gracious and lavish life-styles of these agrarian aristocrats.

With the onset of industrialism, a broadening middle class developed. Industrial class structures tended to be more open than earlier agrarian or feudal structures. This open class ideology was especially marked in new societies such as those of America and Australia which had no tradition of entrenched aristocracy or peasantry. However, certain elements of European class distinctions were evident in the colonies. In puritan Massachusetts there were reported to be three classes within the church, and people not in the church ranked below the church members. At the time of the American Revolution, when the new United States Constitution was being drawn up at Philadelphia, propertied leaders such as Alexander Hamilton and John Adams were arguing for government by "the wise, the good, and the rich," to preserve order and to protect the interests of such "natural aristocracies." On the other hand, there is little doubt that the American Revolution had democratizing effects, and that throughout its brief history the United States has had a relatively open class system in which, although distinctions of status and rank are real, individuals and families still may move upward from the class of their origin via effort and good fortune.

Social stratification is important for marriage and family. The family is the basic unit of the class or caste system. The family gives the newborn child an initial class placement, and socializes the child into the culture of that class. Any change in the class position made by the family while the child is young results in a change for the child. Later in life, a person may make a change in position through achievement, which could result in a breaking of ties with the parental family.

Studies of social class in America have found from three to as many as six social classes in communities throughout the nation.[28] These classes are differentiated in terms of criteria such as occupation, sources of income, property, education, lineage, and community participation. Most frequently, three basic divisions are made into upper, middle, and working or lower classes. As will be seen more fully in Chapter 5, there are many significant variations as well as similarities between families in these social classes.

RURAL AND URBAN FAMILY BACKGROUND

American society has been predominantly rural throughout most of its history, actually until World War I. Thus, in order to understand family variations in America, it is necessary to look at the long rural background and development of the family. It was within this rural context, spanning about 300 years, that so many of the family values, norms, and traditions developed which have persisted in varying degrees on into mid-twentieth century.

By 1970 only about 25 percent of American families lived in rural areas, and less than 5 percent on farms.[29] A comparison of rural and urban social and economic environments today shows the pervasive influences of urbanism on family life in rural America. The greatest internal migrations in twentieth century America have been the movement of rural families to American cities, which often produce undreamed-of hardship. Ex-farmers and other workers from the country may not have the skills necessary to compete for jobs in industry. Rural families often find the conditions of family life difficult in crowded urban residential areas as compared with farm or country life. This subject will be explored more fully in Chapter 4.

Historical-Cultural Sources of Family Change in America

FAMILY CHANGE WITHIN THE CONTEXT OF SOCIAL CHANGE

In his well-known book *World Revolution and Family Patterns*, William Goode presents a penetrating analysis of world changes in family patterns, pointing out that:

For the first time in world history a common set of influences—the social forces of industrialization and urbanization—is affecting every known society. Even traditional family systems in such widely separate and diverse societies as Papua, Manus, China, and Yugoslavia are reported to be changing as a result of these forces, although at different rates of speed. The alteration seems to be in the direction of some type of *conjugal* family pattern—that is, toward fewer kinship ties with distant relatives and a greater emphasis on the "nuclear" family unit of couples and children.[30]

As a preface to his analysis of family changes in various major world cultures today, Goode makes explicit a number of broad relevant theoretical issues:

1 Even if the family systems in diverse areas of the world are moving *toward* similar patterns, they begin from different points, so that the trend in one family trait may differ from one society to another. . . .

2 The elements within a family system may be altering at different speeds. . . .

3 Just how industrialization and urbanization affect the family system, or how the family system facilitates or hinders these processes, is not clear.

4 It is doubtful that the amount of change in family patterns is a simple function of industrialization; more likely, ideological and value changes . . . also have some effect on family action.

5 Some beliefs about how the traditional family system worked may be wrong. . . .

6 Correlatively, it is important to distinguish *ideal* family patterns from *real* family behavior and values. . . .

7   Finally . . . it is necessary to examine carefully whatever (data) can be obtained in order to be sure that they are in fact descriptions of reality and not accidents of poor recording procedures. Especially when inquiring into the past, we must question the validity of the data.[31]

While warning against the tendency to oversimplify the correlation between economic or technological development and the different kinds of family systems, Goode feels it is accurate to state that wherever the economic system expands through industrialization, family patterns do change. "Extended kinship ties weaken, lineage patterns dissolve, and a trend toward some form of conjugal system generally begins to appear—that is the nuclear family becomes a more independent kinship unit."[32]

Next Goode examines the "fit" between the conjugal family and the modern industrial system, with special attention to the United States and Europe.[33] First, industry needs workers who are mobile and free to go where the industries are located, and who are not held locally by extended family bonds or restrictions. Second, the smaller conjugal family helps to open mobility channels by reducing the "closure" of class strata which is generally associated with strong extended family or kinship ties and restrictions. Also, by virtue of its emphasis on the emotional relationship between husband and wife, the conjugal family fits the industrial society better. The conjugal family has the task of "restoring the input-output emotional balance" of workers in the structure. Also, the trend is toward equal inheritance by sons and daughters in this family. Such dispersion of property inheritance fits the fluid class system of industrial society. Finally, the conjugal family allows and actually encourages wider variations and more flexibility in family roles, as compared to traditional societies where family status-roles are more rigidly defined. This enables family members to fit the range of demands found in the industrial system.

Social scientists have long been concerned with the contrasts between modern Western societies and their historic predecessors, as well as with the differences between Western and non-Western societies. The identification of contrasting types of societies helps to accentuate such differences, e.g., industrial-preindustrial, modern-traditional, urban-folk, etc. Although scholars often disagree on how to define the basic differences between modern and preindustrial societies, they generally agree that family life is deeply implicated. Transitions to modern society seem to involve changes in the ways people relate to each other in the family, and the way the family fits into the society and articulates with other social institutions.[34]

The cause-and-effect relationships between industrialism and family change are not simple, as Goode warns us. Moreover, a complex of interrelated developments generally accompanies the processes of industrialization, and these should be viewed as a whole if we are to understand the connection between social change and family change. We must take into account not only the changes in technology and power which led to the factory system of production, but also the growth of cities, the spread of democratic and equalitarian ideologies, and the expansion of education and literacy. Also, we must ask just how and how much family life changes during the transition to modern society. Are there continuities in family life that show underlying stability and permanency? What specific aspects of family life do change—the living arrangements, who lives with whom, the economic functions of the family, the ideas and sentiments people have about sex and marriage? Relationships between industrialization and family change will be pursued further in Chapter 8.

IDEOLOGY AND FAMILY CHANGE   Family change does not result in a simple cause-and-effect way from external changes in technology or the economic system. Rather, it is more accurate to view family change and other economic and social changes as a complex system of interrelated processes. Changes in ideologies are generally an important part of this complex system, affecting social actions and relationships between institutions. As Goode points out, one important source of change is the ideology of "economic progress" and technological development in modern societies.[35] Traditional ways of producing goods and services gave way to rationality and expediency as means of maximizing economic gains.

Scholars often point to individualism and "individualistic rationality" as principal characteristics which differentiate modern societies from traditional societies. In traditional folk or "sacred" societies, a strong nonrationality often prevails. This may mean that a man only works long enough to supply his family's minimal needs, or that people stay together in a large extended family group even though the land and the traditional techniques of farming can no longer support everyone. Beliefs in individualism and rationality help set off chain reactions of psychological effects which further the momentum of social change. Traditional beliefs, norms, and authority patterns are challenged, including those found in the family. As George Murdock points out, those changes that emphasize the individual are related to the development of the nuclear family: "Individualism in its various manifestations, e.g., private property, individual enterprize in the economic sphere, or personal freedom in the choice of marital partners, facilitates the establishment of independent households by married couples."[36]

In discussing ideology and family change, it would be appropriate to consider the development of the "ideology of the conjugal family." Goode found advocates of this ideology appearing before any great changes were observable either in industrial organization or in family areas of life.[37]

The ideology of the conjugal family is a radical one, destructive of the older traditions in almost every society. . . . It asserts the equality of individuals, as against class, caste, and sex barriers. . . . [It] proclaims the right of the individual to choose his or her own spouse, place to live, and even which kin obligations to accept. . . . It asserts the worth of the *individual* as against the inherited elements of wealth or ethnic group. . . . It encourages love. . . . Finally, it asserts that if one's family life is unpleasant, one has the right to change it.[38]

In societies with high literacy, the conjugal family ideology is apt to enter via intellectuals and be spread by the media before the material conditions for its actual existence are present. The ideology functions to prepare people for change and adjustment to new demands in a changing society.

One of the principles of the conjugal family ideology is equalitarianism. The spread of the conjugal family has been accompanied by a trend toward equality between the sexes. The main causes of this trend are probably outside the family, and would appear to be related to political and economic ideological developments. This equalitarian trend in the Western world is very real. Women may hold almost any type of job in business, industry, government, or the professions. They may own property and make legal contracts; they may vote, hold governmental office, and serve on juries. Expansion of women's rights in the community was bound to bring pressure for equal rights within the family. Not that full male-female equality has been attained yet in the modern family, except perhaps in a minority of fully emancipated conjugal families where great effort has been made to match reality to equalitarian ideology. Big differences still exist between social classes and between various racial, ethnic, rural, and urban groups in the degree of equality between the husband and wife. These differences will be discussed more in the appropriate chapters to follow.

THE PSYCHOLOGICAL-EMOTIONAL QUALITY OF THE MODERN FAMILY

Arlene Skolnick poses the question: What is it that sets the modern family off from its historical counterparts?[39] Since most family authorities now believe that in colonial America and western Europe of the same period the nuclear family was the predominant type rather than the large extended family, is there any basis to assume that family life today is essentially different from that of the past? Skolnick feels that the answer should be yes.

Modern family life is different, but the size of the household is not what has changed. What seems to have changed is the psychological quality of the intimate environment of family life, and the relation between family and the larger community. Within the home the family has become more intense emotionally, while the ties between home and the outside community have become more tenuous.[40]

The historian John Demos feels that the family today has become more important psychologically to its members partly because it has become more isolated from the larger community.[41] Again, this change needs to be seen in the context of profound changes in the community. Industrialization and the factory system disrupted the "familial texture" of the community—with the removal of economic productive functions from the family to the factory. The world outside the home was transformed from a small, primary "Gemeinschaft" community to an expanding, secondary "Gesellschaft" society made up of large-scale impersonal associations. The gulf between home and community developed, and each came to be perceived as a separate aspect of life. Home and family thus came to represent a kind of idealized retreat from the harsh realities and impersonal relations of the outside world, a place of love, companionship, and emotional solace.

Conceptual Frameworks for Understanding Family Variations and Change

THE IDEAL-TYPE METHOD

Sociological analysis frequently makes use of a particular method of conceptualization that is known as an *ideal type* or sometimes a *constructed type*. Among those who developed these conceptualizations as tools of analysis were the German sociologist Max Weber and the American sociologist Howard Becker.[42] In order to make sense out of the complexity of family phenomena it becomes necessary to select certain elements and processes for study and to ignore the mass of details. This requires conceptualization of the selected elements and processes by the social scientist. Ideal or constructed types are created for this very purpose by conceptualizing the relevant properties into a coherent model.

Weber defines the ideal type as "the construction of certain elements of reality into a logically precise conception."[43] It is derived from both observation and intuition, whereby several important variables have been combined to form a theoretical construction which has a structural harmony.

The ideal-type method is especially suited for both the comparison of family variations and the analysis of family change. Thus, let us examine further the nature of the ideal type as a technique for sociological analysis.

In their well-known book on the family, Ernest W. Burgess and Harvey J. Locke present the ideal-type method in family research.[44] The concept of ideal type may be distinguished by four characteristics:

1 The modifier "ideal" denotes only logical perfection, not evaluation or approval. It does not imply a judgment of what is "good" in a normative sense.
2 An ideal type represents the extremes and not an average. Most of us are familiar with the idea of a continuum, which is a linear scale with each end representing the logical extremes or polar opposites. In psychology the

polar opposite personality types introvert ⟷ extrovert denote logical extremes of certain personality characteristics. In family power structure, patriarchy ⟷ matriarchy would be logical extremes on this one variable (power). In the former, the husband-father would hypothetically have 100 percent of the power, while in the latter, the wife-mother would have 100 percent of the power. Power, as is true of most family phenomena, exists in degrees, and thus is distributed between the father and the mother in varying degrees in actual families. Few such real-life families could ever be found where either the father or the mother possessed 100 percent of the power—which leads us to the next characteristic of the ideal type.

3   The ideal type is a logical construction. It is an abstraction which cannot be found per se in reality. It is constructed by selecting one or more aspects of the phenomena under study (e.g., family power, place of residence, lineage), and carrying these characteristics to their logical extremes in a hypothetical model which has structural harmony (e.g., a patriarchal, patrilocal, patrilineal family type at one end of the continuum and a matriarchal, matrilocal, matrilineal type at the other end). Each type represents a polar opposite of the other, and they exist only as logical constructions.

4   However, the purpose of the ideal type is the measurement and analysis of reality. As a hypothetical model its use is as a reference point against which reality (e.g., real families) may be compared. How do individual cases of families in a given community, for example, approximate or vary from the ideal-type patriarchal family? What would be the distribution of 1,000 randomly selected American families today on the patriarchal ⟷ matriarchal power continuum? The ideal-type method enables us to make meaningful and consistent comparisons of ethnic, racial, class, rural, and urban families in America. And in studying family change from colonial times to the present, we will be using ideal-type constructs of both societies and families as reference points against which to assess change.

IDEAL TYPES OF SOCIETIES   As we examine variety and change in American families it will be helpful to establish and use certain ideal types of the larger society within which families exist and change. Emphasis will be on the logical connections between certain family types and the societal types which constitute the social environments of the families.

THE GEMEINSCHAFT (SACRED) ⟷ GESELLSCHAFT (SECULAR) TYPOLOGY   Certain kinds of social patterns tend to predominate in less developed, nonindustrialized societies, while other patterns have primacy in highly developed, industrial societies. Among the various scholars to observe and explore this theme were Ferdinand Toennies and Howard Becker.[45] Both developed typologies consisting of polar opposite ideal or constructed types of societies. (See Figure 2-1, a schematic outline of these typologies.)

Toennies designated as *Gemeinschaft* that type of society which is "based upon a consensus of wills, . . . rests on harmony, and is developed and enabled by folkways, mores, and religion."[46] He gave the name *Gesellschaft* to a polar-opposite type of society which is "based upon a union of rational wills, . . . rests on convention and agreement, is safeguarded by political legislation, and finds its ideological justification in public opinion."[47] In the Gemeinschaft type of society, human relations are ends in themselves, intimacy and sentiment are expected among members, and values and norms are traditional. On the other hand, the Gesellschaft type of society is characterized by impersonal and affectively neutral relationships, members are not known in their entirety to each other, social relations are used instrumentally as means to other ends, and values and norms are rational rather than traditional.[48]

Becker called his polar opposite types of societies *sacred* and *secular*, corresponding closely to the Gemeinschaft-Gesellschaft typology of Toennies.[49] Becker observed many contrasts quite similar to those of Toennies, but also expanded the contrasts as follows. In a sacred society there is the greatest reluctance to change. The customs and norms, the division of labor, the technology—everything is passed down from earlier generations and is thought to be right and "sacred," and is not to be changed or even questioned. The sacred society is thus characterized by "traditional nonrationality." Not only religious beliefs and practices but also techniques of production and division of labor in the family are adhered to by the present generation because that is the way tradition prescribes. Other ways may be more efficient or practical, but that is not important. The sentimental and reverent attachment to the "old-fashioned ways" is a deeply emotional thing. In the sacred society there are mental and social isolation as well as inaccessibility. The individual is not receptive to new ideas or knowledge, and the community is closed to outsiders whose foreign culture is feared.[50]

By contrast, the secular society is characterized by the greatest readiness to change. New ways of doing things and new experiences are highly valued, while the traditional old-fashioned ways are denigrated. Expedient rationality prevails. Actors are liberated from normative restrictions and may experiment at will at work, at play, at home. The test of a practice is pragmatic—does it work, is it efficient, is it satisfying? In the secular society one finds both mental and social accessibility. The individual welcomes and seeks new ideas and viewpoints. The society is open to outsiders and their culture is welcomed.[51]

Many historically and geographically isolated folk-rural societies have approximated the Gemeinschaft-sacred type. In our present-day American society, communities such as those of the Old Order Amish in Pennsylvania

FIGURE 2-1 IDEAL TYPES OF SOCIETIES AND FAMILIES

GEMEINSCHAFT (SACRED) TYPE ←————→ GESELLSCHAFT (SECULAR) TYPE
SOCIAL SYSTEM: SOCIAL SYSTEM:

A Gemeinschaft-Gesellschaft (sacred-secular) typologies as conceptual frameworks for analysis of variation and change. Types of actions and relationships articulated in the elements, processes, and conditions of social action.*

Particularism ←————————→ Universalism
Affectivity ←————————→ Affective Neutrality
Functional Diffuseness ←————————→ Functional Specificity
Expressive Consummatory ←————→ Instrumental
Ascription (Quality) ←————→ Achievement (Performance)
Traditional ←————————→ Rational
Familistic ←————————→ Contractual
Sacred ←————————→ *Secular*

   1 Greatest reluctance to change   1 Greatest readiness to change
   2 Social and mental inaccessibility   2 Social and mental accessibility

B Family types identified with Gemeinschaft-sacred and Gesellschaft-secular types of social systems.†

Traditional-Patriarchal Family Type ←———→ *Modern-Equalitarian Family Type*
Extended family organization ←———→ Nuclear family organization
(consanguine ties emphasized)   (conjugal ties emphasized)
Familism ←————————→ Individualism
Multifunctional ←————————→ Limited functions
Traditional role and authority ←———→ Flexible roles and equalitarian
patterns (patriarchy)   authority
Strict sex division of labor ←———→ Flexible and experimental sex
    division of labor
Male dominance and masculine ←———→ Equal rights and privileges for
privileges   sexes
Separate and segregated male and ←———→ Husband-wife companionship and
female interests   shared interests
Patrilineal descent ←————————→ Bilateral descent
Primogeniture ←————————→ Equal inheritance
Patrilocal residence ←————————→ Neolocal residence
Large size; fertility emphasized ←———→ Small size; family planning
    emphasized
Subordinate status or rank of women ←→ Equal status or rank of sexes and
and children   ages
Marriages arranged by parents ←———→ Freedom of choice of mate
Age prestige ←————————→ Youth prestige
Marriage a sacred obligation ←———→ Marriage an interpersonal rela-
    tionship of compatibility and
    satisfaction of personal needs
Marriage relatively indissoluble ←———→ Divorce approved if marriage re-
    garded as a failure

*Adapted from Charles P. Loomis, *Social Systems* (Princeton, N.J.: D. Van Nostrand Co., 1960), figure 2, p. 61.
†Developed by Everett D. Dyer.

still closely resemble this type. By contrast, certain segments of modern urban society approximate the Gesellschaft-secular type, such as Hollywood and some of the urban communes today.

Scholars generally agree that the long-range trend of social change in recent centuries has been from the Gemeinschaft-sacred toward the Gesellschaft-secular. This broad trend would encompass industrialism, urbanism, the spread of science, the expansion of literacy, political liberalism, the ideology of individualism, and other changes associated with modernization. The family, as is true of other institutions, has inevitably been caught up in these long-range trends.

IDEAL TYPES OF FAMILIES   We could expect family life to be quite different in a Gemeinschaft-sacred society from that in a Gesellschaft-secular one. Accordingly we have constructed two polar opposite ideal types of families to fit these two contrasting types of societies. (See Figure 2-1 for outline of contrasting characteristics of the family types.)[52]

1   TRADITIONAL-PATRIARCHAL FAMILY TYPE   This family type would logically be found in the Gemeinschaft-sacred type of society. Since consanguine ties are paramount, there is an extended family organization. Nuclear families exist as parts of the larger extended kinship group, familism is strong, and individual family members cooperate for the well-being of the family. There is high family solidarity and cohesion. The family is the basic social institution in the society and is paramount in performing the many functions necessary to the society. Family statuses and roles are ascribed by tradition, with the husband-father having full authority, i.e., patriarchalism. There is a strict division of labor along sex lines, and children are economic assets with important productive roles. There is patrilineal descent, primogeniture, and patrilocal residence. Fertility is highly valued and families are large. Women and children have subordinate rank to men, and age brings increasing prestige. Marriages of children are arranged by parents; marriage is considered a sacred obligation and is virtually indissoluble.

It should be noted that a traditional-matriarchal family type could be similarly constructed, or even a more general traditional-authoritarian family type. The traditional-patriarchal family type was selected here for its historical and culture relevance for the Western world and for its salience for our understanding of variety and change in the American family.

2   MODERN-EQUALITARIAN FAMILY TYPE   In the Gesellschaft-secular type of society we posit a modern-equalitarian type of family having a nuclear family organization with a strong conjugal emphasis. The individual is all important; thus his or her need satisfaction in the family comes first. This family type has very limited functions (i.e., reproduction, socialization,

affection). Family roles are flexible and there is experimentation in the division of labor. The wife shares authority equally with the husband, and there are equal rights and privileges between the sexes. The family is small, since children are economic liabilities, and also they may not fit in with the personal interests of the husband or wife. Family planning is emphasized. There is bilateral descent, equal inheritance by male and female offspring, and neolocal residence. Children are free to choose their marriage partners, and generally have a high degree of freedom and independence. Youth gives prestige, and age brings declining prestige. Marriage is defined as an interpersonal relationship of compatibility and satisfaction of personal needs. Divorce is approved if the marriage is regarded as a failure.

These ideal types of families and societies will serve as valuable reference points throughout the following chapters, as we examine and compare varieties of American families, and as we examine family change from one period to another in American history.

Summary

This chapter examines the two main theses of the book, American family variation and American family change.

Historical and cultural backgrounds and sources of American family variations are reviewed. These include Old World origins and influences, and colonial and frontier New World influences, followed by a brief discussion of the various racial, ethnic, and religious backgrounds and origins of American families.

The ancient Hebrew family was an extended type, strongly patriarchal, patrilineal, patrilocal, and polygynous. Marriage was highly valued, and sons especially desired in order to perpetuate the family line. Children were expected to honor and obey their parents, according to the cultural norm of filial piety.

The ancient Greek family system was also patriarchal, patrilineal, patrilocal, and extended. Only sons were entitled to inherit property. Marriage was a sacred duty, and divorce was rare.

The ancient Roman Republic family was probably the strongest patriarchal family ever known, with sons remaining under their father's power (*potestas*) as long as he lived. Marriage was as important to the Romans as it was to the Hebrews and Greeks, with great stress on the need to continue the family line by having sons.

Early Christian church leaders held mixed views on marriage. Reacting to vices prevailing among the Romans of the time, leaders such as St. Paul championed chastity, and viewed sexual intercourse in marriage as a necessary evil in order to produce Christian children. Women, associated with the evils of sex, suffered a lowered status which continued well into the Middle Ages. However, by this time sex within marriage was blessed by the Catholic church. The Protestant Reformation saw the traditional authority of the church over marriage and family challenged by civil authorities. In Protestant countries marriage was defined as a civil contract.

In the American colonies Old World traditions and family patterns were modified by New World conditions of life. The nuclear family came to predominate, and individual choice in mate selection gained a foothold. However, the colonial family resembled its European progenitor in being quite patriarchal and in being functionally central in colonial society. This was generally true also of the frontier family, in which individual and family survival depended upon family solidarity and cooperation of all family members. Frontier and rural conditions of life were conducive to strong familism.

With the exception of families that are descendants of the native American Indians, American families past and present are descended from people who migrated to America from Europe, Africa, Asia, and North, Central, and South American nations. A brief review of the principal racial, ethnic, or national sources of American families is given, showing that we are truly a heterogeneous nation.

American family variations also reflect social stratification and social-class differences, derived partly from Old World patterns and based partly on socioeconomic differences accompanying American urban-industrial growth. Other family variations reflect the different conditions of life found in rural and urban environments in America.

Family change in America must be seen within its larger social context in order to be understood. Family authorities point out how well the mobile conjugal family fits the modern industrial system, for example. But the nature of the cause-and-effect relationships between industrialism and family change is complex and not fully understood as yet. Family change is also related to changes in ideologies and value systems, such as the contemporary emphasis on the individual and his or her needs as opposed to the interests or needs of the group.

An ideal-type method is presented as a conceptual tool for the study and analysis of family variations and changes in America. Ideal types of societies are illustrated by the Gemeinschaft (sacred) ⟷ Gesellschaft (secular) typology, and ideal types of families by the traditional patriarchal family type and the modern-equalitarian family type.

Notes

1 For good reviews of the history of Western family development, see Gerald Leslie, *The Family in Social Context* (New York: Oxford University Press, 1973), Chaps. 6,7; Clifford Kirkpatrick, *The Family* (New York: Ronald Press Co., 1963), chap. 5; Bert N. Adams, *The American Family* (Chicago: Markham Publishing Co., 1971), chap. 4.

2 Stuart Queen and Robert Habenstein, *The Family in Various Cultures* (Philadelphia: J. B. Lippincott Co., 1967), pp. 143–144.

3 William F. Kenkel, *The Family in Perspective* (Santa Monica, Calif.: Goodyear Publishing Co., 1977), chap. 3; also, Leslie, op. cit., pp. 156–162.

4 Leslie, op. cit., pp. 162–167.

5 Ibid., pp. 167–173.

6 I Corinthians 7:7–9

7 Willystine Goodsell, *A History of Marriage and Family* (New York: Macmillan Co., 1939), pp. 189–210.

8   Kirkpatrick, op. cit., p. 110.
9   Adams, op. cit., p. 38.
10 Kirkpatrick, op. cit., pp. 115–119.
11 Arthur W. Calhoun, *A Social History of the Family*, Vol. II (New York: Barnes and Noble, 1945), p. 149; and Washington Irving, *Diedrich Knickerbocker's History of New York* (New York: G. P. Putnam's Sons, 1880), p. 210.
12 Leslie, op. cit., pp. 208–210.
13 Adams, op. cit., p. 62.
14 Bernard Farber, *Family: Organization and Interaction* (San Francisco: Chandler Publishing Co. 1964), pp. 106–109.
15 Adams, op. cit., p. 63.
16 Calhoun, op. cit., p. 9.
17 Ibid., p. 11.
18 Adam Smith, as quoted in Calhoun, op. cit., pp. 16–17.
19 Frederick Jackson Turner, *The Frontier in American History* (New York: Henry Holt and Co., 1920).
20 Calhoun, op. cit., p. 30.
21 Ibid., p. 145.
22 Ruth S. Cavan, *The American Family* (New York: Thomas Y. Crowell Co., 1953), p. 35.
23 James W. Vander Zanden, *American Minority Relations* (New York: Ronald Press Co., 1966), p. 25.
24 Ibid., p. 26.
25 *The American Almanac* (New York: Grosset & Dunlap, 1972), table 135, p. 92.
26 Ibid. Many people who immigrated to the United States eventually returned to their homelands. Between 1907 and 1930 the ratios of outflow to inflow ranged from 27.7 percent to 32 percent. See Vander Zanden, op. cit., p. 27.
27 Ibid.
28 W. Lloyd Warner, Marcia Meeker, Kenneth Eells, *Social Class in America* (New York: Harper & Brothers, 1960).
29 *American Almanac*, op. cit., table 16, p. 17.
30 William J. Goode, *World Revolution and Family Patterns* (New York: Free Press, 1963), p. 1.
31 Ibid., pp. 1–2.
32 Ibid., p. 6.
33 Ibid., pp. 10–15.
34 See Arlene Skolnick, *The Intimate Environment* (Boston: Little, Brown and Co., 1973), pp. 96–108, for a good discussion of modern society and the modern family.
35 Goode, op. cit., p. 19.
36 George P. Murdock, *Social Structure* (New York: Macmillan Co., 1949), p. 203.
37 Goode, op. cit., pp. 19–20.
38 Ibid.
39 Skolnick, op. cit., p. 105.
40 Ibid., pp. 105–106.
41 John Demos, *A Little Commonwealth* (New York: Oxford University Press, 1970), p. 186.

42 Howard Becker, *Through Values to Social Interpretation* (Durham, N.C.: Duke University Press, 1950), chap. 2; Max Weber, *The Methodology of the Social Sciences*, trans. and ed. by Edward A. Shils and Henry A. Finch (Glencoe, Ill.: Free Press 1949).

43 H. H. Gerth and C. Wright Mills, *Character and Social Structure* (New York: Harcourt, Brace and Co., 1953), p. 59.

44 Ernest W. Burgess and Harvey J. Locke, *The Family* (New York: American Book Co., 1945), pp. 754–756.

45 Ferdinand Toennies, *Community and Society—Gemeinschaft and Gesellschaft*, trans. and intro. by Charles P. Loomis (East Lansing, Mich.: Michigan University Press, 1951); Howard Becker, op. cit., chap. 5.

46 Charles P. Loomis, *Social Systems* (Princeton, N.J.: D. Van Nostrand Co., 1960), p. 59.

47 Ibid.

48 Ibid.

49 Howard Becker and Alvin Boskoff, *Modern Sociological Theory* (New York: Dryden Press, 1957), pp. 133–185).

50 Ibid., pp. 141–165.

51 Ibid., pp. 141–175.

52 Everett D. Dyer, "Family and Kinship Systems," in Charles P. Loomis and Everett D. Dyer, *Social Systems: The Study of Sociology* (Cambridge, Mass.: Schenkman Publishing Co., 1976), pp. 78–79.

SELECTED READING

Calling for more collaboration between historians and sociologists in the study of family life in early American society, Rudy Seward cites the increasing interest in the history of the American family as a good opportunity for such an interdisciplinary effort. Since the colonial family is now receiving a good deal of attention from both historians and sociologists, collaboration should bring more precise knowledge of family life in colonial times.

Drawing from the work of both sociologists and historians, Seward presents and analyzes data which contribute toward a more accurate restoration or reconstruction of family life in colonial America.

THE COLONIAL FAMILY IN AMERICA: TOWARD A SOCIO-HISTORICAL RESTORATION OF ITS STRUCTURE*

Rudy Ray Seward

During the last two decades there have been many advocates for interdisciplinary work between the fields of history and sociology. Despite favorable arguments (listing the advantages of collaboration) and the founding of committees and journals (aimed at aiding or initiating cooperation) a number of writers have noted the aloofness of both fields and the lack of any real commitment to interdisciplinary work. But with an increasing interest in the study of family history over the last decade by both historians and sociologists there does seem to be an opportunity, and to some degree a necessity, for an interdisciplinary effort between these two fields. The focus here is upon one area of family history that has recently received much attention from both fields—the colonial American family. Both disciplines are involved in a restoration of the colonial family which, in the process, is providing the beginnings of an interdisciplinary effort. The presentation of the results produced up to this point and the problems arising in the restoration process are reviewed with the expectation of stimulating further comparable research and collaboration. A growing knowledge and appreciation of the works, concepts, and techniques of both fields should enable meaningful efforts in the future between the two disciplines. The result will be, for this particular area of study, a more precise image and better understanding of the colonial family system. This should eventually lead to a clearer understanding of familial change and societal change, in general.

When exploring past social phenomena of interest, we only too often find an absence of any quantitative information upon which to base analysis that may lead to understanding. Whether we are concerned with family structures, the process of industrialization, or population structure and trends, the "facts" we find are based primarily upon a collection of impressions from various literary sources. These "facts" are supported by "statistical" evidence which is, more often than not, the result of the conjectures (or based upon an observation of a limited number of phenomena) by the authors of these literary sources. When discussing colonial America, for example, one cannot deny the extensive use of the observations and comments of such prominent writers as Franklin, Sewall, Jefferson, and others in forming an image of the various aspects of colonial America.

The focus of this paper will be upon the restoration of the colonial or preindustrial family in America that is presently taking place to portray the colonial family in a more quantitative and precise manner.

Interdisciplinary efforts have been considered as one important means to increase an understanding of past phenomena. Specifically, during the past twenty years there have been many advocates for an interdisciplinary effort between historians and sociologists. It has become very fashionable to propose such a collaboration and outline the resulting advantages. Appeals from sociologists for an interdisciplinary effort have found sounding boards in presentations to learned societies (Erikson, 1968; Baker, 1969; Spreitzer and Riley, 1970), various scholarly journals (Rose, 1956; Thrupp, 1957a; Thrupp, 1957b; Lipset, 1958; Wolff, 1959; Means, 1962), and books of readings dealing with problems of theory, method, and research in the social sciences (Briggs, 1962; Cahnaman and Boskoff, 1964; Lipset and Hofstadter, 1968; Aronson, 1969.)[1] But two recent assessments of these suggestions and actions (Aronson, 1969; Spreitzer and Riley, 1970) conclude that these seeds have borne little fruit. As Aronson (1969:292) observes, "despite the rhetoric of collaboration, both disciplines remain aloof and few sociologists and even fewer historians are really convinced that a relationship between the two will be useful or productive." Yet despite this situation there are some important gains that can and should be made in an interdisciplinary effort between sociology and history.[2]

This paper will look at one area of socio-historical study—the colonial American family—to assess to what extent collaboration does or does not exist. Full collaboration has certainly not been obtained but it appears at least to be initiated and growing. There are not yet any joint efforts, but there is a growing awareness and appreciation of interdisciplinary work.[3]

[1]This is not intended to be an inclusive list of sources and does not include the numerous articles by historians concerning the same subject. For a more inclusive list see Spreitzer and Riley (1970:i–vii).

[2]Smelser (1967:34) cites important advantages for historians who employ some of sociology's theoretical concepts and models; plus, in a later work, Smelser (1968:37) notes important ways that sociologists can gain from the work of historians.

[3]For example, see references to the works of both historians and sociologists in a recent article concerning American family history by Gordon and Bernstein (1970:665–674) and in a recent book concerning English family history by Anderson (1971). Also significant was a meeting held at Cambridge, England, in 1969, organized by the Cambridge Group for the History of Population and Social Structure, which brought together anthropologists, demographers, historians, and sociologists from various countries (including several contributors from the United States) to consider and discuss, comparatively and historically, the structure of the household and the family (Laslett, 1970: 75–87). Finally, there was devotion, recently, of an entire issue to family history by *The Journal of Interdisciplinary History*, II (Autumn, 1971), which included a number of articles related to the study of the American colonial family. Of special interest in this issue is Hareven's (1971:399-414) article in which she assesses the interdisciplinary influences upon the study of family history.

The Study of the American Family

In viewing the colonial family, it is useful to observe briefly and generally the state of American family study. Carl Bridenbaugh (1963:327), in his 1962 presidential address before the American Historical Association, spoke of the need for research in the neglected area of American family history and suggested that priority be assigned to this area. Demos (1968:40) characterizes the area of American family history as an aspect of American history which has been most "badly served by unsystematic, impressionistic methods of handling source materials." Bailyn, in 1966, commenting on the state of most family studies, observed that it was possible "to prove any reasonable theory about the family" (Saveth, 1969:317). Not only historians but sociologists working in the family history area have observed the dismal state of family studies (*cf.* Goode, 1963: 1–23; Lantz *et al.*, 1968:413-426). A prime concern for sociologists lies with documentation of "base lines" for the American family (Lantz *et al.*, 1968:425). In particular, the consensus for many years by most sociologists has been that the processes of industrialization and urbanization have brought important changes in the American family. Because the majority of the data about the early American family are impressionistic, it is impossible to measure what change or changes, if any, have taken place. Documentation of the colonial American family's characteristics would provide "base lines" to measure change. Despite some differences in focus, both disciplines agree concerning a need for detailed and precise information in the family area. An effort is now in process by both disciplines that should aid in the accumulation of this information.

An important element in the recent developments in the study of the American colonial family has been some exciting and important contributions from the field of historical demography. As Greven (1967:438) observes, the "recent discovery of the family as an important subject of historical inquiry must lead, inevitably, to the discovery of the broader field of historical demography."[4] Early American demographic history is just starting to be explored and the techniques of historical demography are proving and should continue to prove to be useful for early American historical studies. In fact, these techniques have played an important role in a number of studies which have presented data which challenge the traditional view of the American colonial family.

Traditional View of the Colonial Family

The traditional view of the colonial family is being challenged by historians and sociologists. Their challenges are aiding in the restoration of the colonial

---

[4]A full account of historical demography's development and techniques is beyond the scope of this paper, but may be obtained from Glass (1965), Wrigley (1966), Henry (1968), and Hollingsworth (1969).

family, resulting in a new image of the family which contrasts sharply with what Goode (1963:6–7) terms "the classical family of Western nostalgia." The evidence for a majority of the aspects presented by the nostalgic traditional view is derived largely from "verbal data" such as diaries, sermons, novels, and other literary sources. In 1919 Arthur W. Calhoun published a social history of the American family which primarily used these literary sources, particularly those written by leading contemporaries for the colonial period. His work, for many years, has been considered the most comprehensive description of the colonial family (*cf.* Edwards, 1969:12). The characteristics of the colonial family as described by Calhoun that have been the focus of recent studies are as follows:

1 The colonial family was viewed as being "extended" rather than "nuclear" the implication being that a number of generations of kin, a number of siblings and their spouses were all a part of the family unit.
2 The number of children per family was large, and when combined with the "extended" nature of the family, the total unit had a very large size. According to Calhoun (1919:87), "Large families were the rule. Families of ten to twelve children were common. Families of from twenty to twenty-five children were not rare enough to call forth expression of wonder."
3 Marriage occurred at a very early age in the colonial family. Although child marriages were not permitted, Calhoun (1919:67) states that women usually married by age sixteen or under and men by age twenty or under.
4 The mortality rate for infants was particularly high (Calhoun, 1919:89).

   The preceding aspects of the colonial family are those which have been under close scrutiny in the last decade. These familial aspects will be of primary interest in this paper although others will be mentioned.

Data for Restoration

KINSHIP STRUCTURE

The assumption that the colonial family was "extended" has come under much attack despite its widespread support. In addition to the views of Calhoun, Greenfield (1967:312) observes it is "generally viewed in sociological theory" that the "small nuclear family found in Western Europe and the United States" is the "consequence of the urban-industrial revolution." Furthermore the "extended" family was the expected form that preceded the urban-industrial revolution (for a typical example of this argument, see Ogburn and Nimkoff, 1950:469–473). Greenfield (1967), through an excellent use of comparative and historical techniques, challenges this assumed relationship between the family and the urban-industrial revolution and even suggests the reverse: the small nuclear family might possibly have helped produce industrialization.

Greenfield makes the important suggestion (1967:322) that the "small nuclear family was brought to the United States from Great Britain by its earliest settlers." He bases this on Arensberg's contention (1955:1149) that "the nuclear' or 'democratic' family . . . came with [the] Yankees from England." But there is also additional support for this contention. In his study of aristocracy between 1558 and 1641, Stone (1967:269) notes there is a lack of evidence that the "sixteenth century household had taken the form of an extended family." There appeared, in fact, to be little "encouragement for younger sons to remain home, and daughters were almost invariably married off at an early age" (Stone, 1967:269). Laslett and Harrison (1963:167), in their study of Clayworth and Cogenhoe during the last quarter of the seventeenth century, found that the family was not extended, because in most cases the "household did not ordinarily contain more generations than two, [and] . . . living with in-laws or relatives was on the whole not to be expected. . . . Most important is the rule that it was unusual, very unusual, to find two married couples within the same family group." Laslett (1969) in a later work expanded the geographical coverage of these conclusions. He supports the contention that the family form brought to the new world by the English settlers was "nuclear" in nature rather than "extended." Thus if the extended family was typical in the colonies, it must have been because of indigenous elements in the new world.

But based upon recent work completed, the "nuclear" family was also typical in the American colonies in contrast to the stereotype. A number of studies completed since 1965 of the colonial family conclude that the extended structure was the exception rather than the rule. Demos (1965:279) notes that in the Plymouth colony "there were not extended families at all, in the sense of 'under the same roof'."[5] Using family wills as a source, Demos (1965:279) observes "that married brothers and sisters never lived together in the same house" and that "as soon as a young man becomes betrothed, plans were made for the building, or purchase, of his own house." In his study of Dedham, Massachusetts, between 1636 and 1736, Lockridge (1966:343) observes that "80 percent of adult, married men had their own house . . . [hence there was] not extensive doubling-up of two families in one house . . . [and] it was most unusual for married fathers with married sons to live together in an extended family group."

In his study of the seventeenth century family structure in Andover,

---

[5]The distinction between an "extended" versus a "nuclear" family unit is determined by membership in the family of residence or the group of persons who are related by blood, marriage, or adoption who share the same dwelling unit. The importance of the interpersonal relationships between all kin whether in the same dwelling unit or not—the family of interaction—cannot yet be dealt with in quantitative terms.

Massachusetts, Greven (1966:254–255) describes what he termed a *"modified extended family*—defined as a kinship group of two or more generations living within a single community in which the dependence of the children upon their parents continues after the children have married and are living under a separate roof." Greven's findings are not, however, at odds with the previous findings. What he terms the *modified extended family* refers to the family of interaction, and to be consistent with the other works, we must use as a basis for the family unit the family of residence. If we apply the latter definition to Greven's families the difference in structure disappears. This distinction made, the family structure as described by Greven is, in fact, nuclear, as the families in the works previously cited.

In a later study by Demos (1968:44) of colonial Bristol, Rhode Island, he supports the predominance of the "nuclear" family by observing that "married adults normally lived with their own children and *apart* from all other relatives." Together, these works provide evidence based upon quantitative data to challenge the contention of the predominance in the colonial period of the "extended" family.

FAMILY SIZE

Another contention under close scrutiny is that the number of children per family was quite large. The assumption of a large number of children, together with the presumption of the "extended" nature of the colonial family, accounts for the widespread image of large colonial family units. In reference to this, there are two aspects to be considered: the number of children per family and the overall family size.

First, let us examine the number of children per family in the colonial period. It is true that colonial families, on the average, had more children than families of the present day. However, the difference between these two periods has been much exaggerated and certainly the difference is much less than indicated by Calhoun. Indeed, if we look at Demos' statistics (1968) there appears to be little variance in the average number of children from the present figure. Demos (1968:45) reports the mean number of children per family in colonial Bristol for 1689 as 3.27 and the median as 3.04. Only two families of those surveyed by Demos had more than seven children. If the mean reported by Demos—3.27—is compared to the mean reported by the United States Census Bureau (1963:1,465) for 1960 which is 1.72 the difference–1.55—is much less than might be presumed. Regardless of whether this figure is considered a significant difference, the figures presented by Demos (1968) certainly challenge the image of the typical colonial family having a large number of children.

However, there are discrepancies between the figures reported for number of children per colonial family in various works which should be noted. In an earlier work Demos (1965:270) reports for the Plymouth colony "an average of seven to eight children per family who actually grew to adulthood." If the children who died before the age of 21 are included in Demos' sample, the average is raised to between eight and nine children. In a recent work dealing only with eighteenth century Quakers, Wells (1971:74–75) reports the average number of children per family is 5.69. Other figures reported include the following: Greven (1966:238) for Andover, Massachusetts, reports an average of 8.5 children per family, with 7.2 children in these families reaching the age of 21 years; Lockridge (1966:330) for Dedham, Massachusetts, reports an average of 4.64 children for each family; Higgs and Stettler (1970:286–287) for 10 different New England towns report an average of 7 children per family; Norton (1971:444) for Ipswich, Massachusetts, reports a mean number of 4.3 children per family where "the date of the end of union is known" and a mean of 6.4 children for those families that were "technically complete.";[6] and Smith (1912:177) for Hingham, Massachusetts, presents a mean number of 6.53 children per family the overall mean for six marriage cohorts that cover a period from 1641 to 1800 but there are significant variations from this average, especially the 1691findfl1715 cohort which had the lowest mean of 4.61 children per family. Hence, even if we accept the highest reported averages, the stereotype is challenged. Still there exists a wide discrepancy between the various figures reported that must be explored.

One explanation for the discrepancy might be that the various figures reported are unique for the particular town or area studied. Thus, just as it is impossible to describe accurately colonial life based only upon observations by Ben Franklin and others, it is also impossible to generalize and relate from the findings of one town in colonial America to an entire area or era. In an attempt to control for this problem, Higgs and Stettler (1970) collected data from a number of different towns. They observe that differences between towns do exist that must be realized and expected. Higgs and Stettler (1970:289), for example, note the average number of children per family varied from "a low of 5.19 in Malden to a high of 7.76 in Brookfield." The difference—2.57—between the average number of children, presented in their study, is still much smaller than the difference—5.23—between figures reported by Greven (1966) and Demos (1968) as previously noted. Geographical differences in sampling then may be a partial explanation for this discrepancy but does not suffice as a complete explanation.

Another factor that accounts for part of the discrepancy is a decline during the colonial period in complete fertility. Smith (1972:177–179) notes a decline in eighteenth century completed fertility, as compared to the seventeenth century, with the lowest rate recorded by those women marrying at the

---

[6]In this instance completed families are those in which the wife remains married at least until the age of 45 or in which the union lasts at least 27 years (Norton, 1971:443).

beginning of the eighteenth century (1691–1715). As Smith suggests, this is a pattern not unique to Hingham and is, to some degree, supported by the rates presented by the other studies—the higher means, in most cases, come from studies of seventeenth century populations and the lower means, usually, come from studies of eighteenth century populations. This decline in completed fertility is a factor in the discrepancy and a factor that must be explored further but there is a simpler explanation for the wide differences reported.

A larger proportion of the difference can be explained in another way. The main reason for the widespread range of figures presented above is the use of varying operational definitions determining the number of children per family. The biggest difference results from the use of different time perspectives by observers of the colonial family unit. Currently the United States Census Bureau (1963:xxiv) reports the number of children per family as only those children residing in a household family of residence at the time of enumeration. Thus children who have left home, died, or are yet to be born are not counted. Plus, included in the calculation of the average number of children per family are childless couples, including newly married and elderly couples, who were usually not included in colonial studies' figures. This represents a cross-sectional view of the family and its characteristics. With only one exception (Demos, 1968), all of the studies reported above with regard to number of children per family take a longitudinal perspective.

Utilization of the longitudinal perspective means observing the completed family when noting the number of children in each family. The completed family includes: a man with his wife and any children born into their union. Although this has been the most common operational definition of the family used to determine the number of children and family size, there are some unique qualifications used by some of the researchers that should be noted. In his earlier study, for example, Demos (1965:270) used only "families in which both parents lived at least to age 50, or else if one parent died, the other quickly remarried." In their study, Higgs and Stettler (1970:284) included only families for which continuous residence in the same town was recorded throughout the entire childbearing period. Also note the difference—2.1— between families that were "technically complete" and those families where the date the union ended was known, as reported by Norton (1971:444). But even the latter and lower mean—4.1—is overstated, as compared to contemporary figures, because it is still based upon a longitudinal perspective and because of restrictions on the sample (Norton, 1971:443).

It becomes obvious that the number of children per family derived from an operational definition, based upon the completed family, gives us a much larger number than the cross-sectional perspective. This is not only the case for the colonial era but also for the United States today. Plus, with the use of additional limitations, like those used by Demos (1965), Higgs and Stettler (1970), and Norton (1971), a representative sample cannot be obtained from the areas being studied. Higgs and Stettler (1970:284 and 288) admit that their estimates of the number of children and family size are overstated. Certainly overstatement must occur in all those other works using a similar type of operational definition. Yet, because of the uneven recording of the data, the qualification of using only those families for which complete data exist seems to be necessary. In addition to overstatement resulting from sample qualifications, smaller, mobile families were less likely to generate the necessary birth, death, and marriage registrations in subsequent years which would assure inclusion in the sample. The fact that these small, mobile families had a lower probability of being included in a sample supports the contention that samples dealing only with completed families using the longitudinal perspective are unrepresentative and their figures overstated.

Another factor can partially account for the higher averages when dealing with completed families. Most studies that deal with the completed family include only parents or couples with children in the sample. Also only these parents were used in the calculation of the average number of children per family. Thus, those families (couples) without children were not included in this calculation of the average and, as a result, the average reported was additionally overstated. Wells (1971:74–75) provided a partial exception in his calculation of figures on the number of children per family. He did include couples without any children but eliminated couples when the bride's age did not fall "within the normal limits of the childbearing stage of life." Thus Wells' figures are still overstated but not as badly as those who excluded all childless couples. It should be noted that the figures reported by Wells are modest in comparison to others reported. Also his figures are more comparable to current census data which includes parents with children, childless couples, and married couples before, during, and after childbearing age in the calculation of averages.

The only colonial data comparable to contemporary census data are provided by Demos' (1968) figures, based upon a census taken of colonial Bristol in 1689, which indicates the least variance between the contemporary and colonial figures (for figures see above). Although differences would still be expected, if we could derive comparable data cross-sectional in nature—from the other colonial studies the average number of children per family would be reduced significantly. The conclusion must be that the number of children per family has been much exaggerated and that the actual number of children per family is not too different from the present figures.

In regard to overall family size it seems reasonably clear that the size of the colonial American family was much smaller than presumed. First, we noted the restricted nature—only two generations—for the family of residence in regard to generational make up. Second, the actual number of children in the colonial family unit at any given time appears to have been smaller than previously presumed. Thus, the exaggerated figures presented for family size—assuming the U.S. Census' present definition of family size—appears to have resulted from most authors using completed families and usually only a portion of these families to determine overall family size.

An additional element which produced an exaggerated family size was the presence of nonrelatives in the family's household who were counted as family members. An extreme example is presented by Demos (1965:285) using the household of Samuel Fuller. At Fuller's death in 1633, there were nine people in his household; five of these were not family members. In addition to his wife, son, and a nephew, there were two servants, a ward, and two "additional children." The "additional children" had been sent from other families to the Fuller household for education. The inclusion of wards, servants, boarders, resident employees, and others as part of overall family size existed in preindustrial England, as well, as noted by Laslett and Harrison (1963:167–169) and Laslett (1965a:589). [It is noteworthy that the practice of counting all household members as members of the same family of residence, regardless of their relationship to one another, was continued by the United States Census Bureau (1949:18) until 1930.]

Considering only studies of colonial families where the exaggeration factors are controlled or eliminated, the family size appears to have been relatively small indeed. Lockridge (1966:343) derives from lists of houses, counting only parents and children, an average family size of six for Dedham, a little under six for Medfield, and less than five for Salem. In colonial Bristol, where Demos (1968:45) also eliminated all servants and counted only parents and children, the average family size was 5.304. If we compare these figures with the average family size for the United States (Bureau of Census, 1963:465) in 1960—3.65—the difference ranges from 2.35 to less than 1.34 persons per family. By these standards, clearly, the presumed large family did not exist in the majority of cases.

AGE AT MARRIAGE

The ages presented by Calhoun appear to be completely erroneous based upon a consensus of the recent works surveyed. Not only is the colonial marriage age much higher than stated by Calhoun, but the ages for both men and women are higher than those of the present day. Demos (1965:275) reports for the Plymouth colony that the average age at first marriage for men dropped from 27.0 to 24.6 years and for women it increased from 20.6 to 22.3 years. This included people born before 1600 and those born by 1700 which were divided into 25-year groups based upon year of birth. Norton (1971:445) found in Ipswich a similar pattern in regard to age at first marriage and, in fact, very similar ages but the similar age levels occurred approximately half a century later than in the Plymouth colony. Lockridge (1966:331) reports for Dedham from 1640 to 1690 the average age at first marriage for men was 25.5 years and for women 22.5, and Greven (1966:240) observes for Andover almost identical results. In Hingham, although the overall trend is the same, the highest ages at first marriage for both sexes increased initially and reached their highest level at the turn of the century (1691–1715) before declining (Smith, 1971:177). For colonial Bristol, Demos (1968:55) reports the lowest ages at first marriage of all the colonial studies yet cited. For those couples in colonial Bristol who married before 1750, the men had an average age of 20.5 and, for those couples who married after 1750, the men had an average age of 24.3 and the women's average age was 21.1. Higgs and Stettler (197:285) report ages remarkably similar to those reported by Demos for Bristol.

Comparability of the above figures with current data is problematical because age at marriage is reported by the United States Census Bureau in terms of medians, not means or averages—the statistics reported by most colonial family studies with the exception of Demos' (1968) study of colonial Bristol in which he reports both the mean and the median age. His data are presented along with other colonial data and more current data in Table 1.

The ages Demos presents from his 1968 study are remarkably similar to ages presented for the contemporary figures. Utilizing this data, in addition to the ages reported by other works, age at first marriage was not extremely early, as contended by Calhoun, but similar to current figures and sometimes higher.

Considering the discrepancies between the ages reported by the various colonial family studies, we should first note that the lower ages presented by Demos (1968) and Higgs and Stettler (1970:285) contrast with the higher ages reported by Lockridge (1966), Greven (1966), and Demos (1965). The difference appears to be related to the century in which the births of the individuals in the sample occurred. The latter group, with the higher marriage ages for men and women, used samples of individuals born in the seventeenth century; while the former group, with lower marriage ages, used individuals born in the eighteenth century. The data presented by Norton (1971:445) and Smith (1972:177), who present figures for both centuries, support these trends—for men the average age at first marriage was higher in the seventeenth century and declined in the eighteenth century and for women the average age was initially lower in the seventeenth century, increased around the end of the seventeenth century and the beginning of the eighteenth century, declined somewhat during the middle of the eighteenth century, and increased slightly toward the end of the eighteenth century. Further there appears to be a return to a higher age for both sexes in the nineteenth century, as represented by the 1890 data in Table 1, that is similar to the higher ages for those individuals born in the seventeenth century. Although the former figure is a median and the latter a mean, at this point there is little basis to suppose a much greater difference would result if the statistics were the same.

A tentative fluctuation pattern for age at marriage emerges. Age at first

TABLE 1 AGE AT FIRST MARRIAGE: FIGURES FROM COLONIAL STUDIES AND THE U.S. CENSUS BUREAU[a]

TIME OF MARRIAGE	AGE OF MEN		AGE OF WOMEN	
	Mean	Median	Mean	Median
1600's				
Before 1624[b](Plymouth)	27.0		20.6	
1640-1690[c](Dedham)	25.5		22.5	
Before 1691[d](Hingham)	27.4		22.0	
1700's				
1691-1715[d](Hingham)	28.4		24.7	
Before 1750[e](Bristol)	23.9	22.4	20.5	20.3
After 1750[e](Bristol)	24.3	23.8	21.1	20.8
1800's				
1890[f](U.S.)		26.1		22.0
1900's				
1930[f](U.S.)		24.3		21.3
1966[f](U.S.)		22.8		20.5

[a]Data for the 1600's and the 1700's have been selected from a number of recent studies dealing with families residing in colonial communities.
[b]Source: Demos (1965:275)
[c]Source: Lockridge (1966:333)
[d]Source: Smith (1972:177)
[e]Source: Demos (1968:55)
[f]Source: Smigel and Seiden (1968:15-16)

marriage was quite high in the seventeenth century colonies but dropped to a lower level during the eighteenth century; the latter age level was remarkably similar to a level obtained during the present century. Then during the nineteenth century there occurred a marriage age remarkably similar to the high levels reported for the colonial seventeenth century.

Focusing on the colonial period there are a number of factors that have been cited as determining age levels at marriage. The high ages for men and the low ages for women at first marriage during the first decades of settlement in the seventeenth century have been attributed to a severely imbalanced sex ratio (Henretta, 1971:387; Smith, 1972:176) as suggested by Moller's (1945:113–153) study of passengers on ships coming to New England. But as Norton (1971:445–446) has noted, the Puritans emphasized from the beginning that Massachusetts—where the majority of the communities studied and cited here are located—must be colonized by family units rather than single men. For Ipswich an excess of males only occurred for a brief period after it was founded. Norton suggests that economic considerations, particularly the demand for male labor, were important in determining age-levels at marriage. In the eighteenth century the role of certain "external pressures"—limited geographical expansion, military threat from the Indians and French, inheritance systems, migration, and overcrowded towns—upon marital age patterns has been emphasized (*cf.* Henretta, 1971:389–391; Smith, 1972:176–180). As with the tentative fluctuation pattern in marital age levels described above, data on the marital age patterns for the colonial period and, in particular, an understanding of the factors determining these patterns, are fragmentary, although they do provide researchers with a basis for further investigation.

A later age at marriage for colonial women, as these studies appear to indicate, has implications for the birth rate and ultimately family size. A later age at marriage for women is a form of family limitation (*cf.* Wrigley, 1966a:82–109) which reduces the birth rate because the number of birth potential years is shortened. Smith (1972:178) notes that 43.3 percent of the decline in completed marital fertility for his 1691–1715 marriage cohort can be accounted for by an increase in female age at marriage.

INFANT MORTALITY RATE

It has been assumed by Calhoun and others that the infant mortality rate was quite high. However, based upon certain preceding challenges of the stereotype view of the colonial family, there is some support even without data that a view of high infant mortality rate should be altered. If the number of children per family (completed families) is less than expected, the majority of children born must survive to maintain a family unit that will survive from generation to generation. Furthermore, the fact that marriage was occurring at a much later age than assumed reduces the number of children that can be born. These two factors would seem to indicate the probability of a lower infant mortality rate than previously assumed.

The infant mortality rates reported by the various works are quite low but each author notes the tentative nature of these findings. Demos (1965:271) observes the rate of infant mortality for Plymouth to have been "relatively low" with only one child in five dying before the age of 21. Demos notes that the exact date of death frequently cannot be established so it is more accurate to speak of infant and child mortality together. This would apply to the other works, as well. Potter (1965:656, 658–660), in a recalculation of data from New Jersey for the latter part of the eighteenth century, found "an astonishingly low infant mortality rate." Greven (1966:237) found in Andover that only 15.7 per cent of the children whose births were ascertained died before the age of 21. Norton (1971:442) for Ipswich found "strikingly low" infant and children mortality rates even after correcting for underrecording.

One major problem that particularly plagues infant mortality data for the colonial period is underrecording. As Lockridge (1966:329) observes, it is "known that still-born infants and infants who died within two or three days of birth were not recorded." Norton (1971:439–443) estimated that 33 percent of all infant deaths were not registered. Yet even after correcting for underrecording, applying estimates and techniques prescribed by Henry *et al.*, and

---

[7]In using family reconstitution to calculate mortality rates, only the mortality of married adults and, usually, only those children that remain in the family of residence can be studied.

using family reconstitution[7] to check upon the level of mortality derived from aggregative analysis, the mortality rates for Ipswich were quite low. Thus, most recent works note a lower infant mortality rate than previously presumed, but the data are limited to approximate levels of infant mortality.

One explanation that has received some support argues that elements in the colonial environment reduced the probability of a high infant mortality rate. Potter (1965:663) and Klingaman (1971:555) describe the food supply for the colonies as generally adequate and increasingly abundant. In his review of mortality rates for Dedham and Watertown, Lockridge (1966:336) notes that these towns went through a century of life "substantially" free of disasters which could have cut deeply into the ranks of the population. This is in sharp contrast to the demographic crises experienced in similar European villages for the same period. Noting the lack of disease and hunger in these towns, Lockridge (1966:337) believes it is "quite possible that the new land had substantial gifts to offer and freedom to bestow other than the freedom from Anglican persecutions." Norton (1971:449–450) suggests that the most important cause in reduced mortality was the apparent marked decrease in death resulting from infectious disease. This appears to be the result of a number of factors related to the environmental conditions of the colonists—there were fewer sources of infection (all had to be imported), a decreased rate of spread of infection (sparse population), and greater survival chances once the infection was contracted. Furthermore, as these conditions changed the mortality rates increased. These elements helped to sustain the health of childbearing-age women and improved the survival chances of infants, thus keeping infant mortality rates down.

Discussion

The foregoing briefly surveys the work being done on the structural characteristics of the colonial family as previously outlined. These studies provide an important step toward the goal of a restoration of the colonial family system but the scope of these works is limited and further efforts are required. As Greven (1967:443) has observed, the fullest development of "early American history . . . cannot focus exclusively upon the accumulation of data from vital records, nor should it be mesmerized by the prospects of quantification." Other sources of a quantitative nature and "verbal data" are essential to add the necessary dimensions to further inquiries concerning the family and communities. A move to add the necessary dimensions is observed by Saveth (1969:326–327) in his discussion of Bailyn's concept and technique of "family style."

Before the last two decades, our image of the colonial family had been based primarily upon the reports of a restricted set of "verbal data." With the development of new techniques and an expanding interest, this earlier image is being revised by quantitative and documented facts. Before complete restoration can occur one final step is necessary. This step involves the better understanding of the complex interrelationships between patterns of demographic characteristics, family size, birth rates, geographical mobility, health conditions—and family patterns which cannot be quantified—authority pattern, sex role definitions, power relationships, *etc*. Dealing with the interrelationships between various demographic characteristics and their effect upon colonial population growth, Smith (1972) provides an excellent basis and example for further work in this direction. Once this final step is obtained, many family observers anticipate that located within the family will be "the basic determinants of historical change" (Saveth, 1969:326).

There are some limitations, which indicate the direction of further study, that should be mentioned in regard to the status of the restoration of the colonial American family. Although dealing with the general subject of the colonial family, the majority of data thus far reported are limited to families located in New England. Hence, it is necessary to provide data on familial variables for the Middle and Southern colonies, especially in light of the substantial demographic differences that existed, which have important implications for the colonial family (*cf.* Potter, 1965). Of course, there are differences to be expected among the families located in the New England colonies. Even the communities which have been studied thus far vary significantly. Certainly there are different factors affecting the family in a coastal settlement like Ipswich, which depended primarily upon maritime industries, than in an agricultural community like Plymouth. In addition, there are virtually no data available for families residing in frontier settlements, although indications are that major differences existed there (Laslett, 1970:85–86). Further study is necessary upon other factors which played a role in the familial behavior of the colonial American population. Some of this work has begun but further efforts are necessary both on the more obvious variables, such as migration (*cf.* Potter, 1965; Norton, 1971:433–436; Smith, 1972:174), landholding customs (Henretta, 1971:389–391), age distribution, sex ratio, and some of the less visible variables, such as family limitation and relative age of husband in relation to wife's fertility (Smith, 1972:180–182). The work that remains to be done seems almost limitless, yet the work already completed plus an apparent increasing interest should result in a better understanding of the colonial family and its surrounding physical and social environment.

The majority of the work on the restoration of the colonial family surveyed thus far has been carried out primarily by historians and a few sociologists. Most of the sociologists, contributing to this restoration or working on related topics, have been working from a different direction. Based upon the development of the two disciplines, one might have expected the quantitative approach used by the authors already surveyed—mostly historians—to be the major orientation of sociologists. Traditionally, historians have shown, in many cases, a distrust of statistics. This is especially true of statistics without relevant "verbal data"—novels, diaries, newspapers, etc.—for support (*cf.* Jaher, 1970:196). A major influence upon this more quantified approach by historians has been the acceptance and use of techniques developed in the field of historical demography. Sociologists are not only taking a different direction but their approach can be characterized as more qualitative than the approach used by most historians working in this area.

Most sociologists working in the colonial family area have been concerned with rediscovering behavior patterns that are supposedly unique to industrialized societies. Concern has been less directly with restoration of the colonial family and more with challenging the presumed influences of industrialization and urbanization upon the familial institution. Works of this nature make important contributions to the restoration process by establishing the stability or change of various family patterns since the colonial period. In addition a number of sociologists are attempting to determine what factors have brought about the changes in family patterns that have occurred. In a recent review of sociologists' work in this area, Adams (1971:75) notes the increasing precision with which the colonial family can be described. Further, he observes that only a few changes in the family "can be directly related to the industrial revolution."

An example of the "sociologists' approach" is offered by Furstenberg's (1966:337) analysis of the written accounts by foreign travelers in the United States. According to his findings there are striking similarities to the contemporary American family in regard to the system of mate selection, parent-child relations, and the marital relationship in the preindustrial American family. Similarly, Lantz *et al.* (1968:424–425), using content analysis of colonial magazines, observed the prevalence of the romantic love complex and the importance placed upon personal happiness as a motive in mate choice. Both of these patterns are contrary to the commonly postulated patterns for a preindustrial society. It is noteworthy that both of these examples provide data derived primarily from "verbal data," not empirical data. Like the more quantitative work already presented, this approach also contributes to the restoration of the colonial family and the establishment of essential base lines. Through the establishment of these base lines, we can differentiate the dimension and the extent of change. This will lead not only to a refining of our understanding of the relationship between industrialization and the family, but also to a better understanding of total societal change.

In summary, "resulting from all the works surveyed, a new, more realistic, image of the colonial family has emerged. In short, the colonial family appears to be structurally similar in many ways to the present family in the United States. Colonial families were predominantly restricted or nuclear units which, at any given point in time, were similar in size to present family units. Although the completed colonial family was larger than the contemporary family, the difference is not as large as previously assumed. Infant mortality did not play the role in affecting family size as commonly assumed. Furthermore, there is mounting evidence that certain behavioral patterns that were presumed unique to the contemporary family existed in the colonial family system. Thus, there appear to be more similarities than differences between these two family systems." It is surprising, but accurate, that this is a recent perspective in regard to family study. This is primarily due to an overemphasis in the past upon the phenomenon of change. This overemphasis has led to the neglect of what has remained permanent in the American family structure. In support, Aries (1962:9) observes that the "historical differences [in the family] are of little importance in comparison with the huge mass of what remains unchanged." Important changes have occurred but the focus must be upon exactly what has changed and the factors which have brought about this change.

This process of restoration is by no means complete; much work remains to be done. Although the emphasis in this paper has been upon the structural similarity between the colonial and the contemporary family system, there are important differences. Changes, occurring in the patterns of premarital sexual behavior and norms, husband and wife roles, and divorce laws, have been widely accepted by family observers (*cf.* Adams, 1971:64–75). A major difficulty is that patterns of this nature lend themselves less to quantification. This becomes even more of a problem because most of the data concerning these patterns can no longer be obtained, and in many cases the data were not initially recorded in the colonial era. The work must continue on these patterns, however, despite the difficulties to provide a full account of what has changed and to what extent since the colonial family.

The surge of interest in the colonial family over the last decade, by both historians and sociologists, indicates that the restoration process is underway. In addition, there appears to be a growing awareness by certain scholars in history and sociology of the efforts being made in both disciplines. This growing awareness ideally will develop into some form of collaboration between historians and sociologists toward a more complete restoration of the colonial family. Also it is anticipated that a sharing of theory, method, techniques, and concepts will occur. If a sharing of techniques and definitions can be developed, then the restoration of the colonial family will be a more precise and fruitful effort. As noted above, a number of problems result when divergent concepts and techniques are applied to similar data.

Summary

It has been the attempt of this paper to survey the present status of the restoration of the colonial family which is being conducted primarily by historians and sociologists. In the past, interdisciplinary efforts have been encouraged but infrequently carried out. In the study of the colonial American family it must be concluded that, in the past, both disciplines have gone their own directions. But a growing knowledge and appreciation by each discipline of the work in both fields is evident in recent publications (Saveth, 1969; Gordon and Bernstein, 1970; Anderson, 1971). An additional aim of this paper is to add to this growing knowledge and appreciation of the works, concepts, and techniques of both disciplines. The final expectation is that this growing knowledge and appreciation will result in a meaningful collaboration in the future. The success of this collaboration will act as an example to other scholars.

References

Adams, Bert N.—1971—*The American Family: A Sociological Interpretation.* Chicago:Markham Publishing Company.

Anderson, Michael—1971—*Family Structure in Nineteenth Century Lancashire.* New York:Cambridge University Press.

Arensberg, Conrad M.—1955—"American communities." American Anthropologist 57 (December):1143–1162.

Aries, Philippe—1962—*Centuries of Childhood.* New York:Alfred Knopf.

Aronson, Sidney—1969—"Obstacles to rapprochement between history and sociology." Pp. 292–304 in M. Sherif and C. Sherif (eds.), Interdisciplinary Relationships in the Social Sciences. Chicago:Aldine.

Baker, Paul J.—1969—"Historical sociology and social action theory." Paper presented at annual meeting of Southern Sociological Society, New Orleans, April 12, 1969.

Bridenbaugh, Carl—1963—"The great mutation." American Historical Review 68 (January):315–331.

Briggs, Asa—1962—"Sociology and history," Pp. 91–98 in A. T. Welford *et al.* (eds.), Society: Problems and Methods of Study. New York:Philosophical Library.

Cahnman, W. J. and Alvin Boskoff (eds.)—1964—*Sociology and History: Theory and Research.* New York:Free Press.

Calhoun, Arthur W.—1919—*A Social History of the American Family: From Colonial Times to the Present.* 3 Volumes. Cleveland, Ohio:Arthur H. Clark.

Committee on Historiography—1954—*The Social Sciences in Historical Study.* Bulletin 64. New York: Social Science Research Council.

Demos, John—1965—"Notes on life in Plymouth Colony." William and Mary Quarterly, Third Series 22 (April):264–286.

————1968—"Families in Colonial Bristol, Rhode Island: an exercise in historical demography." William and Mary Quarterly, Third Series 25 (October):40–57.

Edwards, John (ed.)—1969—*The Family and Change.* New York: Alfred A. Knopf.

Erikson, Kai—1970—"Sociology and the historical perspective."The American Sociologist 5 (November):331–338.

Eversley, D. E. C.—1966—"Exploitation of Anglican parish registers by aggregative analysis." Pp. 44–95 in E. A. Wrigley (ed.), *An Introduction to English Historical Demography from the Sixteenth to Nineteenth Century.* New York:Basic Books.

Furstenberg, Frank F., Jr.—1966—"Industrialization and the American family: a look backward." American Sociological Review 31 (June):326–337.

Glass, D. V.—1965—"Introduction." Pp. 1–20 in D. V. Glass and D. E. C. Eversley (eds.), *Population in History: Essays in Historical Demography.* Chicago: Aldine Publishing Company.

Goode, William J.—1963—*World Revolution and Family Patterns.* New York:The Free Press.

Gordon, Michael and M. Charles Bernstein—1970—"Mate choice and domestic life in the nineteenth-century marriage manual." Journal of Marriage and the Family 32 (November):665–674.

Greenfield, Sidney M.—1961—"Industrialization and the family in sociological theory." American Journal of Sociology 67 (November):312-322.

Greven, Philip J., Jr.—1966—"Family structure in the seventeenth century Andover, Massachusetts." William and Mary Quarterly, 3rd Series 23 (April):234–256.

————1967—"Historical demography and colonial America." William and Mary Quarterly, Third Series 24 (July):438–454.

Hareven, Tamara K.—1971—"The history of the family as an interdisciplinary field." The Journal of Interdisciplinary History 2 (Autumn):399–414.

Henretta, James A.—1971—"The morphology of New England society in the colonial period." The Journal of Interdisciplinary History 2 (Autumn):379–398.

Henry, Louis—1968—"Historical demography." Daedalus 97 (Spring):385–396.

Higgs, Robert and H. Louis Stettler, III—1970—"Colonial New England demography: a sampling approach." William and Mary Quarterly, Third Series 27 (April):282–293.

Hollingsworth, Thomas H.—1969—*Historical Demography.* Ithaca, New York: Cornell University Press.

Jaher, Frederic C.—1970—"Short review of nineteenth-century cities: essays in the new urban history." The Journal of Interdisciplinary History 1 (Autumn):195–198.

Klingaman, David—1971—"Food surpluses and deficits in the American colonies, 1768–1772." The Journal of Economic History 31 (September):553–569.

Lantz, Herman, Raymond Schmitt, Margaret Britton, and Eloise Snyder—1968—"Preindustrial patterns in the colonial family in America." American Sociological Review 33 (June):413–426.

Laslett, Peter—1965a—"The history of population and social structure." International and Social Science Journal 27 (August):582–594.

————1965b—*The World We Lost.* New York:Charles Scribner's and Sons.

————1969—"Size and structure of the household in England over three centuries." Population Studies 23 (July):199–224.

————1970—"The Comparative history of household and family." Journal of Social History 4 (Fall):75–87.

Laslett, Peter and John Harrison—1963—"Clayworth and Cogenhoe." Pp. 157–184 in H. E. Bell and R. L. Ollard (eds.), *Historical Essays 1600–1750: Presented to David Ogg.* London:Adam and Charles Black.

Lipset, S. M.—1958—"A sociologist looks at history." Pacific Sociological Review 1 (Spring):13–17.

————and Richard Hofstader—1968—*Sociology and History:Methods.* New York: Basic Books.

Lockridge, Kenneth A.—1966—"The population of Dedham, Massachusetts, 1636–1736." Economic History Review, Second Series 19 (August):318–344.

Means, R. L.—1962—"Sociology and history: a new look at their relationships." American Journal of Economics and Sociology 21 (July):285–298.

Moller, Herbert—1945—"Sex composition and correlated culture patterns of colonial America." William and Mary Quarterly, Third Series 2 (October): 113–153.

Norton, Susan L.—1971—"Population growth in colonial America: a study of Ipswich, Massachusetts." Population Studies 25 (November):433–452.

Ogburn, W. F. and Meyer F. Nimkoff—1950—*Sociology.* Boston:Houghton Mifflin.

Potter, J.—1965—"The growth of population in America, 1700–1860." Pp. 631–688 in D. V. Glass and D. E. C. Eversley (eds.), *Population in History: Essays in Historical Demography.* Chicago:Aldine.

Rose, A. M.—1956—"The relationship between history and sociology." Alpha Kappa Deltan 26 (Spring):203–214.

Saveth, Edwards N.—1969—"The problems of American family history." American Quarterly 21 (Summer):311–329.

Smelser, Neil—1967—"Sociological history: the industrial revolution and the British working-class family." Journal of Social History 1 (Fall):17–35.

———1968—*Essays in Sociological Explanation.* Englewood Cliffs, New Jersey:Prentice-Hall.

Smigel, E. O. and R. Seiden—1968—"The decline and fall of the double standard." The Annals 376 (March):6–17.

Smith, Daniel S.—1972—"The demographic history of colonial New England." The Journal of Economic History 32 (March):165–184.

Spreitzer, Elmer A. and Lawrence E. Riley—1970—"Another look at the relationship between sociology and history." Paper presented at annual meeting of American Sociological Association, Washington, D.C., September, 1970.

Stone, Lawrence—1967—*The Crisis of the Aristocracy, 1558–1641.* New York:Oxford.

Thrupp, S.—1957a—"History and sociology: new opportunities for cooperation." American Journal of Sociology 63 (July):11–16a.

———1957b—"What history and sociology can learn from each other." Sociology and Social Research 41 (July):434–438.

United States: Bureau of the Census—1949—*Historical Statistics of the United States 1789–1945.*

———1963—*United States Population: 1960: Detailed Characteristics United States Summary.* Final Report PC(1)-1D.

Vinovskis, Marie A.—1971—"The 1789 life table of Edward Wigglesworth." The Journal of Economic History 31 (September):570–590.

Wells, Robert V.—1971—"Family size and fertility control in eighteenth-century America: a study of Quaker families." Population Studies 25 (March):73–82.

Wolff, K.—1959—"Sociology and history: theory and practice." American Journal of Sociology 65 (July):32–38.

Wrigley, E. Anthony—1966a—"Family limitation in pre-industrial England." Economic History Review, Second Series 19 (April):82–109.

———1966b—"Family reconstitution." Pp. 96–159 in E. A. Wrigley (ed.), *An Introduction to English Historical Demography from the Sixteenth to Nineteenth Century.* New York:Basic Books.

PART TWO

Family Variations in America

CHAPTER 3

Racial, Ethnic, and Religious Family Variations in America

The United States of America is a large, western, urban-industrial society with a heterogeneous and complex culture. There are certain cultural traditions and themes that tend to pervade the whole society, such as the emphasis on individualism, human rights, and a democratic ideology. In the realm of marriage and family, one could identify certain societywide cultural forms such as monogamy, joint residence of parents and their dependent children, and parental responsibility for the care and rearing of children. In addition to such societywide patterns which constitute elements of the general American culture, there are also numerous marriage and family cultural variations scattered throughout American society. Such variations are apt to be identified with different historical groups, and the term "subculture" may be used to designate a particular subsystem of cultural traits—beliefs, customs, traditions, material objects, and the like—which is associated with one such historical group within the larger society. An example would be the Louisiana French (or "Cajun") subculture which includes a language dialect of French-Canadian derivation, certain folk legends, and food customs which set this group or subsociety apart somewhat from other people in Louisiana. While

Scandinavian-American family, 1907. (*Fred J. Pearson.*)

seldom completely isolated from other groups around them, members of such subsocieties tend to interact more among themselves than with members of other groups. There are generally certain key cultural characteristics that serve to identify and differentiate these subsocieties, and it is around these characteristics that the "consciousness of kind" of the group is centered and which gives form to their particular subculture. Among the various subsocieties in America whose subcultures are significant for understanding American family variations are social classes, rural and urban subgroups, and racial, ethnic, and religious subgroups. The present chapter is concerned with the latter three categories.

Origins of American Racial, Ethnic, and Religious Groups

SUBCULTURAL PERSPECTIVES AND FAMILY SUBCULTURES IN AMERICA

While recognizing that there are different ways of defining ethnic groups, for the purposes at hand we will define an ethnic group as "any social group, which, as a part of a larger socio-cultural system, is perceived as being somewhat distinctive because its members adhere to a religion that is more or less unique to them, [or] because of some special national origin or language. . . ."[1] Thus the principal defining characteristics of an ethnic group would be its historical-cultural traditions, beliefs, and practices. For some ethnic groups the most salient characteristic could be their particular religion, such as the Jews or the Amish; for other ethnic groups language and national origin could be more important, such as for Italian-Americans or Mexican-Americans. Technically, a race is defined in genetic and physical terms rather than cultural. Thus a race would be a subdivision of mankind "among whose members some genes are more common than among members of other groups, such genes often (but not always) being associated with the appearance of [distinctive] physical traits. . . ."[2] Race is a more inclusive term than ethnic group; within each race there are generally many ethnic groups, each with its own distinctive subculture. Since they are either physically or culturally different from the majority population, racial and ethnic groups may be called "minority groups." Members of such groups may become objects of prejudice or negative discriminatory treatment.

In America, the sources and origins of our racial and ethnic groups (apart from American Indians) are the free and slave immigration over the centuries. Let us review briefly the history of the migration of peoples from Europe, Africa, and Asia to America.

PERIODS OF AMERICAN IMMIGRATION

In Chapter 2 we considered briefly the various racial and national backgrounds of American families. Here the purpose will be to present a more systematic picture of our immigrant family heritage by showing the periods during which certain racial, ethnic, and religious groups came, their length of time in America, and the variations of their culture from the predominant American culture, as these factors relate to their adjustment to and assimilation into American society.

THE COLONIAL PERIOD   The principal sources of population for the original thirteen American colonies were Europe and Africa. European sources were mainly the British Isles and other western European nations. Of the approximately 2 million white people in the thirteen colonies in 1776, the estimate is that 60 percent were English, 17 to 18 percent Scotch-Irish, 11 to 12 percent German, 7 to 8 percent Dutch, and smaller percentages were French, Scottish, Swedish, Irish, Welsh, Danish, and Finnish.[3] And of course there were the Spanish colonists in Florida and in the southwestern and western Spanish colonies, and the French in Canada. These colonial settlers, particularly those from the British Isles, shaped the early Anglo-American culture which became predominant and to which all successive immigrant groups had to adjust.

The other principal group to come to America during the colonial period was from Africa. The earliest recorded Africans to come to America arrived in Virginia in 1619, as indentured servants. Throughout the colonial period, as slavery grew, many thousands were brought by force. They came from many different national and tribal groups, largely from western Africa. Their condition of servitude and their racial distinctiveness probably were more significant in their adjustment in America than were their varied cultural origins. The first official United States census in 1790 showed a population of 757,208 Negroes, constituting about 19.3 percent of the total population.[4]

Technically, American immigration, as opposed to colonization, did not begin until the Declaration of Independence. But even after the establishment of nationhood, the United States government did not begin to keep immigration records until 1820; and it was not until 1907 that such records became really reliable. However, the government's approximate figures for the different periods of immigration are sufficient for our purposes of reviewing the national and racial sources of American families as the various groups ebbed and flowed over the nearly 200 years of immigration to the United States.

IMMIGRATION FROM 1783–1830   A rough estimate is that about 10,000 free immigrants came each year during this period. The largest numbers were from the British Isles, with Germans and Dutch next, and a scattering of people from France, Canada, Switzerland, Sweden, and Mexico.[5]

IMMIGRATION FROM 1830–1882   (The Old Immigration) This period saw a huge increase in migration to America. It is estimated that more than 10 million immigrants came between 1830 and 1880. The opening of large land areas beyond the Mississippi, the building of roads, canals, and railroads, along with increasing industrialization, offered new jobs to immigrant labor and opened new agricultural areas to settlement. English, Irish, German, and Scandinavian immigrants predominated during these decades. The disastrous Irish potato famine of the mid-1840s resulted in a vast exodus. From 1847 to 1854 more than 1,350,000 Irish were recorded as entering the United States. German immigration reached a peak between 1880 and 1892 when more than 1,770,000 arrived; and about 656,000 Scandinavian people arrived in the United States between 1880 and 1890.[6] As in the previous period, here also the immigrants were disproportionately adult, and males greatly outnumbered females. They came principally from the British Isles, western and northern Europe. Referred to as the "Old Immigration," the cultural backgrounds of these immigrants, while varied, tended to be more like those of earlier settlers in America; thus problems of adjustment and assimilation for these immigrants tended to be not so great as for many of the immigrant groups to follow. However, nativistic sentiment was on the rise in America during this period, and groups such as the Irish Catholics and the culturally different Germans became targets of growing antialien sentiment.

It was during this period that Asian immigrants began to arrive on the West Coast, coming largely from China. Many Chinese were attracted by the gold rush of the 1840s and 1850s. Welcomed at first for their needed labor, they soon became the victims of severe race prejudice and discrimination

TABLE 3-1   IMMIGRATION TO THE UNITED STATES, 1820–1970.

PERIOD	IMMIGRANTS	PERIOD	IMMIGRANTS
1820–1830	151,824	1901–1910	8,795,386
1831–1840	599,125	1911–1920	5,735,811
1841–1850	1,713,251	1921–1930	4,107,209
1851–1860	2,598,214	1931–1940	528,431
1861–1870	2,314,824	1941–1950	1,035,039
1871–1880	2,812,191	1951–1960	2,515,479
1881–1890	5,246,613	1961–1970	3,321,671
1891–1900	3,687,564		

SOURCE: Figures from "We the American Foreign Born," no. 15 in a series of reports from the 1970 Census. U.S. Department of Commerce, June 1973, p. 4.

because of their physical and cultural differences and their willingness to work hard for cheap wages. Negative sentiment was so strong that in 1882 Congress enacted the Chinese Exclusion Act. This marked the beginning of federal control of American immigration.

IMMIGRATION FROM 1882 to 1930   (The New Immigration) This was the period of greatest immigration, with more than 22 million people admitted. The year 1882 was a turning point in the history of American immigration. It marked the high point of immigration from northern and western European nations and the beginning of a new influx of peoples from southern and eastern Europe, which included Italians, Poles, Greeks, Russians, Austro-Hungarians, and other Slavic groups. All these came to be called the "New Immigration" as opposed to the earlier "Old Immigration." During 1882, 87 percent of the total immigrants were from northern and western Europe, while only 13 percent were from southern and eastern Europe; by 1907 the ratios were nearly reversed, with 19 percent Old Immigrants and 81 percent New Immigrants.[7] The cultural differences between these newest immigrants and native Americans tended to be more pronounced. The newcomers were predominantly Catholic, Jewish, or Greek Orthodox in religion. They tended to flow to large cities, where they continued to speak their native languages and live much as they had back in their native lands. Public sentiment favoring new immigration restrictions had become intense by the turn of the century. In 1917 literacy tests were added to earlier requirements aimed at preventing entry of criminals and those who were mentally "defective." In 1921 Congress enacted a quota system which favored people from northern and western Europe and discriminated against those from southern and eastern Europe. This law was revised in 1924 to still further favor Old Immigrants, and to bar all Oriental peoples from entering the United States as permanent immigrants. It was not until 1952 that Orientals were assigned an immigrant quota. In 1968 the national origins system was eliminated, and a total of 170,000 immigrant visas a year was allotted for all nations outside the Western Hemisphere on a first-come–first-served basis, with a maximum of 20,000 from any one nation.[8]

The peak period for American immigration was from 1900 to World War I; more than 1 million people a year entered for several years during this time, mostly New Immigrants who settled in ethnic enclaves in large cities where they were subjected to widespread prejudice and discrimination. Their reaction was to turn inward for mutual protection and support, thereby preserving their old country languages and customs longer than would have otherwise been the case. Their family patterns varied according to nationality, religion, social class, and rural or urban background. In addition to the prejudice and discrimination from the native Americans, the immigrants' own ethnocentric reaction to American culture heightened and prolonged their resistance to becoming assimilated into the mainstream of American society, a process that required several generations for many groups. Some of the main factors influencing the cultural and social assimilation of immigrants will be discussed shortly.

PROBLEMS OF CULTURAL AND SOCIAL ASSIMILATION

SOME CONSEQUENCES OF INTERNATIONAL MIGRATION ON FAMILY LIFE If spatial mobility or migration within a society puts strains on the family, then it could be expected that international migration would have even sharper effects. In his analysis of migration and the family, Robert Blood has identified some of these effects.[9]

1 Severed ties with kinfolk International migration generally involves relatively long-distance moves, frequently across oceans for many thousands of miles. Contact with kin back home may be reduced to correspondence, except for the more affluent few who can afford expensive visits. The combination of great distance and the march of time inexorably weakens the ties between the emigrants and their kin back in the homeland. After two or three generations, these ties may be broken completely and kinsmen lost. An example was dramatically portrayed by the Swedish author Vilhelm Moberg in his book *The Last Letter Home.*

2 Strengthening of Nuclear Family Bonds The interdependence of nuclear family members, or of kin who are migrating together, may be intensified by moving together to a foreign land where the culture is strange and the people not always friendly. Family members are forced to depend largely on one another. This internal strength and cohesion may endure for years, or it may be undermined early by internal family conflict which often develops between immigrant parents and their children who are pushing for family change and Americanization.

3 Altered Family Roles The above-described situation suggests that family roles may be altered as the migrating family is thrown upon its own resources and members become dependent on each other in a strange, new environment. Immigrants from rural or peasant backgrounds moving to large American cities generally experience extensive changes in basic economic roles for both husband and wife and often in the homemaking role for the wife. In their study of Polish immigrants, William I. Thomas and Florian Znaniecki found that the husband had to seek employment away from home, and the wife, long accustomed to working side by side with her husband in the fields in Poland, now found herself deprived of any productive economic role and restricted unwillingly to the role of housewife, which made her feel quite useless.[10]

4 Differential Socialization and Family Conflict A family that migrates to a foreign country has a great deal to learn there—a new language, new laws, new customs, new money, new food, etc. Ideally, all family members will learn

these things at the same time and equally well. But it does not often happen this way. Age and sex differences and different daily experiences mean differential socialization among family members. Some will be more exposed to and will come to accept and learn the new culture sooner than others. This sets the stage for family conflict, which may divide husband from wife, and almost always divides parents from children at some point. Thomas and Znaniecki found that Polish parents continued to demand that their children turn over their earnings to their parents even though American culture taught the children that their earnings were their own. The result was apt to be a "complete and painful antagonism" between parents and children, with the young people withdrawing from their parents, and the parents on finding themselves unable to retain control over their sons and daughters often resorting to severe and repressive punishment.[11]

FACTORS AFFECTING CULTURAL AND SOCIAL ASSIMILATION Ruth Cavan makes a distinction between cultural and social assimilation which is very useful in analyzing variation and change among immigrant groups.[12] When immigrants to America have learned and accepted the prevailing American customs, traditions, norms, and values, as well as the new material culture and technology, they may be said to be culturally assimilated. For them to be socially assimilated, however, they must be personally and collectively accepted by the native Americans, and become integrated fully into the informal as well as the formal social life of the American community. External pressures toward cultural assimilation begin for an immigrant family during its early years or months in America. In the past, there were tremendous efforts made to induce immigrant families to give up their foreign ways and to conform to American ways. Public schools, churches, community centers, and settlement houses with their Americanization programs were all active in this effort after the turn of the twentieth century. As suggested above, these Americanization efforts have generally been more successful with the immigrant children than with their parents. Cultural assimilation generally requires more than one generation in America, and differs in rate of speed and extent from one group to another. Social assimilation takes longer, being dependent not only on cultural assimilation as a precondition but also on the social acceptance of the immigrant group by the Americans who were there ahead of them.

Now we will attempt to identify some of the salient factors that have influenced the cultural and social assimilation processes for American immigrants.

1 Settling in Immigrant Neighborhoods in American Cities Newly arrived immigrants quite naturally are attracted to a neighborhood occupied by people from their native land, and if possible by people from their own locality back home. In large cities these immigrant communities grew rapidly during

the periods of heavy immigration and became distinguishable by the dress and language of the people, the names on stores, and various physical characteristics. Such communities would be called "Little Italy" or "Little Greece" or "Polishtown."

These ethnic enclaves have been functional in many ways for their inhabitants, but also could be dysfunctional in the long run for their ultimate assimilation. Such a community may function as a buffer between the new arrivals and the unknown and bewildering larger society.[13] It shields them while they are learning about America; it provides a transitional culture between the old and the new; it reduces culture shock which can occur when new immigrants are plunged cold into a strange, new world. The immigrant community also provides newcomers with social life, companionship, and security by perpetuating as much of the old country informal activities and formal institutional participation as is possible, e.g., ethnic sports clubs, parish churches, stores stocked with native food and clothes. These provide the immigrant family with a reassuring feeling of being at home in an alien world. These communities also help families maintain their solidarity and reduce family and personal disorganization. In the early years of adjustment, the immigrant community helps to reduce the strain on families which often accompanies too rapid a change from one way of life to another. Perpetuation of Old World customs and institutional patterns helps keep parents and children in touch with each other and reinforces parents' efforts to maintain traditional family roles and relationships. Sooner or later, however, many families experience some degree of disorganization in the processes of change and assimilation into American society.

The principal dysfunction of life in the ethnic community is that life there impedes both cultural and social assimilation into the larger American society. This is, of course, a relative matter and needs to be weighed against the more immediate benefits just pointed out. Assuming, however, that eventually the immigrant family needs to become culturally and socially assimilated, its members will probably need sooner or later to move out of the confining ethnic enclave to accomplish this.

2 The Degree of Culture Change Required Depending on what country they came from and how different its culture is from that of America, the new arrivals experience a greater or lesser change in way of life before they become assimilated or Americanized. For a middle-class English family moving from London to Boston the changes required are minor compared with those for a rural Sicilian family moving to New York City. Thus the amount of culture change required of an immigrant group depends on the extent of the difference between its native culture and that of the American community where its members will live. One reason why the problems of assimilation of New Immigrants have often been greater than those of Old Immigrants is that

the folkways, mores, beliefs, institutions, etc., of the former group often have been in sharper contrast to those found in America.

3   Readiness of the American Community to Accept the Immigrants   Historically, native Americans have reacted ethnocentrically toward foreigners entering American communities. As seen earlier, American people, including their political, religious, and educational leaders, have put pressure on newcomers to shed their odd foreign ways and become Americanized, the sooner the better. Here again, the degree of strangeness or "foreignness" of the particular immigrant group in the eyes of the established Americans in that community will be important in determining whether the newcomers are accepted, perhaps tentatively at first, or are rejected at the outset. The post-World War II era has seen some reduction in ethnocentrism in America, with a corresponding increase in tolerance of cultural differences. This is most apt to be true of those Americans with higher education.

4   The Degree of Family Adjustment Required   Immigrant family adjustment processes are closely related to the factors just discussed. Immigrant families of the peasant-patriarchal type arriving from a Gemeinschaft-sacred society will almost inevitably experience a high degree of family disorganization as they move into urban Gesellschaft-secular American society. The traditional patriarchal Old World family organization and relationships just do not fit the new conditions of life in urban secular America, and the age-old family organization breaks down sooner or later—usually by the time the children have learned and accepted the new American ways and have introduced these beliefs and practices into the household. While some families may disintegrate due to severe conflict and disorganization, many are able to weather these rough periods and reach an accommodation that will enable the family to survive. Cavan describes the process of family disorganization and its probable resolution:

The shifting of roles, the declining status of parents and the increasing status of children, the inadequacy of the old family organization, and the need to change personal conceptions and standards of conduct all tend toward family disorganization and personal demoralization. This phase of adjustment is, however, usually a transitory one, and in time increasing familiarity with American culture and enlarged participation in American social groups bring about new family orientation.[14]

Large-scale immigration has contributed greatly to the creation and persistence of family variations in America. We always should keep in mind, as we review selected samples of American family variations, their Old World roots and experiences which, along with their American experience, have made them what they are. The different historical identities of the groups have been vitally important in shaping the destinies and lives of families in each group. Examples would be the Amish and Hutterites, so influenced by their religious identity, African-Americans by their racial identity, German-Americans, Polish-Americans, and Italian-Americans by their ethnic (national) identities. All such groups have had problems of adjusting to and living in American society with its dominant white, Anglo-American, Protestant culture. Most have suffered to some degree from being identified as minority groups.

Selected Racial, Ethnic, and Religious Family Variations

THE OLD ORDER AMISH FAMILY

The Old Order Amish family represents both a religious and an ethnic family subtype in America. (It is also one of the best examples of a traditional rural farm family.) One of the fascinating aspects of the heterogeneity of the

Horses and buggies take Amish families to Sunday religious service. (*Roger Nett.*)

American population and its diverse cultural origins is the wide variety of religious groups found in America. As a haven of religious freedom, America has attracted throughout its history groups of unorthodox religious persuasion who suffered religious persecution in their native lands. Such a group are the Old Order Amish, who are but one sect of the Mennonites. This larger parent religious grouping includes also the Church Amish, the Old Order Mennonites, the Reformed Mennonites, the Mennonite Brethren, and others. Many of these religious groups have quite distinctive family traditions and patterns of organization.

Religion as an independent variable and its impact on the family need more systematic study. Some of the ways in which religious institutions and practices may affect the family have been set down by Blood: (1) the influence of religious values on family beliefs and norms, (2) the sanctification of marriage and family life, (3) the conservation of old practices and traditions, (4) the shaping of attitudes toward sex and reproduction, (5) the emphasis on family and kin solidarity, (6) the establishment of rules to prevent marriage and family dissolution, and (7) the establishment of rules to encourage family growth.[15] In the ensuing review of family life among the Amish many of these religious influences will become very apparent. For the Amish the family system and the religious system are interlaced and mutually supportive in a remarkable and fascinating manner.

HISTORICAL BACKGROUND OF OLD ORDER AMISH   Many Amish communities exist, but the Old Order Amish group under review live in Lancaster County, Pennsylvania. Other Amish settlements are to be found in eighteen other states and in Ontario, Canada. The Lancaster County settlement is the oldest in America and probably still the most strict in its adherence to the traditional way of life brought over from Europe about 2½ centuries ago. The first Amish immigrants settled in Pennsylvania in 1727, attracted by the religious freedom promised by William Penn. They had departed their native Switzerland because of rising religious persecution. In Lancaster County, where the area of the Amish community covers more than 150 square miles, there is a population of over 6,000 people, most of whom live on farms. For about 250 years these Amish people have maintained a Gemeinschaft-sacred type of social and cultural island, surrounded by a secular American way of life which the Amish reject as being sinful, prideful, and otherwise contrary to God's word.

They have always lived a simple, rural way of life. The Amish man explains his adherence to this rural life by reference to biblical passages which promise special blessings to those who till the soil. With few exceptions Amish men are farmers. It has been estimated that 95 percent of the males are agricultural workers.[16] They are excellent farmers, and their Pennsylvania farms are among the very best in the United States.

AMISH CULTURE, COMMUNITY, AND HOMES   Authorities generally agree that the Old Order Amish are among the most conservative and tradition-oriented people in America. The Bible is the Amish people's literal guide to all aspects of life today, just as it has always been. The Amish way of life comes about as close to a full approximation of the Gemeinschaft-sacred type of social order as will be found in America today. Life on an Amish farm today is little different from what it was in early colonial America in the 1700s. William Kephart finds that "The houses they live in, the clothes they wear, the language they speak (German, Pennsylvania Dutch, some English), the hymns they sing, the beliefs they adhere to—few have changed in any significant way. For the Old Order Amish, major change is looked upon as tantamount to extinction."[17]

Kephart remarks that unless one has some firsthand experience with the Amish, it is very difficult to grasp the extent to which they have resisted inroads of modern American society. Their traditional and standardized dress styles for men and women are a case in point. Men wear plain coats with no collars, lapels or pockets, usually worn over a plain vest. Their plain trousers are worn with suspenders; belts are forbidden. Plain shirts are worn without ties. A man's hat, also plain, has a low crown and a wide brim. Women's dresses are ankle length and of a solid color, almost always worn with an apron. Black, low-heeled shoes are worn over black cotton stockings. One worry the Amish girls and boys do not have is that of keeping up with the latest style changes! John Hostetler, a top authority on the Amish comments on the functional significance of the distinctive and unchanging Amish apparel: "Dress styles serve as symbols for the group. The symbols function very effectively in maintaining separatism and continuity. The language of dress forms a common understanding and mutual appreciation among those who share the same traditions and expectations. Dress keeps the insider separate from the world and also keeps the outsider out. These shared convictions are given sacred sanction and biblical justification. . . ."[18]

The Amish reject most modern inventions and technological devices. Among their long list of taboos are electrical lights, telephones, radios, TVs, modern plumbing, bathrooms and inside toilets, washing machines, furnaces, and automobiles. Such things are considered dangerous to the way of living prescribed in the Bible, and ownership is forbidden. Amish are prohibited from attending movies, commercial sports events, taverns or bars, or other types of urban commercial entertainment. Even travel is discouraged, except for business purposes or for visiting relatives and friends in the community. Amish people belong at home on the farm, and unless they have taken the horse and buggy to town on business or are visiting a relative or neighbor, they will be found at home. Visiting is virtually the only form of adult entertainment for the Amish, and both men and women look forward eagerly to visiting time. Frequent visiting serves to strengthen the web of relationships within the community. Unselfish neighborly assistance in times of need or trouble has always been an Amish tradition. In case of an accident, such as a barn fire, the whole district will turn out to rebuild the barn, generally completing the task in one day! Lightning destroys many barns because the Amish believe lightning rods are contrary to God's will.

To the Amish, farm and home are inseparable.[19] The man is an expert farmer, and the Amish-owned farms here produce some of the finest crops in the world. Although he will not use a tractor, he will use some modern farm equipment such as cultivators, binders, and balers. As the Amish man and his sons keep the farm equipment and barns in top condition, so his wife and daughters keep the house. Although lacking in modern conveniences, the house is always in excellent repair and immaculately clean. Furnishings are sturdy, functional, and mostly homemade—often many generations ago. Lace curtains are not allowed, nor are wallpaper or mirrors. While floor rugs are forbidden, linoleum is approved. The Amish may use different colors in decorating, but they must be solid; no plaids, prints, or stripes. Walls, fences, and posts are often brightly colored. Homes, and rooms in the home, are quite large, especially the kitchen where much of the family life is centered. The Amish enjoy good food and they serve excellent and bountiful meals.

It should be noted that the home of the Amish family is also their church. Unlike another sect, the Church Amish, who do build churches for their services, the Old Order Amish religious services rotate from home to home each Sunday among the members of the district. Ideally, the first floor of the Amish home should be large enough to accommodate the whole district membership on a given Sunday morning. The Amish have no paid clergy; their bishop, ministers, and deacons are chosen by lot from the district membership. Heading the congregation is the bishop, a powerful and vigilant religious leader. The Amish feel that the bishop has been chosen by God to fill this role of authority and great responsibility.[20] Services are held in German or Pennsylvania Dutch. Men and women are seated separately. A Sunday service will start about 8:30 A.M. and continue till about noon.

The religious leaders exert strong control over the actions of the Amish people, but in a legitimized and nonarbitrary way. If a member has been charged with deviancy, the deacon makes a formal charge before all the baptized members following the regular church service. Full discussion follows, and a unanimity of decision is sought and generally obtained by vote of the membership, who look to the deacons and the bishop as their source of divine guidance. "Often a bishop is slow to arrive at a decision, but once he nods his head in approval the opinions of the congregation are likely to coalesce in agreement. Thus the 'bishop's nod' has come to be practically synonymous with ultimate decision."[21] The bishop is the group's principal enforcing agent and he will determine the sanction to be applied to the offender. The most powerful sanction among the Amish is the *Meidung*, a form of shunning or social ostracism. The *Meidung* shuts off the offender from any kind of communication or interaction with anyone in the congregation, including friends, neighbors, and family members. An individual under the "shun" usually must eat alone and remain apart from other members of the family. A short period under the "shun" is generally sufficient to produce the required public repentance and an avowal to discontinue the unacceptable behavior. Since conformity is essential to religious salvation, it is understandable that religious leaders exert such a powerful influence on individual behavior. It is "their judgment on conformity or deviation [which] is held to distinguish saint from sinner."[22]

As Kephart notes, the "watchdog" role of the bishop over the actions of the people is a crucial one, for without it Amish society would probably have fallen apart long ago.[23] The bishop sees that his people adhere strictly to the status quo with respect to manners, morals, and established practices, and guards against changes and innovations. No detail of life escapes the watchful eyes of these Amish leaders. Also, since the Amish keep no official written records and have no written codes or "constitution," it is the religious leaders who are the main keepers and guardians of the Amish culture. Amish history, traditions, and moral codes are mostly handed down by word of mouth.

COURTSHIP, MARRIAGE, AND FAMILY RELATIONSHIPS   Amish courtship has changed very little since the early settlers arrived. Their young people do not date non-Amish youth (called "English"). Opportunities for contact with members of the opposite sex among the Amish young people themselves are restricted. Probably the social occasion offering the best opportunity is the Sunday night "singing" specifically for young single people, generally held at the same home where religious services were held that morning. Other less regular occasions for meeting would be during holiday celebrations. A boy generally asks a girl to let him drive her home after the "singing." The next step would be the boy's visiting the girl at her home at night, more or less secretly. They may sit on the porch or in the kitchen after the old folks have retired. Contrary to rumors or myth, Amish youth do not practice "bundling." Young people are free, within certain limits, to select their own marriage partners. They must marry someone within the Amish group, and parental approval is required. When the young man wants to ask for his love's hand, he approaches her father who in turn goes to see the boy's father. Up until then, the courtship has been kept more or less secret by the young couple. The parents give their approval only when the clergy is satisfied that everything is in order, and then the announcement of the forthcoming marriage is made at the Sunday service. Once the couple is "published" in the religious service, the marriage will normally follow about two weeks later.[24] There is nothing corresponding to engagement as it is understood in the larger American society.

Weddings are normally held in the home of the bride, and like the Sunday religious service, may last three hours, with much hymn singing and a long solemn sermon from the bishop. After the final wedding vows are exchanged, then comes the huge wedding feast. It is not uncommon for the bride's family to feed 200 guests at a wedding celebration.[25] This is probably one reason why most weddings take place in November after the fall harvest is in. Kephart describes the bill of fare at one wedding feast to include ". . . one dozen each of chickens, ducks, and geese; fifty loaves of bread; several bushels of potatoes; vats of assorted vegetables and sauces; sixty pies; a dozen large layer cakes; bowls of mixed fruit; and a seemingly endless supply of fresh milk."[26]

Following the wedding festivities, the newlyweds leave for their honeymoon, but not to Niagara Falls. Rather than go away somewhere in private, the typical honeymooners make an extended series of visits in the homes of relatives and friends in the community. It is during these visits that the couple receive many of their wedding gifts, which are usually practical household items. After the honeymoon, the couple settle down as responsible young adults, generally on a farm. The man now grows a beard, sells his "singles" open buggy and buys a closed-top one suitable for a family. The couple no longer attend the Sunday evening singings for single youth; they take up association with the married group.[27] In most cases the couple will live on a farm located as close as possible to that of either his or her family. Their farm will possibly be a gift from his family, or at least purchased with parental help.

There is much evidence of extended familism among the Amish. That is, there is close and continuing contact between a given nuclear family and their parental families. Kephart cites an old Amish saying that the children when they marry should not move further away from their parents "than you can see the smoke of their chimney."[28] One study showed that 92 percent of the Amish brides and grooms were born in the same county in which their fathers were born.[29] This continuous interaction between married couples and their families of orientation provides not only family continuity but also security to each member throughout the life cycle. Both husband and wife are conscientious workers and thrifty managers, taking much pride in developing their farm enterprise and their home. Children are economic assets, but this is not the only reason for the high fertility rates found here. Amish parents know they are raising "the Lord's families," and it is fairly common for eight to twelve children to be born and raised in devout Amish families. Elmer Smith found that the average number of children per family was 7.5 in the late 1950s.[30]

The Amish family remains patriarchal, although the father's authority is tempered by kindness and affection for his wife and children. While women are subordinate, they seem to harbor little desire to alter their traditional status roles in the family. Children also are subordinate to adults, but not unhappily so. Sons at an early age start helping their father with the farm chores, the care of the livestock, and the field work. Daughters assist their mother with the housework and in the kitchen garden. The Amish boy and girl model their lives after those of their father and mother. Childhood is quite happy for boys and girls. Hostetler says that the extraordinary discipline and love they receive in the family prepare them thoroughly for their adult lives in the Amish community. He observes that:

The Amish home is an effective socializing agent, directed at making the child a mature person in the Amish way of life. Early in life the child learns that Amish are "different" from other people. Thus, he must learn to understand not only how to play the role at home and in the Amish system, but also how to conduct himself in relation to the norms of his "English" neighbors.

He cannot have clothes and toys just like the "English" people have. He soon learns to imitate his parents, to take pride in the "difference." . . . The Amish boy or girl is raised so carefully within the Amish family and community that he never feels secure outside it.[31]

Family discussions assume that the children will become farmers. With this clear objective there is little need to attend school beyond grade school. The Amish boy is a well-trained farmer ready to work at farming full time by the time most "English" boys are pursuing sports and studies in high school.

Amish familism is perhaps nowhere more evident than in the treatment of the aged in the family. The contrast between the lot of aging members here and that frequently found in secular, urban middle-class families becomes sharply clear in Walter Kollmorgen's description.

When the time comes to retire from active farming—usually when the youngest son or daughter marries—the aging parents move to a separate part of the house known as "Grossdawdy's house." Sometimes this is an addition to the main house and sometimes it is a separate unit.

Grossdawdy does not retire from all work when he retires to this part of the house. He finds as much work outside as he cares to do. Grossmutter sews during the day for children and grandchildren. This work keeps both of them healthily occupied as long as they are active. If they need attention younger family members are near. It is doubtful that old people anywhere are more contented than the occupants of the Grossdawdy house who can associate daily with their children and grandchildren and yet be separate.[32]

Kephart feels that there is sufficient evidence that the strongest and most stable family system in America is to be found here in the Old Order Amish community.[33] Families are large and highly integrated. Birthrates are high. Illegitimacy, adultery, and divorce are unheard of. Almost everyone marries, and marriages are broken only by the death of one's marriage partner. The children and the aged have useful, satisfying, and dignified positions in the family. Young people seldom leave the community, and rarely marry outside the Amish community. Families are prosperous but not wealthy, and each family takes care of its own ill or indigent members. No Old Order Amish person has ever been on public relief, nor in fact has one ever accepted any kind of state assistance, including old-age pensions or other kinds of social security. Strains do appear sometimes of course. Young people may express discontent with some aspects of the strict way of life, and a few individuals have been known to "secede" and leave the community. But overwhelmingly, the Amish "are willing to forgo personal attainment in exchange for a deeply rewarding system of family and group values."[34]

THE FUTURE   There is a good deal of speculation about the likelihood of future changes in the Amish way of life. How long will they be able to continue their centuries-old ways and hold the line against increasing pressures from the larger American society? They have developed a remarkable ability to resist change over a period of 2½ centuries, and authorities such as Kephart feel that the probability is high that they will go right on following their traditional life-styles into the foreseeable future.[35] Districts vary in the degree of their orthodoxy, and some districts are less strict than others. This enables an Amish family not in agreement with the codes of one group to move to another district more to their liking, whether more liberal or more conservative.

Kephart finds that in most of the Old Order Amish settlements the only changes that have occurred are in some minor details, and that virtually no changes have taken place in major areas such as in occupation, transportation, housing, general attire, moral codes, marital practices, patriarchal emphasis, biblical adherence, pacifism, and general life-style.[36] What may appear to be change to casual observers or outsiders is likely to be an observation made of one of the more "liberal" Amish groups, who, for example, do use more modern farm machinery.

THE ITALIAN-AMERICAN FAMILY

BACKGROUND AND ORIGINS   Americans of Italian descent have, for the past half century or more, constituted the largest European-derived national-ethnic group in America. Of more than 34 million people of "foreign white stock" (i.e., who were themselves foreign-born or who had at least one parent who was foreign-born) in the United States, according to the 1960 Census, 4½ million, or 13.3 percent, were Italians.[37] Due partly to the size of the group and the relative recency of their movement to America, Italian-Americans have tended to adhere to their ethnic identity, and have been slower than many other white ethnic groups in becoming culturally and socially assimilated. Their slower rate of assimilation has also been attributed in part to the fact that: (1) dialect differences between villages or provinces inhibited intergroup communication among immigrants; (2) the majority came with minimal occupational skills, being of illiterate peasant stock; (3) as Roman Catholics, their religion was at variance with the predominant Protestantism; (4) as a people of "Mediterranean" stock, their appearance varied somewhat from that of the allegedly "Nordic" white Americans.[38]

The vast majority of Italian immigrants came from southern Italy and Sicily during the New Immigration period. The peak years were between 1890 and 1900 when more than 2,300,000 arrived. They were generally young, and many young men came with the intention of staying in America only long enough to earn sufficient funds to enable them to return to Italy, buy some land, marry, and live out their lives with their families. Some did return home to stay; others returned to marry and brought their brides back to America. The majority of the immigrants remained in America despite their original hope of returning home to Italy.

New arrivals settled mostly in urban neighborhoods near kinfolk or friends from the same village or province in Italy.[39] Families generally arranged the marriages of the newcomers. Newly arrived singles, usually male, would often move in with either relatives or friends as part of the household. Thus many children grew up in a household which included their parents and also assorted aunts, uncles, cousins, and other "boarders." People from the same village back in Italy clustered together in the same neighborhood, and native Americans soon termed such a community "Little Italy." In addition to the natural inclination to be near people of one's own nationality (and village if possible), this ethnic clustering was also a defense against inhospitality and prejudice displayed by native Americans and other ethnic groups. Here newcomers could get information and aid regarding housing, employment, schools, etc. Identity with and loyalty to Italian kin and fellow villagers was a source of comfort and strength for the newcomers, but these very loyalties were liable to impede their ultimate assimilation into American society.

CULTURAL AND SOCIAL ASSIMILATION   As noted earlier, cultural assimilation normally precedes social assimilation. And immigrant families generally accept the new material cultural items before they will the nonmaterial beliefs and sentiments. Immigrant women, for example, more readily accept American kitchen devices than they would American equalitarian beliefs.

In order to understand the problems of adjustment and change experienced by the Italian-American family as it moved to and became settled in America, it is necessary to review what the Old World Italian family was like in southern Italy and Sicily. It was largely a peasant family, with a localized village or provincial identity, living in an agrarian, semifeudal society. Family organization was patriarchal, and generally patrilocal, with a strong tradition of primogeniture. The eldest son inherited the family property and the status of his father in the community, and generally followed his father's occupation and pattern of community participation. These male-oriented family patterns stemmed in part from the ancient Roman heritage which included one of the strongest patriarchal family systems ever known.[40] A related characteristic of the Italian family was its strong familism, which entailed reciprocal loyalty and mutual support among family members. Historically, the Italian people have not had much trust or confidence in the government or in their rulers. As Francis Femminella notes, "Family loyalty was therefore the only tie that Italians could trust. The Roman paterfamilias not only ruled but protected the members of his family. It was a kind of patron-client relationship."[41] Next to loyalty to family and kin, the Italian peasant gave loyalty to the village, or *paese*. Thus it was natural for the Italian immigrant to continue these strong loyalties as the family moved to America and settled in the Italian-American enclave.

The Italian rural family was typically large, with the wife and children subordinate to the will of the husband-father who ruled the family in a strict and authoritarian manner. He could and often did punish the children severely. Children were expected to be obedient and respectful to parents and to other adults in the kin or friendship circle.[42] Sons and daughters accepted adult responsibilities at early ages. Sons especially were expected to start work early to help support the family and turn their earnings over to their father. The status role of the mother in the family somewhat counterbalanced and tempered the strong patriarchalism of the father. She often intervened on behalf of the children. Her role was more affectionate and protective, and her influence on the husband-father was considerable even if informal and indirect. A kind of patriarchal-matriarchal family structure often existed, where "the patriarchy's direct and conscious, [and] the matriarchy is 'hidden' and unconscious."[43]

Paul Campisi, in his work entitled "The Italian Family in the United States," traces its transformation and acculturation from the Old World peasant type through the first-generation Italian-American period on to the second generation of the family in America. In the process of acculturation or assimilation he identifies three successive stages: (1) the initial contact stage, (2) the conflict stage, and (3) the accommodation stage.[44] We will review briefly Campisi's analysis.

1   The Initial Contact Stage   During its first decade in America the newly arrived Italian-American family generally remains intact, buttressed by the long Italian traditions of familism and solidarity. But pressures and conditions both within and outside the family begin to affect the Old World peasant family patterns, and changes, actual or potential, are in the works. Some conditions and processes that contribute to family change are (a) tenement living, with American household equipment, utensils, and furniture; (b) the father becoming an employee, generally as an unskilled laborer at the bottom of the occupational hierarchy, handicapped with having to learn a new language; (c) the children attending American public school or sometimes a parochial school, where they quickly learn the new language and other basics of

American culture much more rapidly and systematically than their parents possibly can; (d) the informal interaction of the children with American young people in play groups, church groups, clubs, etc.; (e) the recognition by the children and their parents that continuing to live the Italian way means low status, prejudice, and discrimination; and (f) "increasing pressure by American legal, educational, political, and economic institutions for the Americanization of the foreigners."[45] However, during this period the family is generally able to resist much actual change and remain integrated. It is during the following decade in America that "the first generation family experiences its most profound changes and is finally wrenched from its Old World foundation."[46]

2 The Conflict Stage   Now the Italian-American family is torn by increasing conflict between the Italian way of life and the American way of life, and by overt incompatibility between the parents and their children (who are likely to be in their teens now). This phase generally begins during the second decade of living in America, and is manifest "when the children unhesitatingly express their acquired American expectations and attempt to transmit them in the family situation and when the parents in turn attempt to reinforce the pattern of the Old World peasant family. Conflicting definitions . . . threaten to destroy whatever stability the family had maintained during the first period."[47]

This is a time of great misunderstanding and frustration for both parents and children, which rises to the pitch of "an undeclared state of war between the two ways of life." External pressures for change also continue to build up, and it becomes inevitable that the traditional family structure should crumble in its already weakened condition. The father loses much of his traditional status and power; the sons gain in power and importance in the family; daughters gain "unheard-of independence." What happens is that "the children press down upon the first-generation family an American way of life."[48]

3 The Accommodation Stage   Both the parents and their children begin to realize that a continuation of the misunderstandings, hostility, and conflict can break up the family. Fortunately, there are a number of things that tend toward compromise and more tolerant attitudes. Neither parents nor children want a family breakup. The Italian family traditions of loyalty and affection among members, submerged during the conflict period, now surface again as the children grow more mature and the parents come to realize that their worst fears about their Americanizing children going bad have not been borne out. And the parents come to realize that they must sacrifice certain aspects of their old Italian family ways in order to retain ties with their sons and daughters. The children in turn learn that successful interaction in the American world is possible without a complete rejection of all Italian culture. Other factors that help establish a new modus vivendi are (a) recognition by the parents that they will stay in America permanently; (b) with the passage of

years, the diminishing hold of the Italian village culture on the aging parents; (c) the passing by the children of the immigrants into young adulthood, and marriage and establishment of homes of their own; (d) recognition by the parents that economic and social success can come to their grown-up children only as they become more and more like native Americans; and (e) increasing dependence of the aging parents on their Americanized offspring. Such accommodations between the immigrant parents and their offspring enable the second-generation Italian-American family to become increasingly oriented toward the American way of life, and these second-generation families thus typically pattern themselves after contemporary urban American families. The transition is expedited as the family decreases its ties with the Italian neighborhood, and expands its ties and relationships with non-Italians, including intermarriage.[49]

ITALIAN-AMERICAN FAMILY CHANGES   From the time the Italian immigrant families arrived in America through the second-generation Italian-American family, the changes in courtship, marriage, and family patterns were extensive and extreme.[50]

An example of such extensive change is seen in what happened to their courtship practices. The Old World southern Italian courtship system was quite simple and of short duration. Parents arranged marriages of their children to suitable candidates in the same village. The young people were married in their early teens, and strict chaperonage protected the girl's chastity until her marriage. Any premarital contact between boys and girls was closely supervised by adult family members. In the early years in America the occasions for young people to meet and to be together were not too different from those in the old country, i.e., at weddings, christenings, patron saint day celebrations, or Christmas holidays. It was understood that any couple who paid special attention to each other must be seriously interested in marriage. For a boy and a girl to be in a position to get to this point generally meant that their parents knew each other very well and likely came from the same village. Parental approval was sought, and normally readily given. Then a public announcement of the engagement was made, with the marriage taking place in less than a year. In lieu of a formal dowry the couple was given wedding gifts of linen, furniture, and household items.[51]

By the next generation most of these Old World–based courtship practices had been largely abandoned and were replaced by secular American practices. In the second-generation families the teenagers, who were thoroughly sold on the American courtship customs and norms of free dating and individual choice of marriage partners, resisted strongly the traditional Italian prescription of arranged marriages and the proscription of unchaperoned heterosexual relations. A pattern developed that constituted an intermixture of Italian and American customs, described this way by Michael Lalli:

The boy-meets-girl pattern became increasingly secularized. Sacred holidays, weddings, and christenings were still important but public dances, school events, picnics provided many occasions for meetings. Dates were not specifically arranged. Young men and girls would make their appearance as members of separate groups knowing well who exactly would be there. Although such meetings were "accidental," a young man would often have the opportunity of taking a girl home. If the relationship developed to this point where a date or two was arranged in advance and the young man called at the girl's home, there was a strong presumption in the American community that an engagement announcement would be made.[52]

These practices represented an accommodation between the old Italian pattern of separation of the sexes before marriage and the American way of more freedom between young people of the opposite sex. Herbert Gans, in *The Urban Villagers*, reports the persistence of this group pattern as part of the courtship process among lower- and working-class Italian-Americans in the late 1950s. He found very little contact among individual young men and young women.[53] While second-generation youth had more independence and tended to see dating and courtship through American eyes, most still confined their serious courtship and final selection of a marriage partner to the Italian population. And even those who married an outsider would still seek parental approval.[54]

During the years of the Great Depression it was often difficult for a young married couple to find a house of their own they could afford, so they often lived in the home of parents, sometimes for several years. It was not until World War II and after that large numbers of third-generation families were able to become fully independent and move out of the Italian neighborhoods. This residential mobility was often accompanied by social mobility and the achievement of middle-class status. Dating and courtship for boys and girls in these families became very similar to that of the American middle class.[55]

It should be noted that the behavior patterns of the third-generation Italian-American youth varied according to the modes of adjustment of their parental families. Those teenagers whose parents had largely rejected the Italian traditions and sought integration into American society exhibited very few Italian cultural traits and tended to merge with other Americans. Their parents not only may have severed ties with the Italian neighborhood but also may have changed or at least Anglicized their name. At the other extreme were parents who had resisted Americanization and held tenaciously to the traditional Italian culture. Their children were more likely to continue certain traditional courtship practices, although it was in such families that the most severe conflict between children and their parents generally occurred, as described by Campisi. Between these extremes, the majority of second-generation parents would likely fall, gradually becoming Americanized while still retaining some ties with the Italian community and subculture. Their teenaged children (third-generation Italian-Americans) would have experienced much less culture conflict than their parents had at that age and thus were more comfortable in adopting American courtship practices while still maintaining some aspects of Italian-American identity.[56]

PERSISTING OR CONTINUING ITALIAN-BASED FAMILY PATTERNS With all the many changes that have taken place in the Italian-American family over its span of years in the United States, there are still certain Italian traditions and values that have tended to persist. The Italian family has traditionally been adult-oriented, and there is evidence that this continues to be the case especially in working-class families, according to Gans.[57] Children are still subordinate to adult family members and are expected to be obedient and to act in ways to please their parents. Age still carries some status in Italian-American circles. The young are taught to respect and show regard for older people. Elderly people in the family represent symbols of prestige and authority to Italian-American children. There are also certain semipatriarchal remnants today. While the authority of the father has been much diminished, depending on the degree of acculturation and the family's social-class position, the father is still normally the head of the household. The ideal Italian-American father, says Lalli, is sober and hard working; he puts his family name and obligations first. The ideal wife and mother is still the thrifty, affectionate, and faithful protector of her family. The ideal children are obedient and respectful.[58] Thus it may be said that there are elements of familism still persisting in the Italian-American family in mid-twentieth century. Loyalty and affection among family members continue. The degree to which this latter-day familism is due to Italian traditions as opposed to American influences is uncertain. As Femminella points out, social-class differences are probably significant here. "First- and second-generation Italian-Americans in urban ghettos are in effect 'villagers' in that their familism is derived from their ethnic background. Third-generation Italian-Americans (middle class, suburban, and upwardly mobile) are familistic only to the degree that others in their class, regardless of ethnicity, may also be familistic."[59]

THE FUTURE OF THE ITALIAN-AMERICAN FAMILY With each passing generation the Italian-American family has moved further away from the Old World type. The third generation—and subsequent generations—have moved well into the mainstream of American life, to the point of a considerable amount of intermarriage with non-Italians. In their structure and relationships, contemporary American families of Italian derivation differ from those of earlier generations, and in all likelihood changes will continue in the direction of the urban, secular, middle-class American model. The large patriarchal

Italian family structure has given way to a smaller patricentric family structure in the working class, and a child-centered more equalitarian type in the middle class. As families have become more secular and individual-oriented, they have also become more prone to disruption by separation and divorce. While Italian-American families continue their move toward social assimilation, Femminella believes that their ethnic consciousness will not disappear entirely for some time, pointing out that "Italian-Americans in the third generation and beyond, secure in their Americanism, seem to want, consciously or unconsciously, to color and enliven their Americanism with a kind of romanticized but real Italianness. Where the larger community accepts this, those who had previously rejected their heritage now seek to reestablish their former identity socially, if not yet psychologically."[60]

On another plane, occasional encounters with subtle prejudice or discrimination still remind Italian-Americans that some other Americans continue to view them as "different." Recognition of this condition led to the formation in the late 1960s of the Italian-American Anti-Defamation League to help defend the integrity of the more than 22 million Americans of Italian descent. Also, about the same time, the American Italian Historical Association was founded to promote research on the Italian experience in America.[61]

THE BLACK AMERICAN FAMILY

BACKGROUND AND ORIGINS   Black families constitute a large and important segment of American families. The 1970 census showed the American Negro at 22,673,000, and it has been estimated that by 1976 the black population had risen to 24.2 million persons.[62] Black families play an important role in contemporary American society, as their predecessors played a crucial role in the growth and development of America. Yet, as Andrew Billingsley notes, the Negro or black family has been virtually ignored until very recently by historians and scholars of group life in America. Various kinds of biases and prejudices, conscious or unconscious, have been at fault. Billingsley charges that "Scholars have been steered away from the study of the Negro family by their European ethnocentrism and by the nature of their professional disciplines. Where they have treated the Negro family they have done so in a negativistic and distorted fashion for the same reasons."[63]

Whether or not one agrees with Billingsley, most authorities today would agree that social scientists have had great difficulty studying and discussing black Americans, including black families, without bias, subjectivity, and moral judgments coloring their observations and interpretations. Study of both the history of the black family and the contemporary family scene have been subject to these difficulties, as will be evident in the disagreements over the origins and development of the black family, and in controversies today over

the contemporary black family and its much publicized "instability." Billingsley indicts social scientists for their biases, distortions, and selectivity.

For it must be said with all candor that social scientists who have recently discovered
the Negro family have not yet produced a study of that 75 percent of Negro families
who have stable marriages, or that half of Negro families who have managed to pull
themselves into the middle class, or that 90 percent of all Negro families who are
self-supporting, or those even larger portions who manage to keep out of trouble, often
despite the grossest kinds of discrimination and provocation.[64]

HISTORICAL BACKGROUND OF BLACK AMERICAN FAMILIES: TWO VER-
SIONS   The historical background of the black American family not only
embraces the experience throughout American history following the arrival of
the first Africans in 1619, but also its cultural and social origins in Africa. At
least this is what could logically be expected, and has been the case with all
other peoples migrating to America. One of the long-standing controversies
over the nature and development of the black family in America begins with
this very point of the influence or lack of influence of the African cultural
heritage in shaping the black American family. One view, generally identified
with Melville Herskovitz, is that the social and cultural systems found in the
western African societies from which most African-Americans came were
polygynous and mother-centered; thus these people brought with them the
cultural bases for family instability during the slavery period and after, and
also for the black matricentric family.[65] An opposing view advanced by E.
Franklin Frazier is that the cultural backgrounds of Africans brought to
America as slaves had little or no influence on their subsequent marriage or
family relationships because that native culture was largely obliterated due to
their experiences following capture, transportation to America, and life here in
America.[66] Frazier holds that seldom in history has a group been so
completely stripped of its cultural heritage as were the Negroes who were
brought from Africa to America. Families were separated and people from the
same tribal or nationality groups were separated in order to reduce communication among newly captured slaves and lessen the possibility of their
plotting to escape. In America during slavery Negroes were randomly moved
from place to place. Under such conditions it was extremely difficult for
blacks to sustain their native African family traditions and behavior patterns.
Thus, argues Frazier, new forms of marriage and family relations were
developed here in the New World which reflected their experiences and
conditions of life under slavery. Some conditions and experiences were
conducive to stable forms and relationships and others to unstable forms and
relationships.

Historical data are not now adequate to answer the question of how and to what extent African cultural backgrounds contributed to shaping the marriage and family patterns evinced in the New World by African-Americans. The author is inclined to accept the view that the shattering experiences of capture, transportation to the New World, separation of fellow villagers and often of family members by sale to different owners, plus differential experience during the slavery period, all contributed to the destruction of family ties that normally meet the needs of individuals, thus creating loose and unstable male-female and parent-child relations for many black Americans. Some blacks, such as house servants, more fortunate than the masses of plantation field slaves, were able to maintain or establish more stable and conventional marriage and family relationships patterned after those of white people. So, in addition to loss of African cultural family heritage, differential experience during slavery contributed to the variety of black American marriage and family patterns found during the slavery period.[67]

Differential experiences following emancipation resulted in still further variations in family patterns. Especially significant was the mobility of black families and individuals leaving the rural South for the cities of the North and East. Perpetual crises confronted these blacks in their efforts to adjust to the difficult conditions of big-city life for which their rural background scarcely prepared them. Some marriage and family disorganization was inevitable. Data are not adequate to tell us how much though, and there is disagreement among authorities today on this point. Billingsley feels that the extent of black marriage and family disorganization throughout American history has been exaggerated.[68] (This issue will be examined in some detail below.) Throughout their difficult and often tragic history in America, there is evidence that the big majority of black American families were somehow able to survive with a high degree of stability, a truly remarkable achievement.

FAMILY VARIATIONS UNDER SLAVERY   Conditions of life for many blacks led to the "mother-centered family." The destruction of traditional African family patterns for African-Americans began with their experiences in Africa, where slave traders gathered their human property, consisting mostly of young males, for shipment to the New World. The processes of shipment, sale to new owners, and the scattering of slaves throughout numerous farms and plantations, made it difficult to retain or reknit the fabric of their native culture, including marriage and family customs and role relationships. Particularly among slaves who worked in the fields, where the sexes were often segregated in both work and in living quarters, it was difficult to continue any past marriage and family relations. In addition, there were few guidelines or controls established by the white owners to aid slaves in maintaining conventional marriage and family patterns. Furthermore, legalized marriage was denied to slaves, and certain white-imposed conditions of working and living were conducive to new, unconventional forms of relations among black men, women, and children. As Frazier describes it,

Under the system of slavery the Negro family emerged first as a natural organization based upon the physical and emotional ties between the mother and her offspring. The father and husband played a less important role in family relations because his interest in the family was less fundamental and his relations with his wife and children were influenced to a larger extent by the fortunes of the slave regime. The attitudes of both "husband" and "wife" toward "marriage," which had no legal basis, were influenced by the degree to which they had assimilated the sex and family mores of the whites. The process of assimilation proceeded most rapidly with the house servants who lived in close association with the whites and shared in the lives of the latter.[69]

Field slaves were at a big disadvantage in this respect, as noted above, and the development of a loosely organized mother-centered family was the logical result of their living and working conditions. The mother became the central figure in these families. The emotional ties between mother and child were deeper and their relationships more regular and more permanent than between father and child. The slave mother and her children were treated as a group by the white owner, and they were relatively independent of the black husband-father; they looked to the white owner for most of their needs. Accordingly, the black mother developed a keen sense of her status and personal rights. Although the husband-father was frequently a member of the family group, his relationships there were more casual and more easily broken; he was more apt to be sold and separated from his family. So the male field slave was in a particularly difficult position to assert his wishes or to have significant authority in his family. He could not dominate his wife and children, nor even achieve an equal position with his wife in a marital union.

It seems likely, then, that the conditions of slavery, rather than any African cultural origins, were responsible for the emergence and continuation of the mother-centered black family during this period of American history. The matrifocality was imposed by the lack of power and resources of the black male, the control of the white master, and other factors related to the humiliating experiences of slavery.[70]

A "father-centered family" also existed at this time. During the long period of slavery there were many Americans of African descent who lived under conditions more conducive to conventional American family life than was true for the field slaves discussed above. For these more fortunate black Americans, marriage and family life approximated the white American patriarchal or semipatriarchal type of the time. This was true of many in the house-servant category as well as for the "freedmen." The house servants assimilated white culture more readily, including sex morals and marital roles, while living under conditions more conducive to a stable family life. A male who worked in his master's house was more directly under his influence, more trusted, and had more authority and knowledge than his field-worker counterpart. His status was higher among blacks as well as whites, and he could better sustain his position as head of his family.

As the generations passed, an increasing number of house slaves were mulattoes, a condition that generally yielded higher status among both whites and blacks. The lighter skin was not only closer to white physical standards, but also many owners were partial to slaves of mixed ancestry, not infrequently due to the role the owner had in their birth.[71]

The other segment of the black population to develop a family structure approximating the existing white father-centered family type consisted of "freedmen," many of whom were of mixed racial ancestry. In Frazier's words:

The process of assimilating the family mores of the whites was facilitated and accelerated by racial amalgamation under the slave system. The very fact of white ancestry tended to make the mixed-blood identify himself with the whites. Largely as the result of race mixture, a class of free Negroes came into existence, especially in those areas of the South where the economic basis of slavery was being undermined. Among the nearly half-million free Negroes nearly forty percent of whom were mixed blood, there was a substantial element with a secure economic position, especially in the South. It was among this element that the Negro family acquired an institutional character with traditions of conventional sex and family mores.[72]

By 1860 there were almost a half million free blacks in the United States, and they constituted about 11 percent of the total population of black Americans.[73] Among these free blacks were men who had acquired strong proprietary interests in their wives and children by purchasing them from their white owners. This made a freedman the legal owner of his wife and children. Since some black fathers did not free their families immediately, such ownership was one basis for strong patriarchal authority, supported by a threatened sanction over wife and children of possibly being sold for disobedience.[74] In many respects the freed blacks lived under conditions much more favorable to stable and socially approved marital unions, enabling them to avoid the matrifocality which characterized the less fortunate slave families. They sustained a high degree of family stability during the slavery period, although their status was not equal to that of whites. Freed blacks could not vote, were often harassed, and some were forcibly returned to slavery. Anxious for social acceptance, freedmen adopted and followed strictly the moral codes and customs of middle- and upper-class whites, including the prevailing patriarchal family patterns. Their style of life, quite distinct from that of the masses of slaves, has continued among middle- and upper-class blacks into the twentieth century.[75] Research shows that a high proportion of American black leaders have come from families of freedmen background.[76]

The continuation of a segment of the black patriarchal family population after emancipation was supported by the post-Civil War rural economy. Farms and plantations were frequently run by black tenant farmers or contract labor. Work contracts made with plantation owners by black men often included other family members as laborers, for whose work performance the black father was responsible. This situation tended to sustain the father's interest in his family while perpetuating his patriarchal hold over his wife and children.

In summary, the assimilation of white father-centered family patterns during the slavery period by slaves such as the house servants who were in a position to learn and follow these patterns, as well as similar assimilation by the freed blacks, and the rural economic organization of the Reconstruction period, accounted for much of the existence of the father-centered type of black family during this period of American history.[77]

SOME CONSEQUENCES OF EMANCIPATION   It was unfortunate but inevitable that while black Americans welcomed their new freedom, emancipation would produce new problems and bring widespread social disorganization to the black population. Newly freed slaves lived under constant threat of illness and starvation due to a lack of goods and services needed for survival. They possessed few resources or facilities needed to care for themselves, and many lacked normative guidelines and experience necessary for self-direction and self-support. However, in spite of these problems, most families that had a history of stability during the slavery period were not significantly shaken by the traumas accompanying freedom. On the other hand, where loose attachments had prevailed during slavery, marriages were more likely to be disrupted and family members dispersed under the stresses associated with emancipation. Frazier sums up the postemancipation situation this way:

From emancipation to the first decade of the present century, two general tendencies are apparent in the development of the Negro family. In families which had acquired considerable stability during slavery, the father's position was more firmly established, especially if he became a landowner or a home owner. This class grew in importance during the first fifty years of freedom and together with the descendants of the free Negro with whom they intermarried formed what represented the conventional and stable elements of family life of the Negro. On the other hand, among the great mass of rural Negroes, . . . there developed a form of family life based largely upon mutual interests and mutual sympathies. It lacked an institutional basis, since both legal marriage and divorce were not generally observed. The family often grew out of unmarried motherhood and the common interests which developed from the association of men and women in the struggle for existence.[78]

Since legally sanctioned marriage had been denied black slaves before emancipation, the casual marriage and family ties which were prevalent among rural blacks were frequently severed following emancipation as thousands of ex-slaves seized the opportunity to leave the plantations and farms. Many drifted about the South seeking employment or adventure, then eventually moved to other regions. Casual sexual attachments were often formed during these years. Emancipation meant new freedom of movement, especially for men. Where the combined conditions of male mobility, sexual promiscuity, and family irresponsibility existed following emancipation and during the Reconstruction period, wives and mothers suffered. Under slavery, the black woman had the protection and economic security provided by her white owner's family. This security departed with emancipation, and she suddenly had to depend upon her own resources to support herself and her children. Her husband or "man" might be neither prepared nor willing to accept these new family obligations. When this was the case, the black mother found herself burdened with the responsibility of supporting as well as rearing her children. Since she had to find some means of economic livelihood, she was more tied down than the man. She had to accept men on their terms; to have a man even for a short time meant some affection and perhaps some temporary economic support.

Following emancipation, then, it appears that conditions of life for the masses of rural ex-slaves were conducive to the continuation of a mother-centered family. The mother-child relationship remained the core of family life for many rural black Americans.[79]

MOBILITY AND URBANIZATION AND THE BLACK FAMILY   Following emancipation, blacks in the South began to move, first from farms and plantations into Southern towns and cities. Then, over the decades, an increasing stream of blacks began to leave the Southern regions, settling mainly in cities in the North, and to a lesser extent in the West. Well over 90 percent of all black Americans were living in Southern rural areas at the end of the Civil War, and in 1900 about nine of every ten blacks were still living in the South. Thereafter the main black population shifts took place. By 1940 the proportion of blacks residing in the South was 77 percent, and by 1965 it had declined to 54 percent, with 38 percent living in the North and 8 percent in the West.[80]

A fact of great consequence about black migration is that it has been a movement of millions of individuals and families from rural to urban environments. By the start of World War II nearly half of all black Americans lived in cities, and by 1970 nearly three-fourths had become urban dwellers. The bulk of this black migration has been attracted to the large industrial centers of the country. Between 1940 and 1960 the black populations of New York City and Philadelphia doubled, those of Chicago and Detroit tripled, and that of Los Angeles quintupled.[81]

The combined processes of migration and urbanization have created profound new problems of family life for blacks, as well as intensifying older problems. Frazier observed that "As the result of urbanization and widening contacts, Negro family life had to adjust to a new social and economic environment. The type of family life that took shape among the rural folk in the South could no longer function in the urban environment. There has been much family disorganization, but at the same time the family has adjusted itself increasingly to the demands of city living.[82]"

Since Frazier wrote these lines, many problems of urban life have become more acute for blacks, as evidenced by the city riots and disturbances of the 1960s. Most of the early black migrants arrived in the cities without funds and without skills to sell in the urban job market; they were forced to live in the poorest housing in the slum areas of the city. Their swelling numbers and rural ways aroused negative reactions among white residents. Racial discrimination in employment and exploitation and segregation in housing produced the huge black ghettos in which poor families would be trapped for decades. Life in the city for these rurally raised black families became a life of exclusion—exclusion from white neighborhoods, from white schools and other community institutions, exclusion from white politics and government, and often from white churches. This exclusion and discrimination forced blacks to create their own community organizations. It was not until the post-World War II period when the courts began to reinterpret the Fourteenth Amendment of the United States Constitution that any significant improvements in the civil rights of blacks came to pass. These gains and their impact on black American families will be treated more fully later.

F. Ivan Nye and Felix Berardo have summed up the combined impact of migration and urbanization on the poor black family of rural origin in these words: "The strange, impersonal, and often hostile urban environment, the extremely overcrowded and squalid condition of the slums, and low occupational status and poverty—all of these affected further disruption of this already weakened and loose-knit family system. Lacking the ordinary institutional supports and traditional community controls, the Negro family becomes increasingly disorganized when confronted with the bewildering and anonymous urban world.[83]

CONTEMPORARY BLACK AMERICAN FAMILIES: CONTINUITIES AND EMERGING PATTERNS Throughout its history in America, from the long slavery period through emancipation and Reconstruction and the subsequent migrations to large cities, black family life has undergone continuous processes of change and adjustment. In the 1970s, one finds a truly wide variety of patterns of family life among the more than 24 million black American people. These differences in family organization reflect different historical experiences and conditions of living, and different contemporary environments and experiences. Racial prejudice and discrimination continue today, somewhat less overtly or officially than in the past, but no less real in consequences. Rural and urban differences still exist; about 25 percent of

House in black ghetto. (*E. D. Dyer.*)

black families still live in rural areas, mostly on small farms or as tenant farm families or as farm laborers. The 75 percent of blacks who live in cities live under widely varied conditions, ranging from densely crowded ghettos to middle- and upper-class neighborhoods and suburbs.

Perhaps most relevant today for the understanding of contemporary black family life is the socioeconomic dimension.[84] Black American families vary in more important ways today in terms of occupation, income, and education than in terms of any other factors, including race itself. While black families have made significant gains in recent years, most of the gain has been made in the more highly educated middle- and upper-class groups. In 1960, two-thirds of the nonwhite population in the United States were still living below the poverty level. In the mid-1970s, the big majority of blacks were still well below whites in terms of education, occupation, and income.[85]

Family sociologists have identified a number of types of contemporary black American families. Each family type represents a pattern of life worked out as black Americans have struggled to cope with the complex of social forces and conditions impinging on their daily lives. Certain continuities from the past as well as new and emergent characteristics make up the fabric of each family type.

1   The Contemporary Matricentric Family   The urban, lower-class mother-centered family of today is in some ways a survival of the earlier black matricentric family. The mother and children are the durable heart of the family with the husband-father a more peripheral and often temporary member. These families are concentrated mainly in the slum zones of big cities. Effective family functioning and rewarding internal relationships are handicapped by economic insecurity and the chronic problem of the adult male in finding and maintaining adequate employment. For him, intermittent employment at menial and unsatisfying jobs with low pay results in perpetual frustration, pent-up hostility toward society, and low motivation for assuming family roles and responsibilities. To add to his frustration, he sees that a black woman generally has greater employment opportunities than he does, which enables her to be a more reliable source of family income. This adds to the status and power of the wife-mother in the family, and the male may find his effort to maintain a position as head of the household untenable. The stage is set for marital discord and for misunderstandings and tensions in father-child relations. These conditions of life in the poor black population have been conducive to households centering around the mother, called the "adaptive urban matricentric Negro family" by Stuart Queen and Robert Habenstein.[86]

The extent to which such a female-centered family pattern can be attributed to earlier black mother-centered families is not clear. The cultural heritage of the lower-class black male has been an emasculating one, and as a wage earner he has always lagged behind his white counterpart.[87]

It is quite evident, however, that racial discrimination in employment today has contributed powerfully to the inability of the black man to support his family adequately, thus undermining his ability to fulfill conventional husband-father role expectations.

It has been argued that there are special problems of socialization and identity for male youth in these urban matricentric families. Queen and Habenstein describe this situation:

In the adaptive urban matricentric family, the absence or weak presence of the father hampers the development of the masculine ego. Mothers hold most of the power to reward or withhold emotional gratification and often find difficulty in giving equal shares of response and recognition to the male children. In default of a strong father figure, and immersed in an expressive or acting-out subculture, male youth exchange the mother-dominated restricted family life for the peer group street activities, and the colorful, sometimes violent, tenor of life of the adult world.[88]

Male youth seek to enhance their status and self-esteem through participation in peer-group activities; especially important in their success is the pursuit and sexual conquest of as many girls as possible.[89] Without a strong and consistently present adult male role model in the family the black youth lacks socialization in the attitudes and values conducive to conventional marriage and family male roles. This situation contributes to the perpetuation of the female-dominated urban black family.

Care must be taken not to overgeneralize either the extent of mother-centeredness in poor black families, or the degree of family disorganization therein. The 1960 census showed that 79 percent of all black families with children had a man at the head. Even in the lower-class black urban population 53 percent of these families had a male rather than a female at the head. For families with incomes of $3,000 a year and over, fully 93 percent were headed by a man.[90] It may be argued that the characteristic of matricentricity is really a social-class trait rather than a racial trait, as Lee Rainwater does:

Because of the high degree of conjugal role segregation, both white and Negro lower-class families tend to be matrifocal in comparison with middle-class families. They are matrifocal in the sense that the wife makes most of the decisions that keep the family going and has the greatest sense of responsibility to the family. In white as well as Negro lower-class families women tend to look to their female relatives for support and counsel, and to treat their husbands as essentially uninterested in the day-to-day problems of family living.[91]

With respect to family disorganization, a number of current family sociologists including Billingsley and Bert Adams disagree with Daniel Moynihan that the urban poor black family is essentially disorganized and disintegrating. Billingsley points to the large number of stable, law-abiding, poor black families that never make the news and that tend to be ignored by social scientists. He does not see ". . . the Negro family as a causal nexus in a 'tangle of pathology' which feeds on itself. . . . It is, in our view, an absorbing, adaptive, and amazingly resilient mechanism for the socialization of children and the civilization of its society."[92]

Adams concurs that these urban, poor black families are not typically weak or promiscuous in their behavior, but rather "are primarily stable units, struggling together to survive in a white-dominated society."[93]

2 The Contemporary Black Working-Class Family Frazier gave the name "Black Proletariat" to these urban working-class families where typically both parents were present and the family was self-supporting.[94] Up until the World War II period discriminatory practices in employment had kept the masses of black men restricted largely to unskilled, domestic, or personal service jobs. The shortage of labor during World War II opened up more opportunities in the industrial economy. Many blacks now found employment as miners, steel-workers, longshoremen, stockyard workers, construction workers, and truck drivers. In many ways the family life of these black industrial workers resembled that of the white working class. However, racial discrimination has

continued to be a problem for these black families. Even though able to afford better housing, it has been hard for them to escape the confines of the black segregated neighborhoods. In order to find better living quarters they may be forced to pay exorbitant rents. This may necessitate the employment of the wife in order to supplement her husband's income, or the family may take in boarders.[95]

The position of the husband-father in these working-class families—especially his authority—varies according to how adequately and dependably he performs his family-provider role. Where his earnings are sufficient to enable his wife to remain at home, his authority is strengthened in relation to that of his wife. Frazier found that in some of these families the husband asserted his authority in a harsh and repressive manner. In other families, where the wife was employed too, she continued to occupy a position of considerable authority, and was not subordinate to her husband. Sometimes the wife and her mother would join forces to challenge the husband's authority.[96] More recently, Billingsley has found the emerging pattern to be an "expanding equalitarianism," where the husband and wife both participate in decision making, a pattern not unlike that found in many middle-class families.[97]

Black working-class housing project. (*E. D. Dyer.*)

The lot of the child in the black working-class family varies according to the resources of the family and the priorities set by the parents. Frazier observed that they have fewer children than lower-class parents, and that the parents show a deep concern for the welfare and future prospects of their children. Parents often make great sacrifices to give their children an education.[98] They attempt to provide adequate child care where both parents are employed, and encourage and discipline their children toward conformity and ambition. Other parents, who may be equally concerned about the well-being of their children, may be so preoccupied with their own aspirations and struggles for self-improvement that they neglect their children. On the whole, Frazier found a remarkable spirit of cooperation and democratic outlook in many families as they work together to pursue family goals. "It is in these well-organized families where the entire family is working in order to purchase a home or that their children may obtain an education that one finds a spirit of democracy in family relations, and a spirit of self-reliance on the part of the children."[99]

As employment opportunities have increased for black Americans, the number of working-class families has increased. They tend to dissociate themselves from the lower class and pattern their life-style after working-class people in the general population.[100]

3   The Black Middle-Class and Upper-Class Families   During the nineteenth century a small but distinct group of black families emerged with superior status in the black population. Their high status was based on their racially mixed ancestry, a heritage of family traditions, and long-established economic security. Referred to by Frazier as "Old Families," they were differentiated from the masses by "higher standards of morality and superior culture."[101] With urbanization and increasing occupational differentiation among black workers, other criteria emerged as bases for higher social status, resulting in an expansion of the "Black Bourgeoisie," a term used now to include the range of middle- and upper-class people.[102] Middle-class position was now more apt to be based on the criteria of higher education, occupational achievement, and income. However, the diversity in historical background, origins, and class criteria has resulted in a varied and large black middle class in America.

Billingsley identifies at least three subtypes of middle-class families today: (a) the upper-middle class, consisting of families of highly educated professionals and businesspersons, (b) the middle-middle class, composed of white-collar clerks and salespeople, and (c) the precarious lower-middle class, consisting of skilled artisans and small businesspersons. These three groupings are differentiated in terms of education, occupation, and income levels, and to some extent according to family life-styles. Billingsley estimates that these three groupings constitute about 40 percent of all black American families.[103]

The new and expanding black middle-class families have tended to

Home of affluent black family. (*E. D. Dyer.*)

accept the values and norms of white middle-class culture, and have accordingly been termed the "acculturated middle majority Negro family."[104] They believe in monogamy and permanent marriage, but consider divorce an acceptable alternative to an unhappy marriage. The ideal family is a small, independent nuclear family living in a suburban residential area, managing its own affairs without interference from relatives, but maintaining friendly relations with kinfolk on both sides of the family. In these middle-class families:

Children are wanted, socialized, presented with definable male models by the father, given emotional support from mothers, and encouraged to achieve. Since education is so highly valued, both sexes are encouraged to absorb all the learning they can. . . . What seems to be evident is a joint dedication of husband and wife to establish a stable family, to prosper economically, and to bring forth a succeeding generation of children who will suffer fewer of the disadvantages experienced by their parents.[105]

Children are expected to choose their own mates, and mate selection follows the conventional middle-class sequence of dating, going steady,

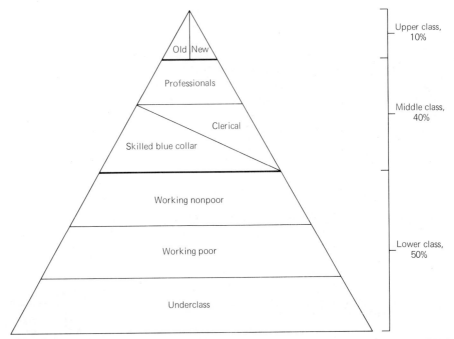

Figure 3-1 The social class distribution of black families. (*Source: Andrew Billingsley*, Black Families in White America, *Englewood Cliffs, New Jersey: Prentice-Hall, 1968, p. 123. Reprinted by permission.*)

engagement, and then marriage. The marriage ceremony may be fairly elaborate, involving many relatives and friends.

Acculturated black middle-class families have attained greater integration into the economic and social systems in America than have the lower- and working-class families. In aspirations and life-styles they approach those of the American middle-class model. These black families have shown that with adequate resources and improved opportunities they can develop and maintain a very stable and satisfying family life.

Summary

In this chapter we have reviewed the origins of American racial, ethnic, and religious groups. These diverse origins are the basis for much of the family diversity discussed in the chapter. The term "subculture" is useful in designating the particular combination of cultural traits and patterns associated with a given racial, ethnic, or religious group. This subculture is reflected directly in the family forms and relationships found in the group.

The sources and origins of racial and ethnic groups in America (other than the American Indians) are the peoples who migrated to America over the centuries, starting with the colonial period, through the Old Immigration (1830 to 1882), then the New Immigration (1882 to 1930), and down to the present. By far the period of greatest immigration was between 1882 and 1930, when more than 22 million people arrived on American shores. The big majority of these "new" immigrants were from south, central, and eastern Europe, and their native cultures were quite different from the dominant American culture, thus posing serious problems of cultural and social assimilation for immigrant families. International migrations may have serious consequences for family functioning and relationships, as ties with kinfolk are severed, roles are altered, and differential socialization among family members occurs in the new country.

The Old Order Amish family illustrates both a religious and an ethnic family subtype. For the Amish people the religious system and the family system are closely tied together. The Old Order Amish still strictly follow a traditional way of life brought over from Europe more than two centuries ago. It is a simple, rural way of life inspired and directed by their interpretation of the Bible. They reject most of the mass American culture, including modern inventions and technology. They live and work hard for their farms and their homes. Farm and home are, for the Amish, inseparable. Their religious leaders, the bishop and the elders, exercise strong controls over the families in their districts. Amish family organization and relationships approximate quite closely the traditional-patriarchal ideal-type family operating in a Gemeinschaft-sacred type of community.

Americans of Italian descent make up one of the largest national-ethnic groups in America. The big majority of Italian immigrants came from southern Italy and Sicily during the New Immigration period. Strongly familistic, patriarchal, and from a rural background, the typical Italian immigrant family experienced many problems in its cultural and social assimilation in American urban communities. By the second or third generation in America, however, changes in courtship, marriage, and family patterns were very extensive. However, certain Italian-derived family traditions and practices have tended to survive, especially in working-class families, such as child subordination, age prestige, and semipatriarchalism.

Black Americans constitute by far the largest social or ethnic group in America today, with over 24 million people. Black American families, past and present, have played vital roles in the development of America. Students of the family disagree as to the amount or nature of the influence that African cultural heritage has had in shaping the black American family. Some believe that the matricentric family can be traced back to western African origins; others disagree and argue that African cultural backgrounds had little or no influence on subsequent marriage and family life in America because African native culture was largely lost due to conditions of life during slavery.

Frazier has identified a number of black family variations, all reflecting different conditions of life during and following the long period of slavery. Mother-centered families were prevalent among the field workers, while father-centered families were more prevalent among the freedmen and the house-servant groups. Emancipation, followed by migration to big cities, created serious problems of family life for black Americans.

Socioeconomic factors are probably most relevant today for understanding the contemporary black American family. Big differences exist in terms of income, occupation, and education. Still, by comparison with whites, the large majority of blacks still are less well educated and do not have as good jobs or incomes. Mother-centered families are still found in the urban lower class, while father-headed families are more prevalent in working-class and middle-class families. Middle- and upper-class families tend to approach the general American middle-class family model.

Notes

1 Thomas F. Hoult, *Dictionary of Modern Sociology* (Totowa, N.J.: Littlefield, Adams & Co., 1969), p. 123.
2 Ibid., p. 261.
3 Donald Taft, *Human Migration* (New York: Ronald Press Co., 1936), pp. 71–72.
4 James W. Vander Zanden, *American Minority Relations* (New York: Ronald Press Co., 1966), pp. 25–27.
5 Ibid., pp. 27–28.
6 Ibid., pp. 29–30.
7 Taft, op. cit., see Table 11, p. 78.
8 Vander Zanden, op. cit., pp. 31–32.
9 Robert O. Blood, *The Family* (New York: Free Press, 1972), pp. 260–268. This section follows Blood closely.
10 William I. Thomas and Florian Znaniecki, *The Polish Peasant in Europe and America* (New York: Dover Publications, 1958), as cited in Blood, op. cit., pp. 262–263.
11 Ibid., pp. 264–265.
12 Ruth S. Cavan, *The American Family* (New York: Thomas Y. Crowell Co., 1969), pp. 155–160. This section follows Cavan closely.
13 Blood, op. cit., pp. 267–268.
14 Cavan, op. cit., p. 160.
15 Blood, op. cit., pp. 103–116.
16 William M. Kephart, *The Family, Society, and the Individual* (Boston: Houghton Mifflin Co., 1966), p. 186. This section follows Kephart quite closely.
17 Ibid., p. 186.
18 John A. Hostetler, *Amish Society* (Baltimore: The Johns Hopkins Press, 1963), p. 138.
19 Walter M. Kollmorgen, *The Old Amish of Lancaster County, Pennsylvania*, p. 59, as cited by Ernest W. Burgess and Harvey J. Locke, *The Family* (New York: American Book Co., 1945), p. 79.
20 Charles P. Loomis and Zona K. Loomis, *Modern Social Theories* (Princeton, N.J.: D. Van Nostrand Co., 1965), pp. 13–14.
21 Ibid., p. 14.
22 William Schreiber, *Our Amish Neighbors* (Chicago: University of Chicago Press, 1962), p. 135.
23 Kephart, op. cit., pp. 191–192.

24 Ibid., pp. 192–193.
25 Richard Gehman, "Amish Folk," *National Geographic*, 128 (August 1965), pp. 243–244.
26 Kephart, op. cit., p. 195.
27 Kollmorgen, op. cit., p. 59.
28 Kephart, op. cit., p. 196.
29 Elmer L. Smith, *Studies in Amish Demography* (Harrisonburg, Va.: Eastern Mennonite College, 1960), p. 85.
30 Ibid., p. 18.
31 Hostetler, op. cit., p. 154.
32 Kollmorgen, op. cit., pp. 62–63.
33 Kephart, op. cit., p. 199.
34 Ibid., p. 202.
35 Ibid.
36 Ibid., p. 203.
37 Michael Lalli, "The Italian-American Family: Assimilation and Change, 1900–1965," *The Family Coordinator*, 18 (January 1969), p. 44.
38 F. Ivan Nye and Felix M. Berardo, *The Family* (New York: Macmillan Co., 1973), p. 76.
39 John S. MacDonald and Leatrice D. MacDonald, "Urbanization, Ethnic Groups, and Social Segmentation," *Social Research*, 29 (Winter 1962), pp. 433–448.
40 Francis X. Femminella, "The Italian-American Family," chap. 6 in Meyer Barash and Alice Scourby, eds., *Marriage and the Family* (New York: Random House, 1970), pp. 128–129.
41 Ibid., p. 130.
42 Lalli, op. cit., p. 47.
43 Femminella, op. cit., p. 132.
44 Paul J. Campisi, "The Italian Family in the United States," as cited by Robert F. Winch and Robert McGinnis, eds., *Selected Studies in Marriage and the Family* (New York: Henry Holt and Co., 1953), pp. 129–137.
45 Ibid., pp. 122–135.
46 Ibid., p. 135.
47 Ibid.
48 Ibid., p. 136.
49 Ibid., pp. 136–137.
50 See Campisi, op. cit., Table 1, pp. 130–135.
51 Lalli, op. cit., p. 46.
52 Ibid.
53 Herbert J. Gans, *The Urban Villagers: Groups and Class in the Life of Italian-Americans* (New York: Free Press, 1962), pp. 36–41.
54 Nye and Berardo, op. cit., p. 84.
55 Lalli, op. cit., p. 47.
56 Nye and Berardo, op. cit., p. 86.
57 Gans, op. cit., p. 66.
58 Lalli, op. cit., pp. 47–48.
59 Femminella, op. cit., p. 138.
60 Ibid., p. 137.

61 Nye and Berardo, op. cit., pp. 87–88.
62 Andrew Billingsley, "The Treatment of Negro Families in American Scholarship," in D. A. Schulz and L. A. Wilson, eds., *Readings on the Changing Family* (Englewood Cliffs, N.J.: Prentice-Hall, 1973), p. 61. Also see U.S. Bureau of the Census, *Current Population Reports: Population Characteristics.* "Population Profile of the United States: 1976," p. 3.
63 Billingsley, op. cit., p. 61.
64 Ibid., p. 69.
65 Melville J. Herskovitz, *The Myth of the Negro Past* (New York: Harper & Brothers, 1941), pp. 167–186.
66 E. Franklin Frazier, *The Negro Family in the United States* (New York: Macmillan, 1957 ed.), pp. 11–12.
67 Ernest W. Burgess and Harvey J. Locke, *The Family* (New York: American Book Co., 1945), pp. 154–155.
68 Andrew Billingsley, *Black Families in White America* (Englewood Cliffs, N.J.: Prentice-Hall, 1968), pp. 137–139.
69 E. Franklin Frazier, "Ethnic Family Patterns: The Negro Family in the United States," *The American Journal of Sociology*, 53 (1948), pp. 435–436.
70 Billingsley, "Negro Families in American Scholarship," op. cit., pp. 61–64.
71 See F. M. Brodie, *Thomas Jefferson: An Intimate History* (New York: Bantam Books, 1974) for a revealing view of Jefferson's relationship with Sally Hennings, one of his slaves.
72 Frazier, "Ethnic Family Patterns: The Negro Family in the United States," op. cit., p. 436.
73 U.S. Bureau of the Census. *Negro Population of the United States, 1790–1915,* (1918), p. 53.
74 Frazier, *The Negro Family in the United States,* op. cit., p. 179.
75 Frazier, *Black Bourgeois* (New York: Free Press of Glencoe, 1957).
76 Billingsley, *Black Families in White America,* op. cit., p. 118.
77 Burgess and Locke, op. cit., pp. 163–164.
78 Frazier, "Ethnic Family Patterns: The Negro Family in the United States," op. cit.
79 Nye and Berardo, op. cit., p. 94.
80 Ibid. Figures taken from various U.S. Census Reports.
81 Gerald R. Leslie, *The Family in Social Context* (New York: Oxford University Press, 1973), p. 292.
82 Frazier, "Ethnic Family Patterns: The Negro Family in the United States," op. cit., p. 437.
83 Nye and Berardo, op. cit., p. 96.
84 Leslie, op. cit., p. 292.
85 U.S. Bureau of the Census, *Statistical Abstract of the United States: 1970,* p. 30.
86 Stuart A. Queen and Robert W. Habenstein, *The Family in Various Cultures* (Philadelphia: J. B. Lippincott Co., 1967), pp. 325–328.
87 Ira L. Reiss, *The Family System in America* (New York: Holt, Rinehart and Winston, 1971), pp. 255–256.
88 Queen and Habenstein, op. cit., p. 335.
89 Lee Rainwater, "Crucible of Identity: The Negro Lower-Class Family," *Daedalus*, 2 (Winter 1966), pp. 172–216.

90 Billingsley, *Black Families in White America*, op. cit., p. 14.
91 Rainwater, op. cit., p. 190.
92 Billingsley, *Black Families in White America*, op. cit., p. 33.
93 Bert N. Adams, *The American Family* (Chicago: Markham Publishing Co., 1971), p. 122.
94 Frazier, *The Negro Family in the United States*, op. cit. see chapter 21.
95 Ibid., p. 342.
96 Ibid., p. 344.
97 Billingsley, *Black Families in White America*, op. cit., pp. 143–144.
98 Frazier, *The Negro Family in the United States*, op. cit., p. 554.
99 Ibid., p. 350.
100 Ibid., p. 355.
101 Ibid., p. 296.
102 Leslie, op. cit., pp. 296–297.
103 Billingsley, op. cit., pp. 131–137.
104 Queen and Habenstein, op. cit., pp. 320–325.
105 Ibid., pp. 323–324.

SELECTED READING

Since space did not permit the inclusion of a full discussion of Oriental-American families in this chapter, the selected reading is an article by John Connor on acculturation and adjustment of Japanese-American families over the generations.

This study illustrates two of the main themes of the present chapter: (1) the processes of cultural and social assimilation experienced by racial, religious, and ethnic families over a period of time and (2) the persistence of certain cultural and social characteristics brought to America from their homeland. Japanese-Americans have a racial as well as an ethnic identity (true also of other Oriental-Americans), which has often made their adjustment to life in America more difficult than has been the case of European-derived ethnic families such as Irish-Americans or Italian-Americans.

Connor interviewed 299 Americans of Japanese derivation living in California. This sample included people who have been in the United States from one to three generations. The first-generation Japanese-Americans (the Issei) came from a rural, agricultural background in Japan, where strong familistic traditions prevailed. Their acculturation has been only marginal, as they cling to their Japanese identity and continue their traditional family practices. The second generation (the Nisei), while becoming much more acculturated than the Issei, still retain many of their traditional Japanese family values and loyalties. The third generation (the Sansei), rate themselves as more than 70 percent acculturated, and many are now marrying non-Japanese. However, Connor found that even in these third-generation Japanese-Americans, there was a greater continuity of Old World–derived attitudes, practices, and traditions than is generally found in comparable Caucasian-American families.

ACCULTURATION AND FAMILY CONTINUITIES IN THREE GENERATIONS OF JAPANESE AMERICANS*

John W. Connor

Family Solidarity and the IE System in Japan

A number of observers have commented on the importance of the Japanese household or *ie* over the individual. Indeed, Beardsley, Hall, and Ward (1959:216–217) note that in rural Japan the household looms over the individual to such an extent that seldom does the individual think of himself or another apart from his role as a household member. Moreover, the importance of the household is reflected in the practice of filing all personal documents in the name of the household; no separate birth or death registers are kept for individuals. Furthermore, the importance of the household or *ie* over the individuals was recognized by law. Before World War II, the *ie* was legally responsible for its members, even while they were away from home (Befu, 1971:40).

The *ie*, then, is a corporate entity that exists through time. As Nakane notes, the *ie* is a continuum from past to future whose members include not only the present generation, but also the dead and those as yet unborn (1970:2–3).

One aspect of the corporate identity of the *ie* is the inculcation of strong emotional bonds and dependency needs in its members. For example, Caudill and Doi (1963:412) state:

In the early stages of infancy (in the traditional oral stage) there is a great deal of gratification given to the Japanese infant in almost all spheres of behavior. This would encourage the development of a very close attachment to the mother, and a sense of trust in others.

Additional evidence can be found in a recent study comparing the behavior of three-to-four-month-old infants in Japan and the United States. In

*Reprinted from *The Journal of Marriage and Family*, 36 (February 1974), pp. 159–165. Copyright © 1974 by the National Council on Family Relations. Reprinted by permission of publisher and author.

their article, Caudill and Weinstein (1969:14–15) came to these conclusions:

In summary, in normal family life in Japan there is an emphasis on interdependence and reliance on others, while in America the emphasis is on independence and self-assertion.

Moreover, in an article on family sleeping arrangements, Caudill and Plath (1966:344–366) were able to demonstrate that the Japanese family sleeping arrangements blurred the distinctions between generations and even between the sexes, and therefore served to emphasize cohesion, strong family bonds, and the interdependence of family members.

This emphasis on the importance of the *ie* over the individual is also to be seen in the care with which the Japanese family members avoid bringing shame to the family. Benedict reports that once a child starts school he becomes in effect a representative of the family. If he engages in behavior that brings shame to the family, he cannot look to the family for support. If the family name has been disgraced, his family will become "a solid phalanx of accusation" (1946:273).

The structure of the *ie* is hierarchical. The authority of the father as household head was enormous and was supported by civil law before World War II. In turn, the importance of hierarchy and the emphasis on the corporate identity of the *ie* leads to the problem of succession. Because of the small size of the land holdings in rural Japan (about two and a half acres) it became common practice to pass the land intact to one son—usually the first born—and ask the remaining sons to seek their fortunes elsewhere. In time, these nonsuccessors would establish branch families of their own and would themselves become household heads.

As successor to the headship the heir was early singled out for special and favored treatment. Siblings were expected to show respect and be deferential to the heir. Indeed, Johnson (1962:91–99) has indicated that the early knowledge of their nonsuccession and their differential socialization, led to an entrepreneurial attitude on the part of the nonheirs.

However, with his favored position the heir was given a number of responsibilities. Upon the assumption of the headship it was his duty to provide for his retiring parents who frequently continued to live with him, his wife, and their children.

Given the importance of the *ie* in Japan it would seem reasonable to assume that those first generation Japanese Americans (Issei) who immigrated to the United States would bring with them not only the belief that the *ie* system was the normal way to organize a family, but they would also have a need to create their own branch families and establish themselves as household heads. In other words, they would attempt to preserve as much as possible of the *ie* ideal and would tend to transmit certain aspects of it to subsequent generations. The subsequent generations would therefore exhibit many of the characteristics associated with the *ie* system in Japan. That is, they would retain a feeling of not wanting to bring shame to the family, they would exhibit a greater sense of hierarchy and order, and have greater dependency and affiliation needs.

The Issei

Reports by a number of authorities (Daniels, 1963; Kitano, 1969; Modell, 1968) on the nature of early Japanese immigration to the United States record many uniformities. By and large the vast majority of the immigrants came from southwestern Japan, were of a rural agricultural background, and did not intend to settle permanently in the United States. This latter characteristic, coupled with the intense anti-Japanese discrimination of the prewar period, resulted in large numbers of the first generation immigrants (Issei) and their offspring living in more or less self-contained Japanese communities on the West Coast. In these communities it was possible to retain many aspects of the Japanese life style (Miyamoto, 1939:57–130).

Our interviews with 90 *Issei* (59 males, 31 females) in the Sacramento area support the conclusions of the earlier writers. That is, the overwhelming majority of our respondents (73 per cent) came from southwestern Japan, they were of a rural, agricultural background, and the level of education was about eight years, while the average age at the time of emigration was about 19 years.

The majority of the Issei we interviewed were not the "pioneer" Issei, or original migrants, but rather the *Yobiyose* or summoned immigrants. That is, they were those immigrants who had been called over by an earlier migrating father or uncle. Indeed, when the present average age of the Issei of 73 years for the males and 71 years for the females is compared with their age at the time of immigration, it can be seen that the majority of the Issei we interviewed arrived here around the time of World War I, or after a substantial number of Japanese had already migrated to the United States.

Despite their being summoned migrants, less than 10 percent stated that they had planned to stay permanently in the United States. The vast majority intended to "make a fortune" and return to Japan. As a matter of fact, most of the Issei maintained some ties with Japan. This can be seen in the fact that 80 percent of them have returned to Japan for at least one visit, and indeed a few have made the trip more than five times.

However, as their ambition of making a fortune proved to be more difficult and take longer than expected, many returned to Japan to obtain a bride, while others relied on relatives to make the necessary arrangements, which often eventuated in "picture-bride" marriages. Well over 90 percent of the Issei we interviewed had their marriages arranged by others.

Given their intent not to settle permanently in the United States, their attempt to preserve as much as possible of the *ie* ideal, their residence in largely self-sufficient Japanese communities, and the often manifested prejudice against them, it is understandable that many Issei would only be marginally acculturated.

The marginal acculturation is apparent not only in their lack of fluency in the English language, but also in their self-evaluation as to the degree of their acculturation. As indicated in Table 1, as part of our interview schedule the Issei were asked to rate themselves on a ten-point scale ranging from a completely Japanese identity (1) to a completely American identity (10). The arithmetic mean score of the Issei was 3.8 for the males and 2.7 for the females.

Once again, an indication of the intent of the Issei to preserve as much as possible of the *ie* ideal can be seen in the fact that over one-half of them state that they see their children and grandchildren daily. Moreover, some 46 per cent of the Issei report that they are living with their children. Of those that do live with their children, approximately 70 percent live with their sons, while the rest live with the daughter's family. This finding is in close accord with

TABLE 1 ARITHMETIC MEAN DISTRIBUTION ON SUBJECTIVE SELF-EVALUATION OF DEGREE OF ACCULTURATION

GENERATION	JAPANESE IDENTITY (I)									AMERICAN IDENTITY (10)
Issei	1	2	3	4	5	6	7	8	9	10
Male (N=59)			3.8							
Female (N=31)		2.7								
Nisei										
Male (N=40)					5.5					
Female (N=40)					5.0					
Sansei										
Male (N=64)							7.2			
Female (N=64)							7.0			

Modell (1968:67–81) who states in his survey of over 1000 Issei that approximately two-fifths of the Issei live with their offspring.

Additional evidence for the preservation of the *ie* ideal in the Issei can be found in the fact that the Issei frequently recorded the birth of their children in the *Koseki* or family register back in Japan. It was this practice that resulted in the problem of the Nisei having dual citizenship before the war. Further evidence can be seen in the responses to the statements depicted in Table 2. These statements were administered to 46 male and 38 female Issei, 94 male and 61 female Nisei, 70 male and 54 female Sansei; and 52 male and 102 female Caucasians, who were of approximately the same age and education as the Sansei. The statements were scored on a five-point scale as follows: strongly agree (5), agree (4), undecided (3), disagree (2), strongly disagree (1). The scoring was further categorized in endorsement of an item on either side of neutrality. This score was on an equal distribution basis. Thus, a strongly positive identification would be greater than 4.20; a positive identification would be greater than 3.40; a neutral, or undecided, identification would range from below 3.39 to 2.61; a negative identification would be below 2.60; and a strongly negative identification would be below 1.80.

A glance at Table 2 discloses that the Issei scored high on all items.

TABLE 2 TOTAL MEAN FAMILY ITEM SCORES

ITEM NO.	ITEM	CATEGORY GROUP AND MEAN ITEM SCORES			
		ISSEI (N = 84)	NISEI (N = 155)	SANSEI (N = 124)	CAUCASIAN (N = 154)
1	Parents can never be repaid for what they have done for their children	3.86*	3.25	2.99	2.86
2	In times of need it is best to rely on your own family for assistance rather than to seek help from others or to depend entirely upon yourself.	3.97**	3.66*	3.05	2.95
3	The best way to train children is to train them to be quiet and obedient.	3.90*	2.72*	2.14	1.93
4	In the long run the greatest satisfaction comes from being with one's family.	4.33	4.38*	3.69	3.52
5	The strongest emotional bond is between a mother and her child.	4.19**	3.85*	3.15**	2.76
6	A man can never let himself down without letting his family down at the same time.	3.85	3.97*	3.31**	2.87

*Significant at the .01 Level (Mann-Whitney U Test)
**Significant at the .05 Level (Mann Whitney U Test)

Items 1, 2, 4, and 6 are family items directly related to the preservation of the *ie* ideal, while item 3 relates to the emphasis on hierarchy and the authority of the father as discussed earlier. Item 5 also provides some support for the previously discussed inculcation of dependency needs in the child.

The Nisei

Given the insularity, the low acculturation of the Issei, and their intention not to reside permanently in the United States, it would seem reasonable to expect that the Issei would attempt to inculcate in their offspring, the Nisei, essentially the same values the Issei had learned in Japan, especially the continued importance of the family or *ie* ideal. Our interviewing of 80 Nisei (40 males and 40 females) by and large bears this out. Indeed, as indicated in the earlier discussion of the importance of the family over the individual, it is understandable that the Issei would emphasize the importance of not bringing shame to the family. As Table 3 indicates, when the Nisei were asked if the family was stressed when they were young, 80 percent of them answered affirmatively. Moreover, when they were asked if they had been told that one must act in such a way as not to bring shame to the Japanese community, 75 percent of the males and 66 percent of the females answered that such a principle had been stressed.

We also have additional evidence as to the importance of the family in the responses a number of Nisei gave during the interviews. When we raised the subject of excluding a child from the family as a means of disciplining him, one Nisei male said that to do such a thing to a child was worse than beating him. Another Nisei female stated with considerable feeling that her father

TABLE 3 PERCENTAGE DISTRIBUTION OF NISEI AND SANSEI REPORTING PARENTAL STRESS ON CERTAIN PRINCIPLES

	NISEI		SANSEI	
PRINCIPLE REPORTED STRESSED	MALE	FEMALE	MALE	FEMALE
1 Avoid bringing shame to the family				
A Stressed	80	80	64	65
B Not stressed	20	20	29	31
C Don't recall	0	0	6	4
2 Must not bring dishonor to the Japanese community				
A Stressed	75	66	44	36
B Not Stressed	20	26	48	58
C Don't recall	5	7	8	6
Number of respondents	40	40	64	64

would lock her in the closet when she was bad. Furthermore, the Nisei had to face this discipline alone. There were no soft-hearted grandparents or kindly aunts from whom they could seek sympathy and comfort.

The values inculcated by the Issei were continually reinforced as the Nisei grew older. Not only did the majority of Nisei attend Japanese language schools, which frequently incorporated within the curriculum the stern moral lessons of the *shushin* or ethics course of the Japanese education system, but the majority of them also resided in the Japanese community. It was the community that was most responsible for the low level of delinquency among the Nisei. As one Nisei who had resided in Sacramento's Japanese community before the war remarked: "You didn't dare step out of line. The first time you did, your parents would be sure to hear about it."

The retention of a number of the values of their parents can be seen in the Nisei responses to several questions they were asked relating to the Sansei. When asked, "What behavior by the Sansei would be most likely to anger or upset you?", the most frequent reply, by 50 percent of the males and 60 percent of the females, was "lack of respect to parents and elders." The next most frequent answer was that of breaking the law or defying authority, which was given by 25 percent of the females and 15 percent of the males. Other opinions given centered upon such subjects as drug taking, demonstrating against the government, and radicalism.

Some indication of the conservatism of many Nisei can be found in their replies to the question, "What Japanese characteristics would you like to see retained in the Sansei generation?" Here again the male-female responses were quite close. The most common response was "respect for parents, elders, and authority," which was given by 60 percent of the males and 58 percent of the females. The achievement orientation of the male Nisei is seen in the reply, "hard work," which was given by 20 percent of the males and 8 percent of the females. A male-female difference was also seen in the response, "humility, endurance, and patience," which was reported by 26 percent of the females and 10 percent of the males. Other responses emphasized the retention of the Japanese language, good manners, and the Buddhist faith.

Additional evidence for the retention of a Japanese identity in the Nisei can be seen in Table 1. When asked to evaluate their degree of acculturation on a ten-point scale, ranging from a completely Japanese identity (1) to a completely American identity (10), the Nisei males rated themselves as 5.5 and the Nisei females 5.0. Once again this supports our other evidence that with their bicultural background the Nisei believe themselves to be unique in that they not only see their generation as being midway between the Issei and Sansei (the average age is about 45), but also that their generation combines the best of both cultures.

Moreover, with respect to the retention of a Japanese identity and the preservation of the *ie* ideal in the Nisei, it can readily be seen from Table 2 that they have retained at the very least a strong feeling for the importance of relying upon the family and the warmth and security that comes from being with the family. Table 2 discloses that in answer to the statement. "In the long run, the greatest satisfaction comes from being with one's family" was scored 4.33 by the Issei and even slightly higher at 4.38 by the Nisei. Furthermore, in answer to the statement, "In times of need it is best to rely on your own family for assistance rather than to seek help from others or to depend entirely on yourself," it can be seen that while the Issei scored 3.97, the Nisei still scored 3.66, as compared to 3.05 for the Sansei, and 2.95 for the Caucasian sample. Finally, the statement "A man can never let himself down without letting his family down at the same time," was scored 3.97 by the Nisei, the highest of any group.

The Sansei

When asked to comment on the Sansei (third generation Japanese Americans) the most frequent response by both the Issei and the Nisei was that the Sansei were "completely Americanized." And indeed, when viewed from the Issei and Nisei perspectives it would seem that the Sansei have retained very little of a Japanese identity. As seen on Table 1, by their own self-evaluation the Sansei, who are largely in their early twenties, now rate themselves as being over 70 percent acculturated. Moreover, in our interviewing of 128 Sansei (64 male, 64 female) we discovered that the majority of them participated rather widely in high school and college extracurricular activities, such as being actively involved in school offices, school athletics, etc. Furthermore, the majority of Sansei now have more non-Japanese than Japanese friends. One result of this, of course, is that there has been an increased incidence of both dating and even marriage to non-Japanese. Our data indicate that in Sacramento County from 1961 to 1970, 28.3 percent of all marriages involving Japanese surnamed males and females were with non-Japanese, and indeed, this trend is increasing in recent years. An article appearing in the December 3, 1971, issue of *The Pacific Citizen* indicates that Sansei marriages are even higher in Fresno, California. In that article, Kuhn reports that since 1964 the intermarriage rate rose to 50 percent and has continued to be about the same rate (Kuhn, 1971).

Yet it would be a mistake to assume with the Issei and Nisei that the Sansei have become "completely Americanized." Our research indicates that when compared with a contemporary Caucasian group of approximately the same age and education, a number of Japanese characteristics remain. For example, as part of our research we also administered the Edwards Personal Preference Schedule or EPPS to 201 Sansei (71 males and 130 females) and to 231 Caucasians (101 males and 130 females) of approximately the same age and education. The results clearly disclose that when compared with the Caucasians, the Sansei are significantly more deferent, more abasive, less dominant, more affiliative, less aggressive, have a greater need for succorance and order, and a markedly lesser need for heterosexuality than do the Caucasians (Connor, 1974).

A further item of contrast may be seen in Table 2, wherein, although the Sansei consistently score lower than the Issei and Nisei on all family items, they, nevertheless, consistently score higher than the Caucasian sample.

A final example of evidence for the continuation of Japanese characteristics among third generation Japanese Americans can be seen in the retention of Japanese patterns of child care in the Sacramento area. This information is available in a study done by Lois Frost under the author's supervision in the spring of 1970 (Frost, 1970). This study was a replication of one conducted by Caudill and Weinstein (1969). The Caudill and Weinstein study consisted of a series of two-day observations made in the homes of 30 Japanese and 30 American first-born, three-to-four-months-old infants, who were equally divided by sex and who were living in middle-class urban families. Information was obtained on the behavior of the mother and the child by means of time-sampling. One observation was made every fifteenth second over a ten-minute period on a predetermined set of categories. This resulted in a sheet containing 40 equally spaced observations. Ten sheets were completed for each of the two days, resulting in a total of 800 observations in each case.

Ms. Frost's sample consisted of 21 infants, 7 males and 14 females. When she was completing her study, I advised her to write to Caudill and advise him of her findings. This she did. He, in turn, was most interested in her study and arranged to conduct a series of observations with her in the homes of four infants in order to have a reliability check for observer bias.

Frost's data were then compared and analyzed with Caudill's Japanese and American samples. In an as yet unpublished paper Caudill and Frost conclude that the Sansei mother is combining both the Japanese and American styles of caretaking (Caudill and Frost, 1973). Moreover, their paper indicates that the Sansei mother does more vocal lulling, more breast and bottle feeding, more carrying, and more playing with the baby than the American mother. In these practices she is more like the Japanese mother. Furthermore, while the mother's overall caretaking style and the behavior of her baby are closer to the American than the Japanese response style, there are still some areas in which the baby seems closer to the Japanese baby's behavior. That is, the Japanese American baby does less finger sucking than the American baby and spends less time playing by himself.

If Frost's findings are seen in conjunction with the higher Sansei needs for succorance, affiliation, nurturance, deference, abasement, and the greater emphasis placed on the family, it is easy to suspect a continuation of dependency needs. Although difficult to demonstrate empirically, all of the above data are clearly supportive of the previously discussed dependency needs fostered in the Japanese family. While not so pronounced as in the Japanese mother, the Sansei mother has retained enough of the Japanese caretaking style so that we are already able to detect discernible differences in her child's behavior at the age of three or four months. Moreover, these differences are exactly the sorts of differences we would expect if we were looking for evidence which would indicate the inculcation of dependency needs.

In conclusion, one can see a continuity in both the importance of the family and an attempt to preserve the *ie* ideal in the three generations of Japanese Americans. While the emphasis on the family and the inculcation of dependency needs in the third generation are considerably attenuated in comparison with first and second generations, the emphasis still remains greater than that found in Caucasian Americans.

Finally, when one compares the Japanese American responses on the EPPS with the Caucasian American responses, a question might be asked. That is, is the continuing emphasis on the family, etc., really evidence of the retention of the *ie* ideal, or is it nothing more than a cultural response to the discrimination and prejudice suffered by the Japanese Americans in the larger American society? In other words, are the higher Sansei EPPS scores on deference, abasement, order, etc., really more a result of their minority status than an indication of continuation of Japanese characteristics? While it is difficult to separate such factors, it can nevertheless be rather quickly demonstrated that when the EPPS has been administered in Hawaii, where the Japanese Americans are the largest ethnic segment and are scarcely treated as minority group, the results are essentially the same as those obtained in our Sacramento Japanese American sample (Arkoff, 1959; Fenz and Arkoff, 1962).

References

Arkoff, Abe 1959 "Need patterns in two generations of Japanese Americans in Hawaii." The Journal of Social Psychology 50:75–79.

Beardsley, Richard K., John W. Hall, and Robert E. Ward 1959 *Village Japan*. Chicago:University of Chicago Press.

Befu, Harumi 1971 *Japan: An Anthropological Introduction*. San Francisco: Chandler.

Benedict, Ruth 1946 *The Chrysanthemum and the Sword*. New York:Houghton Mifflin.

Caudill, William and Takeo Doi 1963 "Interrelations of psychiatry, culture, and emotion in Japan." In Iago K. Goldstone (ed.), Man's Image in Medicine and Anthropology. New York:International Universities Press.

Caudill, William and Lois Frost 1973 "A comparison of maternal care and infant behavior in Japanese-American, American, and Japanese families." To be published in William K. Lebro (ed.), Mental Health Research in Asia and the Pacific. Vol. III. Hawaii:East-West Center Press.

Caudill, William and David W. Ploth 1966 "Who sleeps by whom? Parent-child involvement in urban Japanese families." Psychiatry 29:344–366.

Caudill, William and Helen Weinstein 1969 "Maternal care and infant behavior in Japan and America." Psychiatry 32:12–43.

Connor, John W. 1974 "Acculturation and changing need patterns in Japanese American and Caucasian American students." The Journal of Social Psychology (Forthcoming, August, 1974).

Daniels, Roger 1963 *The Politics of Prejudice.* Berkeley and Los Angeles: The University of California Press.

Fenz, Walter D. and Abe Arkoff 1962 "Comparative need patterns of five ancestry groups in Hawaii" Journal of Social Psychology 58:68–89.

Frost, Lois 1970 "Child raising techniques as related to acculturation among Japanese Americans." Unpublished Masters thesis, California State University, Sacramento.

Johnson, Erwin 1962 "The emergence of a self-conscious entrepreneurial class in rural Japan." In Robert J. Smith and Richard K. Beardsley (eds.), Japanese Culture: Its Development and Characteristics, Chicago:Aldine.

Kitano, Harry 1969 *Japanese Americans: The Evolution of a Subculture.* Englewood Cliffs, N.J.:Prentice-Hall.

Kuhn, Gene 1971 "Hirabayashi challenges Nisei to fight all inequalities." Pacific Citizen (December 3).

Miyamoto, Frank 1939 "Social solidarity among the Japanese in Seattle." University of Washington Publications in the Social Sciences 11:57–130.

Modell, John 1968 "The Japanese American family: a perspective for future investigation." Pacific Historical Review 36:67–81.

Nakane, Chie 1970 *Japanese Society.* Berkeley and Los Angeles:The University of California Press.

CHAPTER 4

Rural and Urban Family Variations

America has been predominantly a rural society throughout most of its history, including the entire colonial period and during almost three-quarters of its 200 years as an independent nation. Actually, it was not until about World War I that urban dwellers began to outnumber rural residents. The United States census of 1920 showed a majority of Americans living in urban areas for the first time. To understand the American family today it is important to look at its long rural background and its development in various rural environments. To some extent this has been done in Chapter 2 as we reviewed the historical and cultural backgrounds of American families.

Background to Rural and Urban Families in America

A brief look at rural and urban population trends is in order here, followed by consideration of differences between rural and urban economic and social environments as they relate to the population trends and family life in rural and urban America.

Four-generation Vermont farm family. (*USDA photo by Byron Schumaker.*)

RURAL-URBAN POPULATION TRENDS

When the first United States census was taken in 1790, about 95 percent of the population lived in rural areas, on farms and in small villages or towns. One hundred years later, the 1890 census showed two-thirds of Americans still living in rural areas. By 1920 the scale had tipped the other way, with more than half of the population now living in cities. The most recent census (1970) shows 73.5 percent living in urban areas and the remaining 26.5 percent in rural areas, including 21.7 percent in nonfarm communities and only 4.8 percent living on farms.[1] The decline in farm population, so long considered the stronghold of the American nation, has been drastic over the past three or four decades. Numerically, it seems that the American farm family, with fewer than 2 1/2 million families counted in 1970, is a diminishing type—perhaps it should now be added to the list of endangered species.

RURAL AND URBAN ECONOMIC AND SOCIAL ENVIRONMENTS

As the above figures indicate, urbanization has been rapid in the twentieth century. Actually, some degree of urbanization has been under way in America throughout most of its history as a nation. The founding of the American nation took place at the time of the industrial revolution in England, and the fledgling United States of America was in continual contact with economic developments in Europe. So American history bears witness to some early industrial development as well as to extensive rural agricultural

FIGURE 4-1 Percentage of rural and urban population, United States, 1790–1970. (*Source: U.S. Bureau of the Census, various published reports.*)

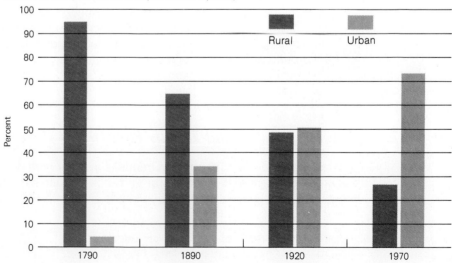

development. In fact, technology and science spurred not only the rise of industrial-urban communities, but also improvement of farming techniques and practices, thereby increasing productivity in the rural segment of the American economy.

We must keep in mind, however, that America was overwhelmingly rural, culturally and socially as well as economically, during its colonial and early national periods. Cities were few and small and were pervaded with "ruralisms." Quite the reverse of what we find today, early American cities were strongly influenced by the surrounding rural culture. Being few and small and encompassed by the rural agricultural countryside, cities experienced rural sights and sounds as a part of their everyday life. Horse-drawn wagons of farmers mingled freely with the carriages of city dwellers, who in turn frequented the countryside regularly.

It was during the first half of the nineteenth century that *ruralisms* or rural cultural influences on city life were probably most pronounced.[2] These rural cultural influences accompanied the migrations of rural Americans to the growing cities and also the migrations of rural European immigrants who settled in American cities. The virtues of gardening and home food preservation have long continued among city families of rural background. Many city people retained rural ties and those who were economically able frequently established a pattern of alternating residence between city and country. The countryside was idealized for its virtues as a kind of counterbalance for the problems and "evils" of the city. City dwellers should return to the sunshine and pure air of the country periodically to revitalize themselves. The values and virtues of agrarianism were deeply entrenched in America, buttressed by traditional and biblical support. Thomas Jefferson, for example, strongly supported agriculture and farm life as superior to industry and city life: "Those who labour in the earth are the chosen people of God, if He had a chosen people, whose breasts He has made His peculiar deposit for substantial and genuine virtue. It is the focus in which he keeps alive that sacred fire, which otherwise might escape from the face of the earth."[3]

Despite the traditional and sentimental attachment to rural life and virtues, the cities grew and became strong, especially following the Civil War. To some Americans the city represented sin and danger; to others it was the epitome of culture and civilization.

Material cultural differences between country and city were probably greatest during the nineteenth century. Inventions such as the telegraph, the telephone, and the incandescent lamp were incorporated into urban culture first, then later filtered outward into rural America. City versus country life-styles and personality stereotypes were drawn, contrasting the urban sophisticate or the "city slicker" with the "country rube" or "rural hick." A differentiated urban culture was well developed by mid-nineteenth century, including theater, opera, museums, clubs, and organized sports.

Well into the early twentieth century, migrations were primarily from rural to urban areas. However, by the end of the nineteenth century there were some countercurrents of migrations from cities out to the country. This movement, though, did not become prominent until after World War II, when it became identified with the suburban movement. The diminishing farm population and the increase in rural dwellers who were not farmers brought about the introduction of the concept "rural non-farm" into the United States census of 1920.[4]

As American population and society grew in size and complexity, social stratification became more pronounced. Again, it was in the cities first that social-class differences were most clearly drawn. But social stratification also developed in rural America as distinctions in education, family background, community participation, and types of farming and farm techniques separated rural populations, and as urban dwellers also introduced their social evaluations into rural communities.[5]

Prior to the industrial revolution, agriculture and industry were still quite closely interrelated in England and the American colonies. Rural-urban differences were small compared with what they were to become later in the nineteenth century. Most industrial production was in the hands of master manufacturers and their apprentice-helpers working together in a small shop or in the home itself. By mid-eighteenth century, master manufacturers were enlarging their operations, and a more authentic urban industry was under way as technology improved, sources of power increased, and markets expanded and also became more centralized.[6] As more and more workers gravitated to these growing industrial centers, urban populations grew rapidly and the urban social environment became quite different from the rural social environment. Urbanism was soon to become a way of life in America.

SOME INDEXES OF RURAL-URBAN DIFFERENCES

Lee Taylor and Arthur Jones feel that among the major rural-urban differences in American society are those found in the areas of occupation, the physical environment, community size, population density, population composition, social differentiation and stratification, mobility, and systems of interaction.[7] The differences involved were more pronounced during the nineteenth and early twentieth centuries than in the second half of the twentieth century. In order to compare rural families of the recent American past with urban families it should prove helpful to examine briefly these indexes of rural-urban differentiation.

OCCUPATIONAL DIFFERENCES   Rural workers have been engaged primarily in agriculture or agriculturally related occupations, while urban workers have participated mostly in manufacturing, trade, commerce, the professions, governing, and other nonagricultural pursuits.

ENVIRONMENTAL DIFFERENCES In the rural world nature tends to predominate over man-made environments. People live in direct contact with nature. In the urban world man becomes more isolated from nature, living and working in a predominantly man-made physical and cultural environment.

COMPOSITION OF THE POPULATION Rural population tends to be more homogeneous socially and culturally, while urban populations are more heterogeneous, especially in large, complex, mobile metropolitan areas.

SOCIAL DIFFERENTIATION AND STRATIFICATION Economic, political, religious, and other social differences are generally fewer in rural than in urban areas. Since these kinds of social differences serve as the bases for social evaluation and ranking, it follows that social stratification is generally more advanced in urban centers.

SIZE OF COMMUNITY AND DENSITY OF POPULATION The rural world consists of open farm lands, small hamlets, villages, and towns, sparsely populated compared with cities. Agrarianism has been correlated with these rural features. Urban communities are normally much larger in size and more densely populated. Urbanization and large size of the community go together, as do urbanity and population density.

MOBILITY AND INTERACTION SYSTEMS In rural areas there are generally fewer spatial, occupational, and other forms of social mobility than in urban areas. Normally, migration currents carry people from the country to the city. There has been some reversal of this trend in more recent times. Urbanity and mobility are generally positively correlated. In rural life there are generally fewer contacts per person, with narrower areas of social interaction, and these are often more of a personal or primary-group nature. In urban life there are more numerous and more varied social contacts per person, many of which are of an impersonal, secondary-group nature.

By way of summing up these rural-urban contrasting characteristics, we may say that taken together, the rural world and its main features approximate the Gemeinschaft-sacred type of society, while the urban world and its principal characteristics approximate the Gesellschaft-secular ideal type of society.

SOME RURAL-URBAN FAMILY DIFFERENCES

In the period between the American Revolution and the Civil War, farming and rural populations continued to expand along with increases in industry and the growth of city populations. Business or commercial farms as well as traditional subsistence farms became more numerous. The predominance of the self-sustaining rural farm family was already being threatened by agricultural specialization and an increasing division of labor in the rural economy.

The difference between rural and urban family life probably reached its peak in the nineteenth century. During the previous centuries, colonial and early American family life was essentially rural, and in the twentieth century family life came to be dominated by urban social organization. But the nineteenth century, say Taylor and Jones, ". . . was characterized by the struggle and vacillation between these two differential ideologies of social organization. Through a contraction and reorganization of its functions the family has shifted from a self-sufficient to a consumption-oriented, egocentric, status-centered way of life."[8]

It was in nineteenth-century cities that family life began to undergo some basic alterations. Economic production moved from the family locus to shops and factories. Other urban institutions and agencies began to assume more and more of the educational, religious, recreational, health, and welfare functions previously centered in the family. At the same time many of these functions and activities were still largely retained by rural families, especially farm families. By the twentieth century many of the urban-born family patterns had come to suffuse family life in rural America too; thus a diminution of rural-urban family differences ensued.

However, certain demographic and social differences between rural and urban families have persisted well into the twentieth century; among these would be differences in birthrates, in infant mortality rates, in marital status, and in age and sex structure.

DIFFERENTIAL BIRTHRATES   Fertility has continued to be higher in rural America than in our cities, although these differences are now narrowing, reflecting urban-secular influences on rural family planning and contraceptive use and diminishing differences in education between rural and urban couples. In a nationwide comparison of birthrates between urban, rural nonfarm, and rural farm families using 1960 United States census data, Charles P. Loomis and J. Allen Beegle found differences in the number of children born per married woman. For urban women: 1.3 percent had three or more children, and 19.2 percent had fewer than two. For rural nonfarm women: 8 percent had three or more children, and 2 percent fewer than two. For rural farm women: 28.6 percent had three or more children and only 0.6 percent had fewer than two. By 1970, 54.7 percent of all urban families had children under age 18, as compared with 55.4 percent of all rural families.[9]

INFANT MORTALITY RATES   The infant mortality rate has been declining over a long period of time, and since 1960 it has declined each year. In 1968 the rate (the number of deaths under one year of age per 1,000 live births) was 21.8. By 1972 the rate had fallen to about 18.9.[10] While here also the gap between rural and urban rates has been declining, the figures show that some differences still persist. In 1968 the more urban middle-Atlantic states showed an infant mortality rate of 18.6 percent for whites and 35.0 for nonwhites, while the largely rural east-south-central states reported rates of 20.9 for whites and 40.5 for nonwhites.[11] (White and nonwhite family differences will be discussed more fully in Chapter 7.)

MARITAL STATUS   Here again, rural-urban differences are declining but some differences linger on. In the early decades of the twentieth century, marriage generally occurred earlier and more frequently for city youth than for rural youth and divorce was less frequent for rural couples. By the 1950s, however, rural-urban differences in age at marriage tended to be insignificant. By 1970, more rural males were married compared to urban males (66.6 percent versus 63.3 percent), and more rural females were married than urban females (65.5 percent versus 56.8 percent). Separated, divorced, and widowed people were more frequently found in the city than in the country.[12]

AGE AND SEX STRUCTURE   The age structure of the rural population in the United States today is still different from that in the urban population. The farm population shows a higher proportion of young people than the city population. Large proportions of males at most age levels are also typical of farm populations, and small proportions at most age levels in urban populations. As Loomis and Beegle point out, the proportions of young people tend to increase as the distance from a Standard Metropolitan Statistical Area increases, and the proportion of elderly people decreases with this change in distance.[13]

Also the sex ratio (number of males per 100 females) tends to increase as the distance increases from the S.M.S.A. Differences in age structure of farm and urban populations become apparent when comparing the ages of heads of households. In 1969 only 28.5 percent of farm family heads of household were 45 years of age, while 71.5 percent were 45 or older. For urban heads of household comparable figures were 44.6 percent and 45.4 percent.[14]

In a thorough review of rural and urban family differences and similarities, Lee Burchinal notes that while idealized views of the rural family abound, until recently there has been a dearth of empirical research on actual rural family patterns.[15] The most systematic and thorough data on family structure and processes in the United States come from studies of urban, white, middle-class families. In the absence of comparable data for rural families, Burchinal feels that descriptive data from urban families may be of value in understanding American rural family variations and change. Accordingly, he has developed a number of propositions as a framework for rural family analysis:

1   In the past century, the foundation of American society has shifted from relatively isolated, self-sufficient rural communities with an agricultural economy to metropolitan complexes with an industrial economy.

2 The American family system, originating in the frontier era, was shaped by and adapted to the rural environment. . . . It has been continuously adjusting to the demands of urban ways of life, which are largely a function of the scientific, technological, and industrial developments in our society.
3 In this process of change, the family system has most frequently been required to adapt to extra-family requirements of change rather than to prompt extra-family system changes. . . .
4 A prototype of the emerging family system can be discerned in urban society. This family type which has as its modal representation among the college educated, professionally employed urban couples, is probably the best gauge of the direction of future change in the American family system.
5 Functionally important linkages connect rural and urban society. These linkages provide the bases for diffusion of knowledge, values, and behavioral patterns from one sector of society to another or from one region of the country to another.
6 It is assumed that most changes in the American family system have been developing in urban communities and have been diffusing to rural communities by means of institutionalized and informal linkages between the rural and urban populations.[16]

These propositions suggest that valuable data for understanding the rural family may be found in the urban family and its development. A review of the data available, Burchinal says, reveals that while rural family organization has tended to follow developments in urban families, there are certain differences remaining between urban and rural family organization and relationships.[17] Among these differences are the following:

DIVISION OF AUTHORITY AND HOUSEHOLD TASKS Family decision-making patterns and household division of labor do not appear to differ very much between urban families and the rural families which have been studied. Joint husband-wife decision-making patterns are prevalent among rural couples, according to Wilkening's research. On the other hand, Murray Straus found evidence of continuation of the traditional pattern of male dominance in the economic aspects of family life among farm families, with a continuation of the older sex division of labor. In their Michigan study, Robert Blood and Donald Wolfe found that both farm wives and city wives defined the majority of household tasks along traditional gender lines, but farm wives were much more apt to perform their gender-defined tasks alone than were the city wives.[18]

EMPLOYMENT OF WIVES OUTSIDE THE HOME Rural wives and urban wives still tend to contribute to the economic support of their families in quite different ways. Studies show that farm wives more frequently make their clothes and do the family baking, as well as raise vegetables, and can and preserve food. City wives much more frequently seek outside employment as a means of helping support the family. Comparison of the employment of farm wives and rural nonfarm wives shows a much higher employment rate among the latter, who were generally better educated and also were more apt to have been employed before marriage.[19]

MARITAL SATISFACTION   Some studies of rural populations dealing with satisfaction in marriage and family relations indicate no real differences between the satisfaction levels of farm and rural nonfarm couples; other studies suggest higher satisfaction among nonfarm couples than farm couples. In general, the findings suggest that farm life may be less conducive to marital and personal satisfaction than nonfarm rural life. In comparing rural with urban marital satisfaction, a number of studies agree that married life seems more satisfying to urban couples than to rural couples. Blood and Wolfe found that farm wives were less satisfied in their love relationships with their husbands than city wives. A. C. Thorpe found greater companionship among urban couples than among farm couples. Other studies show that interpersonal relations in rural families are less often marked by affection than those in urban families. One study showed a much higher proportion of rural than urban wives saying that sexual adjustment was a major problem in their marital happiness or unhappiness.[20]

PRONENESS TO DIVORCE   Despite the evidence of lower satisfaction in husband-wife relations among rural couples, these marriages are less apt to end in divorce than are urban marriages. The author agrees with Burchinal that this is due in large part to greater rural retention of the traditional, sacred value orientation emphasizing the permanence of marriage and priority of family responsibilities over individual interests. This rural-urban difference in divorce rate holds true despite the fact that rural people generally have less education, lower incomes, and a lower level of living conditions. These are generally thought to produce higher divorce rates where found in urban populations.[21] It is hard to say whether this rural-urban difference in divorce rate will continue into the future, as urban, secular, and individual-centered norms for evaluating marital success and permanence become more widely established in rural America.

PATTERNS OF SOCIAL RELATIONSHIPS   Farm husbands and wives generally are less active in community and social organizations than are nonfarm rural couples. However, farm families seem to establish a visiting pattern with relatives more than do rural nonfarm families or urban families.[22] The informal social relationships of these farm families seem still to be centered more in the home.

CHILDBEARING AND CHILD-REARING PATTERNS   Farm families have historically been more fertile than city families. In the United States in recent decades there has been a trend toward narrowing the gap in fertility rates between rural and urban wives, as noted above. Blood and Wolfe suggest the possibility of a future similarity in rural and urban birthrates. Their Michigan study showed that both rural and urban wives wanted approximately the same number of children.[23]

In the area of child rearing, the Detroit study showed that what children mean to their mothers may differ somewhat from the city to the country. City mothers mentioned the emotional satisfaction they derived from having children more often than farm mothers, who in turn were more apt to mention companionship of the child, that the presence of the child helped strengthen the home, and that children helped provide family security by working with their parents.[24] There is some evidence that parent-child relations are less satisfying today in rural homes than in urban homes.

RURAL-URBAN DIFFERENCES IN PREPARATION OF YOUTH FOR ADULT ROLES   A good deal of research supports the conclusion that there are still significant differences in the socialization experiences of rural as compared to urban young people, despite the increasing similarity in rural and urban socialization systems. These differences show up in school achievement levels, occupational aspiration and achievement levels, value orientations, and personality-related characteristics of rural and urban youth.[25] Rural young men still have lower educational levels than city young men. William Sewell found in Wisconsin that farm children, regardless of sex, family class position, or intellectual ability, generally had lower educational aspirations than similar children from rural village homes, and virtually always had lower educational aspirations than comparable urban children[26] Differences in the meaning of or value attached to higher education by rural versus urban people probably accounts for much of the continuing differences in educational ambitions and achievements between rural and urban youth.

From the above comparisons of rural and urban families it becomes quite apparent that rural families are not necessarily as integrated, stable, or familistic as many myths and some of the literature suggest; nor does the urban family by comparison appear to be as unstable, unfamilistic, or necessarily in process of disintegration, as certain long-standing hypotheses have contended. In a study of "Rural-Urban Differences and the Family," William Key questions a number of these old views and hypotheses regarding the alleged disintegration of the family in urban areas, and the view that city people have become so individuated that they have little time to spend with their immediate families, and that in these urban settings in contrast to rural settings there are few intrafamilial cooperative activities.[27] He feels that there is sufficient evidence to support an opposite hypothesis that urban families are gaining in importance by providing their members with affection, companionship, and other primary-group relationships. For one thing, the difficulty of making satisfying personal or primary contact in big, impersonal cities tends to make those ties that do remain with family or kin even more important. Key offers an explanation for the overemphasis found in much of our urban sociology on the alleged disintegration of the extended family in the American city.

It seems likely . . . that the hypothesis of the disintegration of the extended family developed early in the history of urban sociology when attention was focused on recent immigrants to the city. . . . In other words, while there might have been a noticeable lack of contact with relatives during and immediately following the period of greatest immigration to the city, this seems to have been a temporary phenomenon produced by migration rather than by the city as such, and when possible (i.e., after time had elasped and immigrants had attracted more of their kin or had produced and reared children of their own), isolation in the city increased pressure for association with such kin.[28]

Key compared the amount of family participation (with both the immediate family and the extended family) in rural and in urban areas, and found no significant difference in the amount of either immediate family or extended family participation in urban families as compared with rural families.[29] We will return to this and related issues on the urban family later in the chapter.

Rural American Families: Continuities and Variations

First, a brief review of background factors important in shaping rural family life in America.

In order to understand the contemporary rural family in America, it is necessary to comprehend the long history of rural family life in the United States and in the preceding colonial period. In Chapter 2 we reviewed the historical backgrounds and various sources of American families, with attention to the colonial and rural frontier periods. Here it is necessary only to remind ourselves again of certain salient historical, cultural, and environmental conditions that have significantly contributed to shaping family life in rural America.

Families arriving from the Old World during the colonial period found themselves in an eminently rural environment. Whether they lived on isolated farms, in wilderness area settlements, in towns, or in or near one of the few small colonial cities, family patterns and practices tended to be similar in many basic ways, always allowing for racial, ethnic, and class differences.

Each family in the early days of the colonial period, and well into the nineteenth century in frontier areas, was faced with problems of survival, and

Nebraska farm family and truck, 1920. A dual-purpose work vehicle and recreational vehicle. (*Fred J. Pearson.*)

out of necessity developed into a self-sustaining, essentially independent unit. The division of labor was well established between men and women, and each child had important productive roles. Rural children were economic assets to the family, and many children made for a strong family. United States census figures show that in 1790 the median family size was 5.4 members.[30] The man and his sons cleared the land, tilled the soil, cared for the livestock, and often built the family home and other farm buildings. The wife and daughters did the cooking, sewing, spinning, and other domestic chores in the home, as well as frequently helping the menfolk in the fields, as at harvest time.

The principal goals of these rural families were simple and basic: to provide the members with food, shelter, clothing, and protection. Family survival and personal well-being resulted from the cooperative efforts of all members working toward these goals. Training and education were of a practical nature, preparing children and young people to perform useful and productive roles in their parental families and later in their own families. Individual interests were subordinated to family needs and concerns. This kind of rural family life was conducive to a high degree of familism. The individual was circumscribed by family quite literally from the cradle to the grave. In the family, one was not only born and reared, one was also educated and later employed, and in times of illness or trouble, succored by that family; finally, one was buried by the family.

Stemming partly from European traditions and partly from indigenous rural—especially frontier—conditions, the traditional country family tended to be patriarchal, or at least semipatriarchal. However, the need for the services of the wife and children enhanced their importance and status in these rural families. Thus it is likely that rural family life in America may have contributed somewhat to the historical push toward women's and children's liberation. As Ruth Cavan expressed this: "Women were in great demand on the frontier, and men competed for each unmarried woman who appeared. The seeds of equality were thus planted in the pioneer land as a result of the hard conditions of life, at a time when in the East certain women intellectuals were demanding equality with men as a matter of principle."[31]

Valuable insights into the nature and development of the rural family may be gained by examining the life cycle of families in rural America. The conjugal nuclear family begins its life cycle at marriage. As children are added the family grows in size until the last child is born; then the family size remains constant until the first child leaves home. As the children grow up and leave to start their own families, the family size decreases, and finally, with the death of the last parent, the cycle is completed. Each stage in the family cycle brings changes in roles and responsibilities for family members.

Taylor and Jones present an interesting description of the life cycle of the American farm family.[32] The first stage of the cycle lasts up to the birth of the first child, during which time the young couple are generally both engaged in the various farming activities, trying to build up their farm or to acquire a farm of their own. During this stage they may enjoy relative (and often temporary) economic well-being, until the second stage when children begin to arrive. This often brings on a period of economic struggle, since there are additional mouths to feed and the woman's economic productive role is now greatly curtailed. However, the children become economic assets at fairly young ages, assisting with various farm and house chores. In the premechanized farm family this was especially true. In recent times, however, due to farm mechanization and to public pressure for longer periods of formal education for all children, including farm children, farm youngsters tend to spend less time working on their parents' farm. The next period of the family cycle begins when the children leave their parental family to set up homes of their own. Their parents are once again alone (the empty-nest stage), and since there are fewer dependents now and the farm enterprise is apt to be reaching its period of highest productivity, the parental couple may enjoy another period of relative economic security or even some degree of affluence. There comes then the final stage in the cycle when the aging couple reach their declining years. For the farmer, retirement is generally more gradual and somewhat less traumatic than for many urban workers.

It is readily apparent that this family life cycle is closely related to the farming operation cycle. The couple's early years are characterized by a shortage of land and other resources. The farm and the family compete for the limited funds and resources. As the children begin to mature, their relatively inexpensive labor contributes to the expanding farm operation. The farmer's acreage and equipment will likely increase until he is in his mid-50s, after which the farm enterprise levels off and finally slows down as retirement approaches.

FARMING AND FAMILISM

In many ways the independent farm family found in isolated areas throughout American history well down into the twentieth century may be said to approximate the "traditional-patriarchal" family type discussed in Chapter 2. Farming is a family tradition, with all family members participating in it cooperatively, and the status and security of all members are bound up in the success of the farming enterprise. Under these conditions of life, familism may be expected to exist in high degree.

It should be helpful at this point to look more closely at the concept of "familism" as it relates to rural family life. Ernest W. Burgess and Harvey J. Locke specify these characteristics as embraced by this concept:

(1) The feeling on the part of all members that they belong pre-eminently to the family group and that all others are outsiders; (2) complete integration of individual activities for the achievement of family objectives; (3) the assumption that land, money, and other material goods are family property, involving the obligation to support family members and give them assistance when they are in need; (4) willingness of all other members to rally to the support of another member . . . ; and (5) concern for the perpetuation of the family as evidenced by helping an adult child in beginning and continuing an economic activity in line with family expectations, and in setting up a new household.[33]

In the last half of the twentieth century, isolated pockets of rural families may be found in the United States which approximate to a considerable degree this "ideal type" of familism. The Amish families discussed in Chapter 3 are examples, as are the Ozark Highland families described by Carle Zimmerman and M. E. Frampton.[34] The authors found that in these families the individual's "interests and will are fused with those of the family group." A high degree of family stability exists, and strong ties with kin persist throughout life. There is virtually no divorce, and family members stick together in spite of difficulties. Farming is a long family tradition, and there is a deep sentimental attachment to the land.

Today, of course, rural families, both farm and nonfarm, vary greatly throughout America, and taken together would be distributed all across the continuum from the highly familistic traditional-patriarchal type at one end to the modern-equalitarian type at the other end. We will look next at some of these rural family variations.

VARIATIONS IN FARM FAMILIES AND IN FAMILISM AS RELATED TO DIFFERENT TYPES OF FARMING

We see in rural America a historical trend away from the traditional-patriarchal type of family toward the urban-oriented modern-equalitarian type of family. Paralleling this trend is a corresponding decline in familism in rural America, as seen by comparing different kinds of farms and farm enterprises, starting with the traditional, independent, self-supporting family farm, moving through intermediate small or marginal farms, then on to the large-scale commercial, mechanized farms so much in evidence today.[35]

THE TRADITIONAL FAMILY FARM (high familism) These independent family farms, typical of north-central America, are generally large enough (100 to 200 acres) and contain enough good land not only to support the farm family but also to produce for the market. Dairy farms in Wisconsin and fruit farms in Michigan are examples. However, it is not just the size and productivity of the farm that has been conducive to cooperative effort of family members, but also a combination of geographic and social isolation plus a sentimental attachment to the land and to farming as a way of life that has been conducive to high familism.

In a comparison of six rural communities in the United States, Burgess and Locke observed a high degree of familism not only among the Amish, who have large and very productive farms, but also among the poor Spanish-American farm families of El Cerrito, New Mexico, who laboriously eked out a living on their small farms, using old-fashioned agricultural techniques.[36] But these farmers loved their land, resisted modern secular influences, and displayed most of the characteristics of familism. A high degree of family solidarity was also found among independent farm families in Irwin, Iowa, where attachment to the land and to farming was so strong that loyalty of young family members remained high despite recessions and severe droughts.[37] Many of these independent farm families are more recently coming under hard-to-resist influences of the dominant urban-secular trend in America, as we will see in Chapter 8.

Another farm gone, 1975. An auction for a farm going out of business. (*USDA photo by Byron Schumaker.*)

SMALL, MARGINAL FARMS   (declining familism) There are many conditions which may contribute to declines in family solidarity among rural families. If there is not sufficient land to support the farm family, or if the land becomes less productive, or if the farm enterprise is no longer able to compete with larger and more productive farms, then farm sons and daughters are less apt to see their livelihood in farming and begin to look elsewhere for their future. Also, a low value may be placed on farm ownership and on farming, in which case the people have a weak attachment to the land, as was true in Sublette, Kansas, another of the six rural communities compared by Burgess and Locke.[38]

Maybe even more important as a contributor to declining familism among these marginal farm families is the greater influence of urban-secular values and norms as compared with the traditional farm family. Resistance to urban-secular influences has been weakened by the above-mentioned conditions; moreover, many such small, marginal farms are in close proximity to cities, so family members are apt to be in more frequent contact with city people and activities and temptations. How can you keep them down on the farm when they have seen the bright lights of Chicago or Kansas City, where everything's up to date?

Of the six rural communities, Landaff, New Hampshire, best illustrates the decline of rural familism due to these conditions and trends. The impact of urban culture on farm youth was considerable. Personal interests and ambitions were stressed, actually by parents as well as their children, so that when sons wished to leave the farm, their parents made little effort to hold them there. An increasing disparity between the level of living existing or potential on the farm and the aspirations held up to farm youth by their nearby city acquaintances was so great that more and more young people were leaving the farms for the greater promise of the city. Family solidarity declined and family disorganization increased. Sons and daughters migrating to the city were too involved with their personal ambitions and immediate problems to worry much about their parents and other family members back on the farm. Divorce and separation were not uncommon.[39]

LARGE-SCALE MECHANIZED FARMS   (lowest familism) With the coming of mechanization, and more recently computerization, farming methods and techniques have been materially altered. In addition, fundamental changes are apparent in the relationship of the farm family to the community, and in the internal relationships within the farm family itself. The family is less apt to be tied as closely to the rural community or to the land itself as before. The farm crops become more specialized; the farmer deals with specialized agencies, often in a city some distance away, to provide and service farm machinery and give professional advice. Farmer and family not only expand their economic contacts, but their social, recreational, and often educational experiences broaden well beyond the rural community. Mechanization of farming has also been paralleled by improved means of transportation and communication, enabling farm families to reduce both spatial and social isolation and come increasingly under urban-secular influences.[40]

Mechanized and improved farm techniques have resulted in a different and more specialized division of labor on these large commercial farms. Such farming has become a big, efficiently run business enterprise. The farm owner may be the business manager of the enterprise, or may employ a highly trained and experienced professional farm manager to run it. Other family members too may have little to do with the actual farm work, leaving this to hired farm laborers. Also, various specialists and consultants with advanced degrees from agricultural colleges are employed as needed. Consequently, as the farm enterprise becomes larger, more mechanized, and more of a big, impersonal business operation, the old bases for family cooperation and solidarity diminish. There is little place for sentimental attachment to the land or to farming here. The main objective is cash profit, as in any such business enterprise. In many of the very large agricultural operations, such as the Arizona or California vegetable or fruit farms, or the Southern cotton or grain plantations, the owners are generally "absentee"; in fact there is often corporate ownership, with the whole agricultural operation in the hands of highly trained professional people. Few traces of familism survive under these conditions.

MIGRATORY FARM-WORKER FAMILY   This type of farm family, frequently connected to large-scale commercial farming, is that of the migratory agricultural worker. This family does not fit clearly in the picture of declining familism accompanying mechanization and commercialization of agriculture. However, migratory farm labor is associated with large-scale agriculture where seasonal labor is needed, typically at harvest time. While many migratory workers may be unattached, a large proportion of this labor force has always included family groups.[41]

The physical and social conditions of family life have too often been most unfavorable for these families, even when compared with sedentary tenant farm families or urban unskilled workers. Except for a few months each year, the migrant family is on the move following the seasonal need for its services. This makes it very difficult for these families to obtain the normal benefits of citizenship associated with residence in a specific community. Schooling for the children is a chronic problem. Each spring the family starts out on its customary trek, normally following a well-established seasonal route from farm to farm where unskilled farm labor is needed. Usually all family members help with the harvesting except the very young children. They may be left in the camp or small quarters perhaps provided by the employer, often in the care of an older child, while the mother is working alongside the father and the rest of the children in the fields.

Family living quarters are generally poor and crowded, often lacking amenities such as indoor plumbing or even running water. The living area may indeed be a depressing rural slum. All the family energy is bent toward making a living and possibly saving some money to help the family make it through the off-season. Work, long and hard, dominates the family life, leaving little time for informal family activities. Since the family is mobile and thrown on its own resources, there is apt to exist a considerable degree of family unity and solidarity.[42] Thus, in spite of adverse economic and social conditions, many migratory labor families may be more familistic than some other more sedentary rural families where a diversity of viewpoints and goals may strain husband-wife relations or parent-child relations.

As Cavan points out, migratory laborer families have some of the same characteristics as traditional farm families, such as family unity, members working together as a team, and generally close cooperation in matters of work and family living.[43] The migratory family differs, however, in that it has no land or stable base of operation and has little identity with a community, thereby suffering low legal and social status. This rural family type is largely a by-product of large-scale commercial agriculture.

Urbanization and the Urban Family

THE CLASSICAL VIEW OF URBANIZATION AND THE FAMILY

About three decades ago Burgess and Locke identified three factors they considered to be of major importance in reshaping family life in American cities: "(1) industrialization; (2) the transplanting of rural families to cities; and (3) the preponderance of impersonal, formal, and disinterested relationships over intimacy and spontaneous friendliness."[44]

These factors should be helpful as points of departure here as we seek to unravel some of the complexities of the urban environment and its interrelations with family structure.

The industrial revolution brought on basic changes in technology and in

Aerial view of tenement houses, Boston. (*E. D. Dyer.*)

the economic and social organization of production and distribution. When production had been largely by hand, economic organization was on a smaller and more personal basis. Sentiment as well as economic interests entered the relationships of the shop owner and his coworkers. The change from handicraft and small-shop production to machine power and factory production epitomizes the transition from rural and small-village life to urban conditions of life.

Another key factor shaping family life in American cities, say Burgess and Locke, was the transplanting of American and European rural families to American cities.[45] These families, shaped by the social and economic conditions of their rural homeland environments, were suddenly plunged into the new, strange, and often hostile environment of the American city. In most areas of the big city, with the exception of the immigrant neighborhoods, there seemed to be an absence of the spontaneous, intimate friendliness more characteristic of the rural community. Relations among city dwellers were more fragmented and specialized, more formal and impersonal. Also, the physical conditions of life in the big, crowded industrial cities were less conducive to healthy and satisfying family life. In his well-known work "Urbanism as a Way of Life," Louis Wirth identifies some of the salient features of urbanism as a form of social organization and its relationship to the family.

The distinctive features of the urban way of life have often been described sociologically as consisting of the substitution of secondary for primary contacts, the weakening of bonds of kinship, and the declining social significance of the family, the disappearance of the neighborhood, and the undermining of the traditional basis of social authority . . . thus, for instance, the low and declining urban reproduction rates suggest that the city is not conducive to the traditional type of family life, including the rearing of children and the maintenance of the home as the locus of a whole round of vital activities. The transfer of industrial, educational, and recreational activities to specialized institutions outside the home has deprived the family of some of its most characteristic historical functions. In cities mothers are more likely to be employed. . . . Families are smaller and more frequently without children than in the country. The family as a unit of social life is emancipated from the larger kinship group characteristic of the country, and the individual members pursue their own diverging interests in their vocational, educational, religious, recreational, and political life.[46]

In the city social encounters are more numerous than in the country but more transitory and impersonal. The city dweller's work and other activities involve brief contact with many different kinds of people. These contacts depend largely on mutualities of interest in specific associational settings rather than on common humanity. It is this impersonality of city life that has baffled and antagonized newcomers from rural communities. City people may seem very reserved and inhospitable to country people. What they do not understand is that this withdrawal may really be the urbanite's mechanism of self-protection. One feels it necessary to "shut out" the great mass of people in order to stay mentally healthy and to protect oneself against "con-persons" or other types of "secular strangers" who are ready to exploit or use one if given the opportunity. "Caveat emptor" is the watchword here.

Urbanism affects not only personal relations but also one's sense of responsibility for things that are not clearly one's private concern. City people have been known to let calls for help go unheeded, and have been observed to ignore and even walk around a person who has collapsed on a city sidewalk. It is not that they are basically less kind or human than rural people, just more cautious and on guard.

As is apparent by now, social scientists have paid considerable attention to the twin concepts of industrialization and urbanization as explanatory variables for family life patterns and changes in America and elsewhere. Industrialization is generally thought to be antecedent to urbanization (in its modern meaning); and the two processes are then seen as roughly concomitant once industrialization is well under way.[47] Viewed in the context of social change, the family is seen as the dependent variable, reacting and adjusting to the processes and new conditions brought on by industrialization and urbanization. Some sociologists, including Talcott Parsons, have maintained that these twin processes have brought about changes in family life whereby family structure has been altered basically from an earlier, extended, consanguineal type to the current small, nuclear, conjugal type.[48] This theory argues that the earlier extended family, with its emphasis on kinship bonds and familism, restricted the mobility and availability of the labor force required in an industrialized economy. The small, independent nuclear family, on the other hand, is well suited to go anywhere workers are needed in expanding industrializing societies. The family, thus, under the twin influences of industrialization and urbanization, has become a small, mobile, husband-wife–oriented group, relatively isolated from kinfolk, according to this classical view.

REVISED VIEWS OF INDUSTRIALIZATION, URBANIZATION, AND THE FAMILY

Recently, the above classical view of the relationship between industrialization, urbanization, and the family has come under considerable criticism. In *World Revolution and Family Patterns*, William Goode finds a general trend toward the conjugal nuclear family in industrializing societies, but notes too that the nuclear family predates the industrial revolution. He also feels that there has probably been a two-way relationship between the family and industrialization and urbanization.[49] That is, just how these processes influence family systems, or how family systems may influence industrialization and urbanization is not really clearly understood.

Frank F. Furstenberg, in an article titled "Industrialization and the American Family: A Look Backward," shows that the small nuclear family was prevalent in America before the industrial revolution, and finds some remarkable similarities between the family of a century ago and today's family in matters of mate selection, husband-wife relations, and parent-child relations.[50] Many contemporary family problems and strains thought to have resulted from industrialization were quite evident in preindustrial families, according to Furstenberg.

Eugene Litwak, among others, has questioned the older notion of the urban, mobile nuclear family being isolated from its kin.[51] In a Michigan study he found that a large proportion of urban, mobile families manage to maintain ties with their extended family kin to some degree. He argues that "a modified extended family" is prevalent in our present urban society, consisting of two or more related nuclear families bonded together by affectional ties.

There are also many contemporary sociologists who question the older views of Carle Zimmerman, Pitirim Sorokin, and others, that family changes allegedly brought on by urbanization are mostly bad, and that the modern urban family is becoming increasingly unstable and disorganized. They argue that the modern family has shown itself to be resilient and flexible, and in process of change toward a closer approximation of our democratic ideals.[52] These and related issues will be examined more fully in Chapter 6, on social change and family change in America.

Let us sum up our discussion of the "revised" view of the relationship between industrialization and urbanization and the family. While few would deny that the family has been profoundly influenced by urban-industrial processes and conditions, the relationships are complex, and cause and effect are not always clear. (1) It is an oversimplification to say that urban-industrial processes produced the conjugal nuclear family. Rather, the preindustrial nuclear family may well have helped bring about industrialization and urbanism. (2) Many urban family problems found today also existed in preindustrial families. (3) The modern, urban nuclear family is not as isolated from its relatives as previously thought. (4) Urban families today have many strengths as well as certain weaknesses.

URBAN FAMILY VARIATIONS

While many questions still remain as to the interrelations between urbanization and family systems, there is no question that family life in American cities has been richly varied. The different cultural and historical backgrounds of American families reviewed in Chapter 2 attest to this. We noted there that more than 40 million immigrants representing many nationalities and races have come to the United States, and that from the latter part of the nineteenth century onward they settled mostly in American cities. Examples of these diverse families were presented in Chapter 3. Also the social-class family variations to be presented in Chapter 5 largely represent urban class variations. So, in a manner, these other chapters also deal with important urban family variations.

What remains for us here, is to try to show more systematically some of the interrelations between urban processes and environments and family patterns. We will start by reviewing the pioneer work of Ernest W. Burgess and his associates at the University of Chicago, who spent many years studying family life in big American cities. They developed what has become known as the "concentric zone theory" of urban growth and organization.[53] The main idea is that many modern industrial cities grew outward from an inner center in a pattern of concentric zones each of which is different in population composition, social organizations, and institutions. Burgess found different types of families living in most of these zones.

Before continuing, it should be noted that such a theory of urban growth and organization is only a hypothetical model or "ideal construction" of the zones of a large, expanding modern city, and that no real city, not even Chicago, would fit the model exactly. However, for present purposes of trying to sort out the complexity and variety of urban family life and organization, such a model may be very helpful. It enables us to see the ways that during periods of great urban growth and expansion—such as the first half of the twentieth century— human beings, generally in family groups, moved into big cities, became located in certain areas of the city, and interacted with and became adjusted to their particular urban environment.

Burgess and Locke specified six urban zones and a particular type of family identified with each of five of these areas (see Figure 4-2).

ZONE I   THE CENTRAL BUSINESS DISTRICT[54]   Here is found a transitory population. Cheap hotels and flophouses are populated largely by homeless men. This is a nonfamily zone. People living here are apt to have a sad background of broken marriages or severed family ties. Many seek escape in alcohol, drugs, and other vices.

ZONE II   THE ROOMING-HOUSE ZONE[55]   Here is found the emancipated family. Bordering on the central business district are rooming houses and cheap apartment districts populated mostly by mobile young people who are usually temporary residents here just getting started in jobs and who may be going to college or training school. Marriages here are typically childless, and many couples have become emancipated from conventional family and community controls and are seeking new experiences and excitements offered by the city. Their life-style is highly secular and individual-oriented. A variety of unconventional life-styles abound, many associated with artistic, religious, or political cults. Burgess found high degrees of both personal and

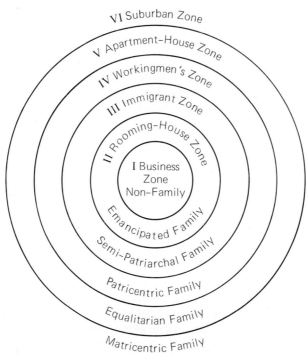

FIGURE 4-2 The theoretical pattern of urban zones and of family types. (*Source: Ernest W. Burgess and Harvey J. Locke*, The Family: From Institution to Companionship, *p. 117. Copyright The American Book Company, 1945. Reprinted by permission.*)

social disorganization among residents here. The more stable couples tend to move out quite soon.

ZONE III   THE IMMIGRANT'S NEIGHBORHOOD AND THE SEMIPATRIARCHAL FAMILY[56]   As seen in Chapter 3, most immigrants transported to America in the nineteenth and early twentieth centuries were of rural background and normally quite patriarchal. Secular influences in American cities tended to weaken the authority of the father; thus the families became semipatriarchal or at a certain point only fictitiously patriarchal. Being foreign-born, and lacking urban job skills needed to compete favorably, these immigrants and their families were frequently forced to live in run-down areas bordering Zone II. Bad housing, overcrowding, and generally unhealthy and unsafe conditions for family life prevailed. In these "foreign" ghettos of the late nineteenth and twentieth centuries were to be found high rates of infant mortality, desertion, juvenile delinquency, and family conflict, as bewildered immigrant parents lost control over their more rapidly Americanizing children.

Among first-generation immigrant families poverty and dependency were high. The needs of these immigrant families gave rise to some community efforts to come to their aid such as the settlement-house movement.

ZONE IV   THE WORKINGMAN'S ZONE AND THE PATRICENTRIC FAMILY[57]
Beyond the crowded immigrant neighborhoods lie the workingmen's living areas. The physical and social environments here are generally better for family living. There is more space and there are more single family homes here. Also the families are better prepared to adjust successfully to urban conditions, being descendants of either earlier immigrants or migrants from rural America. These people are better able to preserve traditional marriage and family norms, while resisting at least some of the urban-secular influences. Family life is more stable, with the father as the head of the family, if no longer the sole or principal authority. Churches, schools, labor unions, and other community groups lend support to these working-class families.

ZONE V   THE APARTMENT-HOUSE ZONE AND THE EQUALITARIAN FAMILY[58]   Burgess feels that the urban way of life is perhaps best exemplified in the apartment-house and residence-hotel districts of the big city. Compared with single-home areas, here the population is much more dense, there is a smaller rate of home ownership, and a higher rate of residential mobility. Certain aspects of family life are quite closely related to these environmental conditions. The dense population, smaller living space, and little play space for the children make child care and upbringing difficult. So the population here is disproportionately adult, with many childless couples and single adults in evidence. A large number of wives in these families are employed, typically working in white-collar jobs.

The families here range from middle class to lower-upper class, with the husband likely pursuing a managerial or professional career. Marriages are more equalitarian than elsewhere, with the wife and husband sharing varied community and family activities, as well as frequently sharing the family provider role. These people, generally with several generations of urban background in their families, are probably best equipped to get the most out of inner-city living.

ZONE VI   THE SUBURBS AND THE MATRICENTRIC FAMILY[59]   Many families who are able to afford it prefer living in the suburban areas which lie beyond the central city zones. They move out there in order to try to get away from some of the less desirable aspects of city life, to have a yard and perhaps a garden, to be closer to the open country, and to enjoy, hopefully, closer Gemeinschaftlike relations with their neighbors. Also they want to live close enough to the main city to enjoy the advantages of employment, shopping, schools, entertainment, and other cultural advantages offered by the large modern city. Perhaps the main reason many families move to the suburbs is their hope that in this kind of environment their children will be healthier, better adjusted, and get a better education. Since many suburbs have been relatively homogeneous with respect to social class and ethnicity, many parents have seen this as a desirable condition for bringing up their children. Family life is normally well supported here by various active community organizations such as church groups, civic clubs, and parent-teacher groups.

Burgess found that the mother is generally the center of the suburban families he observed. The husband-father is absent from the family daily during the workweek from early morning until evening. (Commuting time can be as much as two to three hours a day.) The father's role in the family may be further reduced by weekend business-related commitments, such as golf at the country club. The responsibilities of child care, home management, housekeeping, and other nitty-gritty everyday jobs fall largely on the mother.

More recent research indicates that families in the newer-suburbs may be matricentric in activities, equalitarian or at least flexible in family roles, and perhaps somewhat patriarchal in authority.[60] Ernest Mowrer describes such mother-centered activities and role flexibility:

The suburban wife finds herself constantly occupied with furnishing transportation for other members of the family; . . . to take and meet her husband before and after work, to school and other places . . . to take and bring home the children . . . [and] trips to the neighborhood stores to do the family shopping. Her husband not only finds himself called upon to mow and care for the lawn, but also to become an amateur plumber, house painter, repairer of children's toys and various gadgets about the household, landscaper, and even construction engineer. . . . When the suburban husband turns indoors he is often joined by his wife and together they become interior craftsmen, painting walls and ceilings, hanging paper, and refinishing furniture. Flexibility of role is, in fact, characteristic of suburban family life. . . .[61]

THE SUBURBAN MOVEMENT

Since the time of Burgess and Locke's analysis of city zones and related family types, many changes have taken place in metropolitan America. In big cities such as Chicago, black populations have cut across several zones, and slum clearance and urban renewal projects have introduced new housing designed for middle- and even upper-class families into what used to be Zones II and III.[62]

Certainly one of the most spectacular developments of mid-twentieth century has been the tremendous growth of the suburbs around our big cities, not only the expansion of older suburbs but also the addition of new rings and clusters out beyond them. Before 1920 the central cities had grown more rapidly than the suburbs, reflecting the continuing large immigration from foreign countries and rural areas. By 1930, the outlying areas, particularly

Modern suburban home. (*E. D. Dyer.*)

around large cities, began to grow more rapidly. Following World War II the growth of these outer city areas soared. Between 1930 and 1950 central city growth fell to about two-thirds of this outer-city-area growth, and between 1950 and 1960 further declined to about one-third. Between 1960 and 1970 the suburban areas grew 26.7 percent while the inner cities grew only 6.4 percent.[63] In the early 1970s the suburban trend had slowed, due considerably to soaring transportation costs, and there are indications of a reverse trend as more people opt for inner-city living (see Table 4-1).

Clearly, suburbs have never been entirely middle or upper class, as those studied by Burgess and Locke seem to have been. Especially following World War II, during the period of greatest suburban expansion, families spanning a range from the working class to the top upper class joined the movement. However, by far most of the new suburbanites were middle-class families, either moving out from central city districts or moving in from smaller

TABLE 4-1 U.S. POPULATION INSIDE AND OUTSIDE S.M.S.A. (STANDARD METROPOLITAN STATISTICAL AREAS), 1960 AND 1970

	1960		1970	
	NUMBER	PERCENT	NUMBER	PERCENT
Inside central cities (S.M.S.A.)	59,947,000	33.4	63,797,000	31.4
Outside central cities (S.M.S.A.)	59,648,000	33.3	75,622,000	37.2
Outside S.M.S.A.	59,728,000	33.3	63,793,000	31.4

SOURCE: Figures from *We the Americans: Our Cities and Suburbs,* U.S. Department of Commerce, May 1973, p. 3.

communities or the country. During this period of rapid suburban growth, the suburbs became to some extent idealized as one of the best places for families to live. Life was supposed to be healthier and safer than in the crowded inner city; it was seen as a better place to rear children, to have the security of home ownership, to relax on weekends, and at the same time to have the advantages of city jobs and city services.[64]

While a great many families have undoubtedly had their expectations met by moving to the suburbs, certainly for other families these idealized expectations did not always materialize.

COMPARATIVE CHARACTERISTICS OF SUBURBAN AND CENTRAL CITY FAMILIES AND POPULATIONS

We will conclude this part of our discussion of the family in metropolitan America by drawing some comparisons of suburban families and populations with those living in the inner or central city districts.

Based on their studies of families in suburban and central Detroit, Blood and Wolfe concluded that patriarchal authority may be as high or higher in suburban families as in central city families.[65] Using a constructed index of power, the authors found that the mean power score of the suburban father was consistently higher than that of the central city father. This held true at every social status level. While their findings were quite conclusive for that one city, Detroit, further corroborative studies are needed.

Residential suburbs, in comparison with central cities, generally have a higher sex ratio (the number of men per 100 women), larger families, more home ownership, and more single than multiple dwellings. Specifically, there are more white families found in the suburbs than in the inner city; families are larger, with the average size of 3.66 for the suburbs versus 3.5 for the central city districts; the sex ratio in the suburbs is 96.2 men per 100 women versus

92.9 men per 100 women in the inner city; and there are fewer elderly people and more young adults in the suburbs than in the inner city.[66]

Suburban parents generally have more formal education than central city parents; proportionately there are more family breadwinners in the suburbs employed in high-prestige occupations with higher pay, and conversely more families with low incomes are found in the central city. One study showed not only that three of the leading socioeconomic status indicators—education, occupation, and income—are higher in the suburbs, but also that these differences between suburbs and central cities increase as the size of the metropolitan area increases. "The larger the central city, the more likely it is that the socio-economic status of ring residents will be higher than that of (inner) city residents."[67] United States census data also show that suburbs have the lowest percentage of single men and women, and that more suburban women are married than inner-city women; also, more suburban men are married than either central city men or rural men. Suburban families are less apt to be broken by separation, divorce, or death of a spouse than central city families.[68]

American families have reacted in different ways to suburban living. For many, this environment has been satisfying, while for others there have been frustrations, dullness, uniformity, and lack of cultural stimulation. In Chapter 8 we will examine more fully some of the current reactions to suburban family living and try to see what changes are taking place there today.

GENERAL TRENDS OF URBAN FAMILIES

Are there any broad trends in family patterns that may be discerned among families living in American urban environments? Is it possible to find a prototype of the present-day urban family that would be generally valid without doing violence to the continuing ethnic, racial, social-class or other variations still to be found in American cities today? While fully recognizing that such differences are still present, it may be argued that in keeping with the current Gesellschaft-secular social trend, more and more urban families are coming to resemble the following prototype, as described by Lee Burchinal:

A prototype of urban family organization may be inferred from projections of past changes. This prototype is most clearly represented among families in the urban professional class and, in varying degrees, reflects the following characteristics: enhancement of the welfare, freedom and personality of individual family members by means of family relationships and a flexible family division of labor; differentiation in family and occupational roles . . . ; desire for children based on the opportunities for providing for the personality development of the children and the enrichment which the children bring to the couple; active pursuit and implementation of knowledge (professionalization) related to marital and family roles; use of person-centered criteria in dating, courtship, mate selection, and marriage; and tolerant views toward non-marital sexual experiences.[69]

It cannot now be determined when or if these prototypal patterns will become the modal or predominant characteristics of urban families in America. The above prototype is obviously essentially middle class and it is not known, of course, how far the present middle-class trend will go. More attention will be devoted to these issues in following chapters.

SUMMARY

Since America has been a rural society throughout most of its history, it is necessary to look into its long rural background and development. Comparisons are made of rural and urban economic and social environments. Cultural differences between rural and urban America were probably greatest during the nineteenth century. The values and virtues of rural life and agrarianism were strongly entrenched, and the expanding cities were seen as a threat to good family life by many Americans, while others saw the city as the center of progress and civilization. Among the major rural-urban differences in America—most apparent in the nineteenth and early twentieth centuries—were differences in the physical environments, in population size and density, in community size, and in social differentiation, stratification, and mobility. While rural family organization has tended to follow trends set by urban families, certain differences have remained—at least until very recently—including a more traditional division of labor and authority, less employment of wives outside the home, less divorce, and higher birthrates for rural families.

Rural families are not necessarily as stable and familistic as often thought nor are urban families by comparison as unstable or nonfamilistic as believed by many.

A brief review of historical factors thought to be important in shaping rural family life is presented. The relationship between farming and familism is emphasized. A trend away from the rural traditional-patriarchal type of family toward the urban-oriented modern-equalitarian family type has been accompanied by a corresponding decline in familism in rural America. This change is illustrated by comparing different types of farms and farm families.

The classical view of urbanization and the family emphasized the role of industrialization and the preponderance of impersonal secondary-type relations in reshaping family life for those moving from American and European rural areas into American cities, and the ascendancy of the small, mobile, conjugal family which is prone to instability. Revised views of the relationship between industrialization and urbanization and the family may question parts of the early view, contending that the small nuclear family predates the industrial revolution, that many present-day urban family problems existed in preindustrial families, and that urban families have strengths as well as weaknesses.

American urban family variations are illustrated by reviewing the different family types Burgess and Locke identified with different city zones. The twentieth-century suburban movement is seen as an effort on the part of families who can afford it to move out from the central city to a healthier, safer, and generally more desirable environment.

Notes

1 *The American Almanac* (New York: Grosset & Dunlap, 1972), pp. 16–17, 572.
2 Lee Taylor and Arthur R. Jones, *Rural Life and Urbanized Society* (New York: Oxford University Press, 1964), pp. 55–58. This discussion follows Taylor and Jones quite closely.
3 Paul L. Ford, ed., *The Works of Thomas Jefferson*, vol. IV (New York: G. P. Putnam's Sons, 1904), p. 85.
4 Taylor and Jones, op. cit., p. 57.
5 John Useem, Pierre Tangent, and Ruth Useem, "Stratification in a Prairie Town," *American Sociological Review*, 7 (June 1942), pp. 331–342. Also see Art Gallaher, *Plainville Fifteen Years Later* (New York: Columbia University Press, 1961), chap. 6.
6 Arnold Toynbee, *The Industrial Revolution* (Boston: Beacon Press, 1957), pp. 25–35.
7 Taylor and Jones, op. cit., pp. 50–52.
8 Ibid., p. 348.
9 Charles P. Loomis and J. Allen Beegle, *A Strategy for Rural Change* (Cambridge, Mass.: Schenkman Publishing Co., 1975), table 1, p. 73; U.S. Bureau of the Census, *1970 Census of Population: Characteristics of the Population*, "United States Summary," 1, p. 278.
10 Loomis and Beegle, op. cit., p. 75.
11 *The American Almanac*, 1972, op. cit., table 75, p. 57.
12 U.S. Bureau of the Census, *1970 Census of Population*, op.cit., 1, p. 278.
13 Ibid., 1, p. 413. Loomis and Beegle. op. cit., pp. 79–80.
14 U.S. Bureau of the Census, *Current Population Reports*, ser. P-20, no. 200, 1969, table 17.
15 Lee G. Burchinal, "The Rural Family of the Future," in John N. Edwards, ed., *The Family and Change* (New York: Alfred A. Knopf, 1969), pp. 409–445.
16 Ibid., pp. 409–410.
17 Ibid., pp. 420–439.
18 Ibid., pp. 421–422. Also see Eugene Wilkening, "Joint Decision-Making in Farm Families as a Function of Status and Role," *American Sociological Review*, 23 (April 1958), pp. 187–192; Murray Straus, "Family Role Differentiation and Technological Change in Farming," *Rural Sociology*, 25 (April 1960), pp. 219–228; Robert O. Blood, Jr., and Donald M. Wolfe, *Husbands and Wives* (New York: Free Press of Glencoe, 1960).
19 Ibid., pp. 422–424.

20 Ibid., pp. 425–427. Also see A. C. Thorpe, "Patterns of Family Interaction in Farm and Town Homes," *Michigan Agricultural Experiment Station Technological Bulletin 260*, 1957.

21 Ibid., pp. 427, 436.

22 Ibid., p. 428.

23 Blood and Wolfe, op. cit., p. 429.

24 Ibid.

25 Ibid., pp. 430–431.

26 William Sewell, "Rural-Urban Differences in Educational Aspirations," paper presented at the American Sociological Association Meetings, New York, August 1960.

27 William H. Key, "Rural-Urban Differences and the Family," *Sociological Quarterly*, 2 (January 1961), pp. 49–56.

28 Ibid., p. 54.

29 Ibid., p. 53.

30 U.S. Bureau of the Census, *Historical Statistics of the United States, 1789–1945*, (1949), p. 29.

31 Ruth S. Cavan, *The American Family* (New York: Thomas Y. Crowell Co., 1969), p. 45.

32 Taylor and Jones, op. cit., pp. 352–353.

33 Ernest W. Burgess and Harvey J. Locke, *The Family* (New York: American Book Co., 1950), p. 60.

34 Carle C. Zimmerman and M. E. Frampton, *Family and Society* (New York: D. Van Nostrand Co., 1935).

35 Cavan, op. cit., pp. 46–48; and Burgess and Locke, op. cit., pp. 60–75.

36 Burgess and Locke, op. cit., pp. 66–75.

37 Ibid., p. 67.

38 Ibid.

39 Ibid., pp. 67–73.

40 Cavan, op. cit., pp. 47–48; and Gallaher, op. cit., pp. 32–76.

41 Cavan, op. cit., pp. 55–56.

42 Ibid., pp. 56–57.

43 Ibid., p. 58.

44 Burgess and Locke, op. cit., p. 99.

45 Ibid., pp. 99–101.

46 Louis Wirth, "Urbanism as a Way of Life," *American Journal of Sociology*, 44 (July 1938), p. 20.

47 John N. Edwards, "Industrialization, Urbanization, and the Family," in John N. Edwards, ed., *The Family and Change* (New York: Alfred A. Knopf, 1969), pp. 13–14.

48 Talcott Parsons, "The Social Structure of the Family," in Ruth Anshen, ed., *The Family: Its Functions and Destiny* (New York: Harper & Brothers, 1959), pp. 241–271.

49 William Goode, *World Revolution and Family Patterns* (New York: Free Press, 1963), pp. 1–2.

50 Frank F. Furstenberg, "Industrialization and the American Family: A Look Backward," *American Sociological Review*, 31 (June 1966), pp. 326–327.

51 Eugene Litwak, "Geographical Mobility and Extended Family Cohesion," *American Sociological Review*, 25 (June 1960), pp. 385–394; also see Bert N. Adams, *Kinship in an Urban Setting* (Chicago: Markham Publishing Co., 1968).
52 Edwards, op. cit., pp. 5–6.
53 Burgess and Locke, op. cit., pp. 100–101.
54 Ibid., pp. 102–103.
55 Ibid., pp. 103–105.
56 Ibid., pp. 105–107.
57 Ibid., pp. 107–108.
58 Ibid., pp. 109–111.
59 Ibid., pp. 111–113.
60 Ernest W. Burgess, Harvey J. Locke, and M. M. Thomas, *The Family* (New York: Van Nostrand Reinhold Co., 1971), pp. 73–74.
61 Ernest R. Mowrer, "The Family in Suburbia," in William Dobriner, ed., *The Suburban Community* (New York: G. P. Putnam's Sons, 1958), pp. 156–157.
62 Cavan, op. cit., p. 57.
63 Advisory Commission on Intergovernmental Relations, "The Pattern of Urbanization," in Louis K. Loewenstein, *Urban Studies* (New York: Free Press, 1971), pp. 8–9; and *The American Almanac, 1972*, op. cit., p. 16.
64 E. Gartly Jaco and Ivan Belknap, "Is a New Family Form Emerging in the Urban Fringe?" *American Sociological Review*, 18 (October 1953), pp. 551–557.
65 Blood and Wolfe, op. cit., p. 36.
66 U. S. Bureau of the Census, *1960 Census of Population*, United States Summary, 1, pp. 148–157; also see Burgess, Locke, and Thomas, op. cit., pp. 68–74.
67 L. F. Schnore and D. W. Varley, "Some Concomitants of Metropolitan Size," *American Sociological Review*, 20 (August 1955), pp. 408–414.
68 U.S. Bureau of the Census, *1960 Census of Population*, op. cit., p. 156.
69 Lee G. Burchinal, "The Rural Family of the Future," in John N. Edwards, ed., *The Family and Change* (New York: Alfred A. Knopf, 1969), p. 418.

SELECTED READING

This chapter has stressed the industrialization-urbanization trends in America, and has shown many of the effects of these related processes on family life, both in the city and in the country. Blood's article is addressed to this issue. He examines some of the effects of urbanization on farm families and on city families in Michigan.

Based on data from the Detroit metropolitan area, Blood's findings suggest that modern urban families are quite structurally sound, which enables them to function effectively in their urban environment. While urban living has brought significant changes in family functions, the reduction of some of the older functions has created more time and energy for certain newer functions, such as increased husband-wife companionship and affection.

Blood finds that urban influences now extend beyond the metropolis, and are clearly felt by families living in adjacent rural areas. Thus today rural and urban families are coming to resemble each other more than they did earlier.

IMPACT OF URBANIZATION ON AMERICAN FAMILY STRUCTURE AND FUNCTIONING*

Robert O. Blood, Jr.

In the "good old days," most American families lived on farms, remote and isolated. Pioneer family members clung together with a desperation born of economic necessity. They depended on one another for most essential services. Survival required the cooperation of the entire household. The rudimentary nature of other social institutions imposed religious, political, and educational responsibilities on the family. Divorce was unthinkable, since neither man nor woman could afford to lose the services of the other. Childlessness or even limited childbearing was a hardship to be endured with regret.

The compulsory nature of family life on the frontier is indisputable. The controversial question is whether such family life was not only compulsory but "golden." To many Americans the past has a lustre which the present lacks. Pioneer families seem in retrospect to have found unique satisfaction in working and playing together. Family life then was rewarding and satisfying, vital, and meaningful. By contrast, modern family life seems brittle, tenuous, and often meaningless.

Is this picture true? Unfortunately it is impossible for the methods of social science to be used to measure the family life of the past. However, it is possible to examine contemporary rural and urban families to see whether the "golden past" still survives on the modern farm and whether urban family life is obsolescent. If contemporary rural and urban families do not differ greatly from one another and if urban families have a stable structure and perform vital functions for their members, then the past may not have been so golden, and the present not so tarnished.

Urbanization of the American Farm Family

A total of 178 farm wives were interviewed in southeastern Michigan (a random sample of three counties extending west of Detroit). The information

*Reprinted from *Sociology and Social Research*, 49 (1964), pp. 5–16. Copyright © by *Sociology and Social Research*, 1964. Reprinted by permission of publisher and author.

they provided is fundamentally similar to that derived from the Detroit Area Study. For instance, the city and farm families are equally democratic in their patterns of making family decisions. When the urban families are arbitrarily divided into husband and wife dominated segments of equal size, the farm families have an equally large proportion of equalitarian cases.

The chief way in which these farm and city couples differ is in their division of labor. As tradition suggests, farm wives are move involved than city wives in practical tasks. Farm women engage in such outside tasks as raising poultry and vegetables. They also get less help in the home from their busy husbands. Since city wives are geographically separated from the husband's place of work, they can't assist him directly. Similarly, the fact that the commuter leaves his work behind when he comes home makes him more available to help with household tasks.[1]

Does this greater service of farm wives mean that rural families are better than city families? That depends on the criterion for what is better. If the criterion is divorce rates, farm families score somewhat better. But if it is the wife's satisfaction with her marriage partner, the rural advantage largely disappears. In these samples, farm wives are slightly more satisfied with their standard of living and the husband's understanding, less satisfied with the love and affection received and equally satisfied with the companionship. Since in the American scheme of values, companionship is the crucial test of marriage, the overall evaluation of family life by rural and urban wives is essentially the same.

This brief comparison of contemporary city and farm families suggests that in most respects their family patterns are similar. It gives no conclusive answer to the question whether farm family living in the past was more "golden" than in the present. But it does suggest that city and farm families shine with essentially the same hue today.

Contemporary farm families have become urbanized, at least in Southern Michigan. They read the same newspapers, listen to the same radio broadcasts, and watch the same telecasts as their urban counterparts. Their children attend consolidated schools in urban centers. Their cars and all-weather roads give them access to the city where they participate in community activities. Modern farming has become a business which happens to be located in the country and differs little from urban family businesses in its effect on family life. Viewed in the large, city families and farm families have more common characteristics than differences, for today the metropolitan community and its hinterland are a single social unit.

[1]See Robert O. Blood, Jr., "The Division of Labor in City and Farm Families," *Marriage and Family Living*, 20 (May, 1958), pp. 170–174.

Vitality of the Modern American Family

If farm families resemble city families, perhaps that only proves that they, too, are decadent. Perhaps all American families and not just urban ones have disintegrated. It is not enough to compare city and farm families relative to one another. Some assessment of the actual level of functioning of contemporary families must be made. For the sake of simplicity, this assessment will focus on urban families, but in almost every case, the same findings characterize the farm families studied.

The vitality of family life can be looked at from two points of view. First, how sound is the structure of American family life? Secondly, how effectively do these families carry out their functions.?[2]

Stability of Modern Family Structure

The structure of a family consists of the configuration of positions which the family members occupy. This paper is concerned with the positions which the husband and wife occupy in relation to one another. These positions (or statuses) and the roles attached to them may be analyzed in terms of the power structure and the division of labor in the family.

For present purposes, it is not enough to describe these structural characteristics since no evidence is available that one structure is inherently more stable than another. Rather, the question must be raised as to the basis for contemporary structural forms. Are they based on outmoded conventions undermined by changing times? Or, do they vary randomly with no rhyme nor reason, reflecting chaotic or meaningless social conditions? If, by contrast, family structures are determined by factors which produce efficient results, it may be assumed that they will be stable over a period of time. Efficient social structures create their own rewards, leading the participants to be satisfied with them rather than to wish for change.

An efficient power structure may be defined as one which produces "right" decisions. In the past, husbands were considered the best qualified to make decisions by virtue of being men. However, the improved status of American women has increased their contribution to the decision-making process. Some alarmists suggest that the American wife has already seized domestic power, not necessarily by wresting it from her husband but at least through his abdication of authority.

The Detroit data fail to disclose an American matriarchate. Rather, the

[2]For a complete report and analysis of the Detroit Area Study data on marriage, see Robert O. Blood, Jr., and Donald M. Wolfe, *Husbands and Wives: The Dynamics of Family Living* (New York: The Free Press of Glencoe, 1960).

general mode of decision-making is equalitarian. Around this mode, however, there are significant variations. In some marriages the wife is more dominant while in others the husband dominates.

What is the basis for these variations? Concrete factors which affect the power structure can be summarized under the heading of "competence." Whichever partner has the greater ability to make a decision usually does so. Sometimes competence results from the individual's experience in a certain activity. For example, husbands generally choose their own job and purchase cars whereas wives make decisions about food purchases. However, the crucial question is not the competences husbands generally share but rather the variations which occur between couples.

Table I provides one example of a source of competence affecting marital power structure. In this case, the resource is the time the husband and wife work outside the home. Taken by itself this might not suggest individual competence so much as an economic interpretation of marriage. However, other data show that unpaid participation in the community has a similar relationship to family power structure. For example, whichever partner attends church more often and whichever partner belongs to more organizations tends to make more of the family decisions. Taken together this suggests that participation in activities outside the home provides social experience and knowledge which carry over into marital decision-making. Even more directly reflecting personal competence is the evidence that whichever partner has more education makes more decisions.

If family decisions are made by the best qualified partner, family power structures are geared to the most efficient accomplishment of their objective. Apparently, therefore, these power structures are basically stable and unlikely to be a source of complaint or unrest.

An efficient division of labor gets tasks done with the least effort. This is precisely the pattern which Detroit families follow. In general, the division follows traditional sex lines, with women doing most of the housework and

TABLE 1 HUSBAND'S POWER BY COMPARATIVE WORK PARTICIPATION OF HUSBAND AND WIFE

	WIFE NOT EMPLOYED			WIFE EMPLOYED		
	HUSBAND OVERTIME	HUSBAND FULLTIME	HUSBAND NONE	HUSBAND OVERTIME	HUSBAND FULLTIME	HUSBAND NONE
Husband's mean power score	5.62	5.28	4.88	4.50	4.46	2.67
Number of families*	195	218	25	44	57	3

*White families only

men concentrating on technical repairs and outside work. The fact that these are traditional sex roles does not mean that they are inefficient. Women's tasks are naturally associated with childbearing and child-rearing and men's with muscular strength and mechanical aptitude.

In Detroit, the division of labor at home is drastically affected by the out-of-the-home work schedules of both husband and wife. Housework is primarily the province of the wife, but when she works outside the home, the time left for housework is severely limited. Under these circumstances, the husband tends to come to her rescue, unless he is preoccupied with responsibilities of his own.

It has already been suggested that farm wives do more housework and get correspondingly less help from their husbands because the latter's chores are readily accessible at all hours of the day and every day of the week. Since farmers are seldom far from exterior tasks needing their efforts, they tend to be perennially busy and unable to help around the house.

Although household tasks are generally done by whichever partner has the most time, tasks requiring special skill are less easily interchanged. In Detroit, a task closely linked to personal competence is keeping track of the money and bills. In some families, the wife "has the head for figures," while in others, the husband is the better bookkeeper. In general, whichever partner has more education handles this responsibility, but in the higher income brackets this task is increasingly performed by the husband. Presumably as income exceeds the subsistence level, it is less limited to the wife's usual provinces of consumption and increasingly available for saving, investment, and tax options familiar to the husband from his business experience.

In general, then, the division of labor, like the power structure, is so organized as to accomplish the family's objectives. Hence the modern family's structure is usually stable, no matter what its form.

Quality of Modern Family Services

What about the functions performed by the urban family? They have changed drastically. Old functions have dwindled with the rise of specialized institutions. Protective functions are shared with the police and the army, religious functions with church and Sunday School, educational functions with the school, and recreational functions with the cinema. The once crucial function of home production has shriveled to vestigial proportions in Detroit. Food growing and processing are minority experiences in the metropolitan area, the former because of the unavailability of garden space, the latter because of the ready availability of processed foods at the corner store. Dressmaking has been taken over by the factory, and even the baking company is superseding the housewife in her kitchen. One sixth of our Detroit housewives report that they purchase all their bread and most of their cakes, cookies, and pies, while an additional 7 per cent confess that they never bake at all.

At the same time that economic production has nearly vanished from the urban home, the production of children has dwindled, too. To some extent this results from the children's transformation from useful "hands" into dregs on the family labor market. Partly, however, the decreased number of children born has been offset by the increasing proportion who survive to maturity. Under pioneer conditions, the average family lost at least one child through sickness. Today childhood fatalities are so rare that childbearing can be reduced accordingly.

The emphasis with respect to children has shifted from childbearing to child-rearing, from the quantity of children produced to the quality of children raised. While the emphasis on quality began in the middle class, it is spreading to the masses. As a result of the growing homogenization of parental aspirations for children and of the filtering down of family planning practices to the working class, families at all levels of society are beginning to gear their birthrate to their "ability to pay." For the first time in American history, couples predict that those with greater resources will have more children (see Table II).

People in other countries often wonder what the American wife does with the leisure time provided by her labor-saving devices. One of the important answers is that she spends more time on her children's social development. Whereas she used to be preoccupied with subsistence tasks, today she can focus on her children's personality problems and achievements.

This shift has occurred with respect to parents, too. Whereas the economic and biological functions of the family once monopolized the attention of the parents, today there is time left over for each other's subtler needs. As a result, new functions emerge.

When our Detroit wives were asked to rank several new functions in comparison with the traditional economic and child bearing ones, the shifting pattern of functions appeared. Asked which of five functions they considered

TABLE 2 EXPECTED NUMBER OF CHILDREN BY WIFE'S EDUCATION FOR WIVES UNDER AGE 45

	YEARS OF EDUCATION		
	GRADE SCHOOL	HIGH SCHOOL	COLLEGE
Expected number	2.51	2.64	2.86
Number of families*	50	318	40

*White families only

"the most valuable part of marriage," they most often chose "companionship in doing things together with the husband" (47 per cent). "The chance to have children" was a poor second at 26 per cent, leaving 13 per cent who chose "the husband's understanding of the wife's problems and feelings," 10 percent for "the husband's expression of love and affection," and only 3 per cent for "the standard of living" provided by the husband's income. Exactly how many functions the family performs depends on one's analytic framework but in the light of these statistics there can be no question of the emerging significance of several new ones.

Whereas traditional family functions were directed toward the welfare of the children or of the family as a whole, the new functions focus on the husband-wife relationship. Perhaps for the first time in history, the marriage bond has become important in its own right, even after children arrive. This reflects the emergence of a whole new stage in family living after the departure of the last child from the home.[3] Whereas a few decades ago the typical wife was widowed before her last child married, today's wives experience more than a decade of living alone with their husbands. Under these circumstances, the marital relationship increases in importance.

These new functions are oriented toward the personal needs of the marriage partners. The affectional function meets the need for acceptance and appreciation, the mental hygiene function the need for release from emotional tension, and the companionship function offsets the anonymity and loneliness of urban life.

Two empirical questions can be raised with respect to these functions. (1) How actively do the Detroit couples try to meet these needs? (2) How well do they succeed?

Companionship involves doing things for pure enjoyment through joint use of leisure time. While no overall measure of companionship is available from the Detroit Area Study, several specific facets were measured. A majority of Detroit husbands tell their wives every day or almost every day about things that happened at work. This "informative companionship" reduces the urban gap between the workplace and the home though it does not match the even higher communication level of farm husbands and wives about the business on which they depend for their livelihood.

Other types of companionship require more effort than just talking over the day's events, and therefore cannot be expected to occur so often. Nevertheless the median Detroit couple get together with relatives at least once a week, and with other friends several times a month. This joint

[3]See Paul C. Glick, "The Life Cycle of the Family," *Marriage and Family Living*, 17 (February, 1955), 3–9.

sociability results in shared friendships, for most of the Detroit wives know at least half their husband's friends quite well.

In addition, the typical Detroit male goes to church once or twice a month, almost always with his wife, providing a significant amount of religious companionship. Joint participation in secular organizations, however, is rare beyond a small circle of high status couples.

In general, Detroit married couples engage in a considerable amount and variety of joint activity both inside and outside the home. As a result, 30 per cent of the wives are enthusiastic about their husbands while most of the rest express considerable satisfaction. Should such expressions of satisfaction be discounted as mere rationalizations? Certainly they are subjective evaluations of the marital situation. But they testify to the effectiveness of the marital relationship in meeting the wife's need for companionship.

While no measures of the frequency of expressing affection are available, the wives' enthusiasm about this marital function is even greater. Affection is the one aspect of marriage where urban satisfaction markedly exceeds the rural. Apparently urban husbands particularly excel in giving love. Perhaps they also perform better in the closely related sexual function. In any case, the average Detroit couple is bound together by mutual affection. This interpretation is reinforced by the fact that the majority of urban wives feel that their families are more closely knit than "most other families" they know.

Perhaps the newest family function dealt with is the mental hygiene function. At least this aspect of marriage has seldom been studied. Assuming that peace of mind is a basic human need, what contribution do marriage partners make to it? Particularly after a crisis has disturbed the individual's emotional equilibrium, how does the partner respond?

To be able to respond one must know about the difficulty. The typical Detroit wife tells her husband her troubles about half the time. The rest of the time, she deals with her tensions by herself or turns elsewhere for help. The problems she shares with her husband depend on his availability, his own frame of mind, and the seriousness of the problem. The typical wife relies on her husband for therapeutic assistance whenever she especially needs it and he is capable of giving it.

A majority of Detroit husbands respond with sympathy, advice, or help and the wives feel much relieved as a result. Only a small minority of husbands react so negatively that the wife feels worse or learns that it is better not to tell him at all. Apparently, the mental hygiene function operates effectively when it is really needed.

This brief exploration of three nontraditional functions of marriage reveals sources of strength in modern urban marriages which probably were less effective in the past under more arduous living conditions. In any case, they are rewarding aspects of contemporary family life which reinforce the stability inherent in the modern family's social structure.

Variation in Modern Family Patterns

While it is possible to generalize about "the urban family," there are significant differences between various segments of the population. Detroit's religious and ethnic groups differ little in most aspects of their family life. But educational, occupational, and income groups which involve differential social status produce varying patterns of family structure and functioning.

The Landecker-Lenski Index of Social Status provides a convenient combination of education, occupation, income, and the reported social esteem of ethnic background.[4] Table III shows the direct relationship which exists in Detroit between the husband's social status and the amount of power he wields in the family.

Although the difference between high and low status families in power structure is substantial, there is a regular progression over the social status continuum. Therefore, this is better described as a difference in degree rather than kind. Nevertheless, the difference is great enough at the extremes to become almost qualitative in nature.

Detailed analysis of the Detroit data suggests that high status contributes to the husband's power through increasing his knowledge and skill relevant to decision-making. His wife usually defers to him, recognizing his special competence, rather than being forced to submit to his arbitrary exercise of power. The low status wife frequently finds that she must take over the reins of the family as a result of her husband's incompetence, negligence, or indifference. Insofar as there are matriarchs in America, they are found at the bottom of the social scale. However, they rule by default rather than conquest.

Everything which applies to low status families generally applies in greater degree to Negro families. Table IV shows how much lower Negro husbands' power is than white husbands' within the same occupational category. Extra economic and social disadvantages undermine the Negro husband's morale with the result that he plays a marginal role in family decision-making. This difference in power structure between Negro and white families is correlated with the high incidence of divorce and desertion in low status families generally and Negro families in particular.

In general, high social status is associated with marital satisfaction, though the husband's community responsibilities sometimes conflict with his marital relationship. Especially when the husband is preoccupied with vocational success, companionship with the wife suffers. However, such preoccupation hardly mars the general positive correlation between social status and marital satisfaction.

High social status couples usually do more things together. On all the

[4]Gerhard E. Lenski, "Status Crystallization: A Non-Vertical Dimension of Social Status," *American Sociological Review*, 19 (August, 1954), 405–13.

TABLE 3   HUSBAND'S POWER BY SOCIAL STATUS

	PERCENTILE RANKING ON SOCIAL STATUS				INDEX
	0–19	20–39	40–59	60–79	80–99
Husband's mean power	4.39	4.79	5.00	5.33	5.56
Number of families*	41	147	204	177	86

*Entire urban sample (both white and Negro).

TABLE 4   HUSBAND'S POWER BY OCCUPATION AND RACE

	OCCUPATION			
	BLUE COLLAR		WHITE COLLAR	
HUSBAND'S MEAN POWER BY RACE	LOW	HIGH	LOW	HIGH
White	5.07 (162)	4.98 (161)	5.36 (78)	5.52 (151)
Negro	4.31 (78)	4.60 (20)		5.00 (5)

Numbers in parentheses represent the number of families on which means are computed.

TABLE 5   FREQUENCY WIFE TELLS HUSBAND HER TROUBLES AFTER A BAD DAY, BY HUSBAND'S OCCUPATION

	HUSBAND'S OCCUPATION			
	BLUE COLLAR		WHITE COLLAR	
FREQUENCY WIFE TELLS HER TROUBLES	LOW	HIGH	LOW	HIGH
Always	25%	23%	19%	17%
Usually	23	20	34	24
Half the time	23	26	30	32
Seldom	16	21	10	21
Never	13	10	7	6
Total	100%	100%	100%	100%
Mean	2.32	2.24	2.49	2.26
Number of families*	173	173	88	157

*White families only

types of companionship measured in the Detroit Area Study, high status families report more sharing. However, in the mental hygiene area, high status wives are more selective about telling their troubles to the husband.

Table 5 shows that wives of high status men typically "bother" their husbands half the time whereas wives of low status men are more apt to tell them always or not at all. Perhaps low status extremism reflects greater impulsivity. If the wife is the impulsive partner, she unburdens herself every time. On the other hand, if the husband is the impulsive one, the wife learns it isn't safe to approach him with her troubles. Wives of professional and managerial husbands, by contrast, balance their own needs against the husband's in determining how often to approach him.

Conclusion

Variations between social strata (and the other changes which occur over the family life cycle) are important but fail to alter the basic generalizations about urban families as a whole. In general, data from the Detroit Metropolitan Area suggest that modern urban families possess structural characteristics which enable them to function effectively. The range of functions performed by the family has shifted with the rise of the metropolis, but the reduction of old functions has released time and energy for new ones.

Urbanization, then, has enabled the family to undertake new functions and to make structural alterations appropriate to a new division of labor between the family and other social institutions and to the growing equalization of external participation by the husband and wife. These urban influences extend beyond the metropolis to adjacent farm families with the result that contemporary rural and urban families closely resemble each other in most essential features.

CHAPTER 5

Social-class Family Variations in America

In spite of our equalitarian ideology, American society differentiates between classes of people on the basis of social and economic attributes such as occupation, sources of income, property and wealth, amount of education, and family background. People possessing the attributes most highly valued—higher education, top business or professional occupations, expensive homes in the best residential areas, etc.—come to be ranked higher on the social scale than those possessing less impressive credentials. America is like virtually all other developed societies in this respect, not excepting most of the socialistic societies today. Since we are a very young society historically, with part of our cultural heritage emphasizing equal opportunity and achievement, the American class system is less rigid and more open and flexible than those of many older societies. Neither the social classes nor the boundaries between them are as distinct as is true of many traditional European or Asiatic countries.

Mother and children enjoying outing at the beach. (*Julie Heifetz*.)

Social Class in America

We take pride in our open class ideology, which proclaims that America is a land of opportunity where people may—and perhaps should—strive to improve their economic and social status by study and hard work. Thus we say that America has an *open class system* which allows and encourages upward social mobility, whereby any person, theoretically, may by effort (and good luck) move from the class of his or her birth up to a higher class. Most Americans are aware today that the opportunities for such upward social movement are not equally distributed, but rather may vary according to race, ethnicity, sex, or social-class origin. Studies show that one of the principal effects of social-class origin is how it shapes one's "life chances." The probability of getting a college education and eventually a high-paying and prestigious job are much greater for one born in the middle or upper classes than for one born in the working or lower classes.[1]

The number and the nature of social classes differ from community to community in America. Older and larger communities generally have a wider range of classes than smaller and newer towns. Large cities, with a heterogeneous population and extremes of wealth, educational, and occupational specialties, generally have more classes, and more distinct classes, than smaller towns with a more homogeneous population and a simpler economic organization.

W. Lloyd Warner, a pioneer in the study of social stratification in America, defined social class as "... two or more orders of people who are believed to be, and are accordingly ranked by the members of the community, in socially superior and inferior positions. Members of a class tend to marry within their own order, but the values of a society permit marriage up and down. A class system also provides that children are born into the same status as their parents."[2]

Warner's classification of social classes in America is probably the most widely used, consisting of upper class, middle class, and lower class. In communities of sufficient age and size, each of the three classes may be subdivided, resulting in as many as six classes: upper-upper class, lower-upper class, upper-middle class, lower-middle class, upper-lower class, and lower-lower class.

SOCIAL CLASS AND FAMILY RELATIONS

The family is the principal unit in the social-class system, not the individual. The individual gets his or her initial class identity by being born into a family whose social-class placement is already established in the community; i.e., the person is ascribed an initial class position. This has been referred to earlier as one of the "status-conferring" functions of the family. And, as we have just been discussing above, the individual may change class identity by mobility striving, that is, by achieving the valued attributes which will qualify a person for membership in a class above that of the parental family. Of course the opposite may occur instead, whereby one loses one's initial class identity by moving downward. Such changes normally take place after the individual has grown up and is no longer living in the parental family or family of orientation and is quite likely married. The person has now established a new family of procreation which will be carried up or down with that individual in any future moves.

The family's social-class placement affects the life chances of its members in many ways. It will affect not only their education and earning power, but also their physical and mental health, their marital adjustment and family stability, and their chances of running afoul of the law.[3] The lower the family's class position, the more likely family members are to have serious illnesses, to die younger, to receive less adequate medical care, to get into trouble with the law, and to receive less "equal justice" at the hands of law enforcement officers and in court; they are also more likely to bear illegitimate children, to have less stable marital relationships, and to have more serious problems with their children.[4]

Parental ability to guide and control their children is related both to adequacy of parental education and adequacy of family economic resources. Parents tend to train or socialize their children in the way of life more or less distinctive of their social class. Thus, lower-class children have a harder time in school partly because they have not learned at home the value of "book learning" and have instead had conveyed to them anti-intellectual sentiments. Schoolteachers, generally identified with the middle class, are apt to reward pupils who behave like middle-class children and punish those who do not. Studies show that middle-class parents place value on such things as self-direction, good sense, sound judgment, responsibility, self-reliance, and the ability to face facts and do well under pressure, while working-class parents place more value on conformity, obedience, and staying out of trouble. Melvin Kohn found that these traits fit the types of occupations middle-class and working-class people, respectively, generally have had.[5] Parents in both the working class and the middle class attempt to teach their children the attitudes and values which the parents themselves find useful in their jobs and daily activities.

Such attitudes and values constitute a part of the subculture, or what Weber called the life-style of the different social classes. As societies become differentiated into social-class or caste systems, each stratum comes to develop certain customs, values, norms, role definitions, etc., which set it off as somewhat different from other strata above or below it. These distinctive cultural patterns develop as the result of the unique conditions in each social-class setting. Thus may be found in the social-class life-styles in America significant variations in husband-wife communication, sex-role definitions, infant care and child-rearing practices, birth control attitudes and practices, and contacts and ties with relatives. At the same time there are other cultural traits and patterns that, as basic parts of the cultural fabric of American society, families in all the classes generally follow, such as monogamous marriage, joint residence of husband, wife, and their children, and responsibility of parents for their children.

In the following section some comparisons among family life-styles in the different social classes will be made. Such variations reflect significant differences in the life situations which families experience in their respective social classes.

American Social-Class Family Types

In her work on the American family, Ruth Cavan states that each social class is found to have its own peculiar characteristics, including different family structures and roles and child-rearing patterns.[6] The following profiles of family life in the upper, middle, and lower classes in America will follow Cavan's format in general but will draw from many sources.[7] The profiles may be considered as subcultural models or types of families representative of the different social classes in America. Comparisons will be made of the family unit and kinship ties, cultural and ethnic backgrounds, family organization, courtship and marriage, children and parent-child relations, and value orientations. It should be noted that while the family profiles below are valid in many ways for American families regardless of race or ethnicity, they are derived largely from white family patterns. Black family class differences receive further attention in Chapters 3 and 7.

THE UPPER-CLASS FAMILY

Certain distinctions may be made between the old aristocracies, or elite families, and the "*nouveaux riches*," who have achieved wealth and prominence more recently. Families in the former group, called the upper-upper class, tend to resist encroachment from below, feeling themselves a group set apart by family prominence of long standing, and inherited wealth and position dating back many generations. Thus, in the older communities at least, the upper class may be divided into two parts, the upper-upper and the lower-upper classes. It has been estimated that altogether the upper class accounts for only about 3 percent of the population, with the upper-upper part constituting no more than 1 percent.[8] Since there are important differences in

Upper-class family's country estate. (*E. D. Dyer.*)

family patterns between these two groups, separate attention will be given to the upper-upper-class family and to the lower-upper-class family.

1.   THE UPPER-UPPER-CLASS FAMILY

Although numerically the upper-upper class is small, throughout American history this class has been a most powerful and influential group. Though the American class structure is relatively open and fluid, these properties apply least to the upper-upper class, which is more closed and inaccessible than any other. Families do not generally enter this class on the basis of occupational or financial success alone.

THE FAMILY UNIT AND KINSHIP TIES   While most upper-upper-class families have considerable wealth, it is the great pride in family name or lineage, rather than money or property, that is their distinguishing characteristic. In

Boston names such as Adams, Lowell, Cabot, Lodge, and Saltonstall represent highly honored lineages that trace back ten or more generations in that community. The upper-upper-class family thus has a unique historical dimension. The present generation considers itself only a link (albeit an important one) in the chain of the family's history which extends back many generations and is undoubtedly destined to continue many more generations into the future. Present family members pay homage to those in the early generations who achieved the family prominence which all successive generations have enjoyed. Portraits of these dynasty founders adorn the walls of libraries and drawing rooms in upper-upper-class family homes. Cleveland Amory tells us that family genealogies constitute one of the principal topics at upper-upper-class family gatherings. The "proper Bostonian's" identification with family ancestors is so close that when asked, "How long have you been in Boston?" the reply is likely to be "since 1710."[9]

Since the historical continuity of these old aristocratic families is based on kinship identity over generations, it is only logical that strong kinship bonds exist among members of the present generation bearing the family name. Thus the upper-upper class tends to be very clannish. As Cavan describes the situation:

The upper-upper class family not only has historical continuity, but also functioning lateral relationships. It consists of nuclear units, interconnected by blood ties, marriage, past history, and present joint ownership of property. The great family thus includes uncles, aunts, and cousins of various degrees of closeness, organized into conventional nuclear units, but functioning also as a modified extended family.[10]

The upper-upper class has been characterized by a considerable degree of"genetic closure" as well as social closure.[11] This has resulted from the very strong endogamous marriage norms in this class. The upper-upper class is small in any community, which reduces the field of eligibles for mates. Add to this a desire to keep blood lines "pure" and to keep the family property holdings together, and the result has been a good deal of intermarriage, not only within the class but also within the kin group itself, as cousin with cousin. Family histories of the Lowells, Saltonstalls, Lees, and Roosevelts all show this tendency.[12]

Another factor contributing to extended family identity and solidarity in this social class is the joint ownership of property. Family estates, industries, trust funds, and other forms of wealth are jointly owned so that family members of each generation have tenure in the property and may use it or receive their share of its income, but no one person or nuclear family unit has sole title to the property.[13] Control of such property is generally in the hands of a group of "family elders," thus assuring its wise management—and helping to assure that younger members will conform to family expectations, thereby assuming their continued sharing in the benefits derived from the family holding.

CULTURAL AND ETHNIC CONSTITUENCY AND BACKGROUND Cavan notes that "since, in a given community, all upper-upper class families tend to have established themselves at approximately the same period of time, they represent the same ethnic stock and cultural traditions."[14] In New England they generally had English background, and in the South, English or French ancestry. Amory's "proper Bostonians" illustrate well this cultural and ethnic unity. These families not only have similar ethnic backgrounds, but also show remarkable similarity in family histories. Their original family members came to the New England colonies, and generally the family prominence and fortune were established by the federal period, in the early nineteenth century. Male members were educated at Harvard, then played leadership roles in Boston, and some held state or national governmental offices. Others entered professions such as law, education, or medicine, or continued the family business.[15]

Upper-upper-class cultural unity is maintained by a high degree of social closure. The class establishes and lives within a partially isolated social world which excludes most nonmembers. Only the necessary secondary-group association is maintained with business, educational, and civic groups. Exclusive social clubs serve as an adjunct to these families, supporting the traditions and values of the upper-upper class, as well as functioning to maintain the high social status of the members. It has been said that these private upper-upper-class clubs are perhaps the most exclusive social organizations in America.

FAMILY ORGANIZATION We have seen that kinship ties and loyalties are exceedingly strong in the upper-upper class, so much so that consanguine bonds may predominate over conjugal bonds. In a sense the individual is a member of the extended family first and the nuclear family second. While each nuclear family generally maintains a separate residence, its main concerns and much of its daily life exist within the larger context of the network of relatives. A familistic solidarity prevails. The headship of the larger extended family may be the oldest or strongest person, male or female, or a group of "collateral elders."[16] Family authority thus approximates more the traditional patriarchal or matriarchal type than the patricentric or equalitarian types frequently found in the middle class. Since wives frequently outlive their husbands, the family head may be a woman (e.g., Mrs. Sara Delano Roosevelt). Family elders often wield considerable power over other family members, both young and adult, influencing their choices in education, occupation, and mate selection.[17] In contrast to the middle class, where old age may mean loss of prestige and power, in the upper-upper class senior membership brings or enhances one's power and prestige.

COURTSHIP AND MARRIAGE   Courtship in the upper-upper class is more restricted and circumscribed than in the other classes, especially so for girls. The number of eligible males is quite limited, and dating outside (i.e., below) is discouraged. Violations of the in-class marriage norms are, contrary to movie stereotypes, very few. Upbringing, in-class social experience, future interests, all make it perfectly normal for the upper-upper-class young woman—or man—to court and marry within the class. The debut serves to promote endogamous marriage by identifying for young people the field of proper mate prospects.

Men may have more freedom before marriage, taking advantage of this to have romances with women in classes below them. But should a man become serious about a woman from out of his class, he will soon feel the full weight of family disapproval. Various pressures and sanctions will be applied, and he will most likely change his mind.[18] Actual cases of such marrying out are so rare that they may become big news and provide fodder for gossip columnists for years (e.g., Steven Rockefeller's marriage to Anne Marie Rasmussen, the daughter of a Norwegian grocer). Young people in the upper-upper class generally marry at an age somewhat later than in the other classes, and there is evidence that a high proportion of them do not marry.[19] Divorce rates are lower in the upper-upper class, and there is evidence that marital adjustment is probably better here than in the other classes.[20] Since married couples in this class are at the top of the social hierarchy and are economically secure, they experience fewer of the problems and pressures of economic striving and status seeking, compared with families in the classes below them. The social as well as economic security provided by the large, prestigious extended family is very reassuring to its members.

CHILDREN AND PARENT-CHILD RELATIONS   Children are very important in the upper-upper class. They represent the next generation in the historical family; they are the link between the present and the future. Sons are especially desired, since the families are patrilineal and sons will be the ones to carry on the sacred family name. One or more of the sons normally assumes the responsibility for continuation of the family business or profession. Socialization and education of the children are thus a matter of great concern to upper-upper-class families. The traditions and values of the upper class, as well as the individual's present and future family roles and responsibilities, are impressed upon the growing child in daily living through family rituals and customs. The use of heirlooms and other family symbols helps inculcate a sense of family prestige and continuity. The importance of the family and its place in the top stratum in society is conveyed to the child not only by family members but also by governesses, tutors, camp counselors, and teachers in private schools.

Parental surrogates are responsible for a good deal of the actual rearing of upper-upper-class children, e.g., nurses and governesses during early childhood followed by tutor's and perhaps special teachers later. Formal education may end with a finishing school for the woman; the man will probably attend an Ivy League college.

PERSONALITY OF THE UPPER-UPPER-CLASS CHILD What kind of a personality is shaped by the socialization that the child experiences in the upper-upper-class family circle and social world? Normally the growing child develops a strong sense of personal worth and security. Growing up in the semi-isolated and insulated social mold of the upper-class world, the young woman or man will very likely become a most self-confident individual with a unified personality. As Cavan notes, the fact that one has limited outside contacts and an integrated internal class subculture means that one does not suffer from the cultural inconsistencies or conflict often experienced by youth in the other classes.[21] Youth in this class are taught that they belong to the class with the greatest prestige, and they are treated with respect and deference by servants, teachers, salespeople, and others.

Two of the most important decisions a young person has to make are choice of a mate and choice of an occupation (especially men on the latter). Middle-class and lower-class youth generally experience some anxiety in making these choices. While it would probably be an exaggeration to claim that upper-upper-class youth experience no stress and strain in such matters, the family and class supports and active assistance reduce such anxieties for upper-upper-class youth to a minimum. Cavan expresses it succinctly:

In terms of both economics and future life-goals the upper-class child is secure. Money comes from inherited sources as well as from the present efforts of the family. Often the child's plan of life is fixed from birth. A place awaits him in the family business, or in the professional firm of the elders. Informal family agreements may be made as to marriages between children. If the child is compliant to the family expectations he faces a secure future without the anxiety of deciding for himself what his goals will be or of establishing himself socially or financially.[22]

The upper-upper-class youth does not have to worry as much as other youth about making high grades in school, or about what a college transcript will look like to a prospective employer. The "gentleman's C" is probably still sufficient. The young person does have to show a willingness to learn the family business and be able to fit into it. The young man or woman who cannot meet the expectations of the family may well feel anxieties. However, many individual weaknesses or deviations may be overlooked or tolerated, providing one does not let the family down. One can count on the family for strong support in times of personal trouble or stress.

UPPER-UPPER-CLASS VALUE ORIENTATION   In his analysis of the subcultures of the different social classes in America, Joseph Kahl found that in the old aristocracies the value orientation of "graceful living" is predominant.

The upper-class is always trying to distinguish itself . . . in other terms than money and power. . . . They use the art of graceful living as the criterion. Only those who are used to money know how to spend it "properly", which means spending it almost as though it were unimportant. This is the art peculiar to the old elite. . . . [It] is traditional, like all arts. . . . [One] must appreciate the distinction of an old house or an old painting. To be too modern in style is to identify with the newcomers; to be surrounded by antiques suggests that one has a past of note.[23]

2.   THE LOWER-UPPER-CLASS FAMILY

Families in the lower-upper class are more recent economic and social arrivals than upper-upper-class families. They lack the long historical prominence of the old aristocratic families, and are still seeking to establish themselves by gaining acceptance in the top residential areas, social clubs, etc. They tend to be looked upon by the old families as social climbers or "*nouveaux riches.*"[24] Their life-styles tend toward conspicuous or extravagant consumption, at times overstepping the bounds of good taste prescribed by upper-upper-class family norms. Lower-upper-class families frequently are wealthier than upper-upper-class families, many having gained huge fortunes in the twentieth century in oil, chemicals, publishing, and other businesses.

The family unit is generally the nuclear family, often an upwardly mobile conjugal family which has broken away from less successful kin. More recently derived from the middle class, these new upper-class families represent a wider ethnic and cultural diversity than upper-upper families. They have not yet had time to put down roots in the community, nor have they learned yet to truly appreciate the art of graceful living.

In comparing social-class differences in family stability, August Hollingshead finds the new upper-class family to be very unstable as compared with the old, established upper-class family.[25] The new family lacks the security of established top social position. The economically successful adult family members are full of drive and initiative, relying on themselves rather than on an extended kin group. The result may be "conspicuous expenditure, fast living, insecurity, and family instability."[26] Such a generalization probably needs some tempering. Additional studies are needed before we can say what proportion of the new or lower-upper-class families manifest this instability, and in what degrees. Certainly many new upper-class families are able to maintain their stability in the face of high economic striving and recent success.

THE UPPER-CLASS FAMILY ON THE TRADITIONAL PATRIARCHAL ⟷ MODERN-EQUALITARIAN FAMILY TYPE CONTINUUM (See Figure 2-1, Chapter 2.) We may ask where the upper-class family would be located on the above continuum. Does it approximate either of the ideal-type families at the extremes? In many of its characteristics the upper-upper-class family would appear to approximate the traditional-patriarchal type, probably more closely than do the families of any other social class. With its familism and consanguine emphasis, its patriarchal or matriarchal authority, ages prestige, traditional role definitions, and marriages arranged by parents to some extent this family meets many of the requirements to qualify as a traditional-patriarchal family. However, the lower-upper-class family retains many of the characteristics of the middle-class family from which it has recently sprung, such as a conjugal emphasis, individualism, less clearly defined roles, and free choice of mates. The husband-father may be dominant. Thus the lower-upper-class family is a mixture and cannot be said to approximate either polar type closely. Lower-upper-class families could be found ranging well over the middle half of the continuum.

THE MIDDLE-CLASS FAMILY

The size or proportion of the middle class in America has been estimated variously, by Warner at 38 percent (for Yankee City, Massachusetts), at 30 percent by Hollingshead (for New Haven, Connecticut), and between 40 and 50 percent by Roach (a general estimate).[27] Middle-class families do not have the prominence or wealth enjoyed by upper-class families. They are distinguished from the lower-class families below them by occupation, education, and certain life-style and value orientations. The middle class is often divided into the upper-middle and the lower-middle classes. Upper-middle-class occupations are largely business, managerial, or professional, requiring college or professional school education, while lower-middle-class occupations span the middle and lower ranges of white-collar occupations and some skilled occupations, with education generally ending with high school or perhaps junior college. Distinctions will be made between the upper-middle- and the lower-middle-class families below where appropriate.

THE FAMILY UNIT   The conjugal nuclear family is the family unit for both the upper-middle and lower-middle classes. The family begins with the marriage of the couple, who set up their own home, have and rear their own children, and are relatively independent of their parents or other relatives.[28] The middle-class family values its independence and resents any attempts by relatives (especially in-laws) to control or interfere with its domestic affairs. Various norms of noninterference have become well established.

However, relationships between a married couple and their close relatives may continue on a friendly and mutually supportive basis after marriage. Studies from the 1950s onward have shown that middle-class families tend to be bound together in a loose but persistent, close kin network. In a study in the early 1950s of relationships between 97 middle-class parental couples and their 195 married children living away from the parental home, Marvin Sussman found that these parents desired and made considerable effort to continue close relationships with the children after their marriage.[29] The parents extended financial aid and sent gifts on a fairly regular basis, drawing the line at providing a regular weekly or monthly check. In 154 of 195 cases parents provided either direct financial aid or other material help or services. The aid was often indirect rather than direct. Rather than pay a doctor's bill at the birth of a child, the new grandparents might provide a savings bond in the child's name, as well as send a bassinet or baby clothing. The young couple were very willing to receive such help, and were grateful to their parents for continued interest and support. The parents made it quite clear that they did not expect their children to support them in turn. A number of subsequent studies have supported Sussman's findings,[30] including studies made by the

Middle-class family having lunch at marina. (*Julie Heifetz*.)

author in Sweden and in Texas.[31]

The existence of intergenerational continuity and relationships in middle-class families led Eugene Litwak to apply the term "modified extended family" to such contemporary American families.[32] Litwak's studies show that extended family ties and relations can and do exist in our mobile, industrial, urban society, and are not precluded or too greatly hindered by either occupational or geographical mobility and separation of married couples from their parental families.[33]

Middle-class nuclear families are not as independent or autonomous as previously thought. Despite geographical separation, ties are maintained between parents and their married offspring through letters, phone conversations, exchanges of gifts, etc., although face-to-face reunions may be infrequent. Nevertheless, it should be reiterated that most middle-class families consist of husband, wife, and their children; they live alone and take much pride in their independence and freedom to live their lives as they choose.

CULTURAL AND ETHNIC BACKGROUND OF MIDDLE-CLASS FAMILIES
There is greater cultural diversity in the middle class than in the upper class, and this is reflected in a wider range of life-styles among middle-class families as compared with upper-class families. This cultural diversity in the middle class is logical when we consider the heterogeneous population from which the middle class comes. The greatest diversity is in the lower-middle class, where many families have recently arrived from the working class, which includes many different ethnic, national, and racial stocks. However, with expanding opportunities for economic and social mobility, the upper-middle class has a more diverse population now too. In the 1930s Warner found in Yankee City that the upper-middle class was beginning to include some non-Yankee stock, mostly Irish-Americans, and the lower-middle class included families from a number of ethnic groups, including Irish, French-Canadians, and Jews.[34] The incorporation of more Americans of New Immigration origin has created a greater diversity in religion, tastes in art, music, literature, and marriage and family patterns than existed in the middle class in the nineteenth and early twentieth centuries.[35] Yet today there are countervailing processes afoot making for more cultural uniformity in the middle class—i.e., the spread of mass culture by radio, TV, and movies; increased education; the expansion of travel, etc. These recent influences on middle-class culture will be treated more fully in Chapter 7.

FAMILY ORGANIZATION   Middle-class families are usually less familistic than upper-class families. While ties with parents and other close relatives are not generally severed, as we have just seen, the family unit is the nuclear family, and the emphasis is conjugal rather than consanguine, in comparison with the upper-class family.

Middle-class family authority patterns may range from semipatriarchal (families of recent European, Central and South American, or Asian origin), to patricentric (families of lower-middle-class white-collar workers), to equalitarian (families of college-educated, young working couples), to matricentric (certain suburban upper-middle-class families). While the trend today is definitely toward equalitarianism, middle-class families still tend to be "paternal" in varying degrees. Even when the wife is employed, the husband is generally still considered to be the head of the household, and he still has the primary responsibility for providing for the family. The wife may work if she wishes, but she is not yet under the kind of social and economic compulsion to work that her husband is. It is still contrary to middle-class norms for the husband to stop working and no longer provide for his family. The husband-father's family headship tends to be benevolent and rather low-key. He is deeply concerned with the welfare and happiness of his wife and children and is sensitive to their views and preferences. He seeks family consensus on family decisions and seldom exerts unilateral or arbitrary authority.[36]

Middle-class husbands and wives have functionally differentiated but strongly interrelated roles.[37] The husband is the principal breadwinner with the main responsibility for economic support of the family. He normally also has certain "home-keeping" roles, especially where the family owns its home, which would include caring for the yard and lawn, house maintenance, and minor repair work. When the wife is employed, the husband shares more in housekeeping activities such as meal preparation, dishwashing, and housecleaning—activities traditionally defined as women's work.

The middle-class wife has numerous roles: wife, mother, homemaker, family "social secretary," companion to her husband for their leisure and recreational activities, expanding civic roles, and increasingly a family breadwinner role. It may be argued that the multiple roles of the American middle-class wife-mother today are more demanding and require more time and skills than did those of her grandmother two generations ago. She takes all her roles very seriously, devoting herself to infant and child care with a professional zeal, taking great pride in decorating and caring for the home, and in planning and directing the social activities of her husband and herself and her growing children. She is conscious of the family's social position, and seeks to enhance it by planning and often manipulating the social activities of all family members. She may accept or reject social invitations, as well as tender them, in terms of their significance to the family's social status and its mobility aspirations.[38]

The middle-class wife has been found to play an important role in her husband's career and its progress. She must be able to keep abreast of her husband as he advances in his career and moves upward socially. The successful husband not only needs his wife's personal support and encouragement, he also needs a wife who is prepared psychologically and socially to move into the new social world which opens up to them with the business or professional promotions of her husband. This may require moving into a new neighborhood and giving up certain old friends. William Whyte found that wives failing such "tests" may be in danger of losing their husbands.[39]

Husband-wife relations in the middle class emphasize happiness, communication, and mutual gratification. Even in the area of sex, the stress on equality and mutual needs has created or accentuated a concern for mutual satisfaction. Love is a paramount value, coloring and shaping all husband-wife relationships as well as parent-child relationships.[40]

MATE SELECTION AND MARRIAGE   Middle-class youth generally marry somewhat younger than upper-class young people. In public schools, in colleges, and in work groups, middle-class young men and women are exposed to people from all walks of life, including working-class, lower-class, and occasionally upper-class youth. And within the middle class the range of choice is wider and the number of eligibles is greater than ever before.

As E. E. LeMasters notes, the American courtship system is elaborate and drawn out.[41] The boy or girl starts in the early teens with random dating, moves on to going steady, then to being "pinned" perhaps, then becomes engaged, and finally gets married. Middle-class youth date across class, religious, ethnic, and racial lines more each decade, and more are marrying out of their class than used to do. However, as boys and girls from the middle class move from dating to more serious courtship, they still tend to narrow their field of candidates to members of cliques or close friendship groups made up of people from their own class, and will most likely marry someone from their own class or perhaps one step removed.[42]

CHILDREN AND PARENT-CHILD RELATIONS   There are more children in the middle-class family than the upper-class family, but fewer than in the working- or lower-class families.[43] The emotional bond between child and parents is quite strong. While the family is not as isolated from its relatives as once thought, it still normally lives separate from kinfolk, and the family circle is the immediate nuclear unit of mother, father, and their two or three children. The emotional interdependence between parents and children is intensified by this separation from other relatives and by the small size of the nuclear family.

Middle-class parents as well as upper-class parents are much concerned about the socialization of their children and devote a great deal of time and effort to their proper upbringing. Children are apt to be sheltered from the cares and problems of the adult world during their early years. They are taught to get along with other people, to stand on their own two feet, and to study hard to prepare for future familial, occupational, and citizenship roles. They are taught the value of "deferred gratification," i.e., the postponement of immediate pleasures for the sake of more important goals and satisfactions in the future.

Middle-class parents strive to be intellectual about child care and training, following the methods prescribed by "scientific" child-care experts such as Dr. Spock, and reading up and attending lectures and classes in order to understand the theoretical basis for their practices. Fathers and mothers may curb their natural impulses to caress or slap a child in order to conform to the current theories in child training.

Middle-class children frequently identify with their parents as symbols of success; children are expected to internalize the "success model" and do as well as or better than their parents in school, in sports perhaps, and in careers. All in all, the typical middle-class father and mother expect their children to acquire adequate social skills, to be self-reliant, to be ambitious, to defer gratification, and to be respectable.[44]

VALUE ORIENTATIONS   Certain distinctions may be made here between the upper-middle class and the lower-middle class. As the American middle class developed and expanded during the nineteenth and early twentieth centuries, economic and work values became central in the class subculture. These values were reflected in the "success through pursuit of opportunity" value orientation of middle-class men and women. While this value orientation characterized the whole middle class to a high degree, it was especially strong in the upper-middle-class segment of business and professional people. Thus, in his comparison of the value orientations of the different social classes in America, Kahl found that "career" was the predominant value orientation of the upper-middle class, while "respectability" predominated in the lower-middle class. "The central value orientation for the upper-middle class is 'career'. Their whole way of life—their consumption behavior, their sense of accomplishment and respectability, the source of much of their prestige with others—depends upon success in a career. The husband's career becomes the central social fact for all the family."[45]

The upper-middle-class man is more apt to have the resources to pursue a successful career than the lower-middle-class man: more education, wider experience, solid middle-class background, and a wife with the same background and values. He gets into a career channel that leads upward, and thus career progress and success are realistic expectations for him.

On the other hand, lower-middle-class workers—semiprofessional, semi-managerial, white-collar salesmen, etc.—who also accept the career values and are conscientious and hard-working, come to realize at some point that the likelihood of further career advancement is quite limited. Kahl finds that even though they are constantly striving to get ahead,

Yet most will never get very far. and after they have outlived the romantic dreams of youth, they know it. . . . They cannot cling too strongly to career as a focus of their lives, for their jobs do not lead continuously upward. Instead, they tend to emphasize the respectability of their jobs and their styles of life, for it is respectability that makes them superior to shiftless workers.[46]

Lower-middle-class family respectability is expressed through religion—members of this class are among the most regular churchgoers—and morality, regular school attendance of their children, parental sacrifices to send them to college, and pride in home ownership.

THE MIDDLE-CLASS FAMILY ON THE TRADITIONAL-PATRIARCHAL ⟷ MODERN-EQUALITARIAN FAMILY TYPE CONTINUUM (See Figure 2-1, Chapter 2.) Does the middle-class American family approximate either of the ideal-type families? If not, is it possible to locate a typical or average middle-class family at some point on the continuum? This would be very difficult even were we able to observe all the middle-class families in America, and find a modal family in the distribution. Not only is the American middle class very diverse, it is also undergoing considerable social change, as we have seen and will examine in more detail in Chapter 7. Most middle-class families represent a mixture of the characteristics found in the traditional-patriarchal type and the modern-equalitarian type. Conjugal ties are emphasized, but consanguine ties are not severed. Individualism is stronger than familism, and the number of family functions is diminishing. In the status of women and children, sex division of labor, and role and authority patterns, wide variations exist, related to ethnic or religious background and upper-middle-class or lower-middle-class identity. Some middle-class families still retain the traditional ways of their parental families to a considerable degree, while others have moved rapidly toward equalitarianism. Middle-class families thus would be spread out over the continuum with the majority falling probably in the range between the center of the scale and the modern-equalitarian end of the scale. The twentieth-century trend is certainly for middle-class families to change in that direction.

THE LOWER-CLASS FAMILY

For purposes of analysis and comparison, the lower class may be subdivided into the upper-lower (or working) class, and the lower-lower class. The former is characterized by semiskilled to skilled manual workers and operators, while the latter consists of people who live at or below the poverty line. Workers in these families have minimal skills and little education and are often without regular employment. It is estimated that the upper-lower or working class constitutes between 30 and 40 percent of the American population, while the lower-lower segment accounts for between 15 and 20 percent.[47] Distinctions between family patterns in these two divisions of the lower class will be made where appropriate.

THE FAMILY UNIT The lower-class family unit is normally the immediate nuclear family. However, ties with relatives may be very close and enduring, especially in the working class. In the lower-lower-class family the stable and

Urban lower-class family housing. (*E. D. Dyer.*)

enduring family unit may be the mother and her minor children. The father, especially if unemployed, may be absent or only weakly present in the family. The marriage bond may be weak. In this class, separation, desertion, and divorce occur more frequently than in any other social class.[48]

In the working class the nuclear family unit is tied more closely to its extended family network than is the lower-lower-class family or the middle-class family. In his study *The Urban Villagers*, Herbert Gans found that ". . . the working class sub-culture is distinguished by the dominant role of the family circle. Its way of life is based on social relationships among relatives. The working class views the world from the family circle."[49]

Outside interests and relationships, including work, are of secondary importance to life within the family circle for working-class people. This is less true of the bottom segment of the lower class. Here Gans found that "the lower-lower class sub-culture is distinguished by the female-based family and the marginal male."[50] Where the family circle exists, it consists almost entirely of female relatives.

CULTURAL AND ETHNIC BACKGROUND AND CONSTITUENCY OF LOWER-CLASS FAMILIES   The lower class is probably the most diverse of all classes in its population. It includes old American families who never succeeded or have slipped down the class ladder, newly arrived immigrant families entering at the bottom, rural to urban migrants who have been economically and culturally deprived, and other ethnic and racial minority groups suffering economic and social disadvantages. Wide cultural variations in language, religion, ideology, and family customs have marked the American lower class throughout most of the nineteenth and twentieth centuries. This class thus consists of a kind of crazy quilt of different subcultural groups, each with a group-centered life of its own. This is readily seen where families of the same racial or ethnic stock cluster together in lower-class ghetto communities in large American cities.

FAMILY ORGANIZATION AND RELATIONSHIPS   In its family organizations and patterned relationships among family members, the lower-class family, more than any other, tends to adhere to the image of the traditional family. The husband-father sees himself as the head of the family, often still as a patriarch with authority over his wife and children. He is the final authority and disciplinarian, determines family policy, makes final decisions, and controls the family purse. Only in those lower-lower-class families where the husband-father is chronically unemployed, thereby losing the main support for his authority and esteem, would this patriarchal authority be weakened or possibly even nonexistent. Under these conditions the lower-class family may become matricentric or matriarchal, but rarely equalitarian.

In sex-role division of labor, the lower-class family tends to be more traditional also. The father is the major family provider, while the wife-mother rears the children, cares for the home, and submits to her husband sexually as an obligation. These husband and wife roles are more sharply drawn and separated than in most middle-class families. The man does not expect to participate in housekeeping tasks after he comes home from work.[51]

There is less communication and dialogue between the husband and wife in the lower class than is true in the middle class where such communication is highly valued. In her study of *Blue-Collar Marriage*, Mirra Komarovsky found that the working-class subculture creates barriers to husband-wife communication.[52] Traditional values in this class emphasize separation of the sexes, making it difficult for both, but the male especially, to share his problems and feelings with his wife. He identifies such personal interchange with the feminine world. A strong and self-sufficient man keeps his problems and inner feelings to himself.

Children, while generally welcomed in the lower-class family, still have less family importance than in the middle class. They are clearly subordinate to their parents, who have neither the inclination nor the time to cater to them and nurture their personal and social development as middle-class parents try to do. Until quite recently the expectation has been strong that lower-class children will quit school as soon as they legally can in order to go to work and contribute to the support of the family up to the time of their marriage.[53] Today, however, lower-class parents are more inclined to urge their children to remain in school and get as much education as they can, realizing that this is the best chance their sons and daughters will have to get the skills needed to escape from the lower class.

MATE SELECTION AND MARRIAGE Lower-class young people marry at an earlier age than those in the other classes.[54] Marriages tend to be between young men and women in the lower class, with some marrying out (that is, up) by attractive and ambitious youth. Courtship and mate selection is a less elaborate process than in the middle and upper classes. The criteria of mate selection are personal and sexual attraction, with less consideration given to the personality compatibility or social-status considerations found in the middle-class courtship system. According to Lee Rainwater, lower-class youth often sort of drift into marriage.

[They] do not often show a great deal of enterprize in seeking or choosing marriage partners. Rarely do they express strong feelings about the decision to marry. . . . [And] although it is unlikely that these people would have gotten married without some sense of personal meaningfulness to each other, it does seem that conscious choice and planning play a much smaller role than among middle class men and women.[55]

Lower-class young people are less apt to meet at supervised mixed-group activities than middle-class young people, or even at school since many leave school during adolescence. The place of work, the street corner, the tavern, bring them together. Many lower-class young people may see early marriage as a way to escape a drab or unhappy home life, and are thus inclined to rush through courtship, get married quickly, and perhaps announce their marriage to friends and family after it has taken place.

CHILDREN AND PARENT-CHILD RELATIONS There are generally more children per family in the lower class than in the other classes. In 1964 the average number of children for women having four or more years of college was 1.7, and for those women with one to three years of college the average number was 2.0. However, the average number of children for women with only eight years of school was 2.8, and for those with less than eight years of school it was 3.6.[56] Birth control is less well understood and probably less accepted still by many lower-class couples. Also, children may be viewed as economic assets to the family since they often begin to earn money early in life. As noted above, girls marry young, thus lengthening the total span of their childbearing years. And the general view in many lower-class families is that "children are a natural outcome of marriage."[57] The mother finds much personal satisfaction in producing children, and they will receive a good deal of her affection, especially if her emotional relations with her husband are not very satisfying. To the father, having many children may be symbolic of his manhood, giving him a visible proof of personal accomplishment, something he likely finds lacking in his work role.

Certain differences may be observed in the child-rearing practice of the two divisions of the lower class. Working-class parents teach their children certain traditional values such as respect for adults, honesty, neatness, and obedience—not very different from lower-middle-class parents. They want their children to do well in school, keep out of trouble, and if possible get some higher education as a means to better jobs.[58] In the lower-lower-class family, according to Cavan, the objective of child training:

. . . is to develop a tough-minded, hard-fisted individual, able to compete to the point of personal conflict in support of individual rights and privileges. The little boy is not taught, as is the middle class boy, to wait until he is struck before he fights. . . . He is expected to be able to take care of himself at an early age. The little girl likewise, is taught to be self-sufficient.[59]

The methods of child rearing differ too. The lower-lower-class mother treats her children with a combination of permissiveness and impulsive aggressiveness. Perhaps she treats her children more "naturally" than the working- or middle-class mother, reacting to her child more according to her emotional needs and feelings at the moment. The middle-class mother, especially, will try to control her reactions, seeking to do what is best for her child, according to Dr. Spock perhaps. By comparison, both the lower-lower-class mother and the working-class mother, in relating to their children, are far less concerned than the middle-class mother with "a child-psychologist always peeping over their shoulder".[60]

VALUE ORIENTATIONS OF LOWER-CLASS FAMILIES   The prevailing value orientation of the upper-lower or working class, says Kahl, is simply to "get by."[61] Typical would be a semiskilled automotive worker on the production line in Detroit, who has very little chance for occupational advancement and whose work is monotonous and unsatisfying.

His work has little intrinsic interest, he learns to adjust, to lower his aspirations, to become adept at working without thinking and without dreaming of future advancement. As he retreats from work as a thing of inner importance, he turns to his family and to consumption pleasures. . . . Once he passes beyond the unrealistic visions of youth, he becomes a man primarily interested in merely getting by from day to day.[62]

Kahl finds the value orientation of those poverty-stricken families in the lower-lower class to be "apathy." People in this group:

. . . react to their economic situation and to their degradation in the eyes of respectable people by becoming fatalistic; they feel that they are down and out, and that there is no point in trying to improve, for the odds are all against them. They may have some desires to better their position, but cannot see how it can be done. . . . [They] conclude that the situation is hopeless.[63]

It is often difficult for other Americans to understand this orientation of lower-lower-class people. It requires great effort to really identify with the "down and out" and see the world as they do. It may be argued that their attitudes and reactions represent normal human responses to the lower-class environment in which they live and to the "culture of poverty" in which they have been socialized. These and other related issues will be discussed further in the reading at the end of this chapter by Hyman Rodman, "Middle-Class Misconceptions about Lower-Class Families."

THE LOWER-CLASS FAMILY ON THE TRADITIONAL-PATRIARCHAL↔ MODERN-EQUALITARIAN FAMILY TYPE CONTINUUM (See Figure 2-1, Chapter 2.) As we noted earlier, the lower-class family retains many traditional characteristics. Extended family ties are strong, especially in the working class, sex roles are sharply defined, with "man's place" and "woman's place" clearly understood. Patriarchal authority still prevails, except in some lower-lower-class families, and women and children are subordinate. Children may be expected to contribute to family support. Families are large. Male and female interests tend to be separate and their activities segregated. There is less companionship in the daily life of husband and wife than in the middle class. Lower-class families thus tend to approximate the traditional-patriarchal family type more than do middle-class families or lower-upper-class families. The distribution of lower-class families would likely be from the center over the entire left half of the continuum, with the curve skewed toward the traditional-patriarchal type at the extreme pole.

Social Mobility and the American Family

We have seen some of the differences in family organization and relationships between the social classes. Next we shall examine briefly the phenomenon of family movement from one social class to another. What motivates a family to move from its original class? What happens to the family during the move and after it arrives in a new social class?

SOCIAL MOBILITY AND FAMILY PATTERNS AND PROCESSES

By *social mobility* we mean the movement of an individual or a family up or down the social-class scale or ladder, e.g., from middle to upper class or from middle to lower class. The term *intragenerational mobility* applies to the movement of a nuclear family or an individual during its (or the person's) life-cycle, often referred to as career mobility. *Intergenerational mobility* would mean the movement of a given family over several generations.

In America, as in many other societies, the culture places high value on upward social mobility. This value has been symbolized by expressions such as "the American dream," and extolled by our leaders and in our literature, e.g., the Horatio Alger rags-to-riches theme. Our open class society makes it possible for American families that are ambitious and fortunate to move upward. Other less fortunate families may move downward. It has been estimated that about 25 percent of American families are upwardly mobile, while about 5 percent are downwardly mobile.[64] The average degree of mobility in any one family generation is not great. The rags-to-riches success stories gain much attention because they are unusual. Generally, upward mobility occurs between adjacent classes and takes two or more generations to complete, with the family becoming fully integrated into the new social class. Mobility in either direction may have certain dysfunctional effects upon the family, as we will see below, but downward mobility is likely to be the more destructive.

When a family is slipping downward, as during a depression, with prolonged unemployment of the breadwinner, this can put a severe strain on the relations among family members. The husband-father may lose much of his esteem and authority, since he is no longer able to fulfill his most important family responsibility. A damaging role reversal may take place, with the wife or some other member of the family becoming chief family provider and family authority.[65] However, a downwardly mobile husband's loss of status in the family will probably be lessened if his position is based on sentiments of affection and respect and remnants of the patriarchal tradition.

UPWARD SOCIAL MOBILITY AS A PROCESS   The process of upward social mobility has both sociological and psychological dimensions. It is quite normal for American youth to develop social mobility aspirations. Ralph Turner shows that socialization to this end may take place in a number of ways.[66] A family may be located in one social class, based on occupation and income, but family members may identify with and begin to follow family patterns taken from a higher social class. This constitutes a disjuncture between the family's social-class setting and its private identity. Here the family will be transmitting to its children mobility aspirations and teaching them the means for social ascent. In other families where there is no effectual socialization either for or against mobility striving, the child may, by default, come under the influence of teachers, ambitious age peers, or others in the community who foster his mobility aspirations. In still other families where strong family traditions and neighborhood influences foster class continuity rather than upward mobility, a child may find such restrictions intolerable and seek to escape by striving for upward movement. The child may, in reaction to such frustrations in his family or community environment, and/or for other personal reasons, develop a strong need for achievement which will lead to mobility striving.

The normal pattern of upward social mobility is for one or two young members of a family to move ahead and gradually establish themselves in a new class one or possibly two ranks ahead of that of their parental family. While this is considered normal in America, it tends to create a breach between those upwardly mobile sons and daughters and the rest of the family remaining behind. This creates problems of adjustment in the extended family group.[67] Also the mobile young people and their spouses may face other problems while en route upward and in gaining acceptance into their new social class. Some of these issues will be discussed further below.

SOME CONSEQUENCES OF SOCIAL MOBILITY FOR THE FAMILY

In America, as we noted earlier, a cultural theme idealizing and encouraging upward social mobility exists. Implicit in this theme is the idea that upward social mobility is good or functional both for the individual and for society; that "getting ahead" by one's own efforts and abilities yields earned rewards of higher income, a better style of life, more prestige and power for the individual, and also produces more valuable contributions by the individual to society. In sum, social mobility in this view is right and good and highly functional.

Many social scientists in recent years have come to raise questions about this "happy theme." Studies began to show or suggest that there was another side to the picture—that the consequences of social mobility were not necessarily all good or functional, that there could be also some negative or dysfunctional concomitants for the individual and for social structure.[68]

Julius Roth and R. F. Peck found that upward social mobility often resulted in poor marital adjustment where one spouse was more mobile than the other.[69] Also, Carson McGuire, maintained that marital difficulties were most apt to be found in *divergent families* where there were differences in social-class ambitions and orientations of the husband and the wife. He also found strains and tensions in parent-child relationships in both divergent families and in *mobile families* where both marriage partners are oriented toward moving up in the social-class system.[70]

LeMasters found evidence of strained parent-child relationships in upwardly mobile families. However, families experiencing the greatest disorganization were those whose members were experiencing *differential mobility*, for example, where one spouse was more ambitious than the other. On the other hand, nuclear family integration was strongest in the nonmobile families.[71]

There has been some disagreement among sociologists as to the effects of social mobility on extended family structure and relationships. One point of view sees social mobility as essentially dysfunctional to a stable extended family system. Talcott Parsons holds the view that occupational mobility is antithetical to extended family relations, and that there is accordingly a basic disharmony between modern democratic industrial society and extended family relations.[72]

An opposing view holds that a modified extended family is compatible with social mobility and may be more functional than the isolated nuclear family. The extended family, it is argued, plays an important role for the upwardly mobile person because he or she can achieve status by gaining deference from the extended family. In addition, the extended family may provide aid to young members who are in the initial stages of mobility. One of the proponents of this view is Eugene Litwak, who made a study of occupational mobility and extended family cohesion.[73] He found that the mobile nuclear families visited their relatives as much as the nonmobile families and were not less identified with their extended families than the others. He also found no incompatibility between extended family identity and high "mobility orientation" in his sample.

Representing the opposite view is Robert Stuckert, who studied occupational mobility and family relationships in Wisconsin in 1962, and came to the conclusion that social mobility was indeed detrimental to extended family relationships.[74] Stuckert found an inverse relationship between social mobility and contacts and identity with the extended family.

The literature would appear to indicate that the question is still an open one as to whether or not, or how, social mobility is dysfunctional for the family. The findings are scarcely conclusive, and some are contradictory. More research is needed to seek the various conditions under which social mobility may or may not be dysfunctional for the family.

Enumerated below are some hypotheses on the possible consequences of social mobility for the family.

SOCIAL MOBILITY AND THE NUCLEAR FAMILY: SUGGESTED HYPOTHESES

1 Social mobility is detrimental to nuclear family integration where "differential mobility" exists among nuclear family members. Conversely, social

mobility is less detrimental to the nuclear family where "unit mobility" exists. If the process of "moving up" by some members of the family and not others results in the differences in orientations and associations, nuclear family integration would likely be disrupted to some degree.

2 Social mobility is detrimental to nuclear family integration (specifically, the husband-wife relationship) where "differential mobility orientation" exists between the husband and wife (i.e., where one spouse is more upwardly mobile in aspirations and actions than the other). If both husband and wife share the goals and work together to pursue them, one would expect a better marital relationship than where one partner is more eager and active in trying to "get ahead" than the other.

3 Social mobility is detrimental to nuclear family integration where the marriage partners each have different social-class reference groups and role models (i.e., where the husband's reference groups and role models are in one class and his wife's in another). If social mobility requires changes in orientation from one social class subculture to another, with new values, norms and life-styles to be learned and followed, then one would expect the impact of social mobility to be greater where one marriage partner has adopted individuals and groups in the higher social class as his or her role models and reference groups, and thus has undergone more anticipatory socialization for the new social class, while the other partner still clings to friends and reference groups identified with the earlier (and lower) social class.

4 Social mobility is detrimental to nuclear family integration where:
(a) One marriage partner acculturates to the expectations of the new social class more readily than the other.
(b) The growing children acculturate more readily to the expectations of the new class than do their parents.
(c) The upward mobility is essentially economic rather than social, i.e., where occupational mobility has taken place, but the family is less willing or able to move socially from their present class into a new, higher class.
(d) The upward social mobility is very rapid.

SOCIAL MOBILITY AND THE EXTENDED FAMILY: SUGGESTED HYPOTHESES

1 Social mobility is detrimental to extended family cohesion where differential mobility exists among the nuclear families and individuals making up the extended family. The rationale here is that differential mobility will likely reduce the contacts and communication among nuclear family units and relatives who make up the extended family, and also will result in different value orientations, etc., thus creating loss of ties and loyalties,

and possibly estrangements (e.g., husband and wife versus their siblings or their parents).

2   Social mobility is detrimental to extended family cohesion where differential mobility orientation exists between the husband and the wife.

3   The more rapid and the greater the career mobility of the husband (or the husband and the wife), the more detrimental to extended family cohesion.

4   The greater the intergenerational social mobility, the more detrimental to extended family cohesion.

5   Social mobility is detrimental to extended family cohesion where the nuclear family has experienced rural to urban migration.

6   The negative effects of social mobility will be greater for families moving from the lower class or working class into the middle class than for families moving up in the middle or upper ranges of the hierarchy. The differences between the subcultures of the lower class (and working class) and the middle classes are probably greater and still to some degree antagonistic; the struggle upward is often more intense, and the feelings of those "left behind" toward their more fortunate family members may be a mixture of envy and resentment. And those who are oriented upward may, in turn, find it expedient to reduce their identity with their less fortunate family members. As LeMasters notes, the sociology of "the poor relative" yet remains to be studied systematically.[75]

The author tested some of the above hypotheses in a study conducted in Sweden.[76] As is true of the United States, Sweden is a modern industrial society with an advanced educational system, high per capita income, and a good deal of economic and social mobility. It seems reasonable to expect that consequences for the family would probably be somewhat similar in the two nations.

An investigation of possible dysfunctional consequences of social mobility for nuclear family integration and for extended family cohesion was made by obtaining data from a sample of eighty-nine urban, upwardly mobile families in Uppsala, Sweden.

The findings supported the hypotheses that differential husband-wife mobility orientation and differential generational husband-wife mobility are detrimental to nuclear family integration in these Swedish families. Nuclear family integration may be weakened where the husband and wife do not share or participate together in community organizations, where the wife has low organizational memberships and participation, and perhaps where the husband and wife come from different social-class backgrounds. Social mobility may be dysfunctional for nuclear family integration for those families where the husband is from a rural background, where the couple have experienced high educational and occupational mobility, where the families are moving from the lower into the middle-class ranges, where the husband and wife have different friends and role models, and where the friends and role models of the husband and wife are from different social classes. Nuclear family integration was not appreciably affected by the continued relationships of the husband or wife and their former friends, nor by the couple's rapid upward economic mobility, nor by the extent of intergenerational occupational mobility.

As for the relationship between upward social mobility and extended family cohesion, the findings were not conclusive for this sample of Swedish middle-class families. Some evidence supported the hypotheses that upward social mobility is detrimental to extended family cohesion, but other evidence tended to support Litwak's position that upward mobility today is not necessarily dysfunctional to extended family ties and relationships.

These and other findings tend to support Turner's notion that both "class consciousness" and "prestige identification" exist together in varying degrees in urban, mobile families today.[77] That is, upward social mobility may be dysfunctional for extended family cohesion where class consciousness still exists to the degree that upwardly mobile children develop a new class orientation which is divergent from that of their parents and other nonmobile relatives. Social conditions favoring such class consciousness may lead to strained relationships and even estrangement within the extended family. On the other hand, where class consciousness is low, parents of upwardly mobile offspring may gain some reflected prestige from the success of their children. Such parents—and other relatives too—are happy to continue seeing their ambitious offspring, who also are glad to retain close ties with kinfolk who support and applaud their ambitions and successes. Conditions favoring this kind of "prestige identification" would tend to reduce dysfunctional consequences of upward social mobility for extended family cohesion.[78]

Summary

Social stratification exists in America as it does in virtually all societies. While Americans take pride in having an open class society, one's opportunities and other life chances are still significantly affected by social-class origin. The family is the main unit in the social-class system rather than the individual. One socially inherits initial class status by being born into a family whose class position is already established. Through effort and good luck one may move from one's ascribed status up to a higher class status.

In America, the nature of the social classes as well as the number of them may vary from place to place. Studies have shown from three to as many as six different classes in American communities. Each class has a more or less distinctive set of customs, values, norms, etc., that make up its subculture, often referred to as its life-style. These life-styles both limit and direct the family organization and relationships within the social class.

Comparisons are made between the life-styles of the upper class, the middle class, and the lower class. In the upper class, the old aristocratic (or upper-upper-class) families are distinguished by a long family history of prominence within a given community, dating back many generations. These families tend to be clannish and there is a good deal of intermarriage among them. Kinship ties are strong, and family authority is more patriarchal (or matriarchal) than in most middle-class families. The individual is less free to marry whom he or she pleases. Family life-styles are conservative. Lower-upper-class families that have gained their wealth and prominence more recently tend to have more lavish life-styles, and often less stable marriages.

In the middle class the family unit is clearly the conjugal nuclear family, which, although maintaining some ties with relatives, is very jealous of its independence and freedom to live as it wishes. Middle-class families in America stem from a wide variety of racial and ethnic backgrounds. In family organization, middle-class families range from semipatriarchal to equalitarian to matricentric. The main trend today is toward equalitarianism, with a more flexible division of labor. Middle-class wives are entering the labor force at an accelerated rate. Husband-wife relationships emphasize love, communication, and mutual gratification. Emotional bonds between parents and children are intensified by the separation of the nuclear family from relatives and by its small size.

While the family unit in the lower class is generally the nuclear family, ties with relatives are often close and enduring. This is especially true in the upper-lower class, often called the working class. Lower-class families come from a wide spectrum of racial and ethnic backgrounds. Family organization tends to be more traditional and patriarchal than in the middle class. In those lower-lower-class families where the man may be chronically unemployed, the family may become matricentric or matriarchal. The lower-class family tends to follow the more traditional sex-role division of labor, too. Young people marry earlier and have more children than do middle-class couples, and are less concerned with following the advice of child-rearing experts in bringing up their children. Male and female interests and activities tend to be separate.

American culture places a high value on upward social mobility. Families rather than isolated individuals normally do the moving, whether upward or downward. Thus, what motivates families to move and what happens to them during and after the move is of interest to family sociologists. Some studies show that upward mobility may have some negative consequences for both nuclear family integration and for extended family cohesion. Other studies find little or no negative consequences. Further study is needed to seek the conditions under which social mobility may be helpful or harmful to families.

Notes

1   Melvin M. Tumin, *Patterns of Society* (Boston: Little, Brown & Co., 1973), chap. 3. Also see Ernest Havermann and Patricia S. West, *They Went to College* (New York: Harcourt, Brace and Co., 1952).
2   W. Lloyd Warner and Paul S. Lunt, *The Social Life of a Modern Community* (New Haven: Yale University Press, 1941), p. 82.

3   Melvin M. Tumin, *Social Stratification* (Englewood Cliffs, N.J.: Prentice-Hall, 1967), pp. 56–65.

4   Hyman Rodman, *Marriage, Family, and Society* (New York: Random House, 1966), pp. 213–229.

5   Melvin L. Kohn, *Class and Conformity* (Homewood, Ill.: Dorsey Press, 1969).

6   Ruth S. Cavan, "Sub-cultural Variations and Mobility," in Harold T. Christensen, ed., *Handbook of Marriage and Family* (Chicago: Rand McNally & Co., 1964), p. 541. Also see Ruth S. Cavan, *The American Family* (New York: Thomas Y. Crowell Co., 1969), chaps. 5–7.

7   In addition to Cavan, *The American Family*, see Bert N. Adams, *The American Family* (Chicago: Markham Publishing Co., 1971), chap. 6; Ralph H. Turner, *Family Interaction* (New York: John Wiley Sons, 1970), chap. 18; Gerald R. Leslie, *The Family in Social Context* (New York: Oxford University Press, 1973), chaps. 9, 10; David A. Schulz, *The Changing Family* (Englewood Cliffs, N.J.: Prentice-Hall, 1972) chap. 6; William Kephart, *The Family, Society, and the Individual* (Boston: Houghton Mifflin Co., 1966), chap. 18; Robert O. Blood, Jr. *The Family* (New York: Free Press, 1972), chap. 2; Joseph H. Kahl, *The American Class Structure* (New York: Rinehart & Co., 1957); Jack L. Roach et al., *Social Stratification in the United States* (Englewood Cliffs, N.J.: Prentice-Hall, 1969); and Warner and Lunt, op. cit.

8   Roach et al., op. cit., p. 154; and Cavan, *The American Family*, pp. 74–75.

9   Cleveland Amory, *The Proper Bostonians* (New York: E. P. Dutton & Co., 1947), pp. 15–18.

10   Cavan, *The American Family*, p. 87.

11   For a discussion of closure, see Max Weber, "Class, Status, and Party," in Reinhard Bendix and Seymour Lipset, eds., *Class, Status, and Power* (Glencoe, Ill.: Free Press, 1953), pp. 69–72.

12   Amory, op. cit., pp. 20–21.

13   Ferdinand Lundberg, *America's 60 Families* (New York: Vanguard Press, 1937), pp. 9–22.

14   Cavan, op. cit., p. 89.

15   Amory, op. cit., pp. 12–13.

16   Cavan, op. cit., p. 88.

17   Ibid.

18   American fiction such as Christopher Morley's *Kitty Foyle* and J. P. Marquand's *H. M. Pulham, Esq.* are centered on such alliances between upper-class young men and young women from other classes. In both these stories, the man changed his mind under strong family pressures.

19   E. D. Baltzell, *Philadelphia Gentlemen* (New York: Free Press of Glencoe, 1958), p. 161.

20   Kephart, op. cit., p. 487.

21   Cavan, op. cit., p. 97.

22   Ibid., pp. 97–98.

23   Joseph A. Kahl, *The American Class Structure* (New York: Rinehart & Co., 1957), p. 191.

24   Cavan, "Sub-cultural Variations and Mobility," op. cit., p. 542.

25   August B. Hollingshead, "Class Differences in Family Stability," in Robert F.

Winch, et al., eds., *Selected Studies in Marriage and the Family* (New York: Holt, Rinehart and Winston, 1962), pp. 576–577.

26 Ibid.

27 Roach et al., op. cit., p. 166; and Schulz, op. cit., p. 120.

28 Cavan, *The American Family*, p. 117.

29 Marvin B. Sussman, "Family Continuity: A Study of Factors which Affect Relationships between Families at Generational Levels," unpublished Ph.D. dissertation, Yale University, 1951.

30 See Leslie, op. cit., pp. 319–333 for a review of these studies.

31 Everett D. Dyer, "Upward Social Mobility and Extended Family Cohesion as Perceived by the Wife in Swedish Urban Families," *Journal of Marriage and Family*, 34 (November 1972), pp. 713–724.

32 Eugene Litwak, "Occupational Mobility and Extended Family Cohesion," *American Sociological Review*, 25 (February 1960), pp. 9–21.

33 Eugene Litwak, "Geographical Mobility and Extended Family Cohesion," *American Sociological Review*, 25 (June 1960), pp. 390–394.

34 W. Lloyd Warner and Paul S. Lunt, *The Social Life of a Modern Community* (New Haven: Yale University Press, 1941), pp. 422, 430–431.

35 Ruth S. Caven, *The American Family* (New York: Thomas Y. Crowell Co., 1953), p. 152.

36 Robert O. Blood, Jr., and Donald M. Wolf, *Husbands and Wives: The Dynamics of Married Living* (New York: Free Press of Glencoe, 1960).

37 Cavan, *The American Family*, 1969, p. 118.

38 Ibid., p. 119.

39 William H. Whyte, Jr., "The Wives of Management," *Fortune*, 44 (October 1951), pp. 86–88.

40 Adams, op. cit., p. 104.

41 E. E. LeMasters, *Modern Courtship and Marriage* (New York: Macmillan Co., 1957), pp. 69–95.

42 Cavan, op. cit., pp. 116–117.

43 Ibid., p. 122. Also see fig. 3, p. 97.

44 Adams, op. cit., p. 105.

45 Kahl, op. cit., p. 194.

46 Ibid., p. 203.

47 Roach et al., op. cit., pp. 180, 198.

48 Cavan, op. cit., p. 135.

49 Herbert J. Gans, "Class Sub-cultures in American Society," in Celia S. Heller, ed., *Structured Social Inequality* (London: Collier-Macmillan Co., 1969), p. 270.

50 Ibid.

51 E. E. LeMasters, *Blue-Collar Aristocrats* (Madison, Wis.: University of Wisconsin Press, 1975), chap. 2.

52 Mirra Komarovsky, "Blue-Collar Marriage—Barriers to Marital Communication," in Celia S. Heller, ed., *Structured Social Inequality* (London: Collier-Macmillan Co., 1967), pp. 276–284.

53 Cavan, op. cit., p. 144.

54 Ibid., p. 143.

55 Lee Rainwater, *And the Poor Get Children* (Chicago: Quadrangle Books, 1960), pp. 62–63, as quoted in Kephart, op. cit., p. 497.

56 U.S. Bureau of the Census, *Statistical Abstract of the United States:* 1967, p. 52.

57 Cavan, op. cit., p. 146.

58 Roach, et al., op. cit., p. 181. Also see Urie Bronfenbrenner, "Socialization and Social Class through Time and Space," in Reinhard Bendix and Seymour Lipset, eds., *Class, Status, and Power*, Second Edition, (New York: Free Press, 1966), pp. 362–377.

59 Cavan, op. cit., p. 148.

60 Ibid. p. 149.

61 Kahl, op. cit., p. 205.

62 Ibid., p. 210.

63 Ibid., pp. 211, 213.

64 Carson McGuire, "Social Stratification and Mobility Patterns," *American Sociological Review*, 15 (February 1950), pp. 195–198.

65 Cavan, "Subcultural Variations and Mobility," p. 573.

66 Ralph H. Turner, *Family Interaction* (New York: John Wiley & Sons, 1970). See pp. 478–488 for a good presentation of this issue. The present discussion follows Turner closely.

67 Cavan, *The American Family*, 1969, pp. 189–190.

68 See Melvin Tumin, "Some Unapplauded Consequences of Social Mobility in a Mass Society," *Social Forces* (October 1957), pp. 32–37; Peter Blau, "Social Mobility and Inter-Personal Relations," *American Sociological Review*, 21 (June 1956), pp. 291–295; A. B. Hollingshead, "Class Differences in Family Stability," *Annals of the Academy of Political and Social Sciences* (November 1950), pp. 39–46.

69 Julius Roth and R. F. Peck, "Social Class and Mobility Factors Related to Marital Adjustment," *American Sociological Review*, 16 (August 1951), pp. 478–487.

70 Carson McGuire, "Social Stratification and Mobility Patterns," *American Sociological Review*, 15 (April 1950), pp. 195–204; and "Conforming, Mobile, and Divergent Families," *Marriage and Family Living*, 14 (March 1952), pp. 109–115.

71 E. E. LeMasters, "Social Mobility and Family Integration," *Marriage and Family Living*, 16 (August 1954), pp. 1–8.

72 Talcott Parsons, "The Social Structure of the Family," in Ruth Anshen, ed., *The Family: Its Function and Destiny* (New York: Harper & Brothers, 1959), p. 92; also see Talcott Parsons, "Revised Analytical Approach to the Theory of Social Stratification," in Reinhard Bendix and Seymout Lipset, eds., *Class, Status and Power*, Second Edition, (New York: Free Press, 1963), pp. 166ff.

73 Eugene Litwak, "Occupational Mobility and Family Cohesion," *American Sociological Review*, 25 (February 1960), pp. 9–21.

74 Robert P. Stuckert, "Occupational Mobility and Family Relationships," *Social Forces*, 41 (March 1963), pp. 301–308. See p. 302 for a discussion of the two opposing views.

75 LeMasters, op. cit., p. 8.

76 Everett D. Dyer, "Upward Social Mobility and Nuclear Family Integration as

Perceived by the Wife in Swedish Urban Families," *Journal of Marriage and Family*, 32 (August 1970), pp. 341–350; Everett D. Dyer, "Upward Social Mobility and Extended Family Cohesion as Perceived by the Wife in Swedish Urban Families," *Journal of Marriage and Family*, 34 (November 1972), pp. 713–724.
77 Turner, op. cit., pp. 488–493.
78 Dyer, "Upward Social Mobility and Extended Family Cohesion as Perceived by the Wife in Swedish Urban Families," op. cit., pp. 720–723.

SELECTED READING

We have seen in this chapter that family life-styles may differ considerably from one social class to another, and that people in a given social class may be "class-centric" about their own life-styles. That is, they see their own customs, values, and norms as natural and good, and thus are inclined to view the differing customs, values, and norms found in other social classes somewhat negatively. This situation, plus the fact that people in one social class generally have limited contacts with members of other classes, may lead to misunderstandings and misconceptions on the part of people in one class about families in other classes, especially in the classes below their own. How well can people born and raised in one social class understand others whose lives have been spent in another, quite different, social class? This question seems especially significant for people living in superior classes vis-à-vis those living in inferior classes. Do the values and sentiments of middle-class people, for instance, make it difficult for them to really understand the behavior of lower-class people? Are middle-class families inclined to take a biased and often negative view of lower-class families, characterizing them as unambitious, irresponsible, promiscuous, dirty, and loud?

Rodman examines these questions and finds that such viewpoints and biases are quite widespread among middle-class people, to the point of influencing the investigations and interpretations that social scientists and professional practitioners themselves make of lower-class families. Rodman points out the difficulties that many middle-class people have in overcoming the stereotyped view they have of lower-class people. He feels that many of the different or "deviant" behavior patterns of lower-class people are normal human responses to the deprivations of lower-class life conditions, and are thus quite understandable.

MIDDLE-CLASS MISCONCEPTIONS ABOUT LOWER-CLASS FAMILIES*

Hyman Rodman

How well can middle-class persons understand lower-class life? To what extent do their middle-class values lead them to misinterpret lower-class behavior? It is worthwhile asking these questions about middle-class persons—including social scientists and professional practitioners—who have ideas about members of the lower class. Whyte asked these questions a long time ago when he studied the structure of a lower-class Italian community in Boston,[1] and they have been asked many times since by students of the lower class. But these questions have not usually been asked directly, nor have they been explored in much detail. For the most part, as in Whyte, they underlie the discussions about lower-class life. I therefore propose to focus upon these questions and to discuss their general implications. Although the discussion will be, for the most part, a general one, special attention will be paid to commonly held views about lower-class family life.

Lower-Class and Negro Stereotypes

If we consider the general attitudes of middle-class people toward the lower class, it is clear that there is a great deal of misunderstanding. Members of the lower class often are thought to be "immoral," "uncivilized," "promiscuous," "lazy," "obscene," "dirty," and "loud." Many writers make it clear that this is the way the lower class is frequently viewed within the United States[2] as well as within many other countries.[3] The dominant characterization of the lower class is perhaps in terms of its "immorality," and this reflects the tendency on the part of the middle-class person to judge the lower-class person in terms of his own middle-class values.

Such social class biases are extremely widespread and they appear to be found in most stratified communities. For example, the same biases are found within Negro as well as white communities; thus Davis and Dollard state that "upper-class and middle-class Negroes often criticize lower-class Negroes for being loud, ignorant, black, or dirty persons."[4]

One result of the existence of these biases has been their extension to

*Reprinted from *Blue-Collar World: Studies of the American Worker*, edited by A. B. Shostak and William Gomberg. Copyright © 1964, pp. 50–69. Reprinted by permission of Prentice-Hall, Englewood Cliffs, New Jersey, and the author.

other than a narrowly defined lower-class group. For example, whites often characterize Negroes by the same stereotypes that middle-class people use in characterizing the lower class—obscene, dirty, loud, lazy, promiscuous, irresponsible, happy. Inkeles[5] and Copeland,[6] among others, have commented on the parallel stereotypes applied to the poor and to Negroes. Part of the explanation for the extension of lower-class stereotypes to Negroes as a group is the larger proportion of Negroes who are in the lower class, and the development of a racially competitive tradition in which Negroes are a physically distinguishable, and therefore vulnerable, minority group.[7]

Simpson and Yinger point out that it is not racial difference which leads to these prejudiced stereotypes—indeed, how can it be when similar stereotypes are used toward white Protestant immigrants (from Arkansas and Oklahoma) to California? toward Polish workers in Germany in the late 1800's? and toward minority groups, racial groups, and lower-class groups generally?[8]

The Social Scientist's Biases

It is also worth asking to what extent the social scientist who studies the lower class, and who is himself a member of the middle class, is influenced by his middle-class values.

The question on the bias of the social scientist is much more difficult to answer. Social scientists do not, for example, use labels such as "immoral" or "uncivilized" in writing about the lower class. They do, however, speak of the lower class as being less well socialized, "unintegrated," "immature," "pathological," and more frequently as being "disorganized."[9] In many cases social scientists who use these terms actually have a fairly good understanding of the effect of life's deprivations upon the lower class, but in applying such terms to the lower-class person or to the lower-class family they are temporarily implying middle-class judgments. Why not speak of the total society as being pathological—if it is necessary to use this word—since this is what contributes to the lower-class behavior that we are concerned about? Many years ago Davis and Dollard made a similar point about the bias of social scientists by noting "that it is common practice, even of sociologists, to speak of the lower class as 'unsocialized,' from their middle-class point of view."[10] C. Wright Mills documented this tendency, and pointed to the use of terms like "unadjusted," "demoralized," and "disorganized."[11] These practices have not disappeared.

Another technique that social scientists sometimes use is to describe the lower class by indirection. This is done by giving an account of lower-class behavior as it has been presented by middle-class informants. It is certainly significant that so many middle-class stories and quotations are used to characterize the lower class, and that very few lower-class statements are used to characterize the middle class.

The Professional Practitioner's Biases

It is also of interest to ask to what extent social workers (and professional practitioners generally) are handicapped by their middle-class values in working with and understanding lower-class clients. This is a point that a number of social scientists have raised. For the most part, they have held that social workers do a poor job in contacting or in meeting the needs of lower-class people; for example, this position has been stated by Koos, Whyte, and Spinley,[12] three social scientists who have themselves worked with the lower class. Historically, social workers started out with a moralistic approach to lower-class behavior, and it is only recently that they have become more psychiatric in their approach. This, of course, has paralleled the fact that more and more social workers are being professionally trained, especially within the United States. One of the most significant and promising approaches toward dealing with the lower class has been made by social workers within the past decade, and this is an approach that is beginning to spread to other practicing professions. The approach is best symbolized in the social work literature by such phrases as "hard-to-reach," "hard core," and "multi-problem" families (or individuals or gangs). This approach recognizes the fact that many lower-class clients are difficult to work with, and it emphasizes the need to understand and accept lower-class families or delinquent gangs before making any attempts to reform them.

Social workers have not been alone in having difficulties with lower-class clients. Davis, Hollingshead, Sexton, and Riessman have referred to the cultural differences that underlie the problems that may be faced by teachers and their lower-class pupils;[13] and Hollingshead, Redlich, Overall, and Aronson have made the same point with respect to psychiatrists and their lower-class patients.[14] They have indicated, for example, that lower-class patients frequently expect the psychiatrist to play an authoritarian role, and that this runs counter to the psychiatrist's therapeutic principles. Without really understanding the lower-class patient, the psychiatrist may then label the lower-class patient as being "unable to profit from therapy" or simply as "untreatable."

A fact of great significance, as I have already suggested, is that there has been a trend away from thinking of certain patients or clients as being "untreatable" toward thinking of them as being "resistive" and "hard to reach." This trend reflects the greater realization on the part of professionals that there is a two-way relationship between the professional person and his client, and that the professional shares in the responsibility of establishing a relationship that will be of help to his client. The change from the notion of "untreatable" clients to "resistive" or "hard-to-reach" ones implies that the resistance can be overcome and that the client can be reached. A common saying, in reaction to the strong psychiatric orientation of social work, refers to the need to put the "social" back into social work. The current trend toward seriously trying to reach certain "hard-to-reach" clients may be referred to as putting the "work" back into social work.

Lower-Class Family Behavior

It is lower-class family behavior that presents the greatest challenge to the person who tries to understand lower-class life. The following have all been considered as characteristic of the lower class: "promiscuous" sexual relationships; "illegitimate" children; "deserting" husbands and fathers; and "unmarried" mothers. These characteristics are frequently viewed in a gross manner as, simply, *problems* of the lower class. It makes better sense, however, to think of them as *solutions* of lower-class persons to problems that they face in the social, economic, and perhaps legal and political spheres of life.

How is it that lower-class behavior can so easily be misunderstood? That a middle-class view of lower-class behavior can lead to misunderstanding has already been pointed out. And one of the major ways in which alien values become incorporated into one's view of the lower class is through the use of middle-class terms to describe lower-class behavior. It is little wonder that if we describe the lower-class family in terms of "promiscuous" sexual relationships, "illegitimate" children, "deserting" men, and "unmarried" mothers, we are going to see the situation as disorganized and chock-full of problems. It should be stressed that words like "promiscuity," "illegitimacy," and "desertion" are not part of the lower-class vocabulary, and that it is misleading to describe lower-class behavior in this way. These words have middle-class meanings and imply middle-class judgments, and it is precisely because of this that we ought not to use them to describe lower-class behavior—unless, perhaps, our intention is to judge this behavior in a middle-class manner in order to bolster a sagging middle-class ego.

No claim is being made here, of course, that demographers or social scientists should not discuss rates of desertion or rates of illegitimacy. In a scientific sense these rates have a clear enough meaning and they provide very important pieces of information for certain kinds of analyses. But these terms can also be used in a judgmental sense, and it is this judgmental use that I am cautioning against. I am also cautioning against the rather easy way in which a scientific stance on these matters can buckle under the weight of a middle-class morality. Consider the following example, in which the author rushes headlong into a *non sequitur*:

In my opinion, it is indefensible to write off as "culturally acceptable" to a certain group poverty and its terrible hardships, personality disturbances and their painful results, or the pervasive effect of impaired relationships. How often we have heard that in a particular cultural group it's acceptable for a teen-age girl to have a baby out of wedlock. Whether or not this is a valid generalization is for the sociologist to study. The social worker, on the other hand, must be concerned about the loneliness a teenage girl feels when she has no husband with whom to share her parenthood, when she cannot return to school, when her friends go out on dates while she stays at home to care for the baby, or when her friends get their first jobs and she must apply for public assistance.[15]

The social scientist who studies lower-class families should pay more attention to the language of the lower-class itself. In a practical vein this means that lower-class family patterns are usually best described in lower-class terms:

The language problem is . . . involved in the terms used for the different forms of marital or quasi-marital relationships in the different parts of the West Indies. R. T. Smith has discussed some of the difficulties that develop when the observer sets up his own classification scheme for dealing with lower-class marital unions. In addition, the great variety of terms used by different observers for a marital union that is socially but not legally sanctioned, and the reasons they give for a particular usage, also suggest that the observer's terms may not be the most satisfactory ones. Henriques and R. T. Smith use common-law marriage; Clarke rejects the term "common law" because it suggests legal recognition, and uses concubinage; Stycos rejects "concubinage" and uses consensual union; Matthews, more simply and perhaps more sensibly, uses non-legal union. Although all of these writers recognize the distinctions between the legal and social aspects of the union, it seems to me that in using their own particular terms for the union, they may be causing unnecessary confusion. Would it not make better sense to use the terms that are used by the lower class itself to refer to these unions?[16]

Accordingly, in my own study of lower-class families in Coconut Village, Trinidad, I discuss three different kinds of marital or quasi-marital relationships—"friending," "living," and married. Through a consideration of some of the findings of this study we can come to a better understanding of what I regard as a major middle-class misconception of lower-class families—viewing certain patterns as *problems* when, in reality, they can as easily be viewed as *solutions*.

Although the details that follow refer to lower-class marital relationships in Coconut Village, I believe that the description, in a broad sense, applies to lower-class families in many societies.[17] The "friending" relationship is one in which a man visits a woman at intervals for sexual intercourse, and in which he has certain limited obligations to the woman and to any children of his that she may bear. Although this relationship is not fully acceptable, it is the most frequent type of relationship, and it usually precedes one of the other relationships. The "living" relationship is one in which the man and woman live together under one roof, but in which they are not legally married. It is an acceptable marital relationship and it occurs more frequently than marriage. A married relationship is similar to a "living" relationship, but it involves a church marriage and a legal bond between the man and woman. It occurs least frequently within the lower class. From one point of view, these patterns reflect a reluctance to take on responsibility, since a greater degree of marital responsibility is involved in the "living" than in the "friending," and in the married than in the "living" relationship.

One man put it this way when I asked him why the people were reluctant to marry: "Matrimony is a money that you can't spend." He explained this to mean that it was something you could not easily get rid of. Another man answered the same question this way: "You can buy a penny milk, so what you want with a cow, na?" Such comments are by no means unique to Coconut Villagers, but they do point out for us the reluctance of the villager to enter a strong marital alliance.

What are the reasons for this reluctance, especially on the man's part, to take on responsibilities within the marital relationship? Also, why is there a good deal of "marital shifting" within Coconut Village, such that most villagers in their lifetime will have gone through several "friending" and "living" relationships? Part of the answer to these questions must be sought in the relation of family life to the structure of the society as a whole, particularly to its economy.

Almost all Coconut Villagers are members of the lower class of Trinidad society and face serious economic deprivations. Although someone in approximately half the households of Coconut Village owns some land, not one household is able to earn its living from the land alone. The land is poor and the hoe and cutlass are the only tools used. Transportation is a severe problem because the lands are practically all at a considerable distance from the main road, so that the meager crops are difficult to market. Wage labor must therefore be relied upon by all households within Coconut Village, and here they share, with other members of the lower class, a situation in which wages are low, unemployment and underemployment are high, and geographical mobility is at times necessary in order simply to find a job.[18]

It is the man who is responsible for the financial support of his wife and children. However, since the economic circumstances faced by the lower-class man often make it difficult or impossible for him to meet these responsibilities, it becomes clear as to why there is a reluctance to accept such responsibilities in the first place. We can therefore understand why "friending" occurs more frequently than "living," and "living" more frequently than marriage within lower-class communities. We can also understand why a marital relationship such as "living" becomes such an acceptable lower-class pattern, for it provides the lower-class person with a fluid marital bond.

In addition to the greater number of acceptable marital relationships the lower-class person can choose from, there is also a ready acceptance of a separation when economic circumstances make it necessary for the man to move in order to find employment.* In this way the man can later set up another marital relationship, when he is in a position to do so, while the woman may be able to set up a new marital relationship with a man who can support her.

Fluidity is therefore strategic in marital life. On the one hand there is fluidity with respect to the type of relationship a person enters into, and on the other hand there is fluidity with respect to the permanence of the marital bond such that it is possible to shift from one marital partner to another. Therefore these marital relationships are functional in that they provide the lower-class person with acceptable alternatives which permit him to live with both his conscience and his economic uncertainties.

This fluidity of the marital bond is, I believe, characteristic of lower-class families generally. Within the United States the higher rates of divorce and desertion within the lower class, as well as of "common-law" unions and illegitimacy, are indicative of such fluidity. If, as I am suggesting, these lower-class patterns are responses to the deprivations of lower-class life, and if they are functional for lower-class individuals, then we can see the sense in which many of the lower-class family patterns that are often regarded as problems are actually solutions to other, more pressing, problems.

Concluding Remarks

We have seen that middle-class folk frequently are biased about the lower-class, and that they tend to hold many misconceptions about lower-class family life. Social scientists and professional practitioners may share these biases in some measure. Illustrating this danger is a story told about a social work convention:

A social worker was presenting a paper that included case material about a lower-class client. She reported that her client's husband entered the room during one of her home visits and described him as a burly and taciturn man. One of her colleagues rose to object: "I beg your pardon. That's my husband you're talking about. He's not burly and taciturn. He's strong and silent!"

*Since a separation is easy under such conditions, it often takes place for personal as well as for economic reasons.

This recalls Merton's "engagingly simple formula of moral alchemy":

The proficient alchemist will at once know that the word "firm" is properly declined as follows:

I am firm,
Thou art obstinate,
He is pigheaded.

There are some, unversed in the skills of this science, who will tell you that one and the same term should be applied to all three instances of identical behavior. Such unalchemical nonsense should simply be ignored.[19]

The moral of these stories is obvious. If middle-class persons regard immorality as the special province of the lower classes, then they are not going to be successful in their relations with lower-class people—whether as researchers, practitioners, or in everyday discourse.

There are still many questions in the area of lower-class family relationships and values to which we do not have the answers. With additional research we may eventually begin to get some answers to the many different questions that are being asked about lower-class families. In the meantime, additional research should at least help us to eliminate some of our biases about lower-class families. As Barbara Wootton has said: "The first result of a demand for evidence which will stand up to rigorous scientific examination is the destruction of myths, and such destructive activity is likely for sometime to come to be the main preoccupation of the social sciences."[20]

References

1 It is of interest that in his enlarged edition of *Street Corner Society*, published in 1955 by the University of Chicago Press, Whyte has added a section which deals with the difficulties he had in moving from a middle-class to a lower-class milieu.

2 Herman R. Lantz, *People of Coal Town*, New York: Columbia University Press, 1958, pp. 227–228; Richard Centers, *The Psychology of Social Classes*, Princeton, N.J.: Princeton University Press, 1949, pp. 95–96; W. Lloyd Warner *et al.*, *Democracy in Jonesville*, New York: Harper, 1949, pp. 249–250; August B. Hollingshead, *Elmtown's Youth*, New York: Wiley, 1949, pp. 110–111; St. Clair Drake and Horace R. Cayton, *Black Metropolis*, New York: Harcourt, 1945, pp. 559–563; James West, *Plainsville, U.S.A.*, New York: Columbia University Press, 1945, p. 125; Allison Davis, Burleigh B. Gardner, and Mary R. Gardner, *Deep South,* Chicago: University of Chicago Press, 1941, p. 230.

3 For such views in the West Indies, for example, see F. M. Henriques, *Family and Colour in Jamaica*, London: Eyre and Spottiswoode, 1953, p. 145; Lloyd Braith-

waite, "Social Stratification in Trinidad," *Social and Economic Studies*, Vol. II, Nos. 2 and 3, p. 126.

4   Allison Davis and John Dollard, *Children of Bondage*, Washington, D.C.: American Council on Education, 1940, p. 44.

5   Alex Inkeles, "Industrial Man: The Relations of Status to Experience, Perception, and Value," *American Journal of Sociology*, Vol. LXVI, July, 1960, p. 14.

6   Lewis C. Copeland, "The Negro as a Contrast Conception," in Edgar T. Thompson, ed., *Race Relations and the Race Problem*, Durham, N.C.:Duke University Press, 1939, p. 157.

7   It must also be remembered that the development of prejudiced stereotypes of Negroes, and the often accompanying discrimination, is largely responsible for the greater proportion of Negroes in the lower class. For a more detailed statement of the origin of prejudices toward Negroes see George E. Simpson and J. Milton Yinger, *Racial and Cultural Minorities*, rev. ed., New York: Harper, 1958, pp. 153–154 *et passim*; Gordon W. Allport, *The Nature of Prejudice*, Garden City, N.Y.: Doubleday, 1958.

8   Simpson and Yinger, *op. cit.,* pp. 124, 167–168, *et passim.*

9   Davis and Dollard, *op. cit.,* p. 267; Madeline Kerr, *Personality and Conflict in Jamaica*, Liverpool: Liverpool University Press, 1952, p. 193; Madeline Kerr, *The People of Ship Street*, London: Routledge & Kegan Paul, 1958, p. 156 *et passim*; Dom Basil Matthews, *Crisis of the West Indian Family*, Trinidad: University of the West Indies, Extra Mural Department, 1952, pp. xiii, 19, 125.

10 Davis and Dollard, *op. cit.,* pp. 264–265.
    C. Wright Mills, "The Professional Ideology of Social Pathologists," *American Journal of Sociology*, Vol. XLIX, Sept., 1942, p. 179.

12 Earl Lomon Koos, *Families in Trouble*, New York: King's Crown Press, 1946, pp. 84–86; William F. Whyte, *Street Corner Society*, Chicago: University of Chicago Press, 1943, pp. 98–104; B. M. Spinley, *The Deprived and the Privileged*, London: Routledge & Kegan Paul, 1953.

13 Allison Davis, *Social Class Influences upon Learning*, Cambridge: Harvard University Press, 1952; August B. Hollingshead, *op. cit.*; Patricia Cayo Sexton, *Education and Income*, New York: Viking, 1961; Frank Riessman, *The Culturally Deprived Child*, New York: Harper, 1962.

14 August B. Hollingshead and Frederick C. Redlich, *Social Class and Mental Illness*, New York: Wiley, 1958; Betty Overall and H. Aronson, "Expectations of Psychotherapy in Patients of Lower Socioeconomic Class," *American Journal of Orthopsychiatry*, Vol. XXXIII, April, 1963, 421–430.

15 Carol H. Meyer, "Individualizing the Multiproblem Family," *Social Casework*, Vol. XLIV, May, 1963, p. 269.

16 Hyman Rodman, "On Understanding Lower-Class Behavior," *Social and Ecnoomic Studies* Vol. VIII, Dec., 1959, p. 445. See original article for footnotes.

17 Hyman Rodman, *Lower-Class Families*, in preparation. Cf. Lee Rainwater, Richard P. Coleman, and Gerald Handel, *Workingman's Wife*, New York: Oceana Publications, 1959; Lee Rainwater, *And the Poor Get Children*, Chicago: Quadrangle Books, 1960; Oscar Lewis, *Five Families*, New York: Basic Books, 1959; E. Franklin Frazier, *The Negro Family in the United States*, New York: Citadel Press,

rev. and abridged ed., 1948; Albert K. Cohen and Harold M. Hodges, "Characteristics of the Lower-Blue-Collar Class," *Social Problems*, Vol. X. Spring, 1963.

18 Geographic mobility is therefore not a good index of status mobility. For a brief discussion related to this point see Hyman Rodman, "The 'Achievement Syndrome' and Negro Americans," and Bernard C. Rosen, "Reply to Rodman," *American Sociological Review*, Vol. XXIV, Oct., 1959, pp. 691–692.

19 Robert K. Merton, *Social Theory and Social Structure*, rev. and enlarged ed., New York: Free Press of Glencoe, 1957, p. 428.

20 Barbara Wootton, *Social Science and Social Pathology*, London: Allen and Unwin, 1959, p. 328.

PART THREE

Family Change in America

CHAPTER 6

Social Change and Family Change in America

Most sociologists are interested in the objective analysis of social change—why it occurs, how it occurs, and what are its consequences—rather than in seeking to bring about social change. In their effort to study and understand social change, certain concepts have been developed by social scientists to aid them.[1]

Social Processes and Conditions Influencing Family Change in America

THE STUDY OF SOCIAL CHANGE: CONCEPTS AND PROBLEMS

One long-standing way of conceptualizing social change has been the notion of *evolutionary* change. Societies and their constituent social institutions are envisioned as moving throughout history from a simple or primitive state to a complex and highly developed state. This is essentially a unilinear change idea. Early sociologists such as Comte and Spencer advanced these notions

Four-generation rural family, 1920. (*Fred J. Pearson.*)

Modern couples at beach party, 1970s. (*Julie Heifetz.*)

of social change. Lewis Henry Morgan's theory of family change used this evolutionary approach.[2]

Another way of conceptualizing social change has been the notion of *developmental* or *cyclical* change. This approach views a society or some of its constituent systems as moving through various stages of development or growth to decline and eventual cessation of existence (e.g., from birth to youth to maturity to death). Then the cycle will be repeated. Carle Zimmerman's theory of family change in Western civilization is a good example of this concept applied to family change.[3]

Certain aspects of social change may be analyzed in terms of *functionalism*. This concept assumes that in a given society certain functions and related social structures exist and that these functions and structures change over periods of time. Applied to the study of family change, examples of this functional approach would be found in the theory of William Ogburn on changing family functions in America and in Talcott Parsons' theory on the functionality of the independent nuclear family in modern industrial society.[4]

Another way of conceptualizing certain issues in social change is in terms of the processes of *conflict and tension management*. This approach assumes that constituent groups in a society are in competition for resources, privileges, and power. Those groups possessing more of these things desire to maintain the status quo and thus seek to restrict and limit the amount of change, while groups with less power and privileges seek to expedite social change. Examples in the realm of marriage and family would be (1) the youth movement, focusing on generational differences and the tensions and conflict between parents and their liberated children, and (2) women's liberation, as manifested in tensions and conflict between wife and husband over divisions of labor and power in the family. Sociologists using this approach would direct their attention to the struggles between the pro-change and the anti-change groups, and the ways in which the accompanying tension and conflict are managed.[5]

In Chapter 2 we discussed the ideal-type method of analyzing social variations and social change. This method is especially appropriate for studying social change since it allows us to construct models or ideal types of societies (and their constituent systems such as the family) that vary from one place to another, but also as they vary or change from one time to another in a given place. This idea of social variation or change over time is built into the Gemeinschaft-sacred⟷Gesellschaft-secular typology. The former is a hypothetical model of undeveloped preindustrial society, while the latter is an ideal-type model of modern, highly developed industrial society. Issues and questions of social and family change may be posed and analyzed using these types as reference points.[6] (See Figure 2-1, Chapter 2.) There is general agreement among authorities that in recent centuries the long-range trend in social change has been a movement from the Gemeinschaft-sacred toward the Gesellschaft-secular.[7] Most of the social, economic, political, and ideological processes and conditions to be discussed next as affecting family life in America are encompassed in the broad, general social-change idea conceptualized by this framework.

PROBLEMS IN ASSESSING OR MEASURING SOCIAL CHANGE

Many difficulties arise in trying to assess accurately the nature and extent of social change.[8] One problem lies in separating cause and effect. Many relationships between variables may be reciprocal in nature, making it very difficult or impossible to separate cause from effect. An example would be the emergence of the independent nuclear family along with the rise of industrialization, with each affecting the development of the other. In order for a causal relationship to exist, one variable (X) should precede the other (Y) in time, thus making it possible to explain, at least in part, that what happens to Y as a dependent variable happens because of the influence of X as an independent variable. An example could be the possible relationship between higher education and family birthrates. If it can be shown that couples with a college education at marriage have fewer children than couples without college education, we may assume a causal relationship between college education (*X*) and the birthrate (*Y*). However, further study would be needed to determine if the birthrate fell because of the college education itself or because of other related factors.

Another problem in determining social change lies in the inadequacy and unreliability of historical data. Social science is quite recent, historically, and pre-social-science data are apt to be fragmentary, unreliable, and more subjective than objective. These problems, plus the tendency to idealize the past, make it difficult to establish reliable and accurate base lines in past periods, such as the colonial period, from which to measure changes that have occurred.

Then there are problems of the reliability and validity of the measures or indicators of change. A measure or test procedure is reliable to the extent that it elicits the same results each time it is applied under similar circumstances, and it is valid to the degree to which it measures what it purports to measure.[9] If a test that claims to measure innate intelligence instead actually measures acquired knowledge and skills, it is not a valid test of innate intelligence. Also, if students taking this test a second or third time were to score much lower or higher than they did the first time, the test would not be very reliable.

Problems also may be present in the selection of information and in the way it is reported and interpreted. Figures may be misleading, and it is easy to misinterpret gross figures when comparing those of one time or place to those of another, or when making comparisons between figures that do not have a comparable base. An example of the latter would be in figuring divorce rates. In 1968 there were 2,059,000 marriages and 582,000 divorces in the United States. Some social scientists and many journalists reported that the divorce rate for 1968 was thus a deplorable 28 percent! This "divorce rate," or more accurately "divorce to marriage ratio," is faulty and spurious because almost all divorces granted in a given year, such as in 1968, are awarded to people who were married in the preceding years—from 1 to 25 years or more before. Figures from two different bases are here being compared in a faulty and misleading way. A more accurate estimate of the extent of divorce in 1968 would be to show the number of divorces per 1,000 existing marriages. With about 47 million married couples in 1968, the rate would be about 12.4 divorces per 1,000 marriages, or a bit more than 1 divorce per 100 existing marriages—a much less alarming figure.[10]

Richard Clayton recommends keeping in mind the following points as we seek to assess family change within the larger framework of social change.[11] (1) In using historical macro-level concepts we should resist the temptation to personalize the materials under study. History is larger than individuals. (2) We should realize that much of the historical data needed for a thorough analysis has been lost, and that efforts to recreate lost data often produce idealized or otherwise biased data. (3) Change is a value-laden concept. To some virtually any change is good, while to others most any change is viewed as bad. (4) The family should be seen as a possible source of change itself, not only as a dependent variable being influenced and changed by other social phenomena. In this connection Talcott Parsons said, "I believe profoundly in the importance of the family system, and I furthermore don't think it always follows, but at times it leads, social change."[12]

SOCIAL, ECONOMIC, AND IDEOLOGICAL FACTORS INFLUENCING FAMILY CHANGE IN AMERICA.

TECHNOLOGICAL AND INDUSTRIAL CHANGE   Family change in relation to technological and industrial development has already been introduced in Chapter 2. Only a few points need be made here. America has been in the forefront of the technological-industrial revolution. Therefore, during this period of our history American families could be expected to have come under its influences. We have been warned not to oversimplify the relationship between industrialization and family change. However, most authorities agree that when an economic system expands through industrialization, family patterns do change. Extended family ties and lineage patterns tend to weaken, and some form of a conjugal nuclear family emerges which fits the modern industrial system better by freeing family members from kinship ties so they can go where the industrial economy needs workers. As William Goode emphasizes, however, cause-and-effect relationships between industrialization and family change are very complex.[13] The processes of technological and industrial development are accompanied by a complex of interrelated social changes which themselves affect family life. For example, machine power and factory production brought revolutionary changes in transportation and communication; they also brought the expansion of education and literacy, the growth of cities, rising expectations among the masses, and the spread of democratic and equalitarian ideologies. America has been one of the pioneer societies in industrial development, and it was inevitable that the complex of processes and conditions referred to as industrialization would have profound effects upon the family life of its people.

URBANIZATION AND RURAL-TO-URBAN MIGRATIONS   Industrial development in America was accompanied by the growth of large urban centers where the way of life differed in important ways from that of rural America. Families moving from rural areas to American cities were confronted with dense populations, crowded neighborhoods, limited space in the family dwelling, little or no play facilities for children, and an impersonal and often hostile social environment. Family members dispersed more during the day, with one or both adults going to work and the children going to school. Social life was very different from that in the rural community where more personal

Gemeinschaftlike relationships prevailed; in the big city, the relationships are Gesellschaftlike, impersonal, formal, and circumscribed by norms and status roles in business, commercial, religious, educational, and other types of groups.

As was seen in Chapter 4, the latter part of the nineteenth century and the twentieth century have witnessed vast movements of American families from rural America to our cities. Major adjustments in family life have been required of these new arrivals.

CULTURAL DIVERSITY AND THE MELTING POT   Since American urban populations have been very heterogeneous, including multinational ethnic and racial groups of Old World backgrounds, cultural diversity and social ferment have characterized America, especially the large, dynamic American cities. As was discussed in Chapter 3, the history of families moving from other countries to America has been one of culture contact and culture conflict, followed by varying degrees of cultural and social assimilation. Community pressure by native Americans and community agencies upon these families to shed their foreign culture and become Americanized meant constant agitation for family change. The "melting pot" idea is a vivid image of this scenario for change being experienced by families in the context of population and cultural diversity.

SOCIAL MOBILITY, THE AMERICAN DREAM, AND THE MIDDLE-CLASS FAMILY MODEL   As seen in Chapter 5, American families have since colonial times been subjected to pressures to improve their lot or better themselves. The great American dream has inspired families to work and strive to improve their economic and social position, to move ahead, to provide a better way of life for their children, and to give them advantages and opportunities the parents never had. American families have for generations been oriented toward this upward striving or social mobility goal. And twentieth-century America has seen an increasing proportion of the population pursuing and achieving middle-class goals. As Gerald Leslie says, the mobile, middle-class family may well be the family of the future. Its patterns are the ones held up to us as models to emulate.[14]

IDEOLOGICAL FACTORS   Intermeshed with the above-mentioned processes and conditions conducive to change have been a number of ideological orientations and themes which have provided much of the driving force behind social and family change in America. Emerging ideologies are vital forces in the dynamics of social change, influencing the individual's definitions of situations, the crystallization of group sentiments, beliefs, and goals, and the functioning of social institutions. As Goode observed in his *World Revolution and Family Patterns*, a basic source of social change in modern societies has been the ideology of economic progress and technological development.[15] The ideology of individualism has obviously been important in the economic development of American society, and also in the emergence of the mobile, independent nuclear family. Individualism and individualistic rationality go hand in hand with secularization and modernization. The ideology of equalitarianism has been one of the wellsprings of social change in modern society. Equalitarianism has provided much of the impetus for many of the great social movements of the past century in America, such as feminism and women's liberation, the civil rights movement, and the current youth movements. Equalitarianism has been one of the strongest forces behind many changes in marriage and family, including the emergence of the independent conjugal family freed from extended kin-group controls, the drive for equal rights and authority for women along with men in the family, and the increased employment of married women outside the home. A more detailed discussion of this topic appeared in Chapter 2.

Family Change in America: Themes, Trends, and Emerging Family Characteristics

It can be as misleading to speak of the changing American family as it is to speak of the American family as a uniform entity. As we have seen in Chapters 3 through 5, the historical and cultural bases of American families have been diverse and varied from the earliest days of American history. From colonial times to the present, individual families arriving in the various American colonies, as culture-bearing groups, imported the beliefs, norms, and family customs of their native lands. Here in the New World these variant family ways sooner or later were intermixed and commingled. Such melting pot processes inevitably produced changes in family structure and relationships.

In spite of the great diversity in family life in America historically, one of the most significant processes of change has been the assimilation of families bearing different cultural heritages. True, differences in ethnic, racial, religious, and social-class backgrounds have been extensive and many of these differences still persist, but the processes of assimilation are continuing apace, and a synthesis of family structure and relationships is taking place reflecting these heterogeneous origins.[16]

While some scholars, such as Zimmerman, are concerned mainly with broad macro-level trends of family change, others focus on more immediate pragmatic issues and problems. During the early decades of the twentieth century many family sociologists were concerned with the increasing divorce rates, increasing employment of wives and mothers, declines in birthrates, and loss of family functions. Such family changes were perceived by many to be a threat to the continued well-being or even existence of the American family. A few writers, against the background of the 1920s and the Great Depression, predicted the ultimate disintegration of the American family. In 1941, Pitirim Sokorin wrote, "As it has become more and more contractual, the family of the last few decades has grown ever more unstable, until it has reached a point of actual disintegration."[17] Others, such as Ernest W. Burgess, were far less pessimistic, viewing the changes in family patterns as moves away from rigid traditionalism toward the realization of our democratic ideals.[18] So, while many tend to see evidence of the family's disintegration in higher divorce rates, higher illegitimacy rates, and increases in premarital and extramarital sexual relationships, others say it is equally possible to interpret these changes as newly emergent ways of patterning marriage and family life in response to rapid social change in the outside world. These issues and their ramifications will be considered more fully in Chapters 7 to 10.

It has been said that while the family is one of society's most conservative institutions, it is also very adaptable to changes going on in its social environment. Certainly, American families have been very adaptable historically, and at times have changed quite dramatically in response to developments in American social, economic, and political life. And undoubtedly American families will continue to change in response to even more dramatic changes in technology, science, politics, and ideology in the future. For instance, it is difficult now to foresee the consequences of developments in the biological sciences for the family of the future. They could be very dramatic. It may soon be possible to produce a human being in an artificial womb with the child's sex and other special characteristics predetermined.[19] Should this become technologically possible, it would still require profound changes in our family values and norms before such an alternative would replace the normal biological method of reproduction.

Families change in response to many factors, both outside and inside the family: technological developments, such as the invention of the automobile, telephone, radio, and television; and new situations such as a new job and a home in a new community. Families change in response to public policy changes and new laws, as in the case of some poor families where the father may leave home so his family may be eligible for public support through the Aid to Dependent Children programs. Internally, families may change because family members make decisions to change for certain reasons, such as the wife deciding to seek employment or a young married couple deciding not to have any children at all. On a different level, families change as they move through the family life cycle, normally from the early married state, through childbearing and rearing, to the empty-nest state, and on to the death of one or both of the marriage partners.[20] It should be noted that some of these family changes are more "expected" than others. Each family is expected to develop and move through the life cycle in a manner more or less defined by prevailing family goals and norms. However, because the expanding and changing roles for women in the twentieth century were not all "expected," the implications of the mother's employment outside the home for the rearing of children and for her other domestic roles are such that major role adjustments are often required in the family.

It seems quite likely that the rate of change in family life in America will increase as other changes in our society come along ever more frequently and rapidly. It is all the more important, then, for us to become aware of the nature of these family changes, to seek to understand their significance, and to seek to gain some control over them. Only this way can we have any hope of reducing "future shock" and of influencing family destiny.

SOME GENERAL CHANGES AND LONG-RANGE TRENDS

IDEALIZATION OF THE AMERICAN FAMILY OF THE PAST   In the effort to assess correctly the extent as well as the kinds of changes taking place in the American family today, one needs to examine the recent past. Upon looking into this past, the sociologist or historian may discover, as did William Goode, certain "idealized or stereotyped descriptions of family systems. . . . We must correct such stereotypes in order to measure present-day trends."[21] Goode has labeled this stereotype of the American family of the past "the classical family of Western nostalgia."

It is a pretty picture of life down on grandma's farm. There are lots of happy children, and many kinfolk live together in a large rambling house. Everyone works hard. Most of the food to be eaten during the winter is grown, preserved, and stored on the farm. The family members repair their own equipment, and in general the household is economically self-sufficient. The family has many functions; it is the source of economic stability and religious, educational, and vocational training. Father is stern and reserved, and has the final decision in all important matters. Life is difficult, but harmonious because everyone knows his task and carries it out. All boys and girls marry, and marry young. Young people, especially the girls, are likely to be virginal at marriage and faithful afterward. Though the parents do not arrange their children's marriages, the elders do have the right to reject a suitor and have a strong hand in the final decision. After marriage, the couple lives harmoniously, either near the boy's parents or with them, for the couple is slated to inherit the farm. No one divorces.[22]

This idealized image of the American family of the past can easily lead us astray. Family historians find few actual cases of this "classical" family in recent American history. Most houses were small rather than large and spacious. Not many families remained together as an extended family group working the land jointly, and many farms were not economically self-sufficient. While divorce was rare, it is not really known how happy most marriages were. Lack of data, plus our tendency to look backward to the "good old days," has resulted in a one-sided and probably unrealistic conception of marriage and family life back then. Goode observes, "that in each past generation, people write of a period *still* more remote, their grandparents' generation, when things really were much better."[23]

SOME FAMILY CHANGES SINCE THE COLONIAL PERIOD   What changes have come about in the American family since the end of the eighteenth century? In his work *The American Family*, Bert Adams has attempted to delineate salient family changes since colonial days and to show the extent of the change between 1800 and 1970.[24] Over such a span of time family change has been uneven, fragmentary, often inconsistent, and surely variable within, as well as between, social classes and racial and ethnic groups.

A number of problems plague the sociologist or historian seeking to determine kinds and amounts of family change since colonial times. Already mentioned are the tendency to idealize the past and the related difficulty of putting together an accurate picture of the past. Another problem pointed out by numerous sociologists is the difficulty of determining the relationship between industrialization and family change. There is a good deal of agreement among family sociologists that the relationship between industrialization and family change is highly complex, and that there is no direct cause-and-effect relationship between the process of industrialization and family development and change.[25] Goode feels that "it is doubtful that the amount of change in family patterns is a simple function of industrialization; more likely, ideological and value changes, partially independent of industrialization, also have some effect on family action."[26] Not only ideological and value changes, such as political and social democracy, but also other changes not necessarily subsumed under the term "industrialization," such as the free-enterprise system, agricultural productivity, the knowledge explosion, and communications expansion, all probably relate to family change in important ways. Such factors cannot be ignored, nor the possibility that the development of the nuclear family itself may have been a precondition for the economic and technological changes that gave rise to the industrial revolution.[27]

Causes and effects in family change in American history are not easily sorted out. Some of the difficulties, according to Adams, are that "the argument over change, cause, and effect has raged, but has been persistently contaminated by either an *idealized* view of the colonial or pre-industrial family; by *ignoring other important developments* that were parallel to industrialization and which influenced the family; or by the *selective use of family features* on the part of the individual researcher or writer."[28]

What then are some of the changes that have occurred in the American family since colonial times?[29]

CHANGES IN FAMILY FORMATION, OR PREMARITAL RELATIONS AND COURTSHIP Personal choice of a mate was quite well established among the colonists upon their arrival in the colonies, so the current pattern does not represent a basic change.[30] Only in upper-class families were arranged marriages more apt to occur. However, romantic love was becoming more common as the basis for mate selection, and this was accompanied by major changes in courtship practices and premarital sex norms. Up until the early 1900s courtship had centered largely in the home or in chaperoned social gatherings. The twentieth century brought much greater freedom for young people, especially important for girls, and this freedom combined with the advent of the automobile and more places to go brought about dating as the new and revolutionary form of courtship in America.

As dating became the established pattern of courtship in America, major changes in premarital sex codes have taken place.[31] The extent and significance of these changes have to be viewed in the historical context of the increasing strictness of the sex norms from colonial days through the Victorian era of the nineteenth century, followed by the widespread questioning of these strict codes during the twentieth century. While data are not sufficient for us to know either the true extent of premarital sex during the colonial period when bundling was customary, or during the Victorian period of strict chaperonage, we do know that twentieth-century America "has moved toward an overt and often positive attitude in dealing with sexual matters. . . . An example of this

FIGURE 6-1 Marital status of the population, United States, by sex, 1900 to 1970. (*Source: Department of Commerce, Bureau of the Census and Current Population Reports, Series P-20.*)

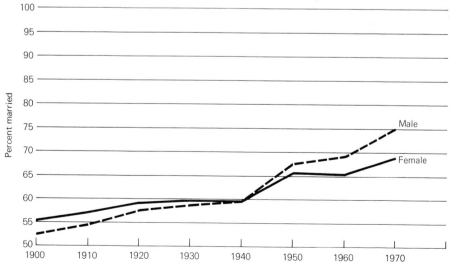

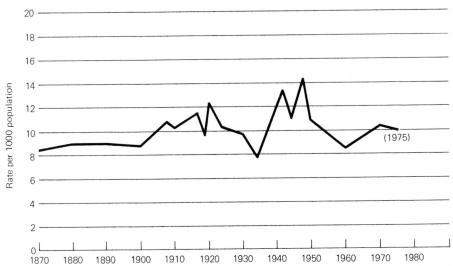

FIGURE 6-2 Marriage rates, United States, 1870–1975. (*Source:* "Marriage: Trends and Characteristics, United States," *U.S. Department of Health, Education and Welfare, Vital and Health Statistics, Series 21, September 1971, p. 2; and Statistical Abstract of the United States, 1976, p. 68.*)

change is that the pros and cons of premarital intercourse are being openly debated . . . by many of the country's religious and moral leaders."[32] Some feel that mid-twentieth-century America has become obsessed with sex, as seen in the popular literature, in the movies and on the stage, and in sex research and sex education.

CHANGES IN INTERNAL FAMILY RELATIONSHIPS AND STRUCTURE   In organization and structure the American family has experienced changes ranging from moderate to great. The nuclear family per se was well established in the colonial period, but the changes that took place in household composition between that time and the twentieth century were a decrease in family size and a decline in the proportion of families which included aging parents in the household.[33] Major changes have occurred in the status of the child and in related socialization processes. Since the twentieth-century family is no longer the basic economic producing unit it once was, parental authority is not now based on socializing and controlling the child as a subordinate in the family work team. The status of the child in the family has thus changed and he is freed from much of the traditional parental authority which could be asserted over a junior member of a work team.[34] This, combined with the decline in moral absolutes in the twentieth century, has increased parental permissiveness toward the child. However, modern parents also show an increasing concern for the child as a growing and developing person.

A considerable change may be seen in the emphasis on the individual in the family. From the Victorian era onward, Adams sees ". . . a decrease in nuclear family values and an increase in the concern with the individual and his needs for adjustment, understanding, personality development, and uniqueness."[35]

Both lack of adequate data and extreme difficulty in ascertaining and measuring power relations between husband and wife make it very hard to determine what the changes really are in this area of family life. Still, there is evidence that the power and influence of the wife have increased, and there is strong evidence that significant changes in power norms or authority expectations have occurred and are continuing today. The patriarchal authority expectations of the colonial family and the Victorian family have, at least in middle-class urban families, given way to equalitarian and democratic norms.[36] As indicated earlier, such changes have been uneven across social-class, racial, and ethnic lines in American history.

Adams argues that there have been only moderate changes in the extent of marital breakup or dissolution from colonial times to the present.[37] The first half of the twentieth century saw substantial increases in the divorce rate, following expansion of the legal grounds for divorce in the nineteenth century. Still, in spite of the increase in divorce, it is difficult to determine the extent of increase in all types of family dissolution since colonial days. A part of the

FIGURE 6-3 Divorce rates per 1000 married women, United States, 1950–1974. (*Source: Statistical Abstract of the United States, 1976, p. 68.*)

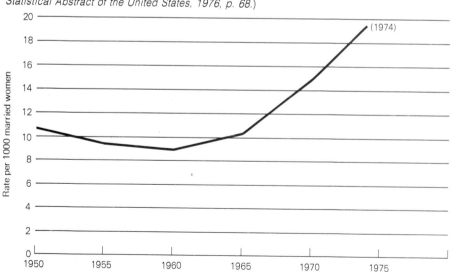

increased divorce rate represents a greater tendency today to legalize marital separation; and in colonial and nineteenth-century periods early death of a spouse frequently precluded possible subsequent desertion or divorce. This is not to say that the stricter marital norms and laws of these earlier periods were not instrumental in preventing marital breakups. A proper historical perspective, however, shows that ". . . while the divorce rate has risen, the rates of family breakup by death, desertion, and separation have declined. In short, change in the legal structures has very likely been greater than change in total rates of marital breakup."[38]

Significant changes have occurred in the status of women since colonial times, and in husband-wife roles and relationships. Over the last century women have gained legally, politically, educationally, and economically. Women can now vote and hold public office, and married women now have the legal right of property ownership. Females now receive the same public education as males, and the twentieth century has brought coeducation to colleges and universities. Economically, more women are becoming wholly or partially independent, with about 36 million women gainfully employed. These represent substantial gains, but do not mean that women have yet gained full equality with men. Employment discrimination against women still exists in hiring and in salaries and promotions.[39] Also, many employed wives (and their husbands) consider their employment as supplementary and not on a par with that of their husbands. Many mid-twentieth-century American husbands still have mixed feelings about their wives' employment.

The feminist movement and changes in the status of women have been accompanied by other changes in husband-wife roles and relationships. There has been a general change from traditional-patriarchal family role and authority patterns of colonial and Victorian times toward a more equalitarian, open, and free-choice orientation to the roles of husband-father and wife-mother in the mid-twentieth-century. Again, this change is most pronounced in emancipated middle-class families, where, lacking any established guides or norms, couples have to work out by trial and error their operating role definitions and division of labor and authority. This change heightens the importance of husband-wife communication and adjustment.

In attempting to compare marital or family adjustment today with that of the colonial period or the nineteenth century, it is well to take notice again of the idealized view we tend to have of the happy and well-adjusted "classical family of Western nostalgia." Early American families were not necessarily happy, close-knit groups. The colonial family was kept together by various traditional practices and legal codes to assure the performance of its many functions, whether or not its individual members were particularly happy or contented. The mid-twentieth-century family lacks many of these traditional cultural supports and social controls, and has fewer societal functions to perform, so its cohesion depends more upon the quality of the relationships among its members.[40] Thus, personal satisfaction, marital happiness, and adjustment become prime goals of the married couple. It may well be that marital adjustment, particularly individual happiness in marriage, is greater today than in colonial or Victorian America, since today's couples probably work at it harder, and more unhappy marriages are weeded out today than before.[41]

CHANGES IN THE RELATIONS BETWEEN THE FAMILY AND THE EXTERNAL WORLD   The twentieth-century American family is characterized by a high degree of residential mobility. Parsons contends that this is related to the tie between the nuclear family and the modern industrial economy, and to the relative independence of this family from its extended kin group.[42] It may be argued, as Adams does, that this high residential mobility today is largely a continuation of patterns found throughout American history. "The history of white colonization and colonial expansion on the American frontier is, in fact, the history of residential mobility."[43] More families may move today than earlier, and some middle-class and upper-class families probably move more frequently than their earlier counterparts, but overall, change in the extent of residential mobility over the periods under consideration has probably been less than heretofore thought.

One central area of family life in which great changes have occurred since colonial days is that of family functions. Many traditional family functions have been transferred over the years to external institutions and agencies. With industrialization, the economic productive function was transferred from the home to the mill, factory, or office. The family remains an economic consumer, but no longer produces goods and services for the market, with a few exceptions such as the diminishing independent farm families. Recreation, protective functions, and health care likewise have departed the family to a large extent, as have educational and religious functions.[44] These changes do not necessarily mean the family is dying out as a social institution. Other important functions remain, including reproduction, care and socialization of children, and fulfillment of the emotional and personal needs of family members. Further discussion of these changes is to be found in the chapters to follow.

Adams offers a succinct summary of family change in America since colonial times.

The most striking changes in family formation or pre-marital conditions since colonial days have been in courtship and sex codes, with an increasing link between romantic love and mate selection. The major change—in reality a complex of changes—in relations between the nuclear family and the larger society is in the expansion and parcelling out of certain traditional functions to other agencies and locations. By far the most numerous large-scale changes have occurred within the family itself. These have included an increase in the number of role options open to both sexes, with a concomitant multiplying of the number of necessary adjustments, and a loosening of divorce laws, making it easier to dissolve a given family unit.[45]

CHANGES IN THE CONTEMPORARY AMERICAN FAMILY

In Chapter 2 we presented some general approaches to family change, and so far in the present chapter we have considered American family changes of a broad historical nature. Now we will attempt to identify some of the current trends and changes which, while having their origins in earlier times, are most pronounced in the twentieth century.

Prominent in the literature on family change in contemporary America is the work of Ernest W. Burgess, Harvey Locke, and Mary Thomes. Their well-known book *The Family: From Tradition to Companionship* carries the theme that certain changes in family organization have accompanied changes in economic growth and organization in America.

A basic theme of this book is that the family has been in transition from a traditional family system, based on family members playing traditional roles, to a companionship family system, based on mutual affection, intimate communication, and mutual acceptance of division of labor and procedures of decision-making. The companionship form of the family is not to be conceived as having been realized but as emerging.[46]

The reader should be reminded that both the "traditional family" and the "companionship family" are ideal types constructed for purposes of comparing and measuring change in actual families, as was discussed earlier in Chapter 2. The *traditional family* system would be maintained by traditional norms and regulations and clearly defined duties and obligations for all family members, while the *companionship family* system is maintained by mutual affection, intimate communication, and mutual acceptance of jointly developed divisions of labor and decision-making patterns.

For many decades the pattern of change, according to Burgess and his associates, has been this:

The American family is moving toward the companionship family system, which may be described as follows: (1) affection is the basis for its existence; (2) husband and wife have mutual acceptance of procedures in decision-making; (3) major decisions are by consensus; and (4) common interests and activities coexist with mutual acceptance of the division of labor within the family and individuality of interests. In most families the control is still moderately patriarchal; in some it is more or less matriarchal; and only in a small proportion is it by consensus of husbands, wives, and children. The proportion that includes participation by children is extremely small.[47]

As an alternative to the concept "companionship family," Daniel Miller and Guy Swanson have proposed the term "colleague family." While agreeing in general with Burgess that women are becoming increasingly equal to men, Miller and Swanson point out that men and women still play many different and specialized roles.

The specialization on the job has entered the home, and the equal partners have been able to see that differences in talent, interest, and function, as long as they are complementary, do not threaten equality. . . . For this reason we call this type of family the "colleague" family. As specialists at work may find in each other skills they lack, but skills they equally need, and as they may defer to one another's judgement on the grounds of differing competence without feeling that they have personally lost in prestige, so husband and wife may now relate in this way.[48]

These writers feel that specialization is one of the distinctive characteristics of the modern bureaucratic order which have led to this new *colleague family*, by creating new conditions for relations in families. Husbands and wives have different or specialized family responsibilities, but such are based on rational decision and consensus.

A somewhat different view of family change in America has been offered by Bernard Farber, who argues that the contemporary American family has been changing in the direction of what he calls a *permanent availability model* or type of family, which is in contrast to the companionship model of Burgess in certain ways. Farber's model assumes that all adults (except those ruled out by the incest taboo), regardless of marital status, are permanently available as potential spouses for all other cross-sex adults. Persons already married remain potential spouses. "The family group takes the form of a voluntary association in which a person continues membership as long as his personal commitments to other family members exceed his commitments elsewhere."[49] This model is consistent with social trends which emphasize personal choice of marriage partner and personal satisfaction and welfare in marriage. Farber contends:

The evidence supports the application of the permanent-availability model to American society. The age span at which people get married is widening, the rate of remarriage is increasing, children are ceasing to be an impediment to divorce, there is a decline of pre-marital chastity and marital fidelity, homogamy in social characteristics is decreasing, there is a growing emphasis upon competence in interpersonal relations, women are growing more independent financially, and the emphasis on youthfulness . . . is increasing.[50]

SOCIAL SYSTEMS ANALYSIS OF FAMILY CHANGE

Using the social systems model developed by Charles P. Loomis, the following analysis focuses on trends and changes in selected elements and processes that make up the family system.[51] Family changes will be analyzed within the larger context of social change, utilizing the ideal types of Gemeinschaft-sacred society and Gesellschaft-secular society presented in Chapter 2.

ENDS OR OBJECTIVES OF THE FAMILY   The ends or objectives of the family are many and varied and relate to societal, community, or individual Individuals may have various objectives for their marriage, such as personal happiness, status improvement, or parenthood. When the husband and wife become parents and start rearing children, we may say that the family is simultaneously satisfying certain individual goals and contributing to the societal needs of replenishing the population and socializing the children to fit into their community and society.

SOME TRENDS AND CHANGES IN FAMILY ENDS OR OBJECTIVES   The trend in contemporary American marriage and family is toward an emphasis on individual needs and goals such as love, individual growth, and companionship, rather than on the more traditional goals of having and rearing many children. One of the results of this trend has been a reduction in family size in

FIGURE 6-4   Annual birthrates, United States, 1937–1976. (*Source: Current Population Reports, U.S. Government Printing Office, 1967 and 1976.*)

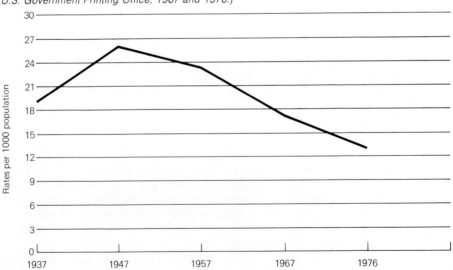

America. A family of two children or less has become a planned goal for large numbers of married couples. Artificial birth control methods are the main means being followed to attain this goal. Increasing concern with overpopulation, coupled with the belief that a family should have only as many children as it can amply provide for, has been a motivating factor in the emergence of the small-sized family goal. Middle-class families have led the way in this trend.

In recent decades there have been many other changes and some reordering of priorities in family goals. For example, the pursuit of upward social mobility and the emphasis on equalitarian values have led to the increased employment of wives and mothers outside the home.

SOME TRENDS AND CHANGES IN FAMILY BELIEF, KNOWLEDGE, AND SENTIMENT As American society becomes more Gesellschaftlike, more families are modifying their beliefs and sentiments in keeping with the secular and scientific trends. A long-term decline in familistic sentiments and beliefs has been noted. Sentiments of loyalty to and belief in obligations to one's family of orientation (parents and kinfolk) have declined in the twentieth century and are being replaced by sentiments and beliefs stressing the reciprocal conjugal obligations between husband and wife. Sentiments of love, happiness, and companionship in marriage have high priority, supported by beliefs that marriage and family life should bring satisfaction of individual needs and yield personal growth. The twentieth century has brought a change from the earlier belief that marriage is primarily a social obligation. The new view is that marriage is a primary means of pursuing individual happiness and that divorce is approved if the marriage does not bring the expected happiness.

Since World War II, and especially during the 1960s, there has emerged a set of beliefs and sentiments called the *new morality*. This viewpoint advocates that one judge all acts in terms of the degree to which such acts promote love between human beings.[52] The new morality supports a premarital sex code of "permissiveness with affection." Also related to the new morality is the wide dissemination of birth control knowledge and the easy availability of more reliable and simpler techniques such as "the pill." Additionally, in the late 1960s abortion was legalized, and information and advice on abortions became accessible to unmarried as well as married women. Thus young people are gaining greater freedom and greater control over sex and reproduction than ever before.

Since the 1960s, there has been a considerable increase in "living together" among young people of this persuasion. Studies by Michael Johnson (1969) and Eleanor Macklin (1972) of college couples living together without benefit of marriage indicate that this may be an alternative form of courtship or "premarriage" rather than a sign of the breakdown of the marriage

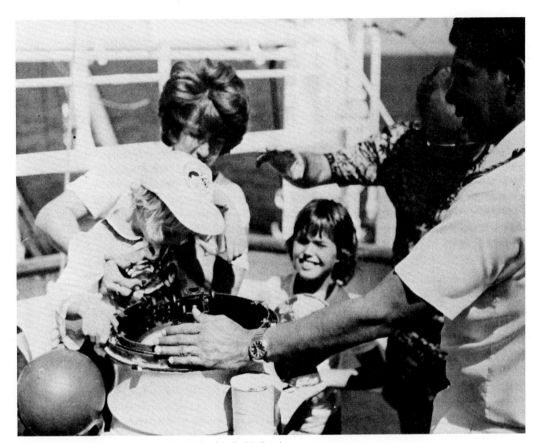

Contemporary family enjoying a boat trip. (*Julie Heifetz.*)

system.[53] Most couples contacted were highly committed to each other, and the likelihood of their marriage in the future was quite high.

What possible effect is the new morality having on premarital and extramarital sexual relations? As to premarital sex, there is evidence that the proportion of nonvirginal unmarried females has been about 50 percent since the 1920s, with some increase since the mid-1960s.[54] Reiss sees a possible rise to 65 or 70 percent of nonvirginal females at marriage before the end of the century. More young people today—women as well as men—are asserting the belief that one has the right to choose one's own sex code. With respect to extramarital sex, new types such as mate swapping (swinging), and mate sharing are being discussed and experimented with by a small minority of married people. However, Ira Reiss feels that old-fashioned adultery is still more prevalent, and will continue to increase somewhat.[55] Alfred Kinsey reported that by age forty, half of the husbands and a quarter of the wives had committed adultery.[56] Research on mate swapping is meager. Estimates are that between 1 and 10 percent of all couples have tried this.[57] We may expect a certain amount of this kind of equalitarian adultery in a society becoming more equalitarian and open in its beliefs and practices.

As to mate-sharing types of communes, reliable conclusions must await careful and more adequate research. Reiss suggests that those couples who believe in "segmental role-relations" are more suited to this (or to mate swapping) than are those whose beliefs and sentiments embrace the ideal, total, self-sharing type of marriage.[58] Reiss concludes:

In sum, if the increased openness on sex and on autonomy has any impact on adultery, I believe it will show itself very largely on increased adultery rates for those who are in process of getting a divorce and for those who are unsatisfied with their marriages and those with narrow self-involvement in their marriages. I do not believe there will be a noticeable impact on happy marriages with diffuse self-involvement.[59]

CHANGES IN FAMILY NORMS With the advent of changes in family beliefs, sentiments, and goals, certain parallel changes in family norms may be expected. For example, the beliefs that a couple should only have as many children as they can well provide for and that there is great danger to the world in overpopulation have led to a change in the family size ideal (and goal) from a large family to a small family. As a result, there has been emerging a set of family norms prescribing family size limitations by means of various birth control methods. These norms have not been uniform in all social classes, however. The middle and upper classes have been the strongest subscribers so far, with the working and lower classes somewhat behind.

Investigation of family planning in the United States shows that family limitation is almost universally approved and is widely practiced, and that education is the most important factor associated positively with differences in family planning.[60] Evidence suggests that the American population is rapidly approaching a point at which a common set of values about family size is emerging.[61] According to Ronald Freedman," . . . the traditionally high fertility of the farm population and of urban couples with low socioeconomic status is no longer supported—if it ever was—by a desire for large families. Lack of knowledge about effective means of preventing conception may always have been the most important reason for the extra children."[62]

TRENDS AND CHANGES IN FAMILY STATUS-ROLES With the long-term development of the urban-industrial secular society have come a number of important changes in marital and family status-roles. A conjugal emphasis has replaced the earlier consanguine emphasis, resulting in a relatively independent nuclear family where the husband-wife status-roles have priority.

Sentiments and norms of individualism, equalitarianism, and feminism—important elements of the secular trend—have brought about redefinitions of status-roles not only for husband and wife, but also for parent and child to some extent.

An important factor in the changing definitions of husband and wife status-roles in the twentieth century has been the increasing employment of married women outside the home. The 1970 United States census found 41 percent of American married women (with husbands present) in the labor force.[63] Of these women 58 percent had children under age 18, and 30 percent had children under age 6. Back in 1920 only 9 percent of American married women were so employed. Increases have been greatest since World War II.[64] From 1947 to 1962, three-fifths of the increase in the entire United States labor force was composed of women. Married women living with their husbands contributed the most to the trend, accounting for more than half the total female labor force.[65] Today, college-educated women are in the forefront of this trend. In 1964, 74 percent of American women who had completed five years or more of college were employed. Of married college-educated women living with their husbands, the figure was 63.4 percent.[66]

Some redivision of labor within the family was inevitable with this massive entry of wives and mothers into the labor force. This redivision involves changes in the status-role definitions of the husband and father as well as the wife and mother. An important aspect of the traditional male family status-role was that the male carried the full responsibility for the economic support of the family. This could now be modified as the wife's earnings took on increasing significance. Another aspect pertains to the traditional definition of "housework" as essentially women's work. In an investigation of working couples in Wisconsin in 1953, the author found that the employment of the wife led to some increased participation by the husband in routine household tasks.[67] At that time, husbands as well as wives were becoming increasingly emancipated from traditional conceptions of "man's place" and "woman's place" in the family. Many recent studies have corroborated these trends.[68] And these changes are now seen in farm families as well as in city families.[69]

Since children are influenced by the sex-role models their parents present, it is logical to expect more overlapping in domestic sex-role definitions and performances as the present generation of children grows up.[70] Some recent studies have also shown that where mothers work, sons as well as fathers share in the traditional household tasks.[71]

Today the trend toward sex equalitarianism and women's liberation is very apparent. The rights of women to work and to equal treatment at work are being advanced and protected by such laws as the Equal Pay Act of 1963 and Title IV of the Civil Rights Act of 1964 prohibiting discrimination in employment on the basis of race, color, religion, sex, or national origin.[72] It is doubtful, however, that complete equalitarianism in gender roles will occur soon. Even in families where the wife is employed full time, there is seldom an equal sharing by the husband in the housework.[73] A study of married couples by Robert Blood, Jr., and Robert Hamblin found that the husband's share of the housework, where the wife was not employed, was 15 percent, and this increased only to 25 percent where the wife was employed.[74] In his study of the equalitarian Israeli kibbutzim, Melford Spiro found that males were prone to avoid the laundry, kitchen, and day care activities.[75] Reiss feels that American husbands and fathers probably will not improve very drastically in their sharing of the various mother and wife roles, and that greater progress toward sex equality will come to American wives and mothers with the increase in collective upbringing facilities, i.e., in day care centers where mothers can bring their preschool children and leave them under proper care while the mothers are at work.[76] It also seems likely that these day care centers will be run mostly by women. This means that the children will still be under the care of women rather than men, and many women will merely be changing scenes, not roles.

What have such changes in status-roles meant for marital adjustment or marital satisfaction? The literature on marriage today reveals that there is a growing acceptance of job-holding wives on the part of men, and that probably the wife's employment is less a source of strain on the marriage than it was earlier.[77] In his study of Wisconsin working couples, the author found a high degree of marital happiness throughout the whole sample. Also, marital happiness was greater where the husband and wife had become partners in other areas of family life as well as in providing for the family. Also, marital happiness was greater where there was a close agreement between the husband and the wife as to the way the family roles should be performed.[78] A positive attitude of the husband toward his wife's employment appears to be a crucial factor in satisfactory marital adjustment for working couples.[79]

TRENDS AND CHANGES IN FAMILY POWER   Some changes in power distribution within American families, especially middle-class families, have accompanied changes in family status-roles. Accompanying the historical trend away from a sacred-type society toward a secular-type society, there has been a corresponding trend away from traditional-patriarchal family power toward democratic-equalitarian power. With the reorganization of family status-roles, American women have been gaining in power within the family. The author learned in his Wisconsin study of married working couples that they had become highly equalitarian in their power or authority patterns. In 84 percent of these families policies were determined and family decisions were made jointly by the husband and wife. Also, a striking feature was that for both husbands and wives there was a similarity between their highly equalitarian performances and their authority expectations.[80] More recent studies show a continuation of this trend toward an equalitarian distribution of power in American families, especially in middle-class families.[81]

These mid-twentieth-century equalitarian trends mean that family life in

America no longer exhibits clear-cut distinctions between the traditional instrumental power role of the father and the expressive role of the mother. Although the middle-class father remains the chief power figure symbolically, the actual power of the father is considerably less than that held by family authority figures earlier. Much of the father's power has been transferred to the mother. These trends are less pronounced in working-class and lower-class families, where the husband-father is still attempting to hold onto his traditional power.[82]

The democratization of family power has spread to the children too, allowing them to share to some extent the power formerly held exclusively by their parents. Again, class differences are apparent here also. Middle-class permissiveness supported by an ideological bent toward "children's liberation" has given middle-class children more freedom and power than is generally found as yet in families in other social classes.

TRENDS AND CHANGES IN FAMILY SOCIAL RANK AND SOCIAL MOBILITY
Different families in a community or society may be ranked differently, depending upon the extent or degree to which they possess or exhibit certain valued qualities or activities. Similarly ranked families are seen as constituting a social class, and the families in a given class pursue somewhat similar life-styles. When a family changes its rank, moving either to a higher or lower class position, we call this process *social mobility*. In a secular society such as America, stressing universalism, achievement, and a readiness to change, it is inevitable that there will be much social mobility, with many families in the process of moving either up or down on the social-class ladder.

Sentiments and goals of success through ambition, hard work, and "right living" are basic parts of the American heritage.[83] Horatio Alger heroes who personify the American dream are still being extolled in America. Although the opportunities for upward social mobility have never really been equal in the United States, and the extent of upward movement for any individual or family in one generation is more likely to be one rung rather than from bottom to top of the ladder in rags-to-riches fashion, still, upward social mobility rates have been high in many periods of American history.[84] Downward mobility occurs also, however, as individuals or families are unable to maintain their social rank, or otherwise fail in their efforts. In either upward or downward mobility, the family experiences a change in social rank, associates with new families, and normally must change its style of life and otherwise adjust to its new class position.

One of the principal means to upward mobility for the family is success in an occupation by one or more members of the family. This responsibility has traditionally been borne by the husband-father, but the wife-mother is now joining her husband more frequently in this effort, as noted above. Their combined occupational efforts may enable the family to "move up" faster and further than would be possible through the husband's efforts alone. The importance of success in occupational careers for the social ranking of families points out a very important systemic linkage between the family system and the economic productive system.[85]

TRENDS AND CHANGES IN FAMILY SANCTIONS   As changes take place in family sentiments, beliefs, norms, and status-roles, issues may arise as to what sanctions are appropriate or acceptable within the family. As society becomes less traditional and the old norms weaken, the modern parent is less often certain of exactly what constitutes desirable and undesirable behavior. Consequently, the parent may use punishment inconsistently, and children may become adept in helping the parent to feel guilty over punishment that neither is sure is justified. The modern secular society, too, offers many alternative ways of behaving in a seemingly simple situation. Questions arise as to what clothes to wear, how late the children should stay out, what activities are appropriate for certain ages, and the like.

Modern parents find themselves often in competition with youth peer groups in their efforts to direct and control their children. In a study of social life in ten high schools, James Coleman was impressed with the power of informal teenage society.[86] While these students did not necessarily ignore or reject the values of their parents, they frequently put the values and norms of the peer group first. As a result, the parents found themselves in constant competition with the teenage society, and they were never sure that their wishes would prevail with their children.

In his studies of parent-child relations in modern America. E. E. LeMasters finds that many American parents are having a difficult time with their teenagers. Part of the blame for the parental problems is attributed to the mass media and part to the pervasive youth society and its experimental subcultures.[87]

CHANGES AND TRENDS IN FAMILY FACILITIES   *Facilities* are the means by which a social system achieves its ends. Examples of family facilities are space-saving, time-saving, and labor-saving devices. The nuclear family's household and surrounding property cannot be bigger than the family can easily take care of; its facilities are thus often multipurpose and compact. Time- and labor-saving devices permit the efficient performance of household activities, a necessary arrangement for the small labor force represented in the modern nuclear family.

Not only are American families today ready and often eager to adopt new time- or labor-saving or space-saving facilities, they are also presented with a plethora of such devices and techniques to choose from by our ever-expanding technology. Innovations in housekeeping methods and materials, in transportation and communication not only affect the life-styles and role performances of family members, but also may have consequences for family integration or solidarity. Facilities which have freed family members from onerous duties may have a dual effect on family integration. These devices may have reduced the need for family teamwork in the production of goods and the rendering of services and thus have allowed family members still further to splinter their activities. On the other hand, these facilities may provide time which otherwise would not be free for families to be together in leisure.[88]

TRENDS AND CHANGES IN FAMILY COMMUNICATION Communication pervades all the elemental and processual aspects of family life. The secular trend in America has meant that family members have become more readily accessible to new ideas and are more amenable to changes based on rational or emotional persuasion. Such trends were generally felt earliest in the more educated middle-class families, but are now being felt in working-class families too. Family members of all ages and classes are peppered with information, opinions, cosmopolitan views, and sales pitches from the various media. Higher education for girls as well as boys, and increasingly now for working-class youth, means the introduction of advanced secular knowledge and ideas into family circles where parents and other older relatives may still be clinging to more traditional orientations and narrower views, as illustrated in the TV show "All in the Family." Although such generation gaps are not really new, they seem especially acute since mid-twentieth century. "Family planning" also is an area of family life that well illustrates the process of intimate family communication for the purpose of achieving a rationally determined goal, the restriction of family size. Rational planning of when and how many children to have probably is based on a composite of information and attitude, both of which are influenced by the efficiency of the communication process.[89] The specific knowledge of contraceptive methods is diffused widely among the better educated groups, as is training in positive attitudes concerning people's control over the universe—including the sizes of their own families.[90]

Within the larger society some groups are more aware than others of the social and economic climate in which they live. Those with superior communication facilities are likely, other things being equal, to be more aware than are the more isolated.

In the area of parent-child communication the well-known generation gap is especially pertinent. Kingsley Davis points out in his article "The Sociology of Parent-Youth Conflict" that there is a basic birth-cycle differential between parents and their children since each generation is born into a different period of social history.[91] This situation creates a problem for parent-child relations and communication, especially in times of rapid social change, such as we have witnessed in recent American history. American young people coming of age in the 1970s have to cope with social problems relating to the atomic age, space exploration, population explosion, and our involvement in many foreign wars, whereas their parents had to cope with problems arising from the introduction of the automobile, the airplane, the Depression, and World War II.

Also, in our increasingly complex modern life, traditional parental authority is often undermined by the secular emphasis on freedom, individualism, and change. A breakdown in parental control often accompanies a breakdown in communication between parents and their sons and daughters.[92]

TRENDS AND CHANGES IN FAMILY SYSTEMIC LINKAGE   *Systemic linkage* is the process whereby some element or elements of two or more systems, such as goals, norms, or status-roles, are articulated in a way that the two systems become joined or linked for certain purposes.[93] Two nuclear family systems become joined through the marriage of the son of one to the daughter of the other. Within the community, any given family system becomes linked with the school system when its sons and daughters become students in the school.

Historically, family life was more restricted and outside contacts more limited for rural traditional families than for urban, modern families. Most of the needs and interests of family members in traditional societies were met within the family system itself. This has changed drastically with the modern, secular emphasis on functional specificity, instrumental roles, and contractual relationships. As we have seen, linkages between the family system and the economic productive system are increasing as females join males in the labor force. Women and children as well as men in the family are increasing their contacts and memberships in a variety of educational, recreational, cultural, civic, health, and military groups, or in various other voluntary organizations.

The nature of the family's linkages will change as it moves through its life cycle. The linkage between the family system and the school system will logically be strong during the child-rearing stage of the family cycle but diminish thereafter. Even linkages which are not children-based, such as those between families and churches, are frequently strengthened and broadened during the period of the life cycle when the children are growing up.[94]

CHANGES IN FAMILY BOUNDARY MAINTENANCE   *Boundary maintenance* is the process whereby the identity of the social system is preserved and its characteristic interaction patterns are maintained.[95] Family systems often experience problems of boundary maintenance in the face of disruptive forces in the society and certain conditions related to social change. The trend from a rural, sacred society toward an urban, industrial, secular society has been conducive to some long-range changes in family systems bearing directly on family boundary maintenance. The familistic solidarity and member-dependence that were characteristic of the earlier rural, traditional family type have given way to the independence and mobility of the small, urban-oriented family type.[96] Urban nuclear families are less apt than traditional rural families to have sentimental attachment to land, to community, or even to their homes—if indeed they have such ownership at all. The family property-inheritance system is considerably weakened as a family boundary-maintenance device in such families.

In contemporary secular societies, the emphasis upon universalism and achievement has been accompanied by a trend away from familistic particu-larism and nepotism as a boundary-maintaining device. Also, in traditional-sacred societies family power arrangements were generally patriarchal and quite rigid. Changes in traditional family power alignments may weaken family boundary maintenance. For example, in the contemporary equalitarian American family the redistribution and diffusion of power make it more difficult for the husband-father—or any family member—to use authority as an effective means of holding family members together. Characteristics of the emerging equalitarian nuclear family include emphasis on personal needs and goals and the definition of marriage as a freely entered-upon interperson-al relationship which must be mutually satisfying to both marriage partners. Accordingly, freedom to choose one's mate has become a very strong norm in Gesellschaft-secular type societies. Most Americans, for example, have taken this "right" of free choice for granted for many decades. Not that American parents do not exert various kinds of influence upon their children's mate selection, but the idea that American parents should have the power to actually choose the mate for their son or daughter would probably strike most Americans as very un-American. An exception to this would be in upper-class families—the old aristocratic families—where the parents and other adult relatives may still exert considerable control over mate selection of sons and daughters, with family boundary maintenance as a definite goal.

Secular trends may affect family boundary maintenance in other ways. For example, there is some concern today that current rejection of middle-class beliefs, sentiments, and norms by many American youth may pose a threat to established marriage and family systems in American society. Rejection of traditional marriage and family roles and responsibilities has contributed to the rising number of broken marriages and of marriage and family dropouts and desertions. This rejection has also led to an increase in the number of couples living together without marriage and has been instrumental in the rise of variant life-styles. Some of the possible effects of such deviations and variations on marriage and family systems will be examined in Chapter 9.

CHANGES IN FAMILY SPACE OR TERRITORIALITY The secular trend has brought about greater freedom of choice of mates, more equality of the sexes, an emphasis on individual needs, and greater social and mental accessibili-ty. A consequence of such changes for the family has been a diminishing of many traditional endogamous marriage prescriptions. More young people are dating and marrying across social-class, religious, ethnic, and even racial lines. This "marrying out" trend makes a widening of the territory over which family linkages are made by marriage.

In older, sacred societies the types of family residence are generally either patrilocal or matrilocal.[97] These types fit with the patrilineal or matrilineal descent and inheritance systems, and the patriarchal or matriarchal authority patterns found in traditional family systems. Then as societies become more secular, the typical residence pattern becomes neolocal. This fits the independent, socially and spatially mobile nuclear family which is concerned with being independent from relatives and which has its eye on economic and social advancement. Such a family must be willing and able to move over a wide range of territory, its destinations generally determined by the occupational opportunities beckoning the husband-father or, more recently, the wife-mother. Business and professional opportunities may now take American families anywhere in the United States, or in fact, in the world. The world is now becoming the territory of such modern, mobile families.

Recent developments in population-space interrelations have brought about many changes in the residential patterns of American families. Urban industrial trends of the nineteenth and twentieth centuries brought mass migrations of families from rural areas to American cities. Their residential space in the city was generally small and crowded compared with farm and other rural residential space, especially for lower- and working-class families. Urban residential neighborhoods became differentiated and often segregated according to the social-class, ethnic, or racial identities of their families. Economic and social life chances as well as family life-styles were strongly affected by these urban residential and ecological conditions. Since World War II the movement of urban families out to suburban and commuter residential zones has been the predominant trend. This has tended to perpetuate social-class, ethnic, and racial residential separation, since the more affluent, white middle and upper classes are most able to move out to seek more living space for their families, while the poorer families, many identified with minority groups, tend to remain behind in the older, more crowded parts of the cities. In the 1970s there are signs that the suburban trend is slowing somewhat, due in part to higher transportation costs and to very high home construction prices. What this will do to urban families remains to be seen.

Summary and Conclusions

In the area of courtship and mate selection, or family formation, several major changes have taken place since colonial times. Although American youth have long had some voice in the selection of their mates, changes have occurred in the primacy given to romantic love as a criterion for mate selection and in the broadening of the field of eligibles across social-class, religious, ethnic, and now, somewhat more frequently, racial lines. Another major change is in the area of sex codes, with the pendulum swinging from premarital continence and strict marital fidelity norms of the Victorian era to premarital permissiveness and greater tolerance of extramarital relations and altogether a more open and positive view of sex in the twentieth century.

In the family's relationship to the community or larger society, perhaps the most significant change has been the loss or transfer of certain traditional family functions to various other institutions and agencies in the community. Following the industrial revolution, the family changed from an economic producing and consuming unit to an economic consuming unit only, as productivity moved from the home or family locus to mills, factories, and offices. Public education took most of the educational function away from the family. Recreation in large part moved from the home to specialized community activities and commercialized entertainment agencies. Religious worship and activities moved to church groups; protective functions became the responsibility of police, firemen, and other such specialized community agencies; health care became the responsibility of doctors, nurses, and pharmacists in community clinics and hospitals. Such changes do not mean that the family has now "run out" of important functions. The family still brings new members into the world, and then has the first and main responsibility for their nurturance and socialization during infancy and childhood.

Probably the most numerous and salient changes in the American family in recent years have taken place in the internal organization or patterning of the relationships among family members. The outstanding change here has been the trend toward greater equality in relations. This relates directly to the long-term trend toward emancipation of women, and to the more recent movement for emancipation of children. Such trends, however, have been felt unevenly up and down the social-class structure. Husband-wife equalitarianism is more advanced in middle-class families than in lower-class or working-class families. This is equally true for liberal or permissive norms in parent-child relations. While equal status for women has yet to be fully realized, predominant middle-class values and norms, supported by trends in law and the economy, are pushing for such equality in marriage and family relations. Internally, this equalitarian trend has been manifest in the emergence of the companionship family and the colleague family and in the increasing flexibility in the division of labor in the family. These changes have been accompanied by attitudes questioning the traditional family role definitions, and in some circles by an outright rejection of stereotyped views of men's work and women's work in the family. Both marital and family adjustment now focus on the welfare and personal satisfaction, happiness, and growth of all family members. Thus the emergence of interpersonal criteria of success in marriage and family relationships.

Notes

1   See Richard R. Clayton, *The Family, Marriage, and Social Change* (Lexington, Mass.: D. C. Heath and Co., 1975), chap. 4, "The Family and Social Change," for a good discussion of concepts and difficulties in studying social change.

2 Lewis Henry Morgan, *Ancient Society* (Chicago: Charles H. Kerr, 1877).

3 Carle C. Zimmerman, *Family and Civilization* (New York: Harper & Brothers, 1947).

4 William F. Ogburn and Meyer F. Nimkoff, *Technology and the Changing Family* (Boston: Houghton Mifflin Co., 1965); Talcott Parsons, "The Social Structure of the Family," in Ruth N. Anshen, ed., *The Family: Its Function and Destiny* (New York: Harper & Brothers, 1949), pp. 173–201.

5 Clayton, op. cit., p. 69.

6 Gerald R. Leslie, *The Family in Social Context* (New York: Oxford University Press, 1972), pp. 72–75.

7 Charles P. Loomis, *Social Systems* (Princeton, N.J.: D. Van Nostrand Co., 1960), pp. 57–63.

8 Clayton, op. cit., pp. 70–74. The present discussion follows Clayton on the difficulties of measuring social change.

9 Thomas F. Hoult, *Dictionary of Modern Sociology* (Totowa, N.J.: Littlefield, Adams & Co., 1969), pp. 271, 343.

10 Clayton, op. cit., p. 72.

11 Ibid., pp. 73–74.

12 Talcott Parsons, "The Normal American Family," in S. M. Farber et al., eds., *Man and Civilization: The Family's Search for Survival* (New York: McGraw-Hill, 1965), p. 52.

13 William J. Goode, *World Revolution and Family Patterns* (New York: Free Press, 1963), pp. 6–15.

14 Leslie, op. cit., pp. 256–257.

15 Goode, op. cit., p. 19.

16 John M. Edwards, ed., *The Family and Change* (New York: Alfred A. Knopf, 1969), p. 5.

17 Pitirim Sorokin, *The Crisis of Our Age* (New York: E. P. Dutton & Co., 1941), p. 187.

18 Ernest W. Burgess, "The Family in a Changing Society," *American Journal of Sociology*, 53 (May 1948), pp. 417–422.

19 Albert Rosenfeld, *The Second Genesis* (Englewood Cliffs, N.J.: Prentice-Hall, 1969).

20 David A. Schulz, *The Changing Family* (Englewood Cliffs, N.J.: Prentice-Hall, 1972), p. 9.

21 Goode, op. cit., p. 6.

22 Ibid.

23 Ibid., p. 7.

24 Bert N. Adams, *The American Family* (Chicago: Markham Publishing Co., 1971), pp. 64–76.

25 See Sydney Greenfield, "Industrialization and the Family in Sociological Theory," *American Journal of Sociology*, 67 (November 1961), pp. 312–322; Frank F. Furstenberg, "Industrialization and the American Family: A Look Backward," *American Sociological Review*, 31 (June 1966), pp. 326–337.

26 Goode, op. cit., p. 2.

27 Adams, op. cit., p. 65.

28 Ibid.

29 Ibid. See table 1, p. 66.
30 Ibid., pp. 66–67. This section follows Adams quite closely.
31 Ibid., p. 67.
32 Ibid., pp. 67–68.
33 Ibid., p. 68.
34 Neil J. Smelser, "The Social Challenge to Parental Authority," in Farber et al., op. cit., pp. 70–71.
35 Adams, op. cit., p. 69.
36 William G. Dyer and Dick Urban, "The Institutionalization of Equalitarian Family Norms," in John N. Edwards, op. cit., pp. 201–211.
37 Adams, op. cit., p. 70.
38 Ibid.
39 "Women: Still Number 2 But Trying Harder," *Time* (May 26, 1975), pp. 40–41.
40 Arlene Skolnick, *The Intimate Environment* (Boston: Little, Brown & Co., 1973), pp. 105–106.
41 Adams, op. cit., p. 72.
42 Parsons, op. cit., p. 35.
43 Adams, op. cit., p. 73.
44 See William F. Ogburn, "The Family and Its Functions," *Recent Social Trends* (New York: McGraw-Hill, 1933), chap. 13.
45 Adams, op. cit., p. 75.
46 Ernest W. Burgess, Harvey J. Locke, and Mary M. Thomes, *The Family* (New York: Van Nostrand Reinhold Co., 1971), p. 7.
47 Ibid., p. 9.
48 Daniel R. Miller and Guy E. Swanson, *The Changing American Parent* (New York: John Wiley & Sons, 1958), pp. 199–200.
49 Bernard Farber, *Family: Organization and Interaction* (San Francisco: Chandler Publishing Co., 1964), p. 110.
50 Ibid., p. 120.
51 See chap. 2, "Family and Kinship Systems," in Charles P. Loomis and Everett D. Dyer, *Social Systems: The Study of Sociology* (Cambridge, Mass.: Schenkman Publishing Co., 1975). The present discussion follows this chapter closely, using the PAS Model (Processually Articulated Structural Model), developed by Charles P. Loomis, to analyze trends and changes in family and kinship systems today. Also see chap. 1, "Social Systems: Their Elements, Processes, and Patterns," for a detailed discussion of this social systems PAS Model.
52 Ira L. Reiss, *The Family System in America* (New York: Holt, Rinehart and Winston, 1970), p. 407.
53 Michael P. Johnson, "Courtship and Commitment: A Study of Cohabitation on a University Campus," master's thesis, University of Iowa, Iowa City, 1969; Eleanor D. Macklin, "Heterosexual Cohabitation Among Unmarried College Students," *Family Coordinator*, 21 (October 1972), pp. 463–471.
54 Reiss, op. cit., p. 407.
55 Ibid., p. 408.
56 Alfred C. Kinsey, et al., *Sexual Behavior in the Human Male* (Philadelphia: W. B. Saunders Co., 1948), p. 587; Alfred C. Kinsey, et al., *Sexual Behavior in the Human Female* (Philadelphia: W. B. Saunders Co., 1953), p. 442.
57 Reiss, op. cit., p. 409.

58 Ibid.
59 Ibid.
60 Ronald Freedman, et al., *Family Planning, Sterility, and Population Growth* (New York: McGraw-Hill, 1959), pp. 7–8.
61 Ibid., p. 403.
62 Ibid.
63 *World Almanac, 1972*, table 332, p. 203.
64 U.S. Bureau of the Census, *Current Population Reports: Labor Force*, no. 662, 1955, p. 50.
65 Esther Patterson, "Working Women," *Daedalus*, 92 (Spring 1964).
66 Ruth E. Hartley, "American Core Culture: Changes and Continuities," in Georgene H. Seward and Robert C. Williamson, eds., *Sex Roles in Changing Society* (New York: Random House, 1970), p. 128.
67 Everett D. Dyer, "Some Trends in Two-Income Middle-Class Urban Families," *Southwestern Social Science Quarterly*, 39 (September 1958), p. 127.
68 Hartley, op. cit., p. 129.
69 Eugene Wilkening and Lakohnu Bharadwaj, "Dimension of Aspirations, Work Roles and Decision-making of Farm Husbands and Wives in Wisconsin," *Journal of Marriage and Family*, 29 (November 1967), pp. 703–711.
70 Ruth E. Hartley, "Children's Concepts of Male and Female Roles," *Merrill-Palmer Quarterly of Behavior and Development*, 6 (1959–1960), pp. 83–91.
71 Robert O. Blood, Jr., "Long Range Causes and Consequences of the Employment of Married Women," *Journal of Marriage and Family*, 28 (February 1965), pp. 43–47.
72 Reiss, op. cit., p. 403.
73 Dyer, op. cit., p. 127.
74 Robert O. Blood, Jr., and Robert Hamblin, "The Effects of the Wife's Employment on the Family Power Structure," *Social Forces*, 36 (May 1958), pp. 347–352.
75 Melford E. Spiro, *Kibbutz: Venture in Utopia* (Cambridge, Mass.: Harvard University Press, 1956).
76 Reiss, op. cit., p. 404.
77 Robert O. Blood, Jr., "The Effect of the Wife's Employment on the Husband-Wife Relationship," in Jerold Heiss, ed., *Family Roles and Interaction: An Anthology* (Chicago: Rand McNally & Co., 1968), pp. 255–269.
78 Everett D. Dyer, "Marital Happiness and the Two-Income Family," *Southwestern Social Science Quarterly*, 40 (Supplement, 1959), p. 102.
79 Harvey J. Locke and Muriel Mackeprang, "Marital Adjustment and the Employed Wife," *American Journal of Sociology*, 54 (May 1949), pp. 536–538.
80 Dyer, "Trends in Two-Income Middle-Class Urban Families," p. 129.
81 Robert O. Blood, Jr., and Donald M. Wolfe, *Husbands and Wives: The Dynamics of Married Living* (New York: Free Press of Glencoe, 1960). Robert O. Blood, Jr., *Marriage* (New York: Free Press, 1969). Bert N. Adams, *The American Family* (Chicago: Markham Publishing Co., 1971).
82 Harold D. Lasswell, *World Politics and Personal Insecurity*, p. 230; bound with *Political Power*, by Charles E. Merriam, and *Power and Conscience Beyond Conscience*, by T. V. Smith. Separately paged and carrying the overall title *A Study of Power* (Glencoe, Ill.: Free Press, 1950).
83 R. Richard Wohl, "The 'Rags to Riches Story': An Episode of Secular Idealism," in

Reinhard Bendix and Seymour M. Lipset, eds., *Class, Status, and Power* (Glencoe, Ill.: Free Press, 1953).

84 Seymour M. Lipset and Reinhard Bendix, *Social Mobility in Industrial Society* (Berkeley, Calif.: University of California Press, 1959).

85 Talcott Parsons, "The Social Structure of the Family," in Ruth Anshen, ed., *The Family: Its Function and Destiny* (New York: Harper & Brothers, 1959), pp. 241–274.

86 James S. Coleman, *The Adolescent Society* (New York: Free Press of Glencoe, 1961), chap. 1.

87 E. E. LeMasters, *Parents in Modern America: A Sociological Analysis* (Homewood, Ill.: Dorsey Press, 1970).

88 George C. Homans, *The Human Group* (New York: Harcourt, Brace and Co., 1950).

89 Freedman, et al., op. cit., p. 100.

90 Ibid., p. 101.

91 Kingsley Davis, "The Sociology of Parent-Youth Conflict," *American Sociological Review*, 5 (August 1940), pp. 523–535.

92 Clifford Kirkpatrick, *The Family as Process and Institution* (New York: Ronald Press, 1963), p. 266.

93 Loomis, op. cit., p. 32.

94 J. B. Lansing and Leslie Kish, "Family Life Cycle as an Independent Variable," *American Sociological Review*, 22 (October 1957), p. 512ff.

95 Loomis, op. cit., p. 31.

96 Burgess, Locke, and Thomes, op. cit.

97 George Peter Murdock, "Family Stability in Non-European Cultures," *Annals of the Academy of Political and Social Science* (November 1950), p. 197.

SELECTED READING

One of the main purposes of the present chapter is to establish the social context for family change in America. We have identified and reviewed briefly various social, economic, demographic, and ideological factors which have influenced family change in American society. The present reading continues in this same vein, showing in greater detail how American families are continuously adapting and adjusting to powerful forces and environmental conditions that are themselves in process of change and development.

Professor Yinger is concerned with identifying some of the principal social forces and conditions in our mobile, urban society that are influencing family change. Students of family life too often are inclined to lament most family change, which is unfortunate, Yinger feels, because this attitude impedes their understanding of what actually is transpiring. Family practitioners as well as family theorists need better knowledge of the ways in which family patterns are related to the larger social structure, its institutions, and the directions of change therein.

The family, Yinger emphasizes, is a creature of its social environment. Thus, the family in America must be studied within its total social context, if progress is to be made toward amelioration of family problems and the rebuilding of families able to cope with a changing society.

THE CHANGING FAMILY IN A CHANGING SOCIETY*

J. Milton Yinger

This presentation is primarily concerned with exploration of the ways in which family patterns are modified by the social setting in which they are found. By considering some of the forces affecting the whole kinship system, we may be able to formulate a helpful interpretation of the place of the family in a mobile, urban society.

Changes in family patterns are not necessarily either happy or unhappy facts. Among students of the family there is a strong tendency to lament most changes, sometimes with the implication that the family seems to be dying out altogether. We need to draw a distinction between "the family" and particular family systems. When a student of government traces the changes in the forms through which political power is expressed, he does not contend that government is disappearing. Economic patterns can change, through many stages, from subsistence operations in isolated villages to complex interdependent processes binding together several nations. We may applaud or lament the facts, but we are not likely to say that economic institutions are disappearing. When we study the family or religion, however, we are more likely to equate change with deterioration or even disappearance. We are more likely to be concerned with form than with function. This attitude is unfortunate, in my judgment, because it impedes the understanding of what is actually happening.

Students of the family have contributed to the confusion, both because they have allowed their own values to intrude into their interpretations, and because they have done little to bring family studies into the framework of systematic theories. Only very recently has this situation begun to change. In the last several years, the primarily descriptive and practical approach to family studies has been supplemented to some degree by a number of attempts to relate family patterns to social structure. Some of the ablest theorists (Parsons, Davis, Murdock, and Goode, for example) are involved in this effort.

It would be a mistake to think of this development as unrelated to the activities of a family service agency. Firm scientific knowledge about the ways in which a family system affects and is affected by the society of which it is a part can greatly strengthen the work of the clinician, especially in his

*Reprinted from *Social Casework*, 40 (October 1959), pp. 419–428, by permission of *Family Service Association of America* and J. Milton Yinger.

long-range planning. Knowledge of culture and subculture, of role definitions and role conflicts, of socialization and the forces that impede it can be of great value to the practitioner. A recent comparative study, for example, demonstrates that as the woman's contribution to subsistence goes up, the economic aspects of marriage change—from a dowry system, to minor gift exchange, to bride-price.[1] This fact may seem to be far removed from any problem likely to be faced by a family counselor. But who can doubt that the dramatic change in the place of women in the economics of the family in the last twenty-five years has produced some new forces of great significance for family stability? Perhaps what we need is more basic research to identify the underlying principles involved.

Influence of Social Institutions

The central proposition of contemporary family theory is scarcely new or startling. It is that the family cannot be understood as an isolated phenomenon. It must be seen in the context of the economic and political institutions, the religious influences, the population facts of the society of which it is a part. It is not by chance that a static agricultural society will emphasize the extended family, will often permit or encourage plural marriage, and will give to parents the power to make choices of partners for their children. Such elements as these fit into a stable social structure, just as emphasis on the conjugal family, romantic love, and separate households is likely to characterize urban, mobile societies. Powerful forces create the kind of family system to be found in a particular setting. If the identity of these forces can be discovered, a family agency can work to maintain or secure the desirable elements. It seems likely, for example, that a still further shrinking of the importance of the extended family is inevitable in the United States. The nuclear family maintains or even increases its significance, but other aspects of the kinship system become weaker. "This means that the family has become a more specialized agency than before, probably more specialized than it has been in any previously known society."[2]

This shift does not make the family any less important. Indeed, its central functions remain. Granted the long period of helplessness of the human infant, the fact that man is a "culture-bearing animal" and requires, therefore, a long period of training; granted the need for a process for placing individuals in their various positions in society—to name only a few of the functions of the family—we can see its fundamental place in all societies. Revolutionary movements sometimes try to destroy the family in order to break the continuity of generations that ties a population to its past traditions. But before long every such movement—in the Soviet Union for example—begins to re-emphasize the importance of the family. On the basis of the evidence of the

1920's it seemed wholly unlikely that by 1940 leaders of Russia would be declaring that the family is the foundation of the state; but that is what happened. (Neither family nor state withered away.)

To stress the vitality of the family is not to contend that there are no serious strains. In a society that is changing as rapidly as is our own, almost every aspect of family life is subject to severe disturbance. We can see very clearly the way in which a family system is affected by its social setting if we look at the various levels of interaction in a family and note the ways in which they are changing. In a sense, the urban industrial revolution through which the United States has been passing for the last century has been breaking up established family structures, unwittingly and slowly, just as other kinds of revolutions do in a more explicit fashion. Culturally established attitudes toward the extended circle of kinfolk, toward the proper roles of men and women, and toward the training of children are being drastically revised. It will doubtless be two or three more generations before our society evolves a family pattern that fits into a mobile, urban, democratic situation. This type of family pattern, after all, is a major social invention—and like most complicated inventions, the early models are pretty crude, and sometimes don't work at all.

Role Expectations

Stable societies train most of their members to accept a particular role definition of what a good husband and a good wife are supposed to be. They also train each person to expect and want the characteristics in the other person which the other has been socialized to exhibit. There is little role ambiguity, either within an individual or between individuals. That this is often not the case in the United States, any member of the staff of a family agency can quickly testify. Our cultural heroes associated with romance are almost all glamorous, handsome, rich, and poised. If this has not become the established cultural definition of the good mate, at least such an image has mingled with older notions of domesticity. Most American men may feel most at ease with "the girl next door," but they have been half-trained to expect a little of the Marguerite Higgins career pattern, with a dash of Brigitte Bardot. Not only is this a difficult combination to find, but it is not at all clear that many men would be really ready to accept it as the appropriate role for their wives if they should find it. Moreover, the girls themselves are taught different role patterns that are at least partially mutually exclusive. To say that many women are taught two roles—one involving a career and the other the older wife-and-mother image—is an oversimplification, but it points to the ambiguity in cultural training. There is probably nothing inevitably contradictory about these different patterns, but our society has only partially invented the ways of institutionalizing their blending into a more complicated but unified single role. Until this blending is accomplished, both men and women will feel the strain.

In an interesting study, Mirra Komarovsky reports the feelings of role ambiguity among 153 young women whom she interviewed. Almost half of them, under the constraints of the older role conception, had "played dumb" on dates, concealed some honor, or pretended ignorance on some subject, playing down some skill "in obedience to the unwritten law that men must possess these skills to a superior degree. At the same time, in other areas of life, social pressures were being exerted upon these women to 'play to win,' to compete to the utmost of their abilities. . . ."[3]

The difficulties associated with role ambiguity in our society are increased by the fact that, in mobile society, young men and women with different role expectations are more likely now than formerly to meet, to court, and to marry. A romantic ideal that holds that love alone counts makes it a little bit indecent to worry about such things as common values, interests, and role definitions; love should override any such minor separating facts. This is not to imply that romantic love is an American invention. William Goode has shown recently that it is found in a very large number of societies, if not in all, but it is much more hedged about by social controls in some than in others. In a society in which marriage has most of the elements of a governmental treaty and an economic contract between large family groups, one is not likely to find anything quite so capricious as romance determining who shall be marriage partners. By such various devices as child marriage, specific definition of potential mates in terms of their group membership, enforced physical separation of adolescents, or strong chaperonage, various societies keep romantic love at a minimum as the determining fact in mate selection.[4] Only in a society where isolated married couples, relatively unrelated to wider circles of kinfolk, are the primary family structure, can romantic love be permitted to operate as freely as it does in the United States. And even here it runs into the stubborn fact that successful marriage requires many shared values and role expectations, that love cannot conquer everything. Too often one of the persons concerned has discovered that the little plan to reform and remake the partner, once he has been caught, proves to be impossible— partly because the partner probably started out with the same hope of doing the reforming. It is better to get a good match to start with.

And even a good match is not without problems, for we demand so much more of a marriage than is true in many societies. As Kurt Lewin pointed out, a husband wants his wife to be—at the same time—sweetheart, comrade, housewife, mother, manager of his income, perhaps co-supporter of the family, representative to the community, and so forth. A wife expects her husband to be sweetheart, comrade, support of the family, father, caretaker of the house, serious but carefree, a good provider but romantically reckless.

Most of us are not so versatile. Moreover, the specialization of urban life tends to create differences in values and needs between husband and wife. In a rural society, marriage partners are influenced by more of the same forces, they often work side by side, they change together. In the city, a large share of the work life and even of the recreation of husband and wife is likely to involve the partner scarcely at all. The man, because of wider contacts and greater mobility, is likely to change more; the wife, with a more restricted range of activity, retains more of her earlier perspectives and values. As *Fortune* magazine once put it, she has stayed home literally and figuratively. A couple that was well mated at the beginning of marriage may be faced with important differences in desire and outlook on life after ten or fifteen years. Even if there is no long-run drifting apart, the differences in schedule and routine create different needs, let us say at the end of the day. The wife is ready for some adult contacts and a little variety; she wants to go out. The husband has *been* out. Our contemporary family patterns have only partially begun to deal with the need for "mutual mobility" of husband and wife through the years and mutual interests and schedules through the days.

Child-Training Methods

The aspect of family life that has been most intensively studied is doubtless the relations between parents and children. Here is a problem on which the psychologist and psychiatrist have a great deal to offer, but a sociological point of view may also be of some value. Child-training methods, to an important degree, are cultural facts; but they vary among classes and other groups, and they change through time—in our society with quite amazing speed. In stable societies, there is no question about how one should respond to his children. The rules are in the folkways and they have been largely internalized through the slow process of learning. But in our time, parent-child relations have become problematic. A young mother cannot turn to her mother for guidance, for they probably live a thousand miles apart—or some equivalent distance in cultural training and inclination. The federal Children's Bureau or the redoubtable Dr. Spock takes over as a grandmother substitute.

Having become self-conscious about our child-training methods, we have also become uncertain and at least slightly anxious. How many of us have felt dismay at the practices we used with our first or second child, in the name of "scientific management," only to discover that the authorities on whom we depended had reversed themselves a little later. Fortunately, children are resilient and survive most of our efforts to make them civilized. What we are witnessing is the development of child-training methods appropriate to the roles and experiences of an urban, changing, democratic society. The pendulum swings are testimony to the difficulty of working out new methods. The strains and conflicts are sometimes severe, but failure to redefine roles and methods of training in a society that has experienced so much change would impose even more severe strains.

In their recent study, Daniel Miller and Guy Swanson have described the child-training methods of earlier days and then studied, by careful interviews with 582 Detroit-area mothers, the range of methods today.[5] The observation that stands out is that parents, for the most part unaware of the choices they are making, treat their children in such a way as to try to prepare them for the kind of adult existence they are likely to face. In sociological terms, child-training methods are part of a complex social system; they both reflect and support economic, political, religious, and stratification facts. If important aspects of the system change, and there are not significant adjustments in the ways in which we socialize our children, the family can be the sources of serious mal-preparation.

It can well be argued, for example, that changes in the economy which have taken the father away from the home for the greater part of the day have left many boys without adequate adult male models. We tend to compound the difficulty by having boys taught primarily by women teachers in the early years. There are many subtle implications to this which we cannot explore here, but it seems reasonable to suppose that some of the difficulties of boys and male adolescents are associated with this shift in patterns of interaction. The resulting behavior seems sometimes to be the essence of anarchy; or it may be an effort on the part of boys who are uncertain of their own manhood—for they have not been helped to learn what it is to be a man—to overcome their own inner doubts. The problem is not made easier by the fact that girls grow up a year or two sooner, placing their agemates among the boys in inferior positions. The over-compensation that often results is not a very graceful response, but its sources in the social structure are not difficult to find.

In comparison of the advice by the authors of *Infant Care* (issued by the Children's Bureau) in the 1914 edition with that given in 1942 and 1945, Martha Wolfenstein shows the extent to which new methods redefine the parental role. It is almost as if we were seeking to sweep away any vestiges of the personalities that resulted from the earlier methods in order to develop people adjusted to an "other-directed" world, ready to take their places as "organization men," skilled at the soft sell. The swing of the pendulum was doubtless much wider in the books of advice than it was in practice, but there is little doubt that in the course of a generation, significant changes occurred. In 1914, the parent was told that the child is endowed with strong and dangerous impulses. The child rebels fiercely if blocked but, since the impulses may easily grow beyond control and may wreck the child for life, he must be blocked. Mechanical restraints to prevent him from exploring his body or sucking his thumb were described. By the 1940's these fierce pleasures became unimportant incidents to be treated casually.[6]

Should a baby be picked up when he cries? Only if he has "real" needs the early authorities agreed—if he is ill or hungry or has the proverbial pin sticking in him—otherwise let him cry. John Watson set the tone for much of this. In 1914, he wrote:

There is a sensible way of treating children. Treat them as though they were young adults. Dress them, bathe them with care and circumspection. Let your behavior always be objective and kindly firm. Never hug and kiss them, never let them sit in your lap. If you must, kiss them once on the forehead when they say good night. Shake hands with them in the morning. Give them a pat on the head if they have made an extraordinarily good job of a difficult task. . . .

If you expected a dog to grow up and be useful as a watch dog, a bird dog, a fox hound, useful for anything except a lap dog, you wouldn't dare treat it the way you treat your child. . . . [7]

Thirty years later, however, the advice was quite different: babies need lots of attention; this is just as important as food and the absence of pain; the need is just as real. Play with your child; enjoy him; teach him the pleasures of human association.

When Vincent studied the methods of infant discipline recommended by three women's magazines, he found amazing shifts from one period to another. In 1890, 100 per cent of the articles recommended flexible scheduling. In the next thirty years this rule began to be supplanted by the advice that schedules should be fixed, that the child should be allowed to cry it out if he demanded attention when he was "not supposed to." By 1920, 100 per cent of all the articles took this position. But soon that advice began to be supplanted so that, by 1948, 100 per cent of all the articles recommended self-regulated schedules for the child. [8]

I doubt very much that such diversity of advice is best explained as a series of fads or the caprices of specialists who have built their ideas on too little evidence. What we see are the agents of a society struggling to rework the child-training methods they have received, in the face of overwhelming changes in the kinds of experience that individuals face. The kind of training that might equip one to deal effectively with life on a frontier—the creation, perhaps, of a tough self-sufficiency and individualism—might be a real handicap in a society of enormous bureaucracies, where one must feel at home with strangers, able to work with the team and to sell himself. I am not suggesting that millions of parents have developed this insight into an articulate philosophy. The simple fact is that in their own experience they have found that certain tendencies helped them to respond to situations they met; other tendencies made life awkward. Gradually this insight is woven into the patterns of interaction between parents and children.

Parent-Child Relationships

It is significant that Miller and Swanson found important differences between what they called individuated and entrepreneurial parents and the welfare-bureaucratic parents. By these terms they are drawing a distinction between those who earn their living in jobs that are "sharply affected by the risks and vicissitudes of the market place," and those who work in large, bureaucratic structures within which they have specialized tasks but no major risk-taking decisions to make. They described the transition from a society in which a large proportion of workers were independent farmers, craftsmen, or businessmen, to one in which the great majority of workers—from unskilled to professional—are part of large organizations over which they have little control. In the new situation, the need is not so much for boldness as for togetherness.

For students of the family the most interesting aspect of the Miller and Swanson book is the effort to see if this shift has affected parent-child relationships. On the basis of a wealth of material, the authors demonstrate some interesting trends that cut across class lines and religious lines (although these also affect family interaction of course). ". . . the parental practices that we believe are becoming conspicuous since 1940 look as if they were peculiarly in harmony with the values and ideas—with the way of life—of a new middle-class person whose numbers are rapidly increasing."[9]

An earlier emphasis on self-denial, rugged independence, and the postponement of satisfactions is fading most rapidly in those families, whatever their class or religion, who are part of the large bureaucratic structures so prevalent in our cities. Although Miller and Swanson do not use Riesman's[10] terms, they present good evidence to support the idea that the prevailing advice (if not practice) of forty years ago was the kind likely to produce an inner-directed person, one who could hold his own in "the jungle," as Upton Sinclair called the city. Both knowingly and unwittingly parents tended to train their children for life in a sea of strangers, to make them able to postpone, to save, to plan, to look after themselves without much dependence on the groups to which they belonged.

In recent years, however, more and more parents have begun to experience the need for close co-operation in large organizations. Many have moved away from the rapidly changing areas of cities to the less anonymous suburbs. They have felt the shift from an emphasis on production to a stress on consumption of goods, as the economy lifted large numbers above the subsistence level. Not surprisingly, the advice and, at least in some measure, the practice of parents have shifted. They have become more permissive. Parents are more likely today to be unhappy over signs that their children do not fit into the group than over signs of lack of individual accomplishment.

Everywhere we hear the lament that schools have deteriorated in the last quarter of a century. In my judgment, the changes that have occurred are a manifestation of the kind of preparation for life that children experience on every hand. Every man is a salesman in our society, whether he be a business man, a minister, or a politician. If a choice has to be made between a capacity for smooth human relationships and an excellence that might be accompanied by a few "knobby" characteristics that cut one off from his fellows, better far, say most of the voices of our society, to choose the former.

I am not at all certain that the details of this shift from individualism to togetherness are correctly described—nor even that in the last analysis the thesis defended by Riesman, by Miller and Swanson, and others is correct. I do believe, however, that recent studies make clear how thoroughly a family system is embedded in the whole society, how it responds to changes therein and can be understood only in its total social context.

There is no better way to describe how deeply the experiences of the child within the family shape his adult tendencies and values than to make some comparative analyses. It is not possible, however, to do so within the limits of this presentation. I should like merely to mention a comparative approach made in an interesting study by Martha Wolfenstein, "French Parents Take Their Children to the Park." Although we shall have to leave unanswered the question of the representative quality of her observations, they seem to harmonize well with other studies of France. Wolfenstein notes how the mother or nurse trains the child to feelings of privacy, self-sufficiency, restraint. While the American child is being taught to share and to play in groups of children his own age, the French child is kept within the family circle, playing only with his own toys, and avoiding contact, pleasant or aggressive, with the children around him. There are arguments, of course, but they are primarily verbal, restrained from developing into fights by the stock parental injunction, "Disputez, mais ne vous battez pas." There is a seriousness about childhood in France that contrasts sharply with the widely held idea in America that childhood is primarily a time for fun. Our children will grow up soon enough, many American parents feel—time enough then for them to take on serious obligations. But many French parents make serious business even of the play that their children carry on. It is not enough to ride the carrousel because it is fun. The sign in the Luxembourg Gardens proclaims: "Chevaux Hygieniques. Jeu gymnastique pour les enfants developpant la force et la souplesse."[11]

What we see in this description is a somewhat extreme form of what Miller and Swanson called entrepreneurial family training. Undoubtedly there are wide variations in France. Perhaps some one of us can get a foundation grant to sit in the parks of Paris to see if more permissive child-training methods are developing, and if so, among whom. It would be important to discover whether such shifts have affected the famed ability of French adults to enjoy life. This ability, although probably exaggerated by the American's stereotype of the Frenchman, can scarcely be doubted. It stems from a well-disciplined childhood that both taught the restraints necessary to the achievement of many satisfactions and created a sense that one has earned the right to enjoy life as an adult without feelings of guilt because one is not working hard enough or is indulging himself too much. The stern training that characterized, and still characterizes, many American families did not seem to produce this same result. In this difference we see again how a family system is intricately tied to the whole society.

Sibling Interaction

A sociological point of view can also contribute something to the understanding of the interaction among the children within a family. The position, "eldest child," for example, may have some aspects that are shared everywhere. Much more clearly, however, it is a position within a particular society, with specified role requirements and privileges, and with certain kinds of personality consequences for those who hold that position. It is one thing to be the eldest child in a society which emphasizes primogeniture, or in the context of an extended family system where there are, so to speak, many fathers and mothers. It is something else in a small, urban, democratic family which draws many of its traditions from an extended family pattern, but places its members in new relationships.

The result, until new role definitions can be worked out, is often a great deal of strain, particularly for the eldest child. Our present family structures are ill-equipped to help him struggle with the jealousy that almost inevitably hits him when a younger brother or sister arrives. Our democratic traditions even lead us to deny that it exists or to declare that it is the result of individual wilfulness, deserving only censure. In fact, however, our small, child-centered families seem almost designed to create a problem of jealousy. The first child is not only much loved but also the only loved. Then along comes a noisy competitor who manages to command a great deal of mother's time and even to be rewarded by attention for doing the very things that he, the older child, is now being punished for. If the latter wakes in the middle of the night and cries, his mother may well shout to him to go back to sleep; if baby wakes, mother gets up and soothes him. If the older child dirties himself he may well be sharply reprimanded or punished; but baby is patiently cleaned and cooed over. It's enough to make a body angry. To a two- or three-year-old, the whole affair is a basic injustice, and he is scarcely equipped to respond to it philosophically. He opposes the newcomer directly or indirectly, frequently with the result that he is punished for hurting baby—which only confirms his suspicions that this strange child that his mother has brought home is the cause of all his troubles. After a little while he gives up hope that the competitor is a temporary visitor, and turns to other strategies to win reassurance. He demands things selfishly, seeking for a sign that he is still loved; he is "bad," by mother's definitions, in order to test her; he regresses, hoping that by acting like a baby he can win the same attention.

Whether this is a small problem, easily smoothed over after a few years, or a basic fact in the personality formation of the individuals involved depends on the warmth and expressiveness of the parents, the presence of other adults, the comparative talents of the children, and many other factors—but there seem to be few situations in our small urban families where jealousy does not arise to some extent. Most first children experience a struggle for several years during which time they are likely to exhibit selfishness, antagonism to other children, and failure to use their full capacities. These should not be seen as fixed traits, but as tendencies, which become more or less inflexible depending upon how the situation is handled within the family and community. In fact, the tendencies vary day by day, even hour by hour, as every parent knows who has felt the peace of having only one child in the house while the others are visiting friends. Nor are the tendencies necessarily fixed at a four- or an eight-year-old level. The unexpressed sense of injustice may be a factor in the later achievements of the eldest, who often demonstrates a capacity for responsible work and for understanding.

There are, of course, many other aspects of sibling interaction. By this brief reference to the jealousy problem I have been trying only to illustrate how changes in the family structure (in this case, a decrease in the importance of the extended family and a reduction in size of the immediate family) create new kinds of influences within the group. By being aware of such developments, a society may be better prepared to devise forms of interaction to deal with them.

The Lack of Normal Family Patterns

To the student of social structure, some of the most interesting aspects of family life are related, not to the kind of redefinition of roles that we have been discussing, but to the appearance of situations where a viable family system is almost lacking. In such a setting we see all too clearly the significance of the family for personality formation, for socialization—in short as an agent for the creation of adults able to live in the society around them and able to achieve personal satisfactions. We are well aware of the extent to which family inadequacy is related to personality disorder, to prejudice, and to delinquency. The need for repression and projection that looms so large among the mentally disturbed can often be traced to a neglectful and cruel home, a setting in which self-acceptance is difficult to achieve. The most intense prejudices are frequently the displaced hostility generated in a frustrating family situation. In commenting on the life histories of prejudiced adults, Selma Hirsh writes:

It is startling to see how often the anger expressed by the prejudiced adult turned out to be nearly as old as he was himself. Usually he had acquired it in the first years of his life when he was forced to learn the most difficult lessons life has to teach long before he could understand them. He had learned too early, for example, that instincts are not always for expression, that love is not necessarily reciprocal, that promises are not always fulfilled, nor punishments always just. Usually these were the first things he had learned, and since he had no other reassuring experiences to cushion him against the shock of their discovery, they had served for him as a lasting introduction to the ways of the world.[12]

The same constellation of ego-alienating and hostility-creating conditions may, of course, lead to delinquency. We speak more cautiously about the cases of delinquency than we did a few years ago. The influence of broken homes, of class status of the family, of neighborhood patterns is not so simple as it once seemed. The value of a home in reducing delinquency is exaggerated by the official statistics, since two children committing the same violation, one with a home, the other without, are often given different sentences. One may be sent home, the other given a police record. In his recent study, Nye found somewhat more delinquency from broken than from non-broken homes, but he wisely notes the need for more careful study of families that have been internally split without a formal break. He found a small but non-significant relationship between the employment of the mother and child delinquency.[13] Such a finding only accents the need for more study to isolate the conditions under which the changing patterns of women working affect family structure.

Although one must speak with caution, because of the intricate network of forces relating an individual to a family and a family to a community, few of us would doubt that many of the trends in our cities today are creating areas in which normal family patterns are very rare. The population of the large cities has been expanding by about 400,000 per year for the last several years, while housing for about 250,000 per year has been built. Since approximately that same amount of housing has been removed, our cities have been getting vastly more crowded. The 400,000 have to be absorbed somehow into a constant amount of housing.[14] The results are well known to all of us: division of houses into apartments, break-up of apartments into one-room units, absorption of additional families into already overcrowded quarters. As Morton Grodzins asks: "How does a mother keep her teen-age son off the streets if an entire family must eat, sleep and live in a single room? What utility can be found in sobriety among a society of drinkers and a block of taverns?"[15] We are talking about the richest nation in the world in the richest period of its history. This may be "the affluent society," but we are not even holding our own in creating a physical setting within which stable family life is possible.

Even the urban renewal programs are sometimes destructive of the lines of communication, the social groups, the political organizations of an area. The result is *anomie*—normlessness, except as the residents improvise a culture of their own. This often takes the form of a gang, whose style of life has recently been described as sub-cultural, but which might more appropriately be thought of as contra-cultural—as a contrast conception by means of which confused and relatively powerless persons try to create a set of values that will place them on top, at the same time that it makes their lowly status unimportant in terms of dominant values.

Conclusion

On many aspects of family analysis there are large areas of disagreement. On this basic fact, however, I imagine that all will agree: the family is, to a vital degree, the creature of its environment. Whenever value confusion, physical blight, and inadequate institutions are the rule, the family will be weak. Whenever social change imposes new requirements and new potentialities, but when revised role-definitions have not yet been worked out, intra-family tensions will mount. A family agency, which has an enormous job simply to work with some of the results of these forces, may nevertheless gain by stepping back from the job occasionally to see the family as part of the whole society.

We in the United States have not yet completed the shift from life in small, face-to-face, stable communities to life in the city. We are confronted with many cultural lags, not least of all in family matters. It is to such groups as family service agencies that we must look for the leadership and skill necessary not only for the amelioration of problems but also for the imaginative rebuilding of a family equipped for a changing society. If the short-run aim is to help families manage and reduce the tensions they carry, the long-run aim must be to prevent tensions from reaching an unmanageable level. To this end we must study the family in its total social context.

References

1 Dwight Heath, "Sexual Division of Labor and Cross-Cultural Research," *Social Forces*, Vol. 38, No. 1 (1958), pp. 77–79.
2 Talcott Parsons and Robert F. Bales, *Family—Socialization, and Interaction Process*, Free Press, Glencoe, Ill., 1955, p. 9.

3   Mirra Komarovsky, "Cultural Contradictions and Sex Roles," *American Journal of Sociology*, Vol. 52, No. 3 (1946), p. 187.
4   William J. Goode, in Merton, Broom, and Cottrell, *Sociology Today*, Basic Books, New York, 1959, pp. 178–196. "The Theoretical Importance of Love," *American Sociological Review*, Vol. 24, No. 1 (1959), pp. 38–47.
5   Daniel Miller and Guy Swanson, *The Changing American Parent*, John Wiley and Sons, New York, 1958.
6   Martha Wolfenstein, "The Emergence of Fun Morality," *Journal of Social Issues*, Vol. VII, No. 4 (1951), pp. 15–25.
7   John Watson, *Psychological Care of Infant and Child*, 1914, pp. 81–82.
8   Clark Vincent, "Trends in Infant Care Ideas," *Child Development*, Vol. 22, No. 3 (1951), pp. 199–209.
9   Miller and Swanson, *op. cit.*, pp. 30–31.
10 David Riesman, *The Lonely Crowd*, Yale University Press, New Haven, 1950.
11 Martha Wolfstein, in Mead and Wolfenstein, *Childhood in Contemporary Cultures*, University of Chicago Press, Chicago, 1955.
12 Selma Hirsh, *The Fears Men Live By*, Harper and Bros., New York, 1955, p. 110.
13 Francis Ivan Nye, *Family Relationships and Delinquent Behavior*, John Wiley and Sons, New York, 1958.
14 Editors of Fortune, *The Exploding Metropolis*, Doubleday, New York, 1958, p. 101.
15 Morton Grodzins, "The New Shame of Cities," *Confluence*, Spring, 1958, p. 40.

CHAPTER 7

Changes and Trends in Racial, Ethnic, and Social-class Families

In Chapter 6 we reviewed some of the social processes and conditions influencing family life change in America. Since class, racial, and ethnic families cover virtually the whole span of American society, the effects of almost all these processes and conditions would be felt in these families. Technological advances, industrialization, urban growth, social and spatial mobility, increased education, expanding economic opportunities and political rights, equalitarianism, individualism, and related secular trends have all influenced family change within these segments of American society. Especially important for racial and ethnic families is the drive for fuller assimilation into the mainstream of American life, resulting in their increased pursuit of the American dream and their rising aspirations to share in "the good life" with more firmly established American families. Rising expectations also affect lower-class families, many of whom are striving to improve their lot and are aspiring to at least some middle-class success goals.

Other specific ideological and social movements contributing to family change among racial, ethnic, and social-class families in recent times would be feminism and women's liberation, the civil rights movement, and the various youth and counterculture movements of the post-World War II period.

American kids playing in the park. (*Julie Heifetz.*)

Ethnic Family Change: The Changing Mexican-American Family

It makes sense to choose the Mexican-American family to illustrate family change among ethnic groups in America today. Mexican-Americans constitute one of the largest and still growing ethnic populations in the United States, with over 6.6 million members.[1] Most live in the border states of California, Arizona, New Mexico, Texas, and also Colorado, but more are now living in northern industrial centers such as Chicago.

Mexican-Americans are far from being completely assimilated into American society. A number of circumstances retarded their assimilation. (1) Mexican culture was in existence in the American Southwest for many centuries prior to the coming of Anglo-Americans to that area. (2) The proximity of old Mexico to southwestern United States has provided continual reinforcement of cultural traditions and customs from the motherland for Mexican Americans. No other ethnic group in the United States, excepting American Indians and perhaps French-Canadians, encounters this situation. A major difference between the assimilation of Mexican immigrants and European immigrants is that each European national group tended to arrive in America in one or more waves and became assimilated more or less together over a span of years, while Mexican immigration has been a constant stream. While earlier arrivals were becoming adjusted in America, newcomers from Mexico were taking their place; and the flow of new immigrants in recent years has been greater than the numbers of Mexican-Americans being assimilated into American life.[2] A great many Mexican immigrants retain close familial and cultural ties with their motherland. (3) Another factor retarding Mexican-American assimilation is the "racial" element. About 95 percent of Mexicans are part Indian and nearly 40 percent are full-blooded Indians. These racial differences which set Mexican-Americans apart from Anglo-Americans cannot be made to disappear quickly by Americanization processes.[3] (4) Another barrier to cultural and social assimilation is that while Mexican-Americans want to be a part of the larger American society, they are very reluctant to give up their Mexican cultural heritage. Anglo-Americans tend to withhold social acceptance as long as Mexican-Americans remain "different." Social assimilation is a function of both the dominant group's behavior and the ethnic group's behavior, requiring a sufficient degree of mutual acceptance.[4] (5) Another factor affecting the assimilation of Mexican-Americans is the amount or degree of difference between the culture of the mass of Mexican immigrants and that of the dominant native American population. The bulk of Mexican immigrants who cross the border are rural, lower-class peasants from a folk society approximating the Gemeinschaft-sacred ideal type. They come quite unprepared into a highly industrialized and urbanized

Gesellschaft-secular society. Ordinary Mexicans have learned to protect themselves from the hostility of the world by being suspicious and mistrustful, especially of those in authority. History has taught them this. The dissimilarity of the two cultures, Mexican and American, is seen in the Mexican *La Raza* concept. *La Raza* is a reference to all Latin Americans who are united by cultural, historical, and spiritual bonds.[5] It connotes a pride in this heritage; it also connotes a fatalistic outlook which is quite contrary to the Anglo-American view of human ability to control nature and human destiny by rational action. What the Anglo-American strives to overcome, the Mexican tends to accept with resignation. "Acceptance and appreciation of things as they are constitute the primary values of *La Raza.* . . . The Latin lacks the future-orientation of the Anglo and his passion for planning ahead."[6] William Madsen contends that *La Raza* has served as the main unifying force of the Mexican people. The spiritual bond of hopes, fears, and needs it has perpetuated over the years cannot be forgotten by simply wading across the Rio Grande. Loyalty to *La Raza* by Mexican-Americans is an indication of their feeling that their cultural heritage is too important and valid to be abandoned. This is a strong impediment to assimilation.[7]

The impression should not be left that little or no acculturation or assimilation has taken place or is presently going on. While the above factors have slowed and tempered change for the Mexican-American and produced different rates of change among various groups in different communities, there are other factors promoting cultural and social assimilation. Among these are better education for Mexican-American children, and more college education for young men and women; also, increasing political awareness and participation, and expanding employment opportunities as more men and women become better qualified to compete in the job market, and as the Mexican-American population becomes largely urban.[8]

TRADITIONAL MEXICAN-AMERICAN FAMILY PATTERNS

An underlying base of the traditional Mexican-American family, directly derived from its Mexican cultural source, has been its strong familism. Madsen writes:

The family is the main focus of social identification in all classes of Mexican-American society. Only with the most Anglicized Latin does individual desire become a more powerful, motivating force than concern for the family. The upper class rancher and the lowly crop picker both think of themselves first as family members and secondly as individuals. Mexican-American society as a whole classifies the individual first as a member of a particular family and secondly as a person with certain talents and shortcomings. "One is thought of first as a Garcia or a Cantu and second as a Paul or a Maria," a Mexican-American explained.[9]

Also found in the traditional Mexican-American family, directly derived from its Mexican heritage, is the pattern of strong patriarchal male dominance. This derives from the centuries-old Mexican belief that males are superior to females. This belief has a deep historical base and has been firmly entrenched in the Mexican normative order, according to Tatcho Mindiola.

This normative pattern purports that males are superior to females biologically, intellectually, and socially. This has been extended to include the subjection of the young to the old and the domination of the father over the entire family. The structure and value systems of Mexican culture strongly support these norms.[10]

Along with this male superiority goes a sharp division of labor and authority between the sexes in the traditional family.

HUSBAND-WIFE RELATIONS   Traditionally, the husband plays the authoritarian role and the wife the submissive role. As stated by William Madsen:

While the Mexican-American male may be a second-class citizen in an Anglo dominated world, he can be a king in his own home. He is entitled to unquestioning obedience from his wife and children. He is above criticism due to his "superior" male strength and intelligence. *En mi casa yo mando* (in my house I command) is the by-word of the Mexican-American husband no matter who gives the orders outside his home.[11]

By contrast, the wife is "ideally submissive, unworldly, and chaste." Her interests are primarily the welfare of her husband and children and secondarily her own needs. Her place is in the home and she is expected to devote her life to her husband and her children, in that order. Madsen finds:

The wife sets the tone of the home atmosphere, ideally by radiating love and understanding. In her role as wife and mother she is frequently compared with the Virgin of Guadalupe. By extension but rarely by direct comparison the husband is seen as a human image of God. He is aloof, absolute and forceful in administering justice.[12]

The husband is traditionally the sole breadwinner and the protector of his family, and his *machismo* (manliness) and authority are not to be violated nor questioned. He is the unquestioned *jefe de la casa* (head of the household).

PARENT-CHILD RELATIONS   Arthur Rubel represents the father in the traditional family as being "gruff and firm, yet neither capricious nor tyrannous."[13] The father tells the child only once what to do, and it is done. He manages all the affairs, social and financial, engaged in by the children. His relationship with the younger children may be extremely affectionate, yet as the children grow older, the father becomes more stern and exercises strict

"La Quinceanera." Traditional Mexican-American family celebration of the daughter's fifteenth birthday. (*Dorothy Dominguez.*)

discipline, especially with his sons. The mother-daughter relationship is extremely close and may remain so throughout life. The mother is the main role model for the growing girl, who learns from her mother the traditional modes of femininity and the household duties she will need to know and perform all her life. The daughter learns that her destiny is to serve and fulfill men's needs. The father is highly protective of his daughter, whose freedom outside the home is severely restricted. This is in sharp contrast with the freedom the sons are encouraged by the father to pursue in order to become men. It is believed that daughters must be secluded and protected not only from predatory males but also from their own weak wills.[14]

The traditional mother-son relationship is also one of deep affection; in fact the adolescent son tends to idolize his mother. However, the mother-son relationship has certain ambivalent aspects, as Mindiola points out. "The son is caught between learning masculinity (which includes viewing females as inferiors) and loving and respecting his mother (the dearest person in the world to him)."[15]

While there is no question of the father's being the head of the household and holding the formal authority in the family, the mother is not without influence, albeit informal, in the traditional family. She is the actual center of family life, the one who sets the tone of the home atmosphere. While her husband is the authority symbol, she is the "love" symbol, in that she is self-sacrificing and affectionate in ministering to her husband and children. According to Beatrice Griffith:

The role of the mother in the Mexican family is a fundamental one based on the feudal concept of the mother doing the work, accepting the suffering, and carrying on the responsibility for raising the family—all in a submissive state. Even so, she is really the power behind the family door, for in the eyes of her children she is held in the highest esteem—more so than in American homes.[16]

There is a long tradition of strong family cohesion in the Mexican-derived family. The emphasis on loyalty has helped sustain the close-knit family structure. Loyalty to one's family of orientation is expected of children even after they are married. "Each member is taught that he is a constant visible symbol of his family, and to disgrace the family name is considered a serious offense and must be avoided at all costs."[17]

CHANGING MEXICAN-AMERICAN FAMILY PATTERNS

The pace of change and the degree of change have not been as great among these families as among many other ethnic American families, due to the inhibiting factors reviewed above. Many Mexican-American families are now in a period of change comparable to Campisi's "conflict stage" for Italian-Americans, with overt differences and tension prevailing between the young people and their elders. (See Chapter 3.) While most change in the Mexican-American subculture has been slow and uneven over the past three or more generations, the processes promoting family change have become accelerated since about World War II. The war brought a large flow of people, especially youth, out of the "barrios," or Mexican-American neighborhoods, into industrial jobs and the military services, where they distinguished themselves, winning more congressional Medals of Honor than any other ethnic group. After the war, veterans returned home to find themselves dissatisfied with many of the old ways. The G.I. bill of rights opened educational opportunities for veterans, and occupational skills were upgraded for others by wartime industrial experiences. In his work "The Changing Mexican-American in Southern California," Fernando Peñalosa cites some of the significant changes occurring since World War II.[18] Before the war the Mexican-American population in the Southwest was largely rural. By 1950 it had become two-thirds urban, and by 1960 it was four-fifths urban. In Southern California it has become 83.7 percent urban. Urbanization and mobility have done much to break down ". . . the formerly very rigid inter-ethnic lines of stratification in Southern California. . . . The World War II and post-war periods promoted occupational and geographical mobility to such an extent that rigid caste barriers against intermarriage and equality of employment and housing opportunities have all but disappeared, particularly in urban areas.[19]

Accompanying this urban movement has been a change from rural to urban types of occupations and from unskilled to skilled jobs, primarily benefiting the younger people.

While some progress has been made in the area of education, improvements have been slow. Bilingualism, a potential asset in the world today, has been considered a handicap by many Southern California school authorities. Peñalosa found that between 1950 and 1960 the average number of years of schooling for Mexican-Americans in California increased by only about one year, from 7.6 to 8.9 years for males and from 8.0 to 9.2 years for females.[20] Peñalosa, writing in 1967, concluded that current changes indicated a metamorphosis of the Mexican-American group from "a lower-ethnic caste to a minority-group resembling a European immigrant group of a generation or two ago such as, for example, the Italian-Americans in New York, Boston, or San Francisco."[21]

Peñalosa found that the family has been one of the focal points of social change among Mexican-Americans in Southern California.

In urban areas of southern California at least, the traditional extended family group including siblings and their children is no longer found to any significant extent. The *compadrazgo* or ritual co-parenthood relation no longer has any significance as a fictive kinship relation. Related to the increased emphasis on individualism is the move away from traditional Mexican values and toward the Anglo-American values of achievement, activity, efficiency, and emphasis on the future.[22]

Let us turn now to some studies dealing with specific aspects of Mexican-American family change.

In his study of changing patterns of Mexican immigrant families in Detroit, Norman Humphrey found that exposure of the family to urbanization and American culture alters many traditional family patterns.[23] Those family roles most affected are those of the father, son, and daughter. The degree of role change is an index of the degree of the family's acculturation. The role of the father as sole family provider and family protector is jeopardized when he is unable to find employment or must take seasonal employment. This leads to a reduction in authority and respect accorded the father in the family. Also threatened is his role of moral leader and protector of the females in the family. He becomes unable to enforce the traditional norm forbidding contact with males outside the family, and he fears that his daughters will become "Americanized." The father's loss of status here depends in part on the degree of acculturation attained by his wife and children. As the father's authority declines, that of his son increases, especially that of his oldest son. He is the one who generally learns English first, which gives him a special vantage point in the family and makes his Spanish-speaking parents dependent on him to guide the family in an English-speaking world. If the son is also employed to help support the family, he may achieve a position equal to or even superior to that of his father in the family. Humphrey found that daughters in these families are still subordinate to the males, but exposure to American culture has increased their independence considerably. If the daughter is working, this increases her freedom. In general the daughter's position is about equal to that of the mother, whose status in the family has remained relatively unchanged. Humphrey concluded that the traditional Mexican status hierarchy within the family becomes significantly changed after the family migrates to an urban area in the United States. The son's status moves above that of his mother and equals that of his father; the mother's status remains about the same, while that of her daughter moves up and equals that of the mother. Instead of four status levels as in the traditional family, there are now only two. These status changes may be seen as an index of the family's acculturation, and they are directly related to the degree of exposure to and participation in American society by family members.

In her study of a Mexican-American community in California, Margaret Clark described changing patterns of family life among lower-income Mexican-Americans.[24] Although the average size of these families was still quite large, younger couples were restricting the number of children, feeling that by so doing they were conforming with Anglo norms. Family discipline patterns were changing, with older children being disciplined less often than younger ones. Girls were still quite closely supervised and not allowed to start dating at an early age. This restriction was a source of conflict in many families, and more girls were openly defying their parents by meeting their boy friends in secret. Under pressure, some parents were reluctantly giving in and allowing their teenage daughters to date in keeping with the "Anglo way." Boys were accorded a larger degree of freedom, often to the point of being excused from routine family chores after becoming teenagers. Although most wives still acknowledged male superiority, Clark found instances of the wife openly challenging her husband's authority. Some wives were employed full time or part time to help support the family, thus becoming less financially dependent on their husbands. Wives in general were exercising considerable influence on the conduct of family affairs. Clark interpreted these changes as indicating a significant move toward a more equalitarian relationship between husband and wife in contemporary Mexican-American families.

Studies of Mexican-Americans in Texas by William Madsen and Arthur Rubel yield additional evidence of the changing nature of Mexican-American families today.[25] Their findings tend to corroborate those of Humphrey and Clark that under the influences of Anglo-American society there is a lessening of strict parental supervision of children and a trend toward more equality between husband and wife. Mexican-American women in these Texas families were reported to be commiserating among themselves about the way they were mistreated by their husbands, complaining that changes benefiting them were not coming about fast enough. The studies showed that such changes were under way in all social-class levels, with middle-class families leading the way.

A study of Mexican-Americans in East Chicago, Indiana, by Julian Samora and Richard Lamanna revealed that among families there many of the traditional family patterns have been sustained despite migration, urban life, and other Anglo cultural influences.[26] Although some change was apparent, the families' stability, self-sufficiency, and cultural distinctiveness were impressive even after many years in a big, urban industrial center. Considering the great distance between Mexico and East Chicago and the lack of "Mexican reinforcement" as is found in the Southwest, it is not surprising that the author refers to the Mexican-American family in East Chicago as a "Bulwark of Tradition."

Most evidence, however, tends to support the hypothesis that as Mexican-Americans become more acculturated there is a general movement toward family equalitarianism and greater freedom for individual family members. In a study of "Changes in Marriage Roles Accompanying the Acculturation of the Mexican-American Wife," Roland Tharp and his associates found this to be true.[27] Comparing two groups of wives in the Southwest, one group relatively unacculturated and the other considerably acculturated, Tharp found that "during acculturation, marriage roles change toward a more equalitarian-companionship pattern, or . . . from a segregated to a joint conjugal role pattern."[28] The more acculturated wives, as compared with the less acculturated, engaged in a wider range of social activities with their husbands. They felt it less important that the husband should "wear the pants" in the family; felt it more important that the husband be one hundred percent faithful to his wife, and felt it less important that the wife be a good housekeeper. They said their husbands did more housekeeping chores; they did more things together with their husbands in the home and enjoyed more recreational activity outside the home with their husbands, and they visited less with relatives. These more acculturated wives also thought it more important that their children's wishes be considered when family decisions were made, and less important that their children be good and well behaved at all times.[29]

In his investigation of *The Mexican-American Family*, Tatcho Mindiola sought the extent to which exposure to Anglo-American culture in the schools has altered traditional Mexican family values among Mexican-American college students.[30] He drew his samples from four colleges and universities in Texas. The students were queried on their attitudes toward father-dominance and authority, loyalty to the family, parent-child relations, and respect for elders. The data revealed that these students had departed considerably from many traditional Mexican family values, but on certain ones, such as father dominance and authority, a large majority of the students held to the traditional view that the father should always be respected, have the main say, and be the final authority in the family. However, the idea of female inferiority was strongly rejected, as was the belief that there should be a strict separation of sex roles in the family. Marriage roles were seen as being more equal, and it was considered proper for the wife to be employed outside the home. The majority of male students did not consider this a threat to the traditional male role of sole breadwinner. Attitudes toward parent-child relations were also changing. While the mother was still considered the dearest person in the world to a son or daughter, the respondents disagreed that the stricter the parent the better for the child, nor did they agree that it helps the child in the long run to be made to conform to the parents' ideas. As to respect for elders, while the students agreed that all adults should be respected as a rule, they did not agree that older people are wiser than the young, and they definitely disagreed that the word of an adult should never be questioned. Respondents also disagreed that a girl should not date a boy unless her parents approve of him, and even more strongly disagreed that if a boy's or a girl's family does not approve of one's boy or girl friend they should not be considered as possible marriage partners. Mindiola concluded that while the students still offered lip service to the value of family loyalty, " 'loyalty to the family before self' appears to be a thing of the past to these students."[31]

By way of concluding our discussion of Mexican-American family change, it is quite obvious that significant changes are being experienced by families within this large ethnic group today. While changes are uneven from family to family and vary according to length of time in the United States, the type of community, and social class, nevertheless the weight of evidence reveals that some basic changes are occurring in family attitudes and behavior. The direction of change is toward the dominant Anglo-American family model. The trend is clearly one of movement away from the traditional-patriarchal family type derived from the Mexican folk (Gemeinschaft-sacred) society, toward the modern-equalitarian family type predominant in our Gesellschaft-secular American society today.

The family changes reviewed suggest that cultural and social assimilation of Mexican-Americans is probably accelerating. The family change taking place will bring Mexican-Americans more in conformity with Anglo-American culture values and norms, and thus enhance this group's acceptance in the larger American society, Intermarriage is on the increase but has been inhibited by both cultural and "racial" differences between Mexican-Americans and other Americans. Complete social assimilation of an ethnic group requires not only acceptance of the group in question by the host society, but also acceptance by the ethnic group of the host people and a desire to integrate socially with them. The question of whether to assimilate or not to assimilate is a lively issue today in Mexican-American circles. Many feel strongly about retaining their identity, their biculturalism, and bilingualism. The Chicano movement of the 1960s and 1970s has stressed these values, symbolized by the idea of *La Raza Unida*. As Peñalosa notes, this view

Chinese-American children. (*Julie Heifetz.*)

does "in fact lead to problems in a society ostensibly committed to cultural pluralism but in reality sustaining the melting-pot ideology."[32]

John Burma sums up the current situation on Mexican-American acculturation and assimilation:

Mexican-Americans have not responded uniformly to the acculturating agents and agencies in the North American culture. Some largely rejected the new culture; some have not rejected it but only passively and accidentally acquired its patterns. Still others actively sought acculturation as a rational method of adjusting to the new situation but rejected assimilation; and others have become fully assimilated. It is probably correct to say that today the great majority of Mexican-Americans seek the full measure of acculturation consistent with cultural pluralism and that in so doing not a few of them achieve assimilation either intentionally or unwillingly. The increasing intermarriage of Anglos with third or more generation Mexican-Americans is one index of increasing assimilation.[33]

Racial Family Change: Black American Family Changes and Trends

FACTORS CONTRIBUTING TO CHANGE IN BLACK AMERICAN FAMILIES

Our discussion of the black family in Chapter 3 focused on historical and contemporary variations in family structure and relationships. Here the focus will be on the changing contemporary black American family with attention to some of the conditions and processes inducing family change, and on certain problems and issues relating to black family change today.

In Chapter 3 we found that there were many historical and cultural conditions and processes which had contributed to the shaping of black American family life: the involuntary move from Africa to America, the loss of much African cultural heritage, the transition from slavery to emancipation, the migrations from rural to urban areas and from southern communities to northern and western communities. More recently, changes from negative to more positive social status and from negative to positive self-images among black people, and their struggle for equality have all significantly affected black family relations and organization. Educational and occupational opportunities are expanding and incomes are increasing, but there is still a wide social-class differential among black families benefiting from these improvements. Recent decades have brought a remarkable change in the self-image of American blacks, from the negative image that "black is inferior" to a positive one that "black is beautiful" and that being black is in every way as worthy as being white.

In their work on the *Transformation of the American Negro*, Leonard Broom and Norval Glenn identify the forces behind the transformation:

An improvement in education, occupation and economic condition has marked the transformation of the Negro American, and in these respects the gap between Negroes and whites has been considerably reduced in the past half century. Once predominantly a southern agricultural population, Negroes are now predominantly urban, highly concentrated in the largest metropolitan areas, 40 percent living outside the South. Negroes now live longer and healthier lives, although not so long nor as healthy as whites. Negro-white cultural differences have diminished. All these are changes of great significance, and they have important bearing on the future. But the most pronounced and striking aspect of the transformation has been a sharp rise in Negro aspirations, and a shift from accommodation and quiet resignation to an urgent demand and struggle for equality.[34]

SOME CONTEMPORARY CHANGES AND TRENDS

It has been widely observed that the structure and functioning of the black family in America today are probably more significantly associated with socioeconomic status than with any other factor.[35] Most of the notable gains over the past several decades have been made by the rising number of black middle-class families, while the large lower class of blacks has benefited far less and still remains economically and socially deprived by comparison. As Andrew Billingsley and others have pointed out, it is the less stable family in the lower or "under class" that has been widely publicized, while the stable and productive working- and middle-class families have been largely ignored.[36] In these families most marriages are stable, the children have two parents to support and care for them, the husband has a high school education or better and is employed full time in a skilled or white-collar occupation. The parents work and sacrifice for their children's education and socialize them to work hard in pursuit of the American dream. These families have achieved in high degree those characteristics which are emphasized in the white middle-class-family model. On the other hand, in the lower-class-family population one still finds more families with only one parent present, higher illegitimacy and desertion rates, children having greater difficulties meeting the demands of the public school system, high rates of unemployment, and jobs that are low in both pay and prestige. It is here that negative images and stereotypes of the black family are perpetuated.[37]

While urban middle-class families have made substantial economic gains during the 1960s and early 1970s, there still remains a sizeable gap between the economic status of black and white middle-class families. In fact, when compared with whites, blacks remain relatively deprived irrespective of social class. United States census figures show that blacks are more than three times as likely to be poor, twice as likely to be unemployed, and three times as likely to die in infancy or during childbirth.[38] From 1960 to 1971 median annual family income for blacks increased from $3,233 to $6,714, and for white families from $5,835 to $10,672. The dollar gap between black and white income had increased from $2,602 in 1960 to $3,958 in 1971.[39] In education blacks made solid gains during the same period but remained substantially below white educational levels. In 1960, 24 percent of blacks twenty years old and over had completed four years of high school as compared with 45 percent of whites; by 1971, 40 percent of black adults had completed high school as compared to 62 percent of white adults.[40] There is considerable evidence that marriage and family stability increase as education increases and as family economic conditions improve.

SOME TRENDS IN BLACK HUSBAND-WIFE AND PARENT-CHILD RELATIONS John Scanzoni investigated husband-wife relations in a study of stable black American families in 1968.[41] Relations between the spouses were characterized by a definite emphasis on companionship in leisure and nonwork activities, by empathy, physical affection, and the need of "someone to love" and "someone to talk to or confide in." Many of these families came from a lower-class background where female dominance prevailed. Scanzoni found that this tradition "appears to be expiring" in the stable families where the husband was employed full time. In fact, the husband's authority participation in the family increased as his occupational rank increased, and both husband and wife felt that this increased authority for the husband was right and proper. Scanzoni summed up the trends in authority patterns thus:

Perhaps the picture can be summarized in this fashion. Although in the lower class black family the female may indeed have considerable power because the male has few resources to "earn" deference, this is not the case in the two-thirds of black American families above the under class. Because the husband is working steadily, he has achieved a certain level of authority within the family. But in contrast to trends within the white family where females are pressing for equalitarian participation, it is the black male who is pressing for and has largely achieved equal authority with his wife. Indeed, it may be that equal participation in conflict-resolution is now generally more evident in stable black families than in comparable white families.[42]

Scanzoni found no significant effects of the employment of the wife on the family authority patterns. Whether the wife worked or not made no significant difference in the essentially equalitarian family authority structure. This is in contrast to white society where the working wife has generally been found to have more authority in the family than the nonworking wife.[43] On the question of why employment changes the authority position of white wives but not black wives, Scanzoni speculates that possibly it is because the white wife starts from a position of relative powerlessness compared with her husband.

Working can only increase her bargaining position and yet not necessarily threaten her husband. On the other hand, the black wife inherits a long tradition of power in the family that, according to Scanzoni,

probably enables her to start from a position of equal bargaining "strength" vis-a-vis her husband. If in addition to this tradition, she would utilize her "work resources" as a means to bargain for still more power, the result could be extremely threatening to the husband and to the total marital relationship. Perhaps, therefore, above the lower class the black wife does not use her resources in this fashion. Power based on a more equalitarian tradition may be sufficient for her, whether she works or not. In the lower class, however, where the husband provides little or no resources, the employed wife very likely does add the full weight of her work resources to her traditional power in order to dominate almost totally.[44]

The study revealed that black parents in this segment of the population are socializing their children to believe in and pursue the American dream. Parents hold high aspirations and expectations for their children's occupational and social attainment, stating that chances were good or excellent that their children would be able to achieve their desired goals and get ahead in life. Over 80 percent of these black parents were quite optimistic about their children's chances to advance within the "status structure" of our society.[45] In spite of being black, these parents have accepted the success goals of American society as far as their children are concerned. As to the means for goal attainment available to their children, these parents see the same means which have proved effective for whites, i.e., faithful school attendance and being a good student on the part of the child, parental direction of children in choice of peers, instilling religious values into their children, and encouraging their children to go to college.

Scanzoni concluded that, based on this study of black American families above the lower class, the trend within the family structure in this population is clearly toward convergence with family patterns existing in the dominant white society. This trend is very evident in husband-wife relations and in parent-child relations. These families want to be a part of modern American society and share its economic and social benefits. They believe that despite continuing white discrimination this participation in American society is possible for themselves and their children.

In a study of social-class differences in socialization among black mothers living in urban Michigan, Constance Kamii and Norma Radin found that the child-rearing goals of middle-class mothers and lower-class mothers do not differ fundamentally, but their methods or practices of socialization do differ considerably.[46] The two groups of mothers gave the same priority to the qualities of honesty, happiness, obedience to parents, and a good education as child-rearing goals. These findings suggest that lower-class black child-rearing goals may be changing significantly. Earlier studies, such as those by Allison Davis and Robert Havighurst, found lower-class black parents tended toward apathy, often lacking both the energy and the incentive to urge their children toward economic or social aspirations.[47]

As to child-rearing practices, Kamii and Radin found that middle-class mothers use "bilateral" techniques more than do lower-class mothers in order to obtain desired behavior from their children (e.g., gently requesting, explaining, psychologically manipulating, etc.), while lower-class mothers use "unilateral" techniques more (e.g., ordering, bribing, coercing, and physically enforcing).[48] Middle-class mothers also rewarded their children for favorable behavior more often than lower-class mothers.

In a study of urban black adolescents from the working class and the middle class, David Nolle examined the young people's perceived orientations toward their parents over a three-year period (from 1964 to 1967).[49] He examined their attitudes toward their parents on closeness, openness, and respect for each parent, and their susceptibility to moral influences of each parent. Results showed very few differences over the time period in perceived orientations of the adolescents toward their parents. The only significant changes in attitudes were in perceived diminishing closeness toward the father among working-class sons and daughters and among middle-class daughters. The findings suggest that these young people tend to feel less close to their fathers as years go by, while retaining closeness toward their mothers. This may imply negative changes in the socioemotional aspects of father-son and father-daughter relations during adolescence. As fathers play roles that are primarily instrumental, while mothers play the expressive family roles, the changes observed here may indicate a sloughing off of a low-priority expressive role by the father as the adolescent grows older and approaches the time for disengagement from the parental family.[50]

SOME ISSUES IN THE STUDY OF BLACK FAMILY CHANGE

1 ARE THERE TWO BLACK AMERICAN CULTURES? We have seen evidence of great diversity in black family patterns, past and present. The disparities have seemed so great on some points as to suggest the existence of two or more divergent cultural patterns. Jessie Bernard has in fact presented the argument that the Negro world in America today is separated into two quite different cultures.[51] They consist of (1) the world of those blacks who have acculturated and internalized the values and norms of white American society, and (2) the world of those blacks who have only become externally adapted to these white cultural values and norms, but do not really accept them and instead develop other values and standards of their own. Blacks identified with the former are respectable, maintain a stable family life, and conform to high sex standards; those identified with the latter are not

concerned about appearing respectable, are pleasure- and consumption-oriented, display irregular sexual behavior, and produce illegitimate children. Bernard contends that these two cultural patterns are to be found in all black social classes, although "the acculturated" are more prevalent in the middle and upper classes while "the externally adapted" are more prevalent in the working and lower classes.[52] According to Bernard, these differences have created a "great chasm between the two Negro worlds [which] is so great as to be for all intents and purposes all but unbridgeable, at least until now."[53] The existence of these two worlds and the cleavage between them would help explain what at times are confusing and seemingly incompatible phenomena among black Americans, such as low achievement and high achievement, strict morality and illegitimacy, marital instability and marital and family stability.

Not all agree, however, that such a chasm of separation and mutual rejection exists between any two segments of the black population. Billingsley argues that there is an increasing sense of identity and community today among black Americans in spite of any differences among them. Those achieving middle-class positions are not withdrawing from those who are less fortunate, but rather are identifying with these people and their problems.[54]

Which view is correct? Perhaps both, suggests Bert Adams, since each represents a different dimension of a historical process. The "Black Bourgeoisie" families described by Frazier were concentrating on becoming respectable and different from the lower-class blacks; today however, professional and white-collar families are taking a broader view and admitting their shared African heritage with other blacks in America. "In other words, the 1960s may be seen as the decade when the 'Negroes' became 'Afro-Americans.' "[55] While obvious social and cultural differences still exist among black Americans, the direction of change in recent years seems to be toward an increasing sense of racial and ethnic identity among them.

2   IS THERE A "RACIAL" EXPLANATION FOR FAMILY INSTABILITY AMONG BLACKS?   Adams points out that SES factors—education, occupation, income differences—do not completely close the gap in marital stability that exists between blacks and whites.[56] Is there a "racial" factor operating here? Among the answers that have been suggested are those that hold that racial prejudice and discrimination, especially in the occupational structure, act to the disadvantage of poor blacks as compared to poor whites. Also, the negative effects of ghettoization on the self-image of the lower-class black man make it difficult for him to fulfill conventional marital and family roles. There is agreement among writers such as Billingsley and Daniel Moynihan that conditions of life for black families in the ghettos are bad and appear to be getting worse.[57] They differ, though, as to what should be done about it. Lee Rainwater and William Yancey, in *The Moynihan Report and the Politics of*

Controversy, hold that Moynihan was arguing that "the socio-economic system constrains the family in ways that lead to disorganization, and that family disorganization then feeds back into the system to sustain and perpetuate social and economic disadvantage."[58] Moynihan's critics feel he is saying that if the structure of the black family were strengthened, especially by returning a strong father to the family, then the other problems of poor black families would disappear. These critics feel that a reverse approach is needed; that the first thing to do is stop discrimination against blacks in the job market, and then the family will eventually stabilize. Since white Americans control the economy this is really a white problem, not a black problem. Black leaders point out that the real problem here is one which can only be solved by the white community—that of its own racism and prejudice.[59]

Adams offers the following comments by way of summing up the current situation for the contemporary black American family:

For substantial numbers within the ghetto community, family instability is perpetuating itself, even intensifying. For even larger numbers, however, the Afro-American family appears to have been a buffer between the individual and the more debilitating aspects of racism. The majority of black households are nuclear family units, with the husband holding a steady job. . . . The problem for blacks in America has differed greatly from that of . . . the European ethnic groups. The problem for the black has been that, *after incorporating much of the dominant culture, they have not been allowed into the dominant society.* The solution hardly seems . . . to be some program directed primarily at black families. Rather, the crucial issues revolve around white attitudes and behavior, as well as around various black efforts which must assume that there will be little *voluntary* change in the white community.[60]

FUTURE PROSPECTS FOR BLACK AMERICAN FAMILIES

As seen above, crucial issues bearing on the future of black Americans center around the attitudes and actions of white Americans as well as around the efforts of black Americans themselves. It is generally conceded that the black matricentric family will continue within the urban lower-class population until the larger society allows and aids black males to obtain the education and training needed to achieve steady employment in decent, adequately paying jobs. There must be occupational opportunities to enable the man to fulfill his family provider role, which is all important to his status as head of his family. Until this is achieved there will likely be continued evidence of marriage and family disorganization among *some* of these families. However, it should be emphasized that an increasing number of these poor black families have shown an impressive ability to adjust to economic and social deprivations and maintain a strong sense of family solidarity.[61]

The number of working-class black families—the "urban proletariat"—

Contemporary black American couple. (*Julie Heifetz.*)

has increased steadily in mid-twentieth century and will in all likelihood continue to expand as more black Americans continue to move into the industrial labor force. Such families become better able to move away from the urban ghetto; the father achieves greater authority under these conditions, and the "ideals and patterns of family life approximate those of the great body of industrial workers."[62]

The middle-class, acculturated black family will surely continue to grow—again, providing that the opportunity structure continues to broaden, and that discrimination and prejudice continue to erode. The values, goals, and life-styles of these black families closely resemble those of the middle majority of white Americans. These black families have demonstrated that, given adequate resources and opportunities, they are well able to develop and sustain a highly stable and functional family and home life.[63]

Social-Class Family Changes and Trends

CHANGES AND TRENDS IN UPPER-CLASS FAMILIES

Although data on upper-class families are rather sparse, some signs suggest that changes are afoot, even though gradual and undramatic. Emphasis on achievement rather than ascription, and on equalitarianism, the expansion of higher education, and greater sophistication of middle-class people have undermined many of the traditional supports of the old aristocracies. In public life, in government, and in business, prominent men and women from middle-class backgrounds now swell the ranks of the new upper class. Their families, representing a newer "aristocracy of achievement," move freely in top social circles, both national and international, often overshadowing the more static and provincial older aristocracies identified with specific American communities. The lines separating these two segments of the upper class appear to be weakening, and the trend is toward a merging or fusing of the two groups through, first, business, professional, and governmental association, followed by increasing primary-group relations including intermarriage. Ruth Cavan describes the trend thus:

Upper-class isolation is less complete today than formerly; and the break in the cultural wall permits contacts with those of other classes. The trend is now for middle- and even aspiring and especially capable lower-class children to attend college and university. Although these young people may not belong to the same clubs or fraternities as the upper-upper-class youths, nevertheless there is an exchange of ideas and information.

Although the upper-upper-class children and young people have more privileges . . . they often have less freedom of individual choice. Some upper-upper-class children and young people therefore attempt to throw off the restraints of their kinship and class group and seek individual freedom outside the prescribed behavior of their class. . . . Marriage outside the class is probably the final sign of rebellion.[64]

In view of these trends in American society, it will be more difficult for the upper class to continue to be "a closed, caste-like domain based on family name, inherited wealth, and an extensive kin network."[65] Strong criticisms of certain upper-class practices have been made by American writers such as F. Scott Fitzgerald and John Phillips Marquand, as well as by numerous social scientists including C. Wright Mills and E. D. Baltzell. Baltzell argues that "a crisis in moral authority has developed in modern America largely because of the white Anglo-Saxon Protestant establishment's unwillingness or inability to share and improve its upper class traditions by continuously absorbing talented and distinguished members of minority groups into its privileged ranks."[66] He feels, however, that upper-class isolation is being threatened through the American courtship system. As more middle-class young people mix with upper-class youth on college campuses, there will be mutual attraction "on the basis of intellectual affinities as against the traditional affinities of caste and class." The extent to which such interclass courtship and marriage is actually taking place now is not really known yet. This requires more empirical study.

One of the few recent studies on upper-class marriage trends was done by Paul M. Blumberg and P. W. Paul, as reported in their article "Continuities and Discontinuities in Upper-Class Marriages."[67] They analyzed 413 of the most prominently featured marriage announcements appearing in the society pages of the Sunday *New York Times* from 1962 to 1972, comparing various individual and family characteristics of the bride and groom, such as Social Register membership, education, occupation, residence, and the father's occupation. They compared their findings with those of an earlier, similar study by David Hatch and Mary Hatch, who analyzed marriage announcements appearing in *The New York Times* on Sundays in June in the decade 1932 to 1942.[68] Blumberg and Paul found a significant expansion of the upper-class marriage market, especially what they call "horizontal expansion," which is described as follows:

The participation of the upper class in various national arenas—private schools and colleges with national enrollments, exclusive clubs, fashionable vacation resorts, etc.—continues to erode the isolation of strictly local upper classes and leads to elite interaction on a national scale, where friendships are made, courtships develop, and marriages ensue. What happens, consequently, is that the upper class marriage market becomes increasingly national in scope.[69]

The authors also report a possible vertical expansion of the upper-class marriage market. Over time a shift away from attending the upper-class boarding schools and elite universities was discerned, with upper-class youth being scattered among more heterogeneous schools and colleges, which opened opportunities for more cross-class courtship and marriage. These data indicate that it is quite likely that for those upper-class youth who "have increasingly turned away from the elite boarding schools and colleges toward a presumably more mixed-class environment, there has been a concomitant and steady rise in the percentage of Social Register members marrying persons who are not in the Social Register."[70]

The authors conclude that the American upper class, which used to be isolated and local, is now becoming somewhat less isolated and more national in nature. There is more interaction with other classes, which may result in increasing rates of intermarriage. As upper-class young people intermingle more with others in colleges and universities, and then later in life in business and professional groups, and as American equalitarianism makes itself increasingly felt, upper-class family patterns will probably become less distinguishable from middle-class patterns.

TRENDS AND CHANGES IN MIDDLE-CLASS FAMILIES

Cavan has stated that "of the three class levels, middle class families are most involved in the issues of family life occasioned by social change."[71] It has been said that perhaps the most important general trend in family change in the current century has been the change toward greater equality in relations among nuclear family members.[72] While this change has not been restricted to the middle-class family, it is here that the equalitarian trend has been most evidenced in husband-wife relations and in parent-child relations. Let us briefly review some of the highlights, focusing on changing family roles.[73]

CHANGES IN ROLES OF THE MIDDLE-CLASS HUSBAND AND FATHER (1) The husband-father still retains the main family provider role, but is receiving more help in this responsibility from his wife. Each decade of the twentieth century has seen more middle-class wives taking employment outside the home. (2) As a parent, the middle-class father has moved gradually away from a restrictive authoritarian approach with his sons and daughters toward a more permissive approach involving rational appeal and effective communication, and more affectionate relations. (3) F. Ivan Nye and Felix Berardo identify certain emerging male family roles as sexual, therapeutic, and recreational.[74] Recent literature stresses the sexual needs of women, so the middle-class husband now feels it is his duty to satisfy his wife sexually. Therapeutically, the husband as well as the wife feels a responsibility to aid other family members in solving their emotional, intellectual, and ethical problems, as a family counselor. The husband also is accepting a greater responsibility in providing for the recreational needs of members of his family. As a companion to his wife, he especially feels he should make his own recreational interests compatible with hers.

CHANGES IN ROLES OF THE MIDDLE-CLASS WIFE AND MOTHER (1) In recent decades, the middle-class woman has been regaining her family provider role, which she lost temporarily during the latter phase of the industrial revolution. Her new provider role requires her to work away from home, however, which has created public concern about her other traditional family duties, such as child care and training. Issues relating to those changes will be discussed more fully below. (2) The child-care and socialization roles of the middle-class mother have undergone significant changes in the past half century. The social-behavioral sciences have made middle-class parents aware of the importance of social experience in the child's personality development and social adjustment. Educated middle-class mothers are made acutely aware of the importance of mother-child relations for the growing child. In the more or less isolated nuclear family the mother assumes a heavy responsibility for the training and upbringing of her children. (3) The housekeeper or homemaking role is undergoing some changes, but the middle-class wife still retains the main responsibility here. Labor-saving devices and more specialized agencies in the community are reducing some of the time and effort required, and middle-class husbands help some with household tasks. If and when adequate day care facilities become available for preschool children, further attenuation of the housekeeper role is likely. (4) As mentioned above, the middle-class wife's sexual role expectations are changing. She expects to receive pleasure and enjoy sexual relations as well as contributing to her husband's enjoyment. She sees herself as an equal partner with her husband in sharing and enjoying this part of their life together. (5) Nye and Berardo identify emerging female family roles in the areas of therapy and recreation. The middle-class wife serves as a sympathetic listener and counselor to her husband and her children, encouraging and reassuring them when they are frustrated or feel insecure. In recreation, middle-class women feel that they should be companions to their husbands, and that as a couple they should do things together both in the home and outside which they both enjoy. There is evidence that middle-class wives highly value this joint recreation.

SELECTED PROBLEMS AND ISSUES
IN MIDDLE-CLASS FAMILY CHANGE

Change seems to be a way of life for middle-class families in the twentieth century. As they move from one community to another and/or from one social-class level to another, middle-class families must continually be adjusting to new physical and social environments. Studies of family life in middle-class American suburbs show that these families have their share of problems and stresses.[75]

PROBLEMS AND ISSUES IN CHANGING MIDDLE-CLASS MARITAL RELATIONS Middle-class youth have been socialized to expect a great deal from marriage. Love and personal happiness are viewed almost as God-given natural rights in marriage, and so most young people enter marriage with the high expectation that it will bring them greater happiness than they have experienced in their unmarried lives. This, plus the decline in belief that marriage should be permanent, has meant that more middle-class young people are entering marriage on a tentative or trial basis. The widespread sentiment is that if the present marriage does not yield the expected happiness, one is free to consider alternatives, which could include separation, divorce, or extramarital relations.

In a well-known study of middle-class marital relations, John Cuber and Peggy Harroff interviewed 437 men and women in the 35 to 55 age range.[76] They were described by the authors as highly educated, financially successful, and articulate. Five different types of relationships were observed among these couples, ranging from marriages fraught with tensions and conflict to those which were highly satisfying to both partners.

1 Conflict-Habituated Relationships   The conflict is chronic but generally kept under control. At worst there is private quarreling and nagging; at best the couple are discreet and polite about their differences. The conflict itself seems to be a main basis of their continuing relationship, constituting the cohesive factor in the marriage.

2 Devitalized Relationships   Although there is typically no serious tension or conflict in these marriages, the relationship is devoid of zest. There is no serious threat to the marriage, and its perpetuation is reinforced by legal requirements and often religious expectations. "But the relationship between the pair is essentially devoid of vital meaning by comparison to what it was when the mating began."[77] This type of relationship was found to be exceedingly prevalent.

3 Passive-Congenial Relationships   About as common as the previous type, the mode of association here is one of "comfortable adequacy." While claiming to share and enjoy many common interests, it comes out that these interests are not very vital nor do they entail much actual joint participation. Such couples are only passively content, and the relationship shows little evidence of real vitality.

4 Vital Relationships   Here the husband-wife relations exude a vitality manifested through a "vibrant and exciting sharing of some important life experience." It may be sex or child rearing or work or some creative activity. The vitality of the relationship derives from the "feelings of importance about it and that that importance is shared."[78]

5 Total Relationships   This relationship is like the vital relationship with the important addition of being multifaceted. A much wider sharing of experiences occurs here. While such total relationships are quite rare, "one will occasionally find relationships in which *all* important aspects of life are mutually shared and participated in. It is as if neither partner has a truly private existence."[79]

Cuber and Harroff call the first three types of relationships *utilitarian* marriages, and the last two types *intrinsic* marriages. In the latter type much more importance is given to "joyful sex, close companionship, deep emotional involvement." The authors warn that their findings should not be generalized beyond the upper-middle-class population from which this sample was drawn. However, their findings do suggest that more middle-class marriages than we realized may be routinized and unexciting and essentially utilitarian in nature.

CAREER VERSUS FAMILY LIFE: AN ISSUE FOR THE MIDDLE-CLASS MAN   Although he may not always be conscious of it, in upwardly mobile middle-class families where success goals are firmly held, the conscientious husband-father faces a dilemma. Demands of his career and demands of his family compete for his time and energy. It may be extremely difficult for him to satisfy both sets of demands. While some can do it, most men probably have to choose between one or the other, opting for family togetherness at the expense of career, or sacrificing family life for career advancement. For men who choose career, a diminished family life often ensues. The marriage may become what Cuber and Harroff have described as utilitarian, with little intrinsic vitality or reward in the husband-wife relations, or in the father-child relations either. If, on the other hand, the "good life" is his choice, there is a greater likelihood of satisfying and vital relations between the man and his wife and children.

For the business or professional man especially, the social pressure to devote his energies to his career is very strong. As David Schulz notes:

It is society that requires the sacrifice of time and talent at the expense, if necessary, of everything else in a professional's life. Without dedicated professionals our complex system would collapse. . . . , and yet with the necessity of such dedication comes the unintended consequences of the corporation widow and the doctor's son whose personal happiness and development might well be reduced because of the needs of an advanced technological society.[80]

This will likely continue to be a problem for the middle-class man and his family. There is some indication that many middle-class husbands today are tempering the demands of their jobs somewhat in an effort to spend more time with their families.

CAREER VERSUS DOMESTIC ROLES: AN ISSUE FOR THE MIDDLE-CLASS WOMAN   Middle-class women are quite aware that feminism, the women's rights movement, more higher education, and expanding job opportunities for women have worked together to create a dilemma for them. Specifically, should a woman apply her education and talents to a career outside the home, or should she continue to devote her energies to the traditional domestic roles of wife, mother, and homemaker? In her pursuit of social equality, the middle-class woman tends more and more to see job equality as central to her quest.[81] Since World War II especially, increased opportunities for women have opened up in the nation's labor markets, and at the same time the older sentiment that "woman's place is in the home" has significantly diminished in middle-class circles. As they have become more highly educated, middle-class women have become more dissatisfied with being "only housewives." The result has been a sharp upward curve in the number of married women in the labor force. The number has increased from 15 percent in 1940 to 41 percent in 1970, and 58 percent of these employed married women had children at home under the age of eighteen.[82] Concern for the welfare of children of employed mothers has been widely voiced, but according to Alice Rossi, among others, there is no evidence of any negative effects on children that are directly traceable to the mother's employment.[83] Very important to the children's welfare is how they are cared for while the mother is at work.

Research to date supports the contention that if a child is reared by a cold non-nurturant mother or is reared in an institution lacking warmth, he will probably have personality disturbances later in life. On the other hand, if the child shares the love of his mother with a warm surrogate or surrogates in a stable environment, it is probable that he will prosper at least as well as and potentially much better than the child reared more exclusively by his mother.[84]

In middle-class families where the wife is employed, adjustments must be made not only in her other roles, but in those of her husband also. He may have to accept additional housework and child-care responsibilities. His attitudes toward her employment will affect their marital relationship. In a study of employed middle-class wives in Wisconsin, the author found that the marital adjustment of the couple was directly related to a favorable attitude of the husband toward his wife's employment. The best adjusted and happiest couples had achieved a partnership-equalitarian mode in their family roles and were essentially emancipated from traditional views of "man's place" and "woman's place" in the family.[85]

Issues involving role choices and role changes for women in middle-class American families will continue and are likely to wax more intense in the immediate future as the push for women's liberation makes itself more widely felt.

MIDDLE-CLASS YOUTH: SOME ISSUES AND PROBLEMS OF CHANGE
Traditionally, middle-class parents try to socialize their children to accept success goals and acquisitive values. Now there is evidence that the ability of parents to do this has become somewhat problematical in recent years. A survey in the late 1960s showed that a majority of college-age youth wanted something quite different out of life than their parents wanted.[86] As social change accelerates, the experience and views of parents seem to become less relevant as guides for middle-class youth, who turn more to other authorities and reference groups for guidance. This kind of generation gap may be greatest in families of middle-class, college-educated youth.

It was among these college-educated, middle-class youth particularly, during the 1960s and early 1970s, that a growing awareness developed of the possible detrimental effects of our highly competitive technology on the

Some middle-class family traditions continue, such as the bride and groom cutting their wedding cake, and the bride wearing her grandmother's wedding dress. (*E. D. Dyer.*)

quality of human life, including family life. A quest for new values resulted, which often took on the characteristics of a "cause" or a social movement. These new values became an overriding ideology for their young adherents. The new value system included new ways of life, new sex codes, less interest in materialism, an emphasis on self-expression, challenges to authority, a quest for more meaningful personal relations and more meaningful work, and a desire to make a significant social contribution.[87] Middle-class youth seemed to show the greatest concern in these matters.

Whereas alienated youth of the 1950s tended to withdraw (David Riesman called it "privatism"), feeling themselves powerless to fight the "establishment" or effect any significant change, more young people in the 1960s opted for involvement, seeking ways to make their voices heard and seeking effective means to produce desired changes in government, education, business, and the military. Middle-class youth became involved in politics and public affairs through organizations such as the Peace Corps, the Youth Corps, and VISTA. They also became active in the presidential campaigns of 1968 and 1972, in mounting protest against the Vietnam war and against environmental pollution and depletion of our natural resources, and in joining the civil rights movement.

As we saw in Chapter 6, recent years have witnessed significant changes in beliefs, sentiments, and norms relating to sex. And middle-class youth have been heavily involved in these developments, espousing the new morality which stresses love and supports a sex code of premarital "permissiveness with affection." Information on birth control and abortions, the availability of "the pill," and professional help in family planning agencies, clinics, etc., are providing greater control over sex for young people. It may be argued that behind these developments in sex behavior is a basic change in beliefs and norms regarding sex in America—a rejection of traditional norms and a positive belief now in the essential goodness of sex.

It has been suggested that the sexual revolution in America is primarily a middle-class movement dating from the 1920s and connected to the emancipation of women.[88] Women are now expected to have basically the same sexual needs as men, and are considered free to initiate sex relations, the same as men. From his studies of these developments Reiss concludes:

Although there has probably been an increase in the frequency with which females have coitus and a concomitant increase in the lack of guilt and qualms these women feel, there still was little evidence of any radical increase in the proportion of non-virginal females during these last fifty years. The proportion has rested close to fifty percent since the 1920's. Nevertheless I do believe that a rise is occurring now which will increase the rate of non-virginal females at marriage to perhaps 65 or 70 percent.[89]

Reiss finds evidence that there has been an improvement in the quality of sex relations of married people, which probably is a reflection of changes in attitudes and experiences of women and the greater concern now of middle-class men for the sexual satisfaction of their wives. With respect to extramarital relations, Reiss feels that new types such as mate sharing and mate swapping will affect only a very small minority of middle-class people, although some of this equalitarian adultery may be expected in our secular, equalitarian society. Old-fashioned adultery has increased some and will likely increase further among those whose marriages are not happy or satisfying. But since divorce is no longer viewed as deviant behavior by most middle-class people, many potential cases of extramarital relations are now precluded by divorce.[90]

TRENDS AND CHANGES IN WORKING-CLASS AND LOWER-CLASS FAMILIES

With the expanding prosperity of the post-World War II period, many more working-class families have become upwardly mobile. This has meant for them some changes in family life-style, often accompanying a move from an older, working-class neighborhood to a better one, perhaps to a suburb.

In a study of working-class families in suburbia, Irving Tallman found that for these families the move to the suburb often takes on the characteristics of a crisis, especially for the wife. He found evidence that "(1) upward mobility deprives the women of a system of structured supports and therefore increases their sense of social isolation and disaffection; and (2) the sense of social disaffection is associated with a breakdown in primary relations."[91]

The move to the suburbs entails a sequence of events leading to this disaffection. It begins with the family's migration away from their working-class neighborhood and their relatives, and leads to a sense of loss and isolation felt especially by the working-class wife in her new suburban community. Previous findings on blue-collar or working-class family life show that wives tend to maintain close ties with their relatives and women friends, and the men with male peers and work group associates. It is not so much the marriage partner in this class, but the same-sex friends and kin who provide social and psychological support for the wife. Her security and identity thus are tied up very closely with a small primary-group network. She tends to have only minimal outside-the-home contacts, by comparison with her husband, and by comparison with the middle-class wife. Tallman concludes that "when mobility destroys the fabric of their social relations, the results may be particularly devastating for such women, principally because they have no structured nor normative system of support outside their intimate group."[92]

Some negative consequences of mobility for these families were heightened tension between husband and wife, more actual marital conflict, and certain anomic reactions to the new world around them. The findings indicate, however, that such reactions are likely to be transitory and represent only a temporary state of marital and family disorganization. The findings do imply that a move to the suburbs requires some fundamental reorganization of conjugal and community roles for working-class families.

This study tends to support findings by the author in an earlier study that social and geographic mobility are disruptive to marriage and family relations.[93] These negative effects of mobility may be more pronounced in working-class families than in middle-class families who are apt to have a wider experience and more resources to aid them in their new social environment, and who are less closely tied to relatives and a small circle of friends.

TRENDS IN LOWER-CLASS SOCIALIZATION AND CHILD TRAINING Urie Bronfenbrenner's review of studies in childhood socialization and social class covering a span of more than twenty-five years shows that differences in socialization still exist between the middle, the working, and the lower classes, but that the gap is narrowing somewhat, especially now between the middle class and the working class.[94] This change is partly due to the rise in education and in standards of living for working-class families, and partly due to the fact that more working-class parents are now practicing middle-class techniques and using the same sources of information as middle-class parents, such as Dr. Spock and other infant and child-care specialists. ("Spock has now joined the family Bible on the shelf of the working-class family.")[95] Differences still do remain however. While middle-class child socialization stresses independence, interchange, and affection, working-class socialization stresses respectability, neatness, and obedience. But now the working-class parent is also emphasizing values heretofore regarded as middle-class such as cleanliness, conformity, and control.[96]

In his comparison of middle-class and lower-class styles of socialization, Adams has identified some emergent and current patterns in lower-class families.[97] By comparison with the middle-class father whose supporting role in socialization may take many forms, such as discussing goals, teaching skills, or complimenting and encouraging his children, the lower-class father generally leaves most of the child-rearing responsibilities to his wife. Also, by contrast to the middle-class emphasis on verbal skills, lower-class parents, who are less likely to live and work in the realm of ideas, less often seek rational explanations for a child's conduct. These conditions, plus a shortage of verbal skills for both parents, seem to produce more authoritarianism in lower-class parent-child relations, more use of "commands and physical response." While the basis for child discipline in the middle class tends to be "behavioral intent," in the lower class it is more likely to be "behavioral consequences." While the middle-class parent would probably punish a child who spilled milk at the dinner table if the child's intent was judged by the parents to be to get back at them for cutting play time short that evening, the lower-class parent would punish the child because the act showed lack of control and was damaging to the furniture.[98] Lower-class parents are still more likely to punish impulsive behavior of the child when it occurs and to use physical punishment, while middle-class parents tend to employ reasoning, shame, or even at times the threat of withholding love.[99] Table 1 sums up some of the important differences found between middle-class and working- and lower-class socialization.[100]

In an insightful study of family relations and life-styles, E. E. LeMasters examined child rearing and socialization among families of blue-collar skilled workers living in a working-class suburb of Madison, Wisconsin, in the early 1970s.[101]

LeMasters found that these working-class fathers and mothers have quite different—and often conflicting—views of how to bring up their children and of what to prepare them for in life. This is especially true for their sons. The men have very conservative views, are more tradition-bound, and "are trying to preserve their way of life by teaching their boys the same code the men have lived by."[102] The mothers, on the other hand, are oriented more toward the future and toward middle-class values and trends such as women's rights, equalitarianism, and white-collar occupational goals for their children, much

TABLE 7-1 SOME DIFFERENCES BETWEEN MIDDLE-CLASS AND WORKING- AND LOWER-CLASS SOCIALIZATION

ASPECTS OF SOCIALIZATION	MIDDLE CLASS	WORKING AND LOWER CLASSES
Parental warmth and demonstration of affection	High	Low
Role of father	Supportive of child	Little role in socialization
Style of verbal communication	Reasoning and discussion	Much use of commands
Basis for discipline	Behavioral intent	Behavioral consequences
Use of physical punishment	Moderately low	High
Tolerance of children's impulses	High	Moderately low
Demand for responsible independence	High	Moderately low

SOURCES: Among the numerous sources are: Urie Bronfenbrenner, "Socialization and Social Class Through Time and Space," in Eleanor E. Maccoby, Theodore M. Newcomb, and Eugene L. Hartley, eds., *Readings in Social Psychology* (New York: Henry Holt, 1958), pp. 400–425; Melvin L. Kohn, "Social Class and Parent-Child Relationships: An Interpretation," *American Journal of Sociology* 68 (1963), 471–80; Grace F. Brody, "Socioeconomic Differences in Stated Maternal Child-Rearing Practices and in Observed Maternal Behavior," *Journal of Marriage and the Family* 30 (1968), 656–60; Arthur Besner, "Economic Deprivation and Family Patterns," in Lola M. Irelan, ed., *Low-Income Life Styles*, Department of Health, Education, and Welfare, Welfare Administration Publication No. 14 (1966), pp. 15–29; Bronfenbrenner, "The Changing American Child—A Speculative Analysis," *Journal of Social Issues* 17 (1961), 6–18; Maccoby and P. K. Gibbs, "Methods of Child-Rearing in Two Social Classes," in W. E. Martin and C. E. Stendler, eds., *Readings in Child Development* (New York: Harcourt, Brace, 1954), pp. 380–96; Kohn and Eleanor E. Carroll, "Social Class and the Allocation of Parental Responsibilities," *Sociometry* 23 (1960), 372–92; Catherine S. Chilman, "Child-Rearing and Family Relationships of the Very Poor," *Welfare in Review* (1965), pp. 9–19; James Walters and Nick Stinnett, "Parent-Child Relationships: A Decade Review of Research," in Carlfred B. Broderick, ed., *A Decade Review of Research and Action* (Minneapolis: National Council on Family Relations, 1971), pp. 99–140; Stanley B. Messer and Michael Lewis, "Social Class and Sex Differences in the Attachment and Play Behavior of the Year-Old Infant," *Merrill-Palmer Quarterly* 18 (1972), 295–306; Steven R. Tulkin and Bertram J. Cohler, "Childrearing Attitudes and Mother-Child Interaction in the First Year of Life," *Merrill-Palmer Quarterly* 19 (1973), 95–106. Additional references can be found in Chilman's article, Bronfenbrenner's paper in *Readings in Social Psychology,* and Walters and Stinnett's "Parent-Child Relationships."

Adapted from Bert N. Adams, *The Family: A Sociological Interpretation* (Chicago: Rand McNally College Publishing Co., 1974), p. 155. By permission of author and publisher.

of which conflicts with their husbands' traditional male-centeredness and blue-collar world of work orientation.

How should sons be brought up, according to these working-class fathers? (1) A boy must learn to defend himself and his rights physically. "Physical strength and 'guts' are primary male attributes. Any boy who grows up to be a 'sissy' is a failure."[103] (2) A boy must learn "how to handle women." He must be on guard against possible feminine efforts to "make a fool out of him," such as trapping him into a forced marriage, or what would even be worse, "henpecking" him after marriage. According to the male code, one way to protect oneself against such hazards is to learn to seduce women. A seduced woman is believed to be less apt to be able to dominate a man.[104] (3)

A boy should learn "not to be a sucker." These men see the world as a tricky place, and one must be on guard at all times not to be taken. A boy must learn to spot a phony, and "how to distinguish an honest crap game from a crooked one."[105] (4) "Above all, don't spoil a boy." Children, especially boys, have to learn early in life that the world is a rough place. Any kid who has been spoiled by his parents has a disadvantage in trying to make it in today's world.[106]

The wives of these men did not agree with their husbands on how to rear their sons. LeMasters found three sources of disagreement:[107] (1) The mothers have more of a middle-class orientation than their husbands. The women read magazine articles on child rearing, watch middle-class soap operas on TV, and often have more contact with middle-class people in their daily lives than do their husbands. (2) The mother's primary goal is to rear her sons to be good husbands and fathers. She is most concerned with socializing them for future family roles, while their father sees his main task as preparing his boys for roles in the outside world, such as working at a job and participating in the male world of sports. (3) The mothers do not accept their husbands as ideal role models for their sons. The wives feel that their husbands do not devote enough time to their families, seeming to prefer the company of their male work associates or their buddies at the tavern. Thus, the mothers try to rear their sons to be different from their fathers.

Mothers and fathers disagreed somewhat less on rearing their daughters. Fathers feel that girls as well as boys should not be spoiled, and should learn early the hard facts of life. Girls should learn not to trust men, especially where sex is concerned. ("These men feel they know men too well to trust any of them with their daughters.")[108] Mothers were in agreement that their daughters need to learn how to "handle men." The mother wants her daughter to grow up to be a "nice girl," to find a good husband—preferably one with a white-collar job—and to become a good mother. Girls should learn skills to help support themselves, such as typing, bookkeeping, nursing, and hairstyling.

LeMasters' study shows that child rearing in working-class families may still be quite different from that found in the majority of middle-class families today. Working-class parents still emphasize discipline and obedience in their children. They have little patience with permissiveness, "child psychology," or the views of child-rearing experts. This last is especially true of fathers.[109]

It is apparent that within these working-class families significant differences exist between men and women on child rearing, especially in the matter of bringing up sons. These men—"blue-collar aristocrats"—are trying to hold onto a traditional, male dominant, rural-derived way of life, and pass this life-style on to their children. Their wives, more exposed to and more sympathetic toward the prevailing urban, middle-class trends, are agitating for some changes, including more rights and prerogatives for women and children. Thus, *differential change* seems to be endemic in such families today. This differential internal family change has many ramifications for parent-child relations and for husband-wife relations in working-class families at present, and for the immediate future at least.

Summary

Very significant for present-day racial and ethnic family change are the various processes and movements agitating for more complete assimilation and participation in the mainstream of American life for minority groups. Similar rising expectations are affecting lower-class families who are striving to improve their lot.

The Mexican-American family was selected to illustrate ethnic family change. Today these Mexican-American families are in various stages of assimilation into the larger American society. Their assimilation has been slowed by their proximity to Mexico, the racial element, their reluctance to give up many aspects of their Mexican cultural heritage, and their dislike of many things in the Gesellschaft-secular American culture. Factors promoting their assimilation include better education for Mexican-American children and young people, expanding employment opportunities, and increasing political participation.

Traditional Mexican-American family patterns approximate the traditional-patriarchal ideal type family, with a powerful father and subordinate wife and children. In many families today the women and young people are challenging these traditional patterns, thus creating tension and conflict within the family. Studies reviewed show that significant changes are occurring in present-day Mexican-American families. The trend is toward the dominant Anglo-American equalitarian model.

Black American family change should be viewed in a context of improvements in education, occupation, economic condition, the political struggle for equality, and improved self-images. However, beneficial changes from these improvements are being felt far less in the lower classes than in the middle and upper classes. Billingsley points out that the less stable lower-class family has been overpublicized, while the stable and productive working-and middle-class families have been largely ignored. Parents in these families work hard, sacrifice for their children's education and future, and are moving toward the American middle-class, equalitarian family model. Some social-class differences still exist in husband-wife relations and in parent-child relations.

The diversity in family patterns has led Bernard to suggest the existence of two divergent black American cultures: (1) the world of those who have become acculturated into white American society, and (2) the world of those who have become only externally adapted to white America and who have developed a different set of values and standards of their own. Other authorities argue that in spite of any differences among them there is an increasing sense of identity and community among black Americans today. There is evidence that continuing racism and the negative effects of ghetto life are still making it difficult for lower-class males to fulfill conventional marital and family roles. Attitudes and actions of white Americans, thus, as well as efforts of black Americans themselves are crucial for the future of these families. Given adequate resources and opportunities, black Americans are as able as any others to develop and maintain stable marriages and families.

Upper-class family life appears to be changing somewhat. The old hereditary aristocracies are being overshadowed by the newer "aristocracies of achievement," and the trend is toward a merging of the upper-upper class and the lower-upper class through increasing business and professional association and informal relations including intermarriage.

A good deal of family change in America has been instigated by middle-class people. It is in the middle-class family that the equalitarian trend has been most pronounced and the changes in sex roles most apparent. However, with all the change and mobility, middle-class families are subject to various stresses and problems. Men and women enter marriage with high expectations and tend to feel that if a given marriage does not yield the expected happiness and personal fulfillment, it is perfectly right to seek another marriage partner or some other alternative. The middle-class man has to try to balance the demands of career and family, while the middle-class woman has to decide whether to devote herself to the traditional domestic roles or pursue a career outside. More women are trying to do both today. In the 1960s many middle-class youth became dissatisfied with middle-class success and acquisitive values, thus widening the generation gap between themselves and their parents.

Working-class families are undergoing change also. Increasing prosperity enables more of these families to move to the suburbs, where the wives especially may have difficult adjustments to make as they leave their close circle of female relatives and friends behind them. Working-class fathers and mothers may have quite different views of how to raise their children and of what to prepare them for in life. The men are more tradition-bound, while the women are becoming middle class in orientation and desire changes that will improve their lot in life and their status.

Notes

1   U.S. Bureau of the Census, *Current Population Reports: Population Characteristics*, "Population Profile of the United States: 1976," p. 3.
2   Edward McDonagh, "Status Levels of Mexicans," *Sociology and Social Research*, 33 (July 1949), pp. 449–459.
3   John Burma, ed., *Mexican-Americans in the United States* (Cambridge, Mass.: Schenkman Publishing Co., 1970).
4   Ozzie Simmons, "Mutual Images and Expectations of Anglo-Americans and Mexican-Americans," *Daedalus*, 90 (Spring 1961), pp. 286–299.
5   William Madsen, *The Mexican-American of South Texas* (New York: Holt, Rinehart and Winston, 1964), p. 15.
6   Ibid., p. 17.
7   Ibid., p. 16.
8   Burma, op. cit., p. 380.
9   Madsen, op. cit., p. 44.
10 Tatcho Mindiola, "The Mexican-American Family," M.A. thesis, University of Houston, 1970, p. 3.

11 Madsen, op. cit., p. 48.
12 Ibid.
13 Arthur J. Rubel, *Across the Tracks: Mexican-Americans in a Texas City* (Austin: University of Texas Press, 1966), p. 213.
14 Mindiola, op. cit., p. 5.
15 Ibid.
16 Beatrice Griffith, *American Me* (Boston: Houghton Mifflin Co., 1948), p. 94.
17 Mindiola, op. cit., p. 6.
18 Fernando Peñalosa, "The Changing Mexican-American in Southern California," in Rudolph Gomez, ed., *The Changing Mexican-American: A Reader* (El Paso: University of Texas Press, 1972), pp. 137–149.
19 Ibid., pp. 143–144.
20 Ibid., p. 145.
21 Ibid., p. 148.
22 Ibid., pp. 145–146.
23 Norman D. Humphrey, "The Changing Structure of the Detroit Mexican Family," *American Sociological Review*, 53 (December 1964), pp. 622–625.
24 Margaret Clark, *Health in the Mexican-American Culture: A Community Study* (Berkeley: University of California Press, 1959), chap. 6, "The Patterns of Family Life," pp. 118–161.
25 Madsen, op. cit., chap. 6, "The Family and Society," pp. 44–57; and Rubel, op. cit., chap. 3, "The Family," pp. 55–100.
26 Julian Samora and Richard A. Lamanna, *Mexican-Americans in a Midwest Metropolis: A Study of East Chicago* (U.C.L.A. Mexican-American Study Project, Advance Report 8, July 1967), chap. 3, "The Family: Bulwark of Tradition," pp. 27–30.
27 Roland G. Tharp et al., "Changes in Marriage Roles Accompanying the Acculturation of the Mexican-American Wife," *Journal of Marriage and Family*, 30 (August 1968), pp. 404–412.
28 Ibid., p. 404.
29 Ibid., pp. 410–411.
30 Mindiola, op. cit.
31 Ibid., p. 59.
32 Peñalosa, op. cit., p. 147.
33 Burma, op. cit., p. 380.
34 Leonard Broom and Norval Glenn, *Transformation of the Negro American* (New York: Harper & Row, 1965), p. 172.
35 F. Ivan Nye and Felix M. Berardo, *The Family* (New York: Macmillan Co., 1973), p. 97.
36 Andrew Billingsley, *Black Families in White America* (Englewood Cliffs, N.J.: Prentice-Hall, 1968), pp. 137–139.
37 J. Ross Eshleman, *The Family: An Introduction* (Boston: Allyn and Bacon, 1974), p. 213.
38 U.S. Bureau of the Census, *Current Population Reports*, ser. P-60, no. 80, 1971, p. 24.
39 U.S. Bureau of the Census, *Current Population Reports*, ser. 60, no. 85, 1972, p. 34.

40 U.S. Bureau of the Census, *Current Population Reports*, ser. P-20, no. 229, 1971, cover page.

41 John H. Scanzoni, *The Black Family in Modern Society* (Boston: Allyn and Bacon, 1971), chap. 6, "Husband-Wife Relationships," pp. 197–274.

42 Ibid., pp. 242–243.

43 David Heer, "Dominance and the Working Wife," *Social Forces*, 36 (May 1958), pp. 341–347.

44 Scanzoni, op. cit., p. 245.

45 Ibid., p. 279.

46 Constance K. Kamii and Norma L. Radin, "Class Differences in the Socialization Practices of Negro Mothers," *Journal of Marriage and Family*, 29 (May 1967), pp. 302–310.

47 Allison Davis and Robert J. Havighurst, "Social Class and Color Differences in Child-Rearing," *American Sociological Review*, 11 (December 1946), pp. 698–710.

48 Kamii and Radin, op. cit., pp. 306–310.

49 David B. Nolle, "Changes in Black Sons and Daughters: A Panel Analysis of Black Adolescents' Orientations Toward Their Parents," *Journal of Marriage and Family*, 34 (August 1972), pp. 443–447.

50 Ibid., pp. 445–447.

51 Jessie Bernard, *Marriage and Family Among Negroes* (Englewood Cliffs, N. J.: Prentice-Hall, 1966) as cited in Ernest W. Burgess, Harvey J. Locke and Mary M. Thomes, *The Family* (New York: Van Nostrand Reinhold Co., 1971), p. 115.

52 Ibid., p. 58.

53 Ibid.

54 Billingsley, op. cit., p. 39.

55 Bert N. Adams, *The American Family* (Chicago: Markham Publishing Co., 1971), p. 124.

56 Ibid., p. 125.

57 Billingsley, op. cit.; and Daniel P. Moynihan, *The Negro Family: The Case for National Action* (U.S. Department of Labor, 1965).

58 Lee Rainwater and William L. Yancey, *The Moynihan Report and the Politics of Controversy* (Cambridge, Mass.: M.I.T. Press, 1967), p. 309.

59 Adams, op. cit., pp. 126–128.

60 Ibid., p. 130.

61 Nye and Berardo, op. cit., p. 101.

62 Frazier, op. cit., p. 355.

63 Nye and Berardo, op. cit., pp. 104–105.

64 Ruth S. Cavan, *The American Family* (New York: Thomas Y. Crowell Co., 1969), p. 99.

65 William M. Kephart, *The Family, Society, and the Individual* (Boston: Houghton Mifflin Co., 1966), p. 488.

66 E. D. Baltzell, *The Protestant Establishment: Aristocracy and Caste in America* (New York: Random House, 1964), as cited by Kephart, op. cit., p. 489.

67 Paul M. Blumberg and P. W. Paul, "Continuities and Discontinuities in Upper-Class Marriages," *Journal of Marriage and Family*, 37 (February 1975), pp. 63–78.

68 David L. Hatch and Mary A. Hatch, "Criteria of Social Status as Derived from Marriage Announcements in *The New York Times*," *American Sociological Review*, 12 (August 1947), pp. 396–403.

69 Blumberg and Paul, op. cit., p. 74.

70 Ibid., p. 75.

71 Cavan, op. cit., p. 131.

72 John N. Edwards, ed. *The Family and Change* (New York: Alfred A. Knopf, 1969), p. 169.

73 Nye and Berardo, op. cit. This section follows closely these authors' discussion of changing roles of husbands, wives, and parents. See chap. 10, pp. 247–268.

74 Ibid., pp. 252–254.

75 David A. Schulz, *The Changing Family* (Englewood Cliffs, N.J.: Prentice-Hall, 1972). See chap. 7, pp. 139–170.

76 John F. Cuber and Peggy B. Harroff, "The More Total View: Relationships Among Men and Women of the Upper Middle Class," *Marriage and Family Living*, 25 (May 1963), pp. 140–145.

77 Ibid., p. 142.

78 Ibid., p. 144.

79 Ibid.

80 Schulz, op. cit., p. 339.

81 Ibid., p. 340.

82 *World Almanac, 1972*, p. 212.

83 Alice Rossi, "Equality Between the Sexes: An Immodest Proposal," *Daedalus*, 93 (Spring 1964), p. 273.

84 Schulz, op. cit., p. 345.

85 Everett D. Dyer, "Marital Happiness and the Two-Income Family," *Southwestern Social Science Quarterly* (September 1959), pp. 95–102.

86 David A. Schulz and Robert A. Wilson, *Readings on the Changing Family* (Englewood Cliffs, N.J.: Prentice-Hall, 1973), p. 10.

87 Daniel Yankelovitch, *Youth and the Establishment* (New York: John D. Rockefeller 3rd Fund, Inc., 1971), p. 50.

88 Schulz, op. cit., p. 308.

89 Ira L. Reiss, *The Family System in America* (New York: Holt, Rinehart and Winston, 1971), p. 407.

90 Ibid., pp. 408–409.

91 Irving Tallman, "Working Class Wives in Suburbia: Fulfillment or Crisis," *Journal of Marriage and Family*, 31 (February 1969), p. 65.

92 Ibid., p. 72.

93 Everett D. Dyer, "Social Mobility and Nuclear Family Integration as Perceived by the Wife in Swedish Urban Families," *Journal of Marriage and Family*, 32 (August 1970), pp. 341–350.

94 Urie Bronfenbrenner, "Socialization and Social Class through Time and Space," in Reinhard Bendix and Seymour Lipset, *Class, Status, and Power* (New York: Free Press, 1966), pp. 362–377.

95 Ibid., p. 376.

96 Ibid., pp. 375–376.

97 Bert N. Adams, *The Family* (Chicago: Rand McNally & Co., 1975), pp. 105–109.

98 Ibid., pp. 156–157. Also see Viktur Gecas and F. Ivan Nye, "Sex and Class Differences in Parent-Child Interaction: A Test of Kohn's Hypothesis," *Journal of Marriage and Family*, 36 (November 1974), pp. 742–755.

99 Ibid., pp. 156–157.

100 Ibid., p. 155.

101 E. E. LeMasters, *Blue-Collar Aristocrats* (Madison, Wis.: University of Wisconsin Press, 1975), pp. 110–124.

102 Ibid., p. 111.

103 Ibid.

104 Ibid., pp. 111–112.

105 Ibid.

106 Ibid.

107 Ibid., pp. 113–114.

108 Ibid., p. 114.

109 Ibid., pp. 115–116.

SELECTED READING

A good deal of attention has been given in recent years by social scientists and journalists to problems and issues of ethnic, racial, and middle-class family life and change. Somewhat less attention has been paid to working-class family life-styles and changes. LeMasters' study of working-class men and their families helps fill the gap, and accordingly the present reading, which is a chapter from his book *Blue Collar Aristocrats*, was selected. The reader will find it both enlightening and entertaining.

The reader has already been introduced to LeMasters' study of family life in the working class. He got his data from regular patrons at The Oasis, a working-class tavern in Wisconsin. His "Battle of the Sexes" describes male-female relations in these blue-collar circles, where the women are pressing for social change—for improvements in their statuses as wives and as women—and the men are fighting to retain their traditional male prerogatives. As LeMasters puts it, the two sexes here are experiencing "differential social change": The women have had a glimpse of what middle-class equalitarian marriage may be like in soap operas and women's magazines, etc., and the men "have been horrified (or frightened) by the same glimpse," which they see as a threat to their rights as men and as heads of their households. The battle lines are thus drawn, and the stage is set for the struggles between husbands and wives which LeMasters describes so well.

BATTLE OF THE SEXES*

E. E. LeMasters

"Women are so goddamm sneaky."
(*Statement by a man at The Oasis*)

Introduction

In any society one of the functional imperatives is to evolve some system whereby the two sexes can work together effectively. It is my belief that this has not been accomplished in the blue-collar group covered in this study.[1]

In an earlier examination of blue-collar marriages, Lee Rainwater came to this conclusion: "Working class men, even more than men in general, tend to think of women as temperamental, emotional, demanding, and irrational; they are sometimes in deadly earnest when they, with the hero of *My Fair Lady* ask with exasperation, 'Why can't a woman be more like a man?' They think that women do silly things: They cry for no reason, they argue in petty ways about the things a man wants to do, and they are always acting hurt for no apparent reason."[2] Some of these attitudes were found in this study and will be examined in this chapter—as will the ideas the women at The Oasis have concerning men.

This discussion is limited to generic items—males and females looking at each other as two different species. How for example, does women's liberation look at the level of the blue-collar aristocrat? Are blue-collar men and women suffering from differential social change—that is, are the women more contemporary than the men? Specific problems related to marriage, sex, and child-rearing are dealt with in separate chapters.

The Men View the Women

SUSPICION, DISTRUST, AND FEAR OF WOMEN

It is difficult, if not impossible, to talk with the men at The Oasis about the opposite sex without feeling that they view women with suspicion and distrust. In many ways these blue-collar men feel the same way about women as they do about Negroes.

One man said: "The trouble with American women is they don't know their place. I was in Japan after World War II and by God those women know who is boss. You tell one of them babes to jump and all they ask is, 'how high?' But an American woman will say, 'why?' "

Another man said: "You take that woman who wants to run the school board.* Hell, when I moved to this town twenty years ago there weren't any women on the school board—it was all men. Now you go up there and the whole damn room is full of women.† No wonder the taxes are going up."

"Women are so damn sneaky," another man said. "You never know what they're up to."

I asked him to give an example.

"Well, you take my wife—if she wants a new sweeper or stove or something like that for the house she won't come right out and say so. Instead, she starts to drag me around the stores until I finally figure out what she's up to—then we either buy the damn thing or we don't. Sometimes it's weeks before I even know what she's looking for."

I asked him if he thought his wife was extravagant in what she bought.

"No, she's a damn good manager, but she's so sneaky. I never know what's coming next."

I asked one of the wives at The Oasis to comment on the above statement. She was caustic: "That woman's husband is so damn tight with a dollar that she'd never get anything for the house if she let him know what she was up to. Fortunately, he is dumber than an ox and she can usually outsmart him."

You get the feeling that the women, having less power, feel that they have to outmaneuver the men to get what they want.

Some of the men at the tavern seem to resent the position women have won for themselves in American society in recent decades. One man, a plumber, put it this way

"I don't mind their being equal," he said, "but some of them want to run the whole damn show. They're just like the niggers—give them an inch and they'll take a mile."

The men complain that the women are unpredictable and moody.

"I came home the other night and the wife was crying. I figured I must have done something wrong but I couldn't think what it was.

"Anyhow, she was crying so I asked her what the trouble was."

" 'Nothing,' she said.

" 'Then what in the hell are you crying for?,' I asked.

"It took me ten minutes to find out she was crying because she got a letter that her favorite uncle died—Uncle Joe.

"You know how old that old bastard was? Ninety-four! And she's crying because he finally kicked the bucket!"

---

*He was referring to a local woman who was a candidate for the school board.
†Actually, as of the 1960s, men still made up a substantial majority of the local school board.

One man laughed and said: "I'll bet you were scared before you found out what she was crying about."

"Hell, yes, I thought maybe she found out I had ordered that new deer rifle she doesn't think we can afford."

Another man said: "Isn't it funny how women cry over the damndest things?"

Then he added: "The last time I cried was when the Packers lost the championship." The men laughed.

I asked one of the women at The Oasis about this complaint from the men that their wives cry too much.

"Sure, they cry," she said. "If you were married to some of these dumb bastards you would cry too."

She was warming up to the subject.

"These guys don't cry—they get drunk, or chase women, or go shoot a deer or something. But women cry. It's good for them—a hell of a lot better than getting drunk or leaping into bed with somebody."

The men seldom complain that their wives are "dumb": it tends to be the opposite, that the women are crafty, sly, devious, or scheming.

"I never can figure out what in the hell she is up to," one man observed about his wife.

"The other night, for example, I was watching a baseball game on television and I noticed her sitting there in her nightgown brushing her hair—usually she just goes to bed when a game is on but this night she didn't.

"Finally, about the eighth inning, I realized what was up—she was in the mood for some loving.

"I shut that goddam set off in one second flat and in two minutes we were in the sack.

"Now why in the hell didn't she come right out and tell me what she wanted?"

I asked a wife at the tavern to comment on the above incident.

"Well," she said, "women have learned that men like to think of themselves as great seducers. They don't want their wife to chase them all over the house when she wants to go to bed with them, so the women play it coy. They undress in front of their husband, or sit around in their nightgown, as this wife did, and pretty soon the husband gets the message and makes a pass and the wife responds. This makes the guy feel that he is irresistible—which is what they like."

On the positive side the men have certain expressions for a woman they like: she is a "good sport," or a "good mother," or a "good manager," or a "helluva good woman."

One never hears a man at The Oasis make a negative reference to his own mother. He might refer to his father as a "no good sonofabitch" but never his mother. Sisters are usually referred to in a positive tone also. Any hostility the men express toward women is focused either on their wife (or former wife) or on some woman activist in the community.

THE IDEAL WOMAN

What sort of woman do these men really want? What kind can they live with happily? Our material would suggest the following ideal:

1   A woman who is content to live along the lines of what some social scientists have called "segregated sex roles"; in other words, in a female world that is largely isolated or blocked off from the world of men.

    One man put this point into these words: "I hate a goddamn woman messing in my affairs—always asking 'Where are you going?' 'What time you gonna be back?' I always answer: 'Going where I have to and back soon as I can.'"

2   A woman who is willing to spend time and effort on her home and children. "If there's anything I can't stand," a carpenter said, "it's a woman who keeps a dirty house or lets her kids run loose all day. I figure if a woman can't take care of the house and the kids she shouldn't get married."

3   A woman who keeps herself neat and clean. A wife doesn't have to be beautiful, but she must take some pride in her appearance.

4   A woman who is sexually responsive. Her willingness to have sexual relations when the man feels like it is more important than her appearance or her body. In other words, it is absolute guarantee against sexual frustration that these men are looking for, not beauty or some vague sexual ecstasy.

5   A woman who is reliable and faithful. When a blue-collar aristocrat spends a lot of time with his male buddies he likes to be sure that his children are being cared for properly and that his wife is home minding her business. Above all she must not be "running around" with some other man. This would expose the husband to ridicule and lower his status in the male peer group.

In general, it would seem that these men like traditional rather than modern women. There is one striking exception, however: almost all (over 90 percent) of these men are willing to have their wives work outside of the home. This represents a modification of the traditional wife model that these men have learned to live with. For some of the older men this change dates back to the economic crisis of the 1930s when they were unable to support their families and their wives had to find some sort of work. For some of the younger or middle-aged men the acceptance of outside employment by wives and mothers dates back to World War II, when labor shortages and a national crisis made it imperative that wives and mothers hold outside jobs if at all possible.

It could be said that these men have evolved a female model that is extremely functional for them: it allows them great freedom; guarantees them good care of their homes and their children; assures them of sexual satisfaction; protects them against ridicule and gossip; and at the same time gives them economic aid when they need it.

When the writer discussed this wife model with one of the women at The Oasis, her comment was: "Why in the hell wouldn't they like a wife like that? It's a damn good deal for them."

One has the feeling that traditional women of the above type are becoming increasingly scarce in American society and that sooner or later the blue-collar aristocrats will have to face the fact that the slaves are in revolt.

WOMEN'S LIBERATION

To say that the drive to liberate women frightens the men in this study is an understatement. As one man said: "It scares the hell out of me." For centuries men have dominated Western society[3] and now they face the prospect that their world, and their power, may have to be shared with women. This prospect leaves them feeling gloomy—or angry.

"What in the hell are they complaining about?" one man asked. "My wife has an automatic washer in the kitchen, a dryer, a dishwasher, a garbage disposal, a car of her own—hell, I even bought her a portable TV so she can watch the goddamn soap operas right in the kitchen. What more can she want?"

Most of the wives at The Oasis are willing to settle for the "good life" described above. They know they have it better than their mothers had it, and the male-female arrangement gives them enough room to maneuver so that they do not feel "hemmed in" or stifled. As one woman said: "If my husband says 'no' to something I can always take him to bed and get a new vote."

One has the impression, however, that the younger women at the tavern are less philosophical about these issues and are more determined to have sexual equality. One of them told me that she claims the same right to "run around" that the men have; she also says that her husband has as much responsibility for the children as she has. This woman is considered a deviant at the tavern now, but sometimes deviants represent the wave of the future.

The older women—those over forty—have very little, if any, tolerance for the militant women's liberationists. This is because the women at the tavern are "gradualists"; they (and their husbands) do not favor social revolution in any form.

One wonders to what extent the attitudes of the men toward women in this study have been formed by the nature of their work: they spend all day, five days a week, in an exclusively male world. I, in contrast, have worked with women (and even under their supervision) for thirty-five years. It could be argued, of course, that being deprived of the company of women all day would make these men anxious to associate with women after work—but this does not seem to be true of the men at The Oasis. These men seem to prefer the company of men.

The Women View the Men

The most common negative reference to the men is that they are "dumb." I once asked one of the women what she meant by this.

"Well, for one thing, they do everything in the book a woman doesn't like and then they can't understand why she loses her enthusiasm for them."

I asked her to be more specific.

"Well, they drink too much; they spend too much time away from home; they often run around with other women; they spend too much money—is that enough or do you want more?"

"Why do you think women marry these men?"

"Because they don't have any choice—the other men aren't any better."

A frequent complaint by the women is that the men drink "too much."

"How often have you seen a woman drunk in here?" one of the wives asked me.

"Four or five times."

"OK. How often have you seen a man drunk in here?"

"Fifty to seventy-five times."

"OK. How would you like to be the little woman at home when daddy comes in with a snootful?"

"Not much."

"OK. That's what women have to put up with.

"And another thing," she added, "if a woman gets too much in here the men think she's *disgusting*—if a man gets too much he's *funny!* I don't get it." She ordered another beer and stared into her glass, contemplating the sad state of the male-female world.

The women complain that the men are "selfish." One woman put it this way: "These guys would go deer hunting if their mother was on her death bed. They think first of themselves. When our kids were small we could never have a birthday party on the right day for one of them because it was the week that the pheasant season opened. Wouldn't you think that kids are more important than pheasants?"

The women also object to what they consider to be sexual promiscuity in the men. This came out when I took a graduate seminar group to the tavern one evening. In the group was a rather vivacious girl in her twenties who made quite a hit with the men. Several of them, married as well as single, danced with the girl, bought her drinks, and plied her with quarters for the juke box.

A few evenings later one of the wives who had witnessed the above incident made a few comments. "That was quite a student you brought over the other night. I thought some of the older men would have a stroke dancing with her. I think Herman* was the only guy that didn't make a play for her."

It is literally true that an attractive woman can excite most of the men at the tavern just by walking in the door. If she is unattached (not married to a regular patron of The Oasis) the atmosphere will be charged with expectation: who will make the approach first? And how?

It may be that attractive men have a similar impact on women at the tavern but if so the women conceal their reaction—at least most of them do.

During the years of this study two or three women did appear at the tavern with an obvious sexual interest in the male customers. These women did not conceal their sexual interest, nor attempt to be coy. They were like the men in that their attraction to certain men was highly visible.

The reaction of both sexes to these women was interesting: the men regarded them as "whores" or "sluts," while the wives considered them "sick." Nobody could view them the way similar men are viewed at The Oasis: as people with an insistent sexual need that has not been satisfied.

The basic attitude of men and women at The Oasis toward each other seems to be that of wary distrust. They know they need each other, but at the same time they are never sure how an alliance or truce will work out.

Differential Social Change and the Two Sexes

To what extent are the two sexes truly compatible or incompatible? Man's ancestors were mammals and primates, neither of which are noted for close and continuous male-female association. Of course, man's great plasticity makes it possible for him to adapt to almost any cultural system if he has been properly socialized. But at the same time there must be some behavior systems which are more congenial to males than other. As Orville G. Brim, Jr., says, it is easier to make a boy out of a boy than it is to make a boy out of a girl.[4]

Is male-female "togetherness" what men really want or is it something they will have to accept because modern society cannot function under any other arrangement?

It is not being suggested here that males are superior to females, or that

*Herman is about seventy years old.

sexual equality is not a desirable goal. The question is whether men like to spend their free hours with their own sex or the opposite sex.

It is difficult to talk with the men and women who frequent The Oasis without feeling that somehow these two groups of people are not very compatible. The men in this study prefer the company of other men.[5] They are fiercely independent, determined not to be domesticated or henpecked by a "damn woman," and the women are equally determined not to be relegated to some nineteenth-century Victorian family style that their feminine ancestors struggled to overthrow.

To phrase this in sociological language one might say that these two sexes, at the blue-collar level, have experienced differential social change during the last few decades: the women have had a glimpse of equalitarian marriage as portrayed in the soap operas and in women's magazines and have liked what they have seen, whereas the men have been horrified (or frightened) by the same glimpse.

And so the battle lines are drawn, with each couple carrying on the struggle in their own way. One wife said that she first began to feel like a *person* after her marriage when she took a job and established her own checking account. "I was damn sick and tired of being dependent on my husband for every dime I needed," she said. "When I first got my own checking account, opened with my own money, I used to go around town buying little things for the kids and myself and writing a check for every little purchase—I was like a child with its first allowance. It felt wonderful."

With some couples the struggle for equality leads to bitterness, and the marriage may be terminated. In other cases the wife concedes defeat and retires to her home and her children. And in a few, the man surrenders, knuckles under, and is seen at The Oasis no more.

This struggle, or conflict, can best be seen among the young couples who have begun rearing their families. If the man continues to spend a lot of time at the tavern when his wife is busy with preschool children, it is apparent that he has won the struggle and has emerged victorious, his freedom and independence intact. But if the man seldom appears at the tavern after his first or second child has arrived, then it seems likely that his wife has prevailed. If the young father reduces the amount of time he spends at the tavern, then the chances are that some sort of compromise has been reached.

This battle or struggle is often not apparent in young married couples who have not had their first child; at that point the wife is still employed outside of the home, has her own income, and retains much of the freedom and independence she had while single. The big test for these couples comes when they begin to have children—and one has the impression that some of the marriages begin to slide downhill at this point.

Margaret Mead has argued that no human society has ever really achieved sexual equality.[6] Efforts toward this end have characterized American society since at least the latter part of the nineteenth century, reaching a climax at the end of World War I when women won the right to vote.[7]

In subsequent decades they also won the right to smoke, drink liquor, enjoy sex, go to college, work outside of the home, and divorce their husbands for a variety of reasons. Out of this social revolution has emerged the so-called "modern American woman."

In the past this struggle for emancipation on the part of women has been experienced largely at the middle- and upper-class levels in American society, but now it is also being fought out at the blue-collar level. Thus many of the skilled workers at The Oasis are only now facing demands from their wives that white-collar men had to face decades earlier.

It has been stated many times in this book that these blue-collar aristocrats are extremely independent persons—in the mass society they refuse to be homogenized. Maybe it is because they know, or sense, that the computer will never replace a good bricklayer; that toilets will always have to be installed by a plumber; or that only a skilled carpenter can make your house look the way you want it to.

And yet one has the feeling that eventually these men are going to lose their fight against social change (out of deference to them we will not call it progress). They are opposed to sexual equality, racial equality, mass production of houses, and many other features of modern society. In a very real (or literal) sense these men are *reactionary*—that is, they yearn for the America that began to disappear yesterday or the day before. One can see this in their attitude toward women, in their gloomy view of the welfare state, and in their hostility toward blacks demanding equality. Perhaps this generation of blue-collar aristocrats can survive free and undomesticated in their marriages, but their sons may be in for a rude awakening a few years hence.

One thing seems clear: the parents of these men did not prepare them to live happily with modern women, to enjoy them as companions (except in bed), while the women were not properly socialized to be good companions for men (even in bed). One is reminded of a point made by David Riesman and his associates in *The Lonely Crowd*:[8] namely, that some parents socialize their children for a world that no longer exists. This would seem to be what happened to some of these men. It may turn out, as our society changes, that the two sexes will become completely compatible, even at the blue-collar level. But this does not appear to be the case today.

References

1 For a general analysis of the male-female relationship in human society, see Margaret Mead, *Male and Female* (New York: William Morrow & Co., 1949).

2 Lee Rainwater, *And the Poor Get Children* (Chicago: Quadrangle Books, 1960), p. 77.

3   For a scholarly analysis of how men have dominated Western society, see Charles W. Ferguson, *The Male Attitude* (Boston: Little, Brown & Co., 1966). For the feminine version, see Elaine Kendall, *The Upper Hand* (Boston: Little, Brown & Co., 1965).

4   See Orville G. Brim, Jr., *Education for Child Rearing* (New York: Russell Sage Foundation, 1959).

5   In a very controversial book, Lionel Tiger has argued that men tend to seek male companionship because male bonding was crucial for human survival in man's early history. See his analysis, *Men in Groups* (New York: Random House, 1969). For some interesting and provocative replies to Tiger and the men who agree with him, see Michele Hoffnung Garskof, ed., *Roles Women Play: Readings toward Women's Liberation* (Belmont, Calif.: Brooks/Cole Publishing Company, 1971).

6   Mead, *Male and Female*.

7   For an excellent historical analysis of the feminist movement in the United States, see William L. O'Neill, *Everyone Was Brave: The Rise and Fall of Feminism in America* (Chicago: Quadrangle Books, 1969).

8   David Riesman et al., *The Lonely Crowd* (New Haven, Conn.: Yale University Press, 1961).

CHAPTER 8

Changes and Trends in Rural, Urban, and Suburban Families

In Chapter 4 considerable attention was paid to long-range rural and urban population trends, to the historical background of twentiety-century rural and urban economic and social environments, and to general trends which have shaped family life in the country as compared to the city. By way of introducing this chapter, we need only to highlight certain present-day trends and changes in rural America which are believed to be related to changes observed in contemporary rural family life.

Rural Family Change

THE CHANGING RURAL ENVIRONMENT

Lee Taylor and Arthur Jones, among others, point to the continuing diminishing differences today between our rural and urban economic and social environments. While farming is still the basic rural occupation, more and more farmers are operating large, impersonal, business-farming enterprises. The farmer's work, his career, and his economic and social goals are becoming

Grain elevator, Hutchinson, Kansas, 1975. (*USDA photo by Bill Marr.*)

more like those of his urban businessman counterpart. As rural "agribusiness" advances, much farm-related work is being done by specialists who supply farm equipment, advise the farmer on farming techniques, and process the farm products. Such agribusiness specialists contribute an ever enlarging proportion of the rural labor force, while farmers themselves are becoming one of the smaller occupational categories in the nation.[1]

Agribusiness and farm mechanization have brought about many changes in rural communities. Small rural towns are less likely to be able to supply the materials and specialized help needed by modern farmers, resulting in more direct contact between farmers and diversified populations in larger towns and cities farther away. Improved highways and transport have facilitated these expanding contacts and increased rural-urban interaction. For most farm and rural people today throughout America, the physical and social isolation of the past no longer exists. Rural families now share in most of the social and cultural as well as economic interests of American mass society along with urban families.

These kinds of changes in rural American communities have been observed by many social scientists, including Art Gallaher who studied a small, typical, Midwestern rural community in Missouri in the 1950s. What makes his study especially significant for seeing rural changes is that it was a repeat study of the same community fifteen years after the original study done there by James West in the late 1930s.[2]

Plainville represents an excellent example of a typical American rural farming community. Gallaher and West feel that what they saw happening there was only representative of what was also happening in hundreds of other Plainvilles throughout America. Gallaher sums up what he feels to be the most significant cultural and social changes in Plainville between 1939-40 and 1954-55:

Change in the community during this period is best generalized as the result of the following interrelated conditions: the steady disappearance of geographical and cultural isolation; pressure for change from the larger culture surrounding Plainville, involving at some points actual interference; and the acceptance of new living standards focused on material comfort and increased efficiency. We can generalize further and say that the major culture change process is urbanization, that is, that Plainvillers are entering into relationships drawing them into ever-widening circles of awareness of, participation in, and dependency upon the surrounding urban world. Central in this process are the extension of technology from the greater mass culture to Plainville and the subsequent adjustment of Plainville systems of values to altered conditions. . . . [3] [Also] a major result of the Plainviller's increased contact with American mass culture is new expectations of what constitutes the desirable in various areas of his life. Among other things he has developed new standards . . . based on models drawn from urban America. . . . These are mirrored in the dominant pattern of change—a newly defined standard of living involving expectations of material and non-material comfort and efficiency.[4]

The broad forces of cultural and social change observed in Plainville had, Gallaher feels, many implications for the family farm tradition in America.

Plainville, in microcosm, exemplifies many of the changes which have affected rural America . . . , and shows some of the effects of the concern for the family farm tradition in our society translated into action. In broad outline the more important changes in Plainville and the rest of rural America can be stated as follows: socio-cultural linkage between rural and urban communities has proceeded at an unprecedented rate; the welfare of the farmer now depends more on state and national farm policy than on the individual efforts of the farm family itself; and there have been revolutionary changes in technology with concomitant social changes.[5]

Rural communities such as Plainville have been increasingly drawn into the urban sphere of influence, due especially, Gallaher feels, to urban technological and economic dominance. "Farm families in most sections of America now accept values characteristically urban, and these values, in fact, integrate changes in many facets of rural life."[6]

In their article "Rural Society in Transition," O. F. Larson and E. M. Rogers have attempted to identify the major social changes underway in American rural society today. They list seven interrelated changes in process:

1 An increase in farm productivity per man has been accompanied by a decline in the number of farm people in the U.S.
2 Linkage of the farm with the non-farm sector of American society is increasing.
3 Farm production is increasingly specialized.
4 Rural-urban differences in values are decreasing as America moves in the direction of a mass society.
5 Rural people are increasingly cosmopolitan in their social relationships. . . .
6 There is a trend toward centralization of decision-making in rural public policy and in agribusiness firms.
7 Changes in rural social organization are in the direction of a decline in the relative importance of primary relationships . . . and an increase in the importance of secondary relationships. . . .[7]

These changes in the rural social and economic environment are logical and understandable when placed in the larger context of social and economic change in twentieth-century America. Rural and urban America are integrally interlinked, comprising the larger whole that is American society. This larger society is, as we have seen in Chapter 6, in process of changing from the Gemeinschaft-sacred type toward the Gesellschaft-secular type of society. So, as rural America now joins urban America in transition from the traditional toward the modern, we may expect to find in rural communities and populations more impersonality in interpersonal relations, more cosmopolitan and less localistic social relations, less emphasis on local ties and perhaps on kinship ties; also higher levels of literacy and education, increased open-mindedness and more flexibility in roles; also greater emphasis on economic rationality, and a more complex economic division of labor, along with a continuously developing farm technology.[8]

CHANGING CONTEMPORARY RURAL FAMILY LIFE

Convergence of rural and urban family organizational patterns is apparent. As rural families in America have emerged from their relative isolation, as they have reduced their economic independence and other self-sufficient features, and as they have become more directly involved in the larger society outside the local community, they have become more like other families in the larger urban-secular society. In his comparison of rural and urban families in the Detroit area, Robert O. Blood, Jr., saw these pervasive urban influences now extending beyond the metropolis out to adjacent rural families, ". . . with the result that contemporary rural and urban families resemble each other in most essential features."[9] Whether these changes are felt to be good or bad is probably a matter of opinion. As we have seen, traditional rural families have a number of strengths but also certain inflexibilities and related weaknesses. And conversely, urban families with their much-publicized problems also have their strengths.

Lee Burchinal has observed a close relationship between rural family change and urban family change today. A review of the literature reveals that "all empirical data consistently support the generalization that changes in rural family organization have followed those described for the urban family system."[10] Burchinal finds the gap between the rural and urban family attitudes, values, and behavior is being narrowed steadily, as evidenced by declining rural family size, declining familism, increasing family role flexibility, and democratization of rural families. Rising levels of education in rural America will contribute to the convergence of rural and urban family patterns. Increasing secularization of rural populations will likely produce higher divorce rates; and as rural youth go to college in greater numbers, the education-related generation gap so often found between urban children and their parents will likely become more pronounced within rural families.

While increasing rural secularization may contribute to more marital instability by removing or weakening traditional taboos against separation and divorce, and perhaps contribute to tensions in parent-child relations, in other ways expanded experiences and increased knowledge accompanying secularization can yield broader understanding and sophistication, which can in turn contribute to richer and fuller marriages and family stability. In the past, success in rural marriage and family relations was more dependent on propinquity, homogamy, and interdependent family roles such as family teamwork in the farm enterprise. The trend now in rural family life is toward an emphasis on interpersonal competency of the spouses, with marital success defined in terms of the ability of the husband and wife to fulfill companionship or colleague roles based upon mutual respect and love.[11]

SELECTED STUDIES IN RURAL FAMILY CHANGE

One of the best-known studies of change in rural family life was conducted by Robert O. Blood, Jr., and Donald Wolfe in Michigan in the mid-1950s.[12] They compared the division of labor and authority in farm families with those observed in urban families in the Detroit area. They found very little evidence of traditional patriarchal authority in either rural or urban families. The general mode of decision making was equalitarian for both farm and city families. However, around this mode there were significant variations. In some families the husband was dominant while in others the wife was more dominant. Why these variations? Blood and Wolfe feel that differences in competence may explain much of the variation here. Whichever marriage partner has the greater competence to make the decision usually does so. Family power structure is geared to the most efficient means of achieving family objectives.[13]

Farmer's wife helps her husband while balancing six-month-old son on her hip, 1975. (*USDA photo by Michelle Bogre.*)

This surely suggests a move away from traditional authority patterns in these farm families (as well as in the city families).

Blood and Wolfe also found that the division of labor in general was organized to accomplish the family's objectives, but more along traditional sex-role lines, particularly in farm families. Significant differences in the internal division of labor were found between farm and city families. They found that farm wives, in traditional fashion, perform a larger share of the household tasks than city wives. For one thing, the husbands have less time to help with housework, for unlike his city male counterpart with a nine-to-five job, the farmer's farm work is never done. Another rural-urban difference found was that farm wives help their husbands in their occupations more than city wives do, showing some cultural continuity in rural family teamwork. This difference also reflects the obvious difficulty of most city wives in helping their husbands in their away-from-home occupations. So, unlike the essentially similar authority patterns found for both farm and city families, the division of labor picture shows significant differences, with farm families still more traditional, thus indicating less change for them. Blood concludes: "The division of labor in city and farm families has proven significantly different. . . . Farm wives exceed city wives in the work they perform both in traditional feminine spheres and in many masculine role areas. The aggregate effect is to suggest that farm women invest substantially more time and energy in tasks around the home which contribute directly to the physical and financial well-being of other family members."[14]

This study suggests that in the area of sex roles and division of labor farm families have not changed as much as city families. However, in the area of family power structure, farm families, like their urban counterparts, are becoming increasingly equalitarian.

In the mid-1960s Herbert Smith did an intensive study of division of labor and authority in 510 farm families in rural Wisconsin.[15] Smith observed the ways family roles are performed and the extent to which the role performances of husbands and wives are differentiated, equalitarian, or specialized. Findings are presented on role performances and authority patterns of the spouses in farm work, in household and child-rearing tasks, and in decision making.

Smith found a clear-cut traditional sex-role differentiation in the area of farm tasks, with the husband doing most of the heavy field work and caring for the livestock and farm equipment. The wife performs those farm tasks that are more in keeping with her work in the home, such as cleaning the milking equipment. She also shares with her husband the keeping of the farm records and the paying of farm bills. Sex-role differentiation is also evident in the area of housework, with the wife performing most tasks conventionally considered "domestic" in nature, such as buying groceries, preparing meals, and washing dishes. The only household task performed mainly by the husband is making any household repairs needed. Tasks in this general area shared by both husband and wife are budget-related activities such as keeping the financial records and paying household bills. In the area of child rearing, the tasks are performed primarily by the wife. Yet these farm husbands do share with their wives to some extent in disciplining their children and in teaching them facts, skills, and table manners.

In the area of family authority patterns, there is, by comparison with family task performance, a more clear-cut equalitarianism, with husbands and wives jointly involved in decision making in a majority of the areas of family life. Only in farm management and operations decision making is the husband clearly dominant. In the household area, husbands share with their wives in making decisions on such matters as selection of household furnishings and home maintenance, but wives assume the major responsibility in this area. Child-rearing decisions are also jointly made by the husband and wife in a majority of these farm families, with the wife taking the greater responsibility in some things (such as when the children will visit friends), and the husband assuming the responsibility in other matters (such as deciding the farm chores for the children).

Smith's findings tend to support those of Blood and Wolfe, showing both change and continuity for mid-twentieth-century farm families. Traditional patriarchal authority has given way to an essential equalitarianism in family authority. In the division of labor, some change is evident in the greater role-flexibility found today, while at the same time a measure of historical continuity is seen in the persistence of some sex-role differentiation along traditional lines. Smith sums it up in this way:

While the data presented support the expectation that both husbands and wives are jointly involved in decision-making, the data also support the principle of differentiation. There is evidence of joint involvement in financial decisions whether pertaining to farm or household. . . . Equalitarian patterns are also found for child-rearing decisions and for the family decisions. Differentiation is also evident and is along the lines expected when one considers the functions performed by farm husbands and wives in the farm-family social system complex. The husband is dominant in farm decisions. . . . The wife dominates the decisions related to her responsibilities as homemaker. The couples share jointly in those decisions pertaining to the general welfare of the family.[16]

In a comparable study in Iowa about the same time, Lee Burchinal and W. W. Bauder compared family decision making and role patterns of farm families, rural nonfarm families, and urban families.[17] They found that equalitarian decision making predominated regardless of family residence. This would indicate that rural families, both farm and nonfarm, have followed the direction taken earlier by urban families; that equalitarian norms have pretty well replaced earlier semipatriarchal norms in rural Iowa. These findings agree in essence with those of Blood and Wolfe in Michigan and Smith in Wisconsin.

Burchinal and Bauder also found, as did the others, the continued existence of sex-stereotyped division of labor between rural husbands and wives. However, they attribute this less to traditional definitions of male and female roles than to expediency or preference, i.e., to "availability, greater competency, or perhaps personal preference of one sex for doing a particular task rather than on a traditional division of labor based on male-female difference."[18] And unlike Blood and Wolfe, who found big differences in family roles between farm and city wives, the present study showed no significant differences between family role patterns of rural wives and city wives. The authors suggest that this difference in their findings from that of Blood and Wolfe may lie in the differences in the composition of Blood and Wolfe's Detroit-area sample and their Des Moines–area sample. The former was probably more cosmopolitan while the latter was still more rural-minded, thus minimizing differences in female family role patterns between rural Iowa people and those who now live in the city of Des Moines.

It seems safe to conclude from these and other similar studies that rural families are in process of changing toward the modern-equalitarian family type, and have, in the third quarter of the twentieth century, moved well away from the opposite traditional-patriarchal family type. The most pronounced and extensive movement is in the area of family authority, where a high degree of equalitarianism has been achieved in rural families. The degree of change in family role patterns, while significant, is not as great and varies with the amount of exposure to urban-secular influences.

As we have noted earlier, one of the most pronounced patterns of population movement in recent decades in the United States has been the migration of both rural and urban dwellers to the outer fringes of metropolitan cities. Families living in such fringe areas may be neither strictly urban nor rural. Hans Sebald and Wade Andrews investigated the adjustments and changes made in a sample of 303 families living in what they called the *rural fringe* area around Columbus, Ohio.[19] They identify the rural fringe as encompassing "the less densely populated unincorporated areas around the cities where agricultural land uses are still prevalent . . . [as opposed to] the urban fringe [which] comprises the urbanized land areas contiguous to the city . . . , and which falls within the Standard Metropolitan Statistical Area."[20]

The authors found that these families generally felt that residence in the rural fringe offered facilities and conditions favorable to child rearing. The best integrated or adjusted families were those that were becoming more involved in formal social participation in the community, with active memberships in church and civic organizations. A positive correlation was also found between formal education and family integration. The researchers infer from this finding that the rural fringe family is probably significantly different from the traditional rural or semirural family where formal education was presumably deemphasized.[21] Families from rural and urban backgrounds seemed to be equally well adjusted in their rural fringe environment; and length of residence in the rural fringe community was not found to be correlated with family integration. Nor was there any relationship between the age of the parents or the size of the family and family integration.

In sum, the findings of this study show that for these rural fringe families: (1) the more they participate in organized activities in the community, the higher the degree of family integration; (2) active families which are well satisfied with their residential area are better adjusted internally; and (3) education appears to be an important factor in family integration, "and may point to a cultural and systematic means for modern [fringe] family integration."[22] The findings suggest that the modern rural fringe family is neither as isolated nor as withdrawn from the outside social world as thought by some. Rather, this kind of modern family is more actively involved in the social life of the community, and generally shows high satisfaction with life in the rural fringe. This is further evidence of the flexibility and adaptability of the American family to our changing and commingling rural and urban environments.

In a study in the late 1960s of 448 Minnesota families, half of which were farm families and the other half urban, Murray Straus not only made comparisons of the degree to which these families were modernized, but also sought to determine some of the conditions under which the families do become modernized, or show evidence of "modernity."[23] His findings are interesting as they bear upon our concern with processes and conditions of rural family change. The theory being tested by Straus was that significant ties with kinfolk typically act as a deterrent to social change in the nuclear family, that those families who maintain frequent contacts with relatives tend to be more conservative and resist change. So, assuming the existence of a generally traditional orientation of rural kinfolk, Straus felt that "it is reasonable to hypothesize that, until the modernization of world society is far more complete than is now the case, the greater the interaction with kin, the less modern the values or behavior of the individual or the family, and therefore, the greater the impediment to societal modernization."[24] Straus sought data to test the following theorems: (1) that ruralness is associated with higher kinship interaction than urbanness, and (2) that regardless of residence, the greater the interaction with kin, the less the "psycho-social modernity."[25] (*Modernity* is measured by the degree of *active-future orientation* in the family, by higher educational expectations held for sons and daughters, and by a five-item planning index showing the degree to which family members are future-oriented and innovative in their family roles.)

The first theorem was supported by the data. Farm wives had more frequent interaction with relatives than urban wives. Stated differently, the data showed greater isolation from kinfolk for urban wives than for rural wives. With respect to the second theorem, the data showed a strong relationship for these rural families between frequency of interaction with kin and "non-modernization." These farm families were significantly less modernized; specifically, they were less future-oriented, did less planning for the future, and had lower educational expectations for both sons and daughters, as compared with the urban families.[26] These findings definitely supported the hypothesis that the greater the interaction with kin, the less "modern" the family will be, and that this condition is still more to be found in rural than in urban families today. This study suggests that social change for rural families is still moving at a slower pace than is true for urban families.

THE RURAL FAMILY OF THE FUTURE

What may be predicted for rural families in the future? It is hazardous to try to make broad generalizations about *the* rural family, of course, since rural families, as is true for urban families, stem from different sources, live in different environments, and encompass great heterogeneity in ethnic, racial, and class characteristics. Also, the research on which to base predictions is not adequate quantitatively or qualitatively, being based largely on a limited number of mostly middle-class, white, rural families. Still, there is some agreement among the authorities as to certain general trends in rural family change. As Burchinal points out in his article "The Rural Family of the Future," "All empirical data consistently support the generalization that changes in rural family organization have followed those [found] for the urban family system."[27] While this is hardly news, it does provide a valuable perspective for predicting changes in rural family organization and relationships. For example, studies have shown that while changes are taking place in families living in isolated mountain areas in Kentucky, these families are about fifty years behind those in the outside world.[28]

Much evidence indicates that there is a general trend for rural families to become smaller, with more flexibility in family roles, with families becoming more democratic in orientation, and less familistic. Broadening social experience and rising levels of education in rural communities will expedite these trends and narrow the gap still further between rural and urban family patterns. Also to be considered are the homogenizing effects of mass media and the ever-increasing contacts and interaction with urban people in all phases of life.

Stated in the broad terms of our typologies, we may say that rural families in America are in an accelerated process of change from the traditional-patriarchal family type moving toward the modern-equalitarian family type, but that the changes are at uneven rates depending upon the degree and intensity of exposure to urban-secular influences.

A final note is in order as to recent rural population trends. There are signs of some reversal in the long-term migration trend of families moving from rural areas to urban areas. Recent United States census surveys show that nonmetropolitan areas are growing now at a faster rate than metropolitan areas. Data show that nonmetropolitan counties gained 4.2 percent population between April 1970 and July 1973, while metropolitan counties grew by 2.9 percent over the same period.[29] It is too soon to tell if this is really the start of a new trend or only a short-term reversal. Opinion polls show more Americans now reporting a preference to live in the country or in a small town, with very few now stating an actual preference for life in a large city. However, people admit that there are drawbacks to life in the country or in towns, including limited job opportunities and limited educational and cultural facilities. Also, with transportation now becoming increasingly costly due to energy problems, it is likely that fewer families whose breadwinners work in the city will be able to live in the outer rural fringes around our big cities.

Urban Family Change

THE CHANGING CONTEMPORARY URBAN ENVIRONMENT

In Chapter 4 we traced the growth of cities and urban populations throughout American history. Here we are mainly concerned with contemporary changes in the urban environment as such changes affect contemporary urban family life. As we pointed out in Chapter 4, the United States did not become a predominantly urban society until about the time of World War I. The United States census of 1920 showed that, for the first time, over one-half of the American population was living in urban areas.[30] Sharp rises in birthrates added impetus to this urban growth. The advent of the automobile was especially important, not only in the general picture of urban development, but particularly in the mid-twentieth-century suburban expansion. Thus, while earlier urban and suburban expansion tended to follow railroad lines, with the mass production of automobiles this older confinement broke, and "urban sprawl" was under way as an irresistible force. Since World War II, urbanization has accelerated to the extent that the 1970 United States census showed nearly three-fourths of all Americans as urban dwellers. Large cities grew rapidly larger and the populations in the metropolitan areas around these cities grew even faster. By 1970 there were over twenty-five urban complexes each with more than 1 million inhabitants, and over fifty urban areas with more than half a million each.[31] Regionally, the Northeastern part of the country became urbanized first, and is still the most urban part of America. Since 1950, the urban population of the West Coast, particularly California, has grown very rapidly, as have urban areas of the Southwest and, most recently, the South.

The urban sprawl phenomenon and the urbanization of the American population has led to the notion of *metropolitanism*, within which distinctions may be made between central cities and their contiguous suburban areas.

The metropolitan concept includes a large central city and generally an even larger "surrounding geographic area with population whose social and economic activities form a more or less integrated system revolving around the central city."[32] This would include suburbs, satellite communities, and fringe areas. The metropolitan concept has become an official part of the United States census, and since 1960 the term Standard Metropolitan Statistical Area (S.M.S.A.) has been used by the Census Bureau to denote such areas in the United States. Metropolitan areas outside the central cities have grown faster in recent decades than the central cities themselves. This growth differential has slowed down some in the 1970s due in part to the "energy problem" which has greatly increased the cost of gasoline and transportation in general.

In addition to the notion of a city, its suburbs, and urban fringe areas combining to form metropolitan areas, we now also hear of several adjacent metropolitan areas coming together to form a *megalopolis*. An example of such a megalopolis or superurban area would be the string of metropolitan areas along the Northeastern Atlantic seaboard, extending roughly from Massachusetts to Virginia. This continuous urbanized band includes over 50,000 square miles and contains more than one-fifth of the whole American population. Another developing megalopolis would be in California, including Los Angeles–Orange–Riverside–San Bernardino–San Diego counties.[33]

This massive twentieth-century urbanization of America is in part the product of an accelerated technological revolution that has permeated virtually all aspects of American life. A combination of modern communications technology, electric power, and modern transportation, particularly the automobile, has set in motion forces that have diffused population and industry over wide areas and permitted dense agglomerations of each.[34]

Has urbanization gone so far today that it is proper to speak of "America as a city" now? Scott Greer, among others, argues that this is so, that America has become a big metropolitan area, that the spread of people to the suburbs has perhaps obscured the fact that the city has come to dominate the entire society in ways never seen before. The importance and power of the local community has declined and that of the larger society increased. It is possible now to argue that the United States has become a real national community, essentially urban in nature. Greer argues thus: "The culture of the large-scale society is urban in its essence; all ears are tuned to the nationwide communication networks; and behavior is ordered by the large-scale agencies of government bureau, corporation, and national market."[35]

What may be some of the consequences of this "nation-city" development for the family and its members? Arlene Skolnick feels that "this nation-city is an abstract and bloodless community. It has undermined the basis of the local community without providing a substitute for community sociability."[36] Thus, while an urban dweller shares certain interests with others in his "status community," such affiliations fall short of satisfying human needs for real communal relations. So, according to Benjamin Zablocki, one of the problems of the urban dweller today is a dilemma of "freedom versus community." As a member of the larger nation-city, one is freed from the older constraints of the local community and the extended kin group. One is now free to live according to personal tastes, temperament, and interests. However, one pays a price for this new freedom in a loss of the security, permanence, and stability offered by the traditional local community.[37] The revival of communes in recent years is in part an effort to recover and reestablish this lost sense of community.

Another dilemma brought on by this nation-city development, according to Skolnick, is that of "privacy and abundance versus community and poverty." [38] Affluence increases family privacy. The luxuries and conveniences which so many urban families have been able to buy have meant greater privacy, but at the price of reduced daily contacts with others in their community. Is it perhaps only the less affluent urban dwellers who retain a sense of belonging to a local community? As seen earlier, working-class and lower-class families may hold more tenaciously to their larger circles of relations and friends than do the more affluent, mobile, and "private" middle-class families.

THE INTENSIFICATION OF URBAN FAMILY LIFE

With the decline of the local community as a viable influence in their lives, many urban dwellers have been turning more to home and family to meet their social and personal needs. The very high rates of urban marriage and remarriage attest to this. Family life in a sense has become more intensified, and the demands being placed upon the few members included in the nuclear family are considerable. Can the urban nuclear family bear the burden of the emotional and psychological demands asked of it by its members? Viewed in this context, the high divorce rate may be interpreted as a symptom of unmet emotional and psychological needs in marriage on the part of many urban people. Skolnick argues that the high urban marriage and divorce rates may show that people are expecting marriage to fulfill needs that cannot all be met by it.[39] In older, more stable, and permanent communities married people probably did not demand so much of each other. Even today in working-class and ethnic urban neighborhoods, husbands and wives often lead rather separate daily lives, the wife with her female relatives and friends, and the husband with his work group and male buddies. As urban families move up to middle-class status and into middle-class suburbs, ties with people outside the family tend to lessen, and marriage becomes more intense and demanding. This view has been rather emphatically put by P. E. Slater:

In a non-mobile society one expects of marriage only a degree of compatibility. Spouses are not asked to be lovers, friends, and mutual therapists. But it is increasingly true of our society that the marital bond is the closest, deepest, most important, and putatively most enduring relationship of one's life. Therefore, it is increasingly likely to fall short of the demands placed on it and to be dissolved. As emotional alternatives are removed, its limitations become less and less tolerable.[40]

Slater also points out that since the family has come to be the main permanent point of reference for urban dwellers, "heroic efforts" are being made today to find ways to enable the marriage relationship to bear up under the enormous demands we place on it. Thus the proliferation of marriage manuals, marriage counsellors, psychotherapists, magazine articles, and the like.

Has the intensification of urban family life expanded beyond the immediate nuclear family? With the diminishing of social ties, perhaps more urban people are maintaining or reestablishing kin ties after marriage than we realized. These questions relate to an issue discussed more fully in Chapter 4, that of urban nuclear-family isolation versus urban extended-family ties. Marvin Sussman, Eugene Litwak, and others have challenged the older Parsonian thesis of the essential isolation of the mobile, urban nuclear family, contending that while these small conjugal-oriented families generally live apart from their kin, the married couples do retain important ties with their close relatives, and the couple are provided both material services and emotional need satisfaction on a regular basis, especially by their parents. Thus, according to Litwak, it is more correct to speak of an urban "modified extended family" today, consisting of at least one nuclear family and a number of their close relatives living "in a state of partial dependence."[41] Something of a controversy has been carried on between the proponents of this view and those still adhering to the Parsonian view of the predominance of the isolated nuclear family in urban America. The author feels that the truth lies somewhere between these opposing views, as expressed by Straus: "A review and synthesis of the literature on the relationship between urbanization and kinship interaction suggests that interaction with the extended kin of urban middle class families is neither as great as the revisionist critics of the 'isolated nuclear family' theory imply, nor as minimal as the proponents of their theory imply."[42]

Returning now to the questions raised just above, it is probably safe to conclude that the urban nuclear family is not now as isolated as it was thought to be earlier, and that there are aspects of urbanization and the urban social environment that may well foster familial ties beyond the nuclear family. Not only are nuclear family relations of great importance to urban dwellers who have felt the loss of a sense of community and whose other primary-group contacts have faded, but contacts with close relatives are being sustained more now to help meet personal needs and to reinforce the nuclear family. As Greer puts it: ". . . kin relations may be seen as growing in importance just because of the diminished reliance placed upon neighborhood and local community."[43]

FLIGHT FROM THE CENTRAL CITY AND
THE SUBURBAN MOVEMENT

One of the most dramatic changes taking place in the urban environment in the second and third quarters of the twentieth century is the tremendous growth and expansion of suburbs in our big metropolitan areas. While the concept of suburb is rather ambiguous, for present purposes we can identify suburbs as those areas within the Standard Metropolitan Statistical Area (S.M.S.A.) but outside the central city, including those residential areas that are located outside the city but are tied to it economically and culturally.[44] These suburbs are generally dependent upon the central city for goods and services and employment, and there is a large amount of commuting to the main city by suburban dwellers. Some suburbs are somewhat industrialized, while others are essentially residential, serving as dormitories for the central city.

Since 1950 the United States Census Bureau has used the term *urban fringe* to include all territory within urbanized areas but outside the central city. Such areas are normally considered suburbs in standard census usage. In 1950, the United States population was 64 percent urban; in 1960 the proportion of urban dwellers was up to 69 percent, and by 1970 it had increased to 73.5 percent. The greatest urban growth during these decades was in the urban fringe or suburbs, which increased from 13.7 percent of the population in 1950 to 21.6 percent in 1960, to 26.8 percent by 1970. (The actual numbers for these three periods were 1950: 21 million; 1960: 32 million; and 1970: 54 million.)[45] During these same decades the rate of growth of the central cities declined.

Mid-twentieth-century suburbs are more varied than those observed earlier, by Burgess for example, which were virtually all middle or upper class. Today more suburbs are working class, embracing a rich mixture of ethnic and other minority groups. By contrast to the stereotyped middle-class suburbanite, some contemporary working-class suburbanites are described by Bennett Berger: "They were still overwhelmingly Democrats—they attended church as infrequently as they ever did; like most working class people, their informal contacts were limited largely to kin; they neither gave nor went to parties; on the whole they had no great hopes of getting ahead in their jobs; and instead of a transient psychology, most of them harbored a view of their new suburban homes as paradise permanently gained."[46]

Insofar as Berger is correct, it appears that these new suburban dwellers are holding onto their working-class norms and customs. It remains to be seen how fast their children, who will grow up in the suburbs and attend suburban schools, will change.

It is still, however, the white middle-class family that is probably most firmly entrenched in suburbia. Robert Winch sees the great growth of the suburbs as "the family's response to the loss of functions."[47] This has been basically a middle-class reaction to life in the city. Fearing the threat of family disorganization posed by life in the crowded, industrial central city, families that can afford to do so move out to the suburbs in pursuit of a safer, more secure, and, they hope, a more satisfying family life. There has also been a racial dimension to this suburban population movement. As increased numbers of black Americans have moved from rural areas to cities, especially since World War II, the rate of white exodus to the suburbs has accelerated.[48]

Most suburbs still tend to be one-class communities, so the families dwelling in a given suburb normally fall within a rather limited socioeconomic range, and generally share certain norms and practices embraced in the subculture of that social class. Zoning regulations restrict the kind of housing built, and developers generally determine the price range of housing available in a given suburban neighborhood. While the life-styles of families in a particular suburb will vary some according to background and individual family tastes, there is apt to be more cultural homogeneity than in inner-city residential areas. The suburban way of life seems to be attractive to increasingly large segments of the urban population. We will take a closer look at family trends and changes in the suburbs below.

CONTEMPORARY URBAN FAMILY LIFE: TRENDS AND CHANGES

TRENDS IN URBAN KINSHIP RELATIONS   Perusal of the literature reveals that much has been written about the conjugally-oriented, urban nuclear family. The degree to which these nuclear families have severed or have retained ties with parents and other relatives is an issue to which many sociologists have turned their attention in recent years. As noted above, there is considerable evidence that the urban nuclear family is not as isolated or removed socially from its kin as earlier thought.[49]

It would be appropriate here to review briefly what some recent studies have shown to be the trends in kinship ties and relations among urban families.

Marvin Sussman has conducted a number of studies on this matter. Typical would be his study of a stratified random sample of 500 families in Cleveland, Ohio.[50] He found big differences in the amount of contacts and relations between these nuclear families and their kin, ranging along a continuum from isolation from all relatives to continuous and very frequent contact and close relations with relatives. About 75 percent reported ongoing relations with close relatives, including visiting (85 percent had kin living in the Cleveland area), phone calls, exchange of letters, and financial help and other services rendered and received. Especially during the early years of marriage do parents aid their young married children. The amount of such aid is greater in the middle class than in the working class, but the willingness to give and receive aid does not vary significantly by class. Sussman concludes that the majority of urban nuclear families retain ties and carry on relationships with close relatives—especially parents—-to the degree that they are members of an integrated kin network both by propinquity and by functional relationships. These urban kinship ties cut across lines of class, race, education, and occupation.

Bert Adams did a study of kinship relations in an old Southern city, Greensboro, North Carolina, in the mid-1960s. His sample consisted of 799 young-to-middle-aged, white, married men and women, of varied social-class backgrounds.[51] Adams found that relations between young adults and their kin are primarily with their parents. Contact patterns show both mutual affection and continuing feelings of obligation between parents and their adult offspring, with a basic concern for each other's welfare. Relations among adult siblings are based less on mutual concern with one another's mutual welfare than upon "interest," or on a comparison of how well the siblings are doing economically and socially. Relations between young adult siblings are limited or constrained to some extent by divergent interests and values; however, there is a tendency, especially among females, to reaffirm ties when married siblings start to have children.[52] Relations between cousins and other secondary relatives were found to be minimal.

Adams's findings appear to corroborate those of Sussman that urban nuclear families tend to retain ties with close relatives in the middle class as well as in the working class. He also found that certain life-cycle variables influence urban kinship relations, especially the aging of the parents.

Aging parents play a particularly central role both in perpetuating their nuclear families of procreation, i.e., in linking siblings together after they leave the parental home, and in maintaining their family of orientation, or ties with their aging siblings and their children. They further serve to relate their families of procreation and orientation to each other, so that young adults at least keep posted on the activities of, if they don't keep in touch with, aunts, uncles, and cousins, as well as their siblings. After the death of the older generation, there is likely to be loss of interest on the part of young adults in their secondary kin, i.e., their parent's family of orientation. They, in turn, are apt to begin to focus on *their* nuclear families of orientation and procreation, and extensions of these in children, as they grow older. The effective kin network is thus constantly expanding by birth and contracting by death and loss of contact on the part of the aging.[53]

Many other studies have corroborated the findings of Sussman and Adams.[54] In their article "Some Neglected Considerations on the American Urban Family," D. E. Carnes, S. Goldberg, and S. Greer offer an insightful analysis of continuing close kinship ties frequently found in urban families today.[55] They distinguish between (1) *instrumental functionality*, where the parties or groups involved "gain something tangible or useful in the course of the interaction," such as giving or receiving financial aid or exchanges of help in doing housework, and (2) *expressive functionality*, where psychological or emotional support is given and received. They suggest that contact with kin among urban dwellers, especially those with a universalistic-achievement orientation, depends, first, upon the degree of instrumental functionality to be gained by such contacts and ties, and, secondarily, upon kinship ties which may be influenced by expressively functional relations, and perhaps also by a sense of duty. These authors agree with Adams that as long as kinfolk are useful in these ways to each other, they will continue to interact and will maintain kin networks.[56] They go on to argue that if the United States were truly a completely universalistic-achievement society, where everyone had equal access to the means of success, kin contacts would have very little instrumental functionality. But many groups in America, such as "blacks, women, Jews, and recent immigrants . . . have been systematically excluded from the broad range of opportunity structures."[57] Thus, kin ties and relations serve important instrumental purposes for many such relatively disadvantaged urban nuclear families striving for success. These families may turn to relatives for business capital, high-risk credit, trusted labor, etc., as, for example, Greer observed among Jewish Americans, or for sheer survival as has often been the case for black urban families. "The location of these groups in an opportunity structure that defines success in a universal way accounts for much of the strength of kinship ties among these people," the authors conclude.[58]

Theoretically, perhaps only in upper-middle-class or upper-class WASP (White, Anglo-Saxon, Protestant) nuclear families would such instrumental functionality be lacking in relations among kinfolk. All such contacts and ties would ostensibly be based entirely on affection and/or a sense of duty.

TRENDS AND CHANGES IN URBAN NUCLEAR FAMILY ORGANIZATION AND RELATIONSHIPS   In a study aimed at determining urban influences on fertility and on employment patterns of women living in or just adjacent to big metropolitan areas, J. D. Tarver and his associates collected data on all women fourteen years of age and older living in eighty-one counties which contain and surround three metropolitan centers: Atlanta, Georgia; Indianapolis, Indiana; and Omaha, Nebraska.[59] They found that the employment of women is related to urbanism in two ways. First, the percentage of employed women increases consistently with city size, and second, employment decreases consistently with the distance of the family residence from the main city. This finding supports the *gradient principle* which holds that the proportion of women employed increases as the population size of the city increases, but also declines with the distance from the metropolitan center.[60] The gradient principle also implies that fertility of women should decline with urbanism, i.e., as population size of the urban center increases. Findings here also supported this hypothesis, with one qualification. Fertility of these women increased consistently with distance from the metropolitan center, but fluctuated irregularly with increasing size of the central city. It was felt that this fluctuation was due largely to the disproportionate number of black women (who have higher fertility rates) living in the Atlanta area. For white women the gradient principle generally held true; i.e., their fertility rates decreased both as the city size increased and as they lived closer to the central city.[61]

It has been noted above and in earlier chapters that one of the most significant urban nuclear family trends has been the increased employment of married women. An intriguing question is whether or not the urban married woman's new family-provider role has increased her power in the family. Blood and Wolfe, among others, have advanced the theory that the wife's power in family decision making increases as her resources increase, and the employed wife with a paid job has more resources vis-à-vis her husband than the unemployed wife. An attempt to test this "*theory of resources* was made by D. B. Kandel and G. S. Lesser on a sample of 800 American urban families and 403 Danish urban families.[62] While in neither country was marital power found to be consistently or clearly correlated with the resources (specifically, income or occupation) brought to the marriage by each spouse, the employment of the wife, whether part time or full time, definitely contributed to her increased power within the family. When the wife was employed outside the home she had more power vis-à-vis her husband than when she was not employed. The researchers feel that the working wife's job-related contacts outside the home may also be very important in increasing her power within the home, rather than just the material resources themselves. They put it this way: "The importance of socio-economic resources for marital decision-making may not derive primarily from the availability of financial and status rewards as much as from the opportunities for gaining experience in interpersonal and decision-making skills outside the family which an individual can then utilize within the family."[63]

This study is just one of many showing the urban nuclear family trend toward expanding roles and power for married women, and the relationship of her outside experiences and position to her increased power and status within the family. These developments fit into the larger historical trend of twentieth-century family change toward the modern-equalitarian family type.

The author has been observing trends and changes in family roles, role expectations, and authority or power patterns for more than two decades. In 1954, these matters were investigated in a study of a sample of 129 middle-class families in Madison, Wisconsin in which both the husband and the wife were employed. Among the family trends found were these: (1) There was a general movement toward democratic role performance, with the division of labor between the husband and wife being worked out to a considerable degree by experimentation in each given family situation. (2) An even more democratic or equalitarian trend was found for the role expectations of both wives and husbands, with the wives somewhat more emancipated from traditional role expectations than their husbands. (3) In authority patterns, these families were strongly equalitarian (84.5 percent equalitarian versus 3.0 percent traditional-patriarchal). (4) Both husbands and wives were strongly equalitarian in family authority expectations (84.5 percent for husbands and 90 percent for wives). Insofar as this sample is an indication, the trend toward equalitarianism in middle-class, working-couple families was already well advanced over two decades ago.[64]

More recently (in the mid-1970s), the author cooperated with several other sociologists in a study of an inner-city residential area in Houston, Texas in which marriage and family trends in a sample of 199 middle-class, young–to–middle-aged men and women were investigated. Each participant was interviewed, and data were obtained on marriage role expectations, familism, and nuclear family integration. A marriage role expectation measure was used to distinguish between traditional and equalitarian role expectations. Four areas of marriage and family life were covered: Family authority role expectations, homemaking role expectations, child-care role expectations, and employment and family finance role expectations. Findings for both males and females were highly equalitarian in all four areas. Composite M.R.E. (marriage role expectation) scores for males in the above four areas of family life were 11 percent traditional, 12 percent intermediate, and 77 percent equalitarian. As might be expected, the women were somewhat more equalitarian than the men, but not significantly so, with 5 percent traditional, 9 percent intermediate, and 86 percent equalitarian. These findings suggest that urban, middle-class men no longer hold onto traditional marriage and family role expectations; this is even more true for women, who have come to the point of embracing equalitarian role expectations with considerable enthusiasm.[65]

These urban men and women were also found to have a familistic viewpoint to a considerable degree. This finding is in keeping with the views of Sussman and Litwak that kinship ties and relations are still important in urban families today. Among the respondents, 69 percent felt that after marriage there should be a moderate amount of mutual aid and friendly exchange with parents and other close relatives, while 22 percent felt even more strongly about the need to continue these close kin contacts after marriage.

A high degree of nuclear family integration was also found in the sample, as measured by (1) the degree to which spouses agreed on fourteen areas of family life (e.g., handling finances, religious matters, choice of friends, etc.), (2) the importance couples placed on sharing activities and expressing affection for each other, and (3) their success in family problem solving. The findings on these three measures of nuclear family integration show a high degree of cohesiveness present within these urban nuclear families.

These findings, taken together with the evidence obtained on marriage role expectations and familism, suggest that while democratic marriage and family expectations and practices have become a way of life for these urban dwellers, both extended family ties and internal nuclear family bonds are also very important to them. These urban nuclear families do not live in isolation from their relatives; nor, within the nuclear family, is there evidence of atomization or excessive individuation. Rather, close ties and "togetherness" between marriage partners and between parents and children are very apparent.

We have observed above that one of the most significant urban family trends of the twentieth century has been the dramatic rise in the employment of wives and mothers, especially since World War II. The 1970 United States census showed that 41 percent of all married women (with husbands present) were employed, 58 percent of these working wives had children under age eighteen, and 30 percent had children under age six. Figures from the Department of Labor show that as of March 1975 both parents were employed in 41 percent of the nation's two-parent families. In these families lived 22 million children, or about four of every ten under age eighteen in the United States.[66]

A pressing problem for these families is how to cope with dual careers and children too.[67] This problem is most acute for working couples with very young children. A study at Princeton University looked into how young professional couples with young children manage.[68] The study focused on a number of questions raised by young college women preparing for professional careers: How could they combine their careers with satisfying relations with their husbands, who were also committed to serious and demanding work lives? How could a working couple share domestic responsibilities satisfactorily? How could a couple, both employed, rear children successfully? How could they sustain other interests and friendships in addition to work and family?

The working couples under study all agreed that "it is not easy." Parenthood for working couples, they said, brings many rewards but places extra demands and burdens on wife and husband, and requires a willingness to make compromises and occasional sacrifices. Among the necessary adjustments they mentioned were the following: (1) For very young children, full-time care is likely to be necessary, which can cost $100 a week or more. (2) Even with help, one parent may have to stay home with the child during crises or in an emergency. This requires a flexible job and an understanding employer. (3) Housework may have to be divided in unorthodox ways and roles reversed in order to fit everyday household tasks into the employment schedules of the couple. The couples agreed that, in general, all the extra effort was worth it; that their family lives were richer, their marriages more stimulating because they both have outside careers, and that they were probably more enthusiastic parents too.

Here are some specifics as to the way one professional couple was managing. Both husband and wife are in their thirties; she is an M.D. and he is the head of a small investment-management firm. Her long hours at the hospital disturb him at times, for example when she has not come home by 7:30 P.M. and has been unable to call him. He finds himself resenting her long work hours as "an interruption to our family life." They have two boys, ages two and seven. The oldest son is very sensitive, the mother says. "He doesn't understand if I can't take him to school, and he's very angry when I don't pick him up in the afternoon." So she tries hard to arrange her medical rounds so she can take him to and from school. She is fortunate to have "supportive relatives" living nearby. A sister helps with the chauffeuring when needed. "It helps a lot not to isolate yourself from your families if you're going to have two careers," she says. (A good example of the functional value of extended family ties for modern urban nuclear families.) She admits that having children is "a very mixed blessing" for a career woman. She finds it both "a delight" and at the same time "very draining on your personality because you come home from work and are never left alone for five minutes . . . after you've been intense all day."

This couple has worked out a flexible and generally satisfactory division of household tasks. He does the grocery shopping. He likes comparing prices in the supermarkets and is willing to take the time. Also, she admits ". . . he doesn't trust me in the supermarket. He knows I'll buy everything in sight and pay whatever it costs because I don't want to waste time." A trade-off is made. She shops for all the things for the children. "My husband's not going to worry that I have to go shopping at 10 o'clock at night." To ease some of the pressure, and to ensure that someone is constantly with their children, the couple have "live-in help," which costs them about $100 a week.

The couple feel they have "a very tight family unit." They do not go out much, and when they do, they generally "go away with the children and do things with them. . . . We don't have a large social life. Both of us are so involved in our careers that we have to give up external relationships."

While it would be unsound to generalize too far from this couple or the others in the Princeton study, they do provide information and insights on how some urban, middle-class couples are managing to cope with dual careers and with marriage and parenthood all at the same time. More study is needed on this.

Trends and Changes in Suburban Family Life

Change in marriage and family living has been going on in the expanding and changing suburbs as well as within the main cities. We have seen that not only middle-class families but also, more recently, working-class families have been moving out into the suburbs. In a study of "Life Style Differences Among Urban and Suburban Blue-Collar Families," Irving Tallman and Ramona Marotz sought answers to these questions: (1) Do working-class family life-styles change as they move out to the suburbs? (2) If suburban-urban blue-collar differences are found, to what extent are the blue-collar suburban life-styles comparable to those found in white-collar suburban families?[69] The researchers interviewed and compared two samples of working class families: (1) fifty-three couples living in a central city district of Minneapolis, and (2) fifty-one couples living in a homogeneous working-class suburb outside the Twin Cities. These two samples were comparable in occupation, income, prestige, and parents' occupational status.

Previous research on suburban family life had shown quite consistently that suburban dwellers are more likely than urban dwellers to be younger, to have larger families, to be more intimate with neighbors, to participate more

Contemporary suburban home. (*E. D. Dyer.*)

widely in community organizations, and to have more extensive nuclear family involvement and family integration.[70] However, most suburban research has been done on middle-class rather than working-class families.

In comparing life-styles of the suburban blue-collar families with those of blue-collar families living in the central city, the suburban families were found to have (1) significantly more local intimacy with their neighbors, (2) higher church attendance, especially the men, (3) *less* involvement on the part of women with relatives and friends, and (4) some increase in communication between spouses, possibly as a consequence of isolation from former friends and relatives back in the city. Also, the suburban dwellers manifested higher social mobility aspirations than the urban dwellers, especially the men.[71] These findings suggest that blue-collar families who move to the suburbs are in process of changing from the older, urban, working-class "family circle" system of close ties with relatives and intimate friends toward a more conjugal-oriented nuclear family with broadening community participation.

Tallman and Marotz conclude that suburban residence is definitely associated with fundamental differences in life-styles for the working-class families studied. They feel also that social class and class-related cultural factors interact with suburban residence to influence some of the life-style patterns, such as slower integration of the working-class women into the suburban patterns of social participation, as compared with the men. In this connection, suburban working-class wives express feelings of isolation more than urban working-class wives, and certainly more than middle-class suburban wives. Thus, Tallman and Marotz point out, even though the blue-collar suburban family life-styles approximate in many ways those of white-collar families, there may still be important qualitative differences in family behavior between these two groups of suburban dwellers.[72]

The fact that life in the suburbs was viewed more negatively by the women and more positively by the men in these working-class families led Tallman to investigate in more depth the changes experienced by these women in moving from the city to the suburbs, and to look into some of the effects of the new residential environment on their personal lives and on their marriages.[73] Sociological theory suggests that social and geographic mobility may disrupt the lives of those involved, even to the point of creating a crisis for those not adequately prepared for the changes. Such may be the case, Tallman feels, for many of these working-class wives with limited education and restricted social experience, women whose lives prior to the move to the suburbs were very intensely tied to a close-knit network of relatives and lifelong female friends. These intimate female ties are of especial importance to working-class women since there is normally a high degree of conjugal role segmentation and minimal communication between wives and husbands in this class subculture.[74]

While these women generally share with their husbands social mobility aspirations in the abstract, they tend to be less aware of the social costs involved. The move to the suburbs is generally easier for the men, due to their jobs and the fact they normally have more frequent contacts outside the home. Also, the men have been socialized into instrumental male roles which identify them as their family representatives in the community. The working-class women, on the other hand, tend to feel that the world outside their family circle (which includes close women friends) is foreign and beyond their control.[75] Under these circumstances, says Tallman, "When mobility destroys the fabric of their social relations, the results may be particularly devastating for such women, principally because they have no structural or normative system of support outside their intimate social group."[76]

The data from the Minnesota study (described above in the Tallman and Marotz report) supported this position. There was greater social isolation among suburban working-class wives, and they had fewer contacts with relatives and female friends than was true of urban working-class women. Related to this was a higher degree of anomie among those women who had moved to the suburbs.[77]

In order to understand American suburban trends today, we must keep in mind certain continuities from the past, as well as seeking current changes and developments.

The suburbs of main interest to observers of the family are, of course, the residential or dormitory suburbs rather than the industrial type where productive activity is centered. For families living in these dormitory suburbs, the work of most family breadwinners is located elsewhere, most frequently in the central city. The husband-father worker may be said to live in the suburb nights and weekends. During the day the dormitory suburb is occupied mainly by women and children and service and professional persons in their service. Suburban mothers have been largely responsible for the day-to-day care of their homes and the training of their children. These conditions, along with the facts that suburban families are larger and that employment opportunities are less available for women in the suburbs, explain to a considerable extent why employment rates of suburban mothers are lower than of urban mothers. However, this scene may be changing too as suburbs become more diversified economically and socially, and as the general trend toward greater employment of wives and mothers comes to be felt more in the suburbs.

A study of "Labor Force Participation of Suburban Mothers" by George Meyers found significant differences in the employment rate of mothers living in an upper-middle-class suburb and mothers living in lower-middle-class and working-class suburbs in the Seattle area, with fewer mothers employed in the former suburb.[78] He found a very strong correlation between the type of occupation of the husband-father and the employment of the mother: 40 percent of the mothers with working-class husbands were employed, while only 27 percent of those whose husbands held white-collar occupations were employed, and only two-thirds of them worked full time.[79] Meyers feels that economic necessity in the working-class families accounts for a good deal of this difference in employment rates for these suburban mothers.

So, diversity and variety within the residential suburbs appear to be a significant trend, as more and more American families of different socioeconomic statuses and from different ethnic and racial backgrounds become able to move out from the inner-city districts. A given suburb may still be quite homogeneous internally but very different from other suburbs in terms of class, occupational, racial, or ethnic composition.[80] This also is likely to change. The future will probably see a wider diversity in ethnic and racial constituency within a given suburb while that suburb itself may still retain its essential social-class identity. For example, middle-class black and Mexican-American families will be moving out to middle-class suburbs while those of working-class status will probably move into working-class suburbs.

Many of the same reasons for the earlier middle-class "white flight" from inner-city areas out to the suburbs now apply to the current "blue-collar flight" and "black flight." And the suburbs exert the same kind of pull or attraction for these families as for middle-class families, i.e., promise of a safer, healthier, cleaner, more spacious environment for family life, especially for bringing up children. United States census data show that between 1970 and 1976 the black population in the suburbs was increasing faster than the white population in many metropolitan areas, especially in the South. In these areas the average annual rate of suburban increase since 1970 has been 5.2 percent for blacks as compared with 1.4 percent for whites.[81]

Suburban schools, by comparison with inner-city schools, tend to be less crowded, less geared to mass education, and to have higher standards and better teachers. There is greater opportunity for parental participation in the functioning of the school system through P.T.A. and other bodies. Robert Winch observes that not only is parental involvement in the school system greater in the suburbs, but this kind of linkage provides valuable public support for families. He feels "that the public schools support the family through utilizing parents as their agents just as the church did in the Middle Ages."[82]

As the suburbs become more diversified in population we may expect the suburban school systems to encounter more of the problems attending a wider range of social-class, ethnic, and racial constituency—problems city school systems have experienced for many decades. Just as black and Mexican-American families have worked in recent times to get city schools to reflect their interests and needs and to improve instruction for their children, so will suburban schools be expected to respond to the cultural variations and special needs of these more recent arrivals in suburbia.

In the context of both suburban change and increasing cultural diversity, Bennett Berger recommends, in his "Suburbia and the American Dream," that suburban planners carefully consider the *pluralist alternative* as opposed to a "melting pot" or homogeneous ideal of what future suburban communities should be like.[83] This pluralist alternative envisions suburban communities where a special kind of human solidarity would be fostered. "This solidarity is loose and heterogeneous, composed of more or less autonomous groups and neighborhoods formed on the basis of ethnicity and social class; communities attached, perhaps, to the notion that good fences make good neighbors, but necessarily related to one another through those political and economic accommodations long characteristic of urban life."[84]

Planning for pluralism in the suburbs makes sense, Berger argues, in that this goal is honorable and in keeping with the promise of the American dream, and furthermore recognizes the fact of persisting cultural diversities in American life. As people of more diverse identities move out to the suburbs they can be expected to bring their cultural practices with them, if they can. For example, working-class families with a tradition of sex segregation (husbands and wives living somewhat separate lives outside the home) would require some different community facilities compared with those required by middle-class families where husband-wife companionship and family togetherness are more the cultural norm.

One final comment on the continuing suburban movement. Viewed in the larger social-historical context of change, from the Gemeinschaft-sacred type of society toward the Gesellschaft-secular type of society, which has been under way in America for more than a century, the suburban movement and family-life trends in the suburbs represent in a way a reversal of this long-range, historical secular trend. Reacting to the extremes of secularism often manifest in the big, impersonal, highly specialized, unfeeling urban centers, suburban families are in a sense seeking to return to or rediscover a more Gemeinschaftlike semirural society environment where they hope to find a sense of community, and to participate directly in and contribute to community activities such as school system projects, local politics, and other civic enterprises.

Summary

The rural environment has undergone important changes with the establishment of farm mechanization and the development of agribusiness. Rural communities have been drawn into the urban sphere of influence, and rural families are becoming more like urban families all the time. The gap between rural and urban family attitudes, values, and behavior is being narrowed, and rural family change is following urban family change more closely. Thus, increasing rural secularization has meant that rural families are moving away from traditional role and authority definitions. Marital success is now defined in terms of the ability of the husband and wife to fulfill each other's personal needs. Studies show that rural families are becoming increasingly equalitarian and more flexible in the division of labor, while retaining some sex-role differentiation along traditional lines. The outlook is for rural American families to become smaller, more flexible in family roles, more democratic in orientation, and less familistic.

America by the mid-twentieth century had become so urbanized that distinctions had to be made between central cities and their adjoining suburban areas. These large urbanized areas are called metropolises or even megalopolises. Some argue that America has become a "nation-city," and that while urbanized families now have greater freedom and variety of choice, they have lost an earlier sense of community. One result of this loss is the intensification of urban family life. Urban dwellers have been turning inward, looking more than ever to home and family to meet their social and personal needs. Is this burden too heavy for the small urban nuclear family to bear? Is the "modified extended family" a reality today partly because of this intensification of urban family life?

The second and third quarters of the twentieth century saw tremendous growth of the suburbs in the big metropolitan areas, while the rates of growth of the central cities have declined each decade since 1950. From mid-twentieth century onward, suburbs have become more varied than earlier, and include more families of various ethnic and racial backgrounds, as well as more working-class families, all seeking an environment which holds promise of a healthier, safer, and more satisfying way of life than the inner city affords.

Studies suggest that the urban nuclear family is not as isolated from its relatives as thought earlier; that the majority of urban nuclear family members probably retain ties and continue their relationships with close relatives throughout their adult years. This is probably as true for middle-class families as for working-class families. These kinship ties and relationships appear to be very functional for urban families, and serve to help satisfy various personal, social, and economic needs.

One of the most significant trends for urban nuclear families in recent decades has been the increased employment of married women. Studies suggest that an employed wife may have more power in the family vis-à-vis her husband than an unemployed wife. The trend toward equalitarianism seems to be especially well advanced in middle-class working-couple families. Other studies indicate that urban middle-class families have become highly equalitarian in role expectations, show a high degree of nuclear family integration, and have a familistic viewpoint to a considerable extent.

A difficult problem for many urban working couples is how to cope with dual careers and children too. Studies indicate that it takes extra effort, much flexibility in family roles, a willing cooperation on the part of the husband, and personal sacrifices on the part of both wife and husband.

Family life is undergoing changes in the suburbs as well as in the main cities, especially with the increased heterogeneity of suburban populations. Studies suggest that working-class (or blue-collar) families which move out to the suburbs tend to change from the older, urban "family circle" system of close ties with relatives and intimate friends toward a more conjugal-oriented family with expanding participation in the suburban community, thus becoming more like middle-class (or white-collar) suburban families. There is some evidence that many working-class wives have difficulty in adjusting to their new suburban situation, feeling themselves to be socially isolated and giving evidence of anomie.

Diversity and variety within residential suburbs is the trend. The future will likely see greater diversity in ethnic and racial constituency within a given suburb while that suburb will still retain its established social-class identity. Suburban schools and other community agencies need to prepare for their increasingly diversified suburban populations of the future.

Notes

1   Lee Taylor and Arthur R. Jones, *Rural Life and Urbanized Society* (New York: Oxford University Press, 1964), pp. 52–53.
2   Art Gallaher, Jr., *Plainville Fifteen Years Later* (New York: Columbia University Press, 1961); James West, *Plainville, U.S.A.* (New York: Columbia University Press, 1945).
3   Gallaher, op. cit., pp. 225–226.
4   Ibid., p. 228.
5   Ibid., p. 256.
6   Ibid., p. 257.
7   O. F. Larson and E. M. Rogers, "Rural Society in Transition: The American Setting," in James H. Copp, ed., *Our Changing Rural Society: Perspectives and Trends* (Ames, Iowa: Iowa State University Press, 1964), pp. 39–67.
8   Ibid., pp. 59–61.
9   Robert O. Blood, Jr., "Impact of Urbanization on American Structure and Functioning," in P. Meadows and E. H. Mizruchi, eds., *Urbanism, Urbanization and Change* (Reading, Mass.: Addison-Wesley Publishing Co. 1969), p. 417.
10 Lee G. Burchinal, "The Rural Family of the Future," in John Edwards, ed., *The Family and Change* (New York: Alfred A. Knopf, 1969), p. 419.
11 Ibid., p. 438.
12 Robert O. Blood, Jr., and Donald M. Wolfe, *Husbands and Wives* (New York: Free Press of Glencoe, 1960). Also see Robert O. Blood, Jr., "The Division of Labor in City and Farm Families," *Marriage and Family Living*, 20 (May 1958), pp. 170–174.
13 Blood, "Impact of Urbanization on American Family Structure and Functioning," op. cit., pp. 411–412.
14 Blood, "The Division of Labor in City and Farm Families," op. cit., p. 173.
15 Herbert L. Smith, "Husband-Wife Task Performance and Decision-making Patterns," in J. R. Eshleman, ed., *Perspectives in Marriage and the Family* (Boston: Allyn and Bacon, 1969), pp. 500–520.
16 Ibid., p. 514.
17 Lee G. Burchinal and W. W. Bauder, "Decision-making and Role Patterns among Iowa Farm and Non-Farm Families," *Journal of Marriage and Family*, 27 (November 1965), pp. 525–534.
18 Ibid., p. 530.
19 Hans Sebald and Wade H. Andrews, "Family Integration and Related Factors in a

Rural Fringe Population," *Marriage and Family Living*, 24 (November 1962), pp. 347–351.

20 Ibid., p. 347.
21 Ibid., p. 350.
22 Ibid., p. 351.
23 Murray A. Straus, "Social Class and Farm-City Differences in Interaction with Kin in Relation to Societal Modernization," *Rural Sociology*, 34 (December 1969), pp. 477–494.
24 Ibid., p. 481.
25 Ibid., pp. 482–485.
26 Ibid., pp. 483–486.
27 Burchinal, op. cit., p. 419.
28 J. S. Brown, "The Family Group in a Kentucky Mountain Farming Community," Kentucky Agricultural Experiment Station Bulletin 588, 1952.
29 "Migration to Rural America Gaining Momentum," *Houston Post*, June 16, 1975, p. 27C.
30 E. W. Butler, *Urban Sociology* (New York: Harper & Row, 1976), pp. 44–47.
31 Ibid., p. 45.
32 Ibid., p. 46.
33 Ibid., p. 47.
34 Philip M. Hauser, "Urbanization: An Overview," in Philip M. Hauser and L. F. Schnore, eds., *The Study of Urbanization* (New York: John Wiley & Sons, 1965), pp. 1–47.
35 Scott Greer, *The Emerging City: Myth and Reality* (New York: Free Press, 1962), p. 195.
36 Arlene Skolnick, *The Intimate Environment* (Boston: Little, Brown & Co., 1973), pp. 428–429.
37 Benjamin Zablocki, *The Joyful Community* (Baltimore: Penguin Books, 1971), p. 294.
38 Skolnick, op. cit., pp. 430–431.
39 Ibid., pp. 431–432.
40 P. E. Slater, "Some Social Consequences of Temporary Systems," in W. G. Bennis and P. E. Slater, *The Temporary Society* (New York: Harper & Row, 1968), p. 90.
41 Eugene Litwak, "Occupational Mobility and Extended Family Cohesion," *American Sociological Review*, 25 (February 1960), pp. 9–21.
42 Straus, op. cit., p. 488.
43 Scott Greer, "Urbanism Reconsidered: A Comparative Study," in John Edwards, ed., *The Family and Change* (New York: Alfred A. Knopf, 1969), p. 99.
44 Butler, op. cit., p. 110.
45 Ibid., p. 115.
46 Bennett M. Berger, "Suburbia and the American Dream," in S. F. Fava, ed., *Urbanism in World Perspective: A Reader* (New York: Thomas Y. Crowell Co., 1968), p. 435.
47 Robert Winch, *The Modern Family* (New York: Holt, Rinehart and Winston, 1966), pp. 161–162.
48 David A. Schulz, *The Changing Family* (Englewood Cliffs, N.J.: Prentice Hall, 1972), pp. 140–141.

49 Straus, op. cit., p. 488. Also see Bert N. Adams, *Kinship in an Urban Setting* (Chicago: Markham Publishing Co., 1968).

50 Marvin B. Sussman, "Relationships of Adult Children with Their Parents in the United States," in E. Shanas and G. Streib, eds., *Social Structure and the Family: Generational Relations* (Englewood Cliffs, N.J.: Prentice-Hall, 1965), chap. 4.

51 Adams, op. cit., pp. 9–10.

52 Ibid., pp. 164–165.

53 Ibid., p. 167.

54 See Ernest W. Burgess, Harvey Locke, and Mary Thomes, *The Family* (New York: Van Nostrand Reinhold Co., 1971), pp. 63–68.

55 Donald E. Carnes, S. Goldberg, and S. Greer, "Some Neglected Considerations on the American Urban Family," in John Walton and Donald E. Carnes, eds., *Cities in Change: Studies on the Urban Condition* (Boston: Allyn and Bacon, 1973), pp. 226–237.

56 Ibid., p. 232.

57 Ibid.

58 Ibid.

59 J. D. Tarver, C. Cyrus, K. Kiser, C. Lee, and R. Moran, "Urban Influence on the Fertility and Employment Patterns of Women Living in Homogeneous Areas," *Journal of Marriage and Family*, 32 (May 1970), pp. 237–241.

60 Ibid., pp. 237–238.

61 Ibid., pp. 239–240.

62 D. B. Kandel and G. S. Lesser, "Marital Decision-Making in American and Danish Urban Families: A Research Note," *Journal of Marriage and Family*, 34 (February 1972), pp. 134–139.

63 Ibid., p. 134.

64 Everett D. Dyer, "Some Trends in Two-Income Middle-Class Urban Families," *Southwestern Social Science Quarterly* (September 1958), pp. 125–132. Also, Everett D. Dyer, "Marital Happiness and the Two-Income Family," *Southwestern Social Science Quarterly* (September 1959), pp. 95–102.

65 Project Silvercoast: An Inner-City Community Study, 1974–1975, Sociology Department, University of Houston.

66 *World Almanac, 1972*, p. 212. And "They Manage Both Careers and Kids," *National Observer* (January 1, 1977), p. 1.

67 Linda Holmstrom, *The Two Career Family*, (Cambridge, Mass.: Schenkman Publishing Co., 1972).

68 "They Manage Both Careers and Kids," op. cit., pp. 1, 9.

69 Irving Tallman and Ramona Marotz, "Life Style Differences Among Urban and Suburban Blue-Collar Families," in Ira L. Reiss, ed., *Readings on the Family System* (New York: Holt, Rinehart and Winston, 1972), pp. 354–371.

70 Scott Greer, *The Emerging City* (New York: Free Press, 1962); and W. M. Dobringer, ed., *The Suburban Community* (New York: G. P. Putnam's Sons, 1958).

71 Tallman and Marotz, op. cit., pp. 359–366.

72 Ibid., p. 367.

73 Irving Tallman, "Working-Class Wives in Suburbia: Fulfillment or Crisis?" *Journal of Marriage and Family*, 31 (February 1969), pp. 65–72.

74 Mirra Komarovsky, "Blue-Collar Marriage—Barriers to Communication," in C.

Heller, ed., *Structured Social Inequality* (New York: Macmillan Co., 1969), pp. 276–283.

75 Lee Rainwater, R. Colman, and G. Handel, *Working Man's Wife* (New York: Macfadden Books, 1962), p. 198.

76 Tallman, op. cit., p. 67.

77 Ibid., pp. 71–72.

78 George C. Meyers, "Labor Force Participation of Suburban Mothers," *Journal of Marriage and Family*, 26 (August 1964), pp. 306–317.

79 Ibid., p. 309.

80 Butler, op. cit., pp. 117–118.

81 U.S. Bureau of the Census, *Current Population Reports: Population Characteristics*, "Population Profile of the United States: 1976," p. 2.

82 Winch, op. cit., pp. 146–147.

83 Bennett M. Berger, "Suburbia and the American Dream," in S. F. Fava, ed., *Urbanism in World Perspective* (New York: Thomas Y. Crowell Co., 1968), pp. 434–444.

84 Ibid., p. 443.

SELECTED READING

Our review of rural and urban family changes in this chapter shows that in recent years rural families are increasingly resembling urban families. Differences between rural and urban family attitudes and behavior patterns are rapidly being reduced as rural people come under urban-secular influences. Many of the rural changes are especially noticeable among young people. Have rural youth become as secularized and emancipated from traditional values and norms as have many of their urban counterparts? The present reading was selected because it addressed this question by examining premarital sexual attitudes of high school–age youth in a rural community in Mississippi.

Studies of American youth living in urban areas show a trend toward more permissive attitudes toward sex in recent years. Is this trend to be found also among American rural young people? And if such a rural trend is evident, does it hold equally true for black and white youth?

Harrison, Bennett, and Globetti sought answers to these questions in a study of black and white high school students in rural Mississippi. What they found suggests that American rural youth, regardless of race, tend to accept the "permissiveness with affection" norm frequently found today among urban young men and women. Black students tend to be more permissive than white students, but neither group showed a widespread predisposition toward premarital promiscuous behavior.

ATTITUDES OF RURAL YOUTH TOWARD PREMARITAL SEXUAL PERMISSIVENESS.*

Danny E. Harrison, Walter H. Bennett, and Gerald Globetti

A popular theme suggests that a revolution in sex is occurring within American society. There is increased nudity in our advertisements and movies, a more open and frank discussion of sexual matters once considered taboo, a profusion of books and articles dealing with sexual topics, and an increment in premarital sex and births outside marriage. What does all this mean? Obviously, it is difficult to tell. Some experts in the area of marriage and the family say that these occurrences are actually an evolution which points to a change in the American standards and values regarding sex. They say we are changing from a premarital standard of abstinence, or more realistically a double standard, to one of permissiveness with affection.[1] Advanced sexual activity prior to marriage, under an affectionate bond, is becoming acceptable behavior within the courtship system. The evident increase in premarital sexual activity among females, most of which occurs with the intended partner immediately prior to marriage, amply demonstrates this fact.[2]

Studies of youth in the more urban areas of the United States have given empirical support to a trend towards more permissiveness in attitudes toward sex in recent years. These studies have suggested that in reference to urban areas, the cultural aspects of the courtship system contribute to greater permissiveness because fewer restrictions operate to restrain a couple's sexual behavior.[3] There exists, however, a paucity of available data regarding the situation as defined by the culture which encompasses approximately one-third of our nation's youth, all of whom live in rural areas. Some suggest that residence does not differentiate individuals in regard to attitudes and behavior.[4] A logical inference to draw from such a notion is that cultural heterogeneity of premarital sexual attitudes is diminishing. On the other hand, there are ample data demonstrating rural-urban differences in attitudes and behavior.[5]

*Reprinted from the *Journal of Marriage and Family*, 31 (November 1969), pp. 783–787. Copyright © 1969 by the National Council on Family Relations. Reprinted by permission of publisher and authors.

This study is prompted by the fact that in Mississippi, Negro and white youth represent two distinguishable subgroups, or in other words, that particular patterns of behaving and values can be identified in each.[6] Thus, it may be assumed that the variations existing between the two racial systems in terms of the cultural definition of situations will be reflected in the attitudes of the respective participating youth. Previous studies have documented the fact that Negro sexual attitudes are more permissive than those of whites.[7] Close inspection of most of the literature, however, shows that attitudinal differences in regard to premarital sexual permissiveness among southern rural youth are largely speculative. A common notion that pervades the popular mind is that the Negro subculture displays more liberal attitudes toward permissible sexual behavior which, in turn, stereotypes the Negro as unrestrained in patterns of premarital sex.

Accordingly, the focus of this study is a comparative analysis of the premarital sexual attitudes of a sample of rural white and Negro high-school students in a Mississippi community. Two types of data are examined. First, the students were asked a series of questions regarding their attitudes toward sexual activity prior to marriage. The aim in this respect was to see if approval of certain behaviors of a sexual nature would increase under conditions of affection. Then from these questions, the permissive students were identified and examined in order to ascertain their distinguishing personal and social characteristics. In this respect, the interest was in determining the influence of sociocultural factors upon the attitudes of Negro and white adolescents. On the basis of Reiss's analysis of racial differences in permissiveness, it is assumed that differential sociocultural situations of the racial subgroups will reflect differential attitudes toward premarital sex.[8]

Methodology

The sample included 132 randomly chosen students, 83 whites and 49 Negroes, enrolled in the high schools of the community studied. These respondents reported to a large conference room in groups of 25 and completed a structured questionnaire within a one-hour period. A research assistant explained the schedule to the assembled groups and interpreted each item when clarification was requested. The students, however, were not permitted to discuss the questions among themselves nor to collate answers. Furthermore, complete anonymity was assured.

The dependent variable—students' attitudes toward premarital sexual permissiveness—refers operationally to the responses given to two five-item Guttman subscales designed by Reiss to evaluate and measure male and female standards of premarital sex.[9] The objective in utilizing the scales was to identify an ordered continuum that represents a gradation in the respondents' acceptability of petting and coitus under differing states of affection. In American society, two major variables explaining sexual permissiveness are the degree of intimacy of the sexual act and the amount of affection between the couples involved. The scales, therefore, were structured to include two types of sexual behavior—petting and coitus.[10] The acceptability of petting was qualified to include three states of affection: engagement or love, strong affection, and no affection. The statements pertaining to coitus included similar states, with the exception of strong affection.

The items comprising the scales are: (1) I believe that petting is acceptable for the male before marriage when he is engaged or in love, (2) I believe that petting is acceptable for the male before marriage when he feels strong affection for his partner, (3) I believe that petting is acceptable for the male before marriage even if he does not feel particularly affectionate toward his partner, (4) I believe that full sexual relations are acceptable for the male before marriage when he is engaged or in love, and (5) I believe that full sexual relations are acceptable for the male before marriage even if he does not feel particularly affectionate toward his partner. The students responded to similar statements in order to determine permissiveness among females, the only difference being, of course, that the female was the referent in each case.

Findings

PATTERNS OF ACCEPTANCE

In analyzing the attitudes of adolescents toward premarital sexual permissiveness, it is first desirable to compare the Mississippi sample with Reiss's Virginia high-school sample in regard to their acceptance of petting and coitus under different conditions of affection. An examination of Table 1 indicates that the Mississippi respondents were consistently more liberal than Reiss's sample. For instance, among the white males and females, the differences between the Mississippi and Virginia students were significant for both items pertaining to coitus. In addition, the Mississippi females displayed a more permissive predisposition to engage in petting when no affection is present in the relationship. In regard to petting under engagement or love or strong affection, no significant differences were observed between the Mississippi and Virginia samples.

The findings among the Negro students were similar. Negro males in Mississippi were significantly more permissive toward coitus, but no significant differences were observed toward the acceptability of petting. On the other hand, the Mississippi Negro female was more permissive than her Virginia counterpart in attitudes toward both petting and coitus. Among the Mississippi students it is interesting to note also that proportionally more

TABLE 1 COMPARISON OF PERCENTAGE AGREEMENT BY RACE WITH EACH ITEM IN MALE AND FEMALE SUBSCALES IN REISS'S SAMPLE AND THE MISSISSIPPI SAMPLE

	WHITES						NEGROES				
ITEM[a]	REISS'S SAMPLE[b]	MISS. SAMPLE[c]	DIFFER-ENCE	Z[d]	SIGNIFI-CANCE[e]	ITEM	REISS'S SAMPLE	MISS. SAMPLE	DIFFER-ENCE	Z	SIGNIFI-CANCE
				MALE SCALE							
1	.61	.65	−.04	−.5988	.2743	1	.80	.75	.05	.6016	.2743
2	.49	.52	−.03	−.4354	.3300	2	.73	.68	.05	.5500	.2912
3	.24	.29	−.05	−.8278	.2033	3	.32	.43	−.11	−1.1410	.1271
4	.21	.41	−.20	−3.2206	.0006	4	.52	.68	−.16	−1.6276	.0516
5	.08	.23	−.15	−3.1914	.0007	5	.27	.45	−.18	−1.8769	.0301
N	143	82				N	56	44			
				FEMALE SCALE							
1	.52	.61	−.09	−1.3119	.0951	1	.71	.91	−.20	−2.4937	.0064
2	.41	.51	−.10	−1.4598	.0721	2	.73	.82	−.09	−1.0688	.1423
3	.17	.28	−.11	−1.9607	.0250	3	.18	.34	−.16	−1.8475	.0322
4	.19	.40	−.21	−3.4482	.0003	4	.55	.75	−.20	−2.0811	.0188
5	.07	.22	−.15	−3.3039	.0005	5	.18	.34	−.16	−1.8475	.0322
N	145	82				N	56	44			

[a]Four of the original items (5, 6, 9, and 10) in Reiss's scale were combined in the Mississippi subscales. The items pertaining to petting while engaged and in love (5 and 6) were combined to form item 1. The items pertaining to coitus while engaged and in love (9 and 10) were combined to form item 4.
[b]The proportion agreeing with item 1 in Reiss's sample represent the smallest proportion of Virginia students agreeing with either items 5 or 6, and the proportion agreeing with item 4 represent the smallest proportion agreeing with either items 9 or 10.
[c]Six students were dropped from further consideration because of incomplete information given to the scale items.
[d]The Z score was obtained by treating each item as a dichotomous variable and then comparing the two independent random samples by a difference of proportion's test. See Hubert M. Blalock, Jr., *Social Statistics.* New York: McGraw-Hill Book Co., Inc., 1960, pp. 176–178.
[e]The .05 level is employed to determine the significance of the differences using a one-tailed test.

students would accept full sexual relations for either the male or female when love or engagement is present than would accept petting with no affection.

Among whites the Mississippi data do not give strong support to the traditional double standard favoring the male. That is, the percentage differences of approval between the male and female standards in regard to petting and coitus are slight. On the other hand, affectionless sexual behavior among Negroes is more acceptable for the male than the female.

SOCIOCULTURAL FACTORS AND ATTITUDES TOWARD PREMARITAL SEXUAL PERMISSIVENESS

A second line of investigation involved the analysis of the sociocultural characteristics of the liberal and conservative students. The responses to each of the ten statements were dichotomized into "agree" and "disagree" and were scaled according to the Guttman scaling technique.[11] For analytical purposes, an individual was assigned a scale type on the basis of his response pattern to the statements of his own sex, and the sample was then classified into two groups or scale types. Those respondents classified as having a *conservative* attitude toward premarital sexual permissiveness were those who negatively answered all items as well as those accepting petting under the conditions of engagement or love or strong affection. Those accepting coitus under either state of affection and those accepting petting when no affection is present in the relationship were classified as *liberal*. The justification for using a conservative-liberal break rests with two considerations. First, this classification is useful in order that the data may be more comparable to Reiss's analysis; and, second, the relatively small sample size makes this classification more feasible for statistical purposes. The factors

TABLE 2 STUDENTS' ATTITUDES TOWARD PREMARITAL SEXUAL PERMISSIVENESS AND SOCIOCULTURAL FACTORS BY RACE (PERCENT LIBERAL)

FACTOR	WHITE		NEGRO	
	N	%	N	%
Sex				
Male	37	70	19	74
Female	45	16	25	64
	$X^2 = 25.235$		$X^2 = .427$	
	$P < .05$		$P > .05$	
Number of Times Gone Steady				
None	36	28	19	68
One	15	33	10	60
Two or more	31	58	15	73
	$X^2 = 5.376$		$X^2 = .490$	
	$P > .05$		$P > .05$	
Religious Participation*				
Low	34	56	29	83
High	48	29	15	40
	$X^2 = 5.867$		$X^2 = 8.185$	
	$P < .05$		$P < .05$	
Father's Education				
Less than high school	39	38	31	71
High school and above	37	43	2	100
	$X^2 = .176$		Not enough	
	$P > .05$		cases for	
			X^2 test	

ªThe religious participation index was based on: (1) the student's membership and average monthly attendance at Sunday school and other religious organizations; (2) the average number of leadership positions the students held in all religious organizations. Scores of zero to ten were arrayed from low to high on the basis of the median score.

examined in correlational analysis with the students' attitudes toward sexual permissiveness include sex, number of times gone steady, religious participation, and socioeconomic status.

Previous studies have indicated that females are more conservative than males in their attitudes toward premarital permissiveness. Females are inclined to associate love or strong affection in the relationship with their sexual expression.[12] The data of this study support this contention for whites. Among the whites, 70 percent of the males and 16 percent of the females were liberal in their attitudes. On the other hand, no significant differences exist between Negro males and females. For instance, 74 percent and 64 percent of the Negro males and females, respectively, were liberal in permissiveness. Accordingly, it appears that the Negro-white differential is explained in part by the greater permissiveness of the Negro female as compared to the white female.

It is assumed that a positive relationship exists between the number of times gone steady and permissiveness. Because of the stronger affection that is present in steady dating, advanced sexual behavior is likely to be more acceptable, especially since females are more inclined to require affection as a prerequisite to sexual behavior.

The relationship is nonsignificant among the white students, but indicates a trend in the predicted direction. Among Negroes, there is no significant association between permissiveness and number of times gone steady. The percentages indicate that among Negro students, the relationship is curvilinear—that is, those having gone steady once tend to be less permissive than those who have never gone steady or have gone steady two or more times.

Religious involvement is one of the major variables related to premarital sexual standards of youth in American society. Furthermore, religious involvement, especially among rural youth, is assumed to be an indicator of a conservative style of life.[13] On this basis a negative relation between religious participation and permissiveness would be expected. These data support this assumption. For example, among both whites and Negroes, low church participation is associated with liberal attitudes of permissiveness. The relationship, however, is slightly stronger among the Negro sample.

Although socioeconomic status has been regarded as an indicator of sexual permissiveness, several studies among high-school and college students have found little or no relationship between the two.[14] A general contention is that persons of higher socioeconomic status are usually more conservative in their sexual behavior, and, conversely, persons of lower-class status are more liberal.[15] The data of this study, using father's educational attainment as an index of class status, show no significant differences between this variable and permissive attitudes among white and Negro students. This finding, as Reiss has suggested, indicates that permissiveness may be influenced more by a liberal-conservative style of life than by social class itself.[16]

Discussion

A comparison of premarital sexual permissiveness among Mississippi and Virginia adolescents indicates that both whites and Negroes in Mississippi tend to display more permissive attitudes, especially in regard to the acceptability of coitus. It appears that the all-inclusive conception of rural groups as conservative in attitudes toward premarital sex is a misconception. Apparently, restraining influences favoring conservative attitudes toward premarital sex do not operate as effectively as one might expect in rural areas.

On the other hand, this study has demonstrated the feasibility of isolating adolescent subgroups in a Mississippi rural community and examining the differential influence of sociocultural factors upon the attitudes of Negroes and whites toward premarital sex. As indicated by other studies, the degree of affection present in a relationship is a key factor in determining acceptability of advanced sexual activity. Overall, neither racial group displays a widespread predisposition toward promiscuous behavior. Negro students, however, tend to display greater permissiveness. In particular, this is exemplified by the wider acceptance among Negroes of coitus under the condition of engagement or love. A widely accepted explanation of this racial difference suggests that the Negro's experiences with slavery and the subsequent family disorganization contribute to the more liberal attitudes. Further insights, however, can be gained from an analysis of sociocultural influences upon sexual permissiveness.

Traditionally, Negroes have been more permissive than whites, and it was assumed that the factors examined would have a differential influence upon permissiveness in the racial groups. The number of times the students had gone steady supported this assumption. That is, permissiveness among whites was influenced by this factor in a positive direction. Among Negroes, however, steady dating did not change individual levels of permissiveness. The sex of the students had a similar influence. For instance, among whites, females were less permissive than males. Among Negroes, no differences were observed. On the other hand, socioeconomic status was not significantly related to permissiveness. Our data on class status, though insufficient, suggests that class does not clearly differentiate levels of permissiveness. This opposes the findings of Kinsey that there is a negative association between permissiveness and social class.

A reliance upon previous studies would indicate that religion is a more effective control mechanism among whites than among Negroes. This, however, does not appear to be the case. Religious involvement appears to deter liberal attitudes among both whites and Negroes. Increased participation among both groups serves as a deterrent influence to permissiveness. Accordingly, this would bring into question the conception that "Negro religion" acts primarily as a mechanism of emotional gratification rather than contributing to individual morality.

References

1   For a more detailed discussion of future trends, see Ira L. Reiss, *Premarital Sexual Standards in America*, New York: The Free Press of Glencoe, 1964, pp. 218–254; see also Ira L. Reiss, "How and Why America's Sex Standards are Changing," *Trans-action*, 5 (March, 1968), pp. 26–32.

2   Harold T. Christensen and George R. Carpenter, "Timing Patterns in the Development of Sexual Intimacy: An Attitudinal Report on Three Modern Cultures," *Marriage and Family Living*, 24 (February, 1963), p. 31.

3   Ira L. Reiss, *The Social Context of Premarital Sexual Permissiveness*, New York: Holt, Rinehart and Winston, 1967, pp. 74–75.

4   See, for example, Harold M. Hodges, Jr., *Social Stratification:Class in America*, Cambridge, Massachusetts: Schenkman Publishing Co., Inc., 1964, pp. 6, 168–169; and Daniel Bell, *The End of Ideology*, Glencoe, Illinois: The Free Press of Glencoe, 1960, pp. 21–36.

5   Norval D. Glenn and Jon P. Alston, "Rural-Urban Differences in Reported Attitudes and Behavior," *Southwestern Social Science Quarterly*, 47 (March, 1967), pp. 381–400.

6   Gerald Globetti, "A Comparative Study of White and Negro Teenage Drinking in Two Mississippi Communities," *Phylon* (Second Quarter, 1967), pp. 131–138. See also Leonard Broom and Norval D. Glenn, "Negro-White Differences in Reported Attitudes and Behavior," *Sociology and Social Research*, 50 (January, 1966), pp. 187–200.

7   Ira L. Reiss, "Premarital Sexual Permissiveness Among Negroes and Whites," *American Sociological Review*, 29 (October, 1964), pp. 688–698.

8   Reiss, *The Social Context of Premarital Sexual Permissiveness, op. cit.*, pp. 38–55.

9   For a comprehensive discussion of the original scale items, see IraL. Reiss, "The Scaling of Premarital Sexual Permissiveness," *Journal of Marriage and the Family*, 26 (May, 1964), pp. 188–198.

10 *Ibid.*, p. 189.

11 Several measures were calculated to determine the acceptability of the scales. The values of the Coefficient of Reproducibility were .95 and .97 on the male and female scales, respectively. No item on either scale had more than seven-percent error, and no non-scale type contained over five percent of the sample population. Finally, 79.4 percent and 87.3 percent of the respondents on the male and female scales, respectively, were classified as pure scale types.

12 Winston Ehrmann, *Premarital Dating Behavior*, New York: Henry Holt and Company, 1959, p. 269.

13 Contrary to this, John Dollard indicates in his classic study of Southerntown that Negro religious involvement serves as an emotional outlet of guilt rather than a

mechanism of self-control. See *Caste and Class in a Southern Town*, Garden City, New York: Doubleday and Company, Inc., 3rd ed., 1957, p. 249.

14 See, for example, Ira L. Riess, "Social Class and Premarital Sexual Permissiveness: A Re-examination," *American Sociological Review*, 30 (October, 1965), pp. 747–756; Lemo D. Rockwood and Mary E. N. Ford, *Youth, Marriage, and Parenthood*, New York; John Wiley and Sons, Inc., 1945, p. 65; Jean Dedman, "The Relationship Between Religious Attitude and Attitude Toward Premarital Sex Relations," *Marriage and Family Living*, 21 (May, 1959), p. 174.

15 Reiss, "Social Class and Premarital Sexual Permissiveness: A Re-examination," *op. cit.*, p. 747.

16 *Ibid.*, pp. 747-756.

CHAPTER 9

Nontraditional Family Variations and Changes

The long-term social changes which have brought American society from its earlier Gemeinschaft-sacred orientation to its present advanced Gesellschaft-secular state are producing waves of criticism of traditional marriage and family patterns and practices. The growing emphasis on equality, freedom, self-realization, and personal growth has brought on the current rash of experimentation and innovation in relations between the sexes and between parents and children.

The Search for Alternative Marriage and Family Life-Styles

BACKGROUND AND SOCIAL CONTEXT FOR THE DEVELOPMENT OF ALTERNATIVE MARRIAGE AND FAMILY FORMS

Experimentation in alternative life-styles is not new, either in the United States or elsewhere. Nineteenth-century America witnessed many "utopian" experiments in community and family living arrangements, such as the Oneida

Man and two women dancing, Beverly Hills, California. (*Julie Heifetz.*)

Community in New York State; New Harmony, Indiana; and Brook Farm, Massachusetts. The twentieth century has seen more extensive experimentation, such as the Bolshevik collective farms in Russia, the Israeli kibbutzim, and the communes of China.

While recent marriage and family experiments in America in the 1960s and 1970s may bear some relationship to the earlier experiments, they have a distinctive flavor of their own. Certain social processes and demographic conditions which have contributed to their distinctiveness and current development can be identified.[1]

THE SOCIAL UNREST AND TURBULENCE OF THE 1960s AND EARLY 1970s   It was during these years that the civil rights movement exploded, the women's liberation movement greatly accelerated, and the Vietnam war divided the country. The use of drugs increased and many young people dropped out of the "straight" life to begin seeking alternative life-styles and goals.

DEMOGRAPHIC CHANGES IN THE UNITED STATES OF AMERICA IN RECENT DECADES   In his analysis of factors contributing to the upsurge of variant life-styles, Gerald Leslie notes that the decade of the 1960s was demographically unique for the United States. Due to the high birthrates beginning at the end of World War II and lasting about a decade, "each year from 1964 through 1971, the people reaching the age of 17 were more numerous than the year before."[2] The 17- and 18-year-olds formed the nation's "demographic center of gravity" during these eight years. During the decade of the 1960s, some 13.8 million people in the 14-to-24-year age bracket were added to the United States population, representing an increase of 52 percent for this age group in one decade. The impact of such a sheer quantity of young people would make itself felt whenever it existed, but coming as it did in a period of change and turbulence, its effects were massive and widespread. As Leslie says: "The possibility is very real that the emergence of a large-scale emphasis in the late 1960's upon creating alternative life styles was not an historical accident. It was to some degree a predictable outcome of a situation in which young people were so numerous that their values, their standards, and their way of life had major influences upon the whole society."[3]

Since that time the demographic center of gravity has moved up to the 22-to-23-year age group, a period when young people are most apt to marry, take full-time jobs, have children, and thus tend to join the ranks of more conventional segments of American society. So we are already seeing a declining influence of the 17-to-20-year-old youth group.[4]

If we add to the above picture the quite drastic economic reversal from the sustained affluence of the 1960s to the deep recession of the mid-1970s, we see that fewer youth and fewer middle-class adults are now financially able to experiment in unconventional life-styles than earlier.[5]

SOME EFFECTS OF THE TREND TOWARD THE POSTINDUSTRIAL SOCIETY Today, according to Daniel Bell, the scientific-technological revolution is creating an economy in which the need for human labor is being reduced.[6] In consequence, since their services are not immediately needed, many young people have to postpone entering the labor market. This situation has contributed to a prolongation of adolescence. During the 1950s and 1960s American colleges and universities became, in effect, "waiting stations" for large numbers of young people—especially young men—for whom there were no places in the labor market. The relationship between this situation, the affluent economy of the 1960s, and the demographic conditions described above should be apparent. Leslie sums it up thus: "An affluent society, accommodating itself to the tremendous numbers of young people in its midst, could afford as it never has been able to before, to keep a sizeable portion of its young adults in a stage of financial dependence."[7]

Certain problems were virtually certain to result. It is difficult and dangerous for a society to keep young adults sidelined because their labor is not needed. Their pent-up energies and frustrations had to seek outlets. The youth contraculture which emerged in the 1960s provided one such outlet.

THE CONTRACULTURE OF THE 1960s Contrary to what might be expected, the leaders of the youth contraculture, or counterculture, as it is more popularly known, were largely of middle-class background rather than working-class or lower-class. They joined forces with minority group and civil rights movement leaders and those protesting against the Vietnam war. Many of the contraculture adherents were from prosperous middle-class families, free from the need to start earning a living at once, with time and energy to devote to social causes. Alienated from their middle-class background, they became articulate critics of conventional American society and its institutions, including traditional marriage and family institutions. They became idealistic advocates of moral and social reform, seeking new systems of values, norms, and relationships designed to replace those which are found in the "straight" world.

While most of the alternative life-styles found in America today are not entirely new, they show both quantitatively and qualitatively the strong influence of the youth contraculture. Among the values and themes found in the youth contraculture which are reflected in the various alternative marriage and family life-styles are emphases upon (1) individual freedom (do what one wants provided it does not hurt someone else); (2) expressiveness, unencumbered by conventional norms; (3) naturalness in appearance, actions, etc., avoiding the artificial, the processed, the plastic; (4) living in and for the present (the present is too important to be sacrificed for the future); (5) the communal as opposed to the private (a belief that one's needs are best met in the close, intimate communal setting rather than in more private and exclusive relationships predominant in the "straight" world).[8]

From such a value position as this, it is understandable that proponents of the contraculture should assert that traditional marriage and family forms were no longer adequate or relevant in American society. Let us next review some of the specific criticisms leveled in these circles against conventional marriage and family.

CRITICAL REACTION TO TRADITIONAL MARRIAGE AND FAMILY NORMS AND PATTERNS In her essay "Variant Family Forms and Life Styles: Rejection of the Traditional Nuclear Family," Betty Cogswell observes that people live by various myths which they use to guide, judge, and rationalize their behavior. She suggests that certain traditional myths may need to be abandoned and replaced by new ones when current conditions and changes "render too great a break between approximation and attainment, when actual behavior deviates too far from prevalent myths, and when new views of reality become more relevant."[9] She suggests that the recent emergence of experimental family forms may signify an arrival at such a point in our history. "The myth of the idealized nuclear family has become untenable for an undetermined proportion of our society, including both those individuals living in nuclear families and those opting for experimental variant family forms."[10]

No one can say as yet, of course, which if any of these experimental marriage and family forms will become sufficiently accepted and established to become institutionalized, and in turn develop their own myths as guides to human relations.

Critics of the traditional family myths "see the nuclear family as inadequate, restrictive, and counter-productive in meeting individual goals, aspirations, and desired life styles."[11] The nuclear family, it is claimed, is a sentimental model based on two idealized notions: (1) that one man and one woman should marry and in effect contract to satisfy all of each other's emotional and physical needs for the rest of their lives, and (2) that as parents they should have the responsibility for meeting all of the needs of their children.[12] Although this idealized model is very difficult to live up to, and thus probably does not represent a good deal of contemporary reality, still, very many Americans believe in it and use it to judge quality and performance in marriage and family life. From this point of view, most departures from the model are judged as failures.

What are some of the features of the traditional nuclear family that are being most criticized today? Foremost would probably be the restrictions on personal freedom, such as sexual exclusivity, and then the traditional sex division of labor. Another focus of criticism is the emphasis on financial success that is brought about by hard work and deferred gratification and by striving for occupational and social mobility.[13] Yet another reason why advocates of new family forms reject the traditional nuclear family is its structural rigidity and restrictiveness, which contrast with the open, opportunistic, and still evolving structures of the experimental forms. With some oversimplification, it may be argued that while the experimental variant forms offer more opportunities and greater personal freedom at the price of some security, the traditional family offers greater security at the price of some restrictions on opportunities and freedom.[14]

Patrick Conover, in his article "An Analysis of Communes and Intentional Communities with Particular Attention to Sexual and Gender Relations," says that it is the affluent middle-class family with its Protestant work ethic and its social-mobility orientation that is being rejected today by an increasing number of young people, and from which they are trying to escape by experimenting with variant forms of marriage and family.[15] What do they want instead?

Their aspirations . . . include self-actualization, autonomy, gender equality, intimacy in a variety of interpersonal relations, openness in communication, and sexual variety. . . . Warm interpersonal relations and concern with personal growth . . . are highly valued. . . . Work is seen as a means for self-actualization, and the psychic income derived assumes greater importance than the monetary gain. The alternate culture works toward liberating both men and women from a highly competitive approach to life.[16]

From this range of values and goals identified with the contraculture, the various experimental marriage and family forms select and establish their priorities.

THE NEED FOR ALTERNATIVE LIFE-STYLES: SOME ARGUMENTS ADVANCED BY PROPONENTS

Whether one takes the position that conventional marriage and family are in serious trouble and in need of surgical change, or whether one believes that our family institutions are still basically sound, it must be conceded that many people feel that many of their personal needs are really not being met within conventional marriage and family arrangements. David Schulz has attempted to identify some of these unmet needs and related conditions.[17]

THE SURPLUS OF UNMARRIED WOMEN IN THE UNITED STATES   It is true that in our present family system there are large numbers of involuntarily single women. (Estimates run between 5 and 10 million.) Women generally come to a marriageable age earlier than men and also outlive men by about seven years. It is argued that modifications need to be made in the present courtship and marriage systems to enable more women to be married, or some alternatives established to meet their needs and enable them to live richer and more complete lives.

UNMET EMOTIONAL NEEDS   Proponents of alternative family forms maintain with conviction that many emotional needs are not being satisfactorily met today by marriage, and they point as evidence to the high divorce rates. While the increases in broken marriages are partly due both to rising expectations in marriage, and to the new freedom to shed a less-than-satisfactory marriage partner in order to seek a more rewarding relationship with somebody new, there are those who argue that traditional marriage is no longer adequate to meet the emotional and related personal needs of many modern Americans.

DRAMATIC RISE IN ILLEGITIMACY IN THE UNITED STATES   Somewhat ironically, even as the legitimate birthrate has been falling since the mid-1950s, the illegitimate birthrate has continued to rise quite sharply (from 7 per 1,000 population in 1940 to over 25 per 1,000 population in 1970).[18] This trend is related to the "sexual revolution," to the increases in premarital sex relations, and also to the lack of proficiency in pregnancy control. It is argued by many that traditional sex mores have broken down and must be replaced by something new.

WEAKNESS OF THE NUCLEAR FAMILY AS AN EFFECTIVE SOCIALIZATION AGENT   Critics argue that the conventional nuclear family has proved ineffective in meeting its responsibilities to produce adequately socialized and motivated children. Would an alternative family form involving adults other than the parents perhaps do a better job?

THE NEED FOR GREATER SOCIAL JUSTICE IN AMERICAN SOCIETY   It is now being argued that we need greater equity and justice along several dimensions: the redefinition of sex roles to enable women to achieve wider fulfillment; the expansion of the role of children in the affairs of the community and the family; new economic and social priorities to benefit the poor; and finally, the removal of the stigma of deviancy from those who are sexually different, such as homosexuals. Such needs, it is argued, call for new and different modes of marriage and family relationships.

Selected Alternative Marriage and Family Life-Styles

In his article "Can the Family Survive Alternative Life Styles?" Bert Adams identifies three major categories of alternatives to conventional marriage and family:[19] (1) *Parallel alternatives* which are outside of but parallel to marriage and family; (2) *incorporable alternatives*, which would modify the family by being incorporated into its structure; and (3) *alternatives to the family itself*, which would be substitutes or replacements for traditional practices and relationships. These are useful kinds of distinctions to make in reviewing and analyzing the growing array of specific experiments.

ALTERNATIVES PARALLELING MARRIAGE AND FAMILY

Such alternatives are external to marriage and the family, and are either in the premarital or the postmarital periods. Probably the best known and most widely experimented-with example today would be "the arrangement," consisting of an unmarried couple—heterosexual—living together. This kind of arrangement is usually premarital. Eleanor Macklin did a study in the early 1970s of such arrangements among college students at Cornell University. Her findings suggest that "living together unmarried is becoming an increasingly common aspect of campus courtship and is frequently associated with the 'going steady' phase of the relationship."[20] It would seem that such a living-together pattern among college students probably represents a modification of conventional courtship patterns or an interim arrangement more than an actual substitute for marriage. Greater freedom of student action on the campus plus the ready availability of the birth control pill and abortion services have all contributed to the expansion of premarital living together.

How widespread is this practice? Macklin found that 34 percent of the junior and senior women and 28 percent of the freshmen and sophomore women sampled had had such a living-together experience since entering college. (A more recent nationwide study of 2,510 young *men* showed 18 percent had lived with a woman for six months or more outside marriage.[21]) These arrangements were based largely on a strong affectual relationship-which, in the eyes of the women, made the cohabitation all right, according to Macklin. They did not consider themselves married, nor did they consider marriage a viable alternative to their existing arrangement. When asked why such living-together arrangements had become more common and open, the women mentioned the following factors: the search for meaningful relationships with others among today's youth; the loneliness of a large university; the emotional satisfaction derived from "having someone to sleep with who cares for you;" the fact that young people today must wait so long before marriage becomes feasible; and the widespread questioning of the institution of marriage itself.[22]

Various kinds of problems were encountered during cohabitation. Among the most common were problems of sexual maladjustment, the tendency to become emotionally overinvolved, a feeling of loss of identity, feelings of being trapped by the relationship, and problems with parents. On the other side, a large majority of the respondents felt the relationships were "both maturing and pleasant," and more than half rated their living-together relationship as "very successful." All the women who had this living-together experience said they would not consider marriage without first having lived together with a prospective marriage partner.[23]

Another study, carried out at the University of Colorado in the early 1970s, found a number of differences in attitudes toward women on the part of college men who were living together with their girl friends and men who were "going with" their girl friends.[24] The living-together man had less trust and respect for the woman he lived with than the going-together man did for the woman he went with. The satisfactions of the living-together man were more in the area of sexual adjustment than in other areas of the relationship. The authors feel that a holdover of Victorian mentality on the part of many male participants in living-together arrangements inclines them to still view with some disfavor their female partners who have entered into a "disapproved" relationship. It would appear that while this premarital living-together pattern is a product of the current secular-emancipation trend, there may be some remnants of stigma attached to it, or guilt felt by participants, stemming from our earlier sacred cultural norms.

Postmarital living together is another parallel alternative to conventional marriage. This may increase as more people postpone remarriage, as in the case of widows or divorcees. The extent and significance of this alternative will be discussed below under "The Alternative of Remaining Single."

ALTERNATIVES INCORPORABLE INTO THE FAMILY, OR ADJUNCTIVE TO MARRIAGE AND FAMILY

It is possible to reorganize various aspects of marriage and family living without basically changing their structure. By reorganizing family roles, by revitalizing the marriage relationship, the internal patterns may be experimentally altered and adjusted to better meet the needs of family members. By extending the network of intimate relationships to include close friends and neighbors, some feel, the family would be strengthened. Some also feel that unmet sexual needs of married people may be satisfied through extramarital relations.

CHANGING SEX ROLES   In an article titled "Androgyny as a Life Style," Joy Osofsky and Howard Osofsky say that in the near future traditional sex-role differentiation may be replaced by *androgyny*, a condition in which there will be no sex-role differentiation.[25] The trend toward changing sex roles in marriage and family life has been apparent for some time. What the authors propose is to carry these changes to the nth degree, until men and women are completely emancipated from traditional definitions of "man's" place and "women's" place in the family and are free to pursue their personal interests and do what is satisfying to each one. The objective would be an eventual society in which there are no stereotyped differences between the family roles of males and females "on the basis of sex alone." Everyone will not behave the same way, though, or participate in the same roles. Both hereditary differences and acquired differences in interests will be encouraged and given full freedom of expression. Full androgyny will not be achieved in the near future, however. New patterns of education and child socialization must come first, they say.

EXPANDING THE INTIMATE SOCIAL NETWORK A second alternative explored by Frederick Stoller, in "The Intimate Network of Families as a New Structure," suggests expanding the family network to include other intimate persons who would share the nuclear family's responsibilities and heavy emotional load.[26] One of the oft-repeated shortcomings of the independent nuclear family is its paucity of members with whom one can share deep concerns. More such intimate individuals could be found in an expanded network in which three or four nuclear families come together on a regular basis to provide services for one another, to explore new living arrangements, and to exchange intimacies.

The isolated nuclear family places a heavy emotional burden on the husband and the wife to meet each other's needs year after year, and an unrelenting burden on the parents to carry the total responsibility of child care and training. The argument is that husband, wife, and children all need other intimate adults. Sharing could take place in all areas of life except sex, and there would be not just one adult but many with whom one could communicate on matters of deep concern. Stoller notes that these ideas are now being explored in family life workshops.

EXTRAMARITAL SEX RELATIONSHIPS An adjunctive alternative to traditional marriage which has existed for a long time and which is expanding today, in spite of long-standing taboos, is extramarital sexual alliance. Some proposals are being made to redefine marriage in such a way that discreet "open sex" will be the norm of the future. Such, notes Adams, would be tantamount to incorporating extramarital sex into the existing marriage and family structure.[27]

Extramarital affairs vary greatly in intensity and duration, of course, and in their meaning to the participants. Several kinds of long-term extramarital relationships have been identified: (1) the sexual liaison, (2) the "other wife," and (3) spouse swapping, or group sex.[28] The first type is probably the most prevalent, and is usually called "having an affair." Having a "second wife" is a more complex arrangement, generally involving two separate households both supported by the man, only one of which is based on a legal marriage. The third type, spouse swapping or "swinging," is attracting a good deal of media attention these days although its true extent is not known.

In a study of mate swapping done by Duane Denfield and Michael Gordon, it was judged that most swingers are really "deviants" in that, while violating conventional sex norms, they still accept them as legitimate.[29] They do not reject the conventional marriage norms in total, nor do they try to change them as do certain other "utopian swingers" who generally live in communes. The "recreational swingers' " sole deviation from conventional marriage and family norms lies in their sharing of marriage partners. Otherwise, they believe in monogamy and want to retain it. They are mostly highly educated middle-class people with professional and business careers who live respectable lives in other ways, but who seek variety and new experience sexually in a carefully planned and discreet way.

Denfeld and Gordon feel that many mate-swappers see this practice as a strategy for revitalizing their marriages, for bolstering a sagging relationship.

Swingers believe that the damaging aspect in extramarital sex is in the lying and cheating, and if this is removed extramarital sex is beneficial in the marital bond. In other words "those who swing together stay together." Swingers establish rules such as not allowing one of a couple to attend a group meeting without the other. Unmarried couples are left out of some groups, because they "have less regard for marital responsibilities."[30]

Mate-swappers try to keep their sexual deviancy secret from their "square" friends and associates. They seek out other couples sharing their views who will be discreet. A swinging party in a middle-class suburb "differs from a conventional cocktail party only in that it revolves around the sexual exchange of mates." Swingers may locate each other through swingers' clubs, swingers' bars, or through personal reference or recruitment, or even through advertising.

How extensive is this practice? Only rough estimates can be made. One study in 1964 estimated that about 2½ million couples exchange partners on a somewhat regular basis (three or more times a year). This would represent about 5 percent of the married couples in the country at that time.[31] A more conservative estimate by Morton Hunt is that not more than 1 percent of married couples participate in this practice.[32]

Potential problems tend to plague the swinging couple. Jealousy is a constant possibility, even for those who follow the rules and try to sustain a liberated viewpoint (as in the film *Bob and Carol and Ted and Alice*). Other problems are contacts with those having sexual hang-ups, or discovery of sexual hang-ups in oneself, or not being able to live up to one's sexual myths or self-perceptions. There is evidence that the dropout rate among swingers is high.[33]

OPEN MARRIAGE   Another alternative which could be incorporated into the traditional marriage institution has been advocated by Nena O'Neill and George O'Neill. They call it "open marriage."[34] This variation involves some redefinition of the marriage relationship with emphasis on each marriage partner retaining his or her personal identity. It stresses the personal growth of each partner through mutual cooperation, but without most of the restrictions to individual action found in conventional marriage.

Conceptually it attempts to provide options for marriage partners in a complex society which values individual self-fulfillment and provides multitudinous opportunities for individuals to develop identities and find warm and intimate relations with many other persons. Open marriage attempts to build on the past difficulties of traditional marriage and provides guide-lines through an open system model for development of intimate marital relationships which provide the growth of the marital partners in a context of a one-to-one relationship.[35]

In an open marriage the partners are committed to their own and to each other's growth. The relationship is flexible and "is constantly being renegotiated in light of changing needs, consensus in decision-making, in tolerance of individual growth, and in openness of possibilities *for* growth."[36]

Guidelines set forth by the O'Neills for pursuing an open marriage are as follows: living for now, realistic expectations, privacy, role flexibility, open and honest communication, open companionship, equality, identity, and trust. They feel that open and honest communication is perhaps the most important element in an open marriage. Future goals—especially materialistic goals—should yield to "relating to the present" with its immediate emotional and intellectual concerns. There should be no restrictions based on traditional marriage and family role definitions; and "open companionship" includes the right of each marriage partner to have meaningful relationships, including heterosexual relationships, outside their marriage.[37]

The O'Neills conclude that for now only a few couples are fully ready to achieve the open marriage, but many more can use it as a model in seeking to improve their marriages. While open marriages are not advocated as the solution to all marriage problems, the authors feel that such marriages do exchange the less constructive problems of traditional marriage for the more constructive ones of individual growth and learning.

ALTERNATIVE LIFE-STYLES OPPOSED TO CONVENTIONAL MARRIAGE AND FAMILY

COMMUNES   Communes are probably the best known of these alternatives to conventional marriage and family. While it has only been during the past fifteen or twenty years that these present-day communes have emerged and attracted considerable attention, communes per se are not new to America. There are clear records of at least 130 communes operating in the nineteenth century.[38] Communal life has a long history in Christendom—it is as old as Christianity itself, in fact. Communal life was practiced by some of the first Christians, as described in the New Testament (Acts 2:42–47).

Some of the nineteenth-century American communes were intensely familistic and monogamous, while others were polygamous. Most of those which have emerged during the past two decades have sought to eliminate or substantially alter traditional marriage and family beliefs, sentiments, and norms as the bases for close interpersonal relations. Many such communal organizations become essentially "total institutions" in which people can virtually live out their whole lives. Such a group may be largely economically

Communal meal. (*Julie Heifetz.*)

self-sufficient, with men and women sharing the productive work, often with little distinction between male and female work roles. These communes are likely to reduce private property to a minimum—a basic feature of many historical communes—with income from all sources pooled, and expenditures determined on a collective rather than an individual basis. Sharing is emphasized, while possessiveness of things—or of persons—is disfavored.

There are many varieties and types of modern communes. Some are primarily economic, with property and income shared, but other aspects of life are left up to the nuclear family units which make up the communal group. Some communes are based on strong ideological beliefs—often of a revolutionary nature—while others have no creed but emphasize certain kinds of experience, such as sex, or drugs, to be shared by like-minded persons.

Bennett Berger distinguishes between *creedal* and *noncreedal* communes, and between *rural* and *urban* communes.[39] Creedal communes are organized around a doctrine or creed, religious or political, to which members are expected to adhere (e.g., the "Jesus Freaks"). Noncreedal communes lack such an explicit ideology or collective belief system, having instead a taken-for-granted set of beliefs assumed to be known and widely shared by members. The line dividing such types is not always clear, however. Creedal communes generally have a firmer authority structure and more explicit rules of conduct, such as rules against drug use. Noncreedal communes tend to rely more on friendship and personal attachments as a source of solidarity, rather than on commitment to an articulated creed.

A rural commune generally tries to establish a self-sufficient economic base so its members can be independent of the larger society which they have rejected. This requires resources—land, farming equipment, buildings, etc. People who commit themselves and their personal resources to such an enterprise and to a relatively isolated group are likely to be more seriously dedicated to the communal experiment than is true of a good many of the urban communards. Berger feels that "rural communes represent a relatively more advanced stage, a purer form of the 'New Age' movement than urban communes do."[40]

Urban communes are normally easier to start, if not to sustain. It only takes a rented house and some interested people. Because of this, urban communes are apt to have a more fluid membership, and it may be difficult at times to tell who is a member and who is a visitor—or a crasher. The average life-span of an urban commune of the 1960s was estimated to be two years, and of the individual member only eight months.[41]

It is difficult to know—for reasons just mentioned—how many communes there are today in the United States and what their total population is. Estimates run from 2,000 up to 4,500 communal groups. And if these communes have an average of 10 members each, it would mean some 45,000 people at the maximum living in communes, or about two one-hundredths of one percent of the American population.[42]

One may ask how communal living affects the relations between the sexes and between parents and their children. A study of thirty-five urban and suburban communal households done by Rosabeth Kanter and associates in 1972 focused on these questions.[43] These communes were described as "avant-garde middle class" rather than as hippie or student. Some of the main effects of communal household living on a male-female and parent-child relations are summed up by Kanter:

The major effects can be summarized as an initial shift in the focus of social control. When relationships are conducted in the presence of "others," couples and parents experience a loss of control, both over their territory and over their partner. The "others" change the relationship by their presence as an audience, direct intervention, their availability as potential coalition partners, and their claims over the intimate space.

Couples experience pressures toward individuation, autonomy, and equalitarianism, as well as a loss of sovereignty.[44]

When a couple move from their own place into the communal household, they generally experience this loss of control and sovereignty in setting rules and living their own lives as freely as before. While this can be stressful, it also can be a positive experience if it is in keeping with their own ideology. The group puts pressure on each person to deemphasize being a part of a couple and rather to emphasize being part of the commune as an autonomous individual. Under these influences, some couples may drift apart or decide "rationally" to separate. Others may resist and continue their identity primarily as a couple, thereby holding onto their power as a unit. They continue to find in each other the emotional sustenance which single members must constantly seek out from other individual members of the commune. Kanter found that:

The couples we studied set limits to the diffusion of intimacy. While there are many needs that others can satisfy, there are many ways in which the intimacy of the community are expressed, multiple sexual relationships are hard to maintain, and are a regular part of very few communes we studied. Our findings contradict the media view of sexual libertarianism as a central feature, at least of urban communes. Nearly all of our communes show a preference for couple members not developing sexual relationships with their housemates. After a while most groups develop an "incest taboo" which seems to be a source of stability, and sexual experimentation occurs largely outside the commune.[45]

As for parent-child relations in communes, while more data are needed, there are indications that parents experience diminishing ability in control over their own children, and in making and enforcing rules in child rearing. Young children become the recipients of increased rule making by other adults in the commune, especially the childless, single adults who tend to complain that the children's parents are exerting an unfair control over the lives of their own children.

The communal household seems to affect parent-child relations in many ways similar to those in which it affects couple relations, by the parents' diminished sovereignty over the household, by the presence of the larger household audience, and by the pressures for individuation and autonomy. However, the loss of parental sovereignty and authority long associated with the traditional nuclear family is here exchanged for some advantages of the communal household, where the larger membership of adults is available to share child-care and -rearing responsibilities, as well as to share control. This way means a freer and more relaxed parent-child relationship, as illustrated by one mother who reported: "The house took the pressure off. When I was the only mommy I lost my temper a lot more. There was no relief, . . . There was absolutely no one else. Here if I have some problem there is always someone to take care of them. So relating to the children is a lot freer. I do it because I want to, not because I have to."[46]

The presence of others in the household thus both complicates parent-child relations, tending to diminish parental control, while at the same time offering relief from exclusive task responsibilities for parents. Kanter also found that a concern for the opinions of other adults may at times cause a parent to overreact to a child's actual or imagined misbehavior. And where adults held differing views on child rearing, competition or conflict over which techniques or standards to employ were frequent. In all the communes studied, parents tended to hold onto and reserve for themselves certain domains, principally their right to protect their children and to punish them when they deemed necessary. Kanter sums up:

Parenting in the presence of others, then, is complex, and like coupling, involves its own delicate balances: help with child care versus the exclusiveness of parenting; concern for the child versus concern for the reactions of others; children's separate relationships with others versus parents' desire to protect their children; letting go of

Three young people share meal preparation. (*Julie Heifetz.*)

burdens versus losing control. Parents both applaud their children's exposure to a variety of relationships and styles and mourn the loss of parental sovereignty.[47]

It is too soon to predict whether or not these modern communes will fare better than most earlier communal experiments in establishing viable and durable alternatives to conventional marriage and family. The communal movement has included quests of many different kinds of people for many different kinds of goals. Joyce Gardener has identified some of the reasons why so many communes fail to achieve their goals.[48] Some fail because their members try only to get what they want but have little to contribute to others or to the group; some fail because members have aggravated their personal problems through interaction with others who are also laboring under personal difficulties; others fail because they lack a vision or goals to live by or strive for.

GROUP MARRIAGE   Somewhat akin to communes are certain group marriages, or multilateral marriages. A *multilateral marriage* has been defined as "an essentially egalitarian relationship in which three or more individuals (in any distribution by sex) function as a family unit, sharing in a community of sexual and interpersonal intimacy."[49] Since such arrangements are still quite strongly disapproved in the larger society, most group marriages are apt to be somewhat secret, making it difficult to know their extent today. Very few studies have been made of these marriages; probably the best-known ones are by Larry and Joan Constantine, who were able to find and interview participants in only thirty-one multilateral marriages.[50]

Members of group marriages differ from "swingers," who are generally conventionally married people in every way except sexually. In group marriage, by comparison, there is a total life-style commitment, a total emotional involvement with the extended marital group, and an emphasis on personal growth. These alliances are generally more stable and enduring than most communal groups where members come and go rather frequently. The boundaries of a multilateral marriage are clear. Everyone knows who the marriage partners are, and if or when such a marriage ends, the group is dissolved completely.

The Constantines found the median age of members at the time of the formation of the multilateral marriage to be thirty-one, with an age range of twenty-three to fifty-nine years. Most participants were legally married couples who tended to be of middle-class background and well educated. They entered the multilateral arrangement as couples.[51]

In his article "Group Marriage: A Possible Alternative?" Albert Ellis tries to assess the advantages and disadvantages of this variant form of marital union.[52] Some of the advantages over conventional marriage are as follows:

(1) Group marriage offers a considerable degree of sexual opportunity and variety. (2) It widens and enhances love relationships by enabling participants to live with and relate intimately to several members of the opposite sex. (3) The family life can be increased and intensified by sharing it with a larger number of people. (4) Group marriage offers economic as well as social advantages by the group's maintenance of one common residence. (5) It provides opportunities for personal growth and development, and an opportunity to pursue the ideal of the "brotherhood of man."

Some disadvantages of group marriage are: (1) The difficulty in finding a group of four or more adults of both sexes who can truly live together harmoniously. (2) The problem of selecting a group of such adults with whom one would like to enter a group marriage arrangement. (3) The high probability of sex, love, and jealousy problems arising in any group marriage. (4) The need to be at least semisecret, since there is strong community disapproval of group marriages. This means that participants try to conceal much of their life from neighbors and many friends. Concerns with discovery, condemnation, possible loss of job, etc., contribute to the instability of group marriages.

The breakup rate of group marriages appears to be quite high. For the above-stated reasons it seems unlikely that very many people will select this as an alternative life-style in the near future.[53]

SUGGESTED NEW LEGAL TYPES OF MARRIAGE   As substitutes for conventional marriage, a number of new definitions or redefinitions of the legal form of marriage itself are being proposed.[54] (These would differ from the proposals immediately above which were directed toward altering the content of the marriage relationship.) One such suggestion is that marriage be redefined in nonlegal terms to last only as long as the couple remain in love. Another suggestion would make the marriage contract renewable periodically, say every two or three years, or to last until one signatory wants out.

One of the most publicized proposals of this genre has been made by Margaret Mead, who has recommended two types of marriage: (1) an *individual marriage*, which is a first-step marriage contract allowing a couple to live together experimentally, but entailing a greater commitment than does the less-formal living-together arrangement, and (2) the *parental marriage*, a second step, to be embarked on only by those who are prepared to take the full and long-term responsibilities of bearing and rearing children.[55] The first step, the individual marriage, would assure that the couple really got to know each other and were compatible and committed before "being trapped in a fatal mistake" of permanent marriage, and, especially, premature parenthood. (See the Mead article at the end of this chapter.)

Given the conventional orientation of most legislative bodies, it is unlikely that such proposals will be enacted into law in the immediate future.

THE ALTERNATIVE OF REMAINING SINGLE   There are many indications to-day that a greater proportion of adults are choosing to remain single—for a time at least—than ever before. In her article "The Singles in the Seventies," Rosalyn Moran points out that in 1971 there were in the United States nearly 41 million single adults, including 15¹/₂ million men and 12¹/₂ million women who had never been married, and 3¹/₂ million widowed and divorced.[56] Traditionally held attitudes that the single adult must be peculiar or at least "different"—perhaps unappealing, frigid, homosexual, promiscuous, or not quite grown up—appear to be softening today. Until fairly recently, the single adult, especially the woman, was supposed to sublimate her or his desires in order to conform to the sex norms of society. Now, belatedly, society is granting more freedom of choice, making a place for singles, including single females. The single female still is at a disadvantage vis-a-vis the single male, however. While public sentiment allows her more freedom of action now, she still suffers systematic discrimination in many areas, such as employment, salaries, and credit.[52]

The subculture of "singles," if there really is one, has not yet developed to the point of being an established alternative to marriage. Rather, singleness seems to be more a temporary way station for those who are not yet ready to "marry and settle down" and for others who are waiting to remarry. True, some may choose to dwell in this way station year after year, getting satisfaction from various singles' activities, while others will be using these activities and groups to sooner or later find a marriage partner. Rosalyn Moran found this to be the case in the study mentioned above. She found that the expanding singles' organizations—bars, clubs, dating systems, and publications—served as dating and matchmaking facilities for single women and men. Today these singles' publications, like their earlier European counterparts, openly and explicitly provide such matchmaking services.

The emergence of the singles identity has even encouraged the single American to advertise for a mate, a hitherto strictly European custom. One of the largest singles advertising monthlies [carries] more than 500 ads. . . . The interesting thing is . . . that all these ads were placed by the so-called white collar worker or person of higher status. . . . All sought the same thing—a female companion—with the view to ultimate matrimony. Only 5 percent intimated they wanted nothing more than a sexual partner, and even then they hinted that matrimony was not entirely out of the question.[58]

The future of singleness as an alternative to conventional marriage remains to be seen. Voluntarily or involuntarily, more men and women are remaining single longer than ever before prior to marriage. United States census figures since 1960 have shown a decreasing percentage of the population age of eighteen years and older as being married. In 1960, of all those eighteen and over, 76.4 percent of the men and 71.6 percent of the women were married. Comparable figures for 1970 were 75.0 percent for men and 68.5 percent for women. By 1975, only 72.8 percent of American men and 66.7 percent of American women were married.[59] This means that a full one-third of American women aged eighteen and over were either widowed, divorced, or not yet married in 1975. Remaining single indefinitely, though, is still felt to be somewhat contrary to American social expectations.

THE ONE-PARENT FAMILY AS AN ALTERNATIVE TO THE CONVENTIONAL TWO-PARENT FAMILY   While remaining single may become an appealing alternative for more unattached men and women, will the one-parent family or household come to be seen as an acceptable alternative to the conventional two-parent family?

As noted above, there is still social pressure on the single adult to find a mate; such pressure is even stronger on the single parent. At the same time, finding a suitable mate and stepparent is often more difficult for a man or woman who already has one or more children to care for. This, plus a number of interrelated trends, assures the continued existence and probable increase of one-parent families for the foreseeable future. More freedom of action and increased economic independence for women, plus the rises in divorce, desertion, and illegitimacy have all contributed to the growing number of one-parent families. More unwed mothers are opting to keep and raise their children. *Time* magazine commented on this development: "No longer fearful about complete ostracism from society, many single girls who become pregnant now choose to carry rather than abort their babies and to support them after birth without rushing pell-mell into what might be a disastrous marriage."[60]

Liberalized adoption laws also make it easier now for single and divorced men and women to obtain children and to establish a home for them without the presence of a marriage partner.

Stereotypical notions have long existed about the single-parent family. They have been labeled as "broken homes," "disorganized," "unstable," and as constituting a "social problem" for the community. While the demands and responsibilities shouldered by the single parent are many and real enough— such as being both mother and father to the children, being the sole breadwinner, the homemaker, etc.—still "probably the most difficult problem facing the single parent comes from the attitudes and behavior of society which isolates to a degree the single spouse from the mainstream of a former socio-economic way of life."[61]

The possible negative aspects of the one-parent family have been greatly overgeneralized, most authorities agree now. E. E. LeMasters, for example, has shown that it is erroneous to automatically assume that the single-parent home is an abnormal or harmful setting for child rearing. He finds little evidence in the family literature of pathological effects of single parenthood, and concludes that one good parent can probably do a better job of child rearing than two parents who are in serious conflict.[62] Jane Burgess agrees and adds that "there is substantial evidence that children are measurably better off living with one parent than the children of unhappy homes characterized by bitterness, fighting, and physical and mental cruelty, whose parents stay together for the children's sake."[63]

No one really knows how many single parents continue to live that way voluntarily. Our impressions are that the proportion is increasing, as more mothers continue to be employed and as community services such as day care centers expand. United States census data show that remarriage rates are still rising while first-marriage rates are gradually declining.[64] It is probably safe to assume that the large majority of those who have become parents without partners, whether by divorce, desertion, or death of a marital partner—and probably most unmarried mothers too—do not yet see the one-parent family as a permanent alternative to the conventional two-parent family.

Some Conclusions Regarding Alternative Life-Styles

What kinds of evaluative comparisons can now be made between the above-discussed variant or alternative life-styles and conventional marriage and family? What advantages and disadvantages for the individual and for society may be identified for the new alternative forms versus the older forms?

COMPARISON OF THE TRADITIONAL FAMILY AND ALTERNATIVE FORMS

In her article "Variant Family Forms and Life Styles: Rejection of the Traditional Nuclear Family," Betty Cogswell makes some general comparisons between traditional marriage and family and the wide range of experimental life-styles.[65] Our discussion will follow her analysis quite closely.

RESTRICTED VERSUS DIFFUSED RELATIONSHIPS Traditional marriage and family have been expected to meet virtually all the emotional needs of members, thus discouraging intimate relations with outsiders to the point where any extramarital relations are generally defined as infidelities or at least disloyalties. It is to escape this traditional "caging" effect that the O'Neills and others are advocating open marriages and looser commune-type life-styles. Cogswell argues that married couples become "caged in." They are expected to present a "couple front" to the world; this requires them to mesh their interests and expectations and to delete most that are not shared by both wife and husband. In the variant marriage and family forms, by comparison, bonding is based on the assumption that no one person, nor a single nuclear family, can ever be expected to meet all the needs of the individual. Therefore, in the alternative forms, individuals tend to "sectorize" their lives and form meaningful relationships with different persons in each sector such as at home, at work, and at leisure.[66]

The assumption is that one cannot realistically expect one single person to fill all the multiple roles such as fishing partner, protector, therapist, lover, business advisor, intellectual companion, etc., as conventional norms seem to prescribe.

It is obvious that these "sectorized" relationships would offer advantages of variety and flexibility in personal relationships; on the other hand, conventional marriage and the nuclear family generally offer greater personal security and more depth in personal relations.

MULTIPLE VERSUS SINGLE PRIMARY RELATIONSHIPS   While in traditional marriage it is expected that there will be a single bonding relationship between husband and wife for life, in the variant types the expectations are for simultaneous as well as serial multiple relations. Members of variant marriage forms expect and welcome these varied relationships which from the traditional view would be defined as clandestine.[67] Advantages here are the variety and openness in intimate relations encouraged by the alternative forms. Traditionalists would likely see disadvantages in the transitoriness and possible superficiality of such mobile and multiple relations as compared to the opportunity offered in conventional marriage for lifelong and deeper emotional relationships.

PERSON-TO-PERSON RELATIONSHIPS VERSUS ROLE-DEFINED RELATIONSHIPS   In traditional families the relations between members tend to conform to conventional family statuses and roles, such as husband, wife, father, mother, son, or daughter. In the contraculture adopted by many of those experimenting with variant family forms, such "role behavior" is viewed negatively because it is felt to be rigid and restrictive and thus detrimental to "natural" person-to-person relations. Those holding this view oppose "stereotyping" individuals by social characteristics such as sex, age, ethnicity, or social class, contending that one person's behavioral expectations about another should develop naturally as a consequence of continuous person-to-person contact. Such openness and freedom in relations would allow and encourage a broader range of acceptable behavior than is possible where traditional roles prevail.[68]

From the point of view of those who support conventional marriage and the nuclear family with its status and role structure, it may be argued that there is nothing built into these conventional statuses and roles which precludes real intimacy, honesty and openness, and self-revelation, the qualities so valued by advocates of alternative forms of relationships. On the contrary, it may be argued that conventional marriage and family statuses and roles embrace these very values and more. The "more" would include long-term reciprocal commitments and responsibilities to support, protect, and love each other, between husband and wife, parents and children. Such shared family role expectations and norms are conducive to greater personal security and well-being as well as making for greater predictability and efficiency in family relationships.

TEMPORARY VERSUS PERMANENT RELATIONSHIPS It has been widely observed that one of the principal differences between traditional marriage and family and the new variant family forms is in their polar opposite views on the duration of the relationships of members. Individuals normally enter conventional marriage with the expectation that the relationship will be permanent, while most who enter a variant form do so with the expectation that relationships will last only so long as they continue to serve mutual needs of members.[69] The emphasis in variant families on openness and trust can lead to a quicker realization of the need to sever relations that are no longer mutually beneficial. Further responsibilities or obligations of one person to another are either lacking or are of a low priority. The stress is on immediate personal fulfillment rather than long-term obligations.

Conversely, in the traditional family, members carry responsibilities that are expected to last a lifetime, and family members expect to be able to count on each other tomorrow as well as today, in bad times as well as good.

These considerations led Cogswell to raise an important sociological question about the variant or alternative family forms: "Are the goals held by those entering variant families adequate or sufficiently inclusive to sustain individuals over a life-span?" Her response to the question is, "Although there are insufficient data to arrive at an informed opinion, it seems likely that variant family goals are most appropriate in short-term, fair weather contexts. Perhaps goals such as self-actualization and autonomy drop to lower priority in times of personal crises when mere survival must take uppermost priority."[70]

Can the variant family meet individual needs which require substantial group effort over long periods of time or require large financial contributions from savings or from other family resources? Can the variant family provide the intensive daily care needed for many months by a member who is severely ill or disabled? Could or would the variant family contribute the large sums of money needed for such medical services, or for extensive legal fees for a member in trouble with the law? Within the traditional family it is expected that all such needs will be met to the extent of the family's financial and physical abilities. While it is too soon to know from experience if or to what extent variant families would make these efforts and sacrifices, Cogswell presents the following opinion: "On the basis of current information, I would be inclined to think that experimental families would default on heavy responsibilities for the care of other members."[71]

Without doubt the dialogue will continue between the proponents of the new, variant family forms and those who support the more conventional marriage and family patterns. More time and much more empirical data are needed on the alternative forms to provide the necessary factual bases for comparisons with the traditional family. For the present, these tentative comparative generalizations are offered by Cogswell:

In very broad and general terms, . . . the [traditional] family structure appears to be tightly constructed, closed, restrictive, and institutionalized while the experimental family structure appears more loosely constructed, open, opportunistic and still evolving. In gross terms the [traditional] family form emphasizes constraints to the detriment of opportunity, and the experimental variant forms emphasize opportunity to the detriment of constraints.[72]

One final note. Admittedly, the above picture is presented in rather stark "either-or" terms, in order to highlight the comparative advantages and disadvantages of the experimental or alternative forms versus the traditional family forms. Actually, what is probably happening, and what will likely continue to happen in family change, represents a compromise between these two extreme positions. Traditional marriage and family structures are surely being modified by modern secular trends, including equalitarianism, feminism, and individuation. And, experience has shown that after their initial experimental phase, many of the alternative forms tend to lose most of their extreme or radical traits, as in the case of certain communes.

If it were necessary to make a guess as to which of the three major categories of alternative life-styles will most likely survive, our first choice would be the "incorporable alternatives," which may modify conventional marriage and family patterns (e.g., changed sex roles in the family, or "open marriage" in varying degrees), but which do not radically change basic family structure. Second most likely to endure will probably be certain "parallel alternatives," which are outside conventional marriage and family—such as premarital or postmarital living together—but again do not aim at basically changing or replacing marriage and family structure and functioning. While it is quite likely that the alternative forms of the third category, which are opposed to and which aspire to be replacements for conventional marriage and family, such as communes or group marriages, will continue to attract a tiny minority of Americans in the future, their impact on the institutions of marriage and family will probably continue to be very minimal.

Summary

While experimentation in alternative life-styles is not new, the recent surge of variant marriage and family experiments in the United States has a distinctive flavor. The experiments need to be viewed within the context of the social unrest of the past two decades, some demographic trends, and various related economic and social conditions. There was a surplus of young people in the 1960s, many of them at loose ends, disenchanted with mainstream American culture, and ripe for something new. Out of this grew the contraculture, or counterculture, whose proponents argued that traditional marriage and family forms were no longer adequate or even relevant. Such critics see the nuclear family as restrictive and antithetical to individual freedom and growth, and no longer able to meet most individual needs.

The wide array of alternative life-styles may be divided into three broad categories: (1) Those parallel to but outside conventional marriage and family, such as premarital or postmarital living together; (2) those incorporable into marriage and family, such as expanding the family network to include nonrelatives, or mate swapping; and (3) those opposed to conventional marriage and family, such as communes or group marriages. There are indications that more adults, both men and women, are choosing to remain single than ever before. There is also an increase in the number of one-parent families, or "parents without partners."

Some evaluative comparisons of the variant or alternative life-styles and conventional marriage and family are presented. Proponents of alternative life-styles argue that traditional marriage and family structures are overly restrictive for the individual and place too great a burden on one person to meet all the multiple needs of one's marriage partner. Alternative forms would allow or encourage one to "sectorize" one's life and form intimate relationships with different persons in different areas of life. This would offer advantages of variety and flexibility but would probably sacrifice the greater depth in personal relationships and the greater security offered in conventional marriage and family. Traditionalists argue that the multiple and sectorized contacts offered in the alternative life-styles would be more superficial and transitory than conventional marriage and family which entail lifelong and deeper personal commitments. Advocates of the variant forms argue that conventional forms tend to inhibit "natural" interpersonal relations by imposing family roles upon members and by stereotyping individuals according to sex, age, etc. They feel this "role behavior" should be eliminated in order to encourage freedom, openness, and honesty in personal relations. Supporters of conventional marriage and family respond that there is nothing built into the conventional marriage and family roles which precludes openness, honesty, and real intimacy, the very things highly valued by the proponents of new forms of relationships. Conventional marriage and family offer these things and more, such as long-term reciprocal commitments and obligations to support, love, and protect.

One of the main differences between the new alternative life-styles and traditional marriage and family is their opposite views on the duration of the relationships. In conventional marriage the expectation is that the relationship will be permanent, while for most who enter an alternative life-style the expectation is that the relationship will endure only so long as it continues to serve the mutual needs of those involved. The concern is with personal fulfillment rather than long-term obligations.

Some family authorities feel that the variant or alternative life-styles are most appropriate where short-term goals are being pursued, and in "fair weather contexts." More data are needed to tell if or to what extent variant or alternative forms will be willing or able to meet long-term needs, to make the financial commitments and the personal sacrifices which are expected of conventional families in times of crisis or when a family member is in serious trouble.

It seems quite likely that conventional marriage and family structures will continue to be modified in keeping with the Gesellschaft-secular trends, but not be replaced by any present or future alternative life-styles.

Notes

1   Gerald Leslie, *The Family in Social Context* (New York: Oxford University Press, 1976), chap. 11. Present discussion follows Leslie closely.
2   Ibid., p. 385.
3   Ibid.
4   Ibid., p. 386.
5   Peter Drucker, "The Surprising Seventies," *Harper's Magazine* (July 1971), pp. 35–39.
6   Daniel Bell, *The Coming of Post-industrial Society* (New York: Basic Books, 1973).
7   Leslie, op. cit., p. 388.
8   Ibid., pp. 390–392.
9   Betty E. Cogswell, "Variant Family Forms and Life Styles: Rejection of the Traditional Nuclear Family," *Family Coordinator*, 24 (October 1975), pp. 391–406.
10 Ibid., p. 391.
11 Ibid., p. 392.
12 R. L. Birdwhistell, "The Idealized Model of the American Family," *Social Casework*, 50 (1970), p. 195.
13 Cogswell, op. cit., p. 394.
14 Ibid., p. 400.
15 Patrick W. Conover, "An Analysis of Communes and Intentional Communities with Particular Attention to Sexual and Gender Relations," *Family Coordinator*, 24 (October 1975), p. 453.
16 Cogswell, op. cit., p. 394.
17 David Schulz, *The Changing Family* (Englewood Cliffs, N.J.: Prentice-Hall, 1972), pp. 418–420. This discussion follows Schulz closely.
18 Ibid., fig. 15-3, p. 360.
19 Bert N. Adams, "Can the Family Survive Alternate Life Styles?" *Forum* (Nov. 2, 1973) pp. 4–8. This section follows Adams quite closely. Also see J. W. Ramey, "Emerging Patterns of Innovative Behavior in Marriage," *Family Coordinator*, 21 (October 1972), pp. 435–456.
20 Eleanor Macklin, "Heterosexual Cohabitation among Unmarried College Students," *Family Coordinator*, 21 (October 1972), p. 463.
21 Ibid., p. 464. Also see Richard Clayton and Harwin Voss, "Shacking Up: Cohabitation in the 1970's." *Journal of Marriage and Family*, 39 (May 1977), pp. 273, 283.

22 Macklin, op. cit., p. 466.

23 Ibid., pp. 468–470.

24 J. L. Lyness et al., "Living Together: An Alternative to Marriage," *Journal of Marriage and Family*, 34 (May 1972) pp. 305–311.

25 Joy D. Osofsky and Howard J. Osofsky, "Androgyny as a Life Style," *Family Coordinator*, 21 (October 1972), pp. 411–418.

26 Frederick Stoller, in Herbert A. Otto, ed., *The Family in Search of a Future* (New York: Appleton Century Crofts, 1970), pp. 145–159.

27 Adams, op. cit., p. 376.

28 Robert E. Bell and Michael Gordon, eds., *The Social Dimension of Human Sexuality* (Boston: Little, Brown & Co., 1972), pp. 120–143. Also see Morton Hunt, *Sexual Behavior in the 1970's* (New York: Dell Publishing Co., 1974), chap. 5, "Postmarital and Extramarital Sex."

29 Duane Denfeld and Michael Gordon, "Mate Swapping: The Family that Swings Together Clings Together," in Arlene S. Skolnick and Jerome H. Skolnick, *Family in Transition* (Boston: Little, Brown & Co., 1971), pp. 463–475.

30 Ibid., p. 473.

31 William and Jerrye Breedlove, *Swap Clubs* (Los Angeles: Sherbourne Press, 1964), as noted in Bert N. Adams, *The Family: A Sociological Interpretation* (Chicago: Rand McNally College Publishing Co., 1975), p. 378.

32 Hunt, op. cit., p. 271

33 G. D. Bartell, "Group Sex among Mid-Americans," *Journal of Sex Research*, 6 (1970), p. 527. Also see Duane Denfeld "Dropouts from Swinging," *Family Coordinator*, 23 (January 1974), pp. 45–49.

34 Nena O'Neill and George O'Neill, *Open Marriage: A New Life-Style for Couples* (New York: M. Evans and Co., 1972).

35 Nena O'Neill and George O'Neill, "Open Marriage: A Synergic Model," *Family Coordinator*, 21 (October 1972), p. 403

36 Ibid., p. 406.

37 Ibid., p. 406–408.

38 John C. Haughey, "The Commune-Child of the 1970's,"in Jack R. DeLora and Joann S. DeLora, eds., *Intimate Life-Styles* (Pacific Palisades: Goodyear Publishing Company, 1975), p. 310. Also see Raymond Muncy, *Sex and Marriage in Utopian Communities: Nineteenth Century America* (Baltimore: Penguin Books, 1974).

39 Bennett Berger et al., "The Communal Family," *Family Coordinator*, 21 (October 1972), pp. 419–420. Also see Ron Roberts, *The New Communes* (Englewood Cliffs, N.J.: Prentice-Hall, 1971).

40 Berger, op. cit., p. 420.

41 Adams, *Forum*, op. cit., p. 381.

42 Leslie, op. cit., p. 404.

43 Rosabeth M. Kanter et al., "Coupling, Parenting, and the Presence of Others: Intimate Relationships in Communal Households," *Family Coordinator*, 24 (October 1975), pp. 433–452.

44 Ibid., pp. 433–434.

45 Ibid., p. 441.

46 Ibid., p. 443.

47 Ibid., p. 447. Also see Susan Wolf and John Rothschild, *The Children of the Counterculture* (Garden City, N.Y.: Doubleday Publishing Co., 1976).

48 Joyce Gardener, "Communal Living: Economic Survival and Family Life," in Gordon F. Streib, ed., *The Changing Family: Adaptation and Diversity* (Reading, Mass.: Addison-Wesley Publishing Co., 1973), pp. 117–118. Also see Roberts, op. cit.

49 Larry L. Constantine and Joan M. Constantine, "Where Is Marriage Going?" *Futurist* (April 1970), p. 44.

50 Larry L. Constantine and Joan M. Constantine, "Sexual Aspects of Multilateral Relations," *Journal of Sex Research*, 7 (August 1971), p. 205.

51 Ibid., pp. 205–206.

52 Albert Ellis, "Group Marriage: A Possible Alternative?" in Streib, op. cit., pp. 82–85.

53 Ibid., p. 86.

54 Adams, *Forum*, op. cit., pp. 380–381.

55 Margaret Mead, "Marriage in Two Steps," in Herbert A. Otto, ed., op. cit., pp. 75–84.

56 Rosalyn Moran, "The Singles in the Seventies," in DeLora and DeLora, *Intimate Life Styles* (Pacific Palisades, Calif.: Goodyear Publishing Co., 1972), p. 338.

57 Ibid.

58 Ibid., pp. 338–339.

59 *Statistical Abstract of the United States*, 1976, "Vital Statistics, Health, and Nutrition," p. 68.

60 "The American Family: Future Uncertain," *Time* (December 28, 1970), p. 38, as quoted by Jane K. Burgess, "The Single-Parent Family: A Social and Sociological Problem," in Frank D. Cox, ed., *American Marriage* (Dubuque, Iowa: Wm. C. Brown, Publishers, 1972), p. 235.

61 Burgess, in Cox, op. cit., p. 228.

62 E. E. LeMasters, *Parents in Modern America* (Homewood, Ill.: Dorsey Press, 1974), pp. 149–151.

63 Burgess, in Cox, op. cit., p. 229.

64 Paul Glick and A. J. Norton, "Perspectives on the Recent Upturn in Divorce and Remarriage," *Demography*, 10 (1973), p. 302.

65 Cogswell, op. cit. This section draws heavily from Cogswell.

66 Ibid., p. 402.

67 Ibid.

68 Ibid., p. 403.

69 Ibid., p. 401.

70 Ibid.

71 Ibid.

72 Ibid., p. 400.

SELECTED READING

Many different alternatives to conventional marriage and family have been identified and compared throughout the present chapter. Since it was not possible to go into much detail on any one alternative form, the present reading was selected to give the reader a more complete view of at least one new type of marriage that has been advocated, with the reasoning and rationale upon which it was based.

Margaret Mead offers an intriguing alternative to conventional marriage. She points out that the age of first marriage in the United States has declined steadily over the years (until very recently, at least), with the inevitable result that young couples are entering parenthood earlier than in the past. Since we encourage these early marriages, we need to think more clearly about the economic responsibilities and problems such youthful marriages entail. More marriages than ever are broken today, and especially fragile are the marriages of those very young couples who become parents before they really know each other as husband and wife. Can marriage possibly be altered in a way that would both provide young couples a chance to know each other better and also give children a better opportunity to grow up in a stronger and more enduring family? A new type of marriage that could help do these things, Mead believes, would be a two-step or two-stage type of marriage.

The first step of this new kind of marriage would be an *individual marriage*, which would bind a man and a woman together as husband and wife for as long as they wished to remain together. The second step, a *parental marriage*, would be possible for those couples desiring to become parents. This would entail greater responsibilities than the individual marriage, and mean a lifelong commitment of the parents-to-be. One of the main advantages of this innovation, Mead feels, is that every child born would be a child that was both wanted and prepared for.

MARRIAGE IN TWO STAGES*

Margaret Mead

The June bride evokes memory pictures of her mother and her mother's mother as just such a happy girl, caught between tears and laughter. The newest bridegroom, describing his difficulties, awakens memories of other crises, each story a different one, and yet in its happy outcome the same.

For everyone taking part in a wedding each small event, like the solemn ritual of marriage itself, binds the generations in the shared belief that what has been true and lasting in the past is true and lasting today and will remain so safely across time. On such occasions sentiment and loving hope for the young couple—these two who are entering the most important relationship of their adult lives—join in renewing our faith in traditional forms. This, we believe, is how families begin.

But in the cool light of everyday experience a different picture emerges. As a society we have moved—and are still moving—a long way from the kinds of marriage our forefathers knew and believed in. We still define marriage as essentially an adult relationship. But now, in a period in which full participation in adult life is increasingly delayed, the age of first marriage for boys as well as girls has been declining steadily. And although people can look forward to longer years of vigorous maturity, young couples are entering parenthood not later than in the past, but earlier.

We still believe that marriage entails financial responsibility. Yet we indulge in endless subterfuge to disguise the economic dependency of the majority of very young marriages. Significantly, we have devised systems of loans and insurance to ease our financial burden of seeing children through years of higher education. However, we have not invented any form of insurance to cover the care of children born of student marriages, or born to teenage parents who are struggling to find themselves. If we encourage these young marriages, as in fact we do, then we must think more clearly about the long-term economic problems for which we, as parents, may have to take some responsibility.

We still believe that marriage is the necessary prelude to responsible parenthood even though, in every social class, pregnancy is to an increasing extent preceding marriage. We still strongly believe that children born of a marriage should be wanted. In the past, this meant accepting the birth of children no matter what the number and circumstances; but today, with existing methods of conception control, every child could be a chosen child.

We still believe that the continuity of the family, based on marriage, is fundamental to our way of life and to the well-being of every individual child. Yet there is clear evidence of the fragility of marriage ties, especially among very young couples who become parents before they know each other as husband and wife.

The disparities are plain to see and the outlook is unpromising. We might expect this to force us to recognize how great are the discrepancies between our expectations, based on tradition, and what is happening to young American families. The truth is, we have not really faced up to the many conflicts between belief and experience, precept and practice, in our current, muddled style of marriage. It is not enough to say, "Yes, marriage patterns are changing." What we have not fully realized is that we do not have to stand by helplessly while change sweeps over us, destroying our hopes for a better life for our children.

Instead, we can look steadily at the changes that have brought us where we are.

We can ask, "How can we invest marriage forms with new meaning?"

We can move toward a reconciliation of belief and practice that is consonant with our understanding of good human relationships.

Of course, there is no simple way of defining the changes that have already taken place, but two things are crucial in the contemporary attitude—our attitude toward sex and our attitude toward commitment. Today, I am convinced, most Americans have come to regard sex, like eating and sleeping, as a natural activity. We lean toward the belief that persons who are deprived of sex will be tense and crotchety and perhaps unreliable in their personal relationships. We have come to believe also that asking physically mature young people to postpone sex until their middle twenties is neither fair nor feasible. And as we have learned to deal more evenhandedly with boys and girls, most of us have ceased to believe in any double standard of morality. This is in keeping with our belief that sex, like marriage and parenthood, should involve social equals who are close in age. When the age gap widens—when the man is much older than the woman or the woman older than the man—we disapprove. And although we may not express our doubts, we do not have very high expectations for eventual happiness when two people must bridge wide differences in upbringing. We believe that young people should learn about sex together, as equals. But this means that both are likely to be equally inexperienced. Our emphasis, in the ideal, is on spontaneity. It is this combination of beliefs, together with our continuing certainty that sex is safe only in marriage, that has fostered—that has in fact, forced—our present acceptance of very young marriage.

But in accepting early marriage as the easiest solution to the problem of providing a sex life for everyone, we confront new difficulties. No matter how many books adolescent boys and girls have read, or how freely they have talked about sex, they actually know very little about it and are very likely to bungle their first serious sex relations. Certainly, this is not new; an unhappy honeymoon all too often has been a haunting prelude to marriage. What is new is that the young husband and wife are as yet inexperienced in living through the initial difficulties that can enter into any important adult relationship of choice. They are, for example, inexperienced in making friends and living through the give-and-take that adult friendships require. Young men today rarely know how to make friends with girls, and girls, looking for mates, are unlikely to be much interested in a man as a friend. Heterosexual friendships therefore are postponed until after marriage, and then entered into only with other married couples. Thus, friendship, which ideally should precede marriage and help the young man and woman better understand the adjustments that any adult relationship requires, now comes too late to help a first marriage.

Inexperience is one hazard. But it becomes especially hazardous because we also believe that no one should be trapped in a final mistake. Individuals as they grow and develop are permitted to change their jobs and occupations, to move from one part of the country to another, to form new associations, and develop new interests that bring them into contact with new people. And as part of our expectation that people change as they grow, most of us have come also to accept the idea of divorce. When a marriage does not work out most of us believe each partner should have another chance to start over again with a different man or a different woman. We believe in commitment, but we do not believe that commitments are irrevocable.

But divorce also is a hazard. It is true that for two adults without children who now find that they cannot carry out a commitment made at an earlier stage of their lives, divorce can be an end and a beginning; but because of the role children play in the present style of marriage, divorce becomes a widespread hazard. For whereas in the past a man, and especially a woman, might marry in order to have children, now having a child validates marriage. Pregnancy often precedes marriage, and even where it does not, the style is to have a child quickly. It is as if having a child sets the seal of permanence on a marriage that is in truth far from permanent, and that, at this stage, is still in the making.

The child thus becomes a symbol. This use of a child is out of keeping with our belief that each person should be valued as an individual for his own sake. And when the marriage breaks down, the child is sacrificed to the changed needs of the man and woman, who are acting not as parents but as husband and wife. The child—a person in his own right, growing toward the future—stands as a symbol of an unreal past.

Perhaps we can catch a glimpse of what we might make of marriage and parenthood if we think in terms of a new pattern that would both give young couples a better chance to come to know each other, and give children a better chance to grow up in an enduring family. Through what steps might this be accomplished?

It should be said at once that changes as important as those involved in creating a new style of marriage can never be brought about through the actions of a few people, or even all the members of a single group. In a democracy as complex as ours, in which one must always take into account a great diversity of religious, regional, class, and national styles, success will depend on contributions made by all kinds of people. Many ideas will arise out of discussions in the press, from the pulpits of many churches, on television, in the agencies of government, in the theater, and in community organizations. Some will come from those whose work brings them face to face with the failures of the present system and who are aware of the urgent need for new forms. Some will be shaped by the actual experiments in which lively, imaginative young people are engaging. And still others will arise out of the puzzlement and questions of the people who listen to the suggestions made by all those who are trying to become articulate about the issues. Out of all these discussions, carried on over a period of time, there will, I hope, evolve the kind of consensus that will provide the basis for a new marriage tradition. We are still a long way from the point at which we can consider the new tradition in such pragmatic terms as its formal social framework—in law and religious practice. No one, it should be clear, can write a prescription or make a blueprint for a whole society.

What I am doing here is advancing some ideas of my own as one contribution to an ongoing discussion. First I shall outline the goals that I personally hope we may reach.

I should like to see us put more emphasis upon the importance of human relationships and less upon sex as a physical need. That is, I would hope that we could encourage a greater willingness to spend time searching for a congenial partner and to enjoy cultivating a deeply personal relationship. Sex would then take its part within a more complex intimacy and would cease to be sought after for itself alone.

I should like to see children assured of a lifelong relationship to both parents. This, of course, can only be attained when parents themselves have such a relationship. I do not mean that parents must stay married. As long as early marriage remains a practice, it must be assumed that some marriages—perhaps many marriages—will break down in the course of a lifetime of growth, mobility, and change. But I should like to see a style of parenthood develop that would survive the breaking of the links of marriage through divorce. This would depend on a mutual recognition that co-parenthood is a permanent relationship. Just as brother and sister are irrevocably related because they share the same parents, so also parents are irrevocably related because they share the same child. At present, divorce severs the link between the adult partners and each, in some fashion, attempts—or sometimes gives up the attempt—to keep a separate contact with the children, as if this were now a wholly individual relationship. This need not be.

Granting the freedom of partners to an uncongenial marriage to seek a different, individual commitment within a new marriage, I would hope that we would hold on to the ideal of a lifetime marriage in maturity. No religious group that cherishes marriage as a sacrament should have to give up the image of a marriage that lasts into old age and into the lives of grandchildren and great-grandchildren as one that is blessed by God. No wholly secularized group should have to be deprived of the sense that an enduring, meaningful relationship is made binding by the acceptance, approval, and support of the entire society as witnesses.

At the same time, I believe, we must give greater reality to our belief that marriage is a matter of individual choice, a choice made by each young man and woman freely, without coercion by parents or others. The present mode of seeking for sex among a wide range of partners casually, and then, inconsistently, of accepting marriage as a form of "choice" arising from necessity, is a deep denial of individuality and individual love. In courtship, intensity of feeling grows as two people move toward each other. In our present system, however, intensity of feeling is replaced by the tensions arising from a series of unknown factors: Will pregnancy occur? Is this the best bargain on the sex market? Even with sexual freedom, will marriage result? Today true courtship, when it happens, comes about in spite of, not because of, the existing styles of dating and marrying.

These goals—individual choice, a growing desire for a lifelong relationship with a chosen partner, and the desire for children with whom and through whom lifelong relationships are maintained—provide a kind of framework for thinking about new forms of marriage. I believe that we need two forms of marriage, one of which can (though it need not) develop into the other, each with its own possibilities and special forms of responsibility.

The first type of marriage may be called an *individual marriage* binding together two individuals only. It has been suggested that it might be called a "student" marriage, as undoubtedly it would occur first and most often among students. But looking ahead, it would be a type of marriage that would also be appropriate for much older men and women, so I shall use the term *individual marriage*. Such a marriage would be a licensed union in which two individuals would be committed to each other as individuals for as long as they wished to remain together, but not as future parents. As the first step in marriage, it would not include having children.

In contrast, the second type of marriage, which I think of as *parental marriage*, would be explicitly directed toward the founding of a family. It would not only be a second type but also a second step or stage, following always on an individual marriage and with its own license and ceremony and kinds of responsibility. This would be a marriage that looked to a lifetime with links, sometimes, to many people.

In an individual marriage, the central obligation of the boy and girl or man and woman to each other would be an ethical, not an economic, one. The husband would not be ultimately responsible for the support of his wife; if the marriage broke up, there would be no alimony or support. The husband would not need to feel demeaned if he was not yet ready, or was not able, to support his wife. By the same token, husband or wife could choose freely to support the other within this partnership.

Individual marriage would give two very young people a chance to know each other with a kind of intimacy that does not usually enter into a brief love affair, and so it would help them to grow into each other's life—and allow them to part without the burden of misunderstood intentions, bitter recriminations, and self-destructive guilt. In the past, long periods of engagement, entered into with parental consent, fulfilled at least in part the requirement of growing intimacy and shared experience. But current attitudes toward sex make any retreat to this kind of relationship impossible. In other societies, where parents chose their children's marriage partners, the very fact of meeting as strangers at the beginning of a lifelong relationship gave each a high sense of expectancy within which shared understanding might grow. But this is impossible for us as an option because of the emphasis on personal choice and the unwillingness to insist on maintaining a commitment that has failed.

Individual marriage in some respects resembles "companionate marriage" as it was first discussed in the 1920's and written about by Judge Ben Lindsey on the basis of his long experience in court with troubled young people. This was a time when very few people were ready as yet to look ahead to the consequences of deep changes in our attitude toward sex and personal choice. Today, I believe, we are far better able to place young marriage within the context of a whole lifetime.

Individual marriage, as I see it, would be a serious commitment, entered into in public, validated and protected by law and, for some, by religion, in which each partner would have a deep and continuing concern for the happiness and well-being of the other. For those who found happiness it could open the way to a more complexly designed future.

Every parental marriage, whether children were born into it or adopted, would necessarily have as background a good individual marriage. The fact of a previous marriage, individual or parental, would not alter this. Every parental marriage, at no matter what stage in life, would have to be preceded by an individual marriage. In contrast to individual marriage, parental marriage would be hard to contract. Each partner would know the other well, eliminating the shattering surprise of discovery that either one had suffered years of mental or physical illness, had been convicted of a serious crime, was unable to hold a job, had entered the country illegally, already had children or other dependents, or any one of the thousand shocks that lie in wait for the person who enters into a hasty marriage with someone he or she knows little about. When communities were smaller, most people were protected against such shocks by the publication of the banns. Today other forms of protection are necessary. The assurance thus given to parents that their son or daughter would not become hopelessly trapped into sharing parenthood with an unsuitable mate also would serve as a protection for the children not yet born.

As a couple prepared to move from an individual to a parental marriage they also would have to demonstrate their economic ability to support a child. Instead of falling back on parents, going deeply into debt, or having to ask the aid of welfare agencies, they would be prepared for the coming of a child. Indeed, both might be asked to demonstrate some capacity to undertake the care of the family in the event one or the other became ill. Today a girl's education, which potentially makes her self-sustaining, is perhaps the best dowry a man can give his son-in-law so he will not fall prey to the gnawing anxiety of how his family would survive his death. During an individual marriage, designed to lead to parental marriage, a girl, no less than a boy, might learn a skill that would make her self-supporting in time of need.

Even more basic to the survival of a marriage, however, is the quality of the marriage itself—its serenity, its emotional strength, its mutuality. Over long years we have acquired a fund of experience about good marriages through the inquiries made by adoption agencies before a child is given permanently to adoptive parents. Now, if we wished to do so, we could extrapolate from this experience for the benefit of partners in individual marriages but not yet joined in parenthood and for the benefit of infants hoped for but not yet conceived. And in the course of these explorations before parental marriage the ethical and religious issues that sometimes are glossed over earlier could be discussed and, in a good relationship, resolved. Careful medical examinations would bring to light present or potential troubles, and beyond this, would help the couple to face the issue: What if, in spite of our desire for a family, having a child entails a serious risk to the mother, or perhaps the child? What if, in spite of a good prognosis, we, as a couple, cannot have a child? And then, even assuming that all such questions have been favorably resolved, it must not be forgotten that in all human relationships there are imponderables—and the marriage will be tested by them.

As a parental marriage would take much longer to contract and would be based on a larger set of responsibilities, so also its disruption would be carried out much more slowly. A divorce would be arranged in a way that would protect not only the two adults but also the children for whose sake the marriage was undertaken. The family, as against the marriage, would have to be assured a kind of continuity in which neither parent was turned into an angry ghost and no one could become an emotional blackmailer or be the victim of emotional blackmail.

Perhaps some men and women would choose to remain within individual marriage, with its more limited responsibilities; having found that there was an impediment to parental marriage, they might well be drawn into a deeper individual relationship with each other. And perhaps some who found meaningful companionship through parenthood would look later for more individualized companionship in a different kind of person.

By dignifying individual relationships for young people we would simultaneously invest with new dignity a multitude of deeply meaningful relationships of choice throughout life. First and foremost, we would recognize parenthood as a special form of marriage. But we would also give strong support to marriage as a working relationship of husband and wife as colleagues, and as a leisure relationship of a couple who have not yet entered into or who are now moving out of the arduous years of multiple responsibilities.

By strengthening parenthood as a lasting relationship we would keep intact the link between grandparents, parents, and children. Whether they were living together or were long since divorced, they would remain united in their active concern for their family of descendants. The acceptance of the two kinds of marriage would give equal support, however, to the couple who, having forgone a life with children, cherish their individual marriage as the expression of their love and loyalty.

The suggestion for a style of marriage in two steps—individual marriage and marriage for parenthood—has grown out of my belief that clarification is the beginning of constructive change. Just as no one can make a blueprint of the future, so no one can predict the outcome of a new set of principles. We do know something about the unfortunate direction in which contemporary marriage is drifting. But we need not simply continue to drift. With our present knowledge, every child born can be a child wanted and prepared for. And by combining the best of our traditions and our best appraisal of human relations, we may succeed in opening the way for new forms of marriage that will give dignity and grace to all men and women.

CHAPTER 10

Future of the American Family

Sociological prognostications regarding the future of any social phenomena should be couched in terms of degrees of probability, as is true of most efforts at scientific prediction. Certainly this is true of any attempts to predict the future of marriage and family. Social scientists, especially, are dealing with variables over which they have little or no control, and any predictions are subject to the influences of a multiplicity of factors. Their predictions have to be of the "if-then" type—*if* certain present trends and conditions continue, *then* such and such are probable for the future. Short-range predictions are of course more likely to be reliable than longer-range prognostications.

Approaches and Methods for Looking into the Future of Marriage and Family

How do sociologists go about trying to foresee the future of the family in America? Reuben Hill, in his article "The American Family of the Future," identifies four methods for projecting the contemporary American family into

Children at a playground. Racial and ethnic differences will become less important. (*Julie Heifetz.*)

the future:[1] (1) Extrapolation of current family trends, (2) projections from generational changes among several generations of contemporary families, (3) inferences drawn from the impact of current inventions on the family, and (4) inferences from the research and writing of family specialists. Let us see how, according to Hill, these four methods may help us look into the future of family life in America.

1   Extrapolating Family Trends   This method of looking into the future is not very reliable even when the aggregate data themselves are reliable. For example, marriage rates, or birth and death rates, may be quite accurately determined, but their future is subject to many unpredictable or unknown influences, such as economic cycles, war, and changes in values. One of the long-range trends observed in the United States census data has been that the average age of first marriage declined steadily from 1890 to 1960. In the next decade, however, the trend reversed and the average age of first marriage began to rise. While one could argue that the long-run trend is safer to predict from than the recent short-run tendency, most sociologists would probably agree that the new trend is going to continue, due to other present-day influences such as the current sex ratio, fertility rates, the condition of the economy, and the effects of higher education, all of which are influencing young people's decisions of when to get married.

2   Projecting Generational Changes   This method, developed by Professor Hill, identifies changes that have taken place over a period of three generations within the same family.[2] In comparing family patterns and life-styles of a sample of 100 married children (aged 20 to 30) with those of their parents (aged 40 to 60), and those of their grandparents (aged 60 to 80), Hill found a number of significant changes taking place, including these: (a) the average number of years of schooling increased impressively, especially for the husbands; (b) the age of first marriage decreased with each generation; (c) the differences in age of husband and wife decreased each generation; (d) the youngest generation has more children than its parents (who married during the Great Depression), but not as many children as its grandparents; (e) in each successive generation more wives have worked outside the home; (f) the youngest generation is more successful economically, and individuals have advanced more rapidly in their careers; (g) the youngest generation is more future-oriented and more optimistic than earlier generations; and (h) in family authority, the greatest shift to equalitarian patterns took place from the grandparent to the parent generation, but continues to hold up in the married-child generation.

3   Impact of Inventions   This method of looking into the future of the family may be exciting, but it is also very hazardous, Hill says.[3] There is a tendency to overstate the impact of mechanical inventions, such as time-saving kitchen equipment. Such inventions may increase the quality of the service, but not necessarily result in more leisure time in family life. Time-saving inventions and new techniques in housekeeping have played an important part in

releasing women from some of the traditional household activities, thus enabling them to do other things, such as seeking employment outside the home.

4   Inferences from Work of Family Specialists   Hill notes that while this method may not provide any firm predictions regarding the future of the family, still it is interesting to speculate on the possible effects of the research, writings, and teachings of family specialists regarding the future of family life in America. What kinds of marriage and family forms and functions are being advocated by these professional family specialists? Hill identifies "objectives for the American family" as set forth most frequently by family specialists in textbooks and research reports. These include (a) better functioning families, (b) better mate selection, (c) better understanding of sex and reproduction, (d) more companionable and competent marriages, and (e) improved preventive and remedial marriage and family services.[4] Hill emphasizes that these are implicit rather than explicit goals, and that one cannot accurately foresee the effects of such professional activities and recommendations upon family life in the future.

Others have attempted to predict the future of the American family by fore- casting future marriage and family patterns in terms of certain trends and changes afoot in the larger society.

Bernard Farber, for one, finds six major short-run social trends which he feels will significantly influence family life in the future:[5] (1) a decline of the work force in agriculture; (2) increased automation in production and distribution of goods and services; (3) increased number of workers in service occupations; (4) increased population density due to continuing urbanization and migration to cities; (5) increased employee-employer ratios (i.e., more employees and fewer employers); and (6) continued advances in medicine and health care leading to greater control of illness and disease. Some of Farber's specific forecasts of future marriage and family patterns based on these trends will be discussed later in this chapter.

Harold Christensen sees four social trends which he feels will continue to influence family patterns in the near future:[6] (1) increasing rates of technological development and innovations; (2) continued population growth and migration to cities, and continued efforts to control population growth; (3) increasing individualism, and a corresponding decline in familism; (4) increasing secularism and materialism, with a corresponding decline in traditional religious values; and (5) increasing confidence in science as the means of meeting human needs. Christensen and Farber appear to be in close agreement as to the major trends which they see as important in shaping the American family of tomorrow.

F. Ivan Nye and Felix Berardo, in much the same vein, point to three broad trends they feel will be most closely connected with family life in the coming decade or two.[7]

1   The Demographic Revolution   Widespread concern with the population

explosion—itself a result of advances in medical science which have drastically reduced death rates—could lead to increasing governmental regulation of family size, postponement of marriages, increased abortions, and more sterilizations. Also, the continuing urbanization and suburbanization of America will bring about further family changes and adjustments.

2   The Cybernetic Revolution   Current technological advances such as automation and computerization can have far-reaching effects on the family of the future. Work and work roles may become less demanding and less important, and could even disappear as a source of family income. In a cybercultural era,

The job-income link makes no sense at all and will be obsolete. The "jobs" individuals hold will be the means for them to accomplish the work they wish to do, rather than the labor they must perform. . . . Thus the husband's job will be no more important to the survival of the family than the wife's—the children can be educated, rather than trained for their future employment; and the whole fabric of which the family structure is woven will change. . . .[8]

The author feels that the full effects of such a cybernetic revolution lie further in the future, not in the next decade or two.

3   The Human Rights Revolution[9]   American history is a story of the long and dynamic struggle of groups of Americans pursuing full citizenship rights. This struggle has entailed processes which are still profoundly affecting family life and the relationships of many Americans. Economic and political freedom for men has been followed belatedly by increases in such freedoms for women and to some extent for children. American emphasis on individual freedom and personal rights will continue to be reflected in our systems of mate selection, marriage, and family relations. The civil rights movement of the 1960s has brought America further along the route toward its ideal of a democratic society, thereby enabling more families of ethnic and racial background to participate more fully in American society and to enjoy more of its benefits.

F. Ivan Nye, in his article "Values, Family, and a Changing Society," identifies two possible value positions or orientations in terms of which family life may be organized, and which may be predictive of the family of the future.[10]

1   The Intrinsic Value Position   Here the family is seen as having an *intrinsic value* per se, in and of itself, or for its own sake. People holding this view would be expected to maintain that traditional and conventional forms of marriage and family are inherently good and should be maintained and strengthened as a social goal. This position would be in keeping with the Gemeinschaft-sacred orientation.

2   The Instrumental Value Position   This position is opposite to the intrinsic

value position. The family here is seen as having mainly an *instrumental value* in society. That is, it is important mainly for the services or functions it performs for society and its members. It is a means to other ends, such as individual happiness and security. This value position would be expected to prevail in societies with the Gesellschaft-secular orientation. This view favors family change along rational and functional lines.

A third value position has been identified by Bert Adams, one which stresses *individualistic values* as a basis for predicting the family of the future.[11] It has been widely observed that American society is becoming more concerned with the individual and with meeting individual needs, adjustments, development, etc. Where this individualistic value orientation is dominant to the point that it overrides the intrinsic or instrumental value orientations, conventional marriage and family patterns may be altered considerably or rejected outright, and new arrangements tried. From the individualistic position, sex needs may be met by premarital experimentation, or by extramarital arrangements, as well as in marriage. Or, when individual happiness becomes one of the main goals of marriage, any sustained unhappiness of either marriage partner becomes a good and sufficient reason for separation or divorce, thus enabling one to seek a new partner with whom one will be happier—which is only one's natural right after all, according to this value orientation. From the individualistic value position, traditional marriage and family may be seen as potentially standing in the way of the individual's right of the pursuit of happiness; this view would be expected where the Gesellschaft-secular orientation is strongly entrenched.

As Adams says, the future of the family may lie in the interplay of these various sets of values. Despite the present emphasis on individualism and the decline in many circles of traditional idealism regarding the family, the author agrees with Nye when he says:

There is little doubt that the institution of the family is *here to stay*, not because this basic unit of social structure is valuable per se, but because it is instrumental in maintaining life itself, in shaping the infant into the person, and in providing for the security and affectional needs of people of all ages. In fact, the family is so central to the fulfillment of several intrinsic values, that it is anticipated that the family will become an even more competent instrument for meeting human needs and, as a consequence, will become more highly and generally valued throughout society in . . . [the] world of tomorrow.[12]

Most family specialists see the American family as a very adaptable social institution, capable of meeting and adjusting successfully to the above-discussed trends, conditions, and changes and continuing to function as an effective social institution. It is recognized that the family will experience problems and difficulties ahead, entailing a certain amount of disruption if not necessarily disorganization. Most authorities, but not all, assume that the nuclear family and monogamous marriage will persist as the predominant form, while significant changes in internal organization will very likely occur.

As we have seen in the preceding chapter, much experimentation is taking place today. While it is too early to tell what lasting effects the various experiments will produce, an attempt will be made to see what their influence may be on marriage and family in the future.

Assessing the Future of Current Experimental and Alternative Life-Styles

Will marriage and family be fundamentally altered by the various experiments taking place today, and possibly even be replaced eventually by one or more of the alternative life-styles? The answers to these questions are likely to be determined by the relative weight one attaches to various factors that continue to support conventional marriage and family versus other factors and pressures that agitate for change and the substitution of alternatives. What relative weights are to be assigned the intrinsic value attached to the family in the minds and sentiments of many people versus the more secular instrumental or individualistic orientations? How much weight can be given the propaganda of the alternative-promoters versus the admonitions of the religious, legal, and helping professions which generally strongly support traditional marriage and family?

According to the various weights assigned these and other relevant factors, one may come up with three quite different answers, according to Adams.

"No, the family cannot possibly stay alive in the face of the alternatives."[13] This conclusion would likely be reached by those who give considerable weight to the instrumental perspective (i.e., that what works best equals "the good"), and to the propaganda of those who advocate the alternatives while decrying the strains and problems found in many conventional families. Arriving at this conclusion also would seem to require one to accept the goodness of scientific advances taking place in the biological sciences, and their inevitable acceptance and incorporation into new forms of family living (e.g., artificial insemination, control over the sex of the child, incubator births, etc.).

A second answer, "Yes, the family will outlast the alternatives,"[14] would very likely be reached if one gives considerable weight to (1) the strong support which much of society still gives the family, emphasizing its intrinsic value, (2) the reluctance of most people to make or accept radical changes, and (3) a willingness to adjust to and adopt some of the alternatives to the family as safety valves in a period of rapid social change.

A third answer is possible also: "Yes, the family will continue to exist, but it will be alongside a series of increasingly legitimated alternatives."[15] While recognizing the instrumental values—and possibly the intrinsic values of the family to some degree—this view also recognizes that many Americans have found conventional family forms unworkable or unliveable for them.

As internal pressures build within our family system, increasing numbers of persons will begin to look for viable alternatives . . .; the reason is that the overarching value in our society is the individual and his self-actualization. As concern for the individual and his happiness becomes increasingly dominant, so will a multiplicity of alternatives be needed to allow for self-fulfillment of a great variety of individual personalities. Economic and familial values will give ground grudgingly, but the individual and his needs and wants in U.S. society cannot be denied.[16]

Such a view obviously places great weight on the individualistic and the instrumental value positions.

Which of these three answers to the question of whether the family will survive the alternative life-styles seems most plausible? The author tends to agree with Adams that the third answer is most likely true for the foreseeable future. In spite of its historical reluctance to change, the family is adaptable and pragmatic, and the pressures for change are strong. Continuing secularization, new scientific developments, continuing experimentation, will probably bring about the gradual acceptance of several alternatives to conventional monogamous marriage, but will not replace it. Which is to say that while an increasing minority of Americans may accept and try some alternative life-style, the large majority will very likely continue to live in conventional marriage and family arrangements while becoming more tolerant of others who do not.

Some Specific Predictions and Speculations

What are some of the predictions and forecasts regarding the future of the American family that are being made by family specialists?

Robert Winch, addressing a meeting of the National Council on Family Relations in 1969, presented his speculations as to the future of the family. He sees the family in America as continuing to relinquish some of its traditional functions, in varying degrees, while placing more stress upon a few newer functions. The prime function of the family, reproduction, may be reduced to a minimum as the birthrate declines; the trend of deemphasizing sex-role differentiation in the family will continue; the family's role in socializing and educating the young will be still further narrowed as other community agencies expand their educational services; and the importance of the family in conferring status on its children will be reduced. Winch tends to agree with William Ogburn's view, stated in the thirties, that the decline in these family functions will most likely be accompanied by some increase in the emotional gratification or affectional function.[17]

By using United States census data, Robert Parke and Paul Glick have attempted to project certain family demographic trends into the future.[18] Among their predictions are the following: (1) A high proportion of Americans will continue to marry at some time in their lives, with the rate of teenage marriages declining and then leveling off. (2) The relative oversupply of females will tend to produce a further rise in the age at which women marry for the first time. (3) Declines in the age difference at marriage of husband and wife will reduce the frequency of widowhood, and increase the proportion of couples who survive jointly to retirement age. (4) Further reduction of poverty and general improvements in socioeconomic status of the population should help reduce the relative frequency of divorce. (Note: This last has not been borne out. Other off-setting factors such as more emphasis on individual criteria of marital success, women's liberation, etc., have resulted in net increases in divorce in recent years.)

Meyer Nimkoff, in an imaginative article titled "Biological Discoveries and the Future of the Family: A Reappraisal," discusses the various implications of recent research in biology for marriage and family.[19] He feels that scientific discoveries in this field will have a greater impact on family than any other scientific or technological developments. One of the most important developments is in the new knowledge about reproduction and birth control. Nimkoff also points to the rapid advances in the areas of sex control, some gains in the biological problems of aging, and some in the control of sex characteristics. He says:

Our review of developments in the biochemistry of man . . . shows great progress in birth control, promising although much slower achievement in sex control, an intermediate degree of control in sex characteristics via hormonal therapy and of the biological problems of aging. In all these fields there is no major problem of opposition from the mores; rather, American society is favorable to most biological research. . . . The simplest scientific problem is that of birth control; somewhat more difficult from a theoretical standpoint is the problem of the control of the sex of the child; and much more complex are the problems of the control of aging and of sexual characteristics.[20]

Nimkoff's analysis raises many questions about the possible consequences for marriage and family of such scientific developments, those already here and those just ahead. For instance, what may happen to the basic family functions of reproduction and early socialization if incubator birth and sex control become realities, and it is shown that all birth and pregnancy defects could be prevented by keeping the human fetus outside the human body? While Nimkoff may be right that there is no great opposition from the mores to most such biological research, the application of these findings to human beings is another issue. Public opposition will very likely continue here for some time. It is difficult to venture an opinion as to when the secular trend will be far enough advanced for most Americans to accept and approve the application of such biological knowledge for the purpose of modifying human beings and their biological nature.

Ira Reiss sees, in the larger picture of social change in America, several common strands which are playing central roles in shaping the family of the future.[21]

1 Centrality of the Dyad Not only in the continuing conventional nuclear family, but also in most experimental and alternative life-styles, the female-male dyad will be the main or central focus. Reiss says:

It has increasingly become clear to me that in virtually all of the new family forms, there was a continued focus on the dyad. By this I mean that people involved in "swinging" will justify their behavior by saying that it helps build up the strength of the marital relationship and thereby keeps the couple together. People who live together before marriage state that they feel they are thereby avoiding mistakes in dyadic choices that they might make if they did not have this living together experience. Women working at careers will point out that they are more interesting wives and that they will harbor less resentment against their husbands because they have a chance at their own careers.[22]

Reiss suggests that perhaps there has been less change than we thought,since the emphasis in the new alternative family forms is on helping the dyadic relationship, one of the very things stressed in conventional marriage.

2 Love and Personality-Need Fulfillment Reiss feels that what has changed is the basic philosophy of what the dyadic relationship consists of, especially apparent in the area of love and personality-need fulfillment. This new philosophy defines love as a positive affectionate feeling one can have toward several other people of the opposite sex—a *diffuse love focus* rather than a *one-person love focus*. What is important here is personal growth and the development of one's ability to relate intimately to a number of other people. This is not really a contradiction of the emphasis on the dyad, Reiss feels. The original dyad (mate and partner) is still central, but other peripheral relations are established to help maintain it. Many questions remain unanswered, however, as to the possible consequences upon the marital dyad of "diffuse love," especially when carried to the point of extramarital relations.[23]

3 Greater Range of Choices The *legitimation of choice* is a particularly important trademark of the family in the twentieth century. The range of legitimated selections in courtship, marriage, and family is far greater today than earlier in the century, e.g., in the areas of sex, divorce, abortion,

employment of women, etc. Reiss sees certain psychological ramifications of this greater range of choice.

What this legitimation of choices means is that a psychological comfort once available to many Americans is fast disappearing. The comfort was the belief that one's way of life was the one right way of life. We are involved now in a society with a variety of life styles that necessitates that people be able to feel that their life style is proper for them, *even though* it may not be . . . for other people. That position is psychologically much more difficult to live with, and it is part of the reason for the stresses and strains felt by many people today. One of the major causes of divorce today is that the role conceptions of what husbands and wives should do is no longer as standardized, and therefore the potential of conflict and disillusionment is greater.[24]

Reiss sees experimentation as a lasting hallmark of our American family system; and not everyone will end up with the same conclusions as to what family patterns will be best suited for them. He concludes, however, that for most people the older patterns of legal marriage and children will still prevail, even though many will have undergone a period of experimentation with other forms of dyadic interaction beforehand.

Bernard Farber also sees the future American family having a wider range of choices, and a greater ability to make plans and pursue them effectively.[25] Farber points out that a number of social trends in America today, such as increased attention to mental health and personal adjustment problems, and child welfare, suggest that a *welfare strategy* of family organization is emerging. He makes a number of forecasts about the future of the American family with respect to this welfare strategy.

First, he suggests that increases in productivity through technological development and automation, higher incomes, and higher educational levels will enable more families to enjoy higher standards of living and to expand their opportunities for choices in life-styles.[26]

Second, according to Farber, as family income increases, so will the health and longevity of family members, enlarging their abilities to plan in all facets of life.[27] So, as the economic status of families improves, and the health and longevity of members increase, "the prospect is for greater participation of parents in the family life of their married children."[28] This trend has been observed in middle-class families for the past two or three decades. Prosperous parents will most likely continue to provide aid in money, goods, and services to their young married children. Farber feels this suggests that parents are "operating with a welfare norm" in their relations with their married children.

Farber's predictions are based on assumptions of continuing and expanding economic prosperity, as well as further advances in health care. Uncertainties, especially with respect to the future of the economy, and the possible effects of other factors on future family life, such as ideological changes, make all such predictions uncertain.

Leonard Benson makes some predictions for the American family of the future on the basis of several well-established social trends, some general developments in the American culture, and "proposals for change or reform that have been expressed often and loud enough to actually be influential."[29]

1   Family Planning   This is a well-established trend in the United States, as manifested by the declining birthrate. If this trend continues unabated, "we may look forward to a nation where family life is much more rational, where family planning is completely accepted, and where children can be absolutely assured of the right to be wanted."[30] As genetic knowledge increases and is more widely accepted and applied, there may be greater social control over marriage and parenthood, including the right to bear children. Implications of these possible developments for future birthrates, pregnancies, eugenics, and family welfare services are, as Benson says, "staggering in their cumulative impact."

2   Meritocracy   A *meritocracy* may be defined as a society where people succeed on the basis of their abilities, not family or social-class background. We seem to be heading in this direction. Such a society generates strong competition among children across class, ethnic, and racial lines, as expanding education opens up more opportunities throughout American society and as middle-class success values become widely pervasive in all kinds of families. In a society where virtually all children would be planned, we could expect even greater competition among them than exists now. Such a competitive society may prove to be an anxiety-ridden place for both parents and children, Benson feels.[31]

What may this competition and success drive do to family cohesion and the quality of family life? We have some clues in certain negative reactions to these pressures showing up among bright but alienated college students who have "dropped out of the rat race," to the chagrin of their parents. To many American parents the success of their children becomes an obsession. Their school records—report cards, college transcripts—become projective indices of their children's future. Parents often feel forced to look for some kind of failure in themselves if their children do not compete well or succeed. In a society that stresses equal opportunity to the point where people are allowed to reach the level of achievement they deserve solely on their ability and effort, there would logically be an end to all family-linked advantages. Benson notes that there is a general trend in the world today toward a decline of the family's power to determine its children's status. This trend is also seen in stiff inheritance taxes which make it increasingly difficult for affluent families to pass on their wealth intact to their children. However, parents still have a strong desire to pass on their status and possessions to their children, and may be expected to continue to exert social and legal resistance to restrictions on what they consider their rights to do so.

Implicit in the trend toward meritocracy is conflict between those striving to achieve and those who, either through inheritance or their own achievement, already have acquired status and possessions which they wish to pass on to their heirs. Benson concludes that these and other implications of meritocracy for future family life in America need more study and thought.

3 Self-Knowledge Related to family planning and meritocracy is a third trend, that of increasing self-knowledge.[32] With the expansion of higher education, especially in the behavioral sciences, young people will bring to marriage more knowledge than ever before regarding personality, child psychology, interpersonal relations, family dynamics, and the like. As their knowledge increases, marriage partners are apt to become more self-conscious about their roles as husband and wife and more concerned about their performance as parents. Being a good mother, for example, is no longer viewed as essentially a natural expression of femaleness, but rather as something complex and difficult that must be learned and developed through experience. The concept of "responsible parenthood" is getting more attention today and will undoubtedly be emphasized more in the future.

Will we see the time when society sets minimum standards for the right—or privilege—to rear children? Benson notes that today popular negative reaction to such a requirement is still strong and visceral, but that more married couples are voluntarily admitting that they are probably not suited to be parents.[33]

4 Reconstruction of Sex Roles Trends and changes in sex roles in America have received a good deal of attention throughout this book. Benson points to technological and ideological changes which are bringing about new forms of personal identity for children, new ways of preparing for adult sex roles, and increasing competition between the sexes. He sums up these points:

Industrial growth has led to the liberation of women from traditional roles, upgrading the quality of their lives in a sense, but stripping the appeal from the role of the mother. At the same time, it has upgraded both the work and family roles of the father. Industrialization also changes patterns of personal identification for boys and girls, and it changes the way they prepare for adult roles (especially for girls). It has greatly expanded the range of competition between the sexes. Implications for mothering and fathering are far-reaching, but it remains questionable whether husband-wife relations will become different in any basic way from what they have been. Greater equality between the sexes should bring them closer together and open even greater possibilities for monogamous marriage.[34]

5 Biological Time Bomb The potential consequences for marriage and family of developments in the biological sciences are tremendous, as noted

earlier in our review of Nimkoff's article. While the full impact of these scientific advances is difficult to foresee and even to contemplate, the biological revolution already at hand, Benson feels, will bring about changes in patterns of reproduction and longevity, which will in turn produce changes in parenthood, old age, and relations between the generations.[35] The range of sexual, medical, and psychic choices open to mankind could be fantastic in the not so distant future.

While the rational-secular trend in America supports the developments in scientific knowledge, their acceptance and application in family life will continue to be tempered by religious, political, and other traditional-sacred values and norms. A culture lag will undoubtedly continue in this area for some time to come.

J. Ross Eshleman offers the following predictions and projections for the family of the American future, while warning that all such predictions must be considered speculative and tentative rather than exhaustive and final.[36]

1   Continuation of Basic Family Form   Marriage and family living may take various forms both in the near and more distant future, in keeping with our pluralistic and ever-changing society. Eshleman feels, however, that most families in the future will still consist of one husband, one wife, and their biological children. Some variations will most likely include more one-parent families, increases in the "modified extended" family, and, perhaps some time in the future, public acceptance of multiple-spouse marriages (polygamy) and maybe even same-sex marriages.

2   Some Probable Redefinition of the Permanence of Marriage and Family Structures   Divorce rates indicate that such a trend is under way today. It may be that in the future marriages may be formulated that are clearly not "until death do us part." Eshleman feels that we can anticipate future public acceptance of temporary marriages, or marriages that last only until the children are grown.[37]

3   Expansion of New Birth Technologies   As seen above, recent developments in biochemistry provide the potential for revolutionary changes in the physical, social, and psychological aspects of marriage and family life. The new birth technology, Eshleman says, centers around the development of the steroid pill, contraceptive vaccines, the control of children, knowledge of how to control the sex of the child, artificial insemination, preservation of human spermatozoa and ova, and embryo implants, among other techniques.[38] The implications of these developments for parenthood, parent-child relations, the sex ratio, physical and mental characteristics of offspring, family size, and population trends are mind-boggling.

4   Increased Professionalization of Parenthood   Competence in the role of mother or father is extremely important and also difficult. Yet we not only permit but actually require untrained and unprepared persons to perform these tasks without regard for their educational, social, or psychological

qualifications. Eshleman sees some future alleviation here not only in increased education for parents, but also in the expansion of community facilities to aid parents and to actually share with the biological parents some of the responsibilities of parenthood.

The arguments are well recognized for having parents rear their own children. However, as our society becomes increasingly specialized, as an increasing number of women receive specialized training, as more women enter the world of paid employment, and as children increasingly become a matter of choice, part-time parenthood is likely to become increasingly common. Thus the choice is not an either-or situation in which a mother is totally absent from her children or with them on a twenty-four hour basis. Some combination of the two will become increasingly the norm.[39]

Nurseries and day care centers, both private and industrial, operated by better-trained people, will very likely be playing a greater role as part-time parents in the future.

5   Changes in Parent-Child Relations   In line with the preceding, Eshleman sees greater variations in parent-child relations and in child-rearing methods in the future. He predicts an increase in quasi parents who will contribute more to child care and training, including grandparents, siblings, neighbors, friends, baby-sitters, and teachers. Also expected is a continuation of the trend toward informality and flexibility and more voice in family affairs by growing children.

Parent-child relations are likely to reflect a movement from a formal . . . relationship, based on differential status positions with clearly defined roles, toward the informal, varied, and person-centered relations in the modern family. With this will be accompanied a greater participation by children in family decision-making, [and] more conscious efforts to help children develop to their social and emotional potentialities. . . .[40]

6   More Changes in Marital Roles and Division of Tasks   Since the division of labor in the family between the sexes is based more on cultural traditions than on biological capacities and limitations of the sexes, the future is likely to bring greater flexibility in family roles throughout America, with stress on work activities being performed freely by either or both spouses, as is the case now in many middle-class families. Tasks will be divided on the basis of the time, energy, skill, and interest each partner can contribute. Eshleman also sees husbands and wives becoming more professionalized in the performance of their marital roles, with more young people seeking knowledge from family life specialists in colleges, and from counseling and family service centers in their communities. Home and family will continue to be a haven of intimacy and personal security in an increasingly impersonal world.

The husband-wife relationship will continue to serve as the primary source of affection for adults. The marriage and family of the future will increasingly be visualized as a place of informality and intimacy. If the society . . . becomes more impersonal, formal, and bureaucratized, the family will serve as an important outlet for openly expressing one's hopes and fears. This function, although performed today, may possibly be one of the most important performed by the family of the future.[41]

7   More Progress Toward Equality for Women in the Family   A recurring theme throughout this book has been the historical trend away from an earlier traditional-patriarchal family pattern toward a modern-equalitarian family pattern, as manifest in present-day premarital, marital, and parent-child relations. Feminism and the women's liberation movement have brought to the front an increasing awareness of long-standing discriminatory practices and the inferior status ascribed to women for centuries. This belated awareness

Modern couple on a house-boat. Family life-styles for many will become increasingly informal. (*Julie Heifetz.*)

does not, however, mean that women have as yet actually been able to achieve equality with men in such areas as occupation, income, or education, contrary to some popular myths that may exist.[42] Full equality for women in America remains to be achieved, both in the community and in the family. The middle-class family is showing the way, in effect, and some progress toward female-male equality is being made in many different types of American families.

8 Continuing Permissive Sex Norms and a Fuller Appreciation of Sex Within Marriage We have referred earlier (Chapter 6) to the "new morality" emerging in the United States in recent years, often identified with the youth movements of the 1960s. This new morality judges actions in terms of the degree to which the act promotes love between people. Eshleman sees one of the results of this for the future to be "an increasing permissiveness of sexual norms, before, during, outside of, and after marriage."[43] And in keeping with the trend toward equality for women, the immediate future will very likely see an increase in the number of unmarried women demanding the same sexual freedom as men. While within marriage, more couples will place an intrinsic value on sex for its own sake. To the extent that this new morality finds social acceptance, there will also probably be more marital infidelity, as more married people reduce their demands for sexual exclusiveness as a must for marital permanence. This new morality by no means has universal social acceptance at this time, of course. The majority of Americans probably still feel that extramarital sex is morally deviant, and they are likely to continue feeling this way into the immediate future. Thus, we may expect to see evidences of tension and conflict between the advocates of the new morality and those still adhering to the traditional morality for some time to come.

John Scanzoni, in an insightful analysis of the future of marriage, predicts that monogamous marriage will not only survive but thrive in the future.[44] A review of the literature shows that even those people who say that the foreseeable future will witness many different forms of marriage and family experimentation, "freely acknowledge that for the overwhelming majority of people in modern society, monogamous marriage will be the preferred pattern."[45]

A goodly number of persons will continue to be bound together in marriage by their interdependence, based on an exchange of benefits and rewards, in traditional fashion. Others, in increasing numbers, will enter monogamous marriages on a basis of role-interchangeability. These would be equal partners who perceive marriage to be a unique reward-producing center for equals.

Scanzoni sees three factors which, in combination, tend to draw people in modern society into monogamous marriage: (1) the economic-status dimension, (2) expressive gratifications, and (3) gratification through children.[46]

1 The Economic-Status Dimension If we assume that most persons will

continue to accept the achievement values of our society, why would a woman marry who could earn economic and status benefits on her own? The obvious answer, Scanzoni says, is in the advantage of husband and wife pooling their resources. Two good incomes can produce a life-style more affluent than one good income. Also, now there is a greater tendency for the wife's occupational status to count as well as that of the husband as a measure of the family's status. In the future her career will most likely be as important as his in determining their social status in the community.

2 Expressive Gratification Despite the amount of publicity given by the media to the so-called sexual revolution, there is little evidence of any widespread sexual promiscuity in America, Scanzoni claims. Men and women who are still somewhat traditionally oriented, and most who are emancipated, including feminists, "will continue to look to a monogamous marriage relationship for their major fulfillment, not only for sexual gratification, but also for companionship and empathy."[47] Scanzoni also argues that as more women achieve equality and power, they will be better able to resist sexual exploitation, and this could have a braking effect on the trend toward greater sexual permissiveness.

3 Gratification Through Children Most times and places, women have received a sense of achievement, creativity, and identity through motherhood. Children may also provide other kinds of rewards for their parents in modern achievement-oriented societies such as America.[48] Parents may identify with their children, whose achievements tend to reflect back on the parents. Even in families where the wife is an achiever as well as the husband, this may still be true, and even though they may have only one child.

Scanzoni sums up his arguments for the continuation of monogamous marriage thus:

We may say: (1) that unless and until large numbers of modern persons reject achievement values, it is difficult to see how tribal experiments can come to replace, except for a few persons, the clearly identifiable and autonomous husband-wife unit; (2) that these autonomous units have persisted because they have been a source of economic and status gratifications and under conditions of genuine equality may supply still additional socio-economic and novel colleague rewards; (3) that likewise, as these units have in the past supplied certain levels of expressive rewards, interchangeability could conceivably generate even greater levels of these rewards (including sexual); (4) that many dual achiever units will continue to produce at least one child, maintain close and unique ties with it, and seek the dual gratifications that a child can supply to parents in modern society.[49]

Nye and Berardo attempt, in the context of three major social trends in America—in technology, in population growth, and in human rights movements—to make a number of quite specific predictions as to the nature of the American family in the near future.[50]

1 More Family Affluence   Assuming continued economic growth (and not too much inflation), family incomes should continue to rise, with a concomitant decline in poverty.

2 More Employment for Wives   Present trends will most likely continue, with more women joining the labor force. Married women in paid employment now outnumber unmarried working women. With more women receiving higher education and occupational training in a wider variety of fields, with expanding occupational opportunities, and with widening social approval of working mothers, we may expect still more dual-worker families in the future.

3 Expanding Child-Care Services   This will parallel the increased employment of mothers. There is growing concern for the need for more and better child-care services and facilities in American communities. Thus we may expect an expansion of nursery centers and day care facilities.

4 More Standardization of Family Life-Styles   While some differences in family customs and practices will undoubtedly continue in America, Nye and Berardo see a convergence of consumer habits (e.g., in food tastes, in clothing styles, in cars, in recreation) and also family values and norms to some degree, as in sexual behavior, birth control, and treatment of children.

5 More Families   Marriage rates are expected to remain at a high level. Thus there will be more families in the immediate future. A reduction in age difference between husband and wife will mean a greater probability of joint survival of spouses in late middle age and in old age.

6 More Divorce and Remarriage   This trend will most likely continue into the near future at least. Most divorced people may be expected to remarry, as they seek someone else with whom they hope to be happier.

I would qualify Nye and Berardo's prediction here somewhat. Recall that Parke and Glick predicted that there would be a reduction in divorce as the economic condition of the population improves, since the divorce rates are greater in the lower socioeconomic strata. So, as working-class and lower-class people acquire more resources and security, their divorce rates may decrease. On the other hand, middle-class divorce will tend to increase as more women gain independence, and as traditional religious norms prohibiting divorce continue to weaken, thus enabling many people caught in what LeMasters has aptly called "holy deadlock" to dissolve their marriage bonds.

7 Older Age at Marriage   This will probably be influenced by more men and especially more women remaining single longer; in effect postponing marriage in order to do other things first, while still free. For some there will be a premarital period of experimentation in alternative life-styles.

8 More Progress Toward Equalitarian Family Power   Nye and Berardo agree with most other family authorities that the family of the future will be more equalitarian. The women's liberation movement, increasing participation of women in politics and community activities, along with the continued

rise in employment of married women, all are conducive to equalitarian authority patterns in more American families.

9 Continued Trend Toward Single Sex Standard for Men and Women The old double standard favoring men may be expected to continue its decline (especially in middle-class circles) as more women demand equal rights with men in the area of sexual behavior.

10 More Fertility Control The family of the future will be in a much better position to control its own biological processes. Safe, effective, and inexpensive contraceptive techniques will soon become available to virtually all couples. Disapproval of birth control by religious groups will diminish still further.

11 More Family Leisure This prediction assumes continued favorable economic conditions, such as prosperity and control of inflation. Technological advances in industry should increase productivity still further, so that the average work week will shrink in the future, increasing the time available for leisure and recreation in American families. Early retirement and increased longevity mean a larger percentage of the life cycle freed for such activities, at least in those families which are economically secure. This prediction may seem overly optimistic in light of recent history. Problems of economic recessions, unemployment, and inflation need to be brought under better control so that more American families can enjoy relative security, not to mention leisure.

Conclusions Regarding the Future of Marriage and Family in America

There are many difficulties confronting those who seek to make a balanced judgment regarding the future of marriage and family in America, as we have attempted to show in this chapter. Feelings run strong among the American people on many of the family issues and problems confronting them. Heated dialogue between advocates of rapid change and their opponents do not help us to see clearly what may lie ahead. Many journalists and some social scientists are prone to select and distort in order to make their points; and certainly there are many honest differences of opinion among competent social scientists.

Can we discern any agreement among the various family authorities as to the probable future of the American family? What particular future family characteristics and trends are stressed? The author feels that the following tentative predictions are supported by evidence and by informed professional opinion, and should help shed light on the issues and questions pertaining to marriage and family raised in Chapters 1 and 9.

Two couples share a camper. Outdoor family recreation will continue to be popular. (*Julie Heifetz*.)

1 There is strong evidence that the family will survive in America, even though in modified form. Perhaps it would be more accurate to say the family will survive in continuously modifying forms. Change will be an ongoing condition of the American family into the foreseeable future.

2 The nuclear family will remain the predominant family unit, while modified extended family ties will continue to be present also. That is, limited but important ties of an intimate nature will continue to be maintained between married couples and their close kin, especially their parents.

3 Monogamous marriage will predominate in America into the foreseeable future. The big majority of Americans, wherever they happen to be located on the continuum between the traditional-patriarchal⟷ modern-equalitarian

ideal types, will continue to have most of their needs met within conventional monogamous marriage.

4 The long-range trend toward a companionship-oriented, colleague-type marriage will continue. As the larger trend toward equalitarianism continues in American society, wives will move toward fuller equality with their husbands in status and power within the family. This trend will also result in more freedom and power for growing children in the family.

5 There will be more role flexibility and role interchangeability in American families in the future, with a parallel decline of role specialization, especially by gender. Husband-wife relations and parent-child relations will probably continue to become more informal.

6 American families will continue in the foreseeable future to experience many problems and situations requiring frequent adjustment efforts on the part of individual members. For instance, in the inexorable movement toward role equality, marriage will continue to be a long-term, ongoing, confrontation between husband and wife. Also, wider ranges of choice and greater freedom of choice in family matters will impose new burdens and responsibilities on each family member.

7 While the "mass culture" trend throughout American society will lead to more standardization of family life-styles, tastes, and practices, there will continue to be significant differences in American families due to a continuation of historical-cultural differences (along social-class, racial, ethnic and religious lines), and also due to different choices of life-styles by youth groups and others espousing variant value systems.

8 Developments in the biological sciences are providing the means and methods for producing drastic changes in marriage and family functioning and organization. However, prevailing values and norms will probably prevent the widespread implementation of this scientific knowledge in the immediate future.

In conclusion, it may be said that our study of variety and change in the American family tends to confirm the position that the family is a unique social institution and that it will continue to be one of humanity's most resilient and durable social groups. Changes ebb and flow and experiments come and go. The long view shows how adaptable and resourceful the family has been throughout our relatively short American history. People today, as at any given time in history, tend to magnify the seriousness and significance of *their* problems and issues. That is, people tend to be "temporalcentric" as well as ethnocentric. As we noted earlier, the family has survived a variety of experiments and efforts to reshape it in recent history, but always, so far, after the experimental fervor has declined, there has been a gradual return to more conventional family patterns. True, the future will witness continuous change in the American family, but the change will most likely be more evolutionary in nature than revolutionary.

Notes

1 Reuben Hill, "The American Family of the Future," *Journal of Marriage and Family*, 26 (February 1964), pp. 20–28. Also see Reuben Hill et al., *Family Development in Three Generations* (Cambridge, Mass.: Schenkman Publishing Co., 1970).

2 Ibid., pp. 21–24.

3 Ibid., p. 24.

4 Ibid., pp. 24–28.

5 Bernard Farber, *Family: Organization and Interaction* (San Francisco: Chandler Publishing Co., 1964), pp. 232–240.

6 Harold T. Christensen, "Changing Roles of Family Members," paper presented in the fall of 1965 at a workshop at Michigan State University, pp. 1–25, as quoted in F. Ivan Nye and Felix M. Berardo, *The Family* (New York: Macmillan Co., 1973), p. 627

7 Nye and Berardo, op. cit., pp. 628–633.

8 Alice M. Hilton, "The Family in a Cybercultural Era," paper presented at October 1966 Meeting of National Council on Family Relations, as quoted in Nye and Berardo, op. cit., p. 631.

9 Nye and Berardo, op. cit., pp. 632–633.

10 F. Ivan Nye, "Values, Family, and a Changing Society," *Journal of Marriage and Family*, 29 (May 1967), pp. 241–248.

11 Bert N. Adams, *The American Family* (Chicago: Markham Publishing Co., 1971), pp. 357–358.

12 Nye, op. cit., p. 248.

13 Bert N. Adams, *The Family: A Sociological Interpretation* (Chicago: Rand McNally College Publishing Co., 1975), p. 386.

14 Ibid., pp. 385–386.

15 Ibid., p. 386.

16 Ibid.

17 Robert F. Winch, "Some Speculations as to the Family's Future," in Bert N. Adams and Thomas Weirath, eds., *Readings on the Sociology of the Family* (Chicago: Markham Publishing Co., 1971), pp. 460–466. Also see William F. Ogburn, "The Changing Family," *The Family*, 19 (July 1938), pp. 139–143.

18 Robert Parke and Paul Glick, "Prospective Changes in Marriage and the Family," in Adams and Weirath, op. cit., pp. 455–459.

19 Meyer F. Nimkoff, "Biological Discoveries and the Future of the Family: A Reappraisal," *Social Forces*, 41 (December 1962), pp. 121–127.

20 Ibid., p. 127.

21 Ira L. Reiss, *Family Systems in America* (Hinsdale, Ill.: Dryden Press, 1976), pp. 431–440.

22 Ibid., p. 431.

23 Ibid., pp. 433–434.

24 Ibid., p. 438.

25 Bernard Farber, op. cit., pp. 274–280.

26 Ibid., p. 275.

27 Ibid., pp. 275–276.

28 Ibid., p. 277.
29 Leonard Benson, *The Family Bond* (New York: Random House, 1971), pp. 369–396.
30 Ibid., p. 370.
31 Ibid., pp. 375–376.
32 Ibid., pp. 378–379.
33 Ibid., p. 379.
34 Ibid., p. 395.
35 Ibid., pp. 393–394.
36 J. Ross Eshleman, *The Family: An Introduction* (Boston: Allyn and Bacon, 1974), pp. 666–688.
37 Ibid., pp. 671–673.
38 Ibid., pp. 674–676.
39 Ibid., pp. 676–677.
40 Ibid., pp. 679–680.
41 Ibid., p. 681.
42 Ibid., pp. 681–682.
43 Ibid., p. 683.
44 John Scanzoni, *Sexual Bargaining* (Englewood Cliffs, N.J.: Prentice-Hall, Inc., 1972), pp. 104–164.
45 Ibid., p. 156.
46 Ibid., pp. 157–163.
47 Ibid., p. 161.
48 Ibid., pp. 162–163.
49 Ibid., p. 163.
50 Nye and Berardo, op. cit., pp. 633–644.

SELECTED READING

The reading selected continues the main theme of the chapter, which is to examine the probable future of the American family, in this case with special attention to marriage and courtship. While the author is quite optimistic about the survival and continued good health of American marriage and family institutions, he concedes that problem areas exist, but feels that improvements can be made in these areas. Accordingly, he offers a number of suggestions for improvement.

Olson points out that marriage continues to be the most popular voluntary association in America, with more than 90 percent of the population marrying at least once. Such a figure is hardly compatible with some of the current predictions of the imminent demise of marriage as a social institution. That changes are taking place in marriage today is quite obvious, but Olson finds these changes—such as the increasing divorce rate—not to be of a revolutionary nature which poses a threat to the survival of marriage in the near future.

Olson examines the mate selection system—the "dating and mating game"—and finds that while it is quite successful in placing most Americans into marriage at least once, it does not always do as good a job of matching up men and women as compatible, lifelong marriage partners. Part of the problem lies in the myths and unrealistic expectations so many individuals bring into marriage. Just what a successful marriage is today needs some redefinition, Olson feels. Toward this end he presents a list of recommendations which he believes would improve the quality and durability of marriage and family relationships in America.

MARRIAGE OF THE FUTURE: REVOLUTIONARY OR EVOLUTIONARY CHANGE?*

David H. Olson

The land of marriage has this peculiarity, that strangers are desirous of inhabiting it, whilst its natural inhabitants would willingly be banished from thence.–Montigue.

The paradoxical nature of marriage has intrigued and perplexed scholars and laymen alike for centuries. Psychologists such as John B. Watson in 1927 prophesized that marriage would not survive by 1977. About the same time, sociologists like Pitirim Sorokin and Carl Zimmerman also predicted its demise. (Bernard, 1970)

A rather common statement one hears nowadays is that "The last fifty years have apparently changed the marriage relation from a permanent and lifelong state to a union existing for the pleasure of the parties. The change thus swiftly wrought is so revolutionary, involving the very foundations of human society, that we must believe it to be the result not of any temporary conditions." (Thwing and Thwing in Reiss, 1971, 317) The only surprising thing about this statement is that it was made in 1887.

In spite of all the predictions regarding the collapse of the institution of marriage, it continues to survive. In fact, marriage still continues to be the most popular voluntary institution in our society with only three to four percent of the population never marrying at least once. And national statistics on marriage indicate that an increasing number of eligible individuals are getting married, rather than remaining single. (Vital Statistics, 1970) For the third consecutive year, in 1970 there were over two million marriages in the country. The rate of marriage has also continued to increase so that the 1970 rate of 10.7 marriages per 1000 individuals was the highest annual rate since 1950. There has also been very little change in the median age of first marriage between 1950 and 1970, 22.8 to 23.2 years for males, and 20.3 to 20.8 years for females, respectively. (Population Census, 1971)

While getting married has increased in popularity, so has the number of individuals who have chosen to terminate their marriage contract. In 1970, there were 715,000 divorces and annulments in the United States, which is almost double the number in 1950 (385,000). Since 1967, the divorce rate has increased by 30 percent. (Vital Statistics, Vol. 19, 1971) The rate has progressively moved toward a cumulative rate, one divorce for every four marriages. The rate of divorce among those married under 18 is close to 50 percent. The ratio of divorced individuals compared to those married has increased in the last ten years. In 1960, there were 28 divorced men for every 1000 men married, and 35 in 1970. Comparable figures for females were 42 in 1960, and 60 in 1970. (Population Census, 1971) The number of divorces for married women over 15 years of age changed from 9.3 per 1000 in 1959 to 13.4 in 1969. (Vital Statistics, Vol. 20, 1971) Also, the average length of marriage has declined to an average of 7.1 years.

The Dating-Mating Game

In spite of the fact that quantitatively marriage continues to be very popular, the quality of the husband-wife relationship is often far less advantageous than individuals either expect or desire. One of the reasons that the marriage institution does not live up to its expectations is because of the many myths and unrealistic expectations that individuals bring to marriage. Another major factor that contributes to problems in marriage is the lack of preparation that society provides for this major decision in life. Whereas one expects that individuals will take years of schooling to adequately prepare for their occupation choice, it is assumed that individuals need no guidance in making what is probably the most significant decision in their life. For unlike a job, or even an occupation, which is relatively easy to change, it still is legally and emotionally much more difficult to change, or at least dissolve, a marital relationship. Individuals are given few useful guidelines to follow and then wonder why marriages are not as fulfilling as expected or desired.

From the vantage point of society, the present dating system which has evolved in this country is successful in that it effectively places most people into marriage at least once. But one of its major limitations is that it is too effective in that it pushes many into marriage who would not, and perhaps should not, get married. In other words, there are rather strong implicit sanctions against anyone who would prefer to remain single. Society does this by labeling individuals as deviant and maladjusted if they do not conform to societal expectations in this regard. The continuous push by parents and friends alike is rather persuasive and very effective. A more complete discussion of the third parties' influence on marriage is described in greater detail in a recent paper. (Ryder, Kafka and Olson, 1970)

This encouragement of heterosexual involvement begins so early that it is becoming more realistic to talk about dating beginning as early as elementary school. Broderick (1968) has documented a rather advanced level of heterosexual development and activity in fifth and sixth grades. Many children (84 percent of the females and 62 percent of the males) at this stage were already accepting the idea that they would eventually be married. Also, a high percentage (74 percent) of those wanting to eventually marry already had a girlfriend or boyfriend, and of those already having a friend, 66 percent reported having been in love.

What has developed, therefore, in this society is a *laissez faire* approach to the mate-selection process and this has helped to turn the process into a dating-mating game. The goal or major objective in this game is finding a suitable marital partner. The rules of the game are usually implicit rather than explicit and this results in a friendly confrontation, with increasing sexual intimacy (which is used as one of the most lethal weapons). The participants use strategies and counter-strategies within the limits of the unwritten rules in order to attain their goal, i.e., a suitable marital partner. While dating has turned out to be fun for some, it is often a hurtful and destructive game for many.

Although dating has been successful from a functional point of view, of facilitating the mate selection process and placing individuals into marriage, it has failed in a most essential way. It has failed because it does not assist couples in learning how to develop and maintain vital and meaningful relationships. Only recently have more of the youth become aware of the time inadequacies of the current dating system which has evolved in this country. They have become aware of the superficiality of dating and the over-emphasis and misuse of the purely sexual aspects of these relationships. As a result, there are increasing numbers who are trying to break away from the traditional dating-mating game by living together, either as couples or in groups. But simply living together is not *alone* going to prepare them to learn how to relate meaningfully, to adequately cope with differences and conflict, or to deal with long-term commitment. However, it is becoming increasingly clear that alternative models of mate selection are needed to prepare couples for lifelong commitment.

Fortunately, there are a few innovative programs that are just beginning to be used to train couples in more functional communication skills. (Miller and Nunnally, 1970) In some ways, however, this is really like giving birth control pills to a woman who just became pregnant—it is too little, too late. Dramatic changes are needed in the education and emotional preparation provided and changes in the social climate that continues to pressure individuals into marriage so early, so unaware, and so unprepared.

Demythologizing the Myths about Marriage

One of the reasons that the marriage institution does not live up to its expectations is because of the many myths and unrealistic expectations that individuals bring to marriage. One of the most prevalent myths about marriage is the belief that "if an intimate relationship is *not* good, it will *spontaneously* improve with time." This myth not only leads couples into marriage but may keep many couples together in anticipation of change in their relationship. Initially, dating couples begin by saying, "If only we go steady, things will improve and he (or she) won't act this way." At a later stage they say, "If my steady and I were having difficulties, engagement might help resolve some of our problems." The same theme continues during engagement with the assumption that "marriage will help change or reform my fiancée." However, most newlyweds soon find greater difficulty in marriage than they anticipated, for not only do their past problems continue to exist, usually in greater intensity than before, but they also encounter new areas of conflict which result from living together. And many couples then feel that: "Our relationship isn't very fulfilling now that we are married, but if we only had a child, that would bring us closer and resolve many of our difficulties." I have even heard couples optimistically carry this theme further and admit that: "This one child has *not* helped our marriage, but if we had another child, our relationship would really improve." In general, all these myths are examples of the general theme that a relationship will spontaneously improve with increasing commitment and time.

Several other common myths have been described by Lederer and Jackson (1968) in their book on the *Mirages of Marriage*. Myths abound regarding the relationship between love and marriage such as: "People marry because they are in love," "Most married people love each other," "Love is necessary for a satisfactory marriage," and "All problems can be solved if you're really in love."

In search of a fulfilling life, many individuals falsely assume that "marriage is easy, the difficulty is finding the right person." Further, "who they marry is more important than when they marry," and therefore, "there is one best person for them to marry." They also assume that "the only way to be truly happy is to marry." They wishfully assume that "marriage will alleviate their loneliness." What they do not realize is that marriage often intensifies rather than eases loneliness. It is important to realize that if individuals cannot live with themselves, they will probably have considerable difficulty trying to live with someone else. (Ryder, 1970) Couples also assume that "their partner will be able to satisfy all their needs" and, therefore, "the more time and activities that are spent together, the better the marriage relationship."

Once couples begin having difficulty in marriage they falsely assume "that patterns of behavior and interaction they develop are easy to change" and "that a quarrel or disagreement can only be detrimental to their relationship." Many further maintain that "it is best *not* to express negative feelings about one's spouse." Couples assume that "if their spouse loves them, they will know what they are feeling or what they want." When marital problems become more extreme many believe that "for the sake of the children, keeping a conflicted family together is preferable to divorce."

In regard to their sexual relationship, many couples falsely assume that"a good sexual relationship is easy to develop" and that "if there is a good sexual relationship, other problems will take care of themselves" and "sexual adjustment in marriage will result more from proper techniques than from proper attitudes." Couples also overemphasize the value and significance of sex in marriage and believe "sex will be one of the most fulfilling aspects of their marriage."

Unfortunately, too many individuals accept many of these myths about marriage and little is currently being done to demythologize these ideas. As a result, many couples enter marriage with idealistic and unrealistic expectations about what marriage can and will provide. It is usually not until after they have become disappointed and frustrated with their partner that they begin to face the realities of the marital relationship.

For further details about the prevalence of these and related myths, a Premarital Attitude Scale (PMAS) was developed and used to assess the attitudes of family specialists and college students on many of these issues. (Olson, 1967; Olson and Gravatt, 1968)

A Sexual Revolution or Evolution?

In 1938, Terman predicted that: "The trend toward premarital sexual experience is proceeding with extraordinary rapidity . . . In the case of husbands the incidence of virginity at marriage is 50.6 percent in the oldest group and only 32.6 percent in the youngest. The corresponding drop for wives is from 86.5 percent to 51.2 percent. If the drop should continue at the average rate shown for those born since 1890, virginity at marriage will be close to the vanishing point for males born after 1930 and for females born after 1940." (321–22)

Kinsey's data on females (1953) indicates the rate of premarital sex (PMS) was about 49 percent. Comparable data from the Burgess and Wallin research (1953) found about 68 percent of the males and 47 percent of the females had premarital sex. A recent study by Kaats and Davis (1970) has indicated similar results of PMS, 60 percent for males and 41 percent for females. Another recent study (Bell and Chaskes, 1970) of female premarital sex patterns in 1958 and 1968 found only a small increase in rate for females from 31 to 39 percent, respectively. One of the best designed studies of sexual attitudes and behaviors of young people in three cultures was conducted in 1958 and replicated in 1968 by Christensen and Gregg. (1970) They found in their midwest sample a rather prominent increase in PMS in females between 1958 and 1968, 21 to 34 percent respectively, but no change in the rate for males, 51 to 50 respectively. All of these recent studies actually are underestimates of the actual rate of PMS because the individuals studied were middle class college students who were not yet married. These studies are not representative because it is known that lower class individuals have higher rates of PMS than college students. Further, the actual rates of PMS cannot accurately be assessed until the individuals are actually married. This latter fact is particularly important since PMS still occurs most frequently with one's potential spouse. (Bell and Chaskes, 1970)

On the basis of these studies, it is clear that Terman's prediction that virgin marriages would be only a historical fact has not been realized. However, there have been noticeable changes in female attitudes and behavior. The most dramatic change, which might even be called a female revolution, is the increasing PMS rates for females, which Christensen and Gregg (1970) found changed in the last decade from 21 to 34 percent. This has resulted in a growing convergence in the rates of PMS between the sexes (50 and 34 percent for males and females respectively). This study also showed considerable liberalizations in the attitudes toward PMS in the last decade, again most dramatically in females. This has resulted in fewer differences between PMS attitudes and behavior, so that fewer people are violating their own values and, therefore, there is less guilt associated with PMS. Although the rate of PMS increased, there was an increasing tendency to limit their sexual activity to one partner.

Another trend found in the study by Bell and Chaskes (1970) was that PMS was less dependent on the commitment of engagement than it was a decade ago. While more PMS occurred during engagement, from 31 percent in 1958 to 39 percent in 1968, the PMS rates increased more drastically in dating, from ten to 23 percent, and going steady, from fifteen to 28 percent, stages.

MARITAL SEX While there is considerable data on premarital sexual behavior, there is a dearth of empirical data on the sexual relationship in marriage. In fact, little has been done since Kinsey's initial data on the male (1948) and female. (1953) Cuber and Harroff (1965) have described the sexual relationships of *Significant Americans* within the context of a relationship typology. However, they did not provide specific normative data about these couples' sexual relationships. Perhaps the largest sample of data on early marriage and sexual behavior is contained in a longitudinal study of 2000 couples conducted by Robert Ryder and the author. Unfortunately, the data on marital sexual behavior has not yet been analyzed. The major source of information, therefore, comes from therapists who find sexual problems to be both a *cause* and a *symptom* of most marital difficulties. We can only hope that the next decade will provide more substantive normative data on this significant aspect of marital behavior.

EXTRA-MARITAL AND GROUP SEX   Unlike the lack of research on sex in marriage, there have been several recent investigations into the *extra* in extra-marital sex (EMS). Kinsey (1948) provided the first extensive data on EMS and reported that by the age of 40 about one-quarter (26 percent) of the females and one-half (50 percent) of the males had at least one such affair. A more recent study by Whitehurst (1969) was done on 112 upper middle class business and professional men. He found that 67 percent had no EMS, nine percent played around but had no serious sexual involvement, sixteen percent had limited affairs, and only about three percent had rather lengthy affairs. He found that those with the highest levels of EMS more often were alienated, especially showing high levels of social isolation and powerlessness.

Another recent study of EMS was conducted by Johnson (1969) in which 100 middle class couples were investigated. He found 28 percent of the marriages were involved in at least one affair. The marital adjustment of the couple was not related to EMS, for an equal number of couples with high marital adjustment had affairs or passed up the opportunity. However, it was found that husbands, but not wives, who had lower levels of sexual satisfaction were more likely to become involved in affairs. An important finding was the significance of a "perceived opportunity" for having EMS. About 40 percent of those who "perceived" an opportunity took advantage of the situation.

A more expanded discussion on extra-marital sex is contained in a recent book, *Extra-Marital Relations*, edited by Neubeck. (1969) Neubeck offered a useful perspective on EMS when he discussed the unrealistic expectation that marriage will meet all the needs of both spouses at all times. While spouses permit each other some freedom to relate to others, "faithfulness is ordinarily seen as faithfulness in the flesh." (22) The unreality of such expectations is demonstrated by the number of involvements, sexual and emotional, that violate these ideals.

While married individuals typically have had unilateral affairs, recent evidence has indicated that more couples have jointly sought out another couple(s) for group sexual experiences. In a recent book by Bartell (1971) he describes a study of 280 swinging couples. He estimates that perhaps as many as one million couples are presently experimenting within this general context. Many are "respectable" suburbanites who use this experience to relieve boredom. Contacts are made purely for sexual reasons and are usually not maintained for more than a few meetings. It appears, however, that this style of life is seldom maintained permanently because of the large amount of time and energy which is needed to simply locate new partners. Also many come to realize that the experience does not provide the degree of satisfaction they expected.

In conclusion, it appears that while new patterns of relating sexually are evolving, there is not a significant change in the sexual behavior of individuals or couples to label any changes as revolutionary. However, it does appear that there are several trends that have implications for sexual behavior in the future. First of all, there appear to be noticeable changes in both attitudes and behaviors of females which will lead to a greater convergence with the male in society. This could lead to a further decline in the traditional double standard of sexual behavior. Secondly, the openness and frequency with which sexual matters are discussed is increasing, not only in the mass media but also interpersonally. As a result, the discrepancy between attitudes and behaviors in both sexes shows signs of diminishing and as this continues there will be less guilt feelings associated with sexual behavior. Thirdly, there is a trend away from restricting the sexual experience only to a relationship where there is some type of mutual commitment, i.e., engagement or marriage. While a good sexual relationship might still be confined to a love relationship, love has also become more broadly defined to include more than just a marriage relationship. While these are only trends and do, in fact, reflect evolutionary changes in both sexual attitudes and behaviors of individuals in society, they do not indicate any type of sexual revolution that would dramatically affect the institutions of marriage and the family.

Alternative Styles of Living

In an attempt to change the qualitative aspects of marriage, there is a growing interest in re-structuring the mate selection process and the traditional monogamous conjugal marriage where husband and wife live alone in their own apartment or home. Discussion of alternative living styles has lately become rather prominent in the mass media. (*Futurist*, April, 1970)

One trend is the increasing numbers of college students and other young people living in arrangements other than segregated male-female dormitories or sorority or fraternity houses. Some are collectively renting large houses and forming communal arrangements. While the housing arrangement is communal, there is a great deal of diversity in the interpersonal life styles these individual residents adopt. Some legitimately qualify as communal arrangements where expenses, tasks, and experiences are shared. But many communes often revert to being more like traditional boarding houses where there is little cooperative interest or emotional commitment to others in the house.

Likewise, heterosexual cohabitation takes a variety of forms, from simply sharing a room with one or more individuals, to sharing a bed and a room as a couple, either alone or with other individuals. Macklin (1971) found in a survey of 150 under-classmen at Cornell University that 28 percent had recently lived under some form of cohabitation. Some of the reasons for cohabitating given in the Macklin study included: a search for more meaningful relating, avoidance of the dating game, avoiding the loneliness of a large university, and the testing of the relationship. In most of the relationships there was a strong affection but marriage was not seen as an immediate possibility. Macklin indicated that about three-quarters of the relationships involved a girl moving in to share a boy's room in an apartment or house he shared with other males. Usually these arrangements were not planned but simply conveniently available at the time they made the decision. Students in the Macklin survey (1971) had mixed feelings about the success of the experience, but over half felt the advantages outweighed the numerous problems they encountered. Of the problems, a variety of sexual problems was the most pervasive issue. Parental disapproval also was frequently encountered, as was interpersonal issues relating to commitment, communication of feelings, and lack of privacy.

It appears that colleges and universities are becoming more responsive to these changes in student attitudes and behaviors. Universities are now becoming more lax in enforcing their regulations regarding *locus parentis*. There are also increasing numbers of coeducational dormitories that permit a variety of living arrangements.

In addition to new styles of living among unmarried individuals, there are others who are forming multilateral marriages in which usually three or more individuals form a group marriage arrangement. An active proponent of group marriage is Robert Rimmer, author of *The Harrad Experiment* and *Proposition 31*, who feels that new experimentation in sex and marriage is needed to break away from the problems with monogamous marriage. Larry and Joan Constantine (1970; 1971) have attempted to study most of these marriages they could locate, which to date numbers approximately 35 to 40. On the average, these arrangements have not lasted more than a year. The Constantines stated that "We must conclude . . . that multilateral marriage, though a promising growth-oriented form of marriage, is itself a structure limited to a relative few." (1970, 45)

Recently more research has also been done on a small sample of approximately 20 to 30 unconventional marriages that were found in the total sample of 2000 couples who were part of the longitudinal study of early marriage conducted at the National Institute of Mental Health by Robert Ryder and the author. Details of this clinical investigation are contained in a paper entitled Notes on Marriage in the Orbit of the Counter-culture. (Kafka and Ryder, 1972) There are several characteristics which define the ethos espoused by these unconventional couples. There is an intended dominance of feelings over cognition, a present versus future orientation, avoidance of conventional role expectations and traditional patterns of marriage, a high evaluation in "working things out," an intense concern with increasing and maintaining openness and heightened intimacy, disavowal of materialistic goals, and high evaluation of play and travel. In spite of their attempts to build this ethos into their daily lives, they were not able to maintain these ideals without, at times, unwittingly slipping back into many of the traditional problems they wished to avoid. For example, their attempts at role reversal were often difficult to maintain and proved to be at times more than either could cope with and consequently there was a "return to the conventional." Although sexual possessiveness was devalued they found that "hang ups" often interfered; for example, the jealousy they experienced when their partner had an affair with a friend. These couples generally exhibited a more meaningful vital and working relationship than the majority of conventional couples sampled in this study. Both their satisfactions and frustrations were experienced with greater intensity and both extremes occur with greater frequency than in conventional marriage. These couples seldom achieved what they desired and they often found themselves "reverting to the conventional style." These marriages also had a higher rate of divorce than the more conventional sample. Paradoxically, one might conclude that the most vital relationships are the ones that do not last.

In conclusion, although increasing numbers of young people are experimenting with alternative styles of relating as a substitute for the traditional dating game, there is little evidence that this is more than a newly emerging developmental stage in the mate selection process. This newly emerging stage would perhaps come as an extension of the engagement period and might appropriately be called experimental marriage. While this experimentation might delay marriage temporarily for some of them, the vast majority will still adopt a more or less conventional conjugal marriage. While this experience might not result in radically different types of marriages, it might contribute to assisting couples in developing a qualititatively different type of marriage relationship or, at least, more adequately prepare them for the types of problems they will encounter in marriage. According to present evidence, there is only a small percentage of couples who actually attempt to develop and permanently maintain a more unconventional marriage from the traditional monogamous conjugal type.

If any single aspect of marriage is in the greatest state of change, it is the expectations regarding the appropriate role relationship between a husband and wife. And as was true in the area of changing premarital-sexual behavior, it is primarily a female revolution. Women, spurred on by women's liberation groups, are increasingly demonstrating against their second class status in marriage in this society. It is true that our society has prescribed roles for husbands and wives that are based not on interest or ability, but on tradition. Tradition has also helped maintain the double standard in sexual and nonsexual areas.

However legitimate the criticisms regarding the woman's role in marriage, changing expectations do not necessarily result in changing actual role relationships that couples adopt. What is happening as a result of these changing expectations is that couples are increasingly being forced into a situation, primarily by the wife, where they must negotiate or renegotiate the way they will structure their role relationships rather than simply accept the traditional definitions. Although this is creating a crisis situation for some, it is providing the opportunity for others to create a new and, hopefully, more vital relationship for both individuals. If these expectations are not realized, it will cause increasing role conflict and growing dissatisfaction with marriage, especially for women, who have traditionally been the defenders of the marriage institution. This is the revolution in marriage. And to paraphrase Otto (1970), what will destroy marriage is not change but the inability of individuals within it to change.

Redefining a Successful Marriage

While a successful marriage has often been determined by its longevity (i.e., those having twenty-fifth anniversaries) or by how well it fulfills the traditional roles prescribed by society (husband being a good provider and wife being a good housekeeper and mother), there is an increasing awareness that these criteria are not necessarily associated with a successful marriage. Youth has begun to seriously question these criteria and they have become somewhat cynical about marriage because of the alienated, conflicted, and devitalized marriages they see their parents and other adults tolerate. Perceptive as they are, they increasingly see marriage as a relationship that is less often cherished than simply tolerated and endured.

In recent years, there seems to be some change in the criteria used to evaluate the success of a marital relationship. Increasingly, individuals are seeking a relationship that will provide growth for them as individuals and as a couple. More than a companionship marriage as defined by Burgess, there is a search for an authentic and mutually actualizing relationship. Ideally, the successful marriage is seen as a relationship context in which growth and development of both partners is facilitated to a greater extent than it could be for either of these individuals outside the relationship. While this has been one function of marriage that has been implicitly assumed, it has not been explicitly demanded until recently.

Ironically, although more individuals are beginning to evaluate marriage in respect to this criterion, most couples have been unable to achieve this idealized type of relationship. One of the main reasons for this is that society has not adequately prepared individuals to relate in a meaningful way that will facilitate mutual growth within a relationship. As a result, if growth occurs, more commonly it occurs in only one of the individuals. And paradoxically, the greater the growth in one partner in a relationship, the greater the chance the couple will grow further apart rather than closer together. This is often true when both individuals grow also, because they usually do not share the same growth experience and do not use the experience to further develop their relationship. As a result, many couples today are becoming increasingly frustrated because they have rejected the more traditional definition of a successful marriage and yet are having difficulty achieving the type of mutually actualizing relationship that they are striving to achieve. It, therefore, appears that a successful marriage continues to be a difficult and elusive objective to achieve.

Needed: A New Lexicon about Marriage

If nothing else productive comes from considering the alternative styles of marriage, it has certainly demonstrated the inadequacy of our present language for describing and classifying marriage and nonmarriage relationships. Even the language used by anthropologists is insufficient to describe the varieties of heterosexual or homosexual relationships and the range of new life styles and communal arrangements on the contemporary scene. This might be a primary reason that family professionals have been unable to develop an adequate typology of marital relationships and another reason why there has been so little substantive research in this area.

Marriage research has, unfortunately, been too concerned with describing marriage along the elusive dimensions of "marital happiness" or "marital satisfaction" or "marital adjustment." The numerous problems with conceptualizing and operationalizing concepts have been reviewed elsewhere (Hicks and Platt, 1970), but their inadequacy becomes even more apparent when describing and classifying unconventional life styles. Family researchers and theorists alike have also limited themselves to simplistic concepts such as "family decision making" and "family power structures." Recent evidence suggests that not only is family power a difficult concept to define and operationalize, but that the various measures used have almost no relationship to each other (Turk and Bell, 1972), and that these measures also lack validity. (Olson and Rabunsky, 1972)

General dimensions that have emerged from this renewed focus on marriage indicate a need for concern with commitment to a relationship rather than primary attention being given to simply whether the couple remains married, i.e., permanence. Attention also needs to be given to a typology of relationships rather than simply classifying a couple as happy. Some preliminary work in this regard was done by Cuber and Harroff (1965) when they classified marriages according to five relationship categories of vital, total, conflict-habitual, passive-congenial, or devitalized. One also needs to know more about the actual interpersonal dynamics in marriage. Newly emerging system concepts such as circular causality, homeostasis, and transaction may aid in this regard.

What is meant by the concepts of marriage and family must also be clearly defined. Are these relationships best defined as legal contracts, verbal commitments, or a definition based on the structure and functions these relationships develop? There need to be new distinctions, such as between emotional monogamy and sexual monogamy. Also, the adaptability (Vincent, 1966) of individuals and relationships needs to be better understood. Attention should also be given to the effects of institutionalizing affection and commitment. Rather than focusing so exclusively on the type and degree of maladjustment that exists in marriage, more attention also needs to be given to marital health (Vincent, 1967) and ways in which individuals and relationships can be helped to become more self-actualizing.

Recommendations Regarding Marriage

After surveying marriage from a variety of perspectives, it is readily apparent that this institution, like many in this society, has not been the panacea that many have envisioned. Rarely is marriage found to be a vital and fulfilling relationship for both spouses. In part, this might be caused by the way we have institutionalized this affectionate relationship. But it also is a reflection of the inability of individuals to relate in meaningful ways and the unrealistic expectations individuals bring to marriage. The following proposals are offered as guidelines and recommendations that might help make marriage a more meaningful and vital relationship.

1 Individuals should not be encouraged to marry at an early age but should wait until they have matured emotionally and have established themselves in their chosen profession.
2 All individuals should not be encouraged or pressured into marriage.
3 Individuals and couples should be encouraged to experiment with a variety of life styles in order to choose the style which is most appropriate for them.
4 Couples should be encouraged to openly and honestly relate rather than play the traditional dating-mating game.
5 Couples should not get married until they have established a meaningful relationship and resolved their major difficulties; for marriage will only create, rather than eliminate, problems.
6 The decision of parenthood should be a joint decision which should follow, rather than precede (as it does in about one-third of the cases), marriage.
7 Couples should not have children until they have established a strong and viable marriage relationship.
8 Couples should be creative and flexible in how they work out their changing

roles and mutual responsibilities, not only during their initial phases of marriage, but throughout their marriage relationship.

Individuals would have greater freedom to develop in these ways if they were given societal support rather than implicit and explicit restrictions and constraints. There are a few specific ways in which legal and legislative reform would facilitate these opportunities.

1 Marriage laws should be made more stringent in order to encourage individuals to take this major decision more seriously. Presently it is easier in most states to obtain a marriage license than a license to drive a car.
2 No-fault divorce laws should be developed while still providing for adequate support for children. California and Florida have already taken constructive steps in this direction.
3 Premarital, marital, and divorce counseling should be offered to all individuals regardless of their ability to pay.
4 Tax laws should be changed so as not to unduly discriminate against any particular life style.
5 Sex laws which prohibit any form of sexual behavior between consenting individuals should be changed to allow for individual freedom and development.

Future Evolution of Marriage

Historically, the types and variety of ways in which couples arrange their marriages have always been changing and evolving. These emerging styles have been both responsive to societal change and a cause of change. In fact, in some ways the marriage institution is an emotional thermometer of contemporary society and also an indicator of future trends. The fact that there are beginnings of a female revolution is already, and will continue to be, reflected both in marriage and society. There are also indications that youth are increasingly questioning many of the institutions in our society, including the marriage institution. Both these groups are challenging marriage as it has been traditionally defined and they have been actively experimenting with alternative ways of arranging their lives and marriages. This might lead to a greater variety of ways in which couples define their relationship, arrange their living styles, and carry out the traditional functions of marriage.

While some may feel that these attempts at change are the cause of society's problems, these behaviors might more appropriately be seen as a solution to problems in marriage and also in society. Some unrealistically fear that the institution of marriage might be radically changed. There is, however, little need to be concerned because institutionalized forms of behavior are difficult to dramatically change. In addition, highly industrialized society offers strong support for the style of marriage that has evolved. Lastly, emotional development will tend to minimize any excessive change. As Reiss (1970) stated:

Our emotions will continue to close off many avenues of change and our habits will further reinforce this. Thinking is a time-consuming activity that often leads to painful revelations. Habit and emotional responses are our ways of easing that pain.(397)

But one must not be afraid of change or afraid to challenge ideas and traditions, no matter how sacred. A great concern is with facilitating the growth and development of individuals in and out of marriage, as Otto (1970) appropriately stated:

What will destroy us is not change, but our inability to change—both as individuals and as a social system. It is only by welcoming innovation, experiment, and change that a society based on man's capacity to love man can come into being.(9)

References

Bartell, Gilbert D. *Group Sex.* New York: Peter H. Wyden, 1971.

Bell, Robert R. and Jay B. Chaskes. Premarital Sexual Experience among Coeds, 1958 to 1968. *Journal of Marriage and the Family*, 1970, **32**, 81–84.

Bernard, Jessie. Woman, Marriage, and the Future. *Futurist*, 1970, **4**, 41–43.

Broderick, Carlfred B. and George P. Rowe. A Scale of Preadolescent Heterosexual Development. *Journal of Marriage and the Family*, 1968, **30**, 97–101.

Christensen, Harold T. and Christina F. Gregg. Changing Sex Norms in America and Scandinavia. *Journal of Marriage and the Family*, 1970, **32**, 616–627.

Constantine, Larry L. and Joan M. Constantine. Where Is Marriage Going? *Futurist*, 1970, **4**, 44–46.

Constantine, Larry L. and Joan M. Constantine. Group and Multilateral Marriage: Definitional Notes, Glossary and Annotated Bibliography. *Family Process*, 1971, **10**, 157–176.

Cuber, John F. and Peggy B. Harroff. *The Significant Americans.* New York: Appleton-Century, 1965.

Hicks, Mary W. and Marilyn Platt. Marital Happiness and Stability: A Review of the Research in the Sixties. *Journal of Marriage and the Family*, 1970, **32**, 553–574.

Hill, Reuben. The American Family of the Future. *Journal of Marriage and the Family*, 1964, **26**, 20–28.

Johnson, Ralph E. Some Correlates of Extramarital Coitus. *Journal of Marriage and the Family*, 1970, **32**, 449–456.

Kaats, Gilbert R. and Keith E. Davis. The Dynamics of Sexual Behavior of College Students. *Journal of Marriage and the Family*, 1970, **32**, 390–399.

Kafka, John S. and Robert G. Ryder. Notes on Marriage in the Orbit of the Counter-Culture, Unpublished manuscript, 1972.

Kinsey, Alfred C., Wardell B. Pomeroy, Clyde E. Martin, and Paul Gibbard. *Sexual Behavior in the Human Female.* New York: Sanders, 1953.

Kinsey, Alfred C., Wardell B. Pomeroy, Clyde E. Martin, and Paul Gibbard. *Sexual Behavior in the Human Male*. New York: Sanders, 1948.

Lederer, William J. and Donald D. Jackson. *The Mirages of Marriage*. New York: W. W. Norton, 1968.

Maslow, A. H. A Theory of Human Motivation. *Psychological Review*, 1943, **50**, 370–396.

Maslow, A. H. *Motivation and Personality*. New York: Harper and Row, 1954.

Miller, Sherod and Elam Nunnally. A Family Developmental Program of Communication Training for Engaged Couples. Monograph Family Study Center, University of Minnesota, 1970.

Neubeck, Gerhard (Ed.) *Extramarital Relations*. Englewood Cliffs, New Jersey: Prentice-Hall, 1969.

Olson, David H. Student Attitudes Toward Marriage. *College Student Survey*, 1967, **1**, 71–78.

Olson, David H. and Arthur G. Gravatt. Attitude Change in a Functional Marriage Course. *The Family Coordinator*, 1968, **17**, 99–104.

Olson, David H. and Carolyn Rabunsky. Validity of Four Measures of Family Power. *Journal of Marriage and the Family*, 1972, **34**, 224–234.

Otto, Herbert A. (Ed.). *The Family in Search of a Future*. New York: Appleton, Century, Crofts, 1970.

Reiss, Ira L. *The Family Systems in America*. New York: Holt, Rinehart, and Winston, 1971.

Ryder, Robert G., John S. Kafka, and David H. Olson. Separating and Joining Influences in Courtship and Early Marriage. *American Journal of Orthopsychiatry*, 1971, **41**, 450–464.

Ryder, Robert G. An Opinion on Marriage. *Mademoiselle*, (January) 1971.

Satir, Virginia. Marriage as a Human-Actualizing Contract. In Herbert A. Otto (Ed.) *The Family in Search of a Future*. New York: Appleton, Century, Crofts, 1970.

Sussman, Marvin B. and Lee Burchinal. Kin Family Network: Unheralded Structure in Current Conceptualizations of Family Functioning. *Marriage and Family Living*, 1962, **24**, 231–240.

Sussman, Marvin B. Relationships of Adult Children with their Parents in the United States. In Ethel Shanas and Gordon F. Streib (Eds.) *Social Structure and the Family: Generational Relations*. Englewood Cliffs, New Jersey: Prentice-Hall, 1965.

Terman, Lewis M. *Psychological Factors in Marital Happiness*. New York: McGraw Hill, 1938.

Turk, James L. and Norman W. Bell. Measuring Power in Families. *Journal of Marriage and the Family*, 1972, **34**, 215–223.

Vincent, Clark E. Familia Spongia: The Adaptive Function. *Journal of Marriage and the Family*, 1966, **28**, 29–36.

Vincent, Clark E. Mental Health and the Family. *Journal of Marriage and the Family*, 1967, **29**, 18–39.

Whitehurst, Robert N. Extra-Marital Sex: Alienation of Extension of Normal Behavior. In Gerhard Neubeck (Ed.) *Extra-Marital Relations*. New York: Prentice-Hall, 1969.

NAME INDEX

SUBJECT INDEX